RESEARCH HANDBOOK OF INVESTING IN THE TRIPLE BOTTOM LINE

Research Handbook of Investing in the Triple Bottom Line

Finance, Society and the Environment

Edited by

Sabri Boubaker

South Champagne Business School, France

Douglas Cumming

College of Business, Florida Atlantic University, USA

Duc Khuong Nguyen

IPAG Business School, France

Edward Elgar PUBLISHING

Cheltenham, UK • Northampton, MA, USA

Published by
Edward Elgar Publishing Limited
The Lypiatts
15 Lansdown Road
Cheltenham
Glos GL50 2JA
UK

Edward Elgar Publishing, Inc.
William Pratt House
9 Dewey Court
Northampton
Massachusetts 01060
USA

A catalogue record for this book
is available from the British Library

Library of Congress Control Number: 2018935761

This book is available electronically in the **Elgar**online
Business subject collection
DOI 10.4337/9781788110006

MIX
Paper from
responsible sources
FSC® C013056

ISBN 978 1 78643 999 4 (cased)
ISBN 978 1 78811 000 6 (eBook)

Typeset by Servis Filmsetting Ltd, Stockport, Cheshire
Printed and bound in Great Britain by TJ International Ltd, Padstow

Contents

About the editors

Sabri Boubaker is Professor of Finance at South Champagne Business School (Troyes, France) and Research Fellow at the Institut de Recherche en Gestion (University of Paris Est). He holds a PhD in Finance from University of Paris Est (2006) and a HDR degree (Habilitation for Supervising Doctoral Research) in 2010 from the same university. He has recently published several academic papers in international refereed journals including *Journal of Corporate Finance, Journal of Banking & Finance, Journal of International Money and Finance, Financial Management, International Review of Financial Analysis, European Financial Management Journal, Review of Quantitative Accounting and Finance* and *Journal of International Financial Markets, Institutions and Money*. Dr Boubaker has also edited several books on corporate finance and financial markets and serves on the editorial boards of several peer-reviewed finance journals. He is the co-founder (with Duc Khuong Nguyen) of the Paris Financial Management Conference and Vietnam Symposium in Banking and Finance (VSBF).

Douglas Cumming is DeSantis Distinguished Professor of Finance and Entrepreneurship at the College of Business, Florida Atlantic University, USA. He holds a JD/PhD in Economics, Finance and Law from the University of Toronto. He has published over 130 academic papers in international refereed journals including *Journal of Financial Economics, Review of Financial Studies, Journal of Corporate Finance, Journal of Banking & Finance, International Review of Financial Analysis, Economic Journal, Journal of Empirical Legal Studies, Academy of Management Journal* and *Journal of International Business Studies*. Dr Cumming has co-authored books on venture capital and hedge funds with Elsevier Science Academic Press and Oxford University Press. Also, Dr Cumming has edited over a dozen books on entrepreneurial finance, private equity and related topics with Oxford University Press, Wiley, Palgrave, and Springer. Dr Cumming is a co-editor at *Finance Research Letters* and *Entrepreneurship Theory and Practice*, the founding editor of *Annals of Corporate Governance*, and serves on the editorial boards of numerous academic journals.

Duc Khuong Nguyen is Professor of Finance and Deputy Director for Research at IPAG Business School (France). He holds a PhD in Finance from the University of Grenoble II (France) and a HDR (Habilitation for Supervising Scientific Research) degree in Management Science from University of Cergy-Pontoise (France), and completed an executive education programme in 'Leadership in Development' at Harvard Kennedy School (United States). He is also a Non-Resident Research Fellow at the School of Public and Environmental Affairs, Indiana University, and a Research Associate at the Department of Finance, Centre d'Economie de la Sorbonne, University Paris 1 Panthéon-Sorbonne. His research articles are published in various refereed journals such as *Journal of Banking & Finance*, *Journal of International Money and Finance*, *Journal of International Financial Markets, Institutions and Money*, *Quarterly Review of Economics and Finance* and *Review of International Economics*. Dr Nguyen has edited several books on corporate finance and financial markets issues and serves as subject and associate editor of several finance journals. He is the co-founder (with Sabri Boubaker) of the Paris Financial Management Conference and Vietnam Symposium in Banking and Finance (VSBF).

Contributors

Mohammed Amidu is Associate Professor of Accounting and Finance and the former Head of the Department of Accounting, University of Ghana Business School. He earned his PhD in Financial Economics from Southampton Business School, University of Southampton, UK. He is a researcher with African Economic Research Consortium (AERC). He has contributed significantly to the accounting and finance literature in areas such as accounting information quality, financial inclusion and literacy, corporate governance, corporate tax policy, development finance, banking market structure and stability. He is also a Senior Research Fellow of VolkswagenStiftung Foundation, Germany and has also held Visiting Scholar positions at the International Monetary Fund (IMF), Washington DC. Currently, he is part of a collaborative research project on 'Delivering inclusive financial development and growth' funded by the Department for International Development (DFID), and the Economic and Social Research Council (ESRC). The University of Ghana Business School awarded him the 'Best Researcher' for the 2015/2016 academic year. He has published in the *European Journal of Finance*, *Review of Quantitative Finance and Accounting*, *International Review of Financial Analysis* and *Accounting Research Journal*. He has authored more than 30 refereed journal articles, six book chapters and a monograph.

Wei Rong Ang is a research scholar at the Ronin Institute. Ang graduated with a Masters degree in economics from Universiti Sains Malaysia. Ang's research interests are in Socially Responsible Investment and Mutual Funds. He has published in *The North American Journal of Economics and Finance*, *Journal of Asset Management*, *Journal of Sustainable Finance and Investment*, *Journal of Global Responsibility* and *ACRN Oxford Journal of Finance and Risk Perspectives*. Recently, he has focused on Socially Responsible Investment in Korea. He was awarded the best research award of Anugerah Persada Kencana for the Masters Pure Art category in 2012 from Universiti Sains Malaysia.

Mohamed Ariff, PhD holds the Chair in Economics & Finance at the Sunway University. He has worked full-time at three AACSB-accredited business schools (National University of Singapore; Monash University; Bond University) for 27 years and has held a senior administrative position for nine years as Head of Banking & Finance in one. His industry experience includes holding top management positions at a listed firm Singtel and a central bank (Singapore). He held three endowed chair professorships consecutively as a regular visitor over the period 1997–13. During a few years on leave from his employer(s), he worked as a professor/fellow at top universities including Harvard (1994) and Tokyo University (1989, 1991, 2008). He has won dean's awards for research and the best teacher in finance award having supervised 44 doctoral students. He has published widely (*Journal of International Financial Markets, Institutions & Money*, *Japan and the World Economy*, *Journal of Business Finance and Accounting*, *Applied Economics*, *Journal of International Money and Finance*, *Journal of Financial Services Research*, *Journal of the Operational Research Society*, *Journal of Small Business Management*, *International Tax Journal*, *Pacific Basin Finance Journal*, etc.). He is an author of the 2007 edition of the top-selling textbook, *Investments* (Bodie, Ariff, Rosa, Marcus and Kane).

François Aubert is currently serving as a Full Professor of Accounting in the Clermont Auvergne University Ecole Universitaire de Management (CRCGM EA 38 49). He recently published papers in the *Journal of Accounting and Taxation*, *Review of Accounting and Finance*, *Journal of International Financial Management & Accounting*, *Comptabilité-Contrôle-Audit*, *International Review of Financial Analysis*, *Advances in Accounting*, *Journal of Applied Accounting Research* and contributed two chapters to books published by Routledge (London) and ATINER, respectively. He has presented many papers in international seminars in the UK and in the USA or at conferences, including the French Accounting Association, European Accounting Association and American Accounting Association annual meetings. His ongoing research deals with the impact and magnitude of accounting restatements on the ability of US firms to predict managed earnings components and discretionary accruals as well as the analysis of analysts' estimates characteristics and time-series properties of earnings analysts and management forecast errors. Professor Aubert has been teaching at the University of Geneva and has taught at the EM Strasbourg Business School and various other institutions in Europe. He is a member of many professional organizations including the French Accounting Association and the European Accounting Association and serves as an ad hoc reviewer for many academic journals.

Harjap Bassan is a Lecturer in Applied Finance in the School of Commerce within the UniSA Business School. Harjap holds a Bachelor of Science (Honours) (BSc (Hons)) and Master of Science (MSc) from the University of Nairobi, a Master of Statistics (MStat) from the University of Florida, is a Fellow (FCCA) of the Association of Chartered Certified Accountants

(ACCA), a Member of the American Statistical Association (ASA) and a Fellow of the Royal Statistical Society (UK) (FRSS). Harjap's research interests are in the areas of accounting information related to valuation, corporate governance, management control, corporate finance and hotel management.

Flavio Bazzana is full professor in Finance and Director of Studies of the Master in Finance at the University of Trento (Italy) where he teaches Corporate Finance, and Investment and Derivatives. He graduated in Economics at the University of Siena (Italy) under Professor Frank H. Hahn and continued his academic training, achieving an M.Phil. in Economic Theory and Econometrics at the University of Cambridge (UK), an M.Sc. in Banking and Finance and a PhD in Finance, both at the University of Siena (Italy). His main interests are in corporate finance, contract theory, risk management and the microstructure of financial markets.

Kathrin Berensmann is Economist and Senior Research Fellow in the 'World Economy and Development Financing' Department at the German Development Institute/Deutsches Institut für Entwicklungspolitik (DIE) in Bonn. Previously she was also employed at the Institute of the German Economy in Cologne and at the University of Würzburg. Her main areas of specialization are green finance, international finance and development finance. For about 20 years she conducted research and extensive policy advisory work for various public institutions including the German Federal Ministry for Economic Cooperation and Development, the German Federal Ministry of Finance, the Deutsche Börse and the GIZ (Gesellschaft für Technische Zusammenarbeit). Kathrin holds a Master of Economics and a PhD in Economics from the University of Würzburg.

Narjess Boubakri is the first Bank of Sharjah Chair holder in Banking and Professor of Finance at the school of Business Administration of the American University of Sharjah. She received her PhD in Finance from Laval University (2000). Her main research interests are in the areas of privatization, corporate governance, empirical finance, international finance, economic reforms and political economy. Professor Boubakri has authored numerous articles and book chapters. Her research has been published in some of the most prestigious peer-reviewed journals, such as the *Journal of Finance*, *Journal of Financial Economics*, *Journal of International Business Studies*, *Journal of Corporate Finance* and *Journal of Banking & Finance*. She is currently the Finance Editor of the *Quarterly Review of Economics and Finance*. Professor Boubakri has taught in HEC Montreal, Laval University and the American University of Sharjah.

Eleonora Broccardo is Assistant Professor in Finance at the University of Trento (Italy) where she teaches Advanced Corporate Finance. She graduated summa cum laude from the University of Trento (2003) and achieved her PhD in Markets and Financial Intermediaries at the Catholic University of Milan, Italy. Her main interests include credit risk management (securitization and collateral with a focus on SMEs, credit derivatives, and non-performing loans), agency cost theory (public and private debt covenants), small corporate finance (state aid in the form of guarantee and mini-bond) and sustainable finance (cooperative banks and social impact bonds). Dr Broccardo's research has been published in national and international peer-reviewed journals, such as the *Journal of Banking & Finance*, *Journal of Risk Finance*, *Journal of Financial Management, Markets and Institutions* and *Public Money and Management*. She has reviewed numerous articles for many top-tier journals.

Florence Dafe is a fellow in International Political Economy at the London School of Economics and Political Science, and a research associate at the German Development Institute (DIE) in Bonn. She holds a Masters degree in Development Studies from the London School of Economics and Political Science and a PhD in Development Studies from the Institute of Development Studies (IDS) at the University of Sussex. Her research interests revolve around the question to what extent governments in developing and emerging economies have the policy space to govern financial sectors in ways that support sustainable development. Florence has written on the opportunities and risks of the widening of central bank mandates in developing countries, the development of local currency bond markets in Africa and the development of the green bond market. Her research has been supported by the German International Cooperation and the European Commission, among others.

Karen Delchet-Cochet is Professor of Management at ISC Paris School of Management, France. Karen graduated from Université d'Orsay (BA), IAE de Paris/Ecole des Mines (MPhil), and Ecole des Mines Saint Etienne (PhD), France. Karen's main research interests include corporate social responsibility and sustainability. She has published in several peer-reviewed journals such as *Revue Internationale PME* and *International Business Research*. She has also co-authored many book chapters, appearing in, for example: *Compétences pour le développement durable* (ESKA Editions), *Regards croisés sur la RSE* (L'Harmattan Editions) and *Manuel de Gestion du développement durable en entreprise: une approche progressive* (FIDES, Editions). She has had a variety of professional experience, having worked at AFNOR certification group and AFNOR competences group for three and four years, respectively.

Michael Dempsey is currently a Professor of Finance with the Faculty of Finance and Banking at TDT University in Ho Chi Minh City, Vietnam. He was previously a Professor and Head of the Finance Discipline at RMIT University in Melbourne, Australia (from early 2013 to late 2017). Prior to this he was an Associate Professor at Monash University, Australia, before which he was an Associate Professor with Griffith University, Australia, having previously been at Leeds University, UK. He also has many years' experience working for the petroleum exploration industry, in the Middle East, Egypt, Aberdeen and London. He is an active researcher in seeking to understand the interplay between risk and returns as the essential dynamic of market behaviour; the theoretical implications of taxation for stock valuation; and corporate decision-making as socially constructed. His recently published *Stock Markets, Investments and Corporate Behavior* (published by Imperial College Press/World Scientific, 2016) summarizes his work in these areas. His teaching expertise includes corporate and investment finance, international finance, derivatives and financial engineering.

Gang Nathan Dong is an Assistant Professor of Healthcare Finance in the Department of Health Policy and Management at Columbia University, where he teaches the Masters degree course of Healthcare Financial Management. After earning a PhD from Rutgers University, a PD from Columbia University, an MBA from Indiana University and an MS from Illinois Institute of Technology, Nathan has been conducting teaching and research at Columbia University's Mailman School of Public Health and Rutgers Business School. His research focuses on corporate finance, financial intermediation, and the financial management of public, non-profit and healthcare organizations. He has published in *BMC Health Services Research*, *Journal of Banking & Finance, Journal of Corporate Finance, Journal of Empirical Finance*, *Journal of Health Care Finance* and *Journal of International Business Studies*. Nathan has extensive industry experience and prior to his academic career provided consulting services to the Bank of New York, Bear Stearns, Credit Suisse and Reuters.

Kizito Uyi Ehigiamusoe is a Research Officer in the Macroeconomics and Public Finance Unit, Department of Research and Training, National Institute for Legislative Studies, National Assembly, Abuja, Nigeria. He holds a Masters in Financial Economics (MFE) and a Masters in Economics (M.Sc.) from the University of Abuja, a Masters in Education Administration and Planning (M.Ed.) from the National Open University of Nigeria and a PhD in Economics from Universiti Sains Malaysia. Kizito has also attended several Certificate Courses in Econometrics in the University of Pretoria, South Africa as well as the School of Mathematical

Sciences, Universiti Sains Malaysia. His major research areas include financial economics, macroeconomics, public finance and applied econometrics. In these areas, Kizito has presented several papers in academic conferences in Africa, Europe and Asia. He has also published several articles in reputable peer-reviewed journals, including the *Journal of Applied Economic Sciences*, *Contemporary Economics*, *Journal of Economic Cooperation and Development*, *Pertanika Journal of Humanities and Social Sciences*, etc.

Jessica Fouilloux is an associate professor of finance in the University of Paris Saclay, France. She holds a PhD degree in Finance from the University of Sorbonne (France) and a Masters degree in Financial Markets from the same University. Before joining the University of Paris Saclay, she was teaching market finance, derivatives and fixed income at the University of Rennes in France. Her research interests cover models of fixed income, carbon markets and investment. Dr Fouilloux has published her research work in several reputable journals such as *Finance*, *Economic Modelling* and *Energy Policy*.

Roberto Gabriele is Associate Professor of Applied Economics at the Department of Economics and Management at the University of Trento (Italy), where he teaches International Corporate Strategy, Industrial Dynamics and Global Scenarios Analysis. He graduated in statistics at the University of 'La Sapienza' (Rome, Italy) and holds a PhD in Economics and Management from Sant'Anna School of Advanced Studies (Pisa, Italy). His main interests are in industrial dynamics, public policy evaluations and agent-based models for economic analysis.

Jean-François Gajewski is currently Professor of Finance and Head of Research at the University of Lyon (UJML3, IAE lyon School of Management, Magellan). He holds a PhD from the Paris-Dauphine University and was awarded the prize for the best thesis in Finance from the Paris Bourse. He was the Head of Research at the lab IREGE (Institute of Management and Economics) from 2008 until 2012, and in 2013 was invited to be a researcher by HEC Montreal. He has published more than 20 papers, mainly in empirical corporate finance in peer-reviewed academic journals such as *European Financial Management*, *Review of Finance*, *European Accounting Review*, *Journal of Corporate Finance*, *Journal of Banking & Finance* and, more recently, *Financial Management*. His research interests deal with corporate financing, behavioural finance and information and financial markets.

Jocelyn Grira is an assistant Professor of Finance in the UAE University. He holds a PhD degree in Finance from HEC Montreal (Canada) and a Masters degree in Financial Engineering from Laval University (Canada).

Before joining the UAE University, he was teaching quantitative finance in the University of Sherbrooke in Canada. Dr Grira has held several senior positions in international corporations based in Canada: KPMG Canada (Risk Consulting & Advisory Services), Desjardins Group (Risk Modelling), Industrial Alliance Group (Risk Analysis & Audit), Financial Markets Authority (Risk Modelling & Regulation), and the Ministry of Finance of Quebec (Financial Engineering & Portfolio Management). His research interests cover sovereign wealth funds, financial regulation, deposit insurance, corporate governance, portfolio management, and risk management. Dr Grira has published his research work in several reputable journals such as *Emerging Markets Review*, *Journal of International Financial Markets, Institutions and Money* and *Economic Modelling*.

Kartick Gupta is a Senior Lecturer at the School of Commerce, Program Director for the Master of Finance programme at the University of South Australia Business School, and a member of the Centre for Applied Finance and Economics (CAFE), where he researches corporate governance, corporate finance and corporate social responsibility. Dr Gupta holds a Bachelor of Commerce (B.Com) with Honours in Accountancy from the University of Burdwan in India, a Master of Arts (MA) in Finance and Investment from the University of Nottingham in the UK, and a PhD in Finance from the University of Waikato in New Zealand. He is a Chartered Financial Analyst® Charter holder, and a Certified Financial Risk Manager. Dr Gupta's research focuses on corporate finance, corporate social responsibility, product market competition, national culture, corporate governance, corporate social responsibility and energy economics. He has published in a range of refereed journal articles and presented his research at conferences and seminars throughout Europe, Asia, America and Australia, and his papers have been recognized for their high-quality research.

Haruna Issahaku is Senior Lecturer at the Department of Economics and Entrepreneurship Development, University for Development Studies, Ghana, where he lectures in econometrics, microeconomics, development finance and macroeconomics. He holds a PhD in Finance from the University of Ghana, Legon. Haruna's main research interests are in the areas of financial inclusion, agricultural finance, development finance, economic development, monetary policy and financial market development. His research works have been published by Elsevier, Taylor & Francis, Emerald and Springer and have appeared in journals such as *Research in International Business and Finance*, *Review of Development Finance*, *Journal of African Business*, *Agriculture Finance Review*, *Agriculture and Food Economics* and *Agriculture and Food Security*.

Lamya Kermiche is an Associate Professor of Finance at Grenoble Ecole de Management. Her main research interests relate to financial markets and risk management on the one hand, and to auditing and accounting quality on the other hand. She published articles in peer-reviewed journals such as *Finance*, *Comptabilité-Contrôle-Audit* [*Accounting-Auditing-Control*] and *Applied Economics*. She has also presented her works at national and international conferences such as the French Finance Association and the European Accounting Association annual meetings. She holds a PhD in Finance from Grenoble University, a research Masters degree in Financial Management, and an engineering degree in computer sciences and applied mathematics. Before joining Grenoble Ecole de Management, Lamya worked as a quantitative analyst in several financial institutions, and has been a professional researcher attached to the Stephen A. Jarislowsky Chair in Governance at HEC Montréal.

Hooi Hooi Lean is a Professor of Economics at the School of Social Sciences, Universiti Sains Malaysia. Dr Lean has published more than one hundred scholarly articles in many reputed international journals. Her H-index is 32 and there are more than 4000 citations to her works on Google Scholar. Professor Lean is the winner of National Academic Award 2015 and Malaysia's Research Star Award 2017 from the Ministry of Higher Education Malaysia. She was granted the prestigious title of 'Researcher of the Week' in GDNet East Asia in 2012 for her excellent contributions. She was awarded the ASEAN-ROK Academic Exchange Fellowship Programme in 2007, the Democratic Pacific Union (DPU) Visiting Fellowship in 2008, the International HERMES Fellowship Programme in 2009 and a Faculty Exchange Fellowship from Georg-Simon-Ohm University in 2012. Professor Lean serves as an associate editor for the *Singapore Economic Review*, *Capital Market Review* and the *International Journal of Economics and Management*. She is also an editorial board member of the *East Asian Journal of Business Management*, *Journal of Asian Finance*, *Economics and Business* and *Frontiers in Energy*. She also sits on the editorial advisory board of the *Indonesian Capital Market Review* and the *Labuan Bulletin of International Business & Finance*.

K. Thomas Liaw is Professor of Finance at St John's University, USA and formerly chairman of the department. He received his PhD from Northwestern University (1988). His main research interests are capital markets, investment management and corporate finance. Professor Liaw has authored several books in capital markets, the business of investment banking, and investment banking and investment opportunities in China. His research articles are in the areas of dividend forecasting, repurchase agreements, Treasury coupon rolls, emerging markets smart beta ETFs, market risks and investment banking. Professor Liaw teaches finance courses in the undergraduate and graduate programmes in investments, corporate finance, capital markets, investment banking, and commercial banking. He has received invitations to speak at executive programmes in securities business, new financial products and risk management. In addition, he has been invited to speak at the Asia Business Conference at Harvard University and the Asia Tomorrow Conference at Yale University. Professor Liaw served as president of the Chinese American Academic and Professional Society and was director at State Bancorp. He has received corporate assignments in asset management and capital markets and has also served in various capacities at several financial institutions.

Nannette Lindenberg is Economist at The German Aerospace Center (DLR) Project Management Agency. She has been Senior Researcher in the 'World Economy and Development Financing' Department at the German Development Institute/Deutsches Institut für Entwicklungspolitik (DIE) in Bonn and the University of Osnabrück, as well as a consultant for the World Bank and guest researcher at the WTO and at OECD. She specializes in climate economics and international finance, with a focus on green finance. Nannette holds a Master of Science in International Business Administration from the University of Tübingen and a PhD in International Economic Policy from the University of Osnabrück.

Frédéric de Mariz is Adjunct Professor at Columbia University's School of International and Public Affairs (SIPA) and Executive Director at a global investment bank. Frédéric has 15 years of experience in investment banking and is responsible for the coverage of Financial Institutions in Latin America. His professional experience includes senior roles at UBS, JPMorgan and Goldman Sachs. His team has been consistently ranked among the top three in independent industry surveys, such as Institutional Investors and Starmine. His team was also ranked #1 in Impact Investing by Euromoney 2017. His areas of expertise include the banking segment, FinTech and impact investing. Frédéric has Masters degrees from Columbia University (SIPA), La Sorbonne, Sciences Po, and has a MBA from ESSEC, Paris. He earned his PhD in Finance at the University of São Paulo (FEA-USP). He has published a number of academic articles and is a member of the Brazilian private equity association (ABVCAP), the sustainability Committee of the Brazilian Banking Association (FEBRABAN), the Brazilian Social Impact Bonds Committee, and has been an advisor to several microfinance institutions in Brazil.

Joseph R. Mason is the Hermann Moyse, Jr. Professor of Finance at Louisiana State University and Senior Fellow at the University of

Pennsylvania's Wharton School. After earning his PhD in Economics from the University of Illinois at Urbana-Champaign, Joseph worked at the US Office of the Comptroller of the Currency researching emerging risks to financial firms and the economy. Joseph's research interests are in financial institutions and economic growth, specifically dealing with topics involving sophisticated structured financial arrangements and their integral nature in today's financial system. He has published in the *American Economic Review*, *Journal of Business*, *Journal of Financial Intermediation*, *Journal of Money, Credit, and Banking* and other academic journals and books. Joseph has been a consultant to entities like the European Parliament, the International Monetary Fund, the Federal Reserve Bank of Philadelphia, and the Federal Deposit Insurance Corporation, among others, as well as corporations, consulting companies and law firms. Joseph has testified before numerous House and Senate Committees, the European Parliament and the Federal Reserve Board. He has made many television and radio appearances on CNBC, NBC News, Bloomberg Television and National Public Radio, and has been cited extensively in press articles worldwide.

Maria Mazzuca has been, since 2014, an Associate Professor of Banking and Finance at the University of Calabria (Italy), where she teaches Financial System and Financial Institutions Management. Maria graduated summa cum laude from the University of Calabria in 1997. Following a PhD in Banking and Finance, she was enrolled by her Alma Mater first as a Research Fellow, between 2004 and 2007, and then as an Assistant Professor of Banking and Finance from 2007 until 2014. She has worked on several research projects (with research grants from sources such as PRIN – research projects of national interest financed by the Italian Government – and Newfin-Bocconi University). Dr Mazzuca's main research interests are Italian and European banks, securitization, credit risk transfer activity, banks disclosure, corporate social responsibility, cooperative banks, social finance, and non-performing loans. Maria has authored numerous articles published in international journals and book chapters. Her research has been published in several prestigious peer-reviewed journals such as the *European Journal of Finance*, *Corporate Social Responsibility and Environmental Management*, *Sustainable Development*, *Business Ethics: A European Review* and *Public Money and Management*. She has reviewed numerous articles in many top-tier journals.

Ron P. McIver is a Lecturer in Financial Economics in the School of Commerce, University of South Australia, Australia, and member of the UniSA Business School's Centre for Applied Finance and Economics (CAFE). He holds a Bachelor of Economics (BEc), Bachelor of Economics

(Honours) (BEc (Hons)) and Master of Economics (MEc) from The Flinders University of South Australia, a Master of Applied Finance (MAppFin) from Macquarie University and a Post-Graduate Certificate in Education (PGCertEd) from the University of Greenwich. Ron's research encompasses corporate finance, banking and financial education. His publications include works on: the impact of ownership, particularly of the state, on financial performance in emerging-market and transition economies; governance and institutional structures' roles in delivering efficient outcomes in transition and emerging-market economies; state-owned enterprise reform; banking system regulation, reform, rehabilitation and efficiency, particularly in transition economies; the operation of water markets, including for environmental applications; culture and firm environmental performance; and teaching and learning methodologies based on student-centred and activity-based learning.

Christin Nitsche holds a BA in International Business Administration from the Berlin School of Economics and Law, Germany. During her Bachelor studies she spent a semester abroad at the University of California, Santa Barbara. In September 2014, Christin graduated with an MSc in Finance, with a major in Corporate Finance, from the Frankfurt School of Finance and Management, Germany. She earned the 1st advancement award of the 'Interessengemeinschaft Frankfurter Kreditinstitute GmbH' as best student of the 2014 graduates at the Frankfurt School. Her research interests include equity financial markets, especially socially responsible investments, as well as valuation and applied corporate finance. Besides her studies, Christin worked for five years in different finance departments at IBM. Since April 2015, she has been working in the Financial Advisory, Valuation & Modelling Department at Deloitte Stuttgart, Germany.

Giulia Porino holds an MA in Economic Sciences at the University of Turin and a post-graduate specialization at the Solvay Brussels School of Economics & Management. She currently works at Finance Watch, the public interest advocacy group working to make finance serve society, by coordinating their activities with members and a broader group of civil society actors as strategic stakeholders to achieve change in the global debate about financial reform. At the same time, she is a PhD candidate in Socio-Economic and Statistical Studies at Sapienza University of Rome. Her doctoral project aims to show the benefits of a greater diversity in the representation of interests within the financial sector from a gender perspective, by looking at the dysfunctions of its governance structure and behaviours. It stresses the urgent need for a public-interest driven agenda to shift the financial sector towards the generation of positive and long-term sustainable social and environmental externalities.

Julia M. Puaschunder has studied Psychology, Business and Economics, among other subjects. Julia M. Puaschunder has launched and administered research projects in many countries around the world. Apart from academic appointments in Austria, Julia has been a scholar at The Australian National University, Columbia University, Harvard University, Princeton University, Ludwig-Maximilians-University of Munich and The Open Society Institute & Soros Foundation New York. Currently, she is conducting research as a Prize Fellow in the Inter-University Consortium of New York. Throughout her academic career, Julia has been invited to present her research at Harvard University, Princeton University, Columbia University, Brown University, Oxford University and Cambridge University. She has published through Harvard University, Columbia University and Oxford University as well as in other journals. Julia has also organized conferences and public speakers from the Harvard Business School and Princeton University in Vienna. Since 2015 Julia Puaschunder has supported the Economics of Climate Change Project Speaker Series hosted at The Schwartz Center for Economic Policy Analysis of The New School for Social Research in New York City. Julia currently pursues the idea of Eternal Equity – responding to Western world intergenerational equity constraints in the domains of environmental sustainability, overindebtedness and demographic ageing, with a focus on law and mind sciences.

José Roberto Ferreira Savoia is Associate Professor of Finance at the Faculty of Business and Economics of the University of São Paulo. He received his PhD in Business from the University of São Paulo (1996). He is Director of the Center for Studies in Regulation and Public Policies. Previously, he was Adjunct Professor at SIPA – Columbia University (2007 and 2009), and Visiting Professor at The Open University Business School (2012). He has extensive expertise in the public sector, as the Superintendent of the City Pension Institute of São Paulo and Chairman of the Board (2010–2012). He was Secretary of Complementary Pensions, during Cardoso's Government (2000–2002) and took part in all the leading national boards related to Social Security and Pensions in Brazil. Professor Savoia has published articles in journals such as the *Journal of Business Research*, *Corporate Governance*, *Latin American Business Review*, *Journal of Applied Mathematics*, *Journal of Private Equity* and *Journal of Business & Policy Research*. He has also published books and book chapters in the fields of capital markets, social security and infrastructure.

Michael Schröder is Senior Researcher in the International Finance and Financial Management department at the Centre for European Economic Research (ZEW) in Mannheim, Germany. He is also a Senior Research Consultant at the Financial Research Center of the Fudan

University in Shanghai, China. Schröder studied Economics and Business Administration at the University of Mannheim. He was a research fellow at the University of Mannheim. Since 1990 he has held a doctoral degree in Economics from the University of Mannheim and in 2009 he received the *venia legendi* for Business Administration at the University of Stuttgart after finishing his Habilitation. From 2011 to 2015 he was an Adjunct Professor of Asset Management at the Frankfurt School of Finance & Management. His main topics of research in the field of empirical capital market analysis are: capital market regulation and effects on financial stability and the real economy; analysis of the formation of expectations on financial markets; socially responsible investments, corporate social responsibility, and ethical banking; asset management of charitable foundations; and capital markets in China.

Viktoryia Tankoyeva is a Business Development Manager at Sabinsa Europe (Germany). She graduated in Economics from Grodno State University (Belarus) and continued her academic studies, achieving a Masters in International Management at the University of Trento (Italy) with Professor Flavio Bazzana. Her main research interests are in the field of corporate finance and banking, financial modelling and analysis.

Jean-Laurent Viviani is Professor in Finance at IGR-IAE Rennes, and member of the CREM research lab, University of Rennes 1, France. He holds a PhD from University Paris XIII (awarded in 1990). His research areas include risk management in banks (liquidity risk and systemic risk) and companies, CSR-SRI and Islamic Banking, Real Option Theory (applied to sustainable development) and Supply Chain Finance. Professor Viviani has published numerous articles and book chapters in journals such as *Energy Policy*, *European Journal of Agricultural Economics*, *Business Ethics: A European Review*, and *The European Journal of Finance*.

Linh Chi Vo is Professor of Strategic Management at Ecole de Management de Normandie, France. Linh Chi graduated from Queensland University of Technology (BA), Australia, Washington State University (MBA), USA and Ecole Centrale Paris (PhD), France. Linh Chi's main research interests include corporate social responsibility, board gender diversity and John Dewey's philosophy of pragmatism. She has published in various journals such as the *Journal of Organizational Change Management* and *M@n@gement*. She co-authored the John Dewey chapter in the *Oxford Handbook of Process Philosophy and Organization Studies*. Linh Chi has taught at various institutions in different countries, including the University of Northern Iowa, Kozminski University and the University of Economics Krakow.

Olaf Weber is a professor and head of the graduate programme in Sustainability Management at the School of Environment, Enterprise and Development (SEED), University of Waterloo, Canada. Furthermore, he is a Senior Research Fellow at the Centre for International Governance Innovation (CIGI) in Waterloo, Canada. His research fields are sustainable finance, sustainable banking, social banking and impact investment. Recently he has been focusing on the impact of financial sector sustainability regulations and codes of conduct on the stability and sustainability of the financial industry. Before coming to the University of Waterloo he was head of the sustainable finance group at the Swiss Federal Institute for Technology, Zurich, and a managing partner of GOE, a consulting firm for sustainable banking and corporate sustainability. Olaf Weber holds a PhD from the University of Bielefeld, Germany and a Masters degree in psychology from the University of Mannheim, Germany. His research is published in a number of peer-reviewed journals and books, such as *Sustainable Banking*, published by Toronto University Press.

Alireza Zarei is Senior Lecturer at the Sunway University of Malaysia. He holds a PhD in Economics (awarded in 2015). He undertook his tertiary education in Iran, India (Pune University) and Malaysia, where he obtained a PhD at the rated University Putra Malaysia. Among his current research interests are the following: exchange rate dynamics in major and emerging economies; asset pricing within monetary economics frameworks; economic modelling in general; international economics and finance; applied financial econometrics; and Islamic banking and finance. He has published in Web of Science journals: *Open Economies Review*, *The Singapore Economic Review*, *Pertanika Journal of Social Sciences and Humanities* and the *Asian Academy of Management, Journal of Accounting and Finance*.

Introduction

Climate change and ongoing economic and social transformations in the context of increasing digitalization have been posing a number of challenging issues for our societies. On the one hand, the industrialization waves across countries and the emission of greenhouse gases have been recognized as main factors that cause global warming and serious damage to environmental quality, human health and economic activities through natural catastrophes and abrupt weather changes. On the other hand, economic and financial crises over the recent decades have sparked off intense debate about new models for economic growth as well as on the efficient use of natural resources without creating harmful impacts on the living conditions of future generations. These challenges have pushed social stakeholders, businesses and governments around the world to initiate, encourage and adopt sustainable practices.

It is also important to stress that the 2015 United Nations Climate Change Conference in Paris (COP21) has made climate change an issue for the future of the whole finance industry and community. Accordingly, financial research, practices and initiatives should be an efficient pathway to direct investment flows towards sustainable development projects through, among others, low-carbon emission businesses, sustainable finance, renewable energy, clean technology and climate funding. This move is effectively the triple bottom line framework – the concept that has been introduced by John Elkington in his 1997 book *Cannibals with Forks: The Triple Bottom Line of 21st Century Business* and ultimately requires economic agents and policymakers to make decisions with respect not only to the financial dimension, but also to the social and environmental dimensions.

To date, the triple bottom line has become increasingly used as criteria to assess the sustainability of financial markets, industries, institutions and corporations. It particularly concerns: (i) the development of financial services and products to cope with sustainable investing and climate risk management; (ii) a regulation framework that guarantees the stability and resilience of financial markets as far as they provide a vital source of capital for economic growth; and (iii) the governance issues that aim to manage organizational risks, the corporate social responsibility culture, and the social-impact investing culture.

The *Research Handbook of Investing in the Triple Bottom Line* recognizes the growing trends in sustainable finance and investing where social, environmental and financial measures are employed to evaluate the sustainable behaviour of economic actors and institutions. It places a special focus on the increasing research and practical initiatives related to, among other factors, impact investment, finance and sustainable development, socially responsible firms, the stock returns of sustainable firms, and financial instruments connected with sustainability issues.

The *Research Handbook* is composed of 20 topical and high-quality chapters which are grouped into three parts: 'Sustainability, Financial Stability and Fraud' (seven chapters); 'Sustainability and Financial Markets' (eight chapters); and 'CSR and Socially Responsible Investment' (five chapters). Part I treats the link between sustainability issues and system-wide financial stability. Part II is devoted to the role of financial markets in promoting sustainability through the development of impact investing instruments and regulation policies. Part III sheds lights on the emergence of socially responsible investors and the impact of their dedicated portfolio allocation, as well as firms' CSR commitments.

Part I of the *Handbook* begins with Chapter 1, 'Financial Regulation and Fraud in CO_2 Markets', by Joseph R. Mason. This chapter suggests that the inefficacy of the carbon markets in reducing CO_2 emissions could be explained not only by the low carbon allowance prices, but also by non-fundamental factors such as fraud (investors, corporations), counterfeiting and rent-seeking, which altogether influence the pricing of carbon emissions. By analysing the European Union's Emissions Trading Scheme's market for carbon emissions, the author shows that a good functioning of this market could not be guaranteed and the objective of carbon reduction would not be achieved if these various forms of fraud exist. The same situation can occur in other carbon markets, which could lead to their serious disruptions and destruction.

Chapter 2, 'How to Better Detect Cases of Financial Reporting Fraud: Some New Findings from Earnings Restatements', by François Aubert, Jean-François Gajewski and Lamya Kermiche focuses on the detection of frauds based on the managed earnings component (MEC) metric and discretionary accrual-based models. They show, from a comprehensive sample of Accounting and Auditing Enforcement Releases (AAERs) issued by the SEC, that the innovative managed earnings component metric of a firm as an independent variable provides a more relevant indicator of accounting fraud than cross-sectional models based on inspecting abnormal accruals. This finding should help regulators to improve fraud detection by preventing voluntary financial misreporting.

Chapter 3, 'Fostering Green Investment Decisions: The Real Option Approach', by Jessica Fouilloux and Jean-Laurent Viviani argues that green investing decisions can be modelled by the real option approach, given its sequential and irreversible characteristics under uncertainty. Concretely, companies have an option to delay, make or extend a green investment such as a shift from polluting to green technologies. Their analyses show that the 'wait and see' approach of the traditional option theory is not appropriate to judge green investment opportunities.

Chapter 4, 'Exchange Rate Instability: Relative Volatility, Risk and Adjustment Speed', by Mohamed Ariff and Alireza Zarei looks at the issue of exchange rate volatility as it is critical to the management of a possible currency crisis. The authors develop four measures of relative instability (relative volatility; interquartile range; degree of co-integration; and speed of adjustment to benchmark currencies of peers) and show that they are useful for tracking, benchmarking and managing foreign exchange market instability, based on 14 international currencies.

In Chapter 5, 'Financial Instability: Economic and Financial Perspectives', Michael Dempsey reviews the academic research and theoretical models related to the market-wise financial instability issue, given its important impact on growth. The author shows that a better understanding of market instability could only be achieved with the recognition of deviations from market efficiency and equilibrium as well as of endogenous market cycles.

Chapter 6, 'The Stability of the Financial System: An Analysis of the Determinants of Russian Bank Failures', by Viktoryia Tankoyeva, Flavio Bazzana and Roberto Gabriele from University of Trento (Italy) shifts attention to the financial stability of banks and focuses on the case of Russia. The authors employ an early warning system and a contemporaneous model based on the CAMELS (Capital adequacy, Assets quality, Management, Earnings, Liquidity) approach. Their findings suggest that the Central Bank of Russia should have a closer look at the dynamics of CAMELS variables when assessing Russian bank solvency.

On a related issue, Kizito Uyi Ehigiamusoe and Hooi Hooi Lean in Chapter 7, 'Sovereign Wealth Funds and Macroeconomic Stability: Before and After their Establishment', analyse the nexus between SWFs and macroeconomic stability through various economic indicators. Their results suggest that the integration of the SWFs into a country's fiscal policy fosters macroeconomic stability, particularly when the SWFs are created with definitive objectives, effective management, accountability and transparency.

Part II of the *Handbook* addresses sustainability issues in financial markets and begins with Chapter 8, 'Financial Markets like Potter's Hands? Rethinking Finance for Sustainability in a Civil Society Perspective', by Giulia Porino, which discusses new ideas and directions for building a sustainable financial system with a greater commitment from the civil society. The analysis leads the author to conclude that the participation of civil society organizations in the debate about sustainable finance plays a pivotal role in shaping the political agenda for financial reform policies.

Chapter 9 by Eleonora Broccardo and Maria Mazzuca offers 'An Alternative Way to Think of Finance: The Case of Innovative, Sustainable Financial Instruments'. It investigates how financial innovations and financial engineering (particularly green bonds and social impact bonds) can contribute to sustainable development. Risk and challenges related to these newly proposed financial instruments are also discussed.

Chapter 10, 'The Market Premium of Sustainability in Health-Care Sector Firms', by G. Nathan Dong (Columbia University, United States) investigates whether health-care firms simultaneously achieve sustainability and financial performance. Interestingly, the author finds that sustainable firms are awarded a market premium in terms of market valuation, which is discounted for firms that have a higher level of environmental pollution.

In Chapter 11, 'Environmental Sustainability and Inter- and Intra-Industry Variation in Stock Returns: International Evidence', Harjap Bassan, Kartick Gupta and Ron P. McIver question the inter-industry and intra-industry (country-level) differences in terms of stock returns across firms which engage in environmentally sustainable practices. Their results show that market rewards for environmentally sustainable practices are not alike across industries. At the country level, stock returns are found to be negatively associated with low institutional quality.

Chapter 12, 'The Role of Financial Markets in Promoting Sustainability – a Review and Research Framework', by Mohammed Amidu and Haruna Issahaku provides a review of previous research on the link between finance and sustainable development. It shows that the literature mostly focused on sustainability financing and responsible investing as well as sustainable finance. By contrast, little is known about the sustainability implications of Islamic finance and regulation policies.

Chapter 13, 'Financial Innovation with a Social Purpose: The Growth of Social Impact Bonds', by Frédéric de Mariz and José Roberto Ferreira Savoia focuses on the analysis of the structure of social impact bonds, which have been developed to attain sustainable development goals (social outcome) through a public-private collaboration. Their results indicate that socially impact bonds can encourage a sustainable economy, but they need to be standardized and have strong support from the regulation bodies and governmental authorities.

Among the new financial instruments of climate finance, green bonds have been growing rapidly. In Chapter 14, 'Asset Allocation and the

Green Bond Market', K. Thomas Liaw reviews the risk-return characteristics of green bonds as well as their diversifying potential for portfolio investments. Besides the willingness to combat climate change, green bonds would be of great interest to investors if their returns are less than perfectly correlated with other existing financial instruments.

Similarly, in Chapter 15, 'Demystifying Green Bonds', Kathrin Berensmann, Florence Dafe and Nannette Lindenberg examine the potential and challenges of green bonds in making the ecological transition happen. They particularly question whether the rapid growth of green bond issuance is associated with a greener economy. Their analysis concludes with the limited contributions of green bonds to sustainable development under weak governance frameworks, as is the case today.

A large body of the literature and current debates on sustainability have focused on the adoption of CSR by organizations and on Socially Responsible Investment (SRI). Part III of this *Handbook* dedicates five chapters to these issues.

In Chapter 16, 'Models of Corporate Socially Responsible Banks: Financial Cooperatives, Islamic Banks, and Micro-Finance Institutions', Narjess Boubakri and Jocelyn Grira present three CSR models for banking firms: the model of cooperative financial institutions; the model of microfinance institutions; and the Islamic banking model. For each model, the authors discuss successively its distinctive characteristics, its contributions to socioeconomic development, and its role in promoting ethical business standards and practices. Their findings point to a heterogeneity of CSR practices across financial institutions.

Chapter 17, 'CSR Implementation in French SMEs: An Adapted Framework', by Karen Delchet-Cochet and Linh Chi Vo focuses on the CSR engagement of French SMEs and discusses its implementation through two projects: the Global Performance procedure and the SD21000 implementation guideline. The authors stress the need for specific CSR implementation tools that are adapted to SMEs.

Chapter 18, 'The Performance, Volatility, Downside Risk and Persistence of Socially Responsible Investments in Korea and the Impact of the Korean Green New Deal', by Wei Rong Ang and Olaf Weber shows that the performance of SRI in Korea improves with the Korean Green New Deal, and the Korean sustainable portfolios are less sensitive to market downside situations than the conventional portfolios.

Chapter 19 by Christin Nitsche and Michael Schröder asks an intriguing question: 'Are SRI Funds Conventional Funds in Disguise or Do They Live up to Their Name?' It uses the ESG (Environmental, Social and Governance) ratings of three rating agencies (Oekom, Sustainalytics and ASSET4) to examine the rating differences between a European and a global fund universe. Their results indicate a significant difference in ratings between the two funds, with the sustainable fund having higher ratings, while the holdings are relatively similar for both funds. Accordingly, the authors suggest that SRI funds do make investments with respect to their principles.

Chapter 20, 'Socio-psychological Motives of Socially Responsible Investors', by Julia M. Puaschunder seeks to understand the potential socio-psychological motives of socially responsible investors to engage in social impact investing. The author proposes a financial social responsibility framework that combines an SRI framework with social and psychological dimensions. Factors such as innovation and entrepreneurship, self-enhancement through identification and self-consistency, expression of social values, and long-term considerations appear to strengthen the financial social responsibility of economic agents.

Altogether, the diverse lessons and reflections presented in all the abovementioned chapters are obviously indicative of an increasing awareness and application of the triple bottom line principle at various levels (firms, markets and economies). While sustainability makes sense and there is a good chance for SRI and system stability to succeed, many challenges exist, ranging from misconduct behaviour to regulatory frameworks and efficient financial innovations. Social and psychological factors, which influence the decision-making process of different shareholders, are also critical drivers of the move towards sustainability. Finally, it is important to recognize that the 'one-size-fits-all' statement does not apply to all actors involved in sustainable development.

We firmly believe that the *Research Handbook of Investing in the Triple Bottom Line* will provide readers with a comprehensive state of the art and an in-depth reflection on what has been done and what has to be done as far as sustainable and impact finance is concerned. Challenges ahead need to be better analysed and understood. We hope that stakeholders, and particularly investors, fund managers, firm executives and regulators will find this *Handbook* useful for planning their actions and strategies. Likewise, this collection of chapters will help students and researchers be better informed and find valuable materials to develop their research agendas.

We would like to take this occasion to thank all the contributors of this *Handbook* for their excellent commitment and fine contributions.

Sabri Boubaker
Douglas Cumming
Duc Khuong Nguyen

PART I

SUSTAINABILITY, FINANCIAL STABILITY AND FRAUD

1. Financial regulation and fraud in CO_2 markets

Joseph R. Mason

1. INTRODUCTION

Classical literature like that of Rosen (2005), Samuelson (1954), and Baumol and Oates (1988) proposed cap and trade as an alternative to levying usage taxes to curb privately beneficial, but socially undesirable action. In economic terms, the goal of both measures is to curb a recognized and measurable externality.

The idea seems simple, on its face. Public finance, and more specifically the sub-discipline of environmental economics, defines the theoretical optimality of the choice between cap and trade and abatement taxes. The optimal outcome can be achieved either through cap and trade or through a pollution charge. Specifically, capping the quantity of emissions that can be produced results in the equality of marginal abatement costs and the marginal benefits of abatement at a market price to the polluter. On the other hand, by creating a price for every unit of carbon that is emitted, producers have an incentive to reduce the quantity of emissions (n). If the set price lies above the cost of reducing emissions it is less costly to reduce pollutants than to pay the tax. Therefore, an emissions price (or tax) theoretically has the same effect on the market as an emissions quantity cap.

Setting either prices (P) or quantities (Q) with certainty is key to the environmental debate around carbon policy. It is not clear, from a purely theoretical basis, whether cost certainty or benefit certainty is more important in the carbon abatement debate. Some scholars have argued that a focus on benefit certainty is theoretically superior because it puts the emphasis on the environment rather than on the economics (see, e.g., Baumol and Oates, 1988 at 74).

That seemingly straightforward argument favoring benefit certainty, however, ignores key empirical dynamics with regard to carbon prices already demonstrated in the experience of the European Union's Emissions Trading Scheme ('EU ETS').

The pervasiveness of heterogeneous cap and trade programs and growing incidents of fraud in the sector likely exacerbate asymmetric information in the overall product market, creating market price anomalies that can ultimately upend policy development and implementation.

If substantial asymmetric information exists regarding the potential for political risk and fraud to interfere with the use of carbon permits, a greater supply of permits will be necessary to achieve any chosen level of benefit. That is, issuing permits that *exactly* match the desired emissions will overprice the desired benefits.

The remainder of this chapter describes conditions precedent in modern CO_2 markets that would suggest such overpricing will be the norm in current institutional arrangements. Cap and trade markets cannot achieve benefit certainty with substantial price uncertainty arising from factors beyond fundamental supply and demand.

This chapter first describes briefly the relationship between EU ETS development and CO_2 price volatility, showing that volatility has been far higher than expected by economists. Whether modeled as a commodity contract or an option, CO_2 contracts simply do not conform to known price models and expected dynamics. The chapter then suggests a key explanation for such deviations from known pricing models, reviewing many of the known incidents of investor fraud, corporate fraud, and counterfeiting and theft that have interrupted EU ETS CO_2 market operations during the first ten years of its existence. As CO_2 contracts become more widely used – and as prices hopefully rise – such fraud and malfeasance will become more valuable to perpetrators, leading to further incidents similar to the ones described herein. Existing economic theory suggests that markets can be expected to continue to price the probability of such disruptions, upsetting CO_2 price dynamics and potentially destroying the EU ETS and similar systems.

2. WEATHER ANOMALIES AND POLITICAL RISK IN CO_2 MARKET PRICING

Carbon prices under cap and trade systems have been far more volatile than originally envisioned. Part of the problem is related to carbon permit demand that fluctuates with weather conditions that are highly correlated with electric power generation. Equally important, however, is that it has become apparent in recent years that exhibited price anomalies are the result of both weather conditions *and* political uncertainties as well as idiosyncrasies in the carbon permit contract that enable fraud by investors, corporations, and others.

The European Union provides a wealth of information and data on markets that have developed from cap and trade programs. In the EU ETS, both cash and futures contracts are traded in a variety of markets. While trade with EU Allowances ('EUAs') began in 2003, the official EU ETS began in 2005. Prices before 2005 were, therefore, forward prices on a not yet traded underlying asset. In the 'pre-2005' period, the traded volume was quite low, at some days even zero as the highest bidder price was smaller than the lowest seller price. Daily EUA prices between August 27, 2003 and December 29, 2004, before agreement on EU ETS, were generally stable. The price during this entire period was stable during any small time window, and fluctuated between €7 and €13 over the entire 18-month period, with bid-ask spreads that were quite large, often exceeding €4.

By contrast, prices between early 2005 and December 29, 2006 fluctuated greatly. Prices spiked at nearly €30 in July 2005 and again in April 2006, and fell to lows of about €6 by December 2006 (see, e.g., Benz and Trück, 2009 for a detailed review of price dynamics). Figure 1.1 confirms

Source: Thomson Reuters Point Carbon (2016).

Figure 1.1 *EU ETS carbon prices, 2005–2015*

that the price of carbon futures fell significantly during 2006. Prices then rose through 2007 and the first half of 2008, but plummeted after July 2008.

Important drivers of the market seem to be a combination of short-run weather and political policy announcements rather than any long-term economic fundamentals. Before the EU Parliament agreed on the introduction of the EU ETS in July 2003 and before the first suggestions for National Allocation Plans ('NAPs') were published at the end of 2003, prices were stable. Both announcements led to an increase in prices. Because of the initially generous allocation of allowances to the countries, prices calmed down again between February and March 2004. Reviewing and accepting the NAPs in the second half of the year, prices increased to about €9. Benz and Trück (2009 at 11–12) show that as the main framework of the trading scheme became defined, the price determinants became more fundamental after January 2005.

Chief among those fundamentals, however, is the weather. For example, Thomson Reuters Point Carbon (2006) notes that prices fell in 2005 due to mild weather and a high supply of wind energy from Scandinavia and North Germany. At the end of January 2005, cold weather and high gas and oil prices in the United Kingdom, coupled with low coal prices, resulted in a strong price increase of EUAs. This effect was magnified by a dry summer in July 2005 in southwestern Europe. Low rainfall depleted reserves and prevented full utilization of hydroelectric plants. The lack of cooling water for nuclear power plants resulted in greater utilization of high emission-producing assets, which therefore increased the demand for carbon permits. By July 2005, prices peaked at €29.15. During the last four months of 2005, prices fell to €22. By March 2006, however, prices again increased to approximately €27, due to a long and cold winter between 2005 and 2006.

May 2006 marked completion of the first full cycle of the EU ETS. Benz and Trück (2009 at 11–12) note that by April 2006, however, it was apparent that a surplus of allowances of approximately 10 percent existed. As a consequence, EUA prices fell by 60 percent within one week, amid fears that emissions prices would drop to zero. The EUA market recovered during the summer of 2006 as the industrial sector began selling EUAs to utilities investors as a dry and hot European summer increased the demand for high-emissions assets.

The European experience outlined above is important because the primary purpose of a cap-and-trade-based carbon market is to provide long-term incentives for firms to invest in clean-air technologies. Such technologies – nuclear assets or clean-air coal assets, for example – are costly to build and they are large baseload units that are technologically intensive. Private investment in these types of assets only makes sense if the long-term benefits of the investment are clear. With carbon permit prices fluctuating wildly, long-term signals regarding the carbon-reducing benefits of investment in clean-air technology are clouded at best and non-existent at worst. Therefore, it is not apparent that a cap and trade system resulting in a market for carbon permits is helpful in aligning private interests with policymakers' long-term goals: the dissemination of technologies that will reduce carbon emissions.

As it stands, CO_2 prices do not conform to commodity price dynamics or option price dynamics, responding more to weather and political risks than financial market and trading influences. The next two sub-sections describe some of the existing evidence underlying current understanding of emissions permit prices.

2.1 While Carbon Permits Are Usually Thought of as a Commodity Contract Because the Deliverable Is a Factor of Production, Price Dynamics of the Contracts Are Not those Expected for Commodities

Cap and trade contracts – being an input to production – were expected to demonstrate the standard behavior of commodity contracts. A commodity contract is a contract to deliver a raw product or primary input such as food, metal, or energy. Since the allowances are used for production, they are removed from the market as they are consumed. Therefore, the right to emit carbon can be compared with other commodities that are traditionally used as factor inputs in production, and standard commodity pricing models can be applied to the carbon emissions market (Benz and Trück, 2009 at 4–15.)

Commodity markets work on a *spot* and a *futures* basis. The spot market is the market for immediate delivery of the commodity. The futures market is the market for delivering the commodity at some point in the future. The futures market is a derivatives market, meaning that its value is derived from the current spot market for the underlying asset. The spot and futures market for the EU's current cap and trade contracts exists on a number of different commodity exchanges. Empirical data from these exchanges can show whether the real-world pricing of cap and trade contracts conforms to the price behavior of other commodities possessing similar characteristics.

The expected future value of a commodity is equal to the current spot price plus carrying costs. This can be stated as

$$F_t = Se^{(r-\delta)(T-t)}, \tag{1}$$

where F is the future price, S is the current spot price, r is the risk-free rate, δ is the carrying cost, t is today, and T is the maturity of the contract.

The conditions just described are the result of what are commonly referred to as arbitrage conditions. If, for instance, the futures price was above the spot price plus storage, arbitrageurs could sell futures and buy on the spot market, storing the commodity for future delivery at a riskless profit. The opposite also generally holds true.

But Paolella and Taschini (2008 at 13–14) establish that in the case of carbon emissions, the optimal level of emissions is stochastic, so that a firm's demand for emissions allowance contracts is also stochastic. When faced with supply uncertainty, a firm benefits from holding an inventory of the commodity.

The benefit that accrues from holding the underlying commodity rather than the contract for the future is known as the *convenience yield*. The convenience yield keeps spot prices higher relative to futures prices – a pricing structure known as *backwardation*. Backwardation can be expressed in [1] as a condition in which δ represents a positive convenience yield. In other words, the convenience yield is sufficiently large such that the future price is less than the spot price. In addition, the future price decreases as time to maturity increases.

The opposite of a backwardation structure is *contango* – spot prices are less than futures prices. Empirical evidence from the EU carbon market shows that the carbon futures market illustrates characteristics not of backwardation, but of contango, where spot prices are less than futures prices. But the financial economics literature suggests that commodities with contango structures usually have readily available inventories that are easily accessed and stored and stable supply and demand functions (Paolella and Taschini, 2008 at 15).

Those conditions contradict the performance of carbon markets to date. The reason that commodities used for production can demonstrate backwardation is that supply uncertainty varies across time. When such uncertainty is present, allowances for different vintages can have different spot prices at a given point in time. Thus, even if cap and trade contracts have no cost of storage and are easily accessed, levels of supply and demand for carbon emissions are not easily predicted. In addition, the level of inventories for cap and trade contracts is dependent on current emission levels, which are stochastic and unpredictable.

Because the empirically observed convenience yield for cap and trade contracts does not conform to standard finance theory for commodities, a price analysis based on a historically consistent theory of future-spot parity is probably not very useful (see, e.g., Paolella and Taschini, 2008 and Borak et al., 2006.)

2.2 While Carbon Permits Can Be Considered an Option Contract Because the Producer Can Choose Whether to Use the Allowances in any given Settlement Period, Price Dynamics of the Contracts Are Not those Expected for Typical Options

A futures contract only allows for delivery at a specific date in the future. A carbon contract can be used for production at any time within that period, until expiration. A carbon cap and trade contract may therefore be more like an option than a future, potentially with different price dynamics. (For a primer on financial options, see Hull [2006].)

An option is a contract between a buyer and seller that gives the buyer the right, but not the obligation, to buy or sell an asset at a specified price on or before a specified date. The option to buy an asset is known as a call option, and the right to sell an asset is known as a put option. In the context of a carbon market, an emissions contract would be similar to a put option because it allows the contract holder to exercise a right to emit carbon during a specific time period – the owner has the right to 'sell' their CO_2.

A multi-period cap and trade contract can be characterized as a sequence of European put options (options that can be exercised at a specific expiration date in the future) that come into effect sequentially through the life of a contract. The decision of when to exercise each put option is characterized as a real option, an optimal-stopping-time problem, similar to the problem of early exercise on an American option. Consistent with common intuition, early exercise is optimal only when the holder's demand for emissions increases.

One of the most common models to price options is the Black-Scholes model. According to the Black-Scholes valuation model, the value p of a European put on a non-dividend paying asset is estimated by

$$p = Xe^{-r_f T}\Phi(-d_2) - S\Phi(-d_1), \text{ where} \tag{2}$$

$$d_1 = \frac{\ln(S/X) + r_f T}{\sigma\sqrt{T}} + \frac{1}{2}\sigma\sqrt{T}$$

$$d_2 = d_1 - \sigma\sqrt{T}$$

Φ = the standard normal cumulative distribution function;
X = strike price;
S = price of the underlying asset;
T = time to maturity;
r_f = discount rate; and
σ = volatility of the underlying asset value.

The cap and trade 'option' can be traded and a market participant could value the put option using the Black-Scholes model. The Black-Scholes model, however, has numerous shortcuts and anomalies that limit its use in valuing even common stock options for which it was designed.

First, the model is only used to value an option if it were to be exercised at expiration (European options). Therefore, it cannot value American options which can be exercised at any point in time before expiration.

Second, the model also assumes that the return on the underlying asset is normally distributed, which may not be the case for carbon emissions, and has certainly not been the case for stocks. (Historically, stock market returns have been skewed or *leptokurtic* – exhibiting more returns in the 'tails' of the distribution than would be found in a normal distribution) (see, e.g., Mandelbrot, 1963; Fama, 1965; Theodossiou, 1998).

Third, the model assumes a constant discount rate, even though the discount rate could change over the life of the contract. Fourth, the model assumes a constant volatility of the underlying asset, which market experience has already shown to vary substantially over time.

The empirical literature testing the accuracy of the Black-Scholes model is enormous. Although most studies confirm that market prices generally are close to the estimates resulting from Black-Scholes, many important anomalies have been found. Several alternatives to the Black-Scholes exist, but they each have their own problems.

In addition to the established anomalies of Black-Scholes and other models in pricing stock options, the market for carbon emissions has its own anomalies that complicate the valuation of cap and trade contracts as options. As discussed above, cap and trade contracts leave holders with the risk of having too few abatement options at the end of the commitment term when they may need those options. Alternatively, a firm that holds more permits than it expects to need may still hold onto the surplus because those permits have some option value, given that purchasing options in the future may be costly. Illiquidity arises endogenously from the fact that firms cannot emit without having permits and thus fear that they may face a market squeeze at the end of the year. The combination of the general anomalies of commodities and options valuation models with the anomalies in the carbon emissions market seriously complicates the valuation of cap and trade permits.

2.3 Exhibited Characteristics of Carbon Permit Prices Confirm that They Are Tremendously Complex Financial Contracts so that Financial Economics Is Unlikely to Find the True Value of 'Cap and Trade' Permits

Emission allowance prices have exhibited periods of high volatility, arising in part due to the correlation between CO_2 emissions and external events such as seasonal changes and environmental disasters. Those external factors increase the difficulty of modeling emission allowance values, making it difficult for market participants to plan ahead for their future carbon emissions.

Similar dynamics are common in other emissions markets. Producers of SO_2 emissions have been granted allowance permits through the United States Acid Rain Program since 1995. Paolella and Taschini (2008) suggest that the spot price for SO_2, at least from June 2003 until November 2005, could be consistent with a stochastic mean-reverting process with a constant positive drift, as desired by cap and trade policy. The prices dropped precipitously after November 2005, however, suggesting that an assumption that the SO_2 cap and trade market was working correctly and that the policy was responsible for the gradual upward trend in price movement would most likely be wrong (Paolella and Taschini, 2008 at 7–8). The point is that shocks routinely upset even well-functioning emissions markets.

Studies of the European CO_2 markets illustrate similar anomalous collapses. According to market participants, political and regulatory uncertainties, weather, and fuel prices were the most important *and* most volatile factors affecting allowance prices (Uhrig-Homburg and Wagner, 2009). Weather changes (such as temperature, rainfall, and wind speed), fuel prices, and economic growth all affect CO_2 production levels. Unexpected events, such as power plant breakdowns or environmental disasters that shock the supply and demand balance for CO_2, and changes in fuel spreads shock the demand *and* supply side of CO_2 allowances and consequently market prices (Benz and Trück, 2009 at 6).

For example, energy consumption (and hence CO_2 emissions) increases with cold weather. Non-CO_2 power generation is affected by rainfall and wind speed. In addition, the relative costs of coal, oil, and natural gas affect the decision to move forward with CO_2 abatement projects, and fuel switching costs can be high. These sources of price uncertainty have a short or medium-term impact on liquidity, which in turn affects the volatility of emission allowance prices (Benz and Trück, 2009 at 6). In addition, the prohibition on banking emission allowances between distinct phases of the EU ETS significantly affects futures pricing in that market (Daskalakisa, Psychoyiosb, and Markellosa, 2009).

As a result of the complex fundamental dynamics, forecasting models based on fundamentals and future-spot parity of CO_2 yield implausible results due to market complexity and to the particular behavior of the allowances, such as inconsistent behavior of CO_2 allowance convenience yields (Paolella and Taschini, 2008). Other studies have also shown that CO_2 emission allowance prices are nonstationary and exhibit abrupt discontinuous shifts, short periods of high volatility, with heavy tails in the distribution (Daskalakisa, Psychoyiosb, and Markellosa, 2009). One study analyzing the dynamic behavior of CO_2 emission allowance spot prices for the European emissions market demonstrates that steep price increases typically occur when the end of the trading period is approaching, in contrast to a smooth approach to spot prices demonstrated in typical commodity markets (Seifert, Uhrig-Homburg, and Wagner, 2008).

The institutional and financial characteristics described above make the choice of a proper statistical model crucial (albeit perhaps impossible) for purposes of risk management and carbon permit securities valuation. Given the interrelationship of carbon prices with both fundamental and policy variables, emission allowance prices and returns will exhibit different periods of behavior that include price spikes, volatility spikes, and heteroskedastic returns. The 'jumpiness' of price series necessitates using not only traditional time series models, but jump and jump-diffusion models to analyze the statistical properties of the series (Benz and Trück, 2009).

The dynamics discussed above are not limited to the EU. In addition to the EU cap and trade emission allowances, which are government-issued offsets that are limited in supply, other 'low cost' emission credits that will assist the countries that are signatories to the Kyoto protocol in meeting their emission reduction targets include Certified Emission Reductions ('CERs') and Emission Reduction Units ('ERUs'). CERs are created from projects in developing countries such as Brazil, Mexico, China and India that reduce greenhouse gas, whereas ERUs are allowances that have been allocated to mainly Eastern European countries that have already met their emission reduction targets. CERs and ERUs are both fully fungible with the EU emission allowances and can therefore be banked and traded within the EU ETS. According to an early 2006 report, some project developers had already sold forward their CERs for delivery in 2006 and 2007, while others were banking their CERs until the price became more favorable (Borod and Tan, 2006).

An important lesson from the EU's experience with CER and ERUs is the arbitrage opportunities that have arisen due to the significant price difference between EU allowances and CERs. Funds and other entities finance energy projects that result in CERs. Then, those entities aggregate the CERs that are produced and create pools of carbon credits that are diversified across projects and countries (Borod and Tan, 2006). These arbitrage opportunities mitigate both credit and country risk, but further complicate efforts to price emission allowance contracts alone.

Given the number of pricing anomalies that exist in financial markets, and the fact that carbon permits would share properties, at least in part, with many financial assets whose prices exhibit similar – but not identical – anomalies, valuations driven by cap and trade markets are unlikely to uncover the true price of carbon permits in the multiple sources of statistical noise in market prices. Although uncertainty may surround the value of such contracts *ex ante*, one can be sure that market participants will soon discover weaknesses in either the contract terms or the market structure and will seek to exploit any arbitrage opportunities that present themselves. Consequently, the nascent market will have to be monitored closely and carefully regulated. Market regulation itself, however, is far from efficient and fraught with difficulties so that, in fact, such opportunities are already manifest.

3. CO_2 PERMIT FRAUD

CO_2 markets have been embroiled in fraud and market interruptions since their inception, making them unsuitable for managing emissions without exposing the broader economy to the potential for commodity market panics and crashes.

The Interpol Environmental Crime Programme now lists ten classifications of carbon crimes that have already occurred throughout the world and continue to remain a threat (Interpol Environmental Crime Programme, 2013). These include:

- Manipulating measurements to fraudulently claim additional carbon credits (additionality);
- Sale of carbon credits that either do not exist or belong to someone else;
- False or misleading claims with respect to the environmental or financial benefits of carbon market investments;
- Exploitation of weak regulations to commit financial crimes;
- Tax fraud;
- Securities fraud;
- Transfer mispricing;
- Money laundering;
- Internet crimes and computer hacking to steal carbon credits; and
- Phishing/theft of personal information or identity theft.

The important point for the economics of cap and trade is that each market disruption creates greater uncertainty for end users of carbon permits, creating a classic 'lemons' discount on market prices. As the Nobel Prize-winning economist George Akerlof has explained:

> Consider a market in which goods are sold honestly or dishonestly; quality may be represented, or it may be misrepresented. The purchaser's problem of course, is to identify quality. The presence of people in the market who are willing to offer inferior goods tends to drive the market out of existence . . . It is this possibility that represents the major costs of dishonesty – for dishonest dealings tend to drive honest dealings out of the market. There may be potential buyers of good quality products and there may be potential sellers of such products in the appropriate price range; however, the presence of people who wish to pawn bad wares as good wares tends to drive out the legitimate business. The cost of dishonesty, therefore, lies not only in the amount by which the purchaser is cheated; the cost also must include the loss incurred from driving legitimate business out of existence. (Akerlof, 1970 at 495)

In the presence of such quality uncertainty, therefore, prices are bid down to adjust for the probability of fraud, no matter what quantity is supplied via the cap and trade policy.

3.1 Investor Fraud

By 2008, the environmental finance sector already included 90 hedge funds and 80 private equity funds, as well as mutual funds, ETFs, and venture capitalist funds. According to a survey by Carbon Finance, a carbon market data service, over 2008–09, funds under management grew by 20 per cent to $16.1bn. The number of carbon funds and government purchase programs over that period increased from 80 to 88 (*Financial Times*, 2009a). '[T]hirty-eight of the 88 funds listed are governmental carbon purchasing vehicles, or are run by multi-laterals either for governments or emitting companies, or a combination. . . . The majority of the remainder are open to institutional investors . . .' (*Financial Times*, 2009a). The returns can be lucrative. From 2005 to 2008, 'The European Carbon Fund, run by French bank Natixis . . . generated an annual return of 27.8 per cent' (*Financial Times*, 2009a).

In just the US, those vehicles invest across some 38 distinct markets dealing in everything from acid rain emissions permits to California's mobile emissions reductions credits. By just 2007, $64 billion in assets were traded on the global carbon market, growing to roughly $100 billion in 2008 (Conniff, 2008). Total market value recently peaked in 2012 at roughly $145 billion, falling to roughly $70 billion in 2015 (Thomson Reuters Point Carbon, 2016).

The problem is that such returns quickly attract fraudulent schemes. For instance, Interpol reported that in 2009 and 2010, an Australian investment firm ran an aggressive telemarketing strategy advertising false connections to legitimate organizations and environmental standards. Potential investors were offered a high return investment opportunity in carbon credits. The firm is estimated to have defrauded Australian investors of $3.2 million (Australian Competition and Consumer Commission, 2010).

In 2012, FT Alphaville warned of a firm called 'Enviro Associates' that was selling voluntary carbon credits for investment purposes, all the while warning that:

> Voluntary Carbon Credits were not designed to be purchased for investment purposes; for that reason Carbon Credits (VERs) are not for all specifications of Investors due to its high risk and undeveloped market landscape and uncertainty . . .
> Individuals should be aware if they are purchasing for speculative means that there is little or no liquidity at present in the market which in turn would affect your ability to sell/exit from a holding at this time. This may change in the future. (Murphy, 2013)

Enviro Associates claimed to be a 'clearing member' of Gemmax Solutions, a payments and clearing service. Britain's Financial Conduct Authority warns, however, that:

> Several unauthorised firms promoting and selling carbon credits are telling investors that Carbon Neutral Investments Limited (CNI) or Gemmax Solutions, firms authorised by us, will handle the money in their investment. We believe this is done to suggest investors will be protected as though they are dealing with an authorised firm. But this is incorrect. (Murphy, 2013; see also BBC World News, 2012)

Without investor protection and regulatory oversight, carbon schemes continue to proliferate.

Britain's Financial Services Authority ('FSA', now the Financial Conduct Authority, or 'FCA') warned investors about carbon frauds, emphasizing that they do not regulate carbon credits in the same manner as shares of stock (Financial Services Authority, 2012). Still, investors flock to these green 'investment' opportunities.

In November 2013, the FSA reported that it had already shut down 19 companies in the past 15 months for bilking roughly 1,500 investors out of roughly $38.7 million through carbon schemes (Szabo, 2013).

The UK Insolvency Service said the firms mainly targeted the elderly with high pressure sales techniques and promises of hefty returns of more than 40 percent. 'Salesmen played on peoples' [sic] keenness to "do their bit" to save the environment while making an investment at the same time', the Service said in a statement (Szabo, 2013). The FCA has put hundreds of companies under investigation since 2011 and listed many of them on its website (Szabo, 2013).

In June 2016, French courts convicted seven ex-Deutsche Bank traders in a CO_2-based VAT fraud scheme alleged to have defrauded authorities out of €145 million of tax revenues. The case involved police raiding Deutsche Bank three times and the bank, itself, paying some €220 million related to a prior action (Matussek, 2016).

In the US, carbon schemes have prompted several States Attorneys General, including those of California, Vermont, Arkansas, Delaware, Maine, Mississippi, Oklahoma, Illinois, Connecticut and New Hampshire, to back efforts by the Federal Trade Commission to investigate consumer fraud in the carbon offsets market (see, e.g., Environmental News Service, 2008).

In February 2016, the New York State Public Service Commission issued its 'Order Resetting Retail Energy Markets and Establishing Further Process', which, in part, required that companies selling 'renewable' energy packages to consumers actually obtain such energy from such sources rather than just using offsets purchased from the market (Giannasca, 2016).

3.2 Corporate Fraud

Clean Development Mechanism ('CDM') projects generate carbon credits based on the extent to which the project resulted in fewer emissions than would otherwise have occurred. Companies, therefore, have an incentive to either inflate the estimate of emissions that would have occurred without the project or claim that the project will reduce emissions by more than it actually does.

In order to constrain firms from mischaracterizing their projects, the CDM mechanism requires third-party validation and verification before a project receives carbon credits. Third-party verification is carried out by Designated Operation Entities ('DOEs') certified by the CDM Executive Board. Even independent third party auditors, however, may be susceptible to bribes or collusion to manipulate the results.

According to Transparency International, bribery is most common at the project approval stage. 'Although kickbacks to officials have not been reported, a Russian agency reportedly asked for direct monetary payments. In South-east Asian countries, it is fairly common for developers to invite the authorities to workshops (with attractive per diems) before submitting projects for approval. In China, it is not uncommon for project developers to invite experts reviewing their projects to dinner' (Transparency International, 2009 at 44).

In 2008 and 2009, respectively, the UN temporarily suspended two independent organizations – Norwegian company Det Norske Veritas and Swiss firm SGS – after 'spot checks found flaws in their methodologies'. At the time, these two companies were dominating the validation/verification market (see Szabo, 2008). Investigations showed that both companies had approved projects without sufficient review (Fortson and Leake, 2010; Murray, 2009).

> The UN inspection found one company had a flawed review process, inadequate preparation and training of their auditing staff, and an overall failure to assign auditors with the proper technical skills. The other was suspended after an inspection raised concerns about staff qualifications and the quality of its internal reviews. (Interpol Environmental Crime Programme, 2013)

In a follow-up review in 2009, the five largest DOEs' validation processes were scored on an A-to-F scale. None received a score higher than a D (Schapiro, 2010).

3.3 Counterfeiting and Theft

There are many examples of fake or invalid carbon permits being sold to unwitting buyers.

In one infamous example, in March 2010, the Hungarian government took possession of two million carbon credits which had been surrendered to them by Hungarian businesses.

The rules of the EU ETS allowed the Hungarian government to legally sell these carbon credits to others because Hungary anticipated being below its Kyoto Protocol target. However, the EU rules prevented these credits from being re-used within the EU (see EurActiv, 2010). Thus, Hungary sold the carbon credits to Hungarian Energy Power, 'with restrictions that they were ineligible for use in Europe and notified the European Commission of the sale' (Airlie, 2010a).

> Hungarian Energy Power then sold the credits to a British trading company, which resold them to a firm in Hong Kong. The Hong Kong firm, however, then put those same recycled carbon credits on BlueNext, a Paris carbon exchange [*The Economist*, 2010], where a number of European brokers and banks purchased them not knowing the carbon credits had already been used in Europe. (Fortson and Leake, 2010)

When BlueNext discovered the credits were ineligible for use in the EU, the exchange 'immediately suspended trading sending the spot price for

CERs spiraling downward' (*The Economist*, 2010). After shutting down for three days to isolate the problem credits, BlueNext facilitated 'swap backs' (Airlie, 2010a), in which the sellers bought back the credits. Prices rose to their previous levels when trading reopened (*The Economist*, 2010).

While the European Commission has now closed the loophole that allowed the credits to re-enter the EU ETS (*Utility Week*, 2010), the episode highlights the importance of 'strong regulations for monitoring the transfer of carbon credits through several foreign exchanges, particularly cross-checking between those exchanges' (Interpol Environmental Crime Programme, 2013).

Carbon permits are also the target of thieves and – due to their electronic registry – hackers. A hacking attack in November of 2010 resulted in the theft of 1.6 million carbon credits (valued at €23.5 million) from the Romanian registry account of Holcim Ltd, the world's second largest cement-maker (Airlie, 2010b). Holcim immediately posted the identification numbers of the stolen credits on its website and law enforcement efforts between Romania and Liechtenstein were able to track and return 600,000 of the stolen credits (Emissions Handelsregister, 2010). Still, while the unique identification numbers of the carbon credits allowed them to be tracked, not all the credits could be returned to Holcim. As it turned out, some 'jurisdictions required the holder to return the stolen credits to the legal owner at the holder's loss, while other jurisdictions allowed the buyer to keep them, with the original owner carrying the loss' (Airlie, 2010b; Macken, 2011).

In another high-profile incident, the European Union's emissions trading system was shut down for a week after cyber-thieves stole emissions allowances worth €7m from an account in the Czech Republic, while criminals also hacked into trading accounts in Austria, Poland, Greece, and Estonia. 'The Commission proposed tighter security measures in 2010 after discovering that hackers had broken into the registries where allowances are stored', but member states have repeatedly claimed they cannot afford the improvements (Chaffin, 2011). It is easy to imagine a similar situation arising in US markets where states would have to bear such unexpected costs.

4. CONCLUSIONS AND POLICY RECOMMENDATIONS

The ETS has suffered from a drastic oversupply of carbon permits for quite some time. In October 2009, Peter Zapfel, assistant to the deputy director general of the environment department at the European

Commission, stated that the oversupply of government allowances was threatening to overwhelm the system. At the time, many newer EU members from Central and Eastern Europe contributed to a huge oversupply of credits. These countries had excess credits that numbered roughly five times those in the European market, depressing prices and undermining the carbon reduction goals the market was formed to support (*Financial Times*, 2009b).

Since then, little has changed. In fact, by January 2013, record low auction bids from utilities, factories, and banks led Germany to cancel an auction of European Union emission permits for the first time, ever. Connie Hedegaard, the EU's climate chief, said the cancellation should be a 'wake-up call' for those who do not support the plan to strengthen the emissions trading system (*Bloomberg News*, 2013). Throughout 2015, EUA and CER prices remained below €8, far short of the €20 level needed to prompt industry and utilities to invest in greener energy (Thomson Reuters Point Carbon, 2016 at 5–8).

The US faces similar problems with low prices. In 2014, it was reported that California companies bought all 16.95 million allowances to release carbon emissions at the state's May 16, 2014 auction at roughly $11.50 each, slightly higher than the previous two auctions in February and November. An additional 4 million permits that can't be used until 2017, of the 9.2 million that were available, sold at $11.36 (Environmental Leader, 2014). California carbon prices are expected to remain low through 2020 due to excess permits (Environmental Leader, 2014).

Since then, prices have remained stagnant. While North American trading volume roughly doubled across 2015, California auctions settled at a price of roughly $12.50, just above minimum prices. RGGI prices in the Northeast peaked in 2015 at $7.50, although, again, that is still near the minimum allowable price (California Public Utilities Commission, 2016).

5. CONCLUSION

Cap and trade markets are not pricing CO_2 at levels that inhibit emissions. As Akerlof noted, 'dishonest dealings tend to drive honest dealings out of the market. . . . The cost of dishonesty, therefore, lies not only in the amount by which the purchaser is cheated; the cost also must include the loss incurred from driving legitimate business out of existence' (Akerlof, 1970 at 495).

Cap and Trade purists seem to think that CO_2 markets will work without a 'central banker' and market supervisor. While markets offer distinct advantages over fiat policy, recent financial research and economic experience suggest that market monitoring and surveillance still has merits. Over-reliance on unsupervised over-the-counter markets trading in home mortgages created systemic risk and financial crisis around the world in 2008, with the effects lingering in many countries today. Without remediation, therefore, current CO_2 markets risk substantially mispricing emissions – at the least – and potentially market collapse.

REFERENCES

Airlie, C. (2010a), 'BlueNext arranges "swap back" of recycled CO_2 credits after trading halt', *Bloomberg*, 14 April, at http://www.bloomberg.com/news/2010-04-14/bluenext-arranges-swap-backs-of-recycled- CO2-credits-after-trading-halt.html

Airlie, C. (2010b), 'EU carbon dioxide emissions permits stolen from Romanian unit of Holcim', *Bloomberg*, 1 December, at http://www.bloomberg.com/news/2010-12-01/romania-s-holcim-says-eu-carbon-permits-stolen-from-its-account.html

Akerlof, G.A. (1970), 'The market for lemons: Quality uncertainty and the market mechanism', *The Quarterly Journal of Economics*, **84**(3), 488–500.

Australian Competition and Consumer Commission (2010), 'SCAMwatch, Western Field Holdings Inc. carbon credit investment scams', 2 March, at https://www.scamwatch.gov.au/news/westernfield-holdings-inc-carbon-credit-investment-scams

Baumol, W. and W. Oates (1988), *The Theory of Environmental Policy*, Cambridge: Cambridge University Press.

BBC World News (2012), '"Misleading" carbon credit claims by Enviro Associates', 12 October, at http://www.bbc.com/news/uk-england-hampshire-20265034

Benz, E. and S. Trück (2009), 'Modeling the price dynamics of CO_2 emission allowances', *Energy Economics*, **31**(11), 4–15.

Bloomberg News (2013), 'EU carbon permits plunge to record after Germany cancels sale', 18 January, at http://www.bloomberg.com/news/2013-01-18/eu-carbon-plunges-after-german-sale-canceled-on-low-bid-prices.html

Borak, S., W.K. Härdle, S. Trück and R. Weron (2006), 'Convenience yields for CO_2 emission allowance futures contracts', *SFB 649 Discussion Paper 2006–076*, http://dx.doi.org/10.2139/ssrn.2894390

Borod, R. and M. Tan (2006), 'Carbon: Is it just hot or is it a new asset class?', *International Securitization Report*, **9**(11).

California Public Utilities Commission (2016), *Celebrating the Year of Carbon*, 1 May, at http://www.cpuc.ca.gov/uploadedFiles/CPUC_Public_Website/Content/About_Us/Organization/Divisions/Policy_and_Planning/PPD_Work/PPD_Work_Products_(2014_forward)/PPD-COMarkets-5May2016.pdf

Chaffin, J. (2011), 'Cyber-theft halts EU emissions trading', *Financial Times*, 19 January, at http://www.ft.com/intl/cms/s/0/27ee8cb0-2401-11e0-bef0-00144feab49a.html?ftcamp=rss#axzz34XaYYLnS

Conniff, R. (2008), 'Wall Street's carbon conversion', *Environment: Yale Magazine*, **7**(2).

Daskalakisa, G., D. Psychoyiosb and R. Markellosa (2009), 'Modeling CO_2 emission allowance prices and derivatives: Evidence from the European trading scheme', *Journal of Banking and Finance*, **33**(7), 1230–1241.

The Economist (2010), 'The wrong sort of recycling', 25 March, http://www.economist.com/node/15774368

Emissions Handelsregister (2010), 'Millions of EUAs stolen from Romanian registry', 2 December, at http://en.emissionshandelsregister.at/service/recent_info/items/news127.html, cited in Interpol Environmental Crime Programme (2013), *Guide to Carbon Trading*

Crime at https://www.interpol.int/en/Media/Files/Crime-areas/Environmental-crime/Guide-to-Carbon-Trading-Crime-2013

Environmental Leader (2014), *California Carbon Auction Sells All Allowances*, 23 May, at http://www.environmentalleader.com/2014/05/23/california-carbon-auction-sells-all-allowances/

Environmental News Service (2008), *States Seek Fraud Protection for Carbon Offset Market*, 25 January, at http://www.ens-newswire.com/ens/jan2008/2008-01-25-091.asp

EurActiv.com (2010), 'Hungary's sale of "used" CO_2 credits worries carbon trade', 22 March, at http://www.euractiv.com/section/climate-environment/news/hungary-s-sale-of-used-co2-credits-worries-carbon-traders/

Fama, E.F. (1965), 'The behavior of stock market prices', *Journal of Business*, **38**(1), 34–105.

Financial Services Authority (2012), *Carbon Credit Trading*, 5 May, at http://www.fsa.gov.uk/consumerinformation/scamsandswindles/investment_scams/carbon_credit

Financial Times (2009a), *Carbon Funds Grow Despite Problems*, 7 December.

Financial Times (2009b), *Investing in Commodities*, 7 December.

Fogarty, D. (2010), 'Firm accused of carbon scam may face legal claims', *Reuters*, 26 March, at http://uk.reuters.com/article/2010/03/26/us-carbon-investment-fraud-idUKTRE62P19020100326

Fortson, D. and J. Leake (2010), 'Hunt for "rogue trader" over recycled carbon credits', *The Times*, 21 March, at http://www.timesonline.co.uk/tol/news/environment/article7069741.ece

Giannasca, N. (2016), 'New York Public Service Commission's ESCO order set for preliminary injunction hearing', *Energy and Environmental Law Blog*, 4 May, at http://www.energyenvironmentallaw.com/2016/05/04/new-york-public-service-commissions-esco-order-set-for-preliminary-injunction-hearing/

Hull, J. (2006), *Options, Futures, and Other Derivatives*, Upper Saddle River, NJ: Prentice Hall.

Interpol Environmental Crime Programme (2013), *Guide to Carbon Trading Crime*, at https://www.interpol.int/en/Media/Files/Crime-areas/Environmental-crime/Guide-to-Carbon-Trading-Crime-2013

Macken, K. (2011), 'Strengthening credibility in the EU ETS following security and fraud related incidents', International Network for Environmental Compliance and Enforcement Conference Paper, at http://inece.org/conference/9/papers/Macken_Ireland_Final.pdf, cited in Interpol Environmental Crime Programme (2013), *Guide to Carbon Trading Crime* at https://www.interpol.int/en/Media/Files/Crime-areas/Environmental-crime/Guide-to-Carbon-Trading-Crime-2013

Mandelbrot, B. (1963), 'The variation of certain speculative prices', *Journal of Business*, **36**(4), 394–419.

Matussek, K. (2016), 'Seven ex-Deutsche Bank managers guilty in CO_2 tax-fraud case', *Bloomberg*, 13 June, at https://www.bloomberg.com/news/articles/2016-06-13/seven-ex-deutsche-bank-managers-convicted-in-c02-tax-fraud-case

Murphy, P. (2013), 'A carbon comedy', *FT Alphaville*, 15 October, at http://ftalphaville.ft.com/2013/10/15/1666352/a-carbon-comedy/

Murray, J. (2009), 'DNV wins back UN authorisation for CDM project approval', *Business Green*, 16 February, at http://www.businessgreen.com/bg/news/1804681/dnv-wins-un-authorisation-cdm-project-approval

Paolella, M. and L. Taschini (2008), 'An econometric analysis of emission trading allowances', *Journal of Banking & Finance*, **32**(10), 2022–2032.

Point Carbon (2006), *Carbon Market Monitor 2005 Review*, at http://www.PointCarbon.com/research/carbonmarketresearch/monitor/

Rosen, H. (2005), *Public Finance*, Boston, MA: McGraw-Hill Irwin.

Samuelson, P. (1954), 'The pure theory of public expenditure', *Review of Economics and Statistics*, **36**(4), 387–389.

Schapiro, M. (2010), 'Conning the climate: Inside the carbon trading shell game', *Harper's Magazine*, February, at http://harpers.org/archive/2010/02/conning-the-climate/

Seifert, J., M. Uhrig-Homburg and M. Wagner (2008), 'Dynamic behavior of CO_2 spot prices', *Journal of Environmental Economics and Management*, **56**(2), 180–194.

Szabo, M. (2008), 'DNV suspension another jab at battered CO_2 scheme', *Reuters*, 2 December, http://www.reuters.com/article/2008/12/02/us-carbon-dnv-idUSTRE4B04K120081202

Szabo, M. (2013), 'UK watchdog says investors lost 24 million pounds in carbon credit scam', *Reuters*, 6 November, at http://www.reuters.com/article/2013/11/06/us-britain-carbon-fraud-idUSBRE9A50L020131106

Theodossiou, P. (1998), 'Financial data and the skewed generalized T distribution', *Management Science*, **44**(12), 1650–1661.

Thomson Reuters Point Carbon (2016), *Review of 2015 and Outlook 2016–2018*, at https://climateobserver.org/wp-content/uploads/2016/01/Carbon-Market-Review-2016.pdf

Transparency International (2009), *Corruption and the Private Sector*, at http://www.transparency.org/whatwedo/pub/global_corruption_report_2009

Uhrig-Homburg, M. and M. Wagner (2009), 'Futures price dynamics of CO_2 emission allowance – An empirical analysis of the trial period', *Journal of Derivatives*, **17**(2), 73–88.

Utility Week (2010), 'EU closes carbon emissions trading loophole', 21 April, at http://www.utilityweek.co.uk/news/news_story.asp?id=148910&title=EU+closes+carbon+emissions+trading+loophole

2. How to better detect cases of financial reporting fraud: some new findings from earnings restatements

François Aubert, Jean-François Gajewski and Lamya Kermiche

1. INTRODUCTION

In response to a series of scandals in accounting and finance, most notably Enron and WorldCom, and more recently the Ponzi scheme elaborated by Bernard Madoff, the SEC (Security Exchange Committee) has decided to reinforce its structure in order to prevent any possibility of fraud in accounting or asset management. Our intent is to propose a new conceptual framework by estimating a new model and to provide empirical evidence to those who employ the extant discretionary accruals models to study earnings management for detecting extreme cases of misreporting.

Above all, the primary objective of this study is to evaluate the ability of the most popular discretionary accruals models versus our managed earnings component metric (MEC) variable to explain the magnitude of financial statement fraud. In summary, our MEC variable consistently exhibits the largest association with the magnitude of accounting fraud, indicating that the innovative metric is superior to abnormal accruals in detecting the restatement amounts.

Besides the development of a new unit specialized in pursuing fooling investment advisors or asset managers, the SEC has also built a new division whose objective is to detect any fraud in financial reporting. To achieve this goal, they now use a tool, called 'RoboCop', which is based on a new model, the Accounting Quality Model (AQM). This instrument is a fully automated system which analyzes the corporate filings. It helps to identify earnings management along a traditional scheme, by regressing accruals on factors mimicking non-discretionary accruals. The residual part of this regression stands for discretionary accruals, leading to earnings management.

By using this model, the risk of potential error could emerge, even if the AQM compares the obtained results for each firm with the results of a sector, thus limiting the risk of flaw. As a matter of fact, this method is very dependent on the models of accruals and their exactitude. If the models of accruals are not exact, the identification of discretionary accruals may incite the SEC to detect some fraud where there is none. To this extent, the question raised in this chapter is how to develop a new methodology to detect any accounting fraud by using an objective measure taken from the earnings restatement. Dechow et al. (2011) and Hui et al. (2014) develop an accounting fraud prediction model by using a combination of discretionary accruals, earnings variability and other control vectors like leverage and firm size. Although this chapter is complementary to prior literature, it radically departs from relying on the assumption that the clearest and easiest pathway to ex ante prevent fraud reporting is through the examination of abnormal accruals. Going a step further, we use a comprehensive sample of fraudulent firms that have misstated either their reported earnings or one of the components of their earnings among sales, gross income, operating income and EBITDA. We show that the managed earnings component metric is a better proxy of the accounting fraud – proxied with the restated amount – than abnormal accruals measures. Overall, we employ what is thought to be a richer source of information about the possibility of a firm's fraudulent earnings: primarily the magnitude of the managed earnings component derived from the ex post consensus of analysts' estimates. Our approach aims at answering the following question: Are the measures of the managed earnings component versus discretionary accruals associated with the magnitude of the financial statement fraud? This question examines the ability of the various metrics to detect significant frauds. We use the restated amount as a proxy for the degree of discretion exercised by managers to fraudulently inflate incomes. Our results point out that the metric of the managed earnings component (MEC hereafter) is more closely related to the magnitude of the financial fraud than commonly employed measures of earnings management.

As a consequence, our chapter contributes to enhancing prior literature on the detection of accounting misstatements and financial statement fraud (Beneish, 1999) and should be of great interest to regulators, investors and academics.

The chapter is organized as follows. After reviewing the traditional models of discretionary accruals in a first step, the chapter then details the managed earnings component (our measure of earnings manipulation), and finally we will use several OLS regression models to explain the restated amount by the models of accruals and the managed earnings, in order to see which measure is the most associated with the amounts of accounting fraud.

2. THE MAIN MEASURES OF EARNINGS MANIPULATIONS BASED ON DISCRETIONARY ACCRUALS

First, we sum up the main aggregate measures of earnings manipulations (discretionary accruals). We then retain five measures of earnings management that are used in prior literature. Because of sample size restrictions, our measures of discretionary accruals and accrual quality are estimated from cross-sectional models.

So as to measure the magnitude of earnings management, we concentrate on several cross-sectional – industry-specific – OLS accrual models specified by Jones (1991) and modified by Dechow, Sloan and Sweeney (1995), using the modified Jones model with either current-year or prior-year return on assets included as an independent variable (Kothari et al., 2005), the accrual estimation error model of Dechow and Dichev (2002) and Francis et al. (2005) (the same as McNichols, 2002) as follows:

$$TA_t/A_{t-1} = \alpha_0 + \alpha_1(1/A_{t-1}) + \alpha_2(\Delta REV_{t,t-1}/A_{t-1}) + \alpha_3(PPE_t/A_{t-1}) + \varepsilon_t$$

(Jones, 1991 modified by Dechow et al., 1995)

$$TA_t/A_{t-1} = \alpha_0 + \alpha_1(\Delta REV_{t,t-1}/A_{t-1}) + \alpha_2(PPE_t/A_{t-1}) + \alpha_3 ROA_{t-1} + \varepsilon_t$$

(Kothari et al., 2005)

$$TCA_t/A_{t-1} = \alpha_0 + \alpha_1(CFO_{t-1}/A_{t-1}) + \alpha_2(CFO_t/A_{t-1}) + \alpha_3(CFO_{t+1})/A_{t-1}) + \varepsilon_t$$

(Dechow and Dichev, 2002)

$$TCA_t/_{t-1} = \alpha_0 + \alpha_1(CFO_{t-1}/A_{t-1}) + \alpha_2(CFO_t/A_{t-1}) + \alpha_3(CFO_{t+1})/A_{t-1}) + \alpha_4(\Delta REV_t/A_{t-1}) + \alpha_5(PPE_t/A_{t-1}) + \varepsilon_t$$

(Francis et al., 2005)

where

- TA_t are the total accruals defined as *Net Income Before Extraordinaries (NIBE)* minus *Cash Flows from Operations (CFO)*,
- TCA_t are the total current accruals,
- A_{t-1} are the total assets of year *t−1*,
- $\Delta REV_{t,t-1}$ is the change in revenue between year *t−1* and year *t*,
- PPE_t is the gross amount of Property, Plan & Equipment in year *t*,
- ROA_{t-1} is the return on assets in year *t−1*,
- ε_t is the error term capturing the discretionary accruals.

Jones et al. (2008) find that the commonly used measures of abnormal accruals are associated with the magnitude of the accounting fraud. However, they show that the accrual estimation models (i.e., the model of Dechow and Dichev (2002) and the model of McNichols (2002)) consistently exhibit the largest association with the existence of fraud as well as the magnitude of the misstatement.

3. THE MANAGED EARNINGS COMPONENT (MEC)

Instead of concentrating on the traditional models of unexpected accruals, we use a new theoretical metric: the *managed earnings component* based on the 'convergent consensus' of brokers suggested by Aubert and Grudnitski (2012, 2014). The 'convergent consensus' (or 'Broker actual') refers to the ex-post consensus that is re-calculated by analysts after the firm has published its realized GAAP earnings (Bessler and Stanzel, 2009). Gajewski and Quéré (2001) use this ex-post consensus in order to appreciate stock market reaction to turnover announcements in France. As there is no obligation to publish net earnings on the first and third quarters, they calculate the variation of consensus (ex-post minus ex-ante consensus) around the announcements of turnover in France to estimate the degree of surprise.

Aubert and Grudnitski (2012) construct a measure of a firm's opportunistic earnings by taking the difference between the ex-post convergent consensus estimate and the firms' reported earnings. That is, when a firm's convergent consensus earnings remain different after its earnings are reported, Aubert and Grudnitski attribute this difference to an expression of analysts' beliefs about the magnitude of a firm's actual opportunistic earnings, which cannot be empirically observed ex ante by researchers. They use an EPS approach to calculate the MEC, while, to make a relevant comparison with error accrual estimation models, we apply throughout the chapter a 'total assets' transformation to that measure. Consequently, the MEC is derived for each firm as follows:

$$MEC_t = (\text{Reported Net Income}_t - \text{Ex post consensus Net Income}_t)/(A_{t-1})$$

where A_{t-1} represents the total assets of year $t-1$.

The absolute value, rather than actual value between the reported and the ex-post consensus net income is adopted in our project so that the differences consistent with the competing hypotheses of management elevating earnings to meet targets or reverse losses and income smoothing do not compensate. The MEC is measured as the difference between the company's reported earnings and the 'convergence consensus' analyst estimates (Bessler and Stanzel, 2009; Aubert and Grudnitski, 2012, 2014). As a consequence, from a theoretical standpoint, employing the convergence consensus analyst earnings estimated offers a few important and significant advantages. First, abnormal accruals may suffer from an *endogenous bias* because they are the results of running cross-sectional or time series equations. Moreover, the arbitrary choice of the researcher plays an important role in sample selection, which may bias the results significantly. Indeed, these estimations depend on the sampling procedures made by the researcher to estimate the industry-specific residuals, which strongly influences the quality of fit of the model. Second, by using information provided by rational and informed traders (i.e., analysts), the 'convergence consensus' analyst estimates refer to a good proxy for the 'non-manipulated' or 'partially-manipulated earnings' of a firm. Consequently, following Aubert and Grudnitski's setting, we hypothesize that the ex-post estimate incorporates all information about discretionary financial reporting choices conveyed by financial statements and the ex-post estimate converges toward the true 'restated' earnings, allowing us to more accurately identify fraudulently reported earnings.

4. DATA, SAMPLE AND METHODOLOGY

Details of our data set are provided in Table 2.1. Because the chapter focuses on the ex-ante identification of earnings misstatements, the initial sample comprises 3,162 Accounting and Auditing Enforcement Releases (AAERs) issued by the SEC during the reporting period from January 1, 1993 to December 31, 2014. Of these, 2,631 don't involve financial statement misstatements, which reduces the sample to 531 AAERs. In 352 cases, there is a lack of information in FactSet and Reuter's identification. At the end, 179 misstating firms and a total of 562 misstating firm-years remain in the final sample. Two categories of AAER firms are finally included in the final sample. First, we identify 'restating' firms for which the SEC required them to restate the net income. There is an example below of such a restatement done by *Huron Consulting Group Inc.* in 2008. The originally reported net profit amounted at 10.08 $ millions while the restated net loss amounted at −1.22 $ millions. As a result, this firm overstated earnings by 11.3 $ millions. Second, we separate the sample into two, the subsample of 'restating' firms and the subsample of firms that reclassify their financial statements. In the latter case, the firms have reported one component of the net income among sales, gross margin, operating income, EBITDA and pre-tax income fraudulently without any

Table 2.1 Definition of variables and data source

Variable name	Definition	Data source and extraction codes
ACCTG_ CHANGE	Amount of accounting changes reported on the income statement, deflated by the lagged total assets.	RG/Annual/Income Statement/Accounting change
ACCTG_FRAUD	Net Income 'originally reported' minus Net Income 'restated' including reclassification of key figures on the income statement (Sales 'originally reported' minus Sales 'restated', operating income 'originally reported' minus operating income 'restated', EBITDA 'originally reported' minus EBITDA 'restated'), deflated by the lagged total assets.	Derived
ACCOUNTING_ FRAUD	Net Income 'originally reported' minus Net Income 'restated', deflated by the lagged total assets.	Derived
AUDITOR_ OPINION	Auditor opinion ('unqualified', 'unqualified with explanations', 'qualified').	RG/Annual/ Miscellaneous/Auditor opinion
BIGX	Dummy variable taking the value of 1 if the statutory auditor is a BIG X; 0 otherwise.	RG/Annual/ Miscellaneous/Auditor name
DECHOW& DICHEV	Discretionary accruals. Coefficients and residuals are industry-specific and estimated from the cross-sectional regression model of Dechow and Dichev (2002).	$TCA_t/A_{t-1} = \alpha_0 + \alpha_1(CFO_{t-1}/A_{t-1}) + \alpha_2(CFO_t/A_{t-1}) + \alpha_3(CFO_{t+1})/A_{t-1}) + \varepsilon_t$
FRANCIS	Working discretionary accruals. Coefficients and residuals are industry-specific and estimated from the cross-sectional regression model of Francis et al. (2005) employing the version of McNichols (2002).	$TCA_t/_{t-1} = \alpha_0 + \alpha_1(CFO_{t-1}/A_{t-1}) + \alpha_2(CFO_t/A_{t-1}) + \alpha_3(CFO_{t+1})/A_{t-1}) + \alpha_4(\Delta REV_t/A_{t-1}) + \alpha_5(PPE_t/A_{t-1}) + \varepsilon_t$
JONES	Discretionary accruals. Coefficients and residuals are industry-specific and estimated from the cross-sectional regression model of Jones (1991) modified by Dechow et al. (1995).	$TA_t/A_{t-1} = \alpha_0 + \alpha_1(1/A_{t-1}) + \alpha_2(\Delta REV_{t,t-1}/A_{t-1}) + \alpha_3(PPE_t/A_{t-1}) + \varepsilon_t$

Table 2.1 (continued)

Variable name	Definition	Data source and extraction codes
$KOTHARI_{1/0}$	Discretionary accruals. Coefficients and residuals are industry-specific and estimated from the cross-sectional regression model of Kothari et al. (2005) according to different specifications including either the control variable of ROA_t or the variable of ROA_{t-1}.	$TA_t/A_{t-1} = \alpha_0 + \alpha_1(\Delta REV_{t,t-1}/A_{t-1}) + \alpha_2(PPE_t/A_{t-1}) + \alpha_3 ROA_{t-1} + \varepsilon_t$
LEVERAGE	Yearly LT Debt divided by yearly total assets.	RG/Annual/Ratios/ LTDebt%TotalAsssets
MEs	Managed earnings component defined as the (absolute value of) yearly Originally Reported Net Income minus *Ex post* Consensus of Net Income, scaled by lagged total assets.	Derived
MAJOR_ MARKET	Dummy variable taking on the value of 1 if the firm is traded on the NYSE/NASDAQ; 0 otherwise.	
MARKET_CAP	Market value of equity (market capitalization).	QR/Price/Market Cap
Ex post Consensus of Net Income	Brokers generally revise their estimates for a firm every time it publishes its results to take into account new information. *FactSet* terms the consensus of estimates after the publication of results, the 'broker actual'. It is available between one and several weeks after the publication of results, the delay depending on the firm's size and the speed of brokers' adjustments.	FE/Annual/Actual/Net Income median/mean-option 'using Broker Actuals' activated
NUMEST	Number of analysts participating in the convergence consensus.	FE/Annual/Actual/ EPS Num. of Estimates-option 'using Broker Actuals' activated

Table 2.2 Distribution of fraudulent firms/firm-years

	Number of fraudulent firms	Number of frauds	Number of fraudulent firm-years
	1	8	8
	6	7	42
	4	6	24
	10	5	50
	15	4	60
	12	3	36
	14	2	28
	29	1	29
All	91		**277**

impact on the final results. Due to a lack of information on all variables, 285 firm-years were removed from the sample in order to keep the same set of observations across all the models of regression. Table 2.1 describes all the variables used in the models of regression.

A final sample of 277 firm-years (ACCOUNTING_FRAUD variable) and 91 misstating firms (see Table 2.2) remains for the reduced models (containing only the dependent and independent variables). In the extended models including additional control variables, the final sample consists of 230 firm-years. When we only focus on 'restating' firms – by removing the 'reclassifying' firms – those numbers are respectively of 172 and 149 firm-years (ACCTG_FRAUD variable). Table 2.2 describes the sample. It can be said that the firms do not try to commit fraud too frequently. The higher the number of frauds, the lower the number of fraudulent firms. For example, there is only one firm which has defrauded eight times, and one third of all the fraudulent firms have misstated only once. As a consequence, the system of punishment seems to be efficient, as most firms do not continue to commit fraud when there is detection. This does not allow us to consider a panel in order to see if there is a temporal effect in the fraud or not.

The methodology consists in comparing the explanatory power (adjusted R-squared) as well as testing the significance of coefficients when using the traditional measures of discretionary accruals and the managed earnings component in the models of regression of the amount of fraud (ACCOUNTING_FRAUD or ACCTG_FRAUD) on the accruals and the MEC.

Besides the two main independent variables of MEC and discretionary accruals presented above, we conjecture that the fraudulently restated amount of a firm should be explained by other control variables. The first control variable is the presence of a voluntarily change in accounting procedure (ACCTG_CHANGE) that captures managerial discretion in accounting policy. Big X auditor and audit opinion are two other firm-level variables in the vector of influences on the magnitude of a firm misstating earnings. Stemming from the work of Becker et al. (1998), Big X auditors are more likely to object to income-increasing accounting choices than non-Big X auditors because of the higher costs of an investor lawsuit or loss in reputation. Similarly, to mitigate audit risk, auditors are reluctant to give a firm an unqualified opinion when there is even a hint of misreporting (Tsipouridoua and Spathisb, 2012, 2014). Analyst following is the final firm-specific variable supposed to have an influence on the magnitude of the fraud. It is intended to represent the quality or amount of effort expended by analysts in preparing their forecasts and is proxied often by the number of analysts following a firm. The rationale for analyst following as a proxy is that when more analysts follow a firm there will be more effort put into producing accurate forecasts and greater diligence shown in identifying situations where a firm misstates earnings to meet or beat its target (Keune and Johnstone, 2012). We conjecture that earnings management activities by these firms are easier to detect, which, in turn, drives the finding of less opportunistic earnings in these firms. Furthermore, we use firm size (market capitalization) and quotation on a major US market (e.g., NYSE/NASDAQ) as independent regressors. We suppose that investors paid more attention to larger firms which are quoted on a major stock exchange. Finally, we hypothesize that firms facing high leverage are subject to greater manipulation of reported earnings in order to comply with banking covenants and reduce potential agency costs (Cornett, McNutt and Tehranian, 2009; Lambert, 2001). Therefore, the LEVERAGE variable (i.e, long-term debt divided by total assets) is also included. The reduced and extended models are defined under the following form.

$$\begin{cases} ACCTG - FRAUD = f(Discretionary - Accruals, Control\ variables) \\ ACCTG - FRAUD = f(MEC, Control\ variables) \end{cases} \quad (1)$$

$$\begin{cases} ACCOUNTING - FRAUD = f(Discretionary - Accruals, Control\ variables) \\ ACCOUNTING - FRAUD = f(MEC, Control\ variables) \end{cases} \quad (2)$$

5. RESULTS AND INTERPRETATION

Table 2.3 exhibits descriptive statistics. From Table 2.3, the median of the MEC presents the lowest magnitude. So, if the MEC allows for a better

Table 2.3 Descriptive statistics

	Mean	Q1	Median	Q3	Std. Dev.	Obs.
Managed earnings component						
|ME|	0.146	0.007	0.022	0.082	0.883	277
|ME_MEAN|	0.141	0.006	0.020	0.075	0.883	277
Discretionary accruals						
|DECHOW&DICHEV|	0.149	0.019	0.041	0.094	1.125	277
|FRANCIS|	0.072	0.017	0.041	0.089	0.093	277
|JONES|	0.169	0.040	0.086	0.178	0.357	277
$\|KOTHARI_0\|$	0.113	0.025	0.057	0.129	0.187	277
$\|KOTHARI_1\|$	0.120	0.024	0.064	0.145	0.189	277
Dependent variables						
ACCOUNTING_FRAUD	0.040	0.003	0.009	0.024	0.155	172
ACCTG_FRAUD	0.025	0.000	0.002	0.012	0.123	277
Independent variables						
ACCTG_CHANGE	−0.003	0.000	0.000	0.000	0.028	277
AUDITOR_OPINION	0.388	0.000	0.000	1.000	0.488	277
BIGX	0.877	1.000	1.000	1.000	0.329	277
LEVERAGE	0.162	0.001	0.123	0.267	0.172	277
MAJOR_MARKET	0.913	1.000	1.000	1.000	0.282	277
MARKET_CAP	17822.7	471.2	1423.7	7664.3	91494.7	277
NUMEST	5.746	2.000	4.500	8.000	4.678	277

Notes: |DECHOW&DICHEV|, |FRANCIS|, |JONES|, $|KOTHARI_0|$ and $|KOTHARI_1|$ are the absolute values of discretionary accruals variables estimated by employing the model of Dechow and Dichev (2002), the model of McNichols (2002) employed by Francis et al. (2005), Jones's model modified by Dechow et al. (1995) and two specifications of Kothari et al.'s model (2005) using the actual and lagged return on assets, respectively. The absolute value of ME (ME_MEAN) is defined as the difference between the median (mean) value of the reported earnings minus broker actual consensus (consensus ex post) of NET INCOME, deflated by the lagged total assets. ACCOUNTING_FRAUD is defined as the originally reported net income minus restated Net Income, deflated by the lagged total assets. ACCTG_CHANGE is the amount per share of accounting changes reported on the income statement, deflated by the lagged stock price. ACCTG_FRAUD is defined as the originally reported Net Income minus restated Net Income, deflated by the lagged total assets for all firms being impacted by misstatements (sales, gross income, operating income, EBITDA); AUDITOR_OPINION takes the value of 1 if the auditor opinion is 'unqualified with explanations' or 'qualified', 0 if the auditor opinion is 'unqualified'; BIGX takes the value of 1 if the company is audited by a big X firm, 0 otherwise; LEVERAGE is the long-term debt divided by total assets; NUMEST is the number of analysts following a firm before quarterly earnings announcements (analyst coverage); MAJOR_MARKET: dummy variable taking on the value of 1 if the firm is traded on the NYSE/NASDAQ, 0 otherwise; MARKET_CAP is the market value of traded shares (market cap.).

detection, it is not due to the magnitude of the discretionary accruals but to the accuracy of the empirical measure.

Tables 2.4 to 2.8 present the results on regressions which have the same objective but depend on the selected sample and the dependent variable. The objective is to study whether the MEC allows for a better detection of financial statement fraud than traditional measures of accruals.

Tables 2.4 and 2.6 consider the whole sample of frauds (i.e. 277 frauds, if we consider the reduced models and 230 if we consider the control variables) for all firms being impacted by misstatements on sales, gross income, operating income and EBITDA. They present the regressions of variable ACCTG-FRAUD for the traditional measures of accruals as well as the MEC. Table 2.4 (*Table 2.5*) considers the dependent variable in absolute (*numerical*) value. From both tables, it appears that variable ME (in mean or median) exhibits higher adjusted R-squared by comparison with the traditional measures of discretionary accruals. While the MEC (either in mean or median) exhibits strong significance, the coefficients corresponding to the discretionary accruals are not always significant. For example, the model of Dechow and Dichev (2002) does not show any statistical significance. The adjusted R-squared of the corresponding regression is very low (-0.35 percent for the reduced model and 4.96 percent for the extended model).

If we reduce the sample of frauds to the case when the firms have defrauded only on the net income (172 for the reduced model and 149 for the extended model), Tables 2.5 and 2.7 highlight the same result. Whatever the magnitude of the fraud size (either in absolute or in relative terms), the adjusted R-squared is higher when we consider the ME (mean or median).

Finally, Table 2.8 restricts the sample to the case when the fraud is upward, meaning that the firms overstate their net income. The evidence shows that the adjusted R-squared is higher, as in the preceding regressions, but the difference between the adjusted R-squared is the highest. The adjusted R-squared when considering the MEC is always higher than 77 percent.

Finally, these regressions may help us to confirm or reject the different models of discretionary accruals. From Tables 2.4 to 2.7, we may deduce that apart from the models of Francis et al. (2005) and Dechow and Dichev (2002), the other models are validated according to the significance of coefficients.

In summary, whatever the sample, the magnitude of accounting fraud (difference between the originally reported net income and the restated net income deflated by the lagged total assets) is more related to the managed earnings component (the difference between the mean or the median value of the reported earnings minus broker actual consensus of net income

Table 2.4 Restatement impact on sales, gross income, operating income, EBITDA, or Net Income (N = 277) [dependent variable ACCTG_FRAUD]

Panel A: Reduced Models

	Specification 1		Specification 2		Specification 3	
Variable	Coef.	*p*-value	Coef.	*p*-value	Coef.	*p*-value
Intercept	0.0078	0.0650*	0.0083	0.0484**	−0.0127	0.0458**
|ME|	0.1158	0.0000***				
|ME_MEAN|			0.1159	0.0000***		
|JONES|					0.2205	0.0000***
$\|KOTHARI_1\|$						
$\|KOTHARI_0\|$						
|FRANCIS|						
|DECHOW&DICHEV|						
Adjusted-R^2	68.65%		68.82%		40.59%	
F-stat.	605.49***		610.17***		189.56***	
N	277		277		277	

Panel B: Extended Models

	Specification 1		Specification 2		Specification 3	
Variable	Coef.	*p*-value	Coef.	*p*-value	Coef.	*p*-value
Intercept	0.0125	0.6604	0.0114	0.6886	0.0488	0.2142
|ME|	0.1172	0.0000***				
|ME_MEAN|			0.1174	0.0000***		
|JONES|					0.2179	0.0000***
$\|KOTHARI_1\|$						
$\|KOTHARI_0\|$						
|FRANCIS|						
|DECHOW&DICHEV|						
ACCTG_CHANGE	0.1016	0.5754	0.1043	0.5646	−0.0280	0.9098
LEVERAGE	0.0029	0.9250	0.0015	0.9604	0.0216	0.6089
BIGX	0.0131	0.4400	0.0131	0.4374	−0.0096	0.6767
AUDITOR_OPINION	−0.0075	0.4881	−0.0076	0.4830	−0.0098	0.5067
LOG(MARKET_CAP)	−0.0043	0.1670	−0.0042	0.1706	−0.0045	0.2818
LOG(NUMEST)	0.0069	0.4168	0.0072	0.3961	0.0082	0.4826
MAJOR_MARKET	0.0101	0.6378	0.0110	0.6084	−0.0321	0.2703
Adjusted-R^2	68.22%		68.34%		40.70%	
F-stat.	62.45***		62.79***		20.64***	
N	230		230		230	

Specification 4		Specification 5		Specification 6		Specification 7	
Coef.	*p*-value	Coef.	*p*-value	Coef.	*p*-value	Coef.	*p*-value
−0.0018	0.8290	−0.0189	0.0080***	−0.0021	0.8172	0.0245	0.0012***
0.2202	0.0000***						
		0.3840	0.0000***				
				0.3711	0.0000***		
						0.0011	0.8672
11.04%		33.48%		7.54%		−0.35%	
35.24***		139.91***		23.49***		0.02	
277		277		277		277	

Specification 4		Specification 5		Specification 6		Specification 7	
Coef.	*p*-value	Coef.	*p*-value	Coef.	*p*-value	Coef.	*p*-value
0.1309	0.0060	0.0777	0.0556	0.1452	0.0023	0.2042	0.0000
0.2009	0.0000***						
		0.3833	0.0000***				
				0.4124	0.0000***		
						−0.0017	0.8175
−0.0319	0.9152	−0.0908	0.7252	−0.0757	0.8021	−0.0332	0.9156
0.0212	0.6780	0.0575	0.1954	0.0418	0.4226	0.0064	0.9048
−0.0269	0.3327	−0.0233	0.3296	−0.0420	0.1322	−0.0421	0.1511
−0.0067	0.7068	−0.0063	0.6813	−0.0123	0.4945	−0.0078	0.6760
−0.0011	0.8214	−0.0041	0.3498	−0.0012	0.8221	−0.0004	0.9340
−0.0082	0.5556	0.0041	0.7342	−0.0092	0.5146	−0.0133	0.3626
−0.0886	0.0111	−0.0608	0.0429	−0.0921	0.0088	−0.1196	0.0009
13.30%		35.36%		11.80%		4.96%	
5.38***		16.65***		4.82***		2.49**	
230		230		230		230	

Notes: ***, ** and * indicate significance at the 0.01, 0.05 and 0.1 levels, respectively.

Table 2.5 Sensitivity tests: restatement impact on EPS only (N = 172) [dependent variable ACCOUNTING_FRAUD]

Panel A: Reduced Models

	Specification 1		Specification 2		Specification 3	
Variable	Coef.	*p*-value	Coef.	*p*-value	Coef.	*p*-value
Intercept	0.0190	0.0012***	0.0197	0.0008***	−0.0133	0.0782*
|ME|	0.1264	0.0000***				
|ME_MEAN|			0.1265	0.0000***		
|JONES|					0.3434	0.0000***
|KOTHARI1|						
|KOTHARI0|						
|FRANCIS|						
|DECHOW&DICHEV|						
Adjusted-R^2	76.45%		76.64%		40.70%	
F-stat.	556.00***		562.11***		20.64***	
N	172		172		172	

Panel B: Extended Models

	Specification 1		Specification 2		Specification 3	
Variable	Coef.	*p*-value	Coef.	*p*-value	Coef.	*p*-value
Intercept	0.0782	0.0557*	0.0761	0.0616*	0.1060	0.0249**
|ME|	0.1246	0.0000***				
|ME_MEAN|			0.1249	0.0000***		
|JONES|					0.3373	0.0000***
|KOTHARI1|						
|KOTHARI0|						
|FRANCIS|						
|DECHOW&DICHEV|						
ACCTG_CHANGE	0.1201	0.5330	0.1242	0.5178	−0.0158	0.9434
LEVERAGE	−0.0197	0.6110	−0.0215	0.5779	0.0050	0.9110
BIGX	0.0167	0.4265	0.0170	0.4166	−0.0056	0.8167
AUDITOR_OPINION	−0.0156	0.2682	−0.0156	0.2671	−0.0258	0.1158
LOG(MARKET_CAP)	−0.0067	0.0909	−0.0066	0.0921*	−0.0085	0.0635*
LOG(NUMEST)	0.0064	0.5888	0.0068	0.5637	0.0137	0.3208
MAJOR_MARKET	−0.0196	0.5475	−0.0180	0.5795	−0.0613	0.1005
Adjusted-R^2	76.61%		76.77%		68.56%	
F-stat.	61.57***		62.15***		41.34***	
N	149		149		149	

Specification 4		Specification 5		Specification 6		Specification 7	
Coef.	*p*-value	Coef.	*p*-value	Coef.	*p*-value	Coef.	*p*-value
−0.0305	0.0127**	−0.0347	0.0000***	0.0035	0.8020	0.0084	0.5459
0.6341	0.0000***						
		0.7263	0.0000***				
				0.4908	0.0000***		
						0.3929	0.0001***
34.15%		66.51%		10.00%		7.71%	
89.67***		340.57***		20.01***		15.28***	
172		172		172		172	

Specification 4		Specification 5		Specification 6		Specification 7	
Coef.	*p*-value	Coef.	*p*-value	Coef.	*p*-value	Coef.	*p*-value
0.1792	0.0035***	0.1417	0.0011***	0.2965	0.0001***	0.3037	0.0001***
0.6982	0.0000***						
		0.7198	0.0000***				
				0.4757	0.0007***		
						0.3847	0.0022***
−0.0497	0.8640	−0.1459	0.4830	−0.0863	0.8088	−0.0942	0.7933
0.0320	0.5860	0.0625	0.1389	0.0312	0.6694	0.0236	0.7484
−0.0136	0.6668	−0.0279	0.2146	−0.0606	0.1193	−0.0422	0.2777
−0.0234	0.2728	−0.0189	0.2144	−0.0143	0.5851	−0.0098	0.7090
−0.0025	0.6720	−0.0076	0.0762*	−0.0004	0.9536	0.0013	0.8601
−0.0174	0.3223	0.0027	0.8343	−0.0252	0.2447	−0.0248	0.2568
−0.1534	0.0013***	−0.1025	0.0029***	−0.1960	0.0010***	−0.2327	0.0001***
46.74%		72.71%		19.60%		18.38%	
17.23***		50.29***		5.51***		50.29***	
149		149		149		149	

Notes: ***, **, and * indicate significance at the 0.01, 0.05 and 0.1 levels, respectively.

Table 2.6 Signed tests: restatement impact on sales, gross income, operating income, EBITDA, or Net Income (N = 277) [dependent variable ACCTG_FRAUD]

Panel A: Reduced Models

	Specification 1		Specification 2		Specification 3	
Variable	Coef.	*p*-value	Coef.	*p*-value	Coef.	*p*-value
Intercept	0.0050	0.2487	0.0047	0.2805	0.0110	0.0676*
ME	0.1146	0.0000***				
ME_MEAN			0.1149	0.0000***		
JONES					−0.1911	0.0000***
$KOTHARI_1$						
$KOTHARI_0$						
FRANCIS						
DECHOW&DICHEV						
Adjusted-R^2	66.69%		66.90%		36.30%	
F-stat.	553.52***		558.92***		158.29***	
N	277		277		277	

Panel B: Extended Models

	Specification 1		Specification 2		Specification 3	
Variable	Coef.	*p*-value	Coef.	*p*-value	Coef.	*p*-value
Intercept	0.0219	0.4598	0.0215	0.4682	0.1106	0.0053***
ME	0.1149	0.0000***				
ME_MEAN			0.1152	0.0000***		
JONES					−0.1865	0.0000***
$KOTHARI_1$						
$KOTHARI_0$						
FRANCIS						
DECHOW&DICHEV						
ACCTG_CHANGE	0.1672	0.3761	0.1676	0.3738	0.0661	0.7964
LEVERAGE	0.0035	0.9139	0.0039	0.9037	0.0440	0.3151
BIGX	0.0120	0.4964	0.0123	0.4841	−0.0194	0.4129
AUDITOR_OPINION	−0.0053	0.6371	−0.0044	0.6927	−0.0083	0.5868
LOG(MARKET_CAP)	−0.0039	0.2216	−0.0040	0.2170	−0.0041	0.3488
LOG(NUMEST)	0.0015	0.8628	0.0015	0.8682	−0.0060	0.6130
MAJOR_MARKET	0.0034	0.8785	0.0030	0.8928	−0.0475	0.1148
Adjusted-R^2	66.16%		66.32%		37.59%	
F-stat.	56.96***		57.37***		18.24***	
N	230		230		230	

Specification 4		Specification 5		Specification 6		Specification 7	
Coef.	*p*-value	Coef.	*p*-value	Coef.	*p*-value	Coef.	*p*-value
0.0130	0.0717*	0.0039	0.5523	0.0190	0.0125**	0.0191	0.0115**
−0.1722	0.0000***						
		−0.3101	0.0000***				
				−0.0081	0.8993		
						−0.0009	0.8961
9.04%		27.89%		−0.36%		−0.36%	
28.44***		107.73***		0.02		0.02	
277		277		277		277	

Specification 4		Specification 5		Specification 6		Specification 7	
Coef.	*p*-value	Coef.	*p*-value	Coef.	*p*-value	Coef.	*p*-value
0.1826	0.0001***	0.1547	0.0001***	0.2103	0.0000***	0.2107	0.0000***
−0.1688	0.0000***						
		−0.3218	0.0000***				
				0.0190	0.8138		
						0.0017	0.8084
0.0561	0.8520	−0.0095	0.9713	0.0279	0.9294	0.0252	0.9362
0.0374	0.4698	0.0766	0.0952*	0.0089	0.8689	0.0077	0.8861
−0.0314	0.2594	−0.0320	0.1910	−0.0402	0.1703	−0.0404	0.1695
−0.0031	0.8615	0.0030	0.8476	−0.0059	0.7534	−0.0056	0.7671
−0.0025	0.6315	−0.0043	0.3383	−0.0009	0.8673	−0.0008	0.8803
−0.0165	0.2386	−0.0090	0.4663	−0.0163	0.2713	−0.0169	0.2501
−0.1062	0.0023***	−0.0967	0.0016***	−0.1266	0.0005***	−0.1266	0.0005***
13.88%		33.17%		5.89%		5.89%	
5.61***		15.20***		2.79***		2.79**	
230		230		230		230	

Notes: ***, **, and * indicate significance at the 0.01, 0.05 and 0.1 levels, respectively.

Table 2.7 Signed tests: restatement impact on EPS only (N = 172) [dependent variable ACCOUNTING_FRAUD]

Panel A: Reduced Models

	Specification 1		Specification 2		Specification 3	
Variable	Coef.	*p*-value	Coef.	*p*-value	Coef.	*p*-value
Intercept	0.0134	0.0316**	0.0128	0.0398**	0.0175	0.0246**
ME	0.1254	0.0000***				
ME_MEAN			0.1257	0.0000***		
JONES					−0.3053	0.0000***
$KOTHARI_1$						
$KOTHARI_0$						
FRANCIS						
DECHOW&DICHEV						
Adjusted-R^2	73.81%		73.98%		58.96%	
F-stat.	482.94***		487.15***		246.71***	
N	172		172		172	

Panel B: Extended Models

	Specification 1		Specification 2		Specification 3	
Variable	Coef.	*p*-value	Coef.	*p*-value	Coef.	*p*-value
Intercept	0.09087	0.03840***	0.0900	0.0399**	0.1687	0.0013***
ME	0.12218	0.00000***				
ME_MEAN			0.1224	0.0000***		
JONES					−0.2939	0.0000***
$KOTHARI_1$						
$KOTHARI_0$						
FRANCIS						
DECHOW&DICHEV						
ACCTG_CHANGE	0.17520	0.39610	0.1765	0.3915	0.0859	0.7312
LEVERAGE	−0.01102	0.79040	−0.0104	0.8022	0.0399	0.4289
BIGX	0.01487	0.50970	0.0151	0.5009	−0.0192	0.4792
AUDITOR_OPINION	−0.01236	0.41280	−0.0109	0.4686	−0.0136	0.4565
LOG(MARKET_CAP)	−0.00621	0.14100	−0.0062	0.1378	−0.0066	0.1949
LOG(NUMEST)	−0.00020	0.98720	−0.0002	0.9887	−0.0093	0.5413
MAJOR_MARKET	−0.03273	0.34930	−0.0332	0.3406	−0.0698	0.0986*
Adjusted-R^2	73.88%		74.01%		61.56%	
F-stat.	53.32***		53.67***		30.62***	
N	149		149		149	

Specification 4		Specification 5		Specification 6		Specification 7	
Coef.	*p*-value	Coef.	*p*-value	Coef.	*p*-value	Coef.	*p*-value
0.0184	0.0847*	0.0064	0.4388	0.0306	0.0120**	0.0228	0.0653*
−0.4301	0.0000***						
		−0.5854	0.0000***				
				−0.0168	0.8611		
						−0.2093	0.0198**
23.67%		54.23%		−0.57%		2.58%	
54.02***		203.57***		0.03		5.53**	
172		172		172		172	

Specification 4		Specification 5		Specification 6		Specification 7	
Coef.	*p*-value	Coef.	*p*-value	Coef.	*p*-value	Coef.	*p*-value
0.2911	0.0000***	0.2216	0.0000***	0.3929	0.0000***	0.3586	0.0000***
−0.4625	0.0000***						
		−0.5961	0.0000***				
				−0.0763	0.5036		
						−0.2288	0.0311**
0.1129	0.7275	−0.0115	0.9628	−0.0143	0.9694	−0.0304	0.9342
0.0755	0.2558	0.1005	0.0478	−0.0114	0.8802	−0.0029	0.9686
−0.0497	0.1568	−0.0480	0.0736*	−0.0462	0.2550	−0.0330	0.4141
−0.0027	0.9088	0.0120	0.5069	−0.0065	0.8134	−0.0093	0.7302
−0.0029	0.6606	−0.0077	0.1319	0.0009	0.9020	0.0030	0.6961
−0.0310	0.1143	−0.0137	0.3620	−0.0410	0.0754*	−0.0412	0.0651*
−0.1770	0.0009***	−0.1216	0.0030***	−0.2649	0.0000***	−0.2648	0.0000***
35.56%		62.39%		14.25%		16.80%	
11.20***		31.68***		4.07***		4.73**	
149		149		149		149	

Notes: ***, **, and * indicate significance at the 0.01, 0.05 and 0.1 levels, respectively.

Table 2.8 Signed tests: restatement impact on EPS only / Upward (N = 133) [dependent variable ACCOUNTING_FRAUD]

Panel A: Reduced Models

	Specification 1		Specification 2		Specification 3	
Variable	Coef.	*p*-value	Coef.	*p*-value	Coef.	*p*-value
Intercept	0.0262	0.0005***	0.0256	0.0007***	0.0281	0.0033***
ME	0.1264	0.0000***				
ME_MEAN			0.1266	0.0000***		
JONES					−0.3143	0.0000***
$KOTHARI_1$						
$KOTHARI_0$						
FRANCIS						
DECHOW&DICHEV						
Adjusted-R^2	77.08%		77.15%		62.30%	
F-stat.	445.00***		446.76***		219.13***	
N	133		133		133	

Panel B: Extended Models

	Specification 1		Specification 2		Specification 3	
Variable	Coef.	*p*-value	Coef.	*p*-value	Coef.	*p*-value
Intercept	0.0745	0.1263	0.0748	0.1246	0.1505	0.0129
ME	0.1263	0.0000***				
ME_MEAN			0.1264	0.0000***		
JONES					−0.3082	0.0000
$KOTHARI_1$						
$KOTHARI_0$						
FRANCIS						
DECHOW&DICHEV						
ACCTG_CHANGE	0.3193	0.6324	0.3267	0.6243	0.1049	0.9003
LEVERAGE	−0.0105	0.8235	−0.0092	0.8446	0.0522	0.3815
BIGX	0.0270	0.3048	0.0274	0.2971	−0.0053	0.8724
AUDITOR_OPINION	−0.0249	0.1702	−0.0232	0.2021	−0.0268	0.2403
LOG(MARKET_CAP)	−0.0091	0.1019	−0.0092	0.0968	−0.0083	0.2329
LOG(NUMEST)	0.0123	0.4294	0.0121	0.4358	−0.0034	0.8605
MAJOR_MARKET	−0.0056	0.8817	−0.0066	0.8601	−0.0459	0.3249
Adjusted-R^2	77.01%		77.04%		63.80%	
F-stat.	48.72***		48.80***		26.11***	
N	115		115		115	

Specification 4		Specification 5		Specification 6		Specification 7	
Coef.	*p*-value	Coef.	*p*-value	Coef.	*p*-value	Coef.	*p*-value
0.0294	0.0241**	0.0149	0.1381	0.0453	0.0036***	0.0352	0.0289**
−0.5189	0.0000***						
		−0.6219	0.0000***				
				−0.0238	0.8361		
						−0.2217	0.0481**
30.03%		58.86%		−0.73%		2.21%	
57.65***		189.82***		0.04		3.98**	
133		133		133		133	

Specification 4		Specification 5		Specification 6		Specification 7	
Coef.	*p*-value	Coef.	*p*-value	Coef.	*p*-value	Coef.	*p*-value
0.2531	0.0010	0.1987	0.0007	0.3897	0.0000	0.3445	0.0002
−0.5767	0.0000						
		−0.6328	0.0000				
				−0.0874	0.5423		
						−0.2611	0.0635
0.0309	0.9771	−0.0208	0.9798	−0.0045	0.9973	−0.0645	0.9601
0.0846	0.2757	0.1066	0.0728	−0.0256	0.7828	−0.0144	0.8744
−0.0434	0.2987	−0.0534	0.0960	−0.0473	0.3548	−0.0325	0.5235
−0.0139	0.6337	0.0084	0.7055	−0.0145	0.6834	−0.0148	0.6725
−0.0013	0.8856	−0.0054	0.4253	0.0027	0.8059	0.0061	0.5785
−0.0342	0.1657	−0.0135	0.4757	−0.0456	0.1373	−0.0466	0.1172
−0.1411	0.0160**	−0.1053	0.0185**	−0.2509	0.0004***	−0.2553	0.0002***
40.36%		65.15%		11.77%		14.30%	
10.64***		27.63***		2.90***		3.37**	
115		115		115		115	

Notes: ***, **, and * indicate significance at the 0.01, 0.05 and 0.1 levels, respectively.

deflated by the lagged total assets) than to the traditional measures of discretionary accruals.

6. POTENTIAL ENDOGENEITY BIAS OF CORPORATE EARNINGS FRAUD

On the one hand, we assume that the restated amount and the EM variables (e.g., MEC and discretionary accruals) are not determined simultaneously (simultaneous equation bias), such that the managed earnings component would be an exogenous variable (Jones, Krishnan and Melendrez, 2008). On the other hand, according to prior literature (e.g., Beyer, 2008), we should be concerned that some (unobservable) variables that affect both earnings management and the properties of ex-post analysts' forecasts have been omitted from the regression analysis (i.e., correlated omitted variable bias), in which case discretionary accruals would be an endogenous variable. Basically, abnormal accruals might be *endogenous* with the decision of disclosing fraudulently reported earnings. However, fully endogenizing the fraudulent restated amount is likely to complicate the models' structure substantially, as that would require specifying the underlying (and thus unobservable) cost and benefit functions facing the companies' managers who engage in fraudulently overstating their earnings (Hui, Lennox and Zhang, 2014). To test whether MEC/discretionary accruals are endogenous in our restated amount equations, we would have performed an extended regression of the Hausman specification test (Larcker and Rusticus, 2010; Roberts and Whited, 2013),[1] which would have heavily complicated our model. As a result, we voluntarily decided to keep the estimated models quite simple given that our primary objective is to examine the relationships between EM measures, specifically our ME metric, and the financial fraud magnitude.

7. CONCLUSION

Our piece of research contributes to the literature on measurement of earnings manipulation and financial statement fraud in several ways. First, we compare a comprehensive set of discretionary accounting models (Dechow et al., 1995; Dechow and Dichev, 2002; McNichols, 2002; Kothari et al., 2005; Francis et al., 2005) with the innovative 'managed earnings component' measure developed by Aubert and Grudnitski (2012, 2014). The main results of the cross-sectional models that consist of regressing accruals and the managed earnings component against the magnitude of accounting fraud reveal that the MEC is a better indicator of fraudulent financial misstatements, across all the models estimated. Second, we examine the correlation between various discretionary accruals metrics and the size of the restated amount after the discovery of the fraud by the SEC for a sample of companies subject to an enforcement action procedure, employing both absolute and actual values. Fundamentally, we strongly believe that the restatement amount defined as the difference between the 'originally reported' earnings and the 'restated' earnings is the most appropriate measure of the extent of the managerial discretion in financial reporting choices. Overall, our results indicate that the MEC has a greater ability than the discretionary accruals models to detect the amount of fraudulently overstated earnings, thus allowing the SEC to concentrate on the most profitable financial statement frauds. By better understanding these fraudulent characteristics, regulators should be in a better position to identify and curtail misstatement activity in the future. The efficient functioning of financial markets depends crucially on the quality of the accounting information provided to investors.

NOTE

1. By estimating a reduced form, our variables of discretionary accruals could be explained by the exogenous variables of the OLS model and an additional instrumental variable, namely, a leverage variable (proxy for debt covenant violation), which is relevant for explaining the extent to which firms' managers have a strong incentive to report fraudulent earnings (Jones, Krishnan and Melendrez, 2008; Dechow, Ge, Larson and Sloan, 2011).

REFERENCES

Aubert, F. and Grudnitski, G. (2012), 'Analysts' estimates: What they could be telling us about the impact of IFRS on earnings manipulation in Europe', *Review of Accounting and Finance*, 11(1): 53–72.

Aubert, F. and Grudnitski, G. (2014), 'The impact of SOX on opportunistic management behavior', *International Review of Financial Analysis*, 32: 188–198.

Becker, C.L., DeFond, M.L., Jiambalvo, J. and Subramanyam, K.R. (1998), 'The effect of audit quality on earnings management', *Contemporary Accounting Research*, 15(1): 1–24.

Beneish, M.D. (1999), 'The detection of earnings manipulation', *Financial Analysts Journal*, 55(5): 24–36.

Bessler, W. and Stanzel, M. (2009), 'Conflicts of interest and research quality of affiliated analysts in the German Universal Banking System: Evidence from IPO underwriting', *European Financial Management*, 15(4): 757–786.

Beyer, A. (2008), 'Financial analysts' forecast revisions and managers' reporting behavior', *Journal of Accounting and Economics*, 46(2–3): 334–348.

Cornett, M., McNutt, J. and Tehranian, H. (2009), 'Corporate governance and earnings management at large U.S. bank holding companies', *Journal of Corporate Finance*, 15: 412–430.

Dechow, P.M. and Dichev, I.D. (2002), 'The quality of accruals and earnings: The role of accrual estimation errors', *The Accounting Review*, 77: 35–59.
Dechow, P., Ge, W., Larson, C.R. and Sloan, R.G. (2011), 'Predicting material accounting misstatements', *Contemporary Accounting Research*, 28(1): 17–82.
Dechow, P., Sloan, R. and Sweeney, A. (1995), 'Detecting earnings management', *The Accounting Review*, 1970: 3–42.
Francis, J., LaFond, R., Olsson P. and Schipper K. (2005), 'The market pricing of accruals quality', *Journal of Accounting and Economics*, 39: 295–327.
Gajewski, J.-F. and Quéré, B. (2001), 'The information content of earnings and turnover announcements in France', *European Accounting Review*, 10(4): 679–704.
Hui, K.W., Lennox, C. and Zhang, G. (2014), 'The market's valuation of fraudulently reported earnings', *Journal of Business Finance & Accounting*, 41(5): 627–651.
Jones, J. (1991), 'Earnings management during import relief investigations', *Journal of Accounting Research*, 29(2): 193–228.
Jones, K., Khrishnan, G.V. and Melendrez, K.D. (2008), 'Do models of discretionary accruals detect actual cases of fraudulent and restated earnings? An empirical analysis', *Contemporary Accounting Research*, 25(2)(Summer): 499–531.
Keune, M.B. and Johnstone, K.M. (2012), 'Materiality judgements and the resolution of detected misstatements: The role of managers, auditors, and audit committees', *The Accounting Review*, 87(5): 1641–1677.
Kothari, S.P., Leone, A. and Wasley, C. (2005), 'Performance matched discretionary accrual measures', *Journal of Accounting and Economics*, 39(2): 163–197.
Lambert, R. (2001), 'Contracting theory and accounting', *Journal of Accounting and Economics*, 32: 3–87.
Larcker, D.F. and Rusticus, T.O. (2010), 'On the use of instrumental variables in accounting research', *Journal of Accounting and Economics*, 49(3): 186–205.
McNichols, M.F. (2002), 'The quality of accruals and earnings: The role of accrual estimation errors: Discussion', *The Accounting Review*, 77: 61–69.
Roberts, M.R. and Whited, T.M. (2013), 'Endogeneity in empirical corporate finance', in G.M. Constantinides, M. Harris and R.M. Stulz (ed.), *Handbook of the Economics of Finance*. North Holland: Elsevier, Amsterdam.
Tsipouridoua, M. and Spathisb, C. (2012), 'Earnings management and the role of auditors in an unusual IFRS context: The case of Greece', *Journal of International Accounting, Auditing and Taxation*, 21: 62–78.
Tsipouridoua, M. and Spathisb, C. (2014), 'Audit opinion and earnings management: Evidence from Greece', *Accounting Forum*, 38: 38–54.

3. Fostering green investment decisions: the real option approach

Jessica Fouilloux and Jean-Laurent Viviani

1. INTRODUCTION

Calling on the context of modern financial theory to favour green investment decisions may seem a daunting task. Green investments challenge the traditional investment decision models in several aspects. Following financial theory, the traditional objective of investment must be to create value for shareholders, which is not the primary objective of green investments. In the corporate social responsibility literature, financial objectives are clearly distinguished from environmental ones. Socially responsible investments (SRI) are characterized by the separation between financial and extra financial criteria in the portfolio selection process. According to Renneboog et al. (2008), unlike the conventional type of investment, SRI applies a set of filters to select or exclude investment assets based on ecological, social, corporate and even ethical governance.

Following the IMF definition (Eyraud at al., 2011), green investment refers to the investment necessary to reduce greenhouse gas and air pollutant emissions. Taking the environment seriously into account generates new constraints and risks for companies. Risks that the company must learn to manage are related to fluctuations in prices and the quantities of inputs, as well as regulatory risks associated with rapid and unpredictable changes in regulations concerning environmental protection and, more generally, strategic and reputation risk. However, note that the green perspective should not be seen solely as a source of cost; it can also create growth opportunities in the future (McWilliams and Siegel, 2001).

Finance, as a scientific discipline, should expand its conceptual framework to analyse environmental financial decisions taken by a company. Indeed, environmental issues, by their specific characteristics (radical uncertainty, complexity, long-term horizon, ethical objectives and partnership perspective), should stimulate reflection on the current paradigm of finance and the emergence of new concepts and methods. At the least, the characteristics of green investment justify the development of a specific field to study how traditional concepts and methods in finance can incorporate the dimension of the natural environment in the decision-making process. Thus, we define environmental or green corporate finance as a consideration of the dimension of the natural environment in the financial decisions of a company. Coping with the environmental dimension involves modifications in the operational management, the investment strategies (modification of existing plants, the choice of new manufacturing plants and technologies, R&D), and the financing policy of companies.

In this chapter we concentrate on investment decisions. Our objective is twofold. The first is to show that the real option model is well suited to the characteristics of green investment decisions. In effect, a real option is a decision that creates the right, but not the obligation, to pursue a future decision. The main types of options investigated in the green investment literature are the option to defer an investment, to grow (make a first investment (R&D for instance) that can enable the company to make further investments in the future), to extend (transfer technologies or knowledge gained to other projects), to switch from polluting to green technologies, and to abandon. The real options approach is relevant when investments are characterized by sequential, irreversible investments made under conditions of uncertainty (Dixit and Pindyck, 1994). We show that these characteristics are typical of green investing. Second, we question the results obtained in the literature on the application of real option models to green investment by demonstrating that they are obtained on very specific assumptions not necessarily in accordance with green investment specificities.

The chapter highlights the dimensions of green investments (irreversibility, flexibility, and uncertainty) that justify the use of real option models (compared to the traditional discount cash flow model). It criticizes the conventional recommendation to 'wait and see' justified by real option models due to the high level of risk in the context of green investments. This result is in fact not robust and depends mainly on the nature of the risk (specific or systematic, exogenous or endogenous, continuous or discontinuous, ambiguous or not) and on the fact that the competitive environment (strategies of actual or potential competitors) is not taken into account in green investment real option models. Finally, it offers a literature review of recent real option models applied to green investment.

The chapter is therefore organized as follows. In section 2, by examining three important dimensions of green investment decisions – irreversibility, flexibility and uncertainty – we demonstrate that the real option model is suitable for informing decisions in this field. In the third section, we review the decisions recommended by real option models when applied to green investment. The fourth section draws on the consequences of recent developments, and section 5 presents new developments in the real option theory to challenge the previous results. The last section offers a conclusion.

2. DIMENSIONS OF GREEN INVESTMENT DECISIONS

The valuation of an investment project is traditionally performed using the Discounted Cash Flow (DCF) technique. The classical Net Present Value (NPV) criterion incorporates studying the present value of cash inflows less the present value of cash outflows. NPV advocates accepting the project when NPV has a positive value and rejecting it when the calculated value is negative. However, the decisions made at the corporate level are not this simple. Three main dimensions justifying the use of real option models are examined in detail here in the context of green investing: irreversibility, flexibility and uncertainty (Dixit and Pindyck, 1994).

2.1 Irreversibility

Interactions between the company and its natural environment are considered in the literature from two main angles: the management of natural resources and environmental management. The management of natural resources is concerned with resource extraction of the natural environment. The concern stems from the problems raised by irreversible resource depletion. Environmental management focuses on environmental releases by a company. The problem is reducing polluting emissions.

In consequence, two different types of irreversibility (Pindyck, 2007) are taken into account in the environmental field: irreversible damages to nature and the irreversibility of investment needed to reduce these damages. These two streams of the literature, originally distinct, have given rise to two different approaches to the theory of options that were born in approximately the same period.

The first approach (Arrow and Fisher, 1974; Henry, 1974; Hanemann, 1989) aims to warn against projects generating irreversible damage to the environment. The main argument is that, under uncertainty and irreversibility, it may be worthwhile to postpone investment and wait for new information to avoid adverse scenarios. In the case where environmental destruction is irreversible, traditional methods of investment decisions are biased in favour of adopting the project destroying nature. In contrast, option theory permits valuing the cost associated with this irreversible destruction of nature. Later models in this field are interested in more complex cases where the destruction (pollution) of nature is partially reversible (Zhao and Zilberman, 1999).

The second approach is the application of financial real option theory to environmental problems. It is this approach, which is more managerial, that is developed below. The presence of irreversibility is also necessary but it concerns the irreversibility of green investments that reduce damage to nature. In this case, irreversibility is a disincentive to implement green investments. Note that the concept of options used in both approaches is not exactly identical. Indeed, the value of a real option to wait depends on two factors: the value associated with information that will be collected during the waiting period (this value depends on the resolution of uncertainty) and the value because future investment can generate greater or lesser cash flows than current investments (this value does not depend on uncertainty). Arrow and Fisher's approach retains only the first source of value (the option value of waiting is then always positive), which is not the case for the real option approach (see Mensink and Requate (2005) for a clarification of this point).

2.2 Flexibility

The real options theory by giving a financial value to flexibility is ideal in regard to comparing solutions with different degrees of flexibility. It is also intended to exploit the flexibility inherent in the sequential nature of choice processes. We have already exposed that the value given to flexibility (the other side of irreversibility costs) explains why companies are slow to adopt irreversible investment in pollution control. We show here that flexibility is essential to comparing green investment projects.

Economic theory shows that the overall costs of reducing pollution are minimized when the division between the parties is such that it equalizes the marginal costs of abatement. Such allocation of effort can be better achieved by more flexible market mechanisms. This result serves as a theoretical foundation for the establishment of markets for pollutions rights (the US emissions trading markets for SO_2 and NOx and the European Union Emission Trading Scheme, EU ETS, are the most studied in the empirical literature). Markets for pollution rights introduce a global constraint on national or regional economies but leave more flexibility to companies: they must compare the development of solutions, often irreversible, to reduce pollution, with the more flexible solution, which is to buy tradable pollution rights.

To avoid making irreversible green investments, companies are often advised (based on real option theory) to choose a more flexible solution (Gollier et al., 2005; Malchow-Møller and Thorsen, 2005; Kort et al., 2010). Flexible decisions could entail making a flexible sequence of smaller investments rather than a single large investment, buying pollution rights or even reducing production levels to meet quotas of pollutant emissions rather than investing. Cortazar et al. (1998) show that firms with a low output price or high volatility have no incentive to invest and should cut production. Even when they decide to invest in green projects, companies tend to choose more flexible technologies. However, these technologies are often more costly. Case studies (Blyth et al., 2007; Yang et al., 2008) show that the adoption of more flexible technologies depends essentially on the ability of firms to pass their extra costs on in the price of their product.

2.3 Uncertainty

A key insight for understanding real option models is that there is economic value to resolving the uncertainty associated with any decision. Therefore, it is often worthwhile to wait so that some of the uncertainty resolves or to spend money now to gain the necessary time to resolve uncertainty.

It turns out that the existence of a strong environmental uncertainty is widely recognized in the literature in green management (Busch and Hoffman, 2009). Uncertainty concerns the availability of resources in the future and ecosystem dynamics (Chichilnisky and Heal, 1998; King, 1995) and the long-term effect of polluting emissions on the ecosystem. It is also linked to changing social expectations, regulations (Kang and Létourneau, 2016) and industry standards (Ishii and Yan, 2007; McDevitt et al., 2007; Husted, 2005). Risks arise from many sources, affecting the cash flows of a project – price risks, technological risks and financial risks. These different risks interact to affect the optimal technology adoption strategy.

We give only one important example concerning new price risks affecting green projects. Political authorities have encouraged the creation and development of new markets, including energy and carbon markets. One major objective of the creation of these markets (electricity and gas at the initiative of the European Union for instance) is to give a better signal on the scarcity of natural resources (the existence of a market creates a closer link between scarcity and price). However, these markets also have the consequences of increasing the price risk for companies. Several studies show that the traditional DCF approach is obsolete within the new deregulated environment and that the real option approaches must be adopted (Tseng and Barz, 2002; Deng and Oren, 2003). For instance, Reedman et al. (2006) show that the uptake of various electricity generation technologies varies significantly depending on investors' view of carbon price uncertainty.

Environmental uncertainty has several peculiarities. Environmental phenomena are characterized by nonlinearity and discontinuities (Baranzini et al., 2003; Pindyck, 2007), which makes their prediction difficult. It concerns the evolution of systems over long periods, with forecasting requiring long data series. Most of these systems may appear to be relatively stable across financial decisions and therefore do not require a prediction mechanism (Busch and Hoffman, 2009). Uncertainty is 'radical'; it is difficult to model by traditional probability theory. It concerns the long term but involves changes in the business environment which may be rapid and massive ('ecological surprises' (King, 1995)). It is also strategic in nature and depends on social interaction (the reaction of competitors, customers and suppliers, the public, etc.). Finally, it affects not only risk factors but also the impact of these factors on companies. Because of the complexity of causal chains and technical solutions available to the company, the sensitivity of company profit or value to changes in the natural environment is difficult to calculate. We show in the last section that those characteristics are not properly taken into account in traditional real option models and that their inclusion could change recommendations of real option models concerning the decision to invest.

3. WHAT ARE THE RECOMMENDATIONS OF TRADITIONAL REAL OPTION MODELS?

We concentrate on three important predictions in the perspective of fostering green investment. The first one is that when an irreversible investment project is implemented, the company loses the opportunity to take another (eventually better) decision. Therefore, the opportunity cost of an irreversible project is higher than that given by the traditional NPV model. This effect is called the hysteresis phenomenon in the real option literature. The two other ones stem from uncertainty and the arrival of new information. For a large irreversible investment, it could be optimal to make the decision to defer to wait for new information and avoid unfavourable outcomes. However, option models justify early investing in relatively small investments generating new information.

3.1 The Hysteresis Phenomenon

Companies have no incentive to invest in pollution control, even if the marginal gain is above the marginal cost of abatement investments (Dixit, 1992). In other words, green investments require greater returns than the traditional NPV break-even point. Chao and Wilson (1993) use an option value approach to study the effect of a market for emissions allowances on investments to reduce pollution. They conclude that the price of allowances may exceed the marginal cost of scrubbers by an amount that reflects the expected present value of the greater flexibility provided by pollution permits compared with the irreversible commitment of a scrubber. Kjaerland (2007) conducts a real option analysis of hydropower investments in Norway. His simulations show that investment is implemented only for a 'very high' level of electricity price, explaining the low level of investment in the hydropower sector. The conclusions are similar for models based on the assumption of the total irreversibility of investments in pollution control. Some studies try to take into account a greater flexibility of green investments to make them more attractive. For example, Insley (2003) focuses on the choice of either buying emission permits or investing in clean filters (to reduce emissions of SO_2). Inspired by Majd and Pindyck (1987), she introduces the possibility of investing gradually in the filters and several other new features compared to the original model: investment is implemented on existing plants that are often already quite old; therefore, the option is limited to the duration of the plant and does not have an infinite duration, as in Majd and Pindyck (plants integrate the new pollution control mechanism more efficiently or use cleaner energy sources); thus investment did not lengthen the life of the plant, and the investment decision was discontinuous. Even with these more flexible assumptions, she fails to justify green investment except for high prices of carbon.

3.2 Waiting to Invest

The standard model of irreversible investment under uncertainty shows that the value of the option to wait increases with uncertainty and that the threshold for implementation of the investment increases (McDonald and Siegel, 1986). Following this line of argument, because green investments face high uncertainty, their wait option value is high, justifying the 'wait and see' attitude of companies towards green investing. Even governmental mechanisms aimed at reducing pollution, such as markets for pollution rights, can reinforce company inertia because they increase uncertainty by introducing a new price risk (price of carbon). However, uncertainty about the price of pollution rights is only a small part of the uncertainty faced by an investment project to reduce pollution. The main uncertainty lies mostly in the process cost of the proposed pollution reduction (Zhao, 2003).

Most empirical studies are in line with the 'wait and see' argument. Sarkis and Tamarkin (2005) show, using internal data of the company BP, that the project of CO_2 reinjection would be postponed indefinitely unless the carbon price reaches very high levels. In the same vein, Wirl (2006) demonstrates that uncertainty increases the threshold to stop greenhouse gas emissions. Fleten et al. (2007) find that companies should wait for higher electricity prices before investing in wind power generation equipment. Yang et al. (2008) and Fuss et al. (2008) conclude that firms expecting climate policy uncertainty should wait until the uncertainty is resolved.

Moreover, as noted above, progressive investment reduces the degree of irreversibility and therefore the value of the option to wait. However, this higher investment flexibility comes at a cost. There is thus a debate on whether to make the investment once or at several times (Dixit and Pindyck, 1994, pp. 51–54; Huisman and Kort, 2004). The case studies (Laurikka, 2006; Laurikka and Koljonen, 2006; Abadie and Chamorro, 2008) can give a better idea of the importance of these effects in more concrete situations. The findings are generally not very favourable to the realization of green investments (even by steps) because the carbon price has to reach unrealistic levels in order for this type of investment to be implemented.

Blyth (2009) investigates what could be the governmental measures to reduce uncertainty (commitment to regulation stability, price cap and floor) and their impact on the 'wait and see' attitudes in the function of the type of low-carbon technologies implemented in the power sector. He also presents an interesting literature review on what could be the contractual arrangements between governments and producers aiming to reduce uncertainty.

3.3 Timing of the Investment

Real options theory can justify investments in the early stages of green projects (Figge, 2005). In effect, the sequential nature of research and development (R&D) has led managers to reject usual evaluation criteria such as NPV. However, real option models value flexibility in a sequential decision-making process with decision points at various development stages before a technology is commercialized. Therefore, green investments are analysed in a similar way to R&D investments and considered as growth options. They are starting points to future investments that will not necessarily be implemented. McGrath (1997) analyses in this way investments in technologies of pollution control. Lee et al. (2003) conduct a synthesis of how to calculate the option value of renewable energy R&D and the challenges for such an evaluation.

Given the many uncertainties about the nature and profitability of green investment, the early stages of a green investment should be viewed not only as a growth option but also as a learning option. In effect, these initial stages not only generate information but also develop knowledge that will be used in later stages (Yeo and Qiu, 2003). They increase the dynamic capabilities of the company (Kyläheiko et al., 2002). The learning effect could be a justification to accelerate the implementation of green investment.

More sophisticated models, using compound options (option on option first applied in the R&D context by Grenadier and Weiss (1997)), address the problem of a company's optimal migration to green technologies. The switchover to new green technologies takes time, and this amount of time is uncertain. This uncertain 'time to build' is a major justification of the usage of real option models. Davis and Owens (2003) and Siddiqui et al. (2007) apply the technique of compounded options to analyse the federal research programme in renewable energy. They show that, contrary to the traditional analysis by the discounted cash flow approach (which gives a negative NPV for the programme), the real options approach justifies an increased budget.

In conclusion, traditional real options theory leads to conflicting recommendations regarding investment for environmental protection. In effect, the recommendations are as follows:

- To delay investments irreversibly destroying the environment,
- To delay irreversible investments reducing environmental destruction,
- To implement investments that allow the emergence of future green technology.

4. CONSEQUENCES OF RECENT DEVELOPMENTS IN REAL OPTION MODELS

In this section, we want to show how recent developments in real option theory can challenge the famous 'wait and see' recommendation of traditional option models used in the green investment literature.

4.1 Risk in Real Option Models

The traditional conclusion of the positive effect of an increase of risk on waiting depends in fact on the notion of risk that is used.

First, the positive effect of an increase in risk on the duration of the waiting period is far from unambiguous, as claimed by the canonical models of McDonald and Siegel (1986) and Dixit and Pindyck (1994). Recent approaches, based on the classical decomposition of risk into a systematic and a specific component, question this general result (Sarkar, 2000, Lund, 2005; Wong, 2007). If it is the specific (diversifiable) risk that increases the waiting period, in this case the canonical result remains true, but if it is the systematic risk that increases, the results are more complex.

There are in fact two different effects when volatility increases: the classical 'risk effect' enhances the value of the option to invest in the project and thus makes waiting more beneficial, and the 'return effect' arising from the upward adjustment of the discount rate (due to an increase in systematic risk) makes waiting more costly by increasing the opportunity cost of waiting. The return factor dominates for low levels of risk, whereas the risk factor dominates for high levels of risk. Concerning the waiting period of green investments, conclusions are difficult to assess theoretically. On one hand, by their global aspect, environmental risk factors are probably systematic and thus reinforce the 'return effect'. On the other hand, green investments face high uncertainty where the 'risk effect' dominates the 'return effect'.

Second, in traditional option models, stochastic processes used are continuous. However, risk can also come in the form of climate or environmental catastrophes inducing stochastic processes of risk factors, which should introduce jumps. Baranzini et al. (2003) show that this introduction accelerates the implementation of green policies. The main reason is that a reduction of the waiting period reduces the probability that a catastrophe occurs before any preventing action takes place.

Third, Knight's (1921) distinction between risk and uncertainty seems to us very important in the green investment field (see our analysis of environmental uncertainty above). Traditional real option models are well suited for incorporating risk, an uncertain realization from a well-specified probability distribution, but not for coping with the inherent unknowability that characterizes the main aspects of the green investment context. Recent research has tried to incorporate Knightian uncertainty (often named ambiguity) in real option models. In the axiomatic framework of Epstein and Schneider (2003), in the presence of ambiguity, agents face not a single probability distribution but a set of probability distributions. In this case, an ambiguity-averse agent acts using the probability distribution leading to the worst outcome, named the worst scenario.

Option models in the presence of ambiguity can justify a reduction in the waiting time, contrary to the conclusion of traditional option models. The reasoning is the following: if the company perceives the future as ambiguous, then waiting has less value because the expected value of new information is reduced. The intuition is that most information has no effect on the worst scenario and thus on the decisions of companies in this context. Moreover, Trojanowska and Kort (2010) show that ambiguity aversion leads to an erosion of the value of the investment opportunity, which can accelerate the implementation of the investment.

Going even further in the analysis, Miao and Wang (2011) distinguish two types of ambiguity resolution: if the ambiguity is resolved at the time the option is exercised, an increase in ambiguity speeds up investment, but if ambiguity remains after the investment (the option exercise date), the investment date is postponed in the presence of ambiguity. In this last case, the investor is ambiguous about the future profit opportunities of the investment project.

In the context of green investments and policy, Asano (2010) introduces ambiguity to analyse governmental environmental policy. Fouilloux et al. (2015) incorporate ambiguity in a real option model to analyse investment in carbon emissions reduction programmes, and Gao and Driouchi (2013), in the context of infrastructure investment, show that an increase in uncertainty often leads to a decrease in the investment threshold. This unusual relationship is even amplified if we suppose, as in Gao and Driouchi (2013), that agents can be optimistic.

Finally, option models suppose that uncertainty resolution is exogenous. However, if uncertainty resolution emerges as an outcome of firm action, as is probably the case for green investments, the option framework is called into question (Adner and Levinthal, 2004). In the case where new opportunities are identified as a consequence of companies' investments, the 'wait and see' behaviour is no longer justified.

4.2 Strategic Interactions

In traditional real option models, strategic interactions are neglected. In these models, prices follow exogenous stochastic processes that completely shape business decisions. However, concerning the environmental question, strategic interactions often cannot be neglected: first because the real option approach emphasizes irreversibility but also the indivisibility of investments (this characteristic often implies a limited number of players, hence imperfect competition); second, because major polluters are often large companies in the same industry (large utility companies for instance); and third because companies interact with governments and other large organizations concerning environmental regulation and constraints.

Real option models in the presence of interaction are quite complex, and thus their conclusions concerning the impact of interactions on the wait duration appear conflicting and not very robust. Leahy (1993) and Dixit and Pindyck (1994) contend that competition does not necessarily reduce the value of waiting if firms correctly anticipate the strategies of other companies and their impact on the price process and if assets have an infinite lifetime. However, these conditions are hardly satisfied in practice. Caballero (1991) suggests that imperfect competition is vital for predicting a negative relationship between uncertainty and investment. For example, competition might mitigate the value of a real option to wait through the threat of pre-emption, as in Grenadier (2002). Ankum and Smit (1993) and Trigeorgis (1996) associate increased competition with a higher dividend yield from the underlying asset. When the dividend is high enough, it can induce early exercise by reducing the value of the option to wait. Similar results are obtained in the presence of potential competitors with entry options (Perotti and Rossetto, 2001) or for two symmetrical competing firms (Huisman and Kort, 1999). Finally, Grenadier (2002) shows, in a quite general setting, that if exercise strategies must be formed as a part of a strategic equilibrium, the value of the waiting option decreases dramatically. These results suggest that the government could speed up green investments by ensuring a high level of competition among investors and low barriers to entry.

Table 3.1 summarizes the impact of option model characteristics on the waiting time period. As seen, the conventional thinking that real option

Table 3.1 Impact of the parameters of the option model on the waiting period

Parameters	Consequences on the waiting period	References[a] (in bold when applied to green investment or policy)
Life-time of the project	Increase	Gryglewicz et al. (2008); **Abadie and Chamorro (2008)**; **Fouilloux et al. (2015)**
Uncertainty		
Specific risk	Increase	McDonald and Siegel (1986); Dixit and Pindyck (1994), **most papers applied to green investment**
Systematic risk	?	Sarkar (2000); Lund (2005) Wong (2007); **Fouilloux et al. (2015)**
Jump risk	Decrease	**Baranzini et al. (2003)**
Knightian uncertainty	?	Trojanowska and Kort (2010); **Asano (2010)**; Miao and Wang (2011); **Gao and Driouchi (2013); Fouilloux et al. (2015)**
Endogenous uncertainty	Decrease	Adner and Levinthal (2004)
Strategic interactions	Decrease	Caballero (1991); Ankum and Smit (1993); Trigeorgis (1996); Grenadier (2002)
Entry option	Decrease	Perotti and Rossetto (2001); Huisman and Kort (1999)

Note: [a] Far from exhaustive.

models justify a wait-and-see attitude is far from justified if one takes into account all the developments in real option theory. However, we can see that the green investment literature has not yet taken into account all the dimensions of these recent developments (strategic interaction and potential entry, endogenous uncertainty).

5. DEVELOPMENTS OF REAL OPTION MODELS IN GREEN INVESTMENT

Green investment can be classified according to its intermediate objective (Eyraud et al., 2011). Green investment can be defined as strategies that reduce emissions caused by **energy production**, **energy consumption** or **carbon sequestration reduction**. Energy production is challenged by low-emission energy investment for electricity generation (hydropower, nuclear, solar, wind, etc.) or direct sources of energy (biofuel, biomass, solar and geothermal for heating). Energy consumption concerns the energy to produce goods and services. Potential gains can be achieved in the electricity sector, transport, industrial management and construction. Lastly, carbon sequestration, in charge of 20 per cent of total emissions, can be improved by decreasing deforestation, changes in the agriculture sector and the development of carbon capture and storage technologies.

5.1 Real Options and Energy Production

Investing in electric power generation is associated with multiple uncertainties that justify the use of real options. First, the establishment of energy markets generates volatile power prices, and second, the constraints related to the environment lead to lower CO_2 emissions. In addition, other uncertainties exist as internal or external uncertainties that can be managed by real options. For example, wind projects depend on wind resources, which are considered as an external uncertainty. However, other uncertainties can appear as internal uncertainties and should be considered as endogenous if the investment is large enough to have an impact on electricity prices. The price of electricity becomes an endogenous uncertainty (see Martinez Cesena et al. (2013) for an electricity generation project review).

The investment in wind technology depends particularly on the development of a carbon market; a higher carbon price can support wind investment. Mo et al. (2016) show that the carbon market has a significant effect on wind power investment but is not the only factor. Real option simulation results exhibit a price for electricity that should be more than twice the one observed to trigger wind power industry development. A relatively higher carbon price is necessary to deliver investments in wind power, coupled with a carbon price stabilization mechanism, such as a carbon price floor.

Concerning electric power plant investment, Kang and Létourneau (2016) examine the effect of government credibility issues as policy risks on real option decisions. Using an exotic compound American option on multiple strips of European spread option, the authors show that government credibility risk leads to more investment in 'less green' resources. The second impact is additional cash flow variation, which increases the average time to investment (value of waiting). The authors also study an extreme case and show that government credibility can hasten investment because the risk may be more favourable to electric power companies. By considering uncertainty in electric power generation, Barria and Rudnick (2011) find a long-term critical electric price that highlights the threshold at which the investment becomes optimal. The authors also demonstrate that flexibility modelled in real option models contributes to an increase in the value of the investment.

Gas-fired power generation is becoming unprofitable and undesirable but is still needed to balance fluctuations in renewable energy technology (RET) power generation. RET includes weather-dependent sources and is difficult to store, so there is a need for more flexible balancing capacity for gas-fired generation. Hach and Spinler (2016) study the effect of capacity payments on investments in gas-fired power plants in the presence of different degrees of RET penetration. A real-option approach permits the evaluation of investment decisions and timing of a single investor in gas-fired power generation. Their model incorporates multiple uncertainties and assesses the effect of capacity payments under different degrees of RET penetration. Stochastic processes for peak-load electricity prices and natural gas prices are modelled. The authors find that capacity payments are an effective measure for promoting new gas-fired generation projects. Especially in times of high renewable feed-in, capacity payments are required to incentivize peak-load investments.

A Combined Cycle Gas Turbine (CCGT) plant (natural gas) has been considered as clean energy, and the question of switching from a coal-fired power plant to a CCGT one has been evoked by Liu et al. (2011). The authors developed a mathematical model accommodating multiple types of uncertainties (fuel prices, electricity prices and CO_2 emission prices). A numerical exercise studies the relationship between fuel and CO_2 prices and the decision to invest. The total probability of transforming a coal-fired power plant to a CCGT plant over the whole planning time horizon was found to be over 44 per cent.

Hydropower projects are the most economically attractive types of renewable electricity projects because they are typically conventional (with storage) or run-of-the-river (without storage) plants (Martinez Cesena and Mutale, 2011). Martinez Cesena and Mutale maintain that real option theory can be used to assess and hedge the generation risks of hydropower plants or identify flexibility within the design of plant projects. The latter application necessitates the ability to model the technical characteristics of hydropower projects. As was the case with wind power, the uncertainty of hydropower plants is an internal uncertainty because it is mainly a function of the water flows.

5.2 Real Options and Energy Consumption

Energy consumption refers to energy to produce goods and services. Potential gains can be achieved in the electricity sector, transport, industrial management and construction.

Given that companies have the flexibility to decide about the size and timing of a renewable electricity investment, Welling (2016) highlights the existence of four paradox effects. Only the type but not the amount of governmental support has an influence on the optimal capacity of a renewable electricity generating system. A decrease of governmental support over time may result in higher capacities of renewables installed on an industry level, at least in the short term. Likewise, higher uncertainty may encourage an expansion of these capacities. In contrast, technological progress may hamper the expansion of capacities. Linnerud et al. (2014) examine whether the prospect of a market for green certificates affects the timing of investment. They use real options theory to compare the value of immediate investments with the value of postponing the investment decision and possibly being entitled to sell certificates. The theory's main prediction is that firms will delay investments in long-lived irreversible assets whenever there is sufficient uncertainty that takes time to resolve and/or whenever the project value increases over time. Special attention is paid to whether behavioural responses varied between professional and non-professional investors.

Gao and Driouchi (2013) come back to the real option investment problem from a 'Knightian' perspective of uncertainty by examining the decision to invest in rail transit infrastructure (i.e., transport improvement). Sources of risk and ambiguity are modelled by population scale and the attitudes of decision-makers or social planners. The authors' results show that the threshold for investment varies with the ambiguity attitudes (i.e., pessimism or optimism) of decision-makers regarding future population dynamics and show that option value can increase or decrease with uncertainty subject to κ-ignorance and ambiguity. Li et al. (2015) also study transit technology investment issues under urban population volatility. A real option model is proposed to explicitly incorporate the effects of transit technology investment on the urban spatial structure in terms of households' residential location choices and the housing market. The trigger population thresholds for investing in a transit technology project and for shifting from one transit technology to another are explored analytically.

The European Union Emissions Trading System (EU ETS) aims at creating financial incentives for firms to invest in climate-friendly innovations. Using real options, Lukas and Welling (2014) demonstrate that under uncertainty, economic and ecological efficiency continue to be mutually exclusive. This problem is even worse if a climate-friendly project depends on investing in a whole supply chain. They model a sequential bargaining game in a supply chain where the parties negotiate over the implementation of a carbon dioxide (CO_2) saving investment project. They show that the outcome of their bargaining is not economically efficient and even less ecologically efficient. The supply chain becomes less economically efficient and less ecologically efficient with every additional chain link. Fouilloux et al. (2015) highlight the role of Knightian uncertainty and the correlation between carbon prices and the market portfolio on carbon emission reduction programmes in firms. The paper shows that, under a more complex setting, real option theory is not necessarily an obstacle to green investment decisions and can foster green investment.

European Union (EU) regulations aim to ensure that the energy performance of buildings meets the cost-optimality criteria for energy efficiency measures by proposing a methodological framework. Tadeu et al. (2015) consider a multi-objective optimization approach to identify the minimum global cost and primary energy needs of 154,000 combinations of energy efficiency measures. The cost-optimal levels and a return on investment approach are compared for a set of suitable solutions for reference building. The authors select 18 combinations of retrofit measures and analyse the influence of real options on investments. They show that a sound methodological approach to determining the advantages of this type of investment should be offered so that Member States can provide valuable information and ensure that the minimum requirements are profitable to most investors. Kumbaroglu and Madlener (2012) use a real options approach to introduce an advancement in the practice of the economic evaluation of building retrofit investment options. Their case study results indicate that energy price changes significantly affect the profitability of retrofit investments and that high price volatility creates a substantial value of waiting, making it more rational to postpone the investment.

5.3 Real Options and Carbon Sequestration

Carbon capture and storage (CCS, or sequestration) technology permits a reduction of GHG emissions by capturing CO_2 at source points (such as large fossil fuel or biomass energy facilities, industries with major CO_2 emissions, natural gas processing, synthetic fuel plants and fossil-fuel-based hydrogen production plants) and transporting and storing it in various deep geological formations.

Even if CCS has suffered from a lack of attention by the public and policy-makers over the past several years, various mitigation plans continue to emphasize the critical role of CCS in limiting the increase of temperature (CCS, 2014). Investing in a carbon capture project implies costs and success probabilities that depend on many factors, for example the scale and scope of the project, the political and public opinions regarding the technology, the storage situation, available funding, the (expected) availability of technology substitutes such as renewable energy technologies, and (expected) carbon prices (Eckhause and Herold, 2014). Eckhause and Herold focus on the construction of the power plant using CO_2 capture technology and on technical uncertainty (transport and storage are not considered). The model demonstrates improved risk reduction by employing multi-stage competition.

The theory of real options has been widely used to consider the decision to invest in improving the environment. It is quite adequate to account for the uncertainty in both price markets that are key in the decision to invest (electricity, carbon), reflecting the uncertainty of future policy decisions and the irreversibility of investment decisions. It is useful for both the choice of their mode of production of energy as well as future consumption choices.

6. CONCLUSION

In this chapter, we try to show that, contrary to popular belief, finance theory is not necessarily an obstacle to investment in sustainable development. It can even be a source of adopting environmentally friendly behaviours (Scholtens, 2006). The exponential growth of socially responsible investing is a striking example (Heinkel et al., 2001; Sparkes and Cowton, 2004). The analysis of portfolio performance also shows the benefits of investing in companies that benefit from climate change (renewable energy producers, wind, solar, etc.) (Chia et al., 2009). With the concepts and tools it offers, financial theory provides a better understanding of how economic agents react to environmental risks and opportunities.

Real options theory justifies the funding of research and development programmes in this area. We have also tried to show that the famous theoretical justification of 'wait and see' behaviour is questioned when new risk dimensions and strategic interactions are integrated into the real options model.

However, to build a corpus, green finance should not only rely on existing tools and theories of finance but also build a body of theories and methods that is specific and relatively homogeneous. This construction seems to us to go around the inclusion of radical uncertainty, the long term and the integration of different stakeholders. Some authors, though few in number, wonder about the specific characteristics of such a sustainable corporate finance. According to Soppe (2004), this new finance should be based on four pillars: the company taking into account multiple objectives (financial, social and environmental sustainable value creation); agents who are rational but seek cooperation and trust, which are the best ways to achieve multiple goals (Zsolnai, 2002); the inclusion of all stakeholders in the decision-making process; and the ethical framework of utilitarianism evolving into Aristotelianism, that is to say, virtuous behaviour (temperance, courage, prudence and justice) (Dobson, 1999; Van Staveren, 1999).

REFERENCES

Abadie, L.M. and J.M. Chamorro (2008), 'European CO_2 prices and carbon capture investments', *Energy Economics*, **30**(6), 2992–3015.

Adner, R. and D.A. Levinthal (2004), 'What is not a real option: considering boundaries for the application of real options to business strategy', *Academy of Management Review*, **29**(1), 74–86.

Ankum, L-A. and H. Smit (1993), 'A real options and game-theoretic approach to corporate investment strategy under competition', *Financial Management*, **22**(3), 241–50.

Arrow, K.J. and A.C. Fisher (1974), 'Environmental preservation, uncertainty, and irreversibility', *Quarterly Journal of Economics*, **88**, 312–19.

Asano, T. (2010), 'Precautionary principle and the optimal timing of environmental policy under ambiguity', *Environmental and Resources Economics*, **47**, 173–96.

Baranzini, A., M. Chesney and J. Morisset (2003), 'The impact of possible climate catastrophes on global warming policy', *Energy Policy*, **31**, 691–701.

Barria, C. and H. Rudnick (2011), 'Investment under uncertainty in power generation: integrated electricity prices modelling and real options approach', *Latin America Transactions*, **9**, 785–92.

Blyth, W. (2009), 'Risks and uncertainties in low-carbon energy investments', *European Review of Energy Markets*, **3**(2), 1–28.

Blyth, W., R. Bradley, D. Bunn, C. Clarke, T. Wilson and M. Yang (2007), 'Investment risks under uncertain climate change policy', *Energy Policy*, **35**, 5766–73.

Busch, T. and V.H. Hoffman (2009), 'Ecology-driven real options: an investment framework for incorporating uncertainties in the context of the natural environment', *Journal of Business Ethics*, **90**, 295–310.

Caballero, R.J. (1991), 'On the sign of the investment-uncertainty relationship', *American Economic Review*, **81**(1), 279–88.

CCS (2014), 'What lies in store for CCS?' Insight series, International Energy Agency, OCDE.
Chao, H.-P. and R. Wilson (1993), 'Option value of emission allowances', *Journal of Regulatory Economics*, **5**(3), 233–49.
Chia, C-P., L. Goldberg, D.T. Owyong, P. Shepard and T. Stoyanov (2009), 'Is there a green factor?' *Journal of Portfolio Management*, **35**(3), 34–40.
Chichilnisky, G. and G. Heal (1998), 'Global environmental risks', in G. Chichilnisky, G. Heal and A. Vercelli (eds), *Sustainability: Dynamics and Uncertainty*, Dordrecht: Kluwer Academic Publishers.
Cortazar, G., E.S. Schwartz and M. Salinas (1998), 'Evaluating environmental investments: a real options approach', *Management Science*, **44**(8), 1059–70.
Davis, G.A. and B. Owens (2003), 'Optimizing the level of renewable electric R&D expenditures using real options analysis', *Energy Policy*, **31**(15), 1589–1608.
Deng, S.J. and S.S. Oren (2003), 'Incorporating operational characteristics and startup costs in option-based valuation of power generation capacity', *Probability in the Engineering and Information Sciences*, **17**(2), 155–82.
Dixit, A.K. (1992), 'Investment and hysteresis', *The Journal of Economic Perspectives*, **6**(1), 107–32
Dixit, A.K and R.S. Pindyck (1994), *Investment under Uncertainty*, Princeton, NJ: Princeton University Press.
Dobson, J. (1999), 'Defending the stockholder model: a comment on Hasnas and on Dunfees' mom', *Business Ethics Quarterly*, **9**, 337–45.
Eckhause J. and J. Herold (2014), 'Using real options to determine optimal funding strategies for CO_2 capture, transport and storage projects in the European Union', *Energy Policy*, **66**, 115–34.
Epstein, L.G. and M. Schneider (2003), 'Recursive multiple-priors', *Journal of Economic Theory*, **113**, 1–31.
Eyraud, L., C. Zhang, A.A. Wane and B.J. Clements (2011), 'Who's going green and why? Trends and determinants of green investment', *IMF Working Papers*.
Figge, F. (2005), 'Value-based environmental management from environmental shareholder value to environmental option value', *Corporate Social Responsibility and Environmental Management*, **12**, 19–30.
Fleten, S., K. Maribu and I. Wangensteen (2007), 'Optimal investment strategies in decentralized renewable power generation under uncertainty', *Energy*, **32**, 803–15.
Fouilloux, J., F. Moraux and J.-L. Viviani (2015), 'Investing in finite-life carbon emissions reduction program under risk and idiosyncratic uncertainty', *Energy Policy*, **82**, 310–20.
Fuss, S., J. Szolgayová, N. Khabarov and M. Obersteiner (2012), 'Renewables and climate change mitigation: irreversible energy investment under uncertainty and portfolio effects', *Energy Policy*, **40**, 59–68.
Fuss, S., J. Szolgayová, M. Obersteiner and M. Gusti (2008), 'Investment under market and climate policy uncertainty', *Applied Energy*, **85** (8), 708–21.
Gao, Y. and T. Driouchi (2013), 'Incorporating Knightian uncertainty into real options analysis: using multiple-priors in the case of rail transit investment', *Transportation Research Part B: Methodological*, **55**, 23–40.
Gollier, C., D. Proult, F. Thais and G. Walgenwitz (2005), 'Choice of nuclear power investments under price uncertainty: Valuing modularity', *Energy Economics*, **27**, 667–85.
Grenadier, S.R. (2002), 'Option exercise games: an application to the equilibrium investment strategies of firms', *Review of Financial Studies*, **15**(3), 691–721.
Grenadier, S.R. and A.M. Weiss (1997), 'Investment in technological innovations: an option pricing approach', *Journal of Financial Economics*, **44**(3), 397–416.
Gryglewicz, S., K.J.M. Huisman and P.M. Kort, (2008), 'Finite project life and uncertainty effects on investments', *Journal of Economic Dynamics and Control*, **32**, 2191–213.
Hach D. and S. Spinler (2016), 'Capacity payment impact on gas-fired generation investments under rising renewable feed-in – a real options analysis', *Energy Economics*, **53**, 270–80.
Hanemann, W.M. (1989), 'Information and the concept of option value', *Journal of Environmental Economics and Management*, **16**(1), 23–37.

Heinkel, R., A. Kraus and J. Zechner (2001), 'The effect of green investment on corporate behaviour', *Journal of Financial and Quantitative Analysis*, **36**(4), 431–49.
Henry, C. (1974), 'Investment decision under uncertainty: the irreversibility effect', *American Economic Review*, **64**(6), 1006–12.
Huisman, K.J.M. and P.M. Kort (1999), 'Effects of strategic interactions on the option value of waiting', Center Discussion paper 9803, Tilburg University, the Netherlands.
Huisman, K.J.M. and P.M. Kort (2004), 'Strategic technology adoption taking into account future technological improvements: A real options approach', *European Journal of Operational Research*, **159**(3), 705–28.
Husted, B.W. (2005), 'Risk management, real options and corporate social responsibility', *Journal of Business Ethics*, **60**(2), 175–83.
Insley, M.C. (2003), 'On the option to invest in pollution control under a regime of tradable emissions allowances', *Canadian Journal of Economics*, **36**(4), 860–83.
Ishii, J. and J. Yan (2007), 'Does divestiture crowd out new investment? The "make or buy" decision in the U.S. electricity generation industry', *Journal of Economics*, **38**(1), 185–214.
Kang, S.B. and P. Létourneau (2016), 'Investors' reaction to the government credibility problem: a real option analysis of emission permit policy risk', *Energy Economics*, **54**, 96–107.
King, A. (1995), 'Avoiding ecological surprise: lessons from long-standing communities', *Academy of Management Review*, **20**(4), 961–85.
Kjærland, F. (2007), 'A real option analysis of investments in hydropower – the case of Norway', *Energy Policy*, **35**(11), 5901–8.
Knight, F.H. (1921), *Risk, Uncertainty and Profit*, Houghton Mifflin, Boston.
Kort, P.M., P. Murto and P. Grzegorz (2010), 'Uncertainty and stepwise investment', *European Journal of Operational Research*, **202**(1), 196–203.
Kumbaroglu, G. and R. Madlener (2012), 'Evaluation of economically optimal retrofit investment options for energy savings in buildings', *Energy and Building*, **49**, 327–34.
Kyläheiko K., J. Sandström and V. Virkkunen (2002), 'Dynamic capability view in terms of real options', *International Journal of Production Economics*, **80**(1), 65–83.
Laurikka, H. (2006), 'Option value of gasification technology within an emissions trading scheme', *Energy Policy*, **34**(18), 3916–28.
Laurikka, H. and T. Koljonen (2006), 'Emission trading and investment decisions in the power sector: a case study in Finland', *Energy Policy*, **34**(9), 1063–74.
Leahy, J. (1993), 'Investment in competitive equilibrium: the optimality of myopic behaviour', *Quarterly Journal of Economics*, **108**(4), 1105–33.
Lee, R., G. Jordan, P.N. Leiby, B. Owens and J.L. Wolf (2003), 'Estimating the benefits of government sponsored energy R&D', *Research Evaluation*, **12**(3), 183–95.
Li, Z.-C., Q.-W. Guo, W.H.K. Lam and S.C. Wong (2015), 'Transit technology investment and selection under urban population volatility: a real option perspective', *Transportation Research Part B*, **78**, 318–40.
Linnerud, K., A.M. Andersson and S.-E. Fleten (2014), 'Investment timing under uncertain renewable energy policy: an empirical study of small hydropower projects', *Energy*, **78**, 154–64.
Liu, G., F. Wen and I. McGill (2011), 'Optimal timing for generation investment with uncertain emission mitigation policy', *European Transactions on Electrical Power*, **21**, 1015–27.
Lukas, E. and A. Welling (2014), 'Timing and eco(nomic) efficiency of climate-friendly investments in supply chains', *European Journal of Operational Research*, **233**(2), 448–57.
Lund, D. (2005), 'How to analyse the investment-uncertainty relationship in real options model?', *Review of Financial Economics*, **14**, 311–22.
McDevitt, R., C. Giapponi and C. Tromley (2007), 'A model of ethical decision-making: the integration of process and content', *Journal of Business Ethics*, **73**(2), 219–29.
McDonald, R. and D. Siegel (1986), 'The value of waiting to invest', *Quarterly Journal of Economics*, **101**, 707–27.
McGrath, R.G. (1997), 'A real options logic for initiating technology positioning investments', *Academy of Management Review*, **22**(4), 974–96.

McWilliams, A. and D. Siegel (2001), 'Corporate social responsibility: a theory of the firm perspective', *Academy of Management Review*, **26** (1), 117–27.
Majd, S. and R.S. Pindyck (1987), 'Time to build, option value, and investment decisions', *Journal of Financial Economics*, **18**(1), 7–27.
Malchow-Møller, N. and B.J. Thorsen (2005), 'Repeated real options: optimal investment behaviour and a good rule of thumb', *Journal of Economic Dynamics and Control*, **29**, 1025–41.
Martinez Cesena, E.A. and J. Mutale (2011), 'Application of an advanced real options approach for renewable energy generation projects planning', *Renewable and Sustainable Energy Reviews*, **15**(4), 2087–94.
Martinez Cesena, E.A., J. Mutale and F. Rivas-Davalos (2013), 'Real options theory applied to electricity generation projects: a review', *Renewable and Sustainable Energy Reviews*, **19**, 573–81.
Mensink, P. and T. Requate (2005), 'The Dixit-Pindyck and the Arrow-Fisher-Hanemann-Henry option values are not equivalent: a note on Fisher (2000)', *Resource and Energy Economics*, **27**(1), 83–8.
Miao, J. and N. Wang (2011), 'Risk, uncertainty, and option exercise', *Journal of Economic Dynamics and Control*, **35**(4), 442–61.
Mo, J.-L., P. Agnolucci, M.-R. Jiang and F. Ying (2016), 'The impact of Chinese carbon emission trading scheme (ETS) on low carbon energy (LCE) investment', *Energy Policy*, **89**, 271–83.
Perotti, E.C. and S. Rossetto (2001), 'Strategic advantage and the optimal exercise of entry options,' CEPR Discussion Papers series 3061.
Pindyck, R.S. (2007), 'Uncertainty in environmental economics', *Review of Environmental Economics and Policy*, **1**(1), 45–65.
Reedman, L., P. Graham and P. Coombes (2006), 'Using a real options approach to model technology adoption under carbon price uncertainty; an application to the Australian electricity generation sector', *The Economic Record*, **82** (1), 64–73.
Renneboog, L., J. Horst and C. Zhang (2008), 'Socially responsible investments: institutional aspects, performance, and investor behaviour', *Journal of Banking and Finance*, **32**(9), 1723–42.
Sarkar, S. (2000), 'On the investment-uncertainty relationship in a real options model', *Journal of Economic Dynamics and Control*, **24**(2), 219–25.
Sarkis, J. and M. Tamarkin (2005), 'Real options analysis for "green trading": the case of greenhouse gases', *The Engineering Economist*, **50**(3), 273–94.
Scholtens, B. (2006), 'Finance as a driver of corporate social responsibility', *Journal of Business Ethics*, **68**, 19–33.
Siddiqui, A.S., C. Marna and R.H. Wiser (2007), 'Real options valuation of US Federal renewable energy research, development, demonstration, and deployment', *Energy Policy*, **35**, 265–79.
Soppe, A. (2004), 'Sustainable corporate finance', *Journal of Business Ethics*, **53**(1–2), 213–24.
Sparkes, R. and C.J. Cowton (2004), 'The maturing of socially responsible investment: a review of the developing link with corporate social responsibility', *Journal of Business Ethics*, **52**(1), 45–57.
Tadeu, S.F., R.F. Alexandre, A.J.B. Tadeu, C. Henggeler Antunes, N.A.V. Simões and P. Pereira da Silva (2015), 'A comparison between cost optimality and return on investment for energy retrofit in buildings – a real options perspective', *Sustainable Cities and Society*, **21**, 12–25.
Trigeorgis, L. (1996), *Real Options*, Cambridge, MA: MIT Press.
Trojanowska, M. and P.M. Kort (2010), 'The worst case for real options', *Journal of Optimization Theory Application*, **146**(3), 709–34.
Tseng, C.L. and G. Barz (2002), 'Short-term generation asset valuation: a real options approach', *Operations Research*, **50**(2), 297–310.
Van Staveren, I. (1999), *Caring for Economics: An Aristotelian Perspective*, Delft: Eburon.
Welling, A. (2016), 'The paradox effects of uncertainty and flexibility on investment in

renewables under governmental support', *European Journal of Operational Research*, **251**(3), 1016–28.
Wirl, F. (2006), 'Consequences of irreversibilities on optimal intertemporal CO_2 emission policies under uncertainty', *Resource and Energy Economics*, **28**, 105–23.
Wong, K.P. (2007), 'The effect of uncertainty on investment timing in a real options model', *Journal of Economic Dynamics & Control*, **31**(7), 2152–67.
Yang, M., W. Blyth, R. Bradley, D. Bunn, C. Clarke and T. Wilson (2008), 'Evaluating the power investment options with uncertainty in climate policy', *Energy Economics*, **30**(4), 1933–50.
Yeo, K.T. and F. Qiu (2003), 'The value of management flexibility – a real option approach to investment valuation', *International Journal of Project Management*, **21**(4), 243–50.
Zhao, J. (2003), 'Irreversible abatement investment under cost uncertainties: tradable emission permits and emissions charges', *Journal of Public Economics*, **87**(12), 2765–89.
Zhao, J. and D. Zilberman (1999), 'Irreversibility and restoration in natural resource development', *Oxford Economic Papers*, **51**(3), 559–73.
Zsolnai, L. (2002), *Ethics in the Economy*, Oxford: Peter Lang.

4. Exchange rate instability: relative volatility, risk and adjustment speed

Mohamed Ariff and Alireza Zarei

1. INTRODUCTION

The Brexit vote in June 2016 resulted in Britain taking steps to leave the European Union (EU), the world's largest trading bloc. That vote led to the sterling currency declining by about 10 percent. That is a massive correction predicting impending exchange rate volatility for the British currency with consequences likely to linger for decades. In this chapter, we develop a way of measuring the exchange rate volatility *relative to a trading country* or a country's exchange rate relative to a group of trading countries such as the EU. Although the study of exchange rate dynamics has been extensively carried out over a century of research on this subject, there is a dearth of published materials on how to measure exchange rate volatility beyond using the standard deviation (SD) or the coefficient of variation (CoV) of a given currency over a given period or value-at-risk (VaR). These measures are inadequate for two reasons. What matters for tracking the *instability* of a phenomenon such as exchange rate volatility is how to relate one currency's stability *relative* to a class to which that currency belongs. Such a measure would be more appropriate for ranking a given currency against a benchmark of closely linked economies or a closely linked central currency.

That is, a measure of volatility of a currency must be in relation to a country (or group) with which the currency has relevance or importance, say, through trade linkages, as argued in this chapter. The link could well be capital flow or other economic benefits that accrue to a country in relation to another country or group of countries. So the stability of the British pound should be measured relative to, say, the EU currency or US dollar because these latter two nations have intense trade relations with Britain. The other reason why SD or CoV is inappropriate is that these measures are one currency's behavior against itself, so neither of these qualifies as a more accurate ranking device *across* a meaningful group that is the benchmark based on common linkages such as trade. The same is true of the VaR, which measures the impact on, say, an entity's core capital, from an x% depreciation.

For these reasons, a measure relative to a benchmark (be it the currency of a trade-linked country or the average currency value of a group of trade-linked countries such as the NAFTA) is required. This benchmark is illustrated in this chapter by using the US dollar (US$) as the benchmark: any other currency could be used as long as the chosen benchmark currency is appropriate. More details of how this is done is found in the methodology section in this chapter. Using this relative measure, it explains how a given currency's *stability could be mapped relative to the benchmark* as an illustration. Next, we use the interquartile range of the relative volatility as a measure of exchange rate risk of a given currency *relative* to its benchmark country or group of countries.

The rest of the chapter is divided into three more main sections. The next section is about concept development and measurement equations. Following that is a description of how the proposed measures could be used for ranking and other analyses using 14 free floating and basket-managed currencies selected for this chapter. The final section concludes this chapter.

2. CONCEPT DEVELOPMENT

The instability of a phenomenon is usually measured by the volatility in the rate of change of a phenomenon X across time (as ln (X_t / X_{t-1}) with t indicating interval of time – in this study monthly interval – used for measurement. The square root of volatility is then a measure of the instability of the item measured as in:

$$\sigma_{\frac{x_t}{x_{t-1}}} = \sqrt{\frac{\sum\left[\ln\left(\frac{x_t}{x_{t-1}}\right) - \left(\overline{\ln\left(\frac{x_t}{x_{t-1}}\right)}\right)\right]^2}{n-1}} \tag{1}$$

where x represents the ratio of a target currency over the US dollar. This measure of population standard deviation (SD) indicates how volatile a currency is at a given test period. SD has been commonly used as an indicator of instability.[1] Another measure, again limiting to the same currency, is the coefficient of variation (CoV), which is the ratio from dividing the SD of a currency by its own average rate of change in the same test period. CoV is often used as a measure of risk of a currency, meaning the higher this ratio is, the higher is the risk of this currency compared to the CoV of another currency. CoV is measured as:

$$Coefficient\ of\ Variation(COV) = \frac{\sigma_{\ln\left(\frac{x_t}{x_{t-1}}\right)}}{\mu_{\ln\left(\frac{x_t}{x_{t-1}}\right)}} \tag{2}$$

The larger the CoV ratio the greater is the likely instability of the currency. Note that this measure is relative to the first two moments of the same phenomenon, that is, one currency with no regard to how one currency is behaving in relation to another currency of importance to the country of the currency concerned.

The next two measures are preferred when the volatility of a currency is *relativized* to the volatility of another currency of importance (close trade linkage is the basis on which another currency may be important).

There is a slight problem here: the pound is expressed in terms of actual observed US dollar values. For devising a measure appropriate for a trade-linked group, the US dollar Index (US$1) is available as an alternative to the actual US dollar values. So we propose to use the SD of the rate of exchange of the US$1.[2] If both currencies are having the same levels of volatility at a given period, then the relative volatility would equal unity. Otherwise it will either be greater than unity if the given currency is more volatile or less than one if the given currency is less volatile than the benchmarked important currency. It is our assumption that most currencies would have a slightly higher relative standard deviation (RV) than unity, given the lower volatility of the US dollar (US$). Hence, the relative volatility RV can be measured as the standard deviation SD of a currency x divided by the SD of a benchmark currency y:

$$Relative\ Volatility(RV) = \frac{\sigma_{\ln\left(\frac{x_t}{x_{t-1}}\right)}}{\sigma_{\ln\left(\frac{y_t}{y_{t-1}}\right)}} \tag{3}$$

where y represents the ratio of the US dollar in relation to a basket of currencies. This measure is a unit for comparing say the British currency SD with the US currency SD. If the RV of the pound against the dollar is exactly the same across time, then the RV would be 1.00. Any deviation around 1.00 is an indicator of the exchange rate instability of the sterling currency. By measuring the RV of the EU dollar, we would have two numbers respectively for the pound and the EU dollar to compare. The size of this measure would be used to measure the instability of the pound and the instability of the EU dollar. That would show which currency is more unstable, which is a practical and useful measure for ranking a given number of countries with significant trade linkages with the USA. Central banks will find this RV a boon for analysis.

The resulting ranking could be done periodically, say every three months, to create a time series to provide a benchmark-relevant measure for policy-making. In this study, we apply this simply to show what this measure looks like for a sample of 14 countries over 20 years. Banks apply the VaR measure to see how the core capital of a bank may be affected by a given x% depreciation or appreciation of a currency. We believe this RV is a better measure for currency.

The interquartile range of the RV is an appropriate measure of the riskiness of a given currency relative to benchmark. The interquartile range (IQR) is simply the difference in the RV of the third and first quartile values of the computed RVs as the IQR_{RV} of the series:

$$IQR = Q_3 - Q_1 \tag{4}$$

where Q_i is specified as under:

$$Q_i = L_i + W\left(\frac{\frac{(in)}{4} - f_c}{f}\right),\ i = 1,2,3 \tag{5}$$

where:
L_i: lower boundary of quartile group,
W: width of quartile group,
f: frequency of quartile group,
n: total number of observations, and
c: cumulative frequency preceding quartile group.

IQR_{RV} is a measure of riskiness of one currency relative to a benchmark. This measure is superior to the CoV since the former is benchmarked to the relevant exchange rate of importance to a given currency of a given country. Ranking the currencies using the IQR would indicate the relative riskiness of one country's currency against the benchmark country's currency. The resulting ranking of a given number of countries – in this study 14 – would enable a policy-maker to judge the relative riskiness of a given trading partner's currency *stability* relative to other closely linked trading partners. Perhaps this ratio could be used to devise trade policies or currency management strategies or even devise correct exchange rate management policy by the central banks. Central banks are known to estimate forward inflation rates as well as forward interest rates to formulate inflation targeting decisions. The same could be done using IQR to target exchange rate stability.

The ranking of countries by RV and the ranking of countries by IQR are two measures for ranking. The former is a measure of *relative instability* of a currency and the latter is a measure of the innate *riskiness* of a currency of a country trading with another country (or group). Finally, regressing the two rankings would show that there is a high degree of predictability of the instability measure with the riskiness measure. The regression is:

$$r_{(RSD)_i} = \alpha_i + \beta_i r_{(IQR)_i} + \varepsilon_i \tag{6}$$

where r_{RSD} = rank of Relative Standard Deviation (Volatility), and r_{IQR} represents the rank of interquartile range as specified in Equation (5).[3]

The correlation coefficient of a regression of the two rank orders in this regression will be high. The coefficient of the right-hand side variable would be around unity, suggesting that the riskiness and volatility of currencies are highly inter-correlated.

Similar tests could be done using cointegration, as in:

$$RSD_t = \theta_i + \gamma_1\left(\frac{1+i_t^d}{1+i_t^f}\right)_t + \gamma_2\left(\frac{CPI_t^d}{CPI_t^f}\right)_t + \gamma_3\left(\frac{Prodty_t^d}{Prodty_t^f}\right)_t + \gamma_4\left(\frac{NFDI_t^d}{NFDI_t^f}\right)_t$$

$$+ \gamma_5\left(\frac{M2_t^d}{M2_t^f}\right)_t + \gamma_6\left(\frac{BOT_t^d}{BOT_t^f}\right)_t + \mu_i \tag{7}$$

where RV represents the relative standard deviation, i^d denotes the real[4] domestic interest rate, i^f is the real foreign interest rate, and the ratio represents the relative interest rate parity among the two trading partners, CPI stands for the consumer price index, and the relative CPI represents the relative purchasing power parity (PPP) among the two trading partners. The other monetary-relevant variables (see Ariff and Zarei 2015) are productivity, net foreign direct investments, money supply, and balance of trade. If the two series RV and IQR of a given currency over a test period used in this study are cointegrated, then this shows that the two series co-move. By estimating the error correction statistics, the speed of adjustment of instability to the rising and falling risk of a currency could also be estimated. The above test model is based on monetary theories of exchange rate determination. As an extension of the measures proposed in the equations (1) and (5), one could also link these measures to the theory of exchange rate dynamics: a published paper (Ariff and Zarei 2016a) has shown the reliability of this model.

To track (a) the adjustment towards equilibrium in the exchange rate under study, we ran an ARDL (auto-regressive distributed lag) regression. The process is normally used in econometrics to estimate the adjustment process in a series. This would also yield a (b) error correction term (ECT), which should have a negative sign and be significant in the test if there is a significant adjustment towards equilibrium.

The data series are monthly exchange rates, so the coefficient would indicate for a given currency (if measured per country without pooling the series or if a panel regression is not done) the number of months the exchange rate takes to adjust to its equilibrium value in the case of the currency in the test. There are several studies by the authors of this chapter where this procedure has been applied to measure the adjustment speed (Ho and Ariff 2011). We intend to document the adjustment process for the sample of countries in this study. The longer the time for adjustment, meaning that the ECT shows a longer time to equilibrium, then that currency would have *more instability*.

3. FINDINGS AND DISCUSSION

The four measures developed for understanding currency instability as well as tracking them over time are: the relative volatility (RV); the exchange rate risk (RSQ); the rank order using RV and RSQ (and their correlation); and the cointegration tests on time to equilibrium (ECT). These results are presented in that order in this section. The descriptive statistics are shown in the Appendix to this chapter.

A priori value for the RV should be equal to 1.00 for a currency with a similar volatility to that of the benchmark (in this chapter, it is the US$). The 12 graphs, one for each country, are drawn in relation to the unity value of 1.00 if two currencies behave the same way, for each of the 14 currencies tested. The currencies included in Figure 4.1A are those of free-floating regimes (Canada (CAD); British pound (GBP); Japan (JPY); Swiss Franc (CHF); the Swedish Kroner (SEK); and the Philippines Peso (PHP)). The last two have been free-floating since 1997–8.

Scanning these RV plots relative to the base of 1.00 shows that these free-floating currencies have three characteristics. First, it is only the British pound that appears to have exchange rate movement below and above the 1.00 line, indicating that this currency, though volatile like any other currencies, appreciated against the US$ at times (that is, the plots are below the 1.00 line), and at other times it depreciated against the US$ when the plots are above the unity line. All other currencies always plot above the unity line, meaning that those currencies are more volatile and are also depreciating over time against the US$. In the cases of Indonesia and the Philippines – free floating since 1997 – these currencies depreciated significantly against the US$ in 1997–8, and then continued to depreciate further. In the years that these currencies were 'managed' prior to IMF-mandated free floating (see Ariff and Can 2007), there is little volatility (which is a behavior obvious in other managed especially fixed currencies, as seen in Figure 4.1.B too).

The next set of graphs – Figure 4.1B – are for managed currencies starting with the Malaysian Ringgit (MYR). The plots of these currencies are above the equilibrium line 1.00 most of the time since switching from pegged to 'basket management' (except Singapore). That means all the managed currencies (except SGD) have depreciated against the US$ throughout the test period. The exceptions are those of Indian and Indonesian currencies, which are just on the unity line in the period when these currencies were managed as fixed against the US$ prior to some dates before adopting the 'basket pegging' in later years. After the end of fixed regime, basket pegging started, and these currencies started to depreciate as they should. In the case of Singapore (as was the case with Britain's pound) the dollar appreciated at times (so the plot is below 1.00) and often depreciated at other times, as is indicated by the plots hovering above the unity line.

Thus, it appears that the world's favorite US$ as the trade-linked benchmark could be used to *relativize* the movements (appreciation and depreciation) of individual currencies relative to the US$ as the benchmark currency among closely trading countries. If we had used the EU currency, we would have somewhat similar results, as would also be the case if the Indian rupee had been used for the South Asian trading block.

In Table 4.1 (see Panels A and B of results), we provide the mean values of the interquartile scores for the 14 countries. We first ranked the order of 14 currencies using the size of the volatility (RV), shown in Table 4.1, and then calculated the rank order values in terms of IQR values (not shown here).[5] The RV rank is by size of the average RV during the test period of 1990–2015. During that period, the Singapore dollar had the lowest RV value compared to all other currencies – see also the figures in Table 4.1. In fact, the average relative volatility of SGD is slightly below 1.00, meaning that in this period, the SGD appreciated, on average. The next rank is occupied by the Philippines with Indonesia occupying the last place. *The lower the average size of the RV value, the more stable the currency is.* A similar observation could also be made about the interquartile range, IQR.

The rank order by currency risk using IQR also produced similar results. The ranking by this second measure of instability – we call this the

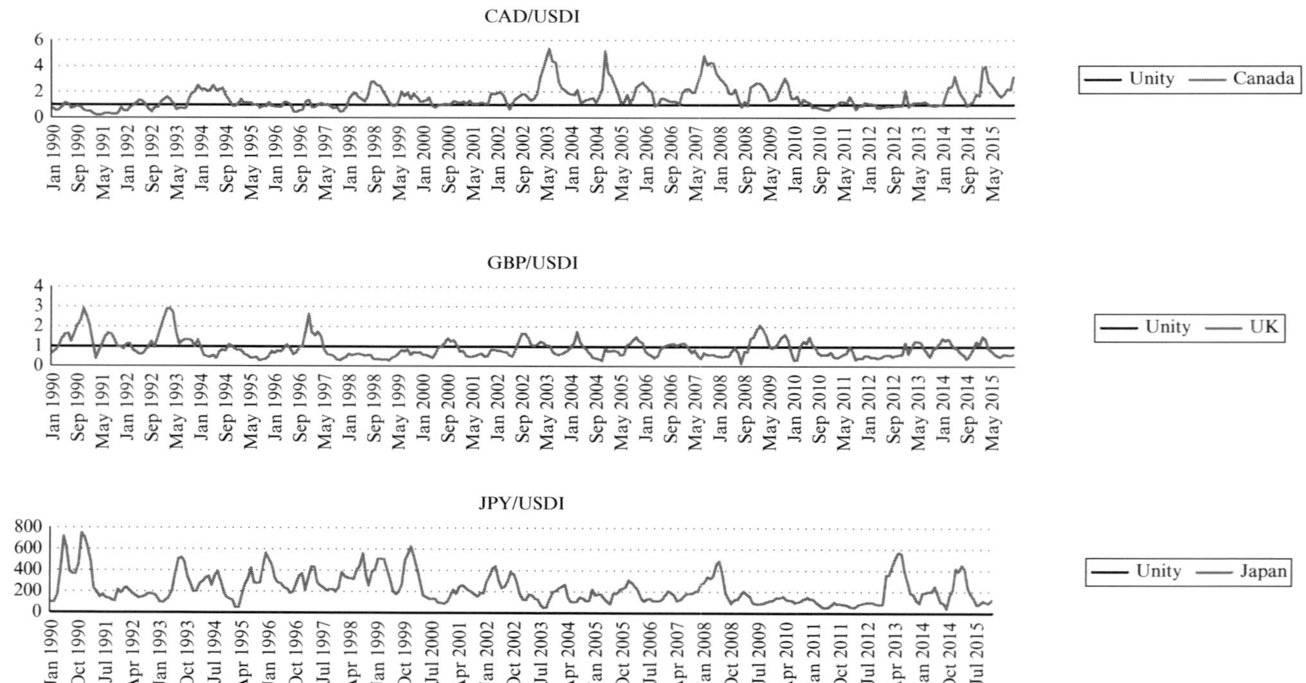

Figure 4.1(a) *Relative volatility to unity of free-floating currencies, 1990–2015*

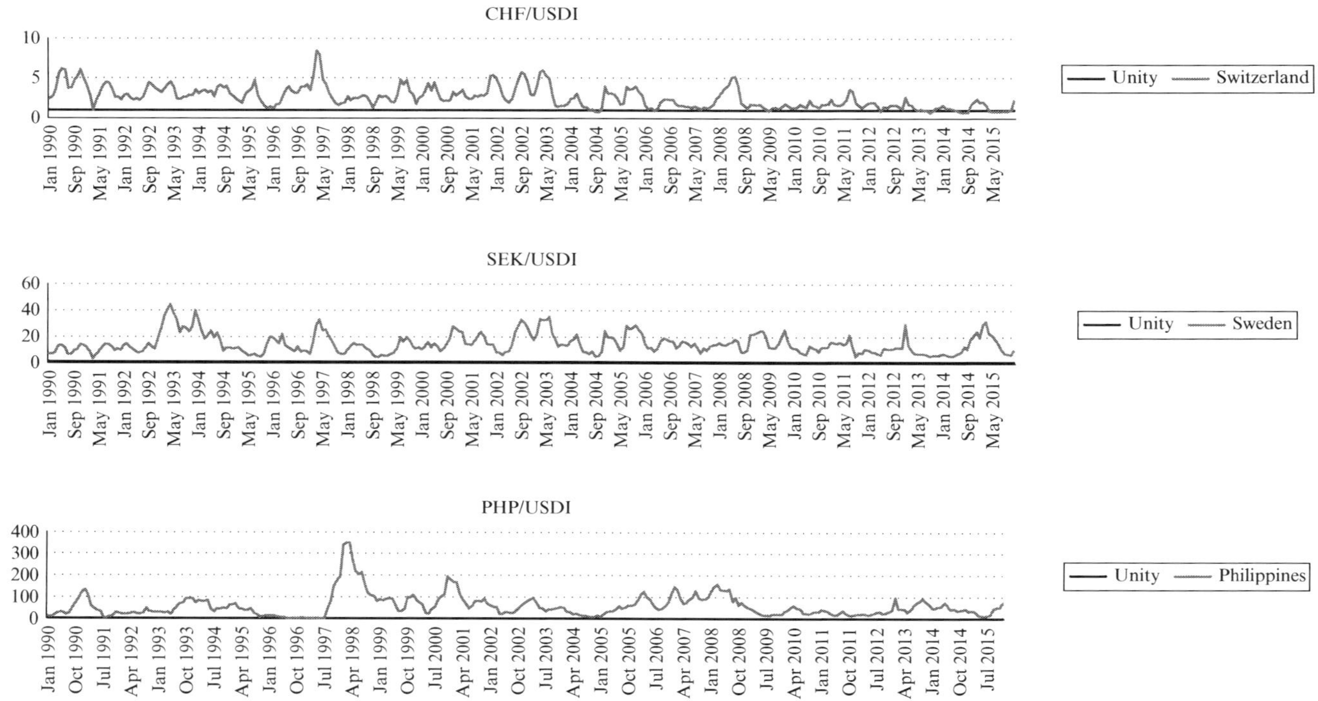

Figure 4.1(a) (continued)

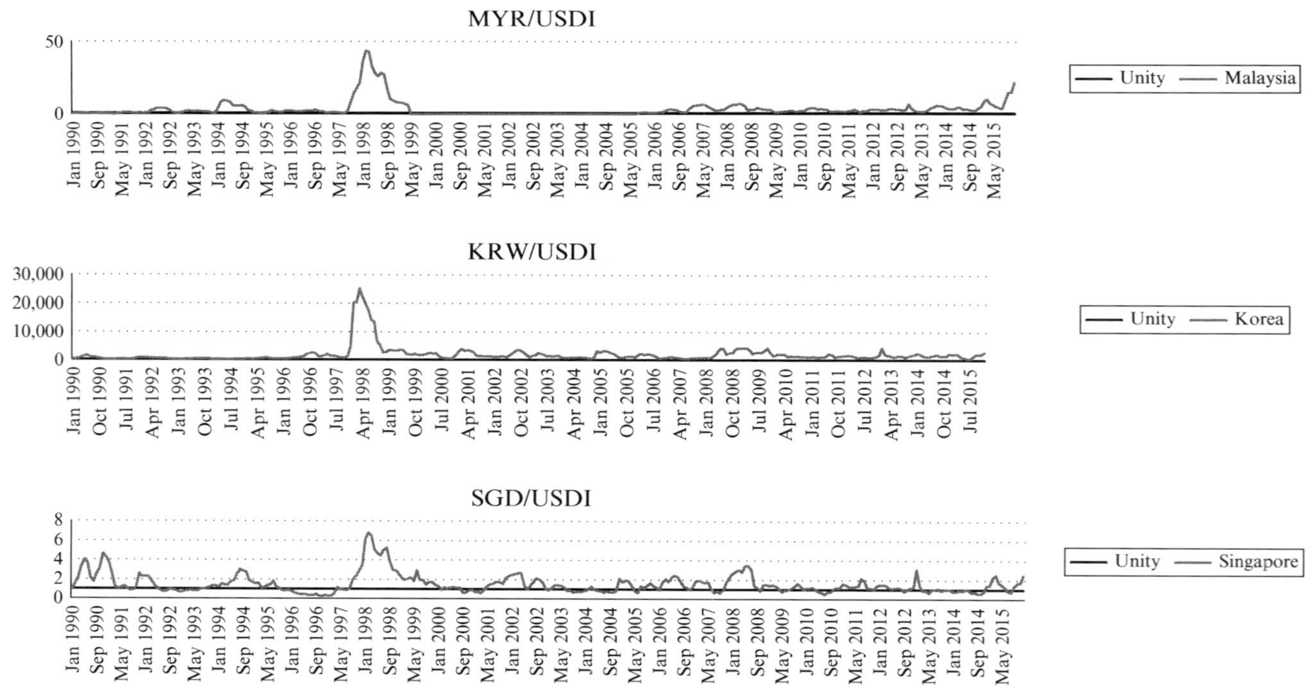

Figure 4.1(b) *Relative volatility to unity of managed currencies, 1990–2015*

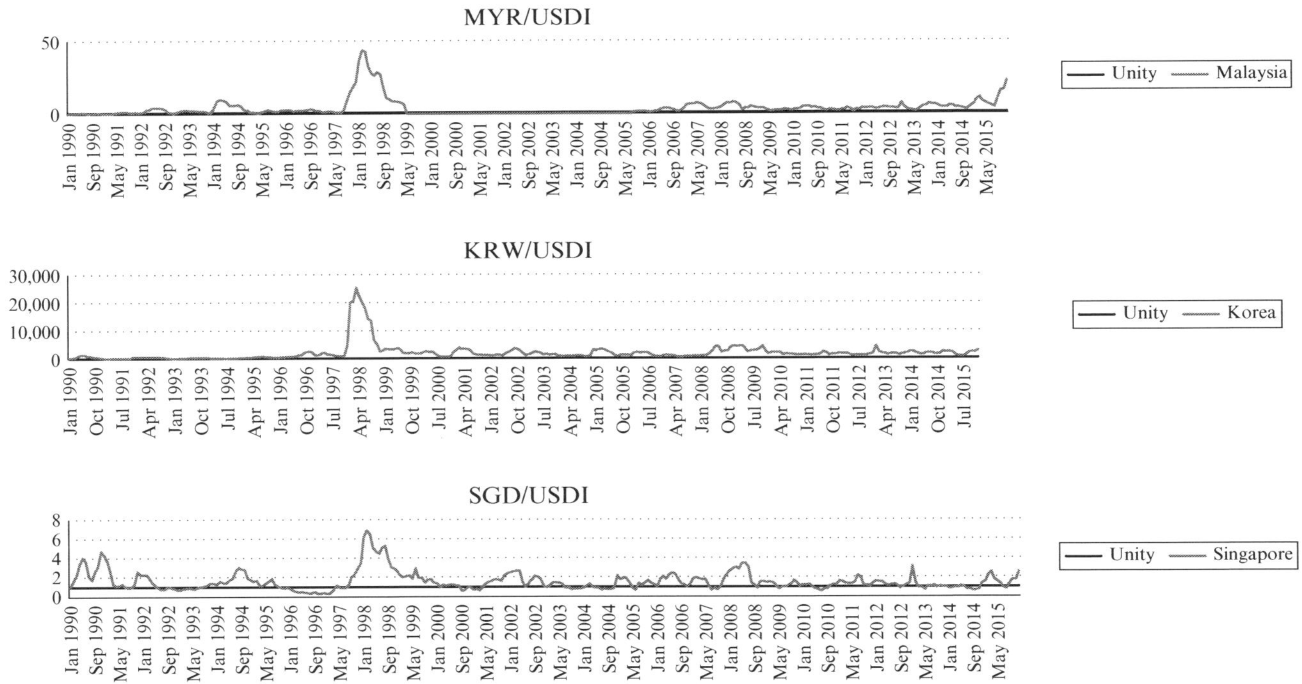

Figure 4.1(b) (continued)

Table 4.1 Ranks (by mean and median) of the 12 countries by relative volatility, 1990–2015

Panel A:	Mean	Median	Std. Dev.
Singapore	0.928 (1)	0.728 (2)	0.568
Malaysia	1.017 (2)	0.695 (1)	1.272
Philippines	1.269 (3)	1.044 (3)	0.900
Canada	1.301 (4)	1.196 (4)	0.661
UK	1.536 (5)	1.377 (6)	0.673
Korea	1.652 (6)	1.244 (5)	1.897
Eurozone	1.790 (7)	1.645 (7)	0.729
Japan	1.807 (8)	1.703 (9)	0.666
Australia	1.867 (9)	1.682 (8)	0.802
Iceland	1.927 (10)	1.768 (10)	1.221
Switzerland	1.962 (11)	1.870 (13)	0.715
Sweden	1.977 (12)	1.807 (11)	0.865
Turkey	2.366 (13)	1.821 (12)	1.858
Indonesia	2.398 (14)	1.169 (14)	3.839

Panel B: Pearson's rank order correlation between volatility and risk

	IQR	RV
	R-squared	0.9999
	p-value	(0.00) ***

Note: The test of the ranks using relative volatility RV and IQR produced a significant (at less than 0.001 level) Pearson's rank order correlation, coefficient r being equal to 0.999. Hence, there is a monotonic relationship between the relative volatility as a measure of *instability* and the riskiness measure of interquartile range for the currencies.

risk measure – is also very similar to the ranking by relative volatility, the first measure of instability. These two ranks could be used to test if these measures are alternatives for the instability measurement. This was done by running the Pearson's rank-order correlation measure (see the note to Table 4.1), which suggests that the two ranks are highly correlated with statistical significance. That is, the relative volatility as a measure is also an indicator of the relative riskiness of a given currency, just as a low beta stock would have a smaller change in stock returns compared to a high-beta riskier stock traded in a stock market. The results of the test on both ranks (RV and IQR) are statistically significant at 0.000 or lower level, as can be seen in Panel B in Table 4.1. As predicted, there is a one-to-one relationship between the two ranks. Either or both measures are excellent to track instability among currencies.

4. COINTEGRATION AND EQUILIBRIUM

The results of the ARDL tests are shown in Table 4.2 for Equation (6). Three test values are given at different significance levels – 0.01, 0.05 and 0.10 – at the bottom of the table. Within the table are test values and the significance test results for all the 14 countries, showing there are cointegrating relationships for each. All 14 currencies pass the test of having a cointegrating relationship. Further, the ECTs have negative

Table 4.2 Long-run relationship (Equation 6) from ARDL tests with ECT values, 1990–2015

Independent Variable: RV	ARDL	F-Statistic	Long-run IQR	ECT
Canada	(8, 0)	4.696**	−0.314 (−0.36)	−0.117 (−3.75)***
Iceland	(8, 2)	4.120***	0.374 (0.78)	−0.135 (−3.52)***
Indonesia	(8, 7)	4.630***	1.073 (1.87)*	−0.127 (−3.74)***
Japan	(5, 5)	9.241***	−0.722 (−1.13)	−0.127 (−5.28)***
Korea	(4, 3)	10.56***	0.277 (0.70)	−0.144 (−5.64)***
Malaysia	(5, 2)	5.364**	−0.868 (−0.37)	−0.042 (−4.02)***
Philippines	(3, 1)	11.393***	0.774 (3.50)***	−0.180 (−5.86)***
Singapore	(8, 3)	11.559***	1.025 (5.67)***	−0.286 (−5.90)***
Sweden	(3, 8)	14.306***	0.377 (1.10)	−0.259 (−6.57)***
Switzerland	(8, 1)	5.179**	−0.901 (−0.80)	−0.098 (−3.95)***
Turkey	(2, 8)	4.846***	1.721 (3.75)***	−0.117 (−3.82)***
United Kingdom	(8, 0)	8.743***	0.347 (1.39)	−0.244 (−5.21)***

Pesaran et al. (2001) Critical Value ($k=1$)	Lower Bound I(0)	Upper Bound I(1)
99% level	3.02	3.51
95% level	3.62	4.16
90% level	4.94	5.58

signs as required, and all are statistically significant. That means that these currencies have different speeds of adjustment to equilibrium: *the higher the value the faster is the adjustment to equilibrium*. Thus, the existence of cointegration between relative volatility RV and interquartile range IQR is upheld in our tests. There is a long-run tendency for both variables to co-move, and be cointegrated as shown by the significant F-ratios for all countries. That means, currencies with high adjustment speed are more stable than those with low adjustment values. This turns out to be a very useful practical indicator on instability for policy judgment.

The test results of the theoretical relationship of relative volatility with monetary-theory-suggested variables are summarized in Table 4.3 for Equation (7). That equation embeds a number of significant factors reported as correlated with the exchange rate movements (Zarei et al., 2015). The ARDL regression results for all countries are significant given the F-ratios are all statistically acceptable at the usual probability levels. Thus, there is a cointegrating relationship between the theory-suggested variables and the measure of currency stability, RV. This is significant: we have RV linked to monetary theory suggested factors as the source of instability, so policy-makers know where the instability comes from.

Finally the error correction values ECT are shown in Table 4.3 to be also significant for all countries. This means all currencies are adjusting to equilibrium values over time, so they co-move. *The larger the ECT values* (monthly values since we used monthly intervals) *the faster is the adjustment to the benchmark US$*. That means such currencies are relatively more stable. For example, the ECT value of 0.244 in Table 4.3 for the British pound or 0.286 for the Singapore currency means that these two are adjusting faster than, for example, Iceland or Canada with values closer to 0.150. One could make an observation that a currency that ranks *lower* using relative volatility and has a *larger* error correction value would be more stable relative to the benchmark used. Thus, there is not one but a pair of relative measures to check the stability of a currency, which is like having robustness testing in scientific research.

5. CONCLUSION: INSTABILITY REVEALED BY RELATIVE MEASURES

Volatility measures as an indicator of instability have a long history in all sciences. In the period since the demise of the orderliness in money markets imposed by the Bretton Woods agreement, currency volatility has been at the center of several episodes of instability, spilling over into the economic and fiscal derailments of countries. Yet, to the best of our knowledge,

Table 4.3 *Long-run relationship (Equation 7) of 12 currencies against benchmark, 1990–2015*

RV = f (IQR, PPP, IFE)	ARDL	F-Statistic	ECT
Canada	(8, 0, 3, 4)	3.441*	−0.153 (−4.17)***
Iceland	(8, 0, 3, 0)	6.281***	−0.115 (−5.56)***
Indonesia	(8, 8, 8, 8)	5.461***	−0.269 (−5.35)***
Japan	(6, 5, 0, 3)	7.659***	−0.207 (−6.24)***
Korea	(3, 8, 1, 4)	3.855**	−0.177 (−4.42)***
Malaysia	(5, 7, 3, 7)	4.362**	−0.094 (−4.70)***
Philippines	(3, 1, 1, 3)	7.892***	−0.181 (−6.32)***
Singapore	(8, 3, 0, 0)	7.742***	−0.279 (−6.18)***
Sweden	(3, 0, 0, 0)	8.113***	−0.256 (−6.50)***
Switzerland	(8, 2, 0, 0)	5.124***	−0.268 (−4.99)***
Turkey	(4, 8, 8, 0)	7.433***	−0.230 (−6.12)***
United Kingdom	(8, 0, 4, 3)	7.852***	−0.288 (−6.35)***
Pesaran et al. (2001) Critical Value (k=3)		Lower Bound I(0)	Upper Bound I(1)
99% level		2.37	3.20
95% level		2.79	3.67
90% level		3.65	4.66

there are no significant publications on how to track the instability emanating from currency using *relative* measures. In mainstream economics, there are models of capacity slack that are a boon to measuring economic instability. What do we have in currency management?

In this chapter, we developed four measures of currency instability and tested these measures with 14 currencies with data over 26 years of monthly observations of real changes in currency values (and US$ Index values). What we have done in this chapter is to show the internal cohesiveness of our models. However, to link these models to the monetary theories on exchange rates (see Equation (6)), which should be expanded further, requires a further research effort for another day. The four measures of relative instability are very likely to be useful for tracking, benchmarking and managing instability in currencies, as shown in this study.

ACKNOWLEDGMENT

We thank the co-editors of the book for their helpful comments on the draft chapter.

NOTES

1. There are several versions of this measure: semi-variance; Parkinson's measure; the Kunitomo measure; etc., all of which are some type of innovation to make the SD appropriate for different purposes. These are found in advanced statistics books. Extreme values at the tails of the frequency distributions could also be used, such as fractiles, cupola, etc. The property of these measures as indicators of instability could be seen by comparing the same measures of another currency to make a judgment about whether the other currency is more or less volatile as measured over a given time period.
2. Currency indices are available for most major and some minor currencies. So for these currencies, it is possible to relativize the measure by using the SD of the rate of exchange in the currency index. In this study, we only use the US Dollar Index as an example. Other indices could well be used as appropriate for different purposes.
3. As a comparison to the finance theory, this equation is equivalent to Sharpe's 1963 Market Model, where the right-hand side variable systematic risk is a risk measure, with the left-hand variable (stock returns) as the responding measure to a unit of risk.
4. The model has included a variable for inflation as the 'ln' on CPI across time. Hence, using the nominal relative interest rate in the test for IFE would mean that the inflation factor is again included in the second variable. To rectify this, we subtracted the expected inflation from the domestic and the foreign nominal interest rates so that we test the IFE on the real relative interest rates.
5. The results are about the same as the results in Table 4.1. The results are available, if needed.

REFERENCES

Ariff, M. and Can, L. (2007). 'IMF Bank-Restructuring Efficiency Outcomes: Evidence from East Asia', *Journal of Financial Services Research*, 35(2): 167–92.

Ariff, M. and Zarei, A. (2015). 'Parity Theorems Revisited: An ARDL Bound Test with Non-parity Factors', *Asian Academy of Management Journal of Accounting and Finance*, 11(1): 1–26.

Ariff, M. and Zarei, A. (2016a). 'Exchange Rate Behavior of Canada, Japan, the United Kingdom and the United States', *Open Economies Review*, 27(2): 341–57.

Ariff, M. and Zarei, A. (2016b). 'One Approach to Resolve the Exchange Rate Puzzle: Results Using Data from the United Kingdom and the United States', *Singapore Economic Review*, 61(1): 1–18.
Atkins, F.J. and Coe, P.J. (2002). 'An ARDL Bounds Test of the Long-run Fisher Effect in the United States and Canada', *Journal of Macroeconomics*, 24(2): 255–66.
Grossmann, A., Love, I. and Orlov, A.G. (2014). 'The Dynamics of Exchange Rate Volatility: A Panel VAR Approach', *Journal of International Financial Markets, Institutions and Money*, 33: 1–27.
Ho, C. and Ariff, M. (2011). 'Sticky Prices and Time to Equilibrium: Evidence from Asia Pacific Trade-related Economies', *Applied Economics*, 43(21): 341–67.
Ho, C. and Ariff, M. (2015). 'Parity and Non-parity Determinants of Exchange Rates in Latin American Economies', *Taylors' Business Review*, 4(2): 182–202.
Moosa, I.A. and Vaz, J.J. (2016). 'Cointegration, Error Correction and Exchange Rate Forecasting', *Journal of International Financial Markets, Institutions and Money*, 44: 21–34.
Pesaran, M.H. and Shin, Y. (1997). 'An Autoregressive Distributed-lag Modelling Approach to Cointegration Analysis', *Econometric Society Monographs*, 31: 371–413.
Pesaran, M.H., Shin, Y. and Smith, R.J. (2001). 'Bounds Testing Approaches to the Analysis of Level Relationships', *Journal of Applied Econometrics*, 16(3): 289–326.
Stosic, D., Ludermir, T. and Stosic, T. (2016). 'Correlations of Multiscale Entropy in the FX Market', *Physica A: Statistical Mechanics and its Applications*, 457: 52–61.
Zarei, A., Ariff, M., Hook, L.S. and Md Nassir, A. (2015). 'Identifying Multiple Structural Breaks in Exchange Rate Series in a Finance Research', *Pertanika Journal of Social Sciences & Humanities*, 23: 155–66.

APPENDIX

Table 4.A Descriptive statistics of relative volatility (RSD) of 14 currencies, 1990–2015

	Mean	Median	Std. Dev.	Observations
Australia	1.867	1.682	0.802	308
Canada	1.301	1.196	0.661	308
Eurozone	1.790	1.645	0.729	200
Iceland	1.927	1.768	1.221	308
Indonesia	2.398	1.169	3.839	308
Japan	1.807	1.703	0.666	308
Korea	1.652	1.244	1.897	308
Malaysia	1.017	0.695	1.272	308
Philippines	1.269	1.044	0.9	308
Singapore	0.928	0.728	0.568	308
Sweden	1.977	1.807	0.865	308
Switzerland	1.962	1.87	0.715	308
Turkey	2.366	1.821	1.858	308
UK	1.536	1.377	0.673	308

5. Financial instability: economic and financial perspectives

Michael Dempsey

1. INTRODUCTION

Academic finance has generally progressed in relation to econometric analyses of markets assumed to be in equilibrium. To a large extent, such exercises have been conducted at an arm's length from the economist's understanding of markets in *dis*-equilibrium. Thus, finance theory has progressed largely independently of the economist's understanding of market fragility and the dynamic (as opposed to equilibrium) implications of debt and leverage in markets and the economy.

Nevertheless, the finance academic's assumptions of markets and market behavior are capable of influencing how financial markets are perceived – both by the general public and by regulatory and supervisory authorities. In which case, we may observe that good assumptions that are endorsed by academics have the potential to influence beneficial behavior, while bad assumptions are likely to legitimize harmful behavior.

Finance theory builds on the assumption that markets are in a fundamental sense efficient. The 'efficient market hypothesis' is a 'good' idea if markets can be held to know best. It is a 'bad' idea, however, when the hypothesis serves to legitimize a free-wheeling hands-off ethos of market behavior while deflecting a more sensible supervision and regulation of markets.

The instability of markets in the global financial crisis (GFC) has led the 'efficient market hypothesis' to be questioned. Nevertheless, such critiques continue to be conducted outside of a traditional understanding of economics, with, if necessary, finance academics prepared to reinvent the economic wheel. Thus, for example, Allen (2012) makes a careful assessment of empirical data to conclude that financial innovation in itself has not been the main culprit leading to financial crises, but, rather, that '[a] common precursor to most of the crises considered was financial liberalization and significant credit expansion', and that '[a]t some point the bubble bursts and the stock and real estate markets collapse. In many cases banks and other intermediaries are overexposed to the equity and real estate markets and about a year later on average a banking crisis ensues' (p. 449). Such statements, of course, were made three decades previously by the economist Hyman Minsky (whose work has been revitalized following the global financial crisis).[1] As another example of where finance has arrived at, Ritter (2012) asks a straightforward question in the title of his paper: 'Is Economic Growth Good for Investors?' We might suppose that such an essential question relating economics to finance theory had been addressed and answered many times over. But, no, we must return to the time of such as Keynes, prior to the advent of modern finance theory, when academics naturally identified their understanding of financial markets in terms of their function in the economic system. The references in the above article by Ritter serve to emphasize how finance articles have preferred to focus on markets at the micro level, rather than their function in shaping the broader economy, as the availability of credit and bull and bear stock markets move through cycles affecting and, in turn, being affected by the real economy.[2]

Prior to the GFC, critiques of finance theory have been the exception. Lo and Mueller (2010, p. 21) – themselves proficient exponents of empirical research – observe that up to the early 1990s, any challenge to the notion of market efficiency was anathema, and that papers claiming to have discovered departures in the data from what was predicted by the capital asset pricing model (CAPM) were 'routinely rejected from the top economics and finance journals, in some cases, without even being sent out to referees for review'.[3]

The aim of this chapter is to argue both (1) that academic finance must recognize its responsibility for an intellectual framework that in its restricted understanding of the market's instability has allowed for and indeed encouraged market practices that have been detrimental to the economy, and (2) that a more effective understanding of – and thereby some greater measure of control over – market instability would benefit from recognizing the economist's understanding of the endogenous cycles of markets and the insights that economists have offered as to the influence of debt and financial leverage in bringing about such cycles. A summary of the papers in support of this chapter is presented in the Appendix.

In developing these ideas, the following section reviews the framework of modern finance theory, highlighting that the theory is essentially a construct that dates from the late 1950s. The section thereafter considers how academic thinking with its commitment to market efficiency and markets in equilibrium has helped shape how markets are perceived and thereby acted upon in practice. The following section considers that academia as the guardian of knowledge succeeds in imposing its ideas on the following generation of students so that a good deal of finance thinking is now hostage to itself in its inability to be more open-minded. The final section concludes with a call for finance to recognize itself as a component of the broader economy to be studied within the wider context of economic theory.

2. THE STRUCTURE OF MODERN FINANCE THEORY

In the late 1950s, the prestige of the natural sciences encouraged the belief that decision making and resource allocation problems could be identified with the elaboration of models and the general extension of techniques from applied mathematics. The writings of Karl Popper had also contributed to exalting the philosophical basis of science as *the* rational process, progressing towards objective truth on the basis of the falsification method of theory selection.

In such a scientific world, the logical structure of corporate decision making implied that practicing managers were likely to make more optimal decisions when supplied with a richer set of positive theories that provided a better understanding of the consequences of their choices. It was natural, therefore, that finance theory (along with other social science disciplines) should seek to identify with the scientific method. It was into this environment in the late 1950s that Merton Miller and Franco Modigliani ushered in their agenda for the modern theory of corporate finance.

Modigliani and Miller pronounced that the 'value' of the firm was its price in the marketplace. As the marketplace was held to be 'efficient', it followed that the firm's key financial decisions must be understood on the basis of providing the firm's investors with a rate of financial return that at least matched their comparable opportunities elsewhere. In this world, investors' required expectation of financial return represents *a firm's cost of financial capital*, on the basis of which all corporate financial decisions must be assessed. The discipline of 'corporate financial management' was transformed thereby from an institutional normative literature – motivated by and concerned with topics of direct practitioner relevance, such as the operations of financial institutions and procedures for raising long-term finance – into a microeconomic *positive* science centered around corporate policy decisions and addressing questions, such as: What are the effects of alternative investment, financing, and dividend policies on a firm's stock price? In this way, corporate financial decision making was formulated as an application of asset valuation models with reference to perfect capital markets.

Against this backdrop, researchers in finance became convinced that markets could and should be made subject to scientific inquiry. The capital asset pricing model (CAPM) of the 1960s held out a concept of US stock markets as having matured from a freewheeling casino in the past, generally held in disdain, to a market of information that allows prices to efficiently clear the market, and which thereby promoted an efficient allocation of capital. The idea underlying the CAPM was developed by various US academics at roughly the same time. The idea was first introduced by Jack Treynor (1962), followed by developments of the idea by William Sharpe (1964), John Lintner (1965) and Jan Mossin (1966), each more or less independently building on the earlier work of Harry Markowitz (1952) on diversification and modern portfolio theory.[4] Such a market represents an important component of a capitalist system. The founders of modern finance theory were anxious to confirm such a reality. In such a world, financial capital circulates to achieve those rates of return that are most attractive to investors, so that when they choose among the securities that represent ownership of firms' activities, they can do so under the assumption that they are paying fair prices given what is known about the firm (Fama, 1976).

Captivated by the CAPM and the Modigliani and Miller propositions, academic finance seeks to understand the behavior of financial markets and commercial companies as a well-ordered response that accords with the principles of the model and the propositions. We are led to imagine corporations and markets as behaving mechanically, with finance as the lubricating oil connecting the moving parts. Unfortunately, there is a problem with these models. Stated simply, it is that *finance is not physics*. The functioning of markets and firms is not represented well by mathematical models applied mechanically. It is the wrong kind of physics: How markets behave today is not necessarily how they will behave tomorrow. The models effectively shut out recognition of first-order effects: decision making under uncertainty, the economic cycles within which the firm operates, the dynamics of financial leverage, the psychology of markets, broader principles of management, the firm as a social construct, and ethical behavior as defining human enterprise. Nevertheless, evidence against the Modigliani and Miller propositions and the CAPM was not what researchers were wishing to hear.

The Modigliani and Miller (1958) irrelevancy of debt proposition (allowing no corporate tax) was followed by their (1963) 'correction proposition' that (due to the corporate tax deductibility of the firm's interest payments) the firm should strive for 100% debt in its capital structure. The implausibility of such a pronouncement necessitated the advancement of counter-balancing bankruptcy and financial distress as balancing with the tax benefits at a certain level of debt.[5] The propositions, however, assume a world of equilibrium in a setting of simplifying assumptions. The propositions fail to recognize the *dynamic* of debt in creating *disequilibrium*.

Thus, the finance community was unable to give warning of the financial instability that emerged from the excessive leveraged positions of banks, which precipitated the global financial crisis. The event, however, had been anticipated by the economist Hyman Minsky. Minsky's response to the 'efficient market hypothesis' was his 'stability is destabilizing' hypothesis (*Stabilizing an Unstable Economy*, 1986). His work builds on the traditional understanding of markets as articulated by Keynes, who recognized how markets become hostage to themselves when self-sustaining optimism or despair is allowed to feed on itself. Minsky articulates the importance of debt in the economic cycle and emphasizes the destabilizing effects of speculative bubbles in asset prices. Thus, when times are good, investors take on debt (and risk); and the longer that times stay good, the more debt they take on; until, inevitably, a point is reached where the cash generated by the assets acquired is no longer sufficient to pay off the mountains of debt that were taken on to acquire the assets. At this point, a *Minsky* moment has arrived in the inevitable collapse of asset values as investors are forced to sell off even their safer positions to make good on their loans. Markets spiral downward and create a severe demand for cash.

The global financial crisis was similarly triggered as, under pressure from shareholders in the good times to increase returns, banks operated with minimal equity, as firms and banks sought to enhance their profitability with cheaply available debt, before discovering to their cost, that while higher levels of debt can indeed prove effective in the good times, such leverage would be responsible for strangling the company to bankruptcy or near bankruptcy when the economic cycle turned downward. Finance, however, holds that one institution's borrowing is simply another institution's lending, so that debt represents a simple distribution of risk between highly sophisticated parties: the market knows best and, as the Modigliani and Miller irrelevancy proposition articulates, the individual firm's debt is fundamentally 'irrelevant'. A rare opposing voice is Stiglitz (2000), who makes the case for regulatory intervention in relation to short-term capital flows.

Likewise, evidence against the CAPM was ignored, as academics collectively responded by resisting any threat that might undermine finance as a domain of economics with its study of 'efficient markets' in terms of econometric sophistication. Thus, notwithstanding that the evidence from the beginning has always been squarely against the notion that investors set stock prices rationally in relation to stock betas, the industry of writing papers in support of the CAPM grew vibrantly over the decades following its inception. A blind eye was purposefully turned to the evidence. Indeed, Dempsey (2013) shows how although earlier work going back to Black, Jensen and Scholes (1972) invalidates the CAPM, a weakly determined positive relation between portfolio returns and their beta was allowed as evidence in support of the CAPM. Fama and French (1992) – while holding to the principle of market efficiency – introduced their paper in the *Journal of Finance* with the pronouncement: 'When the tests allow for variation in β that is unrelated to size, the relation between β and average return is flat'. Nevertheless, they retain beta and the CAPM construct as the basis of their three-factor model (Fama and French, 1996). Lo and Mueller (2010, p. 13) have explained: 'The quantitative aspirations of economists and financial analysts have for years been based on the belief that it should be possible to build models of economic systems – and financial markets in particular – that are as predictive as those in physics'.

3. FINANCE THEORY AS PERFORMATIVE

The philosopher Michel Foucault (1977) has proposed that our institutions progress from being the 'object' of our knowledge base as we attempt to understand them, to becoming ultimately 'subject' to our understanding of them – so that, ultimately, we allow ourselves to be governed by the knowledge base of our institutions rather than by individuals in their own right.

Thus, once imposed, a knowledge base derives almost tangible *power* – as the knowledge base asserts itself as the gatekeeper to subsequent attempts to supervise or regulate – as power resides in the knowledge base *through* which we encounter our institutions. Despite (or, more likely, because of) its removal from a commonplace understanding, academia is capable of exerting a hold on our perceptions as to how the world works, so that its theories are influential in determining how corporate and financial institutions are understood and thereby governed. Keasey and Hudson (2007) observe what they refer to as the *performative* aspect of academic financial economics in its legitimation of external reality – meaning that academic finance affects, rather than merely describes, financial markets.[6] Cai, Clacher and Keasey (2013) expand on the notion that the ideas promoted by academia duly permeate the industry and *do* make a difference. Similarly, Moosa (2013) relates how the perceived status of the 'gurus' to the finance industry succeeded in promoting the belief in markets as efficient and capable of pricing the most complex products of financial engineering through arbitrage.

We observe that academic finance has succeeded in *imposing* the belief that markets are efficient, the markets know best, and that regulations restrict their efficient behavior. Leading up to the global financial crisis, the belief lent support to the spread of ever-increasing complex financial instruments – the derivatives, securitizations, collateralized debt obligations, and credit default swap instruments – that developed without regulatory oversight, while the purchasers of the instruments succumbed to the hype of the bank's promoters who claimed that they were contributing to the building of sophisticated interdependences that allowed investors to transfer risk, when they were in reality creating the house of cards that duly tumbled for everyone.[7]

During the global financial crisis, the idea that the government should be interfering in the business of the big financial banks was anathema to the free market ideology of the Fed chairman, Ben Bernanke and the head of the New York arm of the Fed, Timothy Geithner, as well as other top officials. Such ideology had previously worked to sideline the government and regulators from imposing themselves on market operations – to warn against excesses, to dictate stronger balance sheets for banks, or to curtail executive pay. The denial of market failure has also played a part in discouraging central banks from attempting to curtail asset price bubbles before they might lead to departures of prices from a reasonable assessment of fundamental values.

Prior to the global financial crisis, a belief in markets had also encouraged the accounting profession to see markets as the arbiter of value on the firm's balance sheet. With stock prices rising, 'mark-to-market' valuations or *fair value accounting* (FVA) encouraged banks to increase their financial leverage on their balance sheets. This was linked to the fact that the substantial bonuses for a bank's senior staff were typically linked to the short-term returns to the bank's equity. For the Royal Bank of Scotland (RBS) – the biggest bank in the world prior to the crisis – and Citibank – at the time the biggest bank in the US – the leverage ratios were in the region of 50. In effect, they were capable of absorbing only $2 in losses on each $100 of assets. In reverse, at the outset of the financial crisis, a 'mark-to-market' downgrading of the valuations of the banks' liquid assets required the banks to contract their balance sheets, which provoked contagion in financial markets as banks sold assets at a price below their fundamental value, and the price of the forced sales became relevant to other institutions, which were required by FVA to mark their assets to market, in a rapidly developed downward spiral. The levels of debt of banks and their inherent exposure to illiquid assets when the bubbles burst were such as to cause the banks to lose confidence even in each other. In effect, the regulatory authorities failed to foresee that a significant proportion of the bank's assets must be capable of quickly being wound down in the case that its financial viability is threatened, as well as failing to foresee that, ultimately, provision must be made for a large international bank to go bankrupt without bringing down the whole system (Dempsey and

Jones, 2015). Bear Stearns and Lehman were brought down by an inability to acquire funding in the money markets when other institutions refused to lend to them.

Accredited theories have succeeded in transmitting the firm as a financial entity, transmuting it as an efficient investment counter, rather than an organization with an assortment of broader responsibilities. The outcome is that managers are encouraged by institutionalized bonuses and stock options to treat the firm as such – an investment counter – looking to talk up the firm to the markets, rather than focusing on the long-term direction and financial health of the company with a sense of its broader obligations – while providing information publicly about the firm and thereafter leaving it to the stock markets to get on with *their* job of placing a value on its shares.

Managers at both Lehman Brothers and Bear Stearns were compensated with stock holdings aimed at aligning pay to incentives. Nevertheless, they ran their companies into receivership. Even after having been rescued by government bailouts, investment bankers have continued to pay themselves extravagant bonuses from, in effect, public taxes as subsidies, leading to the observation that banks are allowed 'to capitalize their profits and socialize their losses'. Bonuses may be the worst thing that has happened to industry. The natural response to a bonus is, after all, to play to win the bonus – not because one is greedy necessarily – but as a natural response to a challenge: successfully obtaining a bonus equates with success; failure to do so is identified with, just that, failure. Thus, the bonus encourages managers to aim for a short-term objective independent of any consideration of the long-term impact on the firm. Better, in my view, to reward managers with a salary and allow them to get on with managing the firm to the best of their ability, motivated (like the rest of us) by the incentive of enhancing their reputation. Or are we to understand that the firm's executives are alone amongst its employees in requiring such short-term inducements as share options and bonus targets before they can be expected to align themselves with the firm's success?

Academia, however, has often chosen to champion explicitly the wisdom of executive remuneration packages. An influential paper by Jensen and Zimmerman (1985) concluded that (1) executive compensation is *positively* related to share price performance, as well as arguing that (2) the adoption of new short- and long-term executive compensation plans and golden parachutes is associated with *positive* share price reactions. Jensen and Murphy (1990) went so far as to argue that US CEOs have *insufficient* incentives to increase shareholder wealth, while Conyon and Murphy (2000) argued that incentives among British CEOs 'pale compared to their American counterparts' (p. 668) and recommended that UK remunerations be re-examined to avoid the potential damaging effect to British companies if their managers seek to go abroad. The issue, they argue, is that of selecting the correct performance measure, as well as educating shareholders to understand the relation between executive pay and firm performance (Murphy, 1985). Also in UK studies, Main, Bruce and Buck (1996) and Murphy and Oyer (2001) argue that executive compensation is strongly *positively* related to corporate performance. This is not to say that all academic thinking – even before the financial crisis – had supported executive packages. Several studies had argued that the greater the pay disparity in corporations, the weaker the financial performance, the poorer the internal collaboration, and the lower the product quality (e.g., Cowherd and Levine, 1992; Siegel and Hambrick, 2005). More cynical views are that stock options have been not so much an incentive device but a covert mechanism of self-dealing, which is the process they were supposed to eliminate (Yermack, 1995); and that top managers appear to be an averagely ineffectual officer class who do, however, know how to look after themselves (Froud, Johal, Leaver and Williams, 2006). Dodd and Johns (1999) and Bolton, Scheinkman and Xiong (2006) confirm that executive remunerations have intensified management focus onto pleasing, and at times manipulating, financial markets, motivating them toward stock repurchases and an emphasis on short-term stock market valuation, with consequent reductions on attention to product and service markets and at the expense of long-term corporate value. See also McSweeney (2009) and, for example, Coles, Hertzel and Kalpathy (2006), Ellsworth (1983, 2002), Fuller and Jensen (2002), Graham, Harvey and Rajgopal (2005), Sanders and Carpenter (2003), and Stinchcombe (2000).

Consequently, executives and their remuneration consultants have been able to defend their remuneration increases with the argument that the remunerations are 'set by efficient markets'. It has taken the global financial crisis to bring the disparity between pay and performance into sharp relief. Nevertheless, it has been left largely to non-academic writers to observe that gross pay and bonuses continue to be awarded to managers and executives even when their company does badly or an investment fund performs mediocrely. In *The Myth of the Rational Market* Justin Fox (2009) concludes that options to executives in the bull market of the 1990s made a few superstar CEOs into billionaires and a lot of mediocrities into centi-millionaires (p. 279).

The mantra of 'efficient markets' as espoused by academics also implies an effectiveness and efficiency of the system as steward and protector of common shareholder savings. Against such complacency, John Bogle is a rare outspoken critic.[8] He has repeatedly accused the funds management industry of emphasizing management bonuses driven by short-term performance and salesmanship with an attendant 'churning' of client funds (the holding period is typically less than one year) – with the result that desired outcomes are misaligned with incentives (Bogle, 2005a, 2005b). Bogle concludes that citizens who have entrusted their savings to the care of mutual fund managers have not been well served by the industry. He receives support from Richard Ennis (2005), who considers that for the majority of fund managers, fees are 'beyond the pale of plausibility'.[9] More recently, a report from Britain's regulators, the Financial Conduct Authority (FCA), confirms that the mutual fund industry is not competitive, is adept at hiding its failures, and performs inadequately for its investors (reported in *The Economist* magazine, November 26–December 2, 2016).

4. ACADEMIC FINANCE AS HOSTAGE TO ITSELF

Keasey and Hudson (2007) consider that academic finance succeeds in having its papers published when they are upbeat and confirmatory of the system; in effect, adhering fundamentally to the paradigm of market efficiency. They point out that for finance academics, it is far safer, and more productive, in terms of the research game being played, to narrowly select data from the outside world and produce puzzles on the periphery of what is already established. This keeps the research community busy without seriously threatening the imposed belief system, be it banking or corporate behavior, executive pay or fund management fees.

A good deal of finance is now an econometric exercise in mining data, either for confirmation of a particular factor model or for the confirmation of deviations from a model's predictions as anomalies. The accumulation of explanatory variables advanced to explain the cross-section of asset returns has been accelerating, albeit with little overall understanding of the structure between them. Subrahmanyam (2010) documents more than fifty variables used to predict stock returns. Nevertheless, the papers display little progress in achieving a robust risk-return relationship of markets.

If the question is asked as to why academics are not pursuing more interesting lines of enquiry in their publications, such as the relation between the propensity of banks to offer credit and the cycle of stock markets and the real economy, and the extent to which each is the cause of the other, the answer is that the job of writing papers and achieving citations for papers is most efficiently achieved not by thinking long and hard about financial economic issues, but by mining data until some arguably (statistically) significant relation is found and around which a narrative can be spun so as to have the finding published (and subsequently cited by other academics).[10] Academics do not prosper by experiencing reality and thereby attaining a firsthand understanding of reality. Academics prosper by *writing papers* on perceptions of reality as advanced by other academics.

In a review of the US Center for Research in Security Prices (CRSP) database, *The Economist* magazine (2010) observes that the high level of 'data mining' is the outcome of the opportunity that the CRSP database offers financial economists (it estimates that more than one third of published papers in finance represent econometric studies of the database). Robert Shiller in the same article in *The Economist* is quoted as saying that with the creation of the CRSP database, economists have been led to believe that finance has become scientific, and that conventional ideas about investing and financial markets – and about their vulnerabilities – are out of date. He states that to have seen the financial crisis coming, it would have been better 'to go back to old-fashioned readings of history, studying institutions and laws. We should have talked to grandpa'. For many years, Shiller had been a rare voice advocating the possibility of price movements and bubbles unrelated to information. His work earned him the Nobel Prize for Economics in 2013 (shared with Lars Peter Hansen and Eugene Fama). Shiller (1981) argues that stock market fluctuations show far too much variability to be explained by an efficient market theory of pricing, and that one must look to behavioral considerations and to crowd psychology to explain the actual process of price determination.

Thus, the system that denies the possibility of systematic instability continues to be held hostage to itself, as the aspiring young finance person seeking a PhD and needing to produce a 'job paper' to promote an academic career, is effectively obliged to follow the route of an econometrically sound contribution to empirical data mining, rather than explore the uncertainty associated with endeavoring to contribute to a meaningful understanding of the economic system. And so the self-protecting mechanism of academia continues with the vast majority of top accounting and finance journals ranked primarily on the econometric closure of their contributions rather than the subjective insightfulness of their research.

5. CONCLUSION

Economists recognize the up and down – bull and bear – cycles of market valuations as contributing to a broader economic cycle. In contrast, finance academics have typically preferred to develop their understanding of markets as efficient and tending to equilibrium.

The idea that finance theory must learn to look beyond the limitations of its core precepts continues to be resisted by the vast majority of academics. As a consequence, the need to connect financial markets with economic cycles – each of which is capable of leading the other (up or down) – and thereby to connect with the imperatives of institutional behavior, has received scant academic attention.

Nevertheless, as an outcome of the global financial crisis, the mirror has been held up to academic finance as to how it wishes to see itself – either committed to meaningful and responsible enquiry with regard to the issue of market instability as exemplified by the global financial crisis, or content with the 'business as usual' that embraces an economic foundation that is at arm's length from reality and which is focused on achieving econometric closure within increasingly narrow domains of inquiry, and which finds itself unable to accept the profession's excesses and inefficiencies.

NOTES

1. Arestis, Demetriades and Luintel (2001) and Levine and Zervos (1998) emphasize the role of credit (and stock market) liquidity and banking development, rather than stock market growth, in stimulating economic growth.
2. Arner (2007) confirms that until the late 1990s, the role of the financial sector in economic development was largely ignored (p. 13); and Levine (1997) in an economic journal states, 'I believe that we will not have sufficient understanding of long-run economic growth until we understand the evolution and functioning of financial systems' (p. 720).
3. There have been exceptions. For example, a thin thread of articles critical of the CAPM has appeared in *Critical Perspectives on Accounting* (McGoun, 1995; Dempsey, 1996; Hudson, Keasey, Littler and Dempsey, 1999; Keasey and Hudson, 2007). We also note King (1975), Whitley (1984, 1986) and Durand (1989).
4. Sharpe, Markowitz and Merton Miller jointly received the 1990 Nobel Prize in Economics for their contributions to the field of financial economics.
5. Merton Miller (1977) later dismissed such arguments as reminding him of the fabled horse and rabbit pie: one horse and one rabbit. In effect, a reversal of his correction 1963 paper (with Modigliani), itself a correction to his 1958 paper (with Modigliani).
6. They quote MacKenzie and Millo (2003), who show how the academic modeling of derivatives eventually legitimated derivatives and the means by which they are valued and traded.
7. Ball (2009) argues that attempting to lay the blame for the global financial crisis at the door of a simple proposition – the 'efficient market hypothesis' – is naïve. True, but the point made here is that theories are capable of 'taking hold' and thereafter punching above their intellectual weight in referencing what is considered to be responsible behavior by participants, as well as what is considered to be appropriate interference by those with responsibility as regulators.
8. John Bogle is the founder of the Vanguard Group of Investment Companies – built on principles of low cost. Bogle insists that it is foolish to attempt to pick actively managed mutual funds and expect their performance to beat a low-cost index fund over a long period of time, after accounting for the fees that actively managed funds charge.
9. Richard Ennis is a principal at investment advisory firm, Ennis, Knupp & Associates, Chicago.
10. There is a corrupting influence here when university members vie for prestige and

personal reward on the basis of attaining 'production targets' for their output. Universities might lecture on the merits of free market enterprise, but many of them are governed by centrally planned systems with production quotas for publications handed down to academics.

REFERENCES

Allen, F. (2012), 'Trends in Financial Innovation and their Welfare Impact: An Overview', *European Financial Management*, **18**, 493–514.

Arestis, P., Demetriades, P.D. and Luintel, K.B. (2001), 'Financial Development and Economic Growth: The Role of Stock Markets', *Journal of Money, Credit and Banking*, **33**, 16–41.

Arner, D. (2007), *Financial Stability, Economic Growth and the Role of Law*, Cambridge: Cambridge University Press.

Ball, R. (2009), 'The Global Financial Crisis and the Efficient Market Hypothesis: What Have We Learned?' *Journal of Applied Corporate Finance*, **21**, 8–16.

Black, F., Jensen, M. and Scholes, M. (1972), 'The Capital Asset Pricing Model: Some Empirical Tests', in M.C. Jensen (ed.), *Studies in the Theory of Capital Markets*, New York: Praeger Publishers.

Bogle, J.C. (2005a), 'The Mutual Fund Industry 60 Years Later: For Better or for Worse?', *Financial Analysts Journal*, **61**, 15–24.

Bogle, J.C. (2005b), 'The Relentless Rules of Humble Arithmetic', *Financial Analysts Journal*, **61**, 22–35.

Bolton, P., Scheinkman, J. and Xiong, W. (2006), 'Executive Compensation and Short- Termist Behaviour in Speculative Markets', *Review of Economic Studies*, **73**, 577–610.

Cai, C.X., Clacher, I. and Keasey, K. (2013), 'Consequences of the Capital Asset Pricing Model (CAPM) – A Critical and Broad Perspective', *Abacus*, **49**, 51–61.

Coles, J.L., Hertzel, M. and Kalpathy, S. (2006), 'Earnings Management Around Employee Stock Options Reissues', *Journal of Accounting and Economics*, **41**, 173–200.

Conyon, M.J. and Murphy, K.J. (2000), 'The Prince and the Pauper? CEO Pay in the United States and United Kingdom', *The Economic Journal*, **110**, 640–671.

Cowherd, D.M. and Levine, D.I. (1992), 'Product Quality and Pay Equity between Lower- Level Employees and Top Management: An Investigation of Distributive Justice Theory', *Administrative Science Quarterly*, **37**, 302–320.

Dempsey, M. (1996), 'Corporate Financial Management: Time to Change the Cost of Capital Paradigm?' *Critical Perspectives on Accounting*, **7**, 617–639.

Dempsey, M. (2013), 'The Capital Asset Pricing Model (CAPM): The History of a Failed Revolutionary Idea in Finance,' *Abacus*, **49** (S1), 7–23.

Dempsey, M. and Jones, S. (2015), 'Financial Measurement and Financial Markets', in S. Jones (ed.), *Routledge Companion to Financial Accounting Theory*, Abingdon, UK: Routledge.

Dodd, J.L. and Johns, J. (1999), 'EVA Reconsidered', *Business and Economic Review*, April–June, 13–18.

Durand, D. (1989), 'Afterthoughts on a Controversy with MM, Plus New Thoughts on Growth and the Cost of Capital', *Financial Management*, **18**, 12–18.

The Economist (2010), 'Economics Focus: Data Birth', Nov. 20–26, p. 83.

The Economist (2016), 'Charging the Earth', Nov. 26–Dec. 2, p. 62.

Ellsworth, R.R. (1983), 'Capital Markets and Competitive Decline', *Harvard Business Review*, September–October, 171–183.

Ellsworth, R.R. (2002), *Leading with Purpose: The New Corporate Realities*, Stanford: Stanford University Press.

Ennis, R.M. (2005), 'Are Active Management Fees Too High?' *Financial Analysts Journal*, **61**, 44–51.

Fama, F. (1976), *Foundations of Finance*, New York: Basic Books.

Fama, E. and French, K. (1992), 'The Cross-Section of Expected Stock Returns', *Journal of Finance*, **47**, 427–466.
Fama, E. and French, K. (1996), 'Multifactor Explanations of Asset Pricing Anomalies', *Journal of Finance*, **51**, 55–84.
Foucault, M. (1977), *Madness and Civilization: A History of Insanity in the Age of Reason*, London: Tavistock.
Fox, J. (2009), *The Myth of the Rational Market*, New York: Harper Collins.
Froud, J., Johal, S., Leaver, A. and Williams, K. (2006), *Financialization and Strategy: Narrative and Numbers*, London: Routledge.
Fuller, J. and Jensen, M.C. (2002), 'Just Say No to Wall Street: Putting a Stop to the Earnings Game: Courageous CEOs are Putting a Stop to the Earnings Game and We Will All Be Better Off for It', *Journal of Applied Corporate Finance*, **14**, 41–46.
Graham, J.R., Harvey, C.R. and Rajgopal, S. (2005), 'The Economic Implications of Corporate Financial Reporting', *Journal of Accounting and Economics*, **40**, 3–73.
Hudson, R., Keasey, K., Littler, K. and Dempsey, M. (1999), 'Time Diversification: An Essay in the Need to Revisit Finance Theory', *Critical Perspectives on Accounting*, **10**, 501–519.
Jensen, M.C. and Murphy, K.J. (1990), 'Performance Pay and Top-Management Incentives', *Journal of Political Economy*, **98**, 225–264.
Jensen, M.C. and Zimmerman, J.L. (1985), 'Management Compensation and the Managerial Labor Market', *Journal of Accounting and Economics*, **7**, 3–9.
Keasey, K. and Hudson, R. (2007), 'Finance Theory: A House without Windows', *Critical Perspectives on Accounting*, **18**, 932–951.
Keynes, J.M. (1936), *The General Theory of Employment, Interest and Money*, London: Macmillan and Co.
King, P. (1975), 'Is the Emphasis on Capital Budgeting Misplaced?', *Journal of Business Finance and Accounting*, **2**, 69–82.
Levine, R. (1997), 'Financial Development and Economic Growth: Views and Agenda', *Journal of Economic Literature*, **35**, 688–726.
Levine, R. and Zervos, S. (1998), 'Stock Markets, Banks, and Economic Growth', *The American Economic Review*, **88**, 537–558.
Lintner, J. (1965), 'The Valuation of Risk Assets and the Selection of Risky Investments in Stock Portfolios and Capital Budgets', *Review of Economics and Statistics*, **47**, 13–37.
Lo, A.W. and Mueller, M.T. (2010), 'Warning: Physics Envy May be Hazardous to Your Health', *Journal of Investment Management*, **8**(2), 13–63.
MacKenzie, D. and Millo, Y. (2003), 'Constructing a Market, Performing Theory: The Historical Sociology of a Financial Derivatives Exchange', *American Journal of Sociology*, **109**, 107–145.
Main, B.G.M., Bruce, A. and Buck, T. (1996), 'Total Board Remuneration and Company Performance', *The Economic Journal*, **106**, 1627–1644.
Markowitz, H. (1952), 'Portfolio Selection', *Journal of Finance*, **7**, 77–91.
McGoun, E.G. (1995), 'The History of Risk Measurement', *Critical Perspectives on Accounting*, **6**, 511–532.
McSweeney, B. (2009), 'The Roles of Financial Asset Market Failure Denial and the Economic Crisis: Reflections on Accounting and Financial Theories and Practices', *Accounting, Organizations and Society*, **34**, 834–848.
Miller, M.H. (1977), 'Debt and Taxes', *Journal of Finance*, **32**, 261–275.
Minsky, H. (1986), *Stabilizing an Unstable Economy*, Columbus: McGraw-Hill.
Modigliani, F. and Miller, M. (1958), 'The Cost of Capital, Corporation Finance and the Theory of Investment', *American Economic Review*, **48**, 261–297.
Modigliani, F. and Miller, M. (1963), 'Corporate Income Taxes and the Cost of Capital: A Correction', *American Economic Review*, **53**, 433–443.
Moosa, I.A. (2013), 'The Capital Asset Pricing Model (CAPM): The History of a Failed Revolutionary Idea in Finance? Comments and Extensions', *Abacus*, **49**, 62–68.
Mossin, J. (1966), 'Equilibrium in a Capital Asset Market', *Econometrica*, **34**, 768–783.

Murphy, K.J. (1985), 'Corporate Performance and Managerial Remuneration: An Empirical Analysis', *Journal of Accounting and Economics*, **7**, 11–42.
Murphy, K.J. and Oyer, P. (2001), 'Discretion in Executive Incentive Contracts: Theory and Evidence', available at https://papers.ssrn.com/sol3/papers.cfm?abstract_id=294829
Ritter, J.R. (2012), 'Is Economic Growth Good for Investors?', *Journal of Applied Corporate Finance*, **24**, 8–18.
Sanders, W.G. and Carpenter, M.A. (2003), 'Strategic Satisficing? A Behavioral-Agency Theory Perspective on Stock Repurchase Program Announcements', *Academy of Management Journal*, **46**, 160–178.
Sharpe, W.F. (1964), 'Capital Asset Prices: A Theory of Market Equilibrium under Conditions of Risk', *Journal of Finance*, **19**, 425–442.
Shiller, R.J. (1981), 'Do Stock Prices Move Too Much to Be Justified by Subsequent Changes in Dividends?', *American Economic Review*, **71**, 421–436.
Siegel, P.A. and Hambrick, D.C. (2005), 'Pay Disparities within Top Management Groups: Evidence of Harmful Effects on Performance in High-Technology Firms', *Organization Science*, **16**, 259–274.
Stiglitz, J. (2000), 'Capital Market Liberalization, Economic Growth, and Instability', *World Development*, **28**, 1076–1086.
Stinchcombe, A.L. (2000), 'Social Structure and Organizations: A Comment', in J. Baum and F. Dobbin (eds), *Economics Meets Sociology in Strategic Management: Advances in Strategic Management*, Greenwich, CT: JAI Press.
Subrahmanyam, A. (2010), 'The Cross-Section of Expected Stock Returns: What Have We Learnt from the Past Twenty-Five Years of Research?', *European Financial Management*, **16**, 27–42.
Treynor, J.L. (1962), 'Toward a Theory of Market Value of Risky Assets', unpublished manuscript. A final version was published in R. Korajczyk (ed.) (1999), *Asset Pricing and Portfolio Performance: Models, Strategy and Performance Metrics*, London: Risk Books.
Whitley, R.D. (1984), *The Intellectual and Social Organization of the Sciences*, Oxford: Clarendon Press.
Whitley, R.D. (1986), 'The Transformation of Business Finance into Financial Economics: The Roles of Academic Expansion and Changes in US Capital Markets', *Accounting, Organizations and Society*, **11**, 171–192.
Yermack, D. (1995), 'Do Corporations Award CEO Stock Options Effectively?', *Journal of Financial Economics*, **39**, 237–269.

APPENDIX

Table 5A.1 An overview of studies that have formed the foundation for modern finance theory as well as critiques of such theory

Author(s)	Objective of study	Main findings
Foundations of modern finance theory		
Markowitz (1952)	Theoretical portfolio outcomes as a function of individual portfolio component outcomes.	The development of 'portfolio theory' with the insight that non-market risk can be 'diversified away' by holding many assets.
Treynor (1962) Sharpe (1964) Mossin (1966) Lintner (1965)	The theoretical expected return on an asset as a function of market risk exposure.	The development of the capital asset pricing model (CAPM).
Black, Jensen and Scholes (1972)	Empirically observed returns on an asset as a function of market risk exposure, as a test of the CAPM.	The development of early satisfactory tests of the CAPM (which when examined closely do not actually support the CAPM).
Fama (1976)	The efficiency of capital markets in subsuming available information.	An influential text that makes a robust defense of 'efficient markets'.
Modigliani and Miller (1958, 1963)	The theoretical value of the firm as a function of financial leverage (debt obligations.)	The foundation of a modern theory of corporate capital structure.
Miller (1977)	The value to the firm of the tax deductibility of its interest payments on debt.	A re-assessment of Miller's own argument (with Modigliani, 1963 above) for the tax advantage of corporate debt. Debt is again regarded as 'irrelevant' at the margin of corporate borrowing.
Fama and French (1992)	An empirical examination of the CAPM as a model of share price formation.	An influential demonstration of the *in*-effectiveness of the CAPM as a model of historical share price formation, which motivates Fama and French's own

Table 5A.1 (continued)

Author(s)	Objective of study	Main findings
		three-factor model, and, subsequently, a plethora of models aimed at highlighting 'anomalies' in the data in relation to the CAPM.
Critiques of efficient markets and foundations of finance		
Keynes (1936)	The instability of markets as an outcome of 'fundamental uncertainty' combined with 'the psychology of the marketplace'.	The insights of the economist John Maynard Keynes who recognized the nature of markets as capable of self-fulfilling expectations, leading to prolonged periods of bull and bear market sentiments.
Minsky (1986)	The role of borrowing by individuals, corporations, and the banking industry in stimulating the economy as asset prices rise, before excessive borrowing and price rises inevitably turn as asset and stock prices are 'corrected' in an economic recession.	The insights of the economist Hyman Minsky, who argued that markets are inherently unstable (his work has received revitalized attention following the GFC). His prediction is of a 'Minsky moment', when credit expansion moves from fueling an upward moving economy to precipitating the economy's self-destructive decline.
Durand (1989) Dempsey (1996) King (1975)	The Modigliani and Miller propositions, the cost of capital and capital budgeting.	The foundations of modern finance are recognized as having practical limitations with the observation that the cost of capital is a much more 'nebulous' number than is generally recognized by academics.
Shiller (1981)	The movements of share prices in relation to changes in dividends.	A relatively early critique of the ability of markets to price assets efficiently.

Table 5A.1 (continued)

Author(s)	Objective of study	Main findings
Cai, Clacher and Keasey (2013) Dempsey (2013) Lo and Mueller (2010) Moosa (2013)	The adequacy of the CAPM, and subsequent 'asset pricing models', including the Fama and French three-factor model, as models of asset price formation.	Critiques of academic finance's unthinking adoption of the CAPM, as well as subsequent factor models of asset pricing that incorporate the CAPM.
Subrahmanyam (2010)	The unification of asset pricing models.	A critique of the proliferation of developed asset pricing models with increasingly added 'explanatory variables' that have followed Fama and French's (1992, above) denunciation of the CAPM as adequately describing historical asset prices.
Hudson, Keasey, Littler, and Dempsey (1999) Keasey and Hudson (2007)	The correspondence of academic theory with practitioner approaches to problem solving.	Critiques that argue that academic finance's abstractions have lost relevance with the real world ('outside the window').
MacKenzie and Millo (2003)	The role of academic contributions in justifying the widespread application of derivatives.	Confirmation that academic finance theory determines practice.
Ball (2009)	The role of efficient market theory in the GFC.	A rare defense of efficient markets following the GFC.
Stiglitz (2000)	The question of government regulation of the finance industry.	The argument is made that capital market regulation is required to protect the majority of society against the vested interests of a minority that benefits from market liberalization.
Dempsey and Jones (2015)	The responsibility of standard finance theory in leading to the global financial crisis (GFC).	The argument that finance theory's support of market efficiency encouraged the accountant's marking

Table 5A.1 (continued)

Author(s)	Objective of study	Main findings
		of liquid assets to market, which worked to undermine the integrity of banks and precipitated the GFC.
Levine (1997) Arner (2007) Levine and Zervos (1998) Arestis, Demetriades and Luintel (2001)	The relationships of stock markets, credit and banking expansion to economic growth.	Recognition of the need to understand the evolution and functioning of financial systems as a foundation for long-run economic growth. The role of credit (and stock market) liquidity and banking development, rather than growth in stock markets, in stimulating economic growth.
Allen (2012)	The role of financial innovation in causing financial crises.	The conclusion that credit expansion in the economy, rather than financial innovation as such, is the more likely precursor of financial crises.
Ritter (2012)	The relationship between economic expansion and stock market returns.	The observation that economic growth does not correlate positively with stock market returns.
Philosophy of science		
Foucault (1977)	The role of theory in seeking to understand practice before ultimately controlling practice.	The argument that conceptual explanations ultimately dictate practice as observed practice moves from being the 'object' of theory to becoming 'subject' to theory.
McGoun (1995)	The history of finance.	The observation that modern finance is a construct from the 1960s onwards, and that the development

Table 5A.1 (continued)

Author(s)	Objective of study	Main findings
		has led managers to see their responsibility as 'rewarding shareholders in the immediate term' – as opposed to focusing on the long-term health of the company – with the outcome that managers are overly concerned with share prices.
Whitley (1984, 1986)	The role of academic institutions in theory development.	The observation that academia succeeds in 'perpetuating' its ideas to the next generation of academics by controlling the intellectual scope of its students (undergraduate and PhD students).
Critique of portfolio management		
Bogle (2005a, 2005b) Ennis (2005)	The effective performance and responsibility of mutual fund and portfolio asset managers on behalf of their investors.	Critical assessments of the management of the mutual funds industry with excessive management fees that stifle investors' wealth creation.
Arguments in favor of executive remuneration		
Conyon and Murphy (2000) Jensen and Murphy (1990) Jensen and Zimmerman (1985) Main, Bruce and Buck (1996) Murphy (1985) Murphy and Oyer (2001)	The effectiveness of management remuneration packages in leading to enhanced firm performance and added shareholder wealth.	An argument for the *effectiveness* of (and in the UK the need to increase) the role of executive remuneration packages in enhancing corporate performance.

Table 5A.1 (continued)

Author(s)	Objective of study	Main findings
Arguments against executive remuneration		
Bolton, Scheinkman and Xiong (2006) Coles, Hertzel and Kalpathy (2006) Cowherd and Levine (1992) Dodd and Johns (1999) Ellsworth (1983, 2002) Froud, Johal, Leaver and Williams (2006) Graham, Harvey and Rajgopal (2005) McSweeney (2009) Sanders and Carpenter (2003) Stinchcombe (2000) Siegel and Hambrick (2005) Yermack (1995)	The effectiveness of management remuneration packages in leading to enhanced firm performance and added shareholder wealth.	The argument that executive remuneration packages are actually a feature of inefficient markets, with top management and executive positions only weakly 'contestable' (competitive), so that the system is effectively rigged in favor of top managers and executives who are in a position to 'self-deal' themselves excessive compensation packages at the expense of their shareholders.

6. The stability of the financial system: an analysis of the determinants of Russian bank failures

Viktoryia Tankoyeva, Flavio Bazzana and Roberto Gabriele

1. INTRODUCTION

With the incidence of financial crises, the financial stability of banks has become a matter of great importance. Financial crises may cause massive bank failures, which negatively influence banking system stability and can provoke systemic banking crises. Especially since the global economic crisis of 2008, financial system stability and banking regulation have become more important, principally in economic growth considerations. This correlation has also been deeply discussed in the literature, starting with the connection between financial development and growth (Goodhart, 2014), then introducing the role of financial fragility (Loayza and Rancière, 2006) and finally showing the importance of financial stability (Beck, 2014; Bresser-Pereira et al., 2014). The significant connection between financial system stability and economic growth has also been recently emphasized in monetary policy, as 'a stable financial system is a prerequisite for sustainable economic growth' (W.C. Dudley, President and CEO of the Fed of New York, September 2011), and in fiscal policy, as 'financial stability is a prerequisite for growth' (G. Osborne and V. Cable, Chancellor of the Exchequer and Financial Secretary to the Treasury, UK Government, June 2012). Creating a stable financial system requires regulation of the banking sector to reduce the possibility of bank failure. For this reason, the banking sector is currently strictly regulated by banking supervisory authorities. One important reason for bank regulation is the 'contagion effect' of bank failure. The contagion effect may be compared to the 'domino' effect implying that the effects of a bank failure spill over to other banks regardless of the reasons for such a failure (Aharony and Swary, 1983). Moreover, financial contagion may spread beyond national boundaries and become international. Van Rijckeghem and Weder (2003) provide evidence that 'bank lending contributed to the transmission of currency crises during the recent episodes of financial instability in emerging markets' (Van Rijckeghem and Weder, 2003, p. 483). In light of this fact, the accurate prediction of bank distress has been a matter of great concern to bank supervisory authorities and regulators, and has received much attention in the scientific literature. Both bank regulators and researchers endeavour to develop novel approaches to banking supervision and assessment, which will allow the identification of impaired bank financial positions before a crisis. Such systems may serve as early warning systems (EWSs), signalling regulators if banks' financial positions begin to deteriorate. The adoption of EWSs has developed the supervisory process considerably. At the same time, the incidence of banking crises across the world shows that 'safeguarding the banking system is no easy task' (Demyanyk and Hasan, 2010, p. 319).

As a result of the transformation of the Russian banking system (RBS), a satisfactory level of performance in banking intermediation has been achieved (Karminsky and Kostrov, 2013). The RBS is characterized by high concentration of assets, with the three largest state-owned banks possessing dominant positions in common shares representing approximately 50 per cent of the sector's assets. Russian credit institutions demonstrate moderate profitability, but profit generation is unequal, which increases instability in the RBS. The number of credit institutions has decreased in Russia: of the more than 3,500 licences issued by the Central Bank, only 923 credit institutions were operational as of 1 January 2014. The main threats to the RBS are high levels of systemic risk and dependence on the external environment, regional imbalances in the availability of retail banking services, low diversification of assets and income sources, dependence on a single borrower, and liability base vulnerability (Gudyma, 2013). The efficiency and stability of the RBS is a prerequisite for sustainable economic development in Russia. The stability of the banking system is largely determined by the characteristics and stability of individual banks. Improving service quality and supporting the stable functioning of credit institutions will increase the efficiency of the RBS and will be beneficial to the real sector of the Russian economy.

The Central Bank of Russia (CBR) plays the role of the principal supervisor and regulator of the banking sector by employing 'prudential norms', a series of mandatory financial requirements for capital, liquidity and credit risk exposure. A mix of off-site and on-site inspections ensures compliance with prudential norms. Critiques in the literature have focused on the efficiency of the CBR as a regulator. Among its main limitations are its inexperience, informality in commercial bank supervision, focus on the external aspects of banking activity, inadequate attention to excessive risk-taking, low efficiency and delays in implementing supervisory actions (Lanine and Vennet, 2006; Malyutina and Parilova, 2001). The crisis of

2008–2009 seriously affected the RBS, causing major reductions in asset quality, impairing liquidity and triggering deposits outflows. Under these circumstances, the importance of the role of the CBR as both a regulator and a source of financial replenishment has increased dramatically. The large-scale lending policy of the CBR allowed numerous Russian banks to stabilize their capital ratios and avoid default (Gudyma, 2013). Nevertheless, many banks failed.

The rationale behind identifying the determinants of bank failure and EWS development for the CBR is now straightforward. Numerous cases of bank failure and continuous licence revocation highlight the significance of developing accurate EWS models that predict financial distress and identify problematic banks based on their balance sheet information. Quantitative models of default probability based on banks' financial statements are one such possibility. These models may be of interest to the Central Bank because they would allow the identification and careful monitoring of the most vulnerable credit institutions. Given the frequency of crises in Russia, a series of research papers dedicated to these issues appeared; for example, the works of Kuznetsov (2003) and Styrin (2005) are dedicated to the crisis of 1998. Drobyshevsky and Zubarev (2011) examine the factors determining bank failure during the crisis of 2008, while Styrin (2005) detects the influence of X-inefficiency on the probability of bank default. In most studies dedicated to bankruptcy prediction among Russian banks, authors attribute the probability of failure to profitability, liquidity and capital adequacy ratios. According to Lanine and Vennet (2006) and Konstandina (2006), liquidity ratios are significant predictors that are negatively associated with the probability of Russian bank failure. Profitability ratios are found to be significant predictors of bank financial distress in the works of Lanine and Vennet (2006) and Karminsky and Kostrov (2013). Macroeconomic and institutional variables have also been incorporated into empirical studies of Russian banks' failures. According to Peresetsky et al. (2011) and Karminsky and Kostrov (2013), the use of macroeconomic variables, such as GDP growth rate and inflation rates, improves the predictive power of these models. In contrast, Konstandina (2006) finds that unlike financial indicators, macroeconomic variables are not significant predictors of bankruptcy.

This chapter aims to identify the determinants of bank failure and to develop an accurate EWS model using a sample of Russian banks for 2006–2013 by means of Cox proportional hazard models with time-varying covariates. Beyond the determinants traditionally used in bank distress prediction studies, such as CAMELS indicators, we employ and test the significance of interbank loans for the contemporaneous and early bankruptcy prediction of Russian banks. Our findings suggest that a Cox proportional hazard model with time-varying covariates predicts Russian bank failures well. Compared with the existing studies, the virtue of this chapter consists in its usage of interbank loans for bank failure prediction and its use of the most recent available data for the analysis. The dataset collected includes a time frame long enough to include the recent crises faced by Russian banks. We rely on the most recent publicly available data published on the official CBR website to derive the CAMELS indicators: Capital adequacy, Asset quality, Management, Earnings, Liquidity, and Sensitivity to market risk.[1]

In our analysis, we find that the CAMELS variables, namely, the capital to liabilities ratio and the liquidity ratio, are important predictors of bank financial distress. If we use lagged data to predict early bank failure, we find that different determinants are important. Namely, variables describing profitability and asset quality provide a strong signal of approaching distress. We also find that sensitivity to market risk is an important determinant of bank failure for larger banks. The results of our study suggest that CAMELS and other bank-specific variables can help the stakeholders of Russian banks and regulators to assess the risk of bank failure, as well as to undertake timely actions to avoid and to mitigate the cost of failure.

The remainder of this chapter is organized as follows. In the next section, the methodology employed in the empirical analysis and the data collection are reported. Section 3 'Sample construction and variables' sets forth the description of the sample construction and the variables used in the empirical analysis. In section 4 'Hypotheses', we present the two hypotheses we want to test. The obtained results are presented and interpreted in section 5 'Results'. The final section summarizes our findings and concludes.

2. METHODOLOGY AND DATA COLLECTION

We estimate a series of discrete-time survival models to determine the probability of failure at each point in time, namely, each year. The choice of discrete time is based on the annual collection of the data. Hence, the event 'bankruptcy of a bank' can only occur at discrete points in time identified by calendar year ($y = 2006, 2007, \ldots, 2013$).

Bank default is defined as the date of licence revocation by the CBR, and it is modelled as a dummy variable that takes the value 1 in cases of bank failure in a given year and 0 otherwise. The probability of bank failure is modelled as a function of observable bank characteristics.

We employ a Cox discrete-time proportional hazard survival model in which covariate changes have a multiplicative effect on the hazard rate of bank bankruptcy. More formally, we consider the following hazard function:

$$\lambda(t|\mathbf{x},\beta) = \lambda_0(t)\,\phi(\mathbf{x},\beta)$$

where $\lambda_0(t)$ is the baseline hazard, which is a function of time t, and $\phi(\mathbf{x},\beta)$, which is a function of observed time-invariant and time-varying variables ($\mathbf{x}$). In this discrete-time setting, the probability that a bank exits the market is defined as follows:

$$prob\,(y_{j-1} < T < y_j) = S(y_{j-1}) - S(y_j)$$

where T is a random variable that defines the discrete time of exit (year), y_j is the year, and $S(y_j)$ is the survival function.

The discrete hazard rate is given by:

$$prob\,(y_{j-1} < T < y_j | T < y_{j-1}) = \frac{\phi(\mathbf{x}_j,\beta)}{\sum_{y \in T} \phi(\mathbf{x}_y,\beta)}$$

in which we drop $\lambda_0(t)$ given the parallel assumption.[2] We specify the function $\phi(\mathbf{x},\beta)$ as a function of the series of time-varying covariates introduced above:

$$\phi(x,\beta) = e^{x'\beta} = \beta_1\,\mathrm{FAIL} + \beta_2\,\mathrm{CTA} + \beta_3\,\mathrm{CTL} + \beta_4\,\mathrm{LTA} + \beta_5\,\mathrm{ROC} + \beta_6\,\mathrm{LIQ} + \beta_7\,\mathrm{IBLTA} + \beta_8\,\mathrm{SIZE} + \beta_9\,\mathrm{DER} + \beta_{10}\,\mathrm{INSURANCE}$$

Given the context, we also correct our estimates for left censoring – i.e., late entry – and right censoring – banks that do not fail in the time window under analysis – following the methodology of Cameron and Trivedi (2005).

The data collection process consists of several steps. First, the relevant bank-specific data are retrieved from the financial statements of Russian banks and non-banking credit institutions. Both public and private credit institutions in Russia are required to report to the CBR on a regular basis. The CBR reveals accounting and other relevant information about commercial credit institutions to the public. We collect these data using a focused web crawling application.

The second step consists of semantic treatment of the dataset. The dataset is then hand-checked and cleaned to exclude obvious input errors, inaccurate records and outliers. We excluded banks for which outlier values of the indicators represented likely input errors. Finally, a series of random checks was performed to validate the dataset. Although the official CBR website contains bank accounting information since 1998, we restricted the observation period to 2006–2013 because information on bank failures has only been available since 2006. At the same time, the study period included the most recent available information, including the consequences of the 2008 crisis. As a result, our initial dataset included accounting data for 875 existing Russian credit institutions, as well as for 370 credit institutions whose licences were revoked, cancelled or annulled within the 2006–2013 time frame.

The information on the time of and grounds for licence revocation was collected from orders and letters published by the CBR on its official website and on the official website of the Deposit Insurance Agency. Information on the cases of banks' bankruptcy was obtained from the letters of temporary administrations and liquidators available on the official CBR website.

3. SAMPLE CONSTRUCTION AND VARIABLES

Information on failed credit institutions was taken exclusively from balance sheet data when credit institutions declared bankruptcy simultaneously with or after actual licence revocation. We excluded from this group those credit institutions that lost their licences due to compulsory or voluntary liquidation, merger or acquisition. The group of surviving credit institutions includes banks and non-banking credit institutions successfully operating throughout the analysed period.

We have excluded from the sub-sample of failed credit institutions those institutions whose financial statements were not available for two or more years prior to actual licence revocation to obtain the most recent accounting information for failed credit institutions. Observations with no failures in the subsequent two years were considered part of the surviving bank sample. This method ensures that accounting information is ex ante (up to two years prior to actual licence revocation) available to the public and to regulators and provides early warning of failure.

The sample is composed of 1,020 banks and non-banking credit institutions over the period from 2006 to 2013. After applying the above-mentioned constraints, the sub-sample of failed credit institutions comprised 101 credit institutions, whereas the sub-sample of surviving credit institutions numbered 919 credit institutions. Finally, we excluded from the analysis the subset of non-banking credit institutions to reduce bias from differences in the activities of banks and non-banking credit institutions.

To develop a contemporaneous model, we collected balance sheet data for bankrupt banks as of the date of licence revocation. According to Russian legislation in place since 2010, temporary administrations should disclose financial position information (using Form 0409806) for failed banks as of the date of licence revocation in the official bulletin of the CBR, the *Vestnik Banka Rossii* (*The Herald of the Bank of Russia*). As a result, financial information for 69 Russian credit institutions as of the date of licence revocation was retrieved for the period 2010–2013. Together with the sub-sample of surviving banks for the same period, they constitute the sample for testing the contemporaneous model.

In line with previous studies on Russian bank failure prediction (Lanine and Vennet, 2006), we eliminate the largest state-owned banks (Sberbank, Vneshtorgbank, Gazprombank) from both the contemporaneous and the early warning datasets because of their privileged access to state funds and government financial support (Lanine and Vennet, 2006). According to the literature (Zhao et al., 2009), better results in bank failure prediction have been achieved with the use of constructed financial ratios than with raw accounting information. Therefore, in our study, we focus on retrieving data for financial ratios from the financial statements of Russian banks.

The selection of appropriate variables for bank failure prediction in this study was conducted by referring to the CAMELS rating framework widely employed by supervisory authorities and rating agencies around the world. The definitions of the financial ratios in this framework, as well as the expected signs, are presented in Table 6A.1 in the Appendix. The summary statistics are shown in Table 6.1.

The bank failure indicators used are described below. Capital adequacy ratios measure a bank's ability to cope with financial difficulties, crises and unforeseen losses. Variables associated with capital adequacy include the capital to adequacy ratio (CTA) and the capital to liabilities ratio (CTL). We expect negative relations between the probability of default and capital indicators because better capitalized banks usually possess more reserves to cover possible losses and to meet financial obligations in case of financial difficulty. To capture asset quality, we employ the loans to assets ratio (LTA). The larger the share of loans in the portfolio of a bank, the higher its exposure to credit risk because loans are the riskiest of all the bank's assets. Therefore, positive relations between loan-based variables and the probability of bankruptcy are expected. Management quality is the most intangible part of the CAMELS framework. The approaches of previous studies vary widely. For example, Zhao et al. (2009) use ratios of net income to operating income and net income to total assets, Messai and Jouini (2013) refer to personnel expenses to total operating expenses

Table 6.1 Summary statistics of the dependent variable and of the independent variables used in the analyses

Variable	Variable definition	#	Mean	Std. dev.	Min	Max
Dependent variable						
FAIL	Bank failure indicator (1: failed; 0: not failed)	7,077	0.0213	0.1445	0	1
Capital adequacy						
CTA	Capital to adequacy ratio	7,077	0.2258	0.1722	−0.0281	1
CTL	Capital to liabilities ratio	7,076	46.9279	3,036.10	−0.0273	246.15
Asset quality						
LTA	Loans to assets ratio	7,077	0.6142	0.1857	0	0.9839
Earnings ability						
ROC	Returns on capital	7,077	0.0956	0,2894	−4.9382	16.5562
Liquidity						
LIQ	Liquidity ratio	7,076	36.3129	2,918.79	0.0015	245,435
Sensitivity to market risk						
IBLTA	Share of interbank Loans to total assets	7,026	0.0623	0.1301	0	0.8923
Miscellaneous						
SIZE	Size of a bank (SIZE), as measured by total assets	7,077	14.8267	1.7730	7.4928	21.4311
DER	Debt to equity ratio	7,077	5.6517	4.1498	−36.5563	88.4541
INSURANCE	Deposit insurance scheme	7,077	0.8950	0.3065	0	1

Note: Variables are grouped by CAMELS indicators (Capital adequacy, Asset quality, Management, Earnings, Liquidity, and Sensitivity to market risk). Additional explicatory variables are grouped into the 'miscellaneous' category.

Source: Authors' elaborations on CBR data.

and total operating income to total assets, and Kerstein and Kozberg (2013) consider regulatory enforcement actions against the bank. Because this variable is unavailable for the contemporaneous model and because of differences in the literature, we exclude management quality from our models. For earning ability, we use returns on capital (ROC). Because low profitability is accompanied by higher risk, we expect negative relationships between profitability ratios and the probability of default. For the liquidity part of the CAMELS approach, we use the liquidity ratio (LIQ), which captures the ability of banks to cover unexpected money outflows. The liquidity ratio is expected to be negatively associated with the probability of failure. Finally, to capture sensitivity to market risk, we refer to the share of interbank loans to total assets (IBLTA). Miscellaneous variables include the size of a bank (SIZE), as measured by total assets; the debt to equity ratio (DER); and the presence of a deposit insurance scheme (INSURANCE).

4. HYPOTHESES

The fragility of the financial system is one of the most important factors that researchers cite in discussing crises. In this section, we propose a series of bank-level research hypotheses to test the micro-foundations of the concept of banking system fragility, which in turn are largely responsible for financial system stability.

The first key issue is the identification of the most important factors influencing the probability of default and the survival time of Russian banks. Indeed, the sustainability of the financial and economic system is highly influenced by the ability of the banks to remain active in the market and to support firms' activities. Our approach involves the empirical assessment of the effects of the so-called CAMELS indicators and other bank-specific variables on the probability of bank default by means of a semi-parametric Cox proportional hazard model with time-varying covariates. The dataset compiled from the financial statements of Russian banks offers fertile ground for our research given the frequency of crises and numerous bankruptcy cases. We specify and test two hypotheses based on the contemporary literature.

According to the literature, important predictors of bank default may be summarized according to the CAMELS paradigm. The underlying assumption is that the CAMELS system encompasses all relevant aspects of banking activity, such as capital adequacy, asset quality, earning ability and liquidity. The CAMELS variables are widely employed in bank failure prediction. Empirical evidence (Fiordelisi and Mare, 2013; Karminsky and Kostrov, 2013; Kerstein and Kozberg, 2013) confirms the appropriateness of CAMELS variables for predicting bank failure. Despite being an efficient measure of the current financial positions of credit institutions, the CAMELS system has been criticized because of its limitations. According to Sahaiwala and Van den Bergh (2000) 'the CAMEL systems, and related methodologies, are designed to assess the condition of an institution in a point in time, and they are highly responsive to changes in bank performance and economic conditions' (p. 21). Rojas-Suarez (2002) questions the application of the CAMELS model and the relevance of its indicators in emerging and underdeveloped economies. In addition to the CAMELS variables, we employed other bank-specific variables describing bank performance.

We might also be interested in investigating whether CAMELS can be employed to predict bank failures one year in advance. Such an early warning model (EWM) would allow the anticipation of distress among financial institutions. EWMs have been widely employed by researchers and bank supervisory authorities to identify potentially problematic banks and ultimately to prevent their failure. These models aim at monitoring all relevant information and at assessing banks' financial conditions several years prior to default. We posit that both CAMELS and other relevant bank-specific variables are important determinants of bank failure and can also be employed to predict bank distress one year before the event because problems are quickly recognized in bank financial statements.

Hypothesis 1. The CAMELS variables are important determinants of the probability of bank failure.

Hypothesis 1 is tested using a logit regression model that predicts the probability of bank failure using a group of variables defined in the contemporaneous dataset. This database includes the accounting data of failed banks as of the date of licence revocation during the period 2010–2013. The independent variables included in the model are based on the CAMELS framework presented in Table 6A.1 in the Appendix, in which several indicators are grouped into categories of various aspects of bank health. In particular, our model includes the CTA and CTL ratios to capture capital adequacy, the LTA ratio as a proxy for asset quality, the ROC as a profitability measure, and the LIQ ratio as the liquidity position of a bank.[3] Moreover, the model includes other bank-specific indicators that are relevant for bankruptcy prediction, such as the DER ratio. We control for bank size and participation in deposit insurance. In order to predict bank distress, we use lagged values of the independent variables. It is common practice to lag determinants of bank distress by up to one year. At the same time, Kolari et al. (2002) find evidence that it is possible to accurately predict failure up to two years prior to the event occurrence. In this case, we use the accounting data of banks over the period from 2006 to 2013. In the EWM, financial indicators are lagged. Lags of one year are selected, as financial difficulties quickly recognized via bank balance sheets. Thus, every value of the dependent variable equal to 1 at time *t* corresponds to values of the explanatory variables at *t*-1. The same set of explanatory variables used in the initial model is used to test the EWM.

To meet liquidity requirements, banks may lend and borrow funds on the interbank market. Interbank lending and borrowing have rather ambiguous effects on bank stability and soundness. Thus, strong relationships among banks may benefit a bank or expose it to even more risk. On the one hand, banks benefit from interbank lending and borrowing because this allows the sharing of liquidity risk, eases the allocation of financial resources and helps banks manage their balance sheets efficiently (Ladley, 2013). There is a danger, however, in being exposed to counter-party risk, especially when the counter-party experiences financial problems or fails. In this case, it is impossible for the bank to recover loans.

Depending on the scale and consequences, bank failure may cause severe contagion affecting previously healthy banks. There is no consensus in the research literature on how interbank lending and borrowing affects banks' financial distress. Some studies (Allen and Gale, 2000) show that increased interbank lending facilitates risk sharing and negatively affects failure cascades in the market. Ladley (2013) examines how the interbank loan structure affects the stability of the financial system. Thus, establishing whether and how higher interconnection among banks is related to bank system stability and sustainability is an empirical issue. We aim to provide such a test for the Russian bank system. In our study, we approximate interbank loans as the IBLTA ratio. We are interested in examining the significance of this variable as it relates to the probability of bank failure.

Hypothesis 2. Interbank loans are negatively related to the probability of bank failure, i.e., the more (less) connected a bank is to other banks, the lower (higher) its probability of failure.

To test Hypothesis 2, we investigate the significance of the interbank loans variable in both contemporaneous and EWS models. We assume that the intensity of interbank loans will have a negative influence on the ultimate probability of bank failure because interbank linkages provide insurance and stability through access to liquidity (Ladley, 2013). The underlying logic is that by interacting with other banks and borrowing funds on the interbank market, banks reduce their exposure to liquidity risk. Funds obtained via interbank loans may buffer liquidity shocks. At the same time, defaulting on interbank loans may affect the creditor's stability, leading to bank insolvency.

5. RESULTS

Our first result lends support to Hypothesis 1. The first model (Table 6.2, column (1)) shows that the CAMELS variables, namely, CTL and LIQ, are important predictors of bank financial distress in the contemporaneous model.

This result implies that illiquid and undercapitalized banks have higher probabilities of failure and represent more serious threats to the stability of the banking system. All the significant independent variables in the model exhibit the expected signs. The CTL ratio, which is a proxy for the extent to which a bank's capital can cover its payment obligations, has a negative sign. As expected, the LIQ ratio is a significant predictor and is negatively related to the probability of bank default. The profitability and asset quality ratios are not statistically significant in the contemporaneous model. Our findings provide support for the CAMELS paradigm. Regarding the other bank-specific ratios, debt to equity ratio is a significant predictor of bank distress. The negative correlation in the contemporaneous model can be justified by the fact that in most cases, the capital of failed banks is negative due to their high losses. Thus, the debt to equity ratio is large and negative for failed banks. As soon as the ratio becomes positive, the direction of influence changes according to our expectations. The coefficient for bank size is statistically significant and negative. This implies that larger banks have lower instant probabilities of failure. The concordance test allows us to conclude that the predictive accuracy of the model is very high (96 per cent).

Regarding early bank failure prediction, the results shown in column (2) of Table 6.2 also support Hypothesis 1. However, we find that different determinants are important for prediction one year before a bank failure. Thus, in contrast to the contemporaneous model, in the EWM, the variables describing profitability and asset quality provide strong signals about approaching distress, whereas liquidity and capital adequacy do not.

The coefficient for profitability, as measured by ROC, is strongly significant and negative, indicating deteriorating profitability one year prior to bank distress. The LTA ratio has a positive influence on the probability of default, in line with our expectations. Loans represent the riskiest

Table 6.2 Cox proportional hazard models results (hypothesis 1)

Models	Contemporaneous	Early Warning		
	All banks (1)	All banks (2)	Smaller (3)	Larger (4)
Capital adequacy				
CTA	0.060	−1.697	−0.542	−2.622
	(0.080)	(1.127)	(1.478)	(3.732)
CTL	−3.817***	−0.100	−0.099	−0.701
	(0.529)	(0.112)	(0.108)	(1.223)
Asset quality				
LTA	0.706	1.494**	0.927	2.169*
	(0.761)	(0.621)	(0.773)	(1.118)
Earnings ability				
ROC	−0.0367	−0.642***	−3.600***	−0.537
	(0.033)	(0.211)	(1.350)	(0.327)
Liquidity				
LIQ	−7.912***	0.1000	0.126	0.703
	(3.043)	(0.113)	(0.110)	(1.226)
Miscellaneous				
SIZE	−0.190**	−0.243***	−0.0496	−0.274**
	(0.094)	(0.081)	(0.221)	(0.136)
DER	−0.126***	0.040**	0.072**	0.012
	(0.018)	(0.018)	(0.029)	(0.027)
INSURANCE	−0.443	−0.741**	−0.290	−1.625***
	(0.350)	(0.314)	(0.403)	(0.473)
Observations	3,476	7,042	3,327	3,715
PH assumption test	0.2646	0.6998	0.2723	0.7053
Wald chi2	957.89	40.06	28.93	26.44
Prob. > chi2	0.0000	0.0000	0.0003	0.0004
Log pseudo likelihood	−248.558	−610.7	−305.395	−235.79
Concordance test	0.9897	0.6869	0.6870	0.6733
Prob. > |t|	0.0000	0.0000	0.0000	0.0000

Notes: Results for the contemporaneous model in the period 2010–2013 are in column (1). Early Warning Models (EWM) in the period 2006–2013: column (2) results for all the banks, column (3) for smaller banks and column (4) for larger banks. Dependent variable: probability of bank failure during the current year (Fail). ***, ** and * denote significance at the 1%, 5% and 10% levels, respectively.

Source: Authors' elaborations on CBR data.

portion of bank assets and the most important source of bank income. Maintaining high amounts of loans to total assets exposes banks to high credit risk and is connected with higher probabilities of failure.

These results cast some doubt on the relevance of the CAMELS indicators for early default prediction in line with the previous findings of Cole and Gunther (1998), who have shown that CAMELS rating information becomes obsolete as bank financial conditions change. Regarding the bank-specific variables beyond the CAMELS paradigm, all of them appeared to be strong predictors of bank distress. Thus, bank membership in deposit insurance schemes is negatively related to the probability of failure. The logic behind this result is that banks applying for membership are thoroughly monitored by the Deposit Insurance Agency for soundness. If a bank does not meet soundness requirements, its membership in the insurance scheme is refused. Thus, banks with a priori more stable financial positions participate in deposit insurance systems. Consistent with the results described above, the sign of DER is positive in the EWM. Thus, banks with higher positive values of DER are far more exposed to financial distress and failure. Finally, bank size is negatively related to the default probability, suggesting the relevance of a 'too big to fail' effect among Russian banks. Having assessed the predictive power of the model, we can conclude that the EWM performs relatively well in terms of bank classification (69 per cent of classifications are correct).

To develop more accurate methods of bank default prediction, researchers use clustering approaches. Peresetsky et al. (2011) pioneered the division of Russian banks into clusters. By performing logistic regression analyses for every bank cluster, they show that the influence and significance of explanatory factors differ across clusters. Based on this result, we argue that different determinants should be used to predict failure for banks of different sizes. Consistent with this approach, we divide banks into two subgroups based on their total assets over the period. In particular, we use the median asset value – to 13,586 and to 13,596 for the EWM and the contemporaneous model, respectively – as a threshold. Then, we estimate Cox proportional hazard models for both the smaller and larger bank subgroups, and the results are shown in columns (3) and (4) of Table 6.2, respectively. The results show that ROC and DER are important predictors of small bank distress, whereas LTA, size and membership in a deposit insurance scheme are important predictors for larger banks. However, the predictive accuracy of the model did not increase (0.69 and 0.67 for the sub-samples of smaller and larger banks, respectively).

Turning to the test of Hypothesis 2 (Table 6.3), our results show that interbank loans are negatively related to the probability of failure and statistically significant at the 1 per cent confidence level in both the

Table 6.3 Cox proportional hazard models results (hypothesis 2)

Models	Contemporaneous			Early Warning		
	All banks (1)	Smaller (2)	Larger (3)	All banks (4)	Smaller (5)	Larger (6)
Capital adequacy						
CTA	0.041	0.171***	0.051***	−1.524	−0.470	4.654
	(0.043)	(0.064)	(0.008)	(1.138)	(1.480)	(8.608)
CTL	−3.945***	−4.661***	−4.946***	−0.109	−0.097	−3.915
	(0.473)	(0.741)	(0.874)	(0.110)	(0.103)	(4.300)
Asset quality						
LTA	0.559	0.361	−0.206	1.766***	1.004	2.502*
	(0.562)	(0.635)	(0.753)	(0.680)	(0.801)	(1.305)
Earnings ability						
ROC	−0.038	0.009	−0.078	−0.658***	−3.670***	−0.577*
	(0.035)	(0.046)	(0.064)	(0.216)	(1.424)	(0.326)
Liquidity						
LIQ	−8.513***	−6.499**	−13.98***	0.108	0.120	−0.758
	(3.265)	(2.671)	(3.882)	(0.110)	(0.108)	(2.174)
Sensitivity to market risk						
IBLTA	−0.557**	0.251	−1.135***	−2.949***	−1.846	−4.579***
	(0.235)	(0.611)	(0.171)	(0.836)	(1.289)	(1.203)
Miscellaneous						
SIZE	−0.149	−0.044	−0.299***	−0.172*	−0.035	−0.163
	(0.092)	(0.173)	(0.104)	(0.090)	(0.226)	(0.141)
DER	−0.124***	−0.132***	−0.115***	0.0319	0.0696**	0.020
	(0.017)	(0.026)	(0.021)	(0.020)	(0.030)	(0.030)

INSURANCE	−0.470	−0.578*	−1.959***	−0.872***	−0.323	−1.974***
	(0.347)	(0.347)	(0.355)	(0.329)	(0.406)	(0.499)
Observation	3,438	1,624	1,814	6,991	3,292	3,699
PH assumption test	0.1457	0.9706	0.9606	0.7875	0.2117	0.7095
Wald chi2	824.01	663.60	314.47	53.26	28.08	44.43
Prob. > chi2	0.0000	0.0000	0.0000	0.0000	0.0009	0.0000
Log pseudo likelihood	−246.31	−126.43	−64.189	−593.71	−298.60	−224.90
Concordance test	0.9898	0.9884	0.9904	0.6670	0.6762	0.6671
Prob. > |t|	0.0000	0.0000	0.0000	0.0000	0.0000	0.0000

Notes: Column (1) provides results for the contemporaneous model in the period 2010–2013; column (2) provides those for the contemporaneous model in the period 2010–2013 for smaller banks, and column (3) provides those for the contemporaneous model in the period 2010–2013 for larger banks. Column (4) presents the EWM in the period 2006–2013. Column (5) presents results for the EWM in the period 2006–2013 for smaller banks, and column (6) provides the results for the EWM in the period 2006–2013 for larger banks. Dependent variable: probability of bank failure during the current year (Fail). ***, ** and * denote significance at the 1%, 5% and 10% levels, respectively.

Source: Authors' elaborations on CBR data.

contemporaneous model and the EWM, as shown in columns (1) and (4) of Table 6.3, respectively.

The results suggest that the more funds a bank obtains from counterparties, the lower its probability of failure. In other words, interbank borrowing prevents financial distress and, ultimately, failure. Due to the inclusion of interbank loans in the model, some of the variables, such as SIZE in the contemporaneous model and DER in the EWM lose their significance. The remaining variables maintain their size and significance. Both the contemporaneous model and the EWM maintain high predictive accuracy (99 per cent and 67 per cent, respectively).

The results suggest that the significance of interbank loans varies depending on the bank size. We divide banks into two subgroups according to their average asset value over the period and estimate Cox proportional hazard models for the subgroups of smaller and larger banks and for both the EWM and the contemporaneous model. The results are shown in columns (5) and (6) of Table 6.3 for the EWM and in columns (2) and (3) for the contemporaneous model. Columns (2) and (5) provide the results for smaller banks, while columns (3) and (6) are for larger banks. Thus, IBLTA is statistically significant at the 1 per cent level only for larger banks in the contemporaneous model and the EWM. It is important to note that the coefficient is less important in the contemporaneous model than in the EWM. IBLTA is insignificant for smaller banks in both models.

6. CONCLUSION

In this chapter, we identify the determinant of Russian bank failure using a Cox proportional hazard model with time-varying covariates and a sample of Russian banks for 2006–2013. We use an EWM and a contemporaneous model based on the CAMELS approach for the independent variables.

Overall, we observe the expected signs for the variables, with interesting differences when we compare the two models and smaller and larger banks. We find that the CAMELS variables, namely, CTL and LIQ, are important predictors of bank financial distress in the contemporaneous model. Regarding early bank failure prediction, we find that different determinants are important. In contrast to the contemporaneous model, variables describing profitability and asset quality provide strong signals of approaching distress, whereas LIQ and CTL do not. If we apply the EWM model to different groups of banks, ROC and DER are important predictors of small bank distress, whereas LTA, SIZE and INSURANCE are important predictors for larger banks.

We also test the importance of sensitivity to market risk using the share of interbank loans to total assets as a proxy in both models and for the smaller and larger bank subgroups. The results are as expected, with negative signs and strong statistical significance observed in the two models. We also find that IBLTA is an important determinant of bank failure only for larger banks.

Taking into account the obtained results, the following CBR policies seem reasonable. First, as a supervisory authority, the CBR has to monitor the balance sheet information and financial conditions of Russian banks frequently and permanently to control their evolution. Under current conditions, the financial regulation and control of the CBR seem essential to ensuring the sustainability of the Russian economy in general and of the Russian banking sector in particular. Numerous Russian bank failures highlight the significance of developing accurate models that can predict banking financial distress and identify problematic banks as early as possible. EWSs, such as the model presented here, can provide assistance in doing so. While assessing the solvency of Russian credit institutions, the CBR should draw particular attention to the dynamics of variables describing profitability, liquidity, and asset and capital quality. By doing so, it is possible to accurately predict failures as early as one year before their occurrence and provide financial assistance to banks in trouble to avoid bankruptcy. In addition, it seems reasonable for the CBR to encourage interbank lending and borrowing, as, according to our results, interbank loans decrease the probability of failure and mitigate financial distress. This is particularly true for larger credit institutions.

As the obtained results indicate that bank failure can be predicted in its early stages, we underline the importance of efficient CBR financial regulation and supervision, with support from other relevant authorities. The objective is to support the stability of the banking system to ensure that it is able to withstand internal and external shocks, maintain functioning, maintain equilibrium, and performs its main financial intermediation functions. These policies may increase the stability of the RBS and would benefit the Russian economy in many ways. Consequently, the efficient allocation of financial resources can be achieved to ensure sustainable development and economic growth, in particular by re-distributing resources within the economy, attracting private and public savings, and injecting liquidity into the real sector of the Russian economy facing resource deficits. A sound regulatory and supervisory framework will allow the RBS to efficiently manage and resolve systemic risks and stresses, to predict and prevent financial crises and to identify the vulnerabilities that trigger crises. This is especially relevant for the Russian economy given the frequency of recent financial and systemic crises. Financial regulation is also important for strengthening the RBS in post-crisis periods.

ACKNOWLEDGEMENTS

We would like to thank seminar participants at the IFABS 2015 conference in Hangzhou and at the FEBS 2015 conference in Nantes for providing comments that were helpful in developing this chapter. The usual disclaimer applies.

NOTES

1. The first framework, CAMEL, was defined using five key indicators only. In 1996, sensitivity to market risk was included in the system, and it evolved into CAMELS, whose ratings are designed to provide early signals to supervisory authorities of deteriorating bank financial positions.
2. We formally test this assumption.
3. We avoid incorporating variables related to managerial quality into the analysis because it is not possible to extract them from the financial statements of bankrupt banks.

REFERENCES

Aharony, J. and I. Swary (1983), 'Contagion effects of bank failures: evidence from capital markets', *Journal of Business*, **56**(3), 305–22.

Allen, F. and D. Gale (2000), 'Financial contagion', *Journal of Political Economy*, **108**(1), 1–33.

Beck, T. (2014), 'Finance, growth, and stability: lessons from the crisis', *Journal of Financial Stability*, **10**, 1–6.

Bresser-Pereira, L.C., J. Kregel and L. Burlamaqui (eds) (2014), *Financial Stability and Growth*, London: Routledge.

Cameron, C. and P. Trivedi (2005), *Microeconometrics: Methods and Applications*, New York: Cambridge University Press.

Cole, R.A. and J.W. Gunther (1998), 'Predicting bank failures: a comparison of on- and off-site monitoring systems', *Journal of Financial Services Research*, **13**(2), 103–17.

Demyanyk, Y. and I. Hasan (2010), 'Financial crises and bank failures: a review of prediction methods', *Omega*, **38**(5), 315–24.

Drobyshevsky, S. and A. Zubarev (2011), *Sustainability of Russian Banks in 2007–2009* (in Russian), Gaidar Institute for Economic Policy.

Fiordelisi, F. and D.S. Mare (2013), 'Probability of default and efficiency in cooperative banking', *Journal of International Financial Markets, Institutions & Money*, **26**, 30–45.

Goodhart, C. (eds) (2014), *Financial Development and Economic Growth*, New York: Palgrave Macmillan.

Gudyma, A. (2013), 'The specifics of the Russian banking sector development in the post-crisis period'. Unpublished manuscript.

Karminsky, A. and A. Kostrov (2013), 'Modeling the default probabilities of Russian banks: extended abillities', *Journal of the New Economic Association*, **17**, 64–86.

Kerstein, J. and A. Kozberg (2013), 'Using accounting proxies of proprietary FDIC ratings

to predict bank failures and enforcement actions during the recent financial crisis', *Journal of Accounting, Auditing & Finance*, **28**(2), 128–51.
Kolari, J., D. Glennon, H. Shin and M. Caputo (2002), 'Predicting large US commercial bank failures', *Journal of Economics and Business*, **54**(4), 361–87.
Konstandina, N. (2006), 'Probability of bank failure: the Russian case'. EERC Working Paper Series 1.
Kuznetsov, A. (2003), *Crisis of 1998 and Determinants of Stable Development of a Bank*, New Economic School Working Paper.
Ladley, D. (2013), 'Contagion and risk-sharing on the interbank market', *Journal of Economic Dynamics and Control*, **37**(7), 1384–400.
Lanine, G. and R.V. Vennet (2006), 'Failure prediction in the Russian bank sector with logit and trait recognition models', *Expert Systems with Applications*, **30**(3), 463–78.
Loayza, N. and R. Rancière (2006), 'Financial development, financial fragility, and growth', *Journal of Money, Credit and Banking*, **38**(4), 1051–76.
Malyutina, M. and S. Parilova (2001), 'The determinants of excessive risk-taking by banks in transition'. Unpublished manuscript.
Messai, A. and F. Jouini (2013), 'Predicting banking distress in European countries', *Journal of Economic and Social Studies*, **3**(1), 61–82.
Peresetsky, A.A., A.A. Karminsky and S.V. Golovan (2011), 'Probability of default models of Russian banks', *Economic Change and Restructuring*, **44**(4), 297–334.
Rojas-Suarez, L. (2002), 'Rating banks in emerging markets: what credit rating agencies should learn from financial indicators', in R.M. Levich, G. Majnoni and C.M. Reinhart (eds), *Ratings, Rating Agencies and the Global Financial System*, Boston, MA: Springer, pp. 177–201.
Sahaiwala, R. and P. Van den Bergh (2000), 'Supervisory risk assessment and early warning systems'. Basel Committee on Banking Supervision Working Paper.
Styrin, K. (2005), 'X-inefficiency, moral hazard, and bank failures'. CEFIR Report 1–29.
Van Rijckeghem, C. and B. Weder (2003), 'Spillovers through banking centers: a panel data analysis of bank flows', *Journal of International Money and Finance*, **22**(4), 483–509.
Zhao, H., A.P. Sinha and W. Ge (2009), 'Effects of feature construction on classification performance: an empirical study in bank failure prediction', *Expert Systems with Applications*, **36**(2), 2633–44.

APPENDIX

Table 6A.1 Variables definitions and expected signs in the bank failure prediction models

Attribute	Variable name and definition	Expected sign
Dependent variable		
FAIL	Dummy = 1 when a bank fails in the current year and 0 otherwise	
Capital adequacy		
CTA	Capital to adequacy ratio Equity capital/total assets	–
CTL	Capital to liabilities ratio Equity capital/total liabilities	–
Asset quality		
LTA	Loans to assets ratio Total loans/total assets	+
Earning ability		
ROC	Return on capital Net income/(equity capital – net income)	–
Liquidity		
LIQ	Liquidity ratio Cash and accounts in the CBR/ total liabilities	–
Sensitivity to market risk		
IBLTA	Interbank loans to assets ratio Interbank loans/ total assets	+/–
Miscellaneous		
SIZE	Size Logarithm of total assets	–
DER	Debt to equity ratio Total liabilities/capital	+
INSURANCE	Dummy = 1 when the bank participates in deposit insurance and 0 otherwise	+/–

Source: Authors' elaborations on CBR data.

7. Sovereign Wealth Funds and macroeconomic stability: before and after their establishment

Kizito Uyi Ehigiamusoe and Hooi Hooi Lean

1. INTRODUCTION

Macroeconomic stability describes a situation of an economy that minimizes its vulnerability to external shocks and increases the prospects for sustainable economic growth. Todaro and Smith (2009) posited that the main objectives of macroeconomic stabilization are to control inflation, restore fiscal balance and eliminate current account deficits. The achievement of macroeconomic stability is a serious challenge in many developing economies. This is because inflation variability, interest rates and exchange rates fluctuations, high government deficits and national debts have caused economic crises in several countries. Hence, the International Monetary Fund (IMF), European Union (EU) and other international organizations are focused on assisting these countries to achieve macroeconomic stability.

The five variables of macroeconomic stability identified by Maastricht Criteria[1] are: low and stable inflation rate (capped at 3 per cent); low currency fluctuations (maximum of 2.5 per cent); low and long-term interest rate (maximum of 9 per cent); low fiscal deficits relative to GDP (within 3 per cent); and low national debt relative to GDP (pegged at 60 per cent). Basci (2012) added sustained growth as one of the indicators of macroeconomic stability. Developing economies are now grappling with policy options to stabilize their economies, and one such policy decision is the establishment of Sovereign Wealth Funds (SWFs).

According to Allen and Caruana (2008), SWFs are government-owned investment vehicles that are invested in overseas for a long-term period. They are set up for a variety of macroeconomic purposes as well as the maximization of benefits that are typically funded by foreign exchange assets and commodity-exporting revenues. An investment vehicle can be classified as an SWF if it possesses five basic features, namely: sovereign (is independently managed from official reserves), high foreign currency exposure, absence of explicit liabilities, high risk tolerance, and a long investment horizon (see Gomes, 2008; Jen, 2007). Moreover, Allen and Caruana (2008) highlighted the economic and financial benefits of SWFs in their home countries to include facilitating savings, intergenerational transfer of proceeds from non-renewable resources and helping to reduce boom and bust cycles driven by changes in commodity export prices. Other benefits of SWFs are allowing for a greater portfolio diversification focusing on return, thereby potentially reducing the opportunity costs of reserves holdings. SWFs also help in facilitating a more efficient allocation of revenues from commodity surpluses across countries, enhance market liquidity and alleviate the effects of global financial stress.

SWFs can be traced to the 1950s when the Kuwait Investment Board was established to manage funds that were raised from oil exports with the aim of investing oil revenue surpluses to reduce the reliance on its oil resource. Since then, the world has witnessed a proliferation in the establishment of SWFs, especially in the past three decades. Xie and Chen (2008) asserted that the rapid growth of SWFs is a reflection of rising energy prices, the expansion of fiscal deficits in the US, and a general accumulation of reserves in oil and gas exporting. More than fifty countries across the six continents worldwide have established SWFs in the last decades, including the USA, Canada, Mexico, France, Italy, Ireland, China, Singapore, Indonesia, Malaysia, Australia, UAE, New Zealand, Nigeria, Ghana, Angola, Gabon, Venezuela, Brazil and Chile.

The proliferation and operation of SWFs globally have raised several issues among scholars about motives, transparency, size, operation and investment strategies. Although some researchers welcomed the creation of SWFs, they have argued that SWFs' investments may be affected by political objectives. Other numerous concerns include how SWFs can fit into the domestic policy framework of a country, the expanded role of governments in international markets and industries, and how their investments might affect recipient countries with shallow markets.

Consequently, some studies have examined the potential relationship between SWFs and global financial markets (Beck & Fidora, 2008), SWFs' investments and the return-to-risk performance of target firms (Knill et al., 2012a), SWFs and governance (Aizenman & Glick, 2009; Monk, 2009; Al-Hassan et al., 2013), SWFs' investments and bilateral political relations (Knill et al., 2012b), as well as SWFs and stock prices (Kotter & Lel, 2011). Also, Xie and Chen (2008), Sun and Hesse (2011), Candelon et al. (2011) and Steigum (2012) have examined the potential links between SWFs, macroeconomic determinants, financial stability, and macroeconomic policy alignment.

This chapter differs from previous studies that have mainly focused on the potential influence of SWFs on the economy. It compares the actual performances of six macroeconomic stability variables (i.e. GDP growth rates, inflation rates, exchange rates, interest rates, fiscal deficits relative to GDP, and government debts relative to GDP) before and after the establishment of SWFs in the sample countries covered by this study, namely Algeria, Australia, China, Gabon, Ireland, Malaysia, Mexico, New Zealand, Norway and Venezuela. This is fundamental because it would enable the countries to ascertain whether or not the beneficial effects of SWFs are derived through macroeconomic stability variables. Hence, the main objective of this chapter is to juxtapose the performance of macroeconomic stability variables before and after the establishment of SWFs. Understanding the link between SWFs and macroeconomic stability is crucial in making policy decisions for a country.

This chapter contributes to the existing literature on SWF in two ways. First, it reveals the actual relationship between SWFs and macroeconomic stability. It shows the changes that occurred in GDP growth rates, inflation rates, exchange rates, interest rates, fiscal deficits relative to GDP and government debts relative to GDP after the establishment of SWFs in each country. Second, it puts together the performance of macroeconomic stability variables with Maastricht Criteria recommendations. This would enable the countries to know if the performance of macroeconomic variables is in line with the Maastricht Criteria and the achievement of macroeconomic stability.

It was found that in most countries, the establishment and operation of SWFs resulted in the reduction in GDP growth rates, inflation rates, interest rates, fiscal deficits relative to GDP and government debts relative to GDP, albeit exchange rates depreciated.[2] Also, the performances of these macroeconomic variables reveal that all the variables except exchange rates were within the Maastricht Criteria recommendations. These findings are not sensitive to the level of income of the countries because both developing and developed countries behaved in a similar fashion during the period.

The rest of the chapter is divided into four sections. Section 2 reviews the conceptual and empirical issues, while section 3 contains the analytical framework and methodology. Data analysis and results are presented in section 4, while the final section concludes the chapter with some policy options.

2. CONCEPTUAL AND EMPIRICAL REVIEWS

2.1 Origin and Rationale for Sovereign Wealth Funds

According to Truman (2009), SWFs are separate pools of international assets owned and managed by governments in order to achieve a variety of economic and financial objectives. They could sometimes include domestic assets that are meant to serve multiple objectives, ranging from the accumulation and management of a tranche of reserve assets and the stabilization of the macroeconomic effects of sudden increases in export earnings, to the management of pension assets as well as the transfer of national wealth across generations. Kimmitt (2008) defined SWFs as government investment vehicles funded by foreign exchange assets and managed separately from official reserves – basically the pools of money governments invest for profits. He enumerated four distinctive ways through which countries can hold sovereign wealth: SWFs, international reserves, public pension funds and state-owned enterprises.

Other definitions of SWFs have stressed that the investment of these funds are in a broad portfolio of risky assets including equity, corporate bonds, real estate, infrastructure and alternative investment strategies. Gomes (2008) noted that one basic feature of SWFs is that these foreign reserves are managed independently from official reserves, and can either be financed by revenues from net commodity exports such as oil or revenue generated by a merchandise trade surplus. Typically, SWFs are designed with one or more policy objectives such as stabilization funds, intergenerational savings funds, and reserve management funds.

Since the establishment of the first SWFs, the world has witnessed tremendous growth in the establishment of SWFs. The overall size of global SWFs is above US$4.5 trillion, exceeding hedge funds and private equity, and their growth is likely to further intensify (see Xie & Chen, 2008). Commenting on the global growth of SWFs, Townsend (2008) noted that general interest in SWFs has increased intensely in recent years, particularly with the creation of China's SWF, known as the China Investment Corporation (CIC) and the large, high-profile investments made by many SWFs in Western financial institutions during the global credit crunch.

According to Xie and Chen (2008), five types of SWFs, based on their main objectives, are: stabilization funds (aimed at insulating the budget and the economy against commodity price swings); savings funds for future generations (aiming to convert non-renewable assets into a more diversified portfolio of assets and mitigate the effects of Dutch disease); and reserve investment corporations (often counted as reserve assets and established to increase the return on reserves); as well as development funds (typically to fund socio-economic projects or promote industrial policies that might raise a country's potential output growth); and contingent pension reserve funds (providing from sources other than individual pension contributions contingent unspecified pension liabilities on the government's balance sheet). Despite the objectives and types, SWFs are not uniform in many countries, as some nations have large investments while others have invested little. Table 7.1 shows the global ranking of SWFs based on the value of assets in 2014.

Table 7.1 The global ranking of Sovereign Wealth Funds as at 2014

S/N	Country	Funds	Year of inception	Assets (US$ billion)
1	China	SAFE Investment Company	1997	1,534.7*
2	UAE	Abu Dhabi Investment Authority	1976	1,214.8*
3	Norway	Government Pension Fund – Global	1990	882
4	Saudi Arabia	SAMA Foreign Holdings	1952	762.5*
5	Kuwait	Kuwait Investment Authority	1953	592
6	Singapore	Singapore Investment Corporation	1981	537.6*
7	Hong Kong	Monetary Authority Investment Portfolio	1993	400.2
8	Qatar	Qatar Investment Authority	2005	256
9	Kazakhstan	Kazakhstan National Fund	2000	156.5*
10	United States	Alaska Permanent Fund	1976	140.8*
11	Russia	National Welfare Fund	2008	101.9*
12	Australia	Future Fund	2004	95.3*
13	Libya	Libyan Investment Authority	2006	66
14	Iran	National Development Fund	2011	62
15	South Korea	Korea Investment Corporation	2005	56.6
16	Algeria	Revenue Regulation Fund	2000	50.0
17	Malaysia	Khazanah Nasional	1993	41.6
18	Brunei	Brunei Investment Agency	1983	40
19	Azerbaijan	State Oil Fund of the Rep. of Azerbaijan	1999	37.3
20	Ireland	National Pensions Reserve Fund	2001	27.4
21	France	Strategic Investment Fund	2008	25.5
22	Chile	Social & Economic Stabilization Fund	2007	23.1*
23	New Zealand	New Zealand Superannuation Fund	2003	21.8
24	Oman	Oman State General Reserve Fund	1980	19.0*
25	Iraq	Development Fund for Iraq	2003	18.0
26	Canada	Alberta's Heritage Savings Trust Fund	1976	17.5
27	East Timor	Timor-Leste Petroleum Fund	2005	16.6
28	Bahrain	Mumtalakat Holding Company	2006	10.5
29	Peru	Fiscal Stabilization Fund	1999	9.2
30	Mexico	Oil Revenues Stabilization Fund of Mexico	2000	6.0
31	Italy	Italian Strategic Fund	2011	6.0

Table 7.1 (continued)

S/N	Country	Funds	Year of inception	Assets (US$ billion)
32	Botswana	Pula Fund	1996	5.7
33	Trinidad & Tobago	FEM – Macroeconomic Stabilization Fund	2000	5.5
34	Brazil	Sovereign Fund of Brazil	2008	5.3
35	Angola	Fundo Soberano de Angola	2012	5.0
36	Nigeria	Nigerian Sovereign Investment Authority	2011	1.4
37	Bolivia	FINPRO	2012	1.2
38	Panama	Fondo de Ahorro de Panama	2012	1.2
39	Senegal	FONSIS	2012	1.0
40	Palestine	Palestine Investment Fund	2003	0.8
41	Venezuela	FEM – Macroeconomic Stabilization Fund	1998	0.8
42	Kiribati	Revenue Equalization Reserve Fund	1956	0.6
43	Vietnam	State Capital Investment Corporation	2006	0.5
44	Ghana	Ghana Petroleum Funds	2011	0.45
45	Gabon	Sovereign Fund of the Gabonese Republic	1998	0.4
46	Indonesia	Government Investment Unit of Indonesia*	2006	0.3
47	Mauritania	National Fund for Hydrocarbon Reserves	2006	0.3
48	Mongolia	Fiscal Stability Fund	2011	0.3
49	Equatorial Guinea	Fund for Future Generations	2002	0.08
	Total SWFs			7,367.6

Note: * Summation of all the SWFs in the country.

Source: SWFs Institute: http://www.swfinstitute.org/sovereign-wealth-fund-rankings

2.2 The Nexus Between Sovereign Wealth Funds and Macroeconomic Stability

Allen and Caruana (2008) contended that a well-designed and operated SWF has the potential to support sound fiscal and monetary policies as well as alleviate the effects of Dutch disease. However, it is important to note that SWFs may also create macroeconomic policy challenges. To avert these challenges, therefore, appropriate integration of SWFs into the country's monetary and fiscal policies is fundamental to achieving the overall policy objectives of a nation. The influence of SWFs on macroeconomic stability variables are presented below.

2.2.1 Sovereign Wealth Funds and GDP growth rates

SWFs have the capability to manage capital inflows through the management and transfer of surpluses from large current accounts into investment funds overseas. If capital inflows are not properly managed, it will result in upward pressure on nominal exchange rates, reduce the demand for exports and slow economic growth. Drezner (2008) asserted that through overseas investments, SWFs not only build reserve funds to cushion the adverse effects of commodity boom and bust but they also create assets that provide revenue flow in the long term, thereby promoting economic growth. Furthermore, SWFs may also engender more comprehensive and professional investments and risk management frameworks that can enhance accountability and transparency in the management of government financial assets. They can also result in higher risk-adjusted returns and may help to reduce the opportunity costs of reserves holdings (see Truman, 2009; Allen & Caruana, 2008). However, if they are not properly managed and integrated into a country's fiscal frameworks, SWFs can pose a severe fiscal risk and result in the fragmentation of the budget process. This may have adverse effects on the efficiency and transparency of cash management and resource allocation, and ultimately economic growth.

2.2.2 Sovereign Wealth Funds and inflation rates

The essence of the SWF is to help the government accomplish its fiscal resources and support macroeconomic stability. The domestic economy may not have limitless capacity to absorb large amounts of extra government expenditures that are financed from excess resource revenue. Whenever there is an excessive increase in government spending, aggregate demand may be exacerbated, and this pressure may lead to the high import of goods and services, and ultimately inflation. High inflation is deleterious to the economy because of its capacity to distort savings and investment and reduce the competitiveness of exports (see Bruno & Easterly, 1998; Rousseau & Wachtel, 2002; Rousseau & Yilmazkuday, 2009; Bittencourt, 2011). Also, Steigum (2012) noted that SWFs have positive macroeconomic effects in a democratic welfare state. Therefore, the establishment of SWFs makes it possible for the investment of the excess funds overseas, thereby preventing excessive increases in government expenditures that can lead to inflation.

2.2.3 Sovereign Wealth Funds and exchange rates

The decisions of SWFs' investments have crucial implications on a country's monetary policy since the main aim of monetary policy is to maintain stability in interest rates and exchange rates. If SWFs are invested in assets abroad, the repatriation of returns to the home country involves currency transactions that may influence the exchange rates. Beck and Fidora (2008) noted that SWFs can influence exchange rates and asset prices through pressures on prices or a change in risk aversion. Gomes (2008) noted that for countries that have pegged exchange rates or managed float regimes, the maintenance of competitive exchange rates will increase the attractiveness of their exports, that is, the very source of growth for many of these countries that depend on export-led growth. Therefore, off-shoring capital inflow allows countries that have SWFs to ease the pressure on domestic prices and resist the appreciation of real exchange rates.

2.2.4 Sovereign Wealth Funds and interest rates

Apart from their influence on inflation rates and exchange rates, well-managed SWFs also have a significant influence on stable interest rates, which gives businesses the confidence to make long-term investment plans. Drezner (2008) opined that through consultancy and assets management contracts, financial institutions can benefit from harmonious relations with SWFs which act as a countercyclical stabilizer. This is because their investments in the financial sector are expected to have implications for financial variables, including interest rates. SWFs can also have significant influence on interest rates through their impact on inflation rates. As contended by the Fischer hypothesis and corroborated by Berument and Malatyali (2001), inflation expectation and inflation risks are some of the major determinants of interest rates in an economy. Therefore, by easing the pressures on prices, SWFs influence both inflation and interest rates.

2.2.5 Sovereign Wealth Funds and fiscal deficits relative to GDP

SWFs have the capability for earning higher returns on their investment portfolios because of the diversification with which the funds are invested. SWFs earn better returns than other traditional reserve investments because they spread the risk of their portfolio across a multiplicity of assets, reducing their reliance on a single asset price. Xie and Chen (2008) argue that the higher rate of returns on SWFs' investments provides revenue for government to finance the budget, thereby reducing fiscal deficits. Many commodity exporting countries with fiscal/trade surpluses depend on SWFs to provide a long-term flow of revenue in order to mitigate budget implementation and fiscal deficits.

2.2.6 Sovereign Wealth Funds and government debts relative to GDP

SWFs' investments are able to inject liquidity into the global market, thereby playing a crucial role in the stabilization of financial markets. Truman (2009) remarked that the adoption of the principles of transparency and reputation in the management of SWFs will contribute to the stability of financial markets globally. If the investments are strategic and integrated into the fiscal management frameworks of a country, SWFs are capable of addressing long-term structural issues about the future, such as debt sustainability and economic development. However, SWFs could also potentially generate losses if not properly managed, and this should be considered in public sector solvency and in the assessment of debt sustainability.

2.3 Empirical Issues

Empirical literature on the potential link between SWFs and some variables has been examined in previous studies. Truman (2009) opined that the major objectives of SWFs include: the accumulation and management of a tranche of reserve assets; the stabilization of the macroeconomic effects of sudden increases in export earnings; and the transfer of national wealth across generations.

Gomes (2008) examined the potential relationship between SWFs and international financial stability and concluded that SWFs are long-term investments that can play a stabilizing role in financial markets. SWFs do this through the supply of liquidity and reduction in market volatility, as well as contributing to the gradual unwinding of global imbalances through the gradual diversification of their portfolios. Examining the background and issues surrounding SWFs, Townsend (2008) asserted that SWFs can be used for macroeconomic stabilization, the seeking of higher returns and saving for future generations, as well as restructuring and encouraging domestic industries.

Teslik (2008) examined the implications of SWFs for governments and businesses using analytical and descriptive approaches. He opined that the more efficient the governments' investments through SWFs, the more money governments have to pay salaries and finance research and development. This may also translate into lower taxes in the country, better public works, stronger state-run businesses and sustainable long-term capital growth, as well as long-term economic viability.

Cohen (2009) asserted that although the emergence of SWFs is one of the striking financial developments in recent decades, the concern of many countries where SWFs are invested is the possibility of overt or covert political purposes. SWFs could combine a mixture of business and politics that can be used as a powerful foreign policy tool. Xie and Chen (2008) noted that well-managed SWFs can become an effective tool for fiscal policy, align with the monetary authority, and stabilize the exchange rate and the national balance sheet. Asset allocation of SWFs has significant impacts on the current and capital accounts of both domestic and international balance sheets, as well as impacting on the global financial market and its stability.

Turkisch (2011) corroborated the above view when he examined the opportunities and barriers for SWFs' investments in Africa. He revealed that SWFs can facilitate up to 50 per cent of the investment needs in infrastructure in Africa over the next decade. African economies can benefit greatly from the rising investor interest, which stretches increasingly beyond natural resources. Kotter and Lel (2011) revealed that SWFs have no long-run substantial impact on the performance and governance of firms, albeit they have positive impact on the stock prices of target firms around the announcement date. They also found that SWFs' transparency affects their investment activities as well as their effects on target firm value. Furthermore, In et al. (2013) reported that although SWFs provide significant liquidity in the stock market, SWFs' investments result in destabilizing effects on the stock market. Nevertheless, SWFs that have saving objectives provide stabilizing effects, especially during periods of crisis.

Candelon et al. (2011) revealed that macroeconomic characteristics determine the destination country of SWFs' investments. While exchange rate stability matters to most countries if Europe or North America is their investments' destination, crude oil prices and good governance are the major factors to consider in the rest of the world. Similarly, Knill et al. (2012b) investigated the link between SWFs' investments and bilateral political relations. Although bilateral political relations matter less in how much to invest, they play a fundamental role in determining SWFs' investments. This is because many countries tend to invest their SWFs in countries where they have weaker political relations. Knill et al. also discovered that SWFs' investments have a positive impact on relatively closed economies and a negative impact for relatively open nations.

Al-Hassan et al. (2013) discussed the fundamental role of SWFs in macroeconomic management and stressed the importance of close coordination of SWFs with financial policies, macroeconomic policies and their role in global financial stability. Bernstein et al. (2013) documented that SWFs provide opportunities for countries that have large variations in public revenues to ensure a steady cash flow as well as provide resources for long-term investments.

Bertoni and Lugo (2014) reported that SWFs' investments reduce the credit default swap spreads of target companies. This reduction is greater when SWFs are created by countries that are non-democratic but politically stable. Sun et al. (2014) reported that Chinese SWFs' investment in the energy sector is important for commercial and strategic purposes, especially to support the 'going global' strategy.

Alhashel (2015) showed strong support for economic motives in creating SWFs, albeit there is conflicting evidence on the capacity of SWFs to create value for target firms. Similarly, Megginson and Fotak (2015) also claimed that stock prices rise during the SWFs' announcement period. Bortolotti et al. (2015) reported that during the announcement period, the abnormal returns of SWFs' equity investments in publicly traded firms are positive compared to private investments. Aguilera et al. (2016) developed a framework that fosters a better understanding of the firm-level features and consequences of SWFs.

The above review indicates that previous studies have focused on the relationship between SWFs and economic or non-economic variables without examining the performance of these variables after the SWFs were established. Hence, this chapter tries to fill this gap by comparing the performance or behaviours of these macroeconomic stability variables before and after the establishment of SWFs in the countries studied.

3. METHODOLOGY

The chapter examines the nexus between SWFs and macroeconomic stability variables using an analytical framework and descriptive statistics. The six macroeconomic stability variables are: GDP growth rates; inflation rates; exchange rates; interest rates; fiscal deficits relative to GDP; and government debts relative to GDP. The data for all these six variables are sourced from the World Development Indicator (2015) of the World Bank (https://data.worldbank.org/products/wdi). The sample period is from 1980 to 2013. The performances of the macroeconomic stability variables for each country are compared for two periods. The first period is a minimum of ten years before the establishment of SWFs while the second period is a minimum of ten years after SWFs were established in the countries. Performance in the two periods is also judged against the Maastricht Criteria. Graphical analysis is used to examine the trends and stability of the variables in the two periods.

The chapter finds that out of the 49 countries that are listed in Table 7.1, only 20 countries have operated SWFs for a minimum of ten years. Unfortunately, complete data for 20 years of the six macroeconomic variables are unavailable for all 20 countries. Hence, this chapter is constrained to conduct its analysis on the ten countries that have complete data on the six macroeconomic stability variables. The ten countries are Algeria, Australia, China, Gabon, Ireland, Malaysia, Mexico, New Zealand, Norway and Venezuela. Fortunately, these ten sample countries cut across the continents of Africa, South America, North America, Asia, Europe and Oceania.

4. DATA ANALYSIS AND RESULTS

The performance of the six macroeconomic stability variables during the entire period, the pre-SWFs and post-SWFs establishment eras for each country, is presented in Table 7.2.

4.1 Sovereign Wealth Funds and GDP Growth Rates

The chapter finds seven countries whose GDP growth rates decreased in the post-SWFs establishment period relative to the pre-SWFs era. They are Australia, China, Ireland, Malaysia, Mexico, New Zealand and Venezuela. On the other hand, only three countries have average GDP growth rates increased in the post-SWFs period, i.e. Algeria, Gabon and Norway. This finding confirmed the views of Drezner (2008) and Truman (2009) that the capital outflow associated with SWFs is capable of reducing growth at the initial stage of establishment. However, if not properly managed and integrated into a country's fiscal frameworks, SWFs can pose severe fiscal risk and result in fragmentation of the budget process. This may have adverse effects on the efficiency and transparency of cash management and resource allocation, and ultimately economic growth.

Despite the decrease in average GDP growth rates, the graphical illustration revealed that GDP growth rates were more stable in the post-SWFs era compared to the pre-SWFs period in most of the countries. Since presenting the behaviour of GDP growth rates of the ten countries in a single graph looks clumsy and indecipherable, the study randomly selected four counties based on different results (statistical results in Table 7.2), as well as the proximity of SWFs' establishment year. Hence, the graphical analysis of four countries, namely Algeria, Australia, China and Gabon, are presented in Figure 7.1.

4.2 Sovereign Wealth Funds and Inflation Rates

The behaviour of inflation rates as presented in Table 7.2 revealed that inflation rates decreased in eight of the countries surveyed after the

Table 7.2 The mean performance of macroeconomic variables before and after the establishment of SWFs (%)

Country and year SWF was established	Period	GDP growth	Inflation rate	Exchange rate	Interest rate	Deficits/ GDP	Debt/ GDP
Algeria	Total	2.4	9.76	51.94	0.23	2.42	49.43
2000	Before	1.34	15.76	29.73	0.32	1.05	83.47
	After	3.64	3.77	74.16	0.19	3.58	27.55
Australia	Total	3.40	2.67	1.36	5.22	−0.89	19.93
2004	Before	3.79	2.37	1.55	6.66	−0.16	22.93
	After	2.76	2.79	1.16	4.22	−1.16	16.93
China	Total	10.08	5.49	6.22	1.98	0.96	27.21
1997	Before	10.56	11.59	4.92	1.36	0.59	20.88
	After	9.59	1.74	7.51	2.59	1.33	33.54
Gabon	Total	2.75	3.33	468.43	12.05	2.49	55.29
1998	Before	2.58	5.46	381.89	10.91	−2.64	76.24
	After	2.93	1.41	554.97	14.21	5.58	44.25
Ireland	Total	4.08	2.67	0.79	2.83	−3.29	66.39
2001	Before	6.00	2.68	0.69	4.28	−0.85	77.78
	After	2.17	2.65	0.90	−0.94	−3.38	55.01
Malaysia	Total	6.30	3.18	2.97	4.17	−2.28	48.21
1993	Before	6.86	3.70	2.49	5.44	−0.68	68.53
	After	5.74	2.66	3.43	3.53	−2.59	44.15
Mexico	Total	2.58	24.8	7.92	3.64	−2.81	42.71
2000	Before	2.84	39.76	4.48	6.20	−2.68	45.12
	After	2.32	8.40	11.36	2.36	−2.99	42.01
New	Total	2.82	2.19	1.64	4.62	0.63	33.88
Zealand	Before	3.64	1.80	1.85	5.35	0.48	40.85
2003	After	2.23	2.66	1.43	4.35	0.72	26.92
Norway	Total	3.14	5.19	7.04	6.59	4.69	36.13
1990	Before	2.71	7.96	6.82	7.29	4.75	37.64
	After	3.56	2.41	7.26	5.88	4.64	35.69
Venezuela	Total	3.16	32.58	1.18	−1.93	−3.59	37.07
1998	Before	3.41	41.87	0.13	−1.53	−2.63	34.5
	After	2.89	23.86	2.30	−3.97	−4.58	39.69

Source: Authors' computation from WDI Data 2015.

establishment of SWFs in these countries. The average inflation rate after the establishment of SWFs is not only close to the 3 per cent recommended by the Maastricht Criteria, but is also lower than the average inflation rate in each country for the entire period. After the establishment of

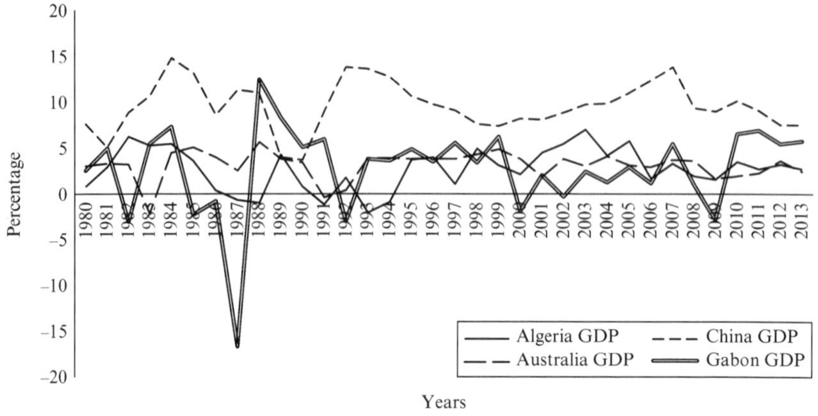

Notes: SWFs were established in Algeria in 1998, in Australia in 2004, in China in 1997 and in Gabon in 1998.

Source: Authors' computation from WDI Data 2015.

Figure 7.1 The pattern of GDP growth rates before and after the establishment of SWFs in Algeria, Australia, China and Gabon

their respective SWFs, inflation rates fell significantly in Algeria, China, Venezuela and Mexico; marginally in Gabon, Ireland, Malaysia and Norway. However, inflation marginally increased in Australia and New Zealand after the establishment of SWFs. Nevertheless, the inflation rates are still within the Maastricht Criteria recommendation in both countries.

This finding agrees with Allen and Caruana's (2008) conclusion that SWFs are capable of assisting the macroeconomic management of large current account surpluses. Countries can alleviate inflationary pressures arising from capital inflows through the transfer of excess revenues into investment funds. Many developing countries are experiencing high growth rates, and there is pressure on assets prices. SWFs can be a requisite fiscal policy tool because it is capable of facilitating fiscal stabilization (see Xie & Chen, 2008; Steigum, 2012). By investing the excess revenues in foreign assets, SWFs ease inflationary pressures in domestic economies and resist real exchange rate appreciation.

From the behaviour of inflation rates in the ten countries, the trends of the four selected countries (i.e. Algeria, China, Gabon and New Zealand) on the basis of the results above and the proximity of the SWFs' establishment year are presented in Figure 7.2. It is obvious that inflation rates performed better after SWFs were established in these countries relative to the pre-SWFs periods.

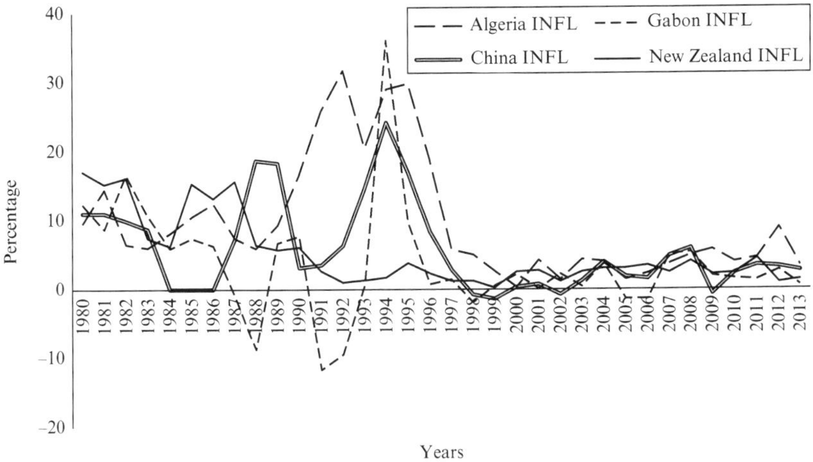

Notes: SWF was established in Algeria in 1998, in China in 1997, in Gabon in 1998 and in New Zealand in 2003.

Source: Authors' computation from WDI Data 2015.

Figure 7.2 The pattern of inflation rates before and after the establishment of SWFs in Algeria, China, Gabon and New Zealand

4.3 Sovereign Wealth Funds and Exchange Rates

The performance of exchange rates before and after the establishment of SWFs is presented in Table 7.3. It was revealed that exchange rates depreciated in eight countries (i.e. Algeria, Mexico, Ireland, Malaysia, Gabon, China, Norway and Venezuela) and appreciated only in Australia and New Zealand in the post-SWFs establishment period relative to the pre-SWFs era. In percentage terms, the exchange rates for these countries were far higher than the 2.5 per cent recommended by the Maastricht Criteria. For instance, exchange rates increased by 43.4 per cent, 45.3 per cent and 52.6 per cent in Venezuela, Gabon and China, respectively. Unfavourable terms of trade and current account deficits are some of possible explanations for the depreciation in the exchange rates, especially in low-income countries.

This finding disproved Beck and Fidora (2008), who noted that SWFs can influence exchange rates and asset prices through pressures on prices or a change in risk aversion. Gomes (2008) also noted that off-shoring capital inflow allows countries that have SWFs to ease pressures on domestic

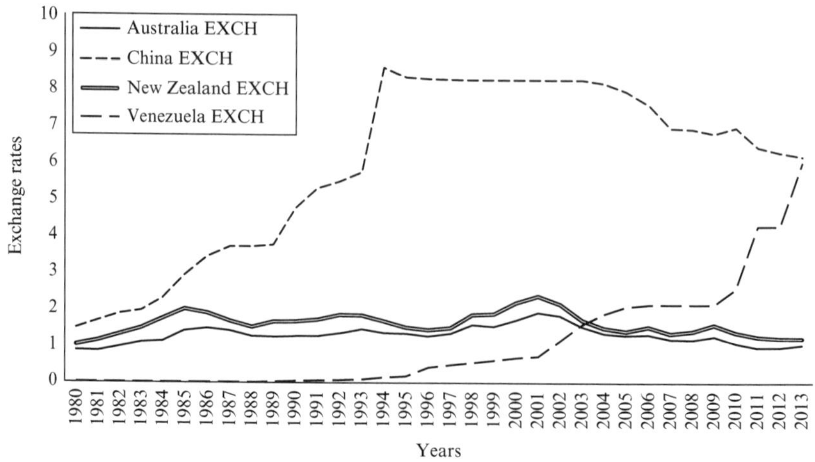

Notes: SWF was established in Australia in 2004, in China in 1997, in New Zealand in 2003 and in Venezuela in 1998.

Source: Authors' computation from WDI Data 2015.

Figure 7.3 *The pattern of exchange rates before and after the establishment of SWFs in Australia, China, New Zealand and Venezuela*

prices and resist the appreciation of real exchange rates. But the decision of where and how SWFs are invested requires effective coordination with the monetary policy or authorities with a view to achieving the goals of monetary policy such as maintaining price stability, which involves a low inflation rate, stable interest rate and exchange rate.

The pattern of exchange rates in the 1980–2013 sample periods as presented in Figure 7.3 shows that exchange rates were higher in most of the countries in the post-SWF establishment era compared to the pre-SWF establishment period. The graphs of four such countries (Australia, China, New Zealand and Venezuela), selected based on the behaviour of exchange rates and the proximity of their SWFs' establishment year, indicated a depreciation trend, except Australia, which witnessed a marginal appreciation.

4.4 Sovereign Wealth Funds and Interest Rates

Table 7.2 revealed the performance of interest rates in ten countries in the 1980–2013 period. Interest rates decreased in the post-SWFs era relative

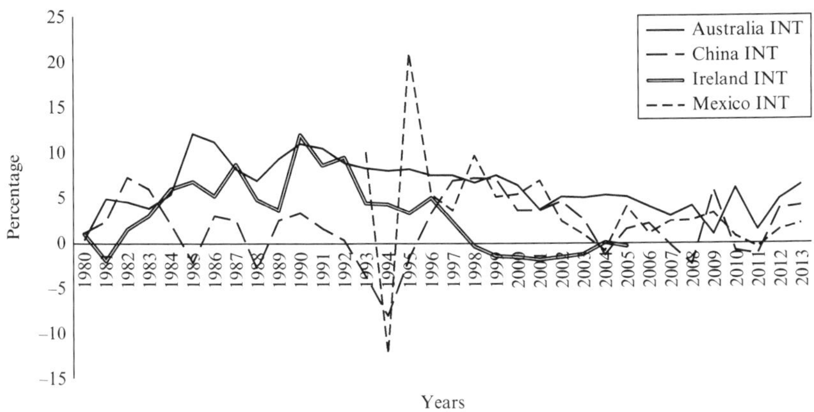

Notes: SWF was established in Australia in 2004, in China in 1997, in Ireland in 2001 and in Mexico in 2000.

Source: Authors' computation from WDI Data 2015.

Figure 7.4 The pattern of interest rates before and after the establishment of SWFs in Australia, China, Ireland and Mexico

to pre-SWFs establishment period in all the countries except China and Gabon. This analysis indicates that the establishment of SWFs could be partly responsible for the decrease in interest rates in these countries.

This finding agreed with Drezner (2008), who opined that the harmonious relations which financial institutions benefit from as a result of SWFs through consultancy and assets management contracts act as a countercyclical stabilizer to their investments in the financial sector, which is expected to have implications for financial variables such as interest rates. Xie and Chen (2008) also noted that well-managed SWFs can be made to align with the monetary authority, which helps to stabilize the interest and exchange rates as well as contributing to the stability of the national balance sheet.

Figure 7.4 demonstrates the behaviours of interest rates in the pre-establishment and post-establishment eras in Australia, China, Ireland and Mexico. These four countries were selected for graphical analysis based on their results and the proximity of the SWFs' establishment year because plotting the ten countries in one graph would look untidy and unreadable. It is clear from the graphs that interest rates were lower after SWFs were established in these countries.

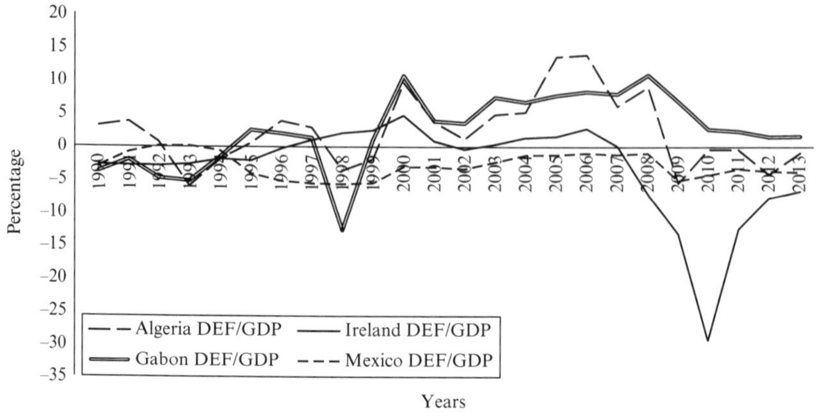

Notes: SWF was established in Algeria in 1998, in Gabon in 1998, in Ireland in 2001 and in Mexico in 2000.

Source: Authors' computation from WDI Data 2015.

Figure 7.5 The pattern of fiscal deficit/GDP before and after the establishment of SWFs in Algeria, Gabon, Ireland and Mexico

4.5 Sovereign Wealth Funds and Fiscal Deficits Relative to GDP

The behaviour of fiscal deficits as a ratio of GDP in the pre-SWFs and post-SWFs eras, as presented in Table 7.2, revealed that five countries experienced improvement in deficits/surplus relative to GDP after the establishment of SWFs. These countries were China, Gabon, Algeria, New Zealand and Norway. However, Ireland and Venezuela experienced deterioration in their fiscal deficits/GDP after the establishment of SWFs in their respective countries. As noted by Gould (2010) the experience of SWFs in the Pacific region has been mixed, with some SWFs facilitating intergenerational equity and macroeconomic stability while others have struggled to bring about improvements in well-being. Figure 7.5 shows the behaviour of four countries (Algeria, Gabon, Ireland and Mexico) out of the ten countries during the pre-SWFs and post-SWFs establishment eras.

4.6 Sovereign Wealth Funds and Government Debts Relative to GDP

The performance of debts as a ratio of GDP presented in Table 7.2 revealed that all countries (except China, Norway and Venezuela) witnessed a reduction in their debts/GDP after the establishment of SWFs.

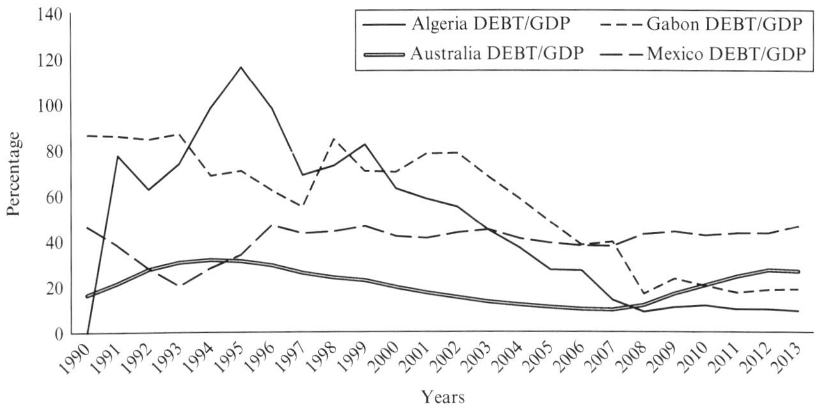

Notes: SWF was established in Algeria in 1998, in Australia in 2004, in Gabon in 1998 and in Mexico in 2000.

Source: Authors' computation from WDI Data 2015.

Figure 7.6 The pattern of government debt/GDP before and after the establishment of Sovereign Wealth Funds (SWFs) in Algeria, Australia, Gabon and Mexico

The Joint Sovereign Wealth Funds Working Group (2010) opined that the major economic and development implications of SWFs include the potential to transform the economy, the opportunity to support national development and to assist in macroeconomic management, as well as the reduction of national debts.

Figure 7.6 shows the behaviour of debts/GDP during the pre-SWFs and post-SWFs establishment eras of four countries, namely, Algeria, Australia, Gabon and Mexico. The behaviours of the other countries are not significantly different from the graphs of these four countries. The graph shows that debt as a ratio of GDP was lower during the post-SWFs era relative to the pre-SWFs establishment period.

5. CONCLUSION AND RECOMMENDATIONS

Several years after the establishment of SWFs in many countries, the relationship between macroeconomic stability and SWFs seems unclear. This chapter adopts analytical and descriptive approaches using available secondary data. The analysis has focused on the behaviours of macroeconomic stability variables, i.e. GDP growth rates, inflation rates, exchange rates, interest rates, fiscal deficits relative to GDP and government debts relative to GDP. Evidence from the chapter suggests that in most countries, the establishment and operation of SWFs resulted in the reduction in GDP growth rates, inflation rates, interest rates, fiscal deficits relative to GDP, and government debts relative to GDP. However, exchange rates depreciated in most of the countries in the post-SWFs establishment era. Furthermore, the performance of these macroeconomic variables revealed that all the variables except exchange rates were within the Maastricht Criteria recommendations. The findings of the study do not vary with developed or developing countries, as all the continents behaved in similar fashion during the period. The chapter contributes to the existing literature by unveiling how these variables performed before and after the establishment of SWFs.

One policy implication of this study is that SWFs have influence and can be used as vehicles for macroeconomic stability. Thus, the establishment, operation and objectives of SWFs should be properly integrated into a country's fiscal and monetary frameworks since they have links with macroeconomic variables with a view to using the funds for the achievement of macroeconomic stability. However, the findings of this chapter should be interpreted with caution because SWFs may not be principally responsible for the performances of these macroeconomic variables. A possible explanation for the reduction in GDP growth rates may not be unconnected with the recent global financial crisis that shrank economic growth across countries worldwide. Conversely, SWFs may be responsible for a temporary slowing down of economic growth because of the outflow of financial resources from individual countries for investment abroad, since most SWFs are invested abroad.

The unavailability of time series data on SWFs and some macroeconomic stability variables in some countries limited the scope and methodology employed in this analysis. SWFs may not be solely responsible for the behaviours of these variables. However, as data become readily available, it is suggested that a more rigorous methodology be utilized to examine the impact of SWFs on these macroeconomic variables. This study has succeeded in stimulating the debate, and it is hoped that future researches will investigate further the nexus between SWFs and macroeconomic stability.

ACKNOWLEDGEMENT

Kizito Uyi Ehigiamusoe wishes to gratefully acknowledge the support of the Universiti Sains Malaysia under the USM Teaching Fellowship.

NOTES

1. The Maastricht Criteria refer to five macroeconomic criteria set by the EU to measure the macroeconomic stability of a country that wants to join the EU and adopt the euro as their currency. The IMF also places a greater emphasis on these variables. The criteria are named after the Dutch city where the convention was hosted.
2. Notwithstanding the findings of this chapter, an alternative explanation is that countries establish SWFs in anticipation of future macroeconomic stability. Hence, the findings of this chapter should be interpreted with caution because SWFs may not be principally responsible for the performances of these macroeconomic stability variables.

REFERENCES

Aguilera, R.V., J. Capape and J. Santiso (2016), 'Sovereign wealth funds: A strategic governance view', *The Academy of Management Perspectives*, **30**(1), 5–23.

Aizenman, J. and R. Glick (2009), 'Sovereign wealth funds: Stylized facts about their determinants and governance', *International Finance*, **12**(3), 351–386.

Alhashel, B. (2015), 'Sovereign Wealth Funds: A literature review', *Journal of Economics and Business*, **78**, 1–13.

Al-Hassan, A., M. Papaioannou, M. Skancke and C.C. Sung (2013), 'Sovereign Wealth Funds: Aspects of governance structures and investment management', IMF Working Paper No. 13/231.

Allen, M. and J. Caruana (2008), 'Sovereign Wealth Funds: A working agenda', Prepared by the Monetary and Capital Markets and Policy Development and Review Departments, IMF.

Basci, E. (2012), 'Financial and macroeconomic stability', Paper presented in the Financial and Macroeconomic Stability Conference held in Istanbul, 4 June.

Beck, R. and M. Fidora (2008), 'The impact of Sovereign Wealth Funds on global financial markets', *Intereconomics*, **43**(6), 349–358.

Bernstein, S., J. Lerner and A. Schoar (2013), 'The investment strategies of sovereign wealth funds', *The Journal of Economic Perspectives*, **27**(2), 219–238.

Bertoni, F. and S. Lugo (2014), 'The effect of sovereign wealth funds on the credit risk of their portfolio companies', *Journal of Corporate Finance*, **27**, 21–35.

Berument, H. and K. Malatyali (2001), 'Determinants of interest rates in Turkey', *Russian and East European Finance and Trade*, **37**(1), 5–15.

Bittencourt, M. (2011), 'Inflation and financial development: Evidence from Brazil', *Economic Modelling*, **28**, 91–99.

Bortolotti, B., V. Fotak, and W.L. Megginson (2015), 'The sovereign wealth fund discount: Evidence from public equity investments', *Review of Financial Studies*, **28**(11), 2993–3035.

Bruno, M. and W. Easterly (1998), 'Inflation crises and long-run growth', *Journal of Monetary Economics*, **41**(1), 3–26.

Candelon, B., M. Kerkour and C. Lecourt (2011), 'Are Sovereign Wealth Funds' investments determined by macroeconomic factors?', Working Paper, University Maastricht, the Netherlands. Accessed 10 June 2015 from https://pdfs.semanticscholar.org

Cohen, B.J. (2009), 'Sovereign Wealth Funds and national security: The great trade-off', *International Affairs*, **85**(4), 713–731.

Drezner, D.W. (2008), 'Sovereign Wealth Funds and the (in)security of global finance', *Journal of International Affairs*, **62**(1), 115–130.

Gomes, T. (2008), 'Sovereign Wealth Funds and international financial stability', Working Paper, International Department, Bank of Canada, Ottawa, Canada. Accessed 10 June 2015 at http://economics.ca/2008/papers/0627.pdf

Gould, M. (2010), 'Managing manna from below: Sovereign Wealth Funds and extractive industries in the Pacific', *Journal of Economic Roundup*, **1**, 63–86.
In, F., J.R. Park, P.I. Ji and B. Lee (2013), 'Do Sovereign Wealth Funds stabilize stock markets?', *Asia-Pacific Journal of Financial Studies*, August.
Jen, S.L. (2007), 'Sovereign Wealth Funds: What they are and what's happening', *World Economics*, **8**(4), 1–8.
Joint Working Group Discussion Paper (2010), 'Possible creation of a Sovereign Wealth Fund', Department of Treasury and Bank of Papua New Guinea. Joint Sovereign Wealth Fund Working Group Discussion Paper.
Kimmitt, R.M. (2008), 'Public Footprints in Private Markets', *Foreign Affairs*, **87**(1), 119–130.
Knill, M.A., B.S. Lee and N. Mauck (2012a), 'Sovereign Wealth Fund Investment and the return-to-risk performance of target firms', *Journal of Financial Intermediation*, **21**, 315–340.
Knill, M.A., B.S. Lee and N. Mauck (2012b), 'Bilateral political relations and Sovereign Wealth Fund investment', *Journal of Corporate Finance*, **18**, 108–123.
Kotter, J. and U. Lel (2011), 'Friends or foes? Target selection decisions of Sovereign Wealth Funds and their consequences', *Journal of Financial Economics*, **101**(2), 360–381.
Megginson, W.L. and V. Fotak (2015), 'Rise of the fiduciary state: A survey of Sovereign Wealth Fund research', *Journal of Economic Surveys*, **29**(4), 733–778.
Monk, A. (2009), 'Recasting the Sovereign Wealth Fund debate: Trust, legitimacy, and governance', *New Political Economy*, **14**(4), 451–468.
Rousseau, P.L. and P. Wachtel (2002), 'Inflation threshold and the finance-growth nexus', *Journal of International Money and Finance*, **21**, 777–793.
Rousseau, P. and H. Yilmazkuday (2009), 'Inflation, financial development and growth: A trilateral analysis', *Economic Systems*, **33**(4), 310–324.
Steigum, E. (2012), 'Sovereign Wealth Funds for macroeconomic purposes', Working Paper Series 4/12. Oslo: Centre for Monetary Economics.
Sun, T. and H. Hesse (2011), 'What do Sovereign Wealth Funds imply for financial stability?', in N. Boubakri and J. Cosset (eds), *Institutional Investors in Global Capital Markets. International Finance Review*, Volume 12, Bingley: Emerald Group Publishing Limited, pp. 245–262.
Sun, X., J. Li, Y. Wang and W.W. Clark (2014), 'China's Sovereign Wealth Fund investments in overseas energy: The energy security perspective', *Energy Policy*, **65**, 654–661.
Teslik, L.H. (2008), 'Sovereign Wealth Funds', Council on Foreign Relations, New York.
Todaro, M.P and C.S. Smith (2009), *Economic Development*, 10th edition, New York: Addison-Wesley Publications.
Townsend, I. (2008), 'Sovereign Wealth Funds', Economic Policy & Statistics Section, House of Commons Library, Working Paper SN/EP/4767.
Truman, E.M. (2009), 'A blueprint for Sovereign Wealth Fund best practices', *Revue d'économie financière* (English edn), **9**(1), 429–451.
Turkisch, E. (2011), 'Sovereign Wealth Funds as investors in Africa: Opportunities and Barriers', OECD Development Centre Working Paper No. 303.
Xie, P. and C. Chen (2008), 'Sovereign Wealth Funds, macroeconomic policy alignment and financial stability', China Investment Corporation Working Paper No 100010.

PART II

SUSTAINABILITY AND FINANCIAL MARKETS

8. Financial markets like the potter's hands? Rethinking finance for sustainability in a civil society perspective

Giulia Porino

'Why did no one see it coming?'
(H.M. Queen Elizabeth II, London School of Economics, November 2008)

1. INTRODUCTION

Several works have tried to quantify the real costs[1] of the financial crisis of 2007–2008 (Furceri and Mourougane 2012; Childress 2012; Pino and Yermo 2010; Gros and Alcidi 2010), to explore how such a global turmoil happened despite warnings from academics and experts,[2] and to identify the lessons that should be learnt (Reinhart and Rogoff 2008; Krugman 2009; Steil 2009; Stucke 2010; Helleiner 2011).

If our understanding of the cocktail of elements that created this crisis is too narrow, we run the risk of facing a comparable mix of ingredients in future, without having developed appropriate tools and backstops to protect taxpayers from paying the bill once again.

The ingredients of the 'crisis-cocktail' included macroeconomic imbalances and profound transformations in the financial system (Lapavitsas 2009; Taylor 2009). This blend became explosive when the massive financial deregulation that had started in the late 1960s combined with the unprecedented financial development that opened the doors to the so-called *commodification of finance* or *financialisation* (Scholte 2013) over the same period.

Indeed, the complexity and multi-layered nature of the interconnections found in the financial system leads to inaccuracy in the estimation of systemic risks (Battiston et al. 2016), and makes the financial system more opaque and difficult to understand.

Despite some important modern twists,[3] this crisis has shown many similarities to those of the past (Bordo 2008; Reinhart and Rogoff 2008). For instance, Kotz (2009a) argues that the current crisis should be seen as a systemic crisis of a particular form of capitalism called neoliberal capitalism,[4] and that this alternation between these two forms seems to have characterised US institutional history from the end of the Civil War until the early 1980s, when neoliberalism replaced regulated capitalism again.

The financial system plays a key fiduciary role in our integrated global society and economy, and its contributions to progress and the real economy are not easily captured by statistics (Epstein and Crotty 2013; Baily and Elliot 2013; Herring and Santomero 1995). It is therefore entrusted with an extraordinary public responsibility. Nevertheless, no single sector should become so powerful that it can repeatedly jeopardise the well-being of society.[5] The fact that the financial sector can still do this is, to borrow a cliché, the elephant in the room.

That being the case, it is in the interests of all civil society stakeholders to have a stable, resilient, transparent, accountable and society-oriented financial system, and citizens should become watchdogs of the vision they want for this sector. A more transparent and inclusive debate around financial reform, especially around accountability, would improve citizens' trust[6] in the financial system and boost the political will to address key societal issues in an ambitious and forward-looking manner.

This chapter will argue that the financial sector should be subject to robust regulatory treatment and that new prudential safeguards are needed to ensure that public resources will not be used in the next financial turmoil. However, to do this properly it is necessary to learn from the missed reform opportunities of the global financial crisis and to involve civil society ahead of time in the debate about a sound reform of the system. Just as private investors have a strong influence over the fate of the troubled companies they rescue, so civil society – who rescued the financial system – should have a say in the debate about the future of finance.

As will be explored further in this chapter, a high level of complexity and technicality still dominate the modern financial sector and its regulation (Aikman et al. 2014). In addition, the disproportionate size of the biggest players of the sector, the so-called Global systemically important banks (G-SIBs) which includes banks considered to be 'too big to fail', allows the financial sector to act as a 'super-sector', calling for government intervention[7] and being extremely vocal in influencing regulations supposed to control their potentially harmful power. Much regulation still favours the business models of large, interconnected banks rather than supporting more traditional banking business models that are more focused on financing the real economy and which tended to be more resilient and less affected by systemic risk in the crisis.[8]

The aim of this chapter is not to present an overly dramatic scenario but to shift the lens to the need to create a public-interest-driven agenda for a sustainable[9] financial sector, both at the European and international level. In fact, notwithstanding the recognised imbalance in the representation of different interests in the debate about finance (Corporate Europe Observatory et al. 2014; Pagliari and Young 2015; Finance Watch 2016c), several civil society actors are already working to unveil the nexus between finance and broader societal issues and how the dysfunctions of the financial sector affect them in a variety of ways. In order to give voice to the work of these civil society organisations working specifically on finance and on related issues such as human rights, sustainability (including the climate dimension), democracy and equality (including the gender perspective), this chapter will offer a first overview of the work of these organisations by presenting their research and concrete alternatives for a sustainable finance sector serving society. If anything, this should sound a wake-up call for experts, policymakers and politicians both at the European and international level to recognise the need to reassess the architecture and functioning of the financial system before another crisis knocks on our doors (Jagger and Hosking 2009).

The chapter is organised as follows. Section 2 briefly analyses the main dysfunctions of the financial sector trying to offer a first analysis of how this affects society in a variety of ways. Section 3 gives voice to civil society concerns about how an excessive 'financialisation' and deregulation of the financial sector are contributing to inequality and preventing the sustainability of the global economic system (OECD 2016). It also highlights alternative solutions and research from civil society organisations focusing on finance as well as a broader group of organisations working on the relationship between broader societal issues and the various ways that the financial sector affects them. Section 4 concludes.

2. FINANCIAL SECTOR DYSFUNCTIONS AND THE CONSEQUENCES FOR SOCIETY – AN OVERVIEW

This chapter has no ambition to challenge the idea that modern financial institutions are crucially important for sustained economic growth. On the contrary, and in light of the critical role that the financial sector plays in empowering local, national and global economies, it is crucial to tackle the practices and trends that have enabled financial institutions to extract (and destroy) value on a massive scale instead of creating it, as well as to understand why the various control systems 'failed so dismally' (Dowd 2009).[10]

Keeping in mind how undeniably no other industry but finance, as stated by Wolf (2008), 'has a comparable talent for privatising gains and socialising losses', the optimistic message from this chapter is the conviction that a financial sector that serves society is not a chimera. To some extent, the process is already underway. Several much-needed regulations have been adopted at European as well as global level after the crisis turmoil, but, as advocated by a number of scholars and civil society organisations focusing on financial issues, the mission of fixing the system is far from being accomplished.[11] Moreover, many voices are raising concerns about the low ambitions as well as 'silo mentality' showed by European and national Member States policymakers and regulators when it comes to challenging the status quo of financial regulation and asking firmly for a robust agenda for change.[12]

As reported by Scholte and Schnabel in the context of the Civil Society and Global Finance Project (2002),[13] when it comes to advocating for the reform of the financial sector and global finance, civil society actors face key choices about their operational strategy and tactics. On the matter of objectives, for instance, civic groups face a choice between supporting the status quo, seeking incremental reform, or pursuing radical transformation of global finance. As for targets, civil society associations must determine whether they best focus their efforts on multilateral organisations, on national governments (particularly of the G8), or on leading financial corporations. Various strategic choices in regard to coalitions must also be made.

Academics have analysed the political and technical factors that facilitated the explosion of the crisis, and which unfortunately are still largely to be addressed (Acharya et al. 2009; Acharya and Richardson 2009; Taylor 2009; Reinhart and Rogoff 2008).

From a civil society perspective, the dysfunctions of the financial sector can be grouped with their direct or indirect relations, and include in particular:

- Innovation and complexity;
- Deregulation and size;
- Credit allocation and dependency.

The aim of this grouping is to show how individual dysfunctions, by affecting a specific part of the financial system as if it were a living body, can weaken it so badly that it becomes a fertile ground for the development of new dysfunctions.

At the same time, and wanting to give an optimistic message, this analysis aims to become a worldwide call for engagement for a much broader group of change-oriented civil society organisations – after having deeply understood the ties and consequences of financialisation, finance-driven globalisation and neoliberal reforms (Epstein 2005; Pianta 2013; Scholte

2013), and so tackle financial issues in the same way they already advocate on issues such as corporate power and influence, sustainable development, labour and employment, environment, transparency and accountability, equality, and so on.

2.1 Innovation and Complexity

Unlike other functions, such as risk management, branch operations or marketing, financial innovation is a relatively new field, even in the banking sector. Indeed, innovation – maximising the use of technology through new products and business models – is a good example of a tool able in principle to make our financial system more efficient and more inclusive, but also harmful if inappropriately applied.

Looking back at the source of the rise of innovation in finance, we can see how it goes hand in hand with a growth in size. Strategic decisions are needed for the financial industry to sustain itself, and innovation enables the sector to boost revenue and reduce costs. In parallel, deregulation, public policies towards credit markets, and broader technological change have facilitated the inflow of innovations and technology to the financial sector, and established the roots of a digital revolution in the functioning and structure of the financial sector.

When it comes to the so-called 'unbanked' and other low-income groups, particularly in the poorest and most peripheral rural areas, innovation can boost financial inclusion by allowing new delivery systems and channels, as shown in the case of microfinance institutions (MFIs). The excitement about alternative delivery channels – so-called 'branchless banking' which includes ATMs, banking agents, online and telephone banking, etc. – can be explained in part by the increased access that unbanked individuals have to financial services, and microfinance institutions benefit from two breakthroughs in this area. First, the possibility of massive outreach to people in locations that remain underserved. Second, the dramatic cost reduction in terms of physical bank branches, which are expensive to maintain and can be difficult for customers to reach, especially in rural and far-flung communities as most branches are located in urban areas. Physical branches are still central to MFI operations, as they are for 'traditional' banks, especially for operating savings products and building customers' trust in the institution. Innovations in branchless banking are therefore valuable for MFIs as well as traditional banks.

Advances in information technology have lowered the costs of collection, processing and disseminating household and business financial data, functions that were once highly localised and are, by today's standards, inefficiently managed.[14] More complex plans may benefit some consumers; for example, pricing that varies according to consumers' credit risk and preferences for certain services may improve access to credit and allow for more customised products.[15]

However, growing complexity becomes an issue if it reduces consumers' ability to identify appropriate financial products.

Just as quantity does not guarantee quality, more information does not guarantee that investment and risk management decisions are well informed (Brunnermeier and Oehmke 2009), even for the most diligent consumers. When complexity reaches the point of reducing transparency, it impedes competition and leads consumers to make poor choices by disguising unfair and predatory practices; an aspect that took extreme forms in the course of the speculative bubble that preceded the crisis exploded in 2007–2008. This has important implications for designing disclosure requirements for consumer protection while taking into account the potential benefits of a digital revolution in finance.

In addition to concerns about consumer protection, financial innovation has led to vast improvements in computer and communications technology that are rendering many traditional institutional arrangements obsolete. Technological breakthroughs have a significant impact on the location of physical facilities, with dramatic effects on job losses, reduced human interface and on the magnitude and speed of market decision-making.

Among the profound transformations involved in the shaping of the modern financial system, financial engineering has surely played an important role as it has created opportunities for banks to trade on their own account (Lapavitsas 2009). In recent years, particularly after the crisis, many commentators identified financial innovation as one of the main causes that led the financial system to become too complex.

While the mainstream authors discussed above have supported the social benefits of financial innovation, some heterodox economists have taken a more critical stance towards them (Epstein and Crotty 2013). Dowd (2009) describes the increased sophistication of the system as a curious paradox at the heart of modern financial risk management, in the sense that the more sophisticated the system, the more unreliable it might be: indeed, sophistication creates greater complexity, less transparency and greater dependency on assumptions (any of which could be wrong) that might consequently generate greater scope for errors that are harder to detect. In addition, Tufano (1989) connected the rush and attention around the technology factor in finance with the fact that innovators become infra-marginal rivals that enjoy lower costs of trading, underwriting and marketing.

Financial institutions benefit from complexity by creating multi-layered networks of contracts among each other and exposures to common assets that link the default probability of one institution to the default probabilities of all the other institutions in the network (Battiston et al. 2016). The complexity of the network can reach such a high level of sophistication and stratification that only 'insiders' are able to fully understand the intermediation chain. From a public interest perspective this has major consequences, as it has been shown that small errors in the knowledge of the network of contracts can lead to large errors in the probability of systemic defaults (Battiston et al. 2016) and therefore in the understanding of whether the prudential safeguards in place will be sufficient to prevent a domino effect in the system if one part of the chain collapses. In this way, when a crisis explodes it is easier to demand a public intervention to rescue the entire network with taxpayers' money, as it is not possible to attribute clear responsibility for the origin of the damage, and at the same time to demand an immediate response to avoid the spread of panic and more irrational behaviour. Just like the smokescreens used by magicians to hide their tricks, complexity and sophistication are used first as a method for shuffling the cards and pushing away civil society from the debate, and secondly as an excuse for pretending that the entire system is too interconnected and therefore has to be saved as a unique and indivisible block. In line with this logic, once the financial sector has been saved through public intervention it is in its interests to lobby[16] against reform proposals that would limit its ability to operate with this level of complexity and sophistication in future. This can be seen both in terms of products, as with securitisation and tranching, and in the balance sheet structures of financial institutions themselves, as with regulations on capital and leverage. Therefore, not only does the financial industry demand to be rescued with public money in case of a crisis, but it then opposes reforms and regulations that aim to avoid a repetition of the mix of ingredients that generated that crisis. This also indicates a clear lack of response to the problem of information asymmetry and moral hazard (Battiston et al. 2013; Farhi and Tirole 2012), powered by the near certainty that the system will be saved because it would be too costly to cope with the collapse of the entire economic system and the dramatic consequences on society in terms of massive job loss, increase of inequality, lack of trust in financial institutions, and so on.

As matters currently stand, the mission of regulating such sophisticated and opaque financial products and mechanisms is still largely unaccomplished.

Moreover, complexity substantially limits the ability of civil society organisations to engage in the debate. If we look at any of the legislative proposals for financial reforms launched recently by global and regional intergovernmental institutions, as well as by the institutions dealing with financial trans-governmentalism,[17] the problem of complexity influences substantially the content of the financial reform proposals, which are so stuffed with technicalities and sophisticated mathematical and econometric models[18] as to become incomprehensible, and are accessible only by a small number of experts and stakeholders, including, unsurprisingly, the financial industry lobby. This obviously creates a significant gap in the ability of civil society organisations that are not directly focused on finance issues to access the democratic debate about such reforms. This creates a two-fold disparity in the representation of the public interest in this debate.

First, it limits the legitimacy of the few civil society organisations – in Europe and beyond – that are able to advocate for reforms that restore the financial sector to serving the needs of society and the real economy. These organisations can count on a very limited number of allies and resources when compared to the size and resources of the financial industry lobby.[19] Their messages and recommendations may be backed by robust evidence, but the limited involvement of a critical mass of civil society organisations limits their effectiveness. The financial industry and its lobby are able to work together to influence legislative decisions through common messages, as the private interests they represent are often quite limited and well-defined. Civil society organisations, by contrast, may not be structured or organised with such efficiencies in mind, as the interests they represent are by definition wider and, as a consequence, they deal with a broader number of topics. Moreover, given the complexity and opacity of the financial sector, it is not easy to define a clear link between the societal issues that different civil society groups focus on and the dysfunctions of the financial sector. As a consequence, it might be harder for policymakers to hear the voices and concerns of civil society organisations seeking to reform finance.

Second, the technical nature of the documentation and public consultations launched by, for instance, the European Commission[20] or the Basel Committee on Banking Supervision,[21] clouds the connection between the ways the financial sector operates and the specific social problems that concern civil society organisations which do not specialise in finance. Unsurprisingly, this further decreases the ability of an organisation engaged in economic development and human rights, for example, to develop advocacy linking the right to food with the financial practice of speculating on commodity derivatives, and the political debate at the EU institutional level about the EU's Review of the Markets in Financial Instruments Directive (MiFID II), which is supposed to prevent excessive 'food speculation'. If such connections are missed, the organisations concerned may also miss the opportunity to engage in advocacy about changing financial practices that negatively affect the social issues they are focusing on.

2.2 Deregulation and Size

The previous section stressed how excessive sophistication and complexity has distanced the financial sector from its original function towards real economy, while postulating on risky financial transactions and speculative activities. In addition, deregulation and liberalisation of finance played a role in the intense growth of cross-border financial transactions, which would not have been possible without the lifting of regulatory restrictions. In fact, the conventional view, part of the so-called Washington Consensus, was quite optimistic regarding the effects of financial liberalisation (Broner and Ventura 2010).

The deregulation of business and finance took place after the 1980s at the national and international level as policymakers offered a red carpet to 'free market' finance, allowing speculative, high-risk activities to proliferate and financial institutions, spurred on by unrestrained competition, to pursue whatever financial activities would bring the highest profits (Crotty 2009; Kotz 2009b).

The combination of deregulation and an unprecedented increase in cross-border financial transactions supported a colossal growth of financial markets, aiding the creation of financial institutions that for proportion and influence had no similar touchstones in contemporary history (Scholte 2013). In this context, traditional financial activities such as taking deposits, issuing and holding loans to small and medium-sized enterprises or households, issuing bonds and selling conventional insurance became less attractive, and a new range of more profitable speculative activities flourished. Multi-layered and highly sophisticated exotic financial instruments such as securitisation of subprime loans, collateralised debt obligations, and credit default swaps (Miller 1986; Crotty and Epstein 2009; Segoviano et al. 2013; Finance Watch 2014a; Battiston et al. 2016) were preferred, despite their high volatility and contribution to systemic risk.

The characteristics of the large banks that emerged from this development (lower capital, high systemic risk, less stable funding, more market-based activities and greater organisational complexity than small banks) suggest that their business model was not solid and their size too large from a social welfare perspective, due to 'too-big-to-fail' subsidies and corporate governance shortcomings (Finance Watch 2014c; Laeven et al. 2016). The fact that large banks were at the centre of the global financial crisis when it started ten years ago, and that the consequences of their distress are still now oppressing society and real economy, supports this idea.

Moral hazard also played a role, since the incentives to generate and propagate risks were higher among those posing the greatest systemic threat. In fact, during the pre-crisis period, too-big-to-fail banks were also operating with weak capital buffers because of the implicit promise of government support, which suggests a positive relationship between bank size and pre-crisis expectations of official sector support (Haldane and Madouros 2014).

Despite the evidence from the crisis and the warning raised by several financial experts, academics, policymakers and civil society organisations (Edmonds 2013; Viñals et al. 2013; European Parliament and Council of the European Union 2014; Finance Watch 2012 and 2016b), including the demand for a review of the rules that allow large banks to use their internal models to calculate their risk weights,[22] the problem of the relationship between global banks' capital ratios and their size is still partially considered unsolved (Haldane 2013; Finance Watch 2014a), since no vaccination against the 'super-spreaders of financial contagion' (Haldane and Madouros 2014) has been implemented.

The current political narrative has, unfortunately, not changed. At the European level, the so-called 'Better Regulation'[23] agenda is working to introduce more restrictive rules about the legislative initiatives that can be taken within the annual European Commission Work Programme. It also pushes the European Parliament and European Council to subject their legislative amendments to more impact assessments which could potentially lead to the withdrawal of legislative proposals that are no longer perceived as useful or which are dragging on for too long in negotiations (Finance Watch 2016a).

While the attempt to cut muddled red-tape and overly complex laws is welcome, without a proper safety net and democratic control this exercise could lead to negative impacts on social, environmental, labour, consumer and public health standards for citizens and the public interest.[24]

The financial industry partially justifies the diminished focus on financing real economy and households with the need to cover costs due to the implementation and compliance with stricter regulation. However, in saying this, it could also be implied that the benefits of regulation in terms of financial stability have less priority than to guarantee that large banks are able to cope with their costs and keep making their investment decisions merely with a short-term profit-focused perspective (Finance Watch 2014a).

Therefore, from a civil society perspective it is crucial to prevent a dangerous new wave of financial deregulation and to safeguard the positive steps achieved with the post-crisis regulation. Civil society initiatives that gather together different stakeholders to advocate a unified message on these issues go in the right direction. However, a stronger citizen-driven movement should emerge, which would affect the direction of economic restructuring and hopefully lead to a second type of 'state regulated capitalism' involving a new social democratic compromise between capital on the one hand, and labour and other popular constituencies on the other (Kotz 2009a).

2.3 Credit Allocation and Dependency

Comparing the financial system with the circulatory system in a human body should not be taken as mere poetic licence.[25] In fact, this image provides a helpful simplification to visualise finance as a branched system that should 'allocate resources' to the entire body, representing our global economic system. If, however, the function of this circulatory system has changed so profoundly that now it is channelling resources only to big organs, leaving what is peripheral unserved because it is considered less useful, then the structure of the entire body will ultimately be affected. The financial system should be called on to channel resources along the entire economic system, and to undertake responsible, transparent and accountable choices on credit allocation for the production of real goods and useful services for society at large and, consequently, to tackle the negative impact that its activity has on global inequality. The allocation of resources and investment decisions following only speculative criteria should be considered a predatory practice since this destroys collective well-being by having an adverse impact on low-income households, that represent the majority of the population, for the benefits of the minority.

Over the past decades the traditional and 'boring' banking model based on providing credit to small and medium-sized enterprises and households, faced an unstoppable weakening (ECB 2013; Darvas 2013). While large companies can fund themselves directly from the capital markets, smaller businesses and families are highly dependent on bank credit. The increased size of financial markets and the introduction of a new range of complex and opaque financial instruments fostered the development of the 'finance for speculation' model, as opposed to the 'traditional boring finance' model (Finance Watch 2014a). If it is true that financial markets facilitate the identification of 'good' investments as well as the incentives to pursue them (Wurgler 2000), then the definition of what is 'good' should be challenged in order to align it better with society's needs. A combination of soft and hard measures to align governance with public interest more systematically could help with this. Voluntary codes of conduct can be considered a good starting point for an internal, culture-based reform of financial behaviour. But soft incentives to 'move the money', for example from brown to green investments, are not enough to address the long-term impacts of capital flows. Without a systematic consideration of the long-term footprints that an irresponsible modus operandi of the financial sector leaves on society – starting from the identification of a harmonised and binding definition of environmental, social and governance requirements to be then introduced in relevant EU legislations – we will keep ignoring the true costs[26] of financial instability – political capture, environmental damage, a decrease in citizens' rights, and increase in inequality, among others.

As identified by Minsky (1993), financial institutions in the neoliberal era shifted away from their traditional activities to pursue higher-profit, more risky speculative activities. The financial crisis left no excuses for ignoring this change. In light of the costs that citizens had borne in recent years, soft incentives to change behaviour in the financial sector do not sound robust or ambitious enough to mitigate the rush of this sector towards its unstoppable growth and influence. Strict and clear rules for transparency, accountability and hard structural reforms are needed to limit the sector's freedom to allocate resources without regard to its responsibilities towards the public sphere.

3. CIVIL SOCIETY ENGAGEMENT FOR A SUSTAINABLE FINANCIAL SECTOR – ALTERNATIVES IN PLACE AND NEW STRATEGIES

This chapter has already stressed the need for a more sizeable engagement of civil society organisations advocating for a sustainable financial service aimed at counterbalancing the status quo and deregulatory pressure.

Notwithstanding the imbalance in the representation of different interests, when it comes to financial regulation it is relevant to note that a significant group of civil society organisations is already working at the frontline of the European institutional (Pagliari and Young 2014, 2015) and public debate through research, advocacy, campaigning and capacity-building efforts.

The legitimacy and relevance of their actions are crucial for a number of reasons. The first reason is the need to point out the key role played by the financial sector in supporting the real economy and households. Looking back at the lessons learnt from the crisis, civil society should demand, at minimum, that financial stability measures are complete, robust and sound. Although this would not tackle the entire set of dysfunctions that the financial sector is able to produce on society, both from a social angle and an environmental angle, it would mitigate the risk of having a new global crisis happen as a 'clone' of the previous one by having the proper backstops in place to protect taxpayers.

This would require that civil society be organised as a more structured voice in the regulatory and political debate about the structure, scope and accountability of banks (among others) and more organised in general on the role that the financial sector plays in our global economy.[27]

In addition, civil society should also adopt a stronger role in determining which financial sector business models are promoted in policy and regulation. The issue of different banking models, namely the shareholder model versus the stakeholder model, opens the debate about ownership and governance of financial institutions. Civil society organisations focusing on these aspects, supported by academic researchers, have been quite vocal in calling for ambitious regulation on bank structure, which remains one of the biggest missed opportunities from the crisis (Finance Watch 2014a, 2014b, 2014c, 2015a; Epstein and Crotty 2013). While this does go in the right direction, much remains to be done to ensure that these initiatives do not remain isolated or sporadic, but merged into an organised and consistent set of civil society demands and advocacy actions.

Comparing again our economy with a human body, civil society organisations can benefit from their geographic 'capillarity' to engage a critical mass of actors that remain otherwise excluded from the debate. Greater engagement would generate two major benefits: first, it would tackle the stereotype that only experts and insiders have legitimacy to debate the financial system given its high complexity; and, second, it would increase the cohesion and collective legitimacy of the civil society organisations that already have a change agenda for a sustainable financial sector. Indeed, as mentioned above, civil society organisations often act with more disparate voices than financial lobby organisations (Pagliari and Young 2015), with the result that these messages are often less well heard in the legislative process.

But then, how to successfully foster civil society engagement in the 'finance topic'? There is a need to consider the blocking factors limiting this broader engagement. Insightful evidence can be found in projects that focus on this specific aspect. The starting point is to investigate why the public interest is not being properly represented in banking and finance and how much this under-representation can be associated with the fact that the European economy is weak and the banking system remains a threat to financial stability.

As an example, the research project 'Representation of Public Interest in

Banking'[28] investigated the numerous ways in which the public is blocked from participating in influencing the activities of banks and from representing its own interests in banking. The aim was to investigate how to deliver better public interest outcomes in banking via an inclusive process with civil society representatives. The innovative twist of this approach came from the wide range of stakeholders involved in raising a number of questions for civil society, public institutions, policymakers and banks themselves about the participation of the public in a highly relevant issue for the population at large. The final policy proposals in this project reflected this broader participation, including strategies for civil society, policies to make banks more open to public interest representation, and changes to the regulatory process to foster broader, more effective participation.

Other projects offer meaningful examples of the synergies generated by a systematic and structured cooperation between different voices of civil society, for instance civil society organisations and academics (Fazi 2016). This kind of synergy facilitates the achievement of a critical mass of stakeholders engaging in the debate, while adding robustness to the civil society messages given by the unique blend of theoretical and granular expertise. As already mentioned above, a more systematic and structured synergy can contribute to decreasing the fragmentation of the messages that civil society conveys in the public and policy debate, fostering the adoption of a holistic and interdisciplinary approach when looking at the nexus between finance and civil society issues as, for instance, the social and environmental dimension.

A comprehensive analysis of lessons from the crisis should also consider the missed opportunity coming from civil society not being prepared to present a unified set of proposals and actions in response to the financial crash nor to advocate with a consistent sort of 'flagship' initiative that could have had influence on the post-crisis agenda of reforms.

In fact, evidence shows that having the right analysis and a robust theory of change is not enough to make an impact and that achieving a high legitimacy requires an agreement on a common narrative, which is able to interlace the several angles of interest through which civil society actors can connect their own mission with an agenda for financial reforms. As already pointed out, the lack of resources and technical expertise represents a blocking factor in this direction, also considering the high complexity and technicalities of the issue at stake. As a result, civil society inclusion remains confined to a limited number of subjects, diminishing its potential impact. In addition, the 'empty space' left by civil society is taken over by the agenda of the financial sector lobby; though with a higher level of harmonisation and much bigger resources, this empty space could have garnered more effective results.

The argument promoting more effective participation of different interests in finance is the common thread of this chapter. On top of this, it remains relevant to explore the level of homogeneity within the internal structure of the financial system and specifically within banks' boardrooms. Group-thinking and herd behaviours had been identified among the causes which led to the financial sector corporate governance failure, and which ultimately led to the crisis. Adequate regulation and guidelines seeking for a more balanced and intersectional representation of diversity in banks' boardrooms are needed to promote the creation of a new financial landscape: the future of banking depends on them (Finance Watch 2015b; Lehmann 2016). Policy proposals endorsed by civil society have been already mentioned, and include ideas[29] such as the separation of bank activities, the revival of 'boring banking' over 'market-based banking', curbing the use of internal models in regulating capital adequacy as well as the greater representation of different interests in banks' business models and governance.[30]

The bottom line for any consideration about financial sector reform should include considerations about cultural and behavioural shifts in terms of scope and incentives that contributed to transform the financial sector into the self-referential sector, heedlessly driving society 'sensu lato' into the foregoing crisis. This would require a long-term strategy to mitigate the risk of behavioural dysfunctions in banks' corporate governance and the consequent risk of governance failure being a trigger for a new systemic financial crisis. The crisis has shown how the issues related to a dysfunctional bank culture need to be tackled in order to achieve a sound improvement of its resilience and long-term sustainability. That would also imply challenging the composition of the decision-making groups inside banks. Indeed, a too homogeneous composition would hardly facilitate a robust culture-based shift when it comes to, for instance, evaluating the consequences that the group's choices have on society at large. On the contrary, a decision-making group with a mixed composition in terms of represented interests and individuals' characteristics and backgrounds can positively affect group thinking and better catalyse the public interest angle into the governance of the organisation. In addition, a 'diversity versus uniformity' policy would provide new empirical evidence to assess bank business models and, ultimately, to improve micro-prudential banking supervision.

A number of promising initiatives coming from synergies between different civil society interest groups are crucial to show the way towards the promotion of the right set of policies, as well as to define a civil society strategy for conveying the change they advocate for.

One civil society contribution in this area involved more than 30 civil society groups across Europe convening to create a prototype Citizens' Dashboard of Finance.[31] This aims to measure how well the financial sector is serving society's needs, by engaging various categories of stakeholders to form a positive vision of how the financial sector is meeting society's needs and then finding data to measure how well the financial system is meeting those needs. It includes indicators on the environment, financial stability, real economy financing and inequality, among other factors. The Dashboard's legitimacy stems from the participation of civil society organisations, academics and finance pioneers, as well as the use of official data.

The ISI Growth[32] project is another example of strong interaction between theoretical and empirical insights by offering comprehensive diagnostics of the relationships between innovation, employment dynamics and growth in an increasingly globalised and 'financialised' world economy. On the basis of such analysis it has been possible to identify the wide range of proposals for policy alternatives developed in recent years by European civil society, including critical analysis, policy alternatives and potential mobilisations – from the perspective of European civil society and of progressive movements in general – of the key problems relating to macro areas of interest. The bottom line of this project stands in the synergy created between a number of European civil society organisations, trade unions, think tanks and scholars associated with them, with particular attention to the organisations that have embraced membership of the Civic Action Network of the ISI Growth project. Other research projects across Europe are implementing similar interdisciplinary approaches to support with empirical evidence how the network perspective plays a critical role in reshaping the policy process to overcome the financial and political crisis faced by the EU.

The 'Financial Systems Simulation and Policy Modelling' project – SIMPOL – carries out initiatives on mapping networks of influence on policies in finance and climate with the objective of developing new methods to assess the systemic importance of market players in complex (climate) financial networks and to investigate which regulations could help to ignite a transition towards a greener economy and a more sustainable financial system.[33] In a complementary way, the 'Distributed Global Financial Systems for Society' or DOLFINS project[34] addresses the global challenge of making the financial system better serve society by placing scientific evidence and citizens' participation at the centre of the policy process in finance. The expected impact is to achieve crucial advances in reshaping the policy process to overcome the financial and political crisis faced by the EU.

By looking at the public interest from a different angle, the European

Legitimacy in Governing through Hard Times: The Role of European Networks[35] project – ENLIGHTEN – explores the legitimacy of European governance in dealing with the so-called fast- and slow-burning crises and investigates them within several areas of societal interest. Again, the cooperation between different civil society actors is at the heart of this investigation.

4. CONCLUSIONS AND RECOMMENDATIONS

The previous sections aimed to offer a high-level overview of the main characteristics of the financial sectors – complexity, opacity, interconnectedness, size – that need to be challenged to mitigate negative externalities affecting society in terms of, among other things, the misallocation of capital, systemic risks, opacity, predatory behaviours and rising inequality. However, while further research is needed in the near future to offer a more in-depth analysis of these issues, the hope is that, if anything, this analytical framework will help to inspire strategies for strengthening the voice of civil society organisations required for a meaningful reform of the financial sector in a public interest perspective.

Indeed, this chapter aims to be a first attempt to open a window for a transversal discussion about the need for an ambitious rethinking of the financial sector in the light of the dramatic consequences paid by civil society in the years that followed the beginning of the last global financial crisis.

A number of civil society organisations, academics, practitioners and experts have been vocal since the beginning of the turmoil – and even ahead of it, although regrettably unheard – providing evidence that the latest transformations of the financial sector have led to a negative shift in the way that it affects directly and indirectly broader societal issues such as, for instance, climate change, inequalities, job losses, and so on.

This chapter is largely based on and inspired by their works and it will hopefully represent only the first of a series of deep insight analyses of their approaches and vision when looking at alternative models and solutions for a financial sector that does not endanger the global economic system while meeting the local needs of the real economy. Nevertheless, there are several clear areas stemming from this analysis in which improvements could be made:

- engaging with different categories of civil society actors to foster a dialogue around a financial reform for the common good, including with financial practitioners that are already implementing sustainable alternatives to more 'casino-like' business models;

- introducing a holistic perspective to unveil the transversal links between finance and society;
- empowering a broader group of civil society organisations and citizens to help legitimise their engagement in the debate by creating a common narrative about finance and society;
- building a common theory of change and agenda of actions to reshape the financial sector for the common good;
- occupying space in the current political and regulatory debate.

If we do not want to disperse the momentum raised by the collective indignation and suffering generated by the crisis, we – as part of civil society – need to advocate together for a robust reform of the internal governance of financial institutions.

However, to shift this debate into a collective call for action, efforts need to start at the roots of economic thinking and culture, where students and young professionals are educated and trained. Universities, business schools and research centres can play a major role in promoting alternative approaches and methodologies against the mainstream mind-set that often presents financial institutions as just like any other for-profit businesses, while dismissing their role of acting for the common good and in the public's interest. In a way it is emblematic that nowadays future bankers and financial experts often come from a restricted group of universities that are globally top ranked for business studies, where the angle of public interest is diluted into a more market-based concept of business administration and shareholder value maximisation.

But we need to go even beyond that. In fact, the gap between the influence of the financial sector in our modern economy and the general participation of citizens in the debate on finance has become simply too big. Not only do the next generations of financial experts and practitioners need to be aware of the mechanisms at the root of the system and how their wrong manipulation can have sinister effects on society, but also the debate about finance needs to become as popular among citizens as the debates on climate change or migration.[36] Stronger and more regular synergies should be established between different actors of civil society, for instance civil society organisations, academics, scholars, researchers and practitioners. In fact each of them, through their own specific angle of research, knowledge and granular expertise, can contribute to the creation of a common civil society narrative about a global reform of the financial sector in terms of its objectives, mechanisms, functions, risk management and governance.

The starting point, however, is the need to go 'back to basics'. Too much complexity in financial markets and products and the technical and lengthy process of making financial regulation[37] (sometimes too long even for financial experts and insiders) are making the participation of non-financial experts almost impossible or highly limited. Until not so many decades ago, financial institutions were 'also' companies – considering also the long-term externalities produced on the local economy – while they are now mainly 'only' companies – prioritising the creation of short-term value for shareholders. This shift happened also because of the 'distraction' of too many of us. The mission drift went so far that the financial sector was allowed to dismiss completely its role of pumping lifeblood into the real economy to blindly focus on short-term vision and profit maximisation.

The chapter started with H.M. Queen Elizabeth II asking, '*Why did no one see it coming?*' A partial reply to this question is that the entire system was focusing only on pursuing the same profit maximisation goal, with no direct consideration of the public interest or indirect consideration of the consequences that a collapse of that 'house of cards' would have on citizens.

A clear lesson from the crisis is that the weight and responsibility of banks and financial institutions have become too big to be left only in shareholders' hands. The interests of financial institutions are too interconnected with those of households and businesses to be isolated and not fully accountable for the damage they can generate. As the mistakes of the financial sector have been fixed with public money in the past, citizens have every right to ask for a clear representation of their interest in the banks' boards of directors. One way of moving towards this could be to include the possibility of having civil society nominees as directors on the boards of banks, given a positive decision from the nomination committee and the ratification of shareholders. In addition, all banks should have an 'independent' ethics committee with binding voting powers.[38]

Such reforms will never come voluntarily to the financial world: as citizens we should be vocal in advocating collectively for them and in supporting the work of civil society actors who are already working on the frontline of the debate. This would be the starting point for a shift towards a new paradigm where civil society plays the role of the potter using a new model of economic democracy as the clay to shape a reformed financial sector that, being robust, accountable and transparent, is able to deliver its mission towards society at large.

ACKNOWLEDGEMENTS

I am deeply thankful to Marcella Corsi and Gary Dymski for insightful and motivating discussions throughout the writing of this chapter, as well as to all my family, friends and colleagues who inspired and encouraged me along the way. Support from Finance Watch and Sapienza University of Rome is gratefully acknowledged. The usual disclaimers apply. This chapter is based on my Ph.D. dissertation in the context of the Euro-PhD in Socio-Economic and Statistical Studies at Sapienza University of Rome.

NOTES

1. The Better Markets Report (2012) stated that the full cost of the crisis is largely unquantifiable, as quantitative figures do not capture many social costs (https://www.bettermarkets.com).
2. A recent example of mobilisation from academics is the letter addressed in 2016 to the Members of the European Parliament expressing concerns about the European Commission's proposal to create an EU market for 'simple, transparent and standardised' (STS) securitisations, as it may push toward a more 'financialised' growth, instead of real growth. Accessed 23 February 2017 at https://crimfi.files.wordpress.com/2016/05/open-letter-to-meps-sts-securitisation.pdf.
3. Bordo (2008) states that many of the financial institutions and instruments caught up in the crisis are part of the centuries old phenomenon of financial innovation as well as the growth of the unregulated non-bank financial sector (shadow banking system).
4. For an analysis of neoliberalism as an ideological expression of the return to the hegemony of the financial fraction of the ruling classes see Duménil and Lévy (2001). For an analysis of how neoliberal reforms and financial powers have impoverished democracy see Pianta (2013).
5. See Childress (2012).
6. Serricchio et al. (2013) observed that the most pronounced increase in Euroscepticism has taken place in countries most affected by the crisis.
7. Erkens et al. (2012) observed that an unprecedentedly large number of financial institutions collapsed or were bailed out by governments during the global financial crisis of 2007–2008.
8. See Finance Watch (2015b, 2014b) and NEF (2013, 2016).
9. The definition of sustainable finance should include the creation of positive externalities for society at large and goes hand in hand with a robust mitigation of the operational and governance dysfunctions of the sector.
10. See also Cull et al. (2006), Campbell (2011), Epstein and Crotty (2013), and Baily and Elliot (2013).
11. See also Cochrane (2009), Stucke (2010), Taylor (2010), Navaretti et al. (2010), Baily and Elliot (2013) and Finance Watch (2014a).
12. After the onset of the global financial crisis, several political scientists and economists called for a wide-ranging discussion about the lessons to be learned. See in particular Buiter (2007), Reinhart and Rogoff (2008), Helleiner (2011), Kirkpatrick (2009), Cochrane (2009), Steil (2009) and Stucke (2010).
13. The Civil Society and Global Finance Project gathered together experts, academics and practitioners all engaged in advocacy, policy and research on questions of global finance.
14. See also Board of Governors of the Federal Reserve System (2007), *Report to the Congress on Credit Scoring and Its Effects on the Availability and Affordability of Credit*, accessed on 23 February 2017 at https://www.federalreserve.gov/boarddocs/rptcongress/creditscore/creditscore.pdf.
15. See Bernanke (2009).
16. Corporate Europe Observatory et al. (2014) estimated that the resources put in place by the financial industry compared to other (public) interests in terms of EU lobbying were

bigger by a factor of more than 30. See also Pagliari (2012) and Pagliari and Young (2014, 2015).

17. For a more detailed analysis of finance governance please see Scholte (2013).
18. Schlefer (2012) stated that economies are too complex to be reduced to simplified assumptions about an imaginary world tested via manipulated econometric models. Minsky (1970) argued that the crisis showed how econometric models alone cannot explain the behaviour of a system that was proved to act in the framework of uncertain psychological assumptions, despite the massive push to reduce it to a purely theoretical perspective through the excessive 'mathematicalisation' of the economic science, which is no longer anchored in reality. On this, see also Dumitrescu (2010).
19. CEO et al. (2014) found that the financial industry lobbied on post-crisis EU regulation using more than 700 organisations, which outnumbered civil-society organisations and trade unions by a factor of more than seven, with an even stronger dominance when numbers of staff and lobbying expenses are taken into account.
20. When developing policy and legislation, the European Commission consults widely with EU citizens and stakeholders through, inter alia, public consultations. Criticisms aimed at the effectiveness of this process come from its complexity and technicality as well as the difficulties of access for citizens.
21. The Basel Committee on Banking Supervision has the mandate to strengthen the regulation, supervision and practices of banks worldwide with the purpose of enhancing financial stability.
22. See Finance Watch (2016d).
23. See http://ec.europa.eu/info/strategy/better-regulation-why-and-how_en
24. Network of 66 EU organisations that follow the European Union's Better Regulation agenda closely, providing input into the processes and debates and challenging the widely held belief that regulation is a burden for society. See http://www.betterregwatch.eu/
25. UNEP and IHRB (2016) defined the financial system as 'the lifeblood of the economy'. Haldane (2013) compared the macroeconomic impact of the 2002 SARS epidemic with the contagious consequences generated by the Lehman Brothers bankruptcy in 2008.
26. See FERN (2016) and Global Witness and Friends of the Earth Europe (2016) for analysis of the influence that banks and investors have over the companies they finance to improve corporate performance on environmental and social issues. Academics have also made recommendations on divestments. See https://oxfordacademicsfordivestment.wordpress.com/.
27. See Finance Watch (2013, 2014b, 2015a) for an overview of the arguments made against regulating the structure of the largest banks as well as an analysis of the very different characteristics of Europe's small, medium and large banks.
28. See Finance Watch (2016c).
29. See in particular Fazi (2016) and Finance Watch (2012, 2016b).
30. See Finance Watch (2014a, 2016c).
31. http://www.citizensdashboardoffinance.org/ (accessed on 23 February 2017).
32. http://www.isigrowth.eu/ (accessed on 23 February 2017).
33. Preliminary examples of these network diagrams are available at https://graphcommons.com/graphs/846f5aca-97c9-46b9-8f6b-db9f5286452d
34. http://www.dolfinsproject.eu (accessed on 23 February 2017).
35. http://enlightenproject.eu/research-themes/banking-crisis-and-financial-sustainability/ (accessed on 23 February 2017).
36. Popular universities such as, for example, the 'Université Populaire de St Gilles' in Brussels, are concrete examples of how to promote debate about financial reform among various stratifications of citizens.
37. The Basel III accord offers a good example of how the issue of complexity is still affecting financial regulation. See Onaran (2013).
38. As it is in the case, for example, of Banca Etica in Italy (see http://www.bancaetica.it/idea-and-principles). See also Finance Watch (2016c) and NEF (2016).

REFERENCES

Acharya, V. and Richardson, M. (2009), 'Causes of the financial crisis', *Critical Review*, **21**(2–3), 195–210.

Acharya, V., Philippon, T., Richardson, M. and Roubini, N. (2009), 'The financial crisis of 2007–2009: causes and remedies', *Financial Markets, Institutions & Instruments*, **18**(2), 89–137.

Aikman, D., Galesic, M., Gigerenzer, G., Kapadia, S., Katsikopoulos, K.V., Kothiyal, A. and Neumann, T. (2014), 'Taking uncertainty seriously: simplicity versus complexity in financial regulation', MPRA Paper No. 59908, 14 November.

Baily, M.N. and Elliot, D.J. (2013), 'The role of finance in the economy: implications for structural reform of the financial sector', The Brookings Institution, 11 July.

Battiston, S., Caldarelli, G., Georg, C.P., May, R. and J.E. Stiglitz (2013), 'Complex derivatives', *Nature Physics*, **9**(3), 123–125.

Battiston, S., Caldarelli, G., May, R.M., Roukny, T. and Stiglitz, J.E. (2016), 'The price of complexity in financial networks', *Proceedings of the National Academy of Sciences*, **113**(36), 10031–10036.

Bernanke, B.S. (2009), 'Financial innovation and consumer protection', speech presented at the Federal Reserve System's Sixth Biennial Community Affairs Research Conference, Washington, DC, 17 April, accessed 23 February 2017 at https://www.federalreserve.gov/newsevents/speech/bernanke20090417a.htm#f2

Better Markets Report (2012), 'The cost of the Wall Street-caused financial collapse and ongoing economic crisis is more than $12.8 trillion', accessed 23 February 2017 at https://www.bettermarkets.com/newsroom/better-markets-report-cost-wall-street-caused-financial-collapse-and-ongoing-economic

Bordo, M.D. (2008), 'An historical perspective on the crisis of 2007–2008', NBER Working Paper Series No. 14569.

Broner, F.A. and Ventura, J. (2010), 'Rethinking the effects of financial liberalization', NBER Working Paper No. 16640.

Brunnermeier, M. and Oehmke, M. (2009), 'Complexity in financial markets', Princeton University, 8, accessed 23 February 2017 at http://scholar.princeton.edu/sites/default/files/complexity_0.pdf

Buiter, W.H. (2007), 'Lessons from the 2007 financial crisis', CEPR Discussion Paper No. 6596.

Campbell, J.L. (2011), 'The US financial crisis: lessons for theories of institutional complementarity', *Socio-Economic Review*, **9**(2), 211–234.

Childress, S. (2012), 'How much did the financial crisis cost?' *Frontline*, 31 May, http://www.pbs.org/wgbh/frontline/article/how-much-did-the-financial-crisis-cost/

Cochrane, J.H. (2009), 'Lessons from the financial crisis', *Regulation*, **32**(Winter), 34–37.

Corporate Europe Observatory (CEO), The Austrian Federal Chamber of Labour and The Austrian Trade Union Federation Report (2014), *The Fire Power of the Financial Lobby: A Survey of the Size of the Financial Lobby at the EU Level*, accessed 23 February 2017 at http://corporateeurope.org/financial-lobby/2014/04/fire-power-financial-lobby

Crotty, J. (2009), 'Structural causes of the global financial crisis: a critical assessment of the new financial architecture', *Cambridge Journal of Economics*, **33**(4), 563–580.

Crotty, J. and Epstein, G. (2009), 'Regulating the US financial system to avoid another meltdown', *Economic and Political Weekly*, 87–93.

Cull, R., Lance, E.D., Lamoreaux, N.R. and Rosenthal, J.L. (2006), 'Historical financing of small- and medium-size enterprises', *Journal of Banking & Finance*, **30**, 3017–3042.

Darvas, Z. (2013), 'Banking system soundness is the key to more SME financing', Bruegel Policy Contribution, No. 2013/10.

Dowd, K. (2009), 'Moral hazard and the financial crisis', *Cato Journal*, **29**(1), 141–166.

Duménil, G. and Lévy, D. (2001), 'Costs and benefits of neoliberalism: a class analysis', *Review of International Political Economy*, **8**(4), 578–607.

Dumitrescu, L. (2010), 'Neoliberalism, the economic theory behind the international financial crisis', *Romanian Journal of Sociology*, New series (1–2), 17–25.

Edmonds, T. (2013), 'The Independent Commission on Banking: the Vickers report', *House of Commons Library*, Standard note SNBT No. 6171. Available at: http://researchbriefings.parliament.uk/ResearchBriefing/Summary/SN06171#fullreport
Epstein, G.A. (ed.) (2005), *Financialization and the World Economy*, Cheltenham, UK and Northampton, MA, USA: Edward Elgar Publishing.
Epstein, G. and Crotty, J. (2013), 'How big is too big? On the social efficiency of the financial sector in the United States', speech presented at the Festschrift Conference in honor of Thomas Weisskopf, University of Michigan, Ann Arbor, 30 September, accessed 23 February 2017 at http://citeseerx.ist.psu.edu/viewdoc/download?doi=10.1.1.370.1630&rep=rep1&type=pdf
Erkens, D.H., Hung, M. and Matos, P. (2012), 'Corporate governance in the 2007–2008 financial crisis: evidence from financial institutions worldwide', *Journal of Corporate Finance*, **18**(2), 389–411.
European Central Bank (ECB) (2013), 'Survey on the access to finance of small and medium-sized enterprises in the Euro area', accessed 23 February 2017 at http://www.ecb.europa.eu/pub/pdf/other/accesstofinancesmallmediumsizedenterprises201311en.pdf
European Parliament and Council of the European Union (2014), Directive 2014/59/EU establishing a framework for the recovery and resolution of credit institutions and investment firms, 15 May, accessed 23 February 2017 at http://eur-lex.europa.eu/legal-content/EN/ALL/?uri=CELEX:32014L0059
Farhi, E. and Tirole, J. (2012), 'Collective moral hazard, maturity mismatch and systemic bailouts', *American Economic Review*, **102**(1), 60–93.
Fazi, T. (2016), 'How can Europe change? Civil Society Proposals for Policy Alternatives on Socially Inclusive and Sustainable Growth', ISI Growth Working Paper, accessed 23 February 2017 at http://www. isigrowth.eu/2016/10/25/economic-policy-alternatives-a-survey-of-civil-society-views/
FERN (2016), 'Financing land grabs and deforestation: the role of EU banks and investors', accessed 23 February 2017 at http://www.fern.org/financinglandgrabs
Finance Watch (2012), *To End All Crises?*, accessed 23 February 2017 at http://www.finance-watch.org/our-work/publications/330-crd4-position-paper-to-end-all-crises.
Finance Watch (2013), *The Importance of Being Separated*, accessed 23 February 2017 at http://www.finance-watch.org/our-work/publications/580.
Finance Watch (2014a), *A Missed Opportunity to Revive 'boring' Finance?*, accessed 23 February 2017 at http://www.finance-watch.org/our-work/publications/998-position-paper-on-ltf.
Finance Watch (2014b), *Structural Reform to Refocus Banks on the Real Economy*, accessed 23 February 2017 at: http://www.finance-watch.org/our-work/publications/898-fw-policy-brief-august-2014.
Finance Watch (2014c), *Too-big-to-fail in the EU*, accessed 23 February 2017 at http://www.finance-watch.org/our-work/publications/912-tbtf-note-fw
Finance Watch (2015a), *Separating Fact and Fiction*, accessed 23 February 2017 at http://www.finance-watch.org/ifile/Publications/Reports/Finance-Watch-note_Separating-fact-from-fiction_March-2015.pdf
Finance Watch (2015b), *Separating Universal Banks from Too-big-to-fail Banks (TBTF)*, accessed 23 February 2017 at http://www.finance-watch.org/our-work/publications/1055-fw-policy-brief-march-2015-en.
Finance Watch (2016a), *Annual Report 2015*, accessed 23 February 2017 at http://www.finance-watch.org/ about-us/governance-and-funding
Finance Watch (2016b), *Response to the BCBS Consultation on 'Reducing Variation in Credit Risk-weighted Assets'*, accessed 23 February 2017 at http://www.finance-watch.org/our-work/publications/1268- response-bcbs-consultation-rwa
Finance Watch (2016c), *Representation of the Public Interest in Banking*, accessed 23 February 2017 at http://finance-watch.org/our-work/publications/1310-report-public-interest-banking
Finance Watch (2016d), *So-called 'Basel IV' Would Help Restore Trust in the Health of the European Banking Sector*, accessed 23 February 2017 at http://www.finance-watch.org/hot-topics/blog/1267

Furceri, D. and Mourougane, A. (2012), 'The effect of financial crises on potential output: new empirical evidence from OECD countries', *Journal of Macroeconomics*, **34**(3), 822–832.

Global Witness and Friends of the Earth Europe (2016), *Regulating Risk*, accessed 23 February 2017 at https://www.globalwitness.org/en/reports/regulating-risk/

Gros, D. and Alcidi, C. (2010), 'The impact of the financial crisis on the real economy', *Intereconomics*, **45**(1), 4–20.

Haldane, A.G. (2013), 'Rethinking the financial network', in S.A. Jansen, E. Schröter and N. Stehr (eds), *Fragile Stabilität–stabile Fragilität*, Springer Fachmedien Wiesbaden, pp. 243–278.

Haldane, A.G. and Madouros, V. (2014), 'Complexity in financial regulation', in V.A. Acharya, B. Thorsten, D.E. Douglas, G.G. Kaufman and R. Portes (eds), *The Social Value of the Financial Sector: Too Big to Fail or Just Too Big. World Scientific Studies in International Economics*, **29**, 455–465.

Helleiner, E. (2011), 'Understanding the 2007–2008 global financial crisis: lessons for scholars of international political economy', *Annual Review of Political Science*, **14**, 67–87.

Herring, R.J. and Santomero, A.M. (1995), 'The role of the financial sector in economic performance', Working Paper No. 95–05-B, Wharton School of the University of Pennsylvania.

Jagger, S. and Hosking, P. (2009), '"Wake up, gentlemen", world's top bankers warned by former Fed chairman Volcker', *The Sunday Times*, December 9, accessed 23 February 2017 at http://business.timesonline.co.uk/tol/business/industry_sectors/banking_and_finance/article6949387.ece

Kirkpatrick, G. (2009), 'The corporate governance lessons from the financial crisis', *OECD Journal: Financial Market Trends*, **2009**(1), 61–87.

Kotz, D.M. (2009a), 'The financial and economic crisis of 2008: a systemic crisis of neoliberal capitalism', *Review of Radical Political Economics*, **41**(3), 305–317.

Kotz, M.D. (2009b), 'The future direction of economic restructuring', University of Massachusetts Amherst, accessed 23 February 2017 at http://people.umass.edu/dmkotz/articles/Possible_Directions_of_Restructuring_09_06.pdf

Krugman, P. (2009), 'How did economists get it so wrong?', *New York Times*, 2 September, accessed 23 February 2017 at http://www.nytimes.com/2009/09/06/magazine/06Economic-t.html?_r=1&pagewanted=print

Laeven, L., Ratnovski, L. and Tong, H. (2016), 'Bank size, capital, and systemic risk: some international evidence', *Journal of Banking & Finance*, **69**, S25–S34.

Lapavitsas, C. (2009), 'The roots of the global financial crisis', CDPR Development Viewpoint Series No. 28, accessed 23 February 2017 at https://www.soas.ac.uk/cdpr/publications/dv/file50940.pdf

Lehmann, M. (2016), 'Volcker rule, ring-fencing or separation of bank activities – comparison of structural reform acts around the world', *Journal of Banking Regulation*, **17**(3), 176–187.

Miller, M.H. (1986), 'Financial innovation: the last twenty years and the next', *Journal of Financial and Quantitative Analysis*, **21**(4), 459–471.

Minsky, H.P. (1970), 'Financial instability revisited: the economics of disaster', paper presented at Steering Committee for the Fundamental Reappraisal of the Discount Mechanism Appointed by the Board of Governors of the Federal Reserve System, accessed 23 February 2017 at http://citeseerx.ist.psu.edu/viewdoc/download?doi=10.1.1.364.2754&rep=rep1&type=pdf

Minsky, H.P. (1993), 'The financial instability hypothesis', The Jerome Levy Economics Institute Working Paper No.74, in P. Arestis and M. Sawyer (eds), *The Elgar Companion to Radical Political Economy*, Cheltenham UK and Northampton, MA, USA: Edward Elgar Publishing.

Navaretti, G.B., Calzolari, G., Pozzolo, A.F. and Levi, M. (2010), 'Multinational banking in Europe – financial stability and regulatory implications: lessons from the financial crisis', *Economic Policy*, **25**(64), 703–753.

New Economics Foundation (NEF) Report (2013), *Stakeholder Banks: Benefits of Banking Diversity*, accessed 23 February 2017 at http://neweconomics.org/2013/03/stakeholder-banks/

New Economics Foundation (NEF) Report (2016), *Taking Control of RBS. People-powered Banking that Puts Communities First*, accessed 23 February 2017 at http://neweconomics.org/wp-content/uploads/2016/10/CONTROL-OF-RBS_BULLETIN_E.pdf

OECD Report (2016), *In It Together: Why Less Inequality Benefits All*, 22–23, accessed 23 February 2017 at http://www.oecd.org/social/in-it-together-why-less-inequality-benefits-all-9789264235120-en.htm

Onaran, Y (2013), 'Basel becomes Babel as conflicting rules undermine safety', *Bloomberg*, 3 January, http://www.bloomberg.com/news/articles/2013-01-03/basel-becomes-babel-as-conflicting-rules-undermine-safety

Pagliari, S. (2012), 'How can we mitigate capture in financial regulation?', in S. Pagliari (ed.), *Making Good Financial Regulation: Towards a Policy Response to Regulatory Capture*, London: Grosvenor House Publishing, pp. 1–50.

Pagliari, S. and Young, K. (2014), 'Leveraged interests: financial industry power and the role of private sector coalitions', *Review of International Political Economy*, **21**(3), 573–610.

Pagliari, S. and Young, K. (2015), 'The interest ecology of financial regulation: interest group plurality in the design of financial regulatory policies', *Socio-Economic Review*, **14**(2), 309–337.

Pianta, M. (2013), 'Democracy lost: the financial crisis in Europe and the role of civil society', *Journal of Civil Society*, **9**(2), 148–161.

Pino, A. and Yermo, J. (2010), 'The impact of the 2007–2009 crisis on social security and private pension funds: a threat to their financial soundness?', *International Social Security Review*, **63**(2), 5–30.

Reinhart, C.M. and Rogoff, K.S. (2008), 'Is the 2007 US sub-prime financial crisis so different? An international historical comparison', NBER Working Paper Series No. 13761.

Schlefer, J. (2012), *The Assumptions Economists Make*, Cambridge, MA: Harvard University Press.

Scholte, J.A. (2013), 'Civil society and financial markets: what is not happening and why', *Journal of Civil Society*, **9**(2), 129–147.

Scholte, J.A. and Schnabel, A. (2002), *Civil society and global finance*, Volume 3, London: Routledge.

Segoviano, M., Jones, B., Lindner, P. and Blankenheim, J. (2013), *Securitization: Lessons Learned and the Road Ahead*, IMF WP/13/255, 3–66, accessed 4 May 2018 at http://www.imf.org/external/pubs/ft/wp/2013/wp13255.pdf

Serricchio, F., Tsakatika, M. and Quaglia, L. (2013), 'Euroscepticism and the global financial crisis', *JCMS Journal of Common Market Studies*, **51**(1), 51–64.

Steil, B. (2009), 'Lessons of the financial crisis', paper presented at Council on Foreign Relations, Council Special Report No. 45, March, accessed 23 February 2017 at http://www.cfr.org/international-finance/lessons-financial-crisis/p18753

Stucke, M.E. (2010), 'Lessons from the financial crisis', *Antitrust Law Journal*, **77**(1), 313–341.

Taylor, J.B. (2009), 'The financial crisis and the policy responses: an empirical analysis of what went wrong', NBER Working Paper Series No. 14631.

Taylor, J.B. (2010), 'Getting back on track: macroeconomic policy lessons from the financial crisis' (Digest Summary), *Federal Reserve Bank of St. Louis Review*, **92**(3), 165–176.

Tufano, P. (1989), 'Financial innovation and first-mover advantages', *Journal of Financial Economics*, **25**(2), 213–240.

UNEP and IHRB (2016), *Human Rights and Sustainable Finance – Exploring the Relationship*, accessed 23 February 2017 at http://web.unep.org/inquiry/publications

Viñals, J., Pazarbasioglu, C., Surti, J., Narain, A., Erbenova, M.M. and Chow, M.J. (2013), 'Creating a safer financial system: will the Volcker, Vickers, and Liikanen structural measures help?', paper presented at the International Monetary Fund Staff

Discussion note, 14 May, accessed 23 February 2017 at https://www.imf.org/external/pubs/ft/sdn/2013/sdn1304.pdf
Wolf, M. (2008), 'Regulators should intervene in bankers' pay', *Financial Times*, 16 January, accessed 4 May 2018 at https://www.ft.com/content/73a891b4-c38d-11dc-b083-0000779fd2ac
Wurgler, J. (2000), 'Financial markets and the allocation of capital', *Journal of Financial Economics*, **58**(1), 187–214.

9. An alternative way to think of finance: the case of innovative, sustainable financial instruments

Eleonora Broccardo and Maria Mazzuca

1. INTRODUCTION

This chapter discusses how finance and financial engineering can contribute to sustainability. The idea is that market-based solutions and financial innovation can aid human welfare. Different channels can be used, for instance issuing social impact bonds (SIBs) that permit the reallocation of risks and responsibilities among interested (private and public) parties (Whitfield, 2012), or issuing green bonds (GBs) that permit the filling of a specific sector's financial gap. The need to rethink finance to take into account environmental and social values is recognized by several international organizations (such as the United Nations Environment Programme Initiative), as well as by private initiatives (such as microcredit and social banking) and academics (Lagoarde-Segot and Paranque, 2017).

The importance of considering innovative financial solutions arises essentially for two reasons, critically influencing the sustainability of firms engaged in social projects. First, the recent global financial crisis has produced severe consequences that have affected worldwide economic growth, in terms of both the availability of funds and the effectiveness of traditional financial channels. Second, the public debt crisis in Europe has drastically changed the channels and the magnitude of intervention by public actors. However, the investors' general distrust of financial engineering instruments has reduced the types of potential financing methods. At the same time, emerging supranational policy concerns have drawn attention to the awareness about globally developing initiatives to support investments addressing social and environmental challenges.

Considering the rapid evolution of the above-mentioned universe, it seems possible to divide financing for sustainability into two macro-areas. The first includes the so-called socially responsible investments (SRIs) that encompass strategies incorporating environmental, social and governance (ESG) criteria to make investment decisions (GSIA, 2015). The second relates to specific financial instruments/asset classes, devoted to responding to particular requests from the public or the private sector. Focusing on the second area, we distinguish at least three broad categories of instruments. The first category comprises the payment-by-results instruments (such as SIBs), which allocate risks and responsibilities among the public sector, social enterprises and investors. Non-profit institutions often act as equity investors and allow the alleviation of risks to debt investors. The second category includes traditional instruments (such as GBs), which mix a traditional financial structure with sustainable purposes, exploiting financial know-how to respond efficiently to environmental issues. The third category comprehends the structured instruments (such as green securitization), which use financial engineering to create asset classes with a risk-returns profile that differs from that of the issuer.

We analyse GB and SIB instruments both because they are rather new instruments, and because they imply the issue of a specific financial asset. We do not discuss these instruments through comparisons with other types of social investments/public interventions. By assuming a financial perspective, we analyse GBs and SIBs, using different approaches.

The unique feature of GBs is the issuer's statement to raise capital to fund investments with specific environmental impacts. Since GBs' technical features are similar to those of conventional bonds, we do not focus on their structure. Instead, we first present both the main standards and the sources of guidelines for GBs and market stakeholders. Next, we investigate the so-called labelled GB market.

SIBs are innovative financial instruments that require the use of sophisticated techniques to fund social investments. We first aim to clarify the dynamics of these instruments, in terms of their structure and participants. Understanding this basic functioning clarifies how it would be readily adaptable to the different needs that might emerge from the affected parties. Successively, we discuss the case study of Newpin SBB. The rationale is that the increased understanding of the market (GBs) and the instruments' functioning (SIBs), also from economic/financial and technical perspectives, can improve their use.

The literature on GBs is mainly empirical and relates mostly to the US market. A consistent number of studies assess the effects of undertaking green investments or adopting green management policies on firms' costs of capital, financial returns or access to finance (Ramiah et al., 2013; Griffin and Sun, 2013; Di Giuli and Kostovetsky, 2013). The empirical literature on SIBs is very scarce, because of exiguous data availability. The evidence on SIBs' implementation is investigated mainly by reports of practitioners and policy makers. The academic literature on SIBs includes studies discussing their contribution to improving public policy and in potentially developing new social programmes (Bolton and Savell, 2010; McHugh et al., 2013; Sinclair et al., 2014), studies focusing on their institutional design (Warner, 2013), and papers that specifically analyse the role of financial innovation in sustaining social purposes (Schinckus, 2015a; Henke, 2016). Our chapter is related to the literature aimed at assessing how financial innovation can be deployed to enhance the development of sustainable investments. We aim to contribute by analysing the risks and challenges posed by both the GBs and SIBs through a common framework and using the financial perspective.

Our study shows that GBs and SIBs can effectively contribute to sustainability. Some critical issues need to be addressed to foster their diffusion, such as those related to the comprehension of their risks and to the challenges that they pose. The remainder of this chapter is organized as follows. Section 2 focuses on GBs, whereas section 3 analyses SIBs. Section 4 discusses the benefits, risks, and challenges of both instruments. Section 5 presents our conclusions.

2. GREEN BONDS

2.1 Structure and Participants

From a financial perspective, GBs' characteristics are identical to those of regular, fixed-income bonds. Accordingly, the issuer (i) raises a fixed amount of capital from investors on the issue date, (ii) reimburses the nominal amount on the maturity dates, and (iii) regularly pays the agreed interests throughout the life of the bond. The key difference between a standard bond and a GB from the same issuer is the issuer's commitment to exclusively allocate the raised capital to financing green projects, assets or business activities. The earmarking of the proceeds is the unique feature of a GB. To what extent a project can be considered green is inevitably an ongoing evaluation process that follows scientific and technical progress. Accordingly, the recent significant increase in the GB market has prompted the debate on the definitions, assessment methodologies and reporting principles needed to improve GBs' transparency and comparability. In June 2016, the Executive Committee of the Green Bond Principles (GBPs)[1] released the updated version of the voluntary process guidelines for issuing GBs. The 2016 GBPs are still framed within four components. The first is the use of proceeds. The bond's documentation should appropriately describe the utilization of the bond's proceeds. The issuer should provide and if feasible, quantify the environmental impact of the financed project. The GBPs identify broad categories of eligible green projects, belonging to four main areas of concern (climate change, natural resource depletion, loss of biodiversity and pollution control). The GBPs do not provide a definition of an eligible green project but consider existing criteria developed by independent institutions. The Climate Bonds Initiative (CBI)[2] has carried out the most relevant industry initiative by defining a taxonomy that identifies green standards under each category of the GBPs. The second component refers to the process for project evaluation and selection. The selection and evaluation of the green project should be performed with high-level transparency and possibly supported by an external reviewer's supplementary analysis. The issuer should outline (i) the process that states how the project fits into the eligible green areas; (ii) the related eligibility criteria; and (iii) the relevant and possibly measurable environmental impact. The third component deals with the management of proceeds. The key element to verify the proper use of the proceeds is the implementation of internal tracking methods that account for the allocation of funds. Various methods are appropriate; the GB proceeds could be credited to a sub-account, moved to a sub-portfolio, or transferred to a separate bank account. The issuer has to outline (i) the process implemented to transparently track the use of the proceeds and (ii) the periodic information disclosure. An external review to verify the internal tracking method is suggested. Lastly, the fourth component relates to the reporting. The GBPs recommend that the GB's issuer should regularly provide both the list and a synthetic description of the financed projects, together with the expected environmental impact. Leading international financial institutions have developed a harmonized framework for impact reporting (ICMA, 2015), which should at least yearly disclose quantitative and qualitative information on (i) when, how long, and according to which process the project should be included in the report; (ii) the amount of the proceeds allocated to eligible projects; (iii) the ex-ante estimate of the project's expected environmental impact; and (iv) when possible, the justified ex-post verification of the completed project's impact.

Within the above-mentioned framework and from a financial perspective, it is possible to identify the two types of GBs. The first type can be defined as a use of proceeds bond (a standard recourse-to-the-issuer debt obligation). The allocation of raised funds targets green projects, while the reimbursement of the GB is backed by all assets of the issuer. This plain vanilla issuance is the most commonly used GB structure. Technically, this type of GB is said to be *pari passu* with conventional obligations of the issuer so that at the issuance no price difference from any other plain vanilla bond from the same issuer is warranted. On one hand, issuers are unable to justify to investors a lower remuneration through green labelling of the bond (BNEF, 2015). On the other hand, investors are unable to express their demand for a higher yield because they are not exposed to additional risks of the financed green project as they finance the issuer's total assets. A few exceptions emerge. As recent research shows, on the secondary market, investors are paying a premium to acquire GBs (OECD and Bloomberg Philanthropies, 2015). This trend has been increasing over time and could be due to opportunistic pricing that follows from the combination of a strong GB demand from environment-focused funds and a constrained GB supply. From a ratings perspective, there is no difference between a standard and a use-of-proceeds GB (KPMG, 2015). The second type of GB can be defined as a use-of-proceeds revenue bond (a non-recourse debt obligation in which specific cash flows are pledged as the basis for GB repayment). Under this type of bond, two subcategories can be specified: the green use-of-proceeds project bond and the green use-of-proceeds securitized bond. The green use-of-proceeds project bond is a project bond for a single project or multiple eligible projects, whose specific revenue cash flows are exclusively allocated to the investors. It may also be issued by a special purpose entity, which refers to a specific project, without recourse to the issuer. The green use-of-proceeds securitized bond is a bond collateralized by a collection of many eligible projects/assets, including covered bonds, asset-backed securities and other structures. The repayment of the GB is ensured by the cash flows generated by the underlying assets.

According to the Organisation for Economic Co-operation and Development (OECD) and Bloomberg Philanthropies (2015), there is a small but significantly growing number of GB issuances whose reimbursement is related to the cash flows generated by the underlying projects. From a financial perspective, the most appropriate projects for the issuance of a use-of-proceeds revenue GB are generally those with high upfront costs but low, long-term and stable maintenance costs. Typical suitable projects guarantee a long-term revenue stream, such as energy production investments combined with a power purchase agreement. When a project's cash flows are implicitly more volatile, a more complex GB structure has to be defined and, potentially, the recourse to an external credit enhancer is required. Moreover, the ratings of a use-of-proceeds revenue bond are lower than those of a vanilla GB, in recognition of the greater risk. The development of a more creative bond structuring, such as green securitization, could be necessary to fund projects with less stable cash flows, such as forest bonds.

Regarding technical characteristics, GBs do not show a typical duration; so far, they are issued with a duration ranging from less than one year to over ten years (CBI, 2016).

A GB's considerable flexibility is reflected in the fact that the green eligibility criteria are not traced to the issuer's profile but are linked only to the financed project. Consequently, although multilateral development banks originally dominated the market, since 2012 various financial and non-financial sectors' issuers have been observed as active players in the

GB market (see subsection 2.2). Nevertheless, the development of the GB market continues to be peculiarly driven by investor demand. In 2008, the World Bank (WB) issued the second GB in response to a specific demand from Scandinavian pension funds, which were committed to effectively integrating ESG criteria into their entire business and aimed to ensure the long-term positive social and environmental sustainability of their investment returns. From the issuer's perspective, the GB issuance could consequently be justified by the opportunity to reach new investors (mostly institutional ones) that are considered cognizant of responsible investments simply because they have integrated ESG criteria into their portfolio allocation processes. To date, the investor base has enlarged to include both institutional (asset managers, insurance companies and pension funds) and corporate types. To satisfy an emerging retail demand, GB issuances have recently been offered to retail investors, such as the solar asset backed securities (ABS) structured by the US company SolarCity in 2016.

Reputational risk is an important issue in the GB market as investors need to be confident that the funds are being used for eligible green projects. To avoid subjective judgments or expensive due diligence checks, the issuer can obtain an external review. Taking the view of KPMG (2015), the external assessment could consist in a second opinion approach or take the form of an independent third-party assurance. Second-opinion assessment is an ex-ante external party review, typically conducted by an environmental consultant, focusing on the criteria applied to select green projects. Second opinions give investors confidence about the issuers' stated intention to invest in appropriate areas, but they do not address whether or not the issuers keep their promise. Providers of second opinions could be ESG research service providers (such as Oekom, Sustainalytics and Vigeo) or scientific experts, such as the Swedish Centre for International Climate and Environmental Research Oslo (CICERO). An independent third-party assurance is a certification based on an external green assessment standard. This is the most rigorous review; it can be performed both ex ante and ex post and is typically conducted by professional auditors, in line with professional standards of relevant quality and independence. The independent third-party assurance provides investors with the highest level of confidence in the issuer's appropriate governance structures to select, monitor and report both the use of the proceeds and the impacts of eligible projects. Regarding climate-related projects, the CBI released the Climate Bond International Standards (CBS) and the Certification Scheme to provide assurances that funds raised using the Climate Bond Certified mark are being allotted to low-carbon resilient (LCR) projects. To date, approved third-party assurance providers under the CBS include (among others) audit firms (such as KPMG and Ernst

& Young), as well as ESG research service providers (such as Oekom, Sustainalytics, Vigeo and DNV GL).

2.2 The Labelled GB Market

Our analysis is based on all self-labelled GBs (LGBs), tracked by the CBI in a dataset that is continuously updated and freely available on its website. Note that a much larger, unlabelled bond market finances green projects. However, LGB issuance has grown rapidly in recent years, representing an increasing proportion of the whole market. As of June 2016, the unlabelled climate-aligned bond universe stood at US$694 billion, whereas the outstanding LGBs amounted to US$118 billion, comprising 17 per cent of the total GB market (CBI, 2016).

The CBI's main dataset information refers to (i) the issuer's name; (ii) the issue date, volume, currency, and maturity date; and (iii) a second opinion (the reviewer's name and the review document). Our elaboration aims to emphasize both the emerging trends in the types of issuers and the main features of the issuances.[3] To allow for comparability, we convert all issuances to US dollars.

Regarding the LGB issuers' profiles (Figure 9.1), from 2007 to 2011,

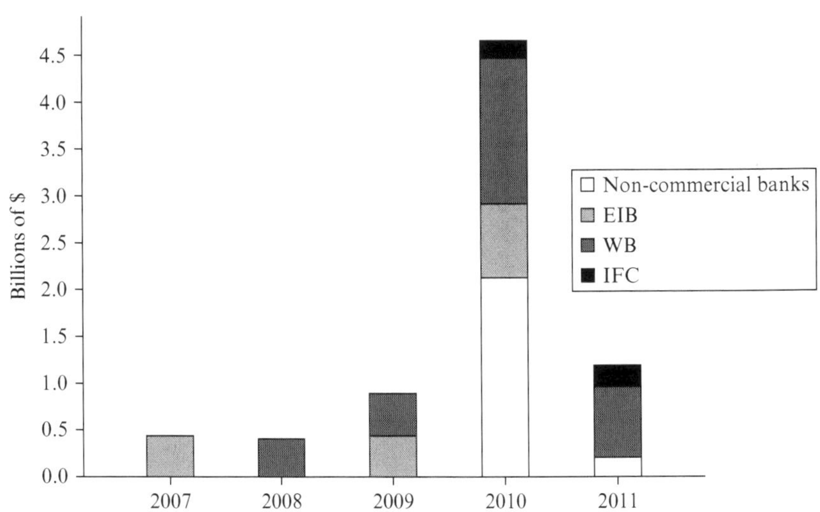

Source: Authors' elaboration from Climate Bonds Initiative (CBI).

Figure 9.1 Annual labelled green bonds' issuance by issuer's sector (2007–2011)

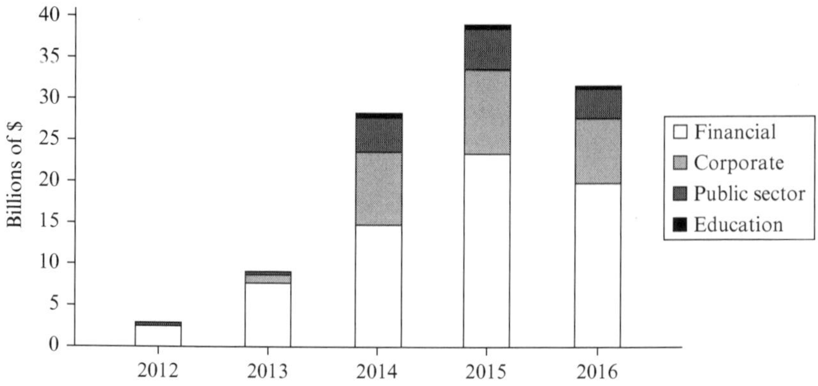

Source: Authors' elaboration from Climate Bonds Initiative (CBI).

Figure 9.2 Annual labelled green bonds' issuance by issuer's sector (2012–mid-2016)

supranational organizations and non-commercial banks (typically development banks) had monopolized the LGB issuances. The pioneering issuers had been the European Investment Bank (EIB) and the WB, which overall issued US$1.8 billion through only six LGBs. In 2010, the International Finance Corporation (IFC) became an active and major player in the market. Other development banks' issuances have constantly grown; the most relevant LGB issuers have been the Asian Development Bank, the Nordic Investment Bank and the African Development Bank. Although new issuers have entered the market, its size has remained small; in total, 92 LGB issuances (59 in 2010 and 33 in 2011) only amounted to US$5.5 billion.

Since 2012, there has been a sharp rise in the LGB market (Figure 9.2). The market has grown rapidly since 2013, with issuances totalling US$42 billion in 2015, almost quadrupling the US$11 billion issued in 2013. Until the end of May 2016, issuances amounted to over US$28 billion, and the CBI estimates that the 2016 figure could reach US$100 billion. Although the financial sector remains important in meeting LGB demand, new issuers have entered the market. In March 2012, the French region Île-de-France issued the first municipal LGBs (also called muni bonds). Since then, the largest issuers have been EU and US municipalities, such as Stockholm Lans Landsting, New York and Massachusetts, and over US$13.6 billion muni LGBs have been issued. The first corporate LGBs were issued by Electricité de France (EDF) in November 2013, and an increasing number of issuances have appeared in subsequent years,

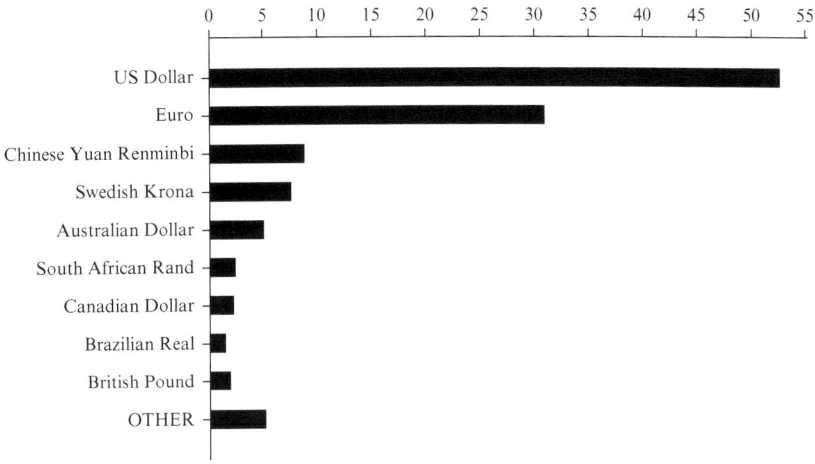

Source: Authors' elaboration from Climate Bonds Initiative (CBI).

Figure 9.3 Total labelled green bonds' volume by currencies (2007–mid-2016)

totalling almost US$28 billion up to June 2016, with a peak in 2015. In September 2014, the new theme of green property for universities emerged, with the Massachusetts Institute of Technology (MIT) issuing the first LGB to refinance green buildings, followed by other US public universities and schools in 2015 and 2016. Banks' issuances climbed steadily to over US$23 billion in 2015, and financial issuers (aggregated in Figure 9.2) have been enhanced by new players. In 2012, commercial banks' issuances started growing constantly. Credit Agricole is an early and the most active issuer; others include the Bank of America, ABN AMRO and Yes Bank.

The issuances are diversified by currency (see Figure 9.3). The bulk of LGB issuances consists of US dollars and Euros. China's yuan renminbi ranks third, due to the 2016 large issuances of over US$ 8 billion by Chinese issuers, mainly development banks. To date, 23 currencies are represented, reflecting the increasing participation of development banks that issue small LGBs in local currencies (such as the Colombian peso, the Indian rupee, and the Malaysian ringgit).

Table 9.1 highlights the main features of the LGBs, classified by type of issuer and in ascending order by year of the first LGB issuance. Outstanding LGBs totalled 701 issuances, amounting to US$118.5 billion as of mid-June 2016. The average LGB maturity term is around five years; in contrast, approximately 70 per cent of the unlabelled GB market has a tenure of ten years or more (CBI, 2016). Almost 60 per cent of LGBs

Table 9.1 The labelled green bonds (LGBs) market by issuer's sector

Issuer's sector	First issuance year	Total LGBs issuances				Total LGBs with second opinion		
		Nr	Volume (US$ bn)	Average size (US$ bn)	Average maturity (year)	%	Most significant external reviewer (ID and %)	
1. Financial	**2007**	**437**	**75.5**	**0.17**	**6.1**	72	**CICERO**	**75**
EIB	2007	50	12.7	0.25	6.7	100	KPMG*	100
WB	2008	129	8.8	0.07	6.6	98	CICERO	100
IFC	2010	35	4.8	0.14	4.7	100	CICERO	100
Non-commercial banks	2010	154	37.6	0.24	6.6	59	CICERO	81
Commercial banks	2012	69	11.7	0.17	4.6	91	Sustainalytics	71
2. Public sector	**2012**	**92**	**13.7**	**0.15**	**6.3**	**51**	**CICERO**	**76**
3. Corporate	**2013**	**159**	**28.0**	**0.18**	**6.5**	**34**	**DNV GL**	**33**
Fully green-oriented	2013	127	17.8	0.14	6.9	35	DNV GL	39
Not fully green-oriented	2014	32	10.2	0.32	4.9	31	Vigeo	33
4. Education	**2014**	**13**	**1.3**	**0.10**	**20.3**	–	–	–
All sectors	**2007**	**701**	**118.5**	**0.16**	**5.1**	**59**	**CICERO**	**68**

Note: * Information from CBI (2016).

Source: Authors' elaboration from Climate Bonds Initiative (CBI).

are evaluated by a second-party opinion; CICERO is the most significant provider of external reviews.

As of mid-June 2016, the financial sector had issued 437 LGBs amounting to over US$75 billion. Non-commercial banks dominate the sector, in terms of both the number of issuances (154) and the volume (US$37.6 billion), while commercial banks' LGBs show on average a shorter maturity term (4.6 versus 6.6 years) and a smaller size (US$0.17 billion versus US$0.24 billion). Historical players tend to structure LGBs differently; the WB's issuances are more than double those of the EIB's (129 versus 50), but the total outstanding amount is smaller (US$8.8 versus US$12.7 billion). These figures reflect the WB's global issuances of small LGBs.

The public sector was the second player that entered the LGB market in 2012. Since then, 92 LGBs (muni bonds) have been structured, totalling US$13.7 billion and with an average maturity term over six years. This broad category includes LGBs used to finance an extensive range of projects, such as urban railroads, renewable energy, sewage treatment and recycling. Accordingly, muni bonds' features differ considerably in terms of volume and maturity date. Infrastructure muni bonds show typically longer maturity terms (up to 20 years), whereas transport muni bond issuances have a larger average volume (US$0.28 billion versus US$0.11 billion in water- and energy-related LGBs).

The third to enter the market in 2013, corporate issuers are the second players in the LGB market, in terms of both the number of issuances (159) and the volume (US$28 billion). Most of the corporate issuances (127) are structured by firms that are fully active in green-related sectors. The LGBs issued by corporations that are not exclusively involved in green investments first appeared in 2014, and since then have amounted to 32 issuances and over US$10 billion. Although overall corporate issuances have steadily increased, corporate LGBs tend to remain small in size, with only three issuances exceeding US$1 billion.

The education sector is the newest entity to enter the market. After the private MIT issuance in 2014, LGB issuances in this sector are currently mainly structured by US public universities (such as Cincinnati, Arizona and Virginia) and other institutions (such as the San Diego Unified School District and the Chicago Board of Education). The proceeds are essentially used to finance green buildings, the average size is very small (US$0.1 billion), and the maturity term is lengthy (over 20 years).

Regarding second opinion providers, CICERO is the most active reviewer, evaluating almost three-quarters of the issuances of the public sector, all WB and IFC issues, and almost 80 per cent of the LGBs issued by non-commercial banks. Sustainalytics is the leader in commercial banks' issuances (71 per cent). The EIB exclusively refers to KPMG reviews, while DNV GL reviews almost one-third of corporate LGBs. The LGBs in the education sector do not seem to seek a second opinion.

Regarding the largest issuers, since 2007, the EIB and the WB, as the pioneering players, have ranked first and second, respectively. The EIB has issued the largest amount of LGBs to date (over US$17 billion) and was the top issuer in 2014 and 2015 (CBI, 2016). However, over the last few years, interesting new trends have emerged. First, the increasing role of the German development bank KfW indicates its explicit mandate in Europe; with over US$6 billion issuances up to June 2016, KfW occupies the third place after eight issuances since 2014. Second, 2016 is a bumper year for Chinese issuers; with only two issuances worth over US$5 billion, the Shanghai Pudong Development Bank was the largest issuer in 2016 and ever. Third, a few large corporations' issuances continue to grow. Among these, Apple's US$1.5 billion LGB in 2016 is the largest GB issued by a US corporation. Apple aims to minimize the environmental impact of business processes by focusing on renewable energy, resource conservation efforts and green buildings. The major corporate players' role shows how the GB market is also becoming of significant interest for firms that are not fully devoted to green issues but are keen to adapt their business processes towards a low carbon economy.

3. SOCIAL IMPACT BONDS

3.1 Structure and Participants

The SIBs are financial instruments issued by using a financial technique, which have mostly been developed in the UK, the US, Australia and Canada[4] since 2010. Within a few years, over 20 SIBs (and development impact bonds [DIBs])[5] have been prepared worldwide, covering several sectors.[6] Despite this growth and the interest in these innovative instruments that has been shown by local governments and different international organizations, so far the amount of capital raised remains minimal relative to their potential, at around US$100 million (SIIT, 2014a).

The SIBs are payment-by-results instruments that involve a contract between public or non-profit service providers and private investors that provide upfront funding for interventions to improve specific targeted social outcomes (Warner, 2013). Figure 9.4 illustrates the basic functioning of a SIB, with the following steps:

1. Investors pay the initial cost (the investment) to finance (partly or fully) the social project.

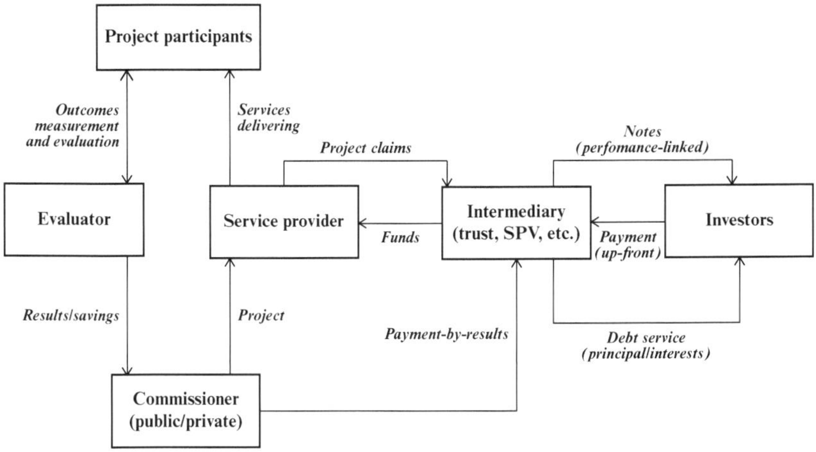

Source: Authors' elaboration.

Figure 9.4 The functioning of a SIB

2. The service provider realizes the commissioned project by delivering the social services.
3. Investors obtain their investment returns when the contracts meet their payment trigger points (the results are achieved).

This complex process involves several actors. The commissioner, typically a public service provider (such as a government or a local authority) or a non-profit organization, is interested in undertaking the project that can bring social benefits. However, it lacks the financial resources needed to implement the project (or does not intend to allocate the financial resources at its disposal). For this reason, the commissioner appeals to private investors to finance the project. If the project's outcomes are achieved, the commissioner will make payments to investors by drawing from the future cost savings that the realization of the project and the achievement of its objectives allow. The commissioner usually sets the terms of the arrangement but ultimately cedes almost all control to an intermediary (making the process design crucial and difficult) (Warner, 2013).

The social service provider carries out the project by implementing the social programme and delivering the social services to the target participants.

Investors pay the up-front cash to finance the programme and receive payments (interest plus principal) if the target outcomes are achieved.

The capital necessary to implement the programme can be raised according to several schemes, based on the risk-return profile that different kinds of investors are willing to achieve. Investors interested in SIBs can be private or non-profit investors, including foundations, high net worth individuals and philanthropists, banks and other financial service firms, and intermediaries (OECD, 2015). To date, the most active social impact investors have been high net worth individuals and family offices (OECD, 2015). Being more flexible in positioning across the risk-return spectrum, foundations have also played an important role (by building the market infrastructure, such as the Rockefeller Foundation, or providing 'catalytic' capital) in the social impact investment market (OECD, 2015). Private investors can range from those who are willing to provide funding for organizations that are unable to generate market returns to more traditional investors interested in having a social impact as well (OECD, 2015). Targeted investors could be institutional investors, such as pension funds, with long-term liability structures and regulated rating requirements for their investments. The past decade has also witnessed individual investors' growing interest in tackling social issues at the local level (OECD, 2015). The investors' interest is related to their objectives (social versus other objectives), their type of liability structures (long-term versus short-term), their risk appetite, their need for portfolio diversification, and other types of needs (for instance, the need for compliance with some social ratings criteria). Other things being equal, the investors' interest increases in the presence of a robust SIB contract, a service provider and an evaluator with a strong reputation. In the presence of critical mass, adequate infrastructure and specialized intermediaries, the investment is facilitated by the creation of social impact funds.[7]

An intermediary coordinates the programme and the bond issuance. In several transactions, the intervention of a trustee or a special purpose vehicle (SPV) is required. The intermediary can be considered the vehicle itself or its manager. In a broad sense, the intermediary is the subject that mitigates the information asymmetries between investors and other actors, such as the service provider and the government. Intermediaries can have both a non-financial and a financial nature. When a financial institution intervenes, it can also contribute by reducing the transaction costs (such as those for preparing the contracts), which are typically high in SIBs, structuring the deals, creating liquidity for the market, facilitating payment mechanisms (agent), and managing the funds. Typically, the social impact investment market is affected by a lack of efficient intermediation, making it difficult to break down historical barriers between philanthropy and investment (Freireich and Fulton, 2009).

The evaluator monitors and measures the programme's results and therefore plays a critical role. The measurement of the outcomes is one of the most debated aspects of SIBs because it determines the project's rate of return and the payment triggers. As emphasized by the literature on performance management systems (Lowery, 1998), some problems may arise due to the difficulty in aligning the goals of different participants. Moreover, potential issues may result from the challenges of uniquely attributing the improvements of the outcomes to the project.

An SIB's life cycle can be imagined as similar to those of other financial instruments (Figure 9.5). During the origination phase, the initiative's feasibility has to be assessed, and the project should be designed. The commissioner, together with the (potential) service provider, should identify the type of financing (choosing between the commissioner's direct financing of the project and indirect financing via an SIB). More sophisticated solutions can be structured in which a non-profit organization invests in the project as an equity provider (but only for a part of the entire project, the equity piece precisely); by doing so the non-profit organization can leverage its investment while the financing of the project is completed by using debt capital via an SIB. The investors' interest is related to the potential returns of the project's outcomes that strictly influence the public sector's cost savings, representing the source of cash flows to the investors.

During the second stage, the notes to be issued have to be structured. Attention is focused on their volume, maturity and cash flows. The volume depends on the type of project. The maturity is related to the type of delivered services (the timing of the investment) and the time lag between the intervention and the possibility to measure its outcomes and the release of savings in the public sector budget. The cash flows are the debt service paid to investors (principal and interest). The repayment period has to be defined also, and its start may be more or less delayed compared to the issuance of the notes. The longer the time lag, the greater the risk perceived by investors, and the higher their expected return on investment (risk premium). The overall risk and the risk premium demanded by investors also depend on other factors, related both to the possible failure of the project itself and to how the project is structured. The first risk factors are related to the possibility that the outcomes' improvements will not be achieved and to the inability/difficulty in measuring the results (impact risks). The other risk factors are associated with the presence/absence of credit enhancement and the (in)completeness of the contracts. From a financial perspective, other risk factors derive from an incorrect pricing of the notes (which determines an inadequate return), as well as the erroneous assessment of the general market conditions that may impact investors' expectations and demand.

The achievement of the results will trigger the payments. Apparently,

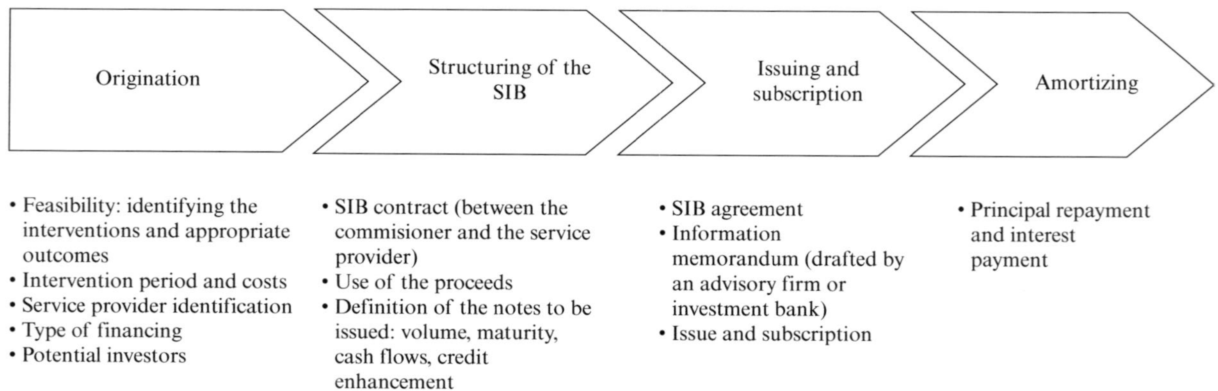

Source: Authors' elaboration.

Figure 9.5 An SIB's process

this feature could be perceived as an element of novelty contributing to increasing an SIB's uncertainty. However, similar instruments have existed in the financial markets for several years. These refer to derivatives, particularly credit derivatives (such as the credit default swap [CDS]) that allow the transfer of the risk from one economic entity (the protection buyer) to another (the protection seller) in exchange for a fee. Similarly, the SIB allows the risk transfer from the originator/service provider (the protection buyer) to investors (the protection sellers) in exchange for a fee in the form of an up-front payment. In both cases, the protection seller's future payments will be triggered by an event, a credit event (for instance the default of the reference entity) in the case of credit derivatives, and the failure to achieve the outcomes in the case of an SIB. As with all derivatives, the SIB permits a better allocation of the risk between the counterparties involved. As with all complex financial techniques involving the participation of different actors and the use of derivative instruments, SIBs can also be considered structured finance instruments.

Before issuing an SIB, the use of the proceeds of the notes should be exactly defined to assure investors that their investment is intended precisely for the project and to help alleviate the informational asymmetries between the service provider and the investors. The transparency with which the project is defined (the completeness and the clarity of the contracts, as well as all the disclosed information) represents a crucial element for the success of the transaction. The more transparent the overall transaction, the lower the risk premium demanded by investors.

During the third stage, the notes are issued, and investors subscribe to them. In best practices, an (informal/confidential) information memorandum is drafted, aimed at soliciting the investors' interest and mitigating the information asymmetries between market participants and the project's proponents. The document discloses the main features of the investment (actors, characteristics of the notes, and risks). Given the SIBs' innovative nature and their special feature that blends social and financial goals, the document typically includes other information (such as the discussion on case studies), with the aim of improving the understanding of the proposed instrument.

The fourth stage consists of the amortizing period, during which cash flows are paid to investors.

3.2 The Case of Newpin SBB

The first one in Australia, the Newpin SBB[8] is a social benefit bond that funds a programme aiming to restore children (who were previously under out-of-home care) with their families and to prevent the need for children

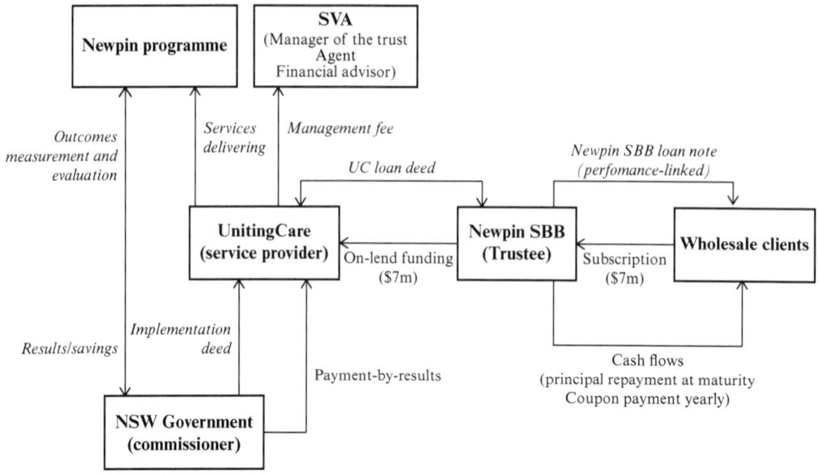

Source: Authors' elaboration based on SVA (2013).

Figure 9.6 Newpin SBB functioning

to enter out-of-home care. The programme's originator is the New South Wales (NSW) Government. The interest in this project comes from both the rapid growth of government spending on out-of-home care and the presence of several stresses for the children concerned (due to their separation from their parents). The idea is that the NSW Government can obtain savings from directly supporting childcare by implementing initiatives that support family reunification and remedy domestic abuse. The investment returns offered by the Newpin SBB reflect the sharing of these savings.

The Newpin SBB is a loan agreement between the investors (wholesale clients) and the Newpin SBB (the Trustee) (Figure 9.6), with the recourse limited to the single material asset of the Trust, namely the UC Loan. The loan note is issued pursuant to the SBB Loan Note Deed Poll, and the aggregate subscription amount is a maximum of US$7 billion. The note has an expected term of seven years and three months, from the targeted financial closing date (June 2013) to maturity (September 2020). Investors pay an up-front cash amount that the Trustee uses to on-lend fund UnitingCare (the service provider), which in turn allocates the proceeds to the implementation of the Newpin programme (under the UC Loan Deed).

The NSW Government and UnitingCare enter into a contract (the Implementation Deed). The government payments to UnitingCare have a payment-by-results nature because they are linked to the expected long-term government savings generated by the programme's outcomes. Likewise, the Trustee's payments to the investors are linked to performance. The principal repayment and interest payments are related to the project's results. Social Venture Australia (SVA) is the manager of the Trustee and receives the fees paid by UnitingCare (which reimburses the Trustee).[9]

The amount of cash flow to investors is linked to the programme's performance, measured by the restoration rate (calculated annually and verified by an independent certifier) – the ratio between the number of children reunited with their families and the total number of children (reunited and not reunited) – based on the number of families that attended the programme.

The principal is repaid upon the maturity by UnitingCare and there is no amortization (bullet). The principal is only partially protected; during the first four years, the principal's losses are limited to 25 per cent (75 per cent protection) and then to 50 per cent after the fourth year. The amount of principal repaid is a proportion determined by the restoration rate; 100 per cent of the principal is repaid if the restoration rate over the full term is greater than 55 per cent, and a minimum of 50 per cent of the principal is repaid on the maturity date.

Interests are paid annually in arrears, with the first payment in 2014. Coupon payments are linked to the restoration rate and are calculated according to the interest rate (and the principal amount). A minimum of 5 per cent is applied over the first three interest payments, with a maximum of 15 per cent.[10]

The key risks for the investors are the following (SVA, 2013):

1. UnitingCare performance risk, depending on the restoration rate;
2. UnitingCare credit risk, due to the limited recourse of the Trustee;
3. Outcomes measuring risks, related to (i) the reliability of the data provided and the calculation of the restoration rate, and (ii) the cohort size because the restoration rate can be impacted by a possible statistical error associated with small sample sizes;
4. Dependence on key personnel risks, related to the capacity to recruit/retain the key staff;
5. Administrative/political risks arising from the following changes that may adversely impact the investment: (i) changes in government policy or in economic conditions that may affect the out-of-home care costs incurred by the government (in this case, the risk is quite limited because if the NSW Government terminates the project, for instance because it considers the programme no longer consistent with its policy strategy, investors would be paid out in full), and (ii) changes in taxation, regulations, laws, accounting policies or valuation methods (so-called regulatory risks);

6. Early termination risk. Several triggers can cause the early termination of the agreement and therefore of the Newpin SBB, prior to the maturity date. The termination payment scenarios are related to the determinants of early termination.[11] Generally, the termination interest payment is based on the restoration rate, while the principal repayment is equal to 100 per cent, with a few exceptions;
7. Liquidity risk, due to the absence of a secondary market (investors rely on principal repayments upon maturity to recover their investments).

4. BENEFITS, RISKS AND CHALLENGES

The GBs and the SIBs enable the achievement of different economic goals, which are separately discussed in this section. They also pose risks and challenges, which we analyse by using a common framework.

4.1 Benefits

The interest in GBs gained momentum at the 2014 Climate Summit, where the finance community showed a strong commitment to becoming a stable partner in addressing environmental issues by supporting low-carbon and climate-resilient investments. As supported by the McKinsey Global Institute (2013), overall green project financing shows a typical debt-to-equity ratio of 70:30. Accordingly, most of the time, a green project can realistically be financed through a fixed-income instrument. Labelling a bond as green could be a win-win solution. From the issuer's perspective, GBs allow funding diversification by attracting investors that otherwise might not have been interested in a standard bond issuance. These new kinds of investors (mostly institutional ones) are aware of responsible investments, often because they have integrated ESG criteria into their allocation processes and are seeking to reduce their portfolios' climate risk exposure. The supply of a transparent GB facilitates the investors' ESG analysis. Despite limited evidence of favourable terms and prices, the attraction of new investors is shown by a GB's oversubscription with respect to regular bonds of the same issuer, such as in the GB issuance of the US State of Massachusetts in 2013.

Another benefit of GBs arises from the possibility of enhancing the reputations of the actors involved. The advantages associated with a better reputation can be justified by the theory of disclosure (Leuz and Verrecchia, 2000), which recognizes the benefits of increasing disclosure due to the reductions in information asymmetry (and the risk premium requested by the investors), agency costs between investors and managers, and other transaction expenses (such as liquidity costs). The GBs build up the reputations of both investors and issuers. As highlighted by Reichelt and Davies (2015), a unique feature of the GB market is the investors' consensus in being associated with a GB issuance. Press releases commonly report an investor's interest declaration to subscribe to a specific GB issuance. By issuing a GB, the issuers demonstrate their commitment to the environment and develop closer relationships with sustainability professionals. Particularly significant is the increasing issuance of GBs by corporations. This shows their deep commitment to implementing sustainable managing processes, controlling their environmental impacts, and optimizing their use of energy and natural resources (see subsection 2.2).

Several commentators point out the main economic goals of SIBs, generally recognized as the possibility to increase the demand for and the supply of social investment, improve the environment for social investment, inspire innovation by incentivizing service providers to enhance their performance, fill the gap in the public financing of social services, encourage the diversity of service providers, and implement a market discipline that rewards effective service providers (Bolton and Savell, 2010; Cabinet Office, 2013; Sinclair et al., 2014). Other authors highlight the critical issues related to such instruments, mainly linked to the unintended consequences for the third sector and to problems of governance (McHugh et al., 2013; Warner, 2013; Sinclair et al., 2014). We can summarize the main economic goals of SIBs according to the following categories of benefits for (i) the community, because SIBs allow the expansion of the range of instruments that can finance social investment, (ii) charities and social enterprises, and (iii) investors. The benefits to the community have been emphasized (Cabinet Office, 2013; OECD, 2015). Less attention has been paid to the other two categories of advantages.

Charities and social enterprises have to face two types of problems, related to the scarcity of available resources and to the blended nature of their returns (that mix social and financial benefits). The SIBs can help social enterprises alleviate these interconnected problems. The projects realized by these enterprises are typically not profitable enough to attract traditional investors. Consequently, these enterprises need financial support from the government, foundations, or other types of donors on which they often depend. If they find a new way to fund their projects, these can become more appealing for private investors as well, who are interested in different asset classes according to their risk-return profiles. By issuing SIBs, social enterprises can leverage the investments and make these more profitable and attractive for private investors (see Bugg-Levine et al., 2012).

Investors can attain several economic goals by investing in SIBs. First, they can move across the risk-return spectrum and achieve their potential for portfolio diversification. We can think of a technique known as pooling and tranching, typical of securitizations, in which the investment's capital structure can be imagined as follows. The project is in the asset side. The liabilities side has the financial sources. The liabilities can be divided into different tranches, from senior (low risk) to equity (high risk); each tranche has its own risk-return profile associated with a priority in the repayment of the principal and the payment of interest, according to a cash flow waterfall. Investors with the highest risk profiles or a strong interest in a project (such as donors or governments) invest in the equity tranche and earn the excess spreads, where available, while the capital repayment is not expected. Investors with lower risk profiles (typically private investors) invest in the other tranches – senior tranches with the lowest risk-return profiles and the highest priority in the cash flow repayments, as well as mezzanine tranches with intermediate risk-return profiles and lower priority in future cash flows. The SIB represents a middle ground between traditional finance and securitization. It links future cash flows to a project's performance and, as such, represents a form of quasi-equity debt. It behaves similarly to a synthetic securitization (that makes use of CDS) because it permits the transfer of risks from the originator to the investors that are interested in a special asset class and in diversifying their portfolios (such as other forms of financial engineering). Potentially interested investors could include institutional investors or, for particularly risky investments/tranches, hedge funds. To increase the attractiveness of these investments, other variants of the basic structure can be implemented. For instance, social impact/investment funds can be used to increase diversification while attenuating risks. Cash or synthetic securitization of SIBs can be considered as well, which pools and subsequently transfers SIBs to third parties.

The second reason why traditional investors can be interested in SIBs is related to the potential for growth, as impact investment naturally lends itself to identifying areas of new and rapid growth in otherwise mature markets (SIIT, 2014b). Furthermore, mainstream investors can be drawn to SIBs because these behave differently from traditional investments; SIBs and DIBs (designed to earn 7–10 per cent returns) offer the prospect of a low correlation with the rate of economic growth in their country, movements in the local stock market, or interest rates (SIIT, 2014a).

4.2 Risks

The typical risks of GBs are similar to those of standard bonds, while SIBs' risk system is more complex. In an effort to classify the GB and the SIB risks, we distinguish between their common and specific risks. Common risks can be grouped into the following four categories. The first relates to risks typically associated with other types of bonds (such as liquidity, early termination and taxation risks). In both GBs and SIBs, these risks appear higher than in standard bonds. The GBs' and SIBs' illiquidity is extremely high because of the absence of standard contracts and the involvement of investors with specific expertise in structured finance and/or social investment. The presence of several events that can trigger early termination also contributes to increasing the risk for investors. The second type of risks are those typically associated with special players (such as those involved in securitization or acting as protection sellers in credit derivative contracts). We refer mainly to the credit risks of the service provider. These risks arise from the limited recourse nature of the instruments, making the credit risks of SIBs and GBs typically higher than those usually arising for bondholders (with unlimited recourse). The third category of risks includes administrative and political risks. Bondholders and shareholders are typically affected by these risks remotely. In the case of GBs and SIBs, these risks appear relevant when a project's commissioner is a public actor, and, therefore, the life of the project/programme could be affected by political events. The fourth category of risks refers to corporate governance risks. These are related to the complex (and often fragile) corporate governance structure, designed to align the different participants' goals and to create stable conditions to encourage investors' interest. The most prominent examples of corporate governance risks are the financial institutions' litigation payments (Henke, 2016).

The GBs' specific risks are reputational. The main investors' concerns involve situations in which (i) the proceeds are not allocated to an eligible green project; (ii) the issuer's core business activities are unsustainable; and (iii) the environmental impact of the financed project is not documented. To minimize the so-called green-washing problem (when a firm operates in a different manner to the announced green initiatives), issuers should first develop clear GB criteria and then put in place strong GB disclosure, robust internal management processes, and control measures. Moreover, they could consider seeking an independent third-party assurance.

The specific risks of SIBs arise from their special nature. The most relevant are the impact risks, typically associated with equity investment (rather than bonds). These risks are related to the payment-by-results nature of the instrument and include risks that may affect the outcomes, specifically, the provider's performance risks, risks in measuring the outcomes, and personnel risks.

4.3 Challenges

The main challenges in enhancing the diffusion of GBs and SIBs are related to several needs that have emerged, linked to the level of standardization, disclosure and transparency, attracting mainstream investors, and strengthening public incentives.

With reference to standardization, there is a need to develop global standards for definitions, data collection, impact measurement and the evaluation of policies. Further, international collaborations associated with experience-sharing among market players are important; international organizations can play a vital role in facilitating the achievement of these goals (OECD, 2015).

Enhancing disclosure and transparency is crucial for GBs' and SIBs' future development. The importance of labelling has already been emphasized for GBs. Labelling is also relevant to SIBs due to the difficulty in precisely defining the boundaries of impact investing.[12]

The challenge related to the need for attracting mainstream investors is especially pertinent to SIBs. The dialogue with investors (particularly institutional investors) has to be structured in a language that they can understand. Initiatives such as the Global Impact Investing Network create a link between mainstream and social impact investors and help increase awareness and interest (OECD, 2015). Furthermore, given the scarcity of significant and high-quality investment opportunities, more products should be developed across the risk-return spectrum, in which institutional investors can deploy social impact investment funds (WEF, 2014; OECD, 2015). A strategy to attract retail investors is also needed, considering citizens' increasing interest in social investments (Triodos Bank, 2014).

The public sector can perform a catalytic function in the social impact investment market, as well as in the GB market (OECD, 2015). Policy actions can differ, depending on each country's legal system and political context. Some countries have addressed regulatory issues (including specific environmental policy mandates, such as clean energy standards or deployment targets) or encouraged the supply of these instruments through fiscal policies or guarantees and subsidies.[13] Other countries have sustained market infrastructures for social impact investment through the creation of specialized intermediaries, trading platforms and other channels to facilitate the links between the supply of and demand for social impact investment.

5. CONCLUSIONS

In this chapter, we have discussed GBs and SIBs by emphasizing their benefits and risks, as well as the main challenges that should be overcome to encourage the future development of these bonds. To conclude, we focus on the last critical issue that could create obstacles to the spread of these instruments. The GBs and the SIBs are financial instruments designed to boost development by addressing the financial weaknesses of some countries. However, in developing countries, the dissemination of these instruments seems more difficult for two reasons. First, these nations' financial sectors are underdeveloped. Second, their risk systems are more complex, and some risks, such as the regulatory risk, are comparatively higher. Implementing initiatives aimed at solving these problems (such as the development of social exchanges or international standards) is challenging due to the different social, economic, political and cultural contexts in which the instruments have to be applied. It seems insufficient to export US or European approaches; what emerges is the need to consider local specificities to shape the instruments in an efficient and effective way.

The practical and policy implications of our results are mainly related to the risks and challenges of GBs and SIBs. The comprehension of the risks is crucial to achieve their diffusion; we argue that the use of the lens and of the language typical of finance can contribute to pursuing this goal. More efforts have to be made to increase both the (global) level of standardization (by reinforcing international collaborations and experience sharing, also among market players) and the disclosure and transparency associated with these instruments. Efforts and initiatives aimed at attracting mainstream investors appear equally necessary. Our study moves in this direction because it helps to clarify some technical and critical profiles of GBs and SIBs and contributes to increasing the awareness and interest of investors. Finally, it highlights the need to strengthen public incentives, necessary to facilitate the links between the demand and supply of GBs and SIBs at the national level.

NOTES

1. The GPB initiatives include issuers, investors, intermediaries and observers active in the GB market, and is administered by the International Capital Market Association.
2. The CBI is an international investor-focused not-for-profit organization, promoting large-scale investment in the low-carbon economy.
3. The labelled GB figures may differ from other studies due to differences in exchanges rates. Because the issuance's date is missing, we convert each GB's volume at the average monthly exchange rate of the corresponding month of each GB.

4. The first SIB was launched by Social Finance in September 2010 at Peterbourgh Prison to fund rehabilitation services for short-sentence prisoners released from the prison.
5. In DIBs the outcomes payers are foundations and international agencies (rather than the domestic government) (SIIT, 2014a). For the purposes of this work SIB, DIB and Social Benefit Bond can be considered synonyms.
6. Child and family welfare; youth employment and care; helping school drop-outs into employment; drop-out rates from girls' primary schools; recidivism; juvenile justice; teen pregnancy prevention and reduction of teenage unemployment (SIIT, 2014a).
7. Recently, fund-of-funds have been created to provide greater scale and diversity for institutional investors (WEF, 2014).
8. We study this case based on secondary data, mainly from the information memorandum (SVA, 2013) and from the Annual Investor Report (SVA, 2014, 2015).
9. The management fee is intended to cover the general expenses and all the services offered by SVA (such as investor reporting, preparing accounts, managing Newpin SBB payments, monitoring the performance of the UC Loan Deed).
10. The interest rate is calculated as 3% + [0.9 x (Restoration Rate – 55%)]. The interest rate is nil (except in the first three years) if the restoration rate is below 55%. Interests are calculated on a cumulative basis.
11. The triggers are termination: (1) by the Trustee on grounds of poor restoration rate; (2) by the Trustee on grounds of a breach of the UC loan deed by UnitingCare; and (3) of the UC loan deed due to the termination of the implementation deed.
12. The European Social Entrepreneurship Funds regulation provides a label for investment funds that address social issues.
13. In the USA the New Markets Tax Credits, the Community Reinvestment Act, and the Low Income Housing Tax Credit greatly increased the capital available to poorer areas. In 2014, the UK government announced the rates of the Social Investment Tax Relief.

REFERENCES

BNEF (Bloomberg New Energy Finance) (2015), 'Green Bonds Buyers Should Pay a Premium, Issuers Say', Bloomberg Brief Clean Energy&Carbon, June.

Bolton, E. and L. Savell (eds) (2010), *Towards a New Social Economy: Blended Value Creation through Social Impact Bonds*, London: Social Finance UK.

Bugg-Levine, A., B. Kogut and N. Kulatilaka (2012), 'A New Approach to Funding Social Enterprises: Unbundling Societal Benefits and Financial Returns Can Dramatically Increase Investment', *Harvard Business Review*, January–February.

Cabinet Office (2013), *Growing the Social Investment Market: A Vision and Strategy*, London: Cabinet Office.

CBI (Climate Bonds Initiative) (2016), 'Bonds & Climate Change: State of the Market 2016', July.

Di Giuli, A. and L. Kostovetsky (2013), 'Are Red or Blue Companies More Likely to Go Green? Politics and Corporate Social Responsibility', *Journal of Financial Economics*, **111**(1), 158–180.

Freireich, J. and K. Fulton (2009), 'Investing for Social and Environmental Impact: A Design for Catalyzing an Emerging Industry', *Monitor Institute*, January.

Griffin, P.A. and Y. Sun (2013), 'Going Green: Market Reaction to CSRwire News Releases', *Journal of Accounting & Public Policy*, **32**(2), 93–113.

GSIA (Global Sustainable Investment Alliance) (2015), '2014 Global Sustainable Investment Review'.

Henke, H. (2016), 'The Effect of Social Screening on Bond Mutual Fund Performance', *Journal of Banking & Finance*, **67**, 69–84.

ICMA (International Market Capital Association) (2015), 'Working Towards a Harmonized Framework for Green Bond Impact Reporting', December.

KPMG (2015), 'Sustainable Insight: Gearing up for Green Bonds', March.
Lagoarde-Segot, T. and B. Paranque (2017), 'Sustainability and the Reconstruction of Academic Finance', *Research in International Business and Finance*, **39**(Part B), 657–662.
Leuz, C. and R.E. Verrecchia (2000), 'The Economic Consequences of Increased Disclosure', *Journal of Accounting Research*, **38**(supplement), 91–124.
Lowery, D. (1998), 'Consumer Sovereignty and Quasi-Market Failure', *Journal of Public Administration Research and Theory*, **8**(2), 137–172.
McHugh, N., S. Sinclair, M. Roy, L. Huckfield and C. Donaldson (2013), 'Social Impact Bonds: A Wolf in Sheep's Clothing?', *Journal of Poverty and Social Justice*, **21**(3), 247–257.
McKinsey Global Institute (2013), 'Infrastructure Productivity: How to Save $1 Trillion a Year', January.
OECD (2015), *Social Impact Investment: Building the Evidence Base*, Paris: OECD Publishing.
OECD and Bloomberg Philanthropies (2015), *Green Bonds: Mobilising the Debt Capital Markets for the Low-carbon Transition*, Paris: OECD Publishing.
Ramiah, V., B. Martin and I. Moosa (2013), 'How Does the Stock Market React to the Announcement of Green Policies?', *Journal of Banking & Finance*, **37**(5), 1747–1758.
Reichelt, H. and C. Davies (2015), 'Getting to Know the Green Bond Market', April, Cheshire, UK: Pension Fund Service.
Schinckus, C. (2015a), 'Financial Innovation as a Potential Force for a Positive Social Change: The Challenging Future of Social Impact Bonds', *Research in International Business and Finance*, **39**, 727–736.
Schinckus, C. (2015b), 'The Valuation of Social Impact Bonds: An Introductory Perspective with the Peterborough SIB', *Research in International Business and Finance*, **35**, 104–110.
SIIT (Social Impact Investment Taskforce) (2014a), 'Impact Investment: The Invisible Heart of Markets', September.
SIIT (Social Impact Investment Taskforce) (2014b), 'Allocating for Impact', September.
Sinclair, S., N. McHugh, E. Huckfield, M. Roy and C. Donaldson (2014), 'Social Impact Bonds: Shifting the Boundaries of Citizenship', in K. Farnsworth, Z. Irving and M. Fenger (eds), *Social Policy Review 26: Analysis and Debate in Social Policy*, Bristol: The Policy Press, pp. 111–128.
SVA (Social Venture Australia Limited) (2013), 'Information Memorandum. Newpin Social Benefit Bond', April.
SVA (Social Venture Australia Limited) (2014), 'Newpin Social Benefit Bond. Annual Investor Report', June.
SVA (Social Venture Australia Limited) (2015), 'Newpin Social Benefit Bond. Annual Investor Report', June.
Triodos Bank (2014), 'Impact Investing for Everyone: A Blueprint for Retail Impact Investing', September.
Warner, M.E. (2013), 'Private Finance for Public Goods: Social Impact Bonds', *Journal of Economic Policy Reform*, **16**(4), 303–319.
WEF (World Economic Forum) (2014), 'Charting the Course: How Mainstream Investors Can Design Visionary and Practical Impact Investing Strategies', World Economic Forum, Geneva, September.
Whitfield, D. (2012), 'The Payments-by-result Road to Marketization', in A. Silvestri (ed.), *Critical Reflections: Social and Criminal Justice in the First Year of Coalition Government*, London: Centre for Crime and Justice Studies, pp. 22–23.

10. The market premium of sustainability in health-care sector firms

Gang Nathan Dong

'Investor-owned health care organizations have social responsibilities beyond those that typify the for-profit world' (Bradford Gray and Walter McNerney,[1] Institute of Medicine, National Academy of Sciences)

1. INTRODUCTION

The concept of corporate social responsibility (CSR) in general and sustainability management in particular is not new. In his famous essay, Friedman (1970) argues that company executives should concentrate on fulfilling the core responsibility of profit making rather than exercising social responsibility. Yet, it is commonly agreed in the literature that corporate social responsibility reflects the social imperatives and the social consequences of business success; therefore, commercial practice should reflect business responsibility for some of the wider societal good. The precise manifestation and direction of the responsibility, however, lie at the discretion of the company. While the literature on corporate social responsibility is large and growing (e.g., Crane et al., 2008; Lockett et al., 2006), there is scant agreement on what corporate social responsibility is and what it is not, partly due to its complex and dynamic nature (Moon et al., 2005; Carroll, 1999). More importantly, corporate social responsibility is an umbrella term, overlapping with some, if not many, conceptions of business-economy-society relations (Matten and Crane, 2005). Therefore, a more practical meaning of corporate social responsibility could be the one that relates corporate social responsibility to a firm's commitment to sustainable economic development and improving the general quality of life (Holme and Watts, 2000). Dyllick and Hockerts (2002) further transpose the notion of sustainable development to the business level, and define corporate sustainability as meeting the needs of a company's direct and indirect stakeholders (e.g., employees, clients, pressure groups and local communities), without compromising its ability to meet the demands of shareholders. For example, a firm can be seen as contributing to sustainable development by operating its business in a way that increases competitiveness whilst ensuring environmental protection. It is therefore suggested that a responsible approach to businesses should take into consideration the environmental, social and economic dimensions of sustainable development (Branco and Rodrigues, 2006; Elkington, 1997; Carroll, 1979, 1991).

A large volume of research has been undertaken to study the strategic relevance of corporate social responsibility and sustainability principles (Dentchev, 2004; D'Amato et al., 2009); however, its impact on the financial performance of organizations is still not well understood. The relationship between CSR and financial performance can be either negative or positive. On the one hand, from the shareholder theory of Friedman (1962, 1970), CSR is often considered as a costly donation from shareholders to stakeholders that would reduce profits, or a wasteful outcome of agency conflict between shareholders and the manager that is driven mainly by the manager's social preferences or intention to benefit stakeholders. On the other hand, the theoretical literature also predicts a positive relation between CSR and financial performance. From the stakeholder theory of Freeman (2010), Agle et al. (2008) and Jones (1995), CSR can benefit both stakeholders and shareholders because the firm can engage in socially responsible activities to improve operational efficiency and business reputation, brand and trust, and, over time, socially conscious customers are attracted to the products and services and hence help increase the company's competiveness and profitability (Barney, 1991; Hart, 1995; Porter and Kramer, 2006; Russo and Fouts, 1997; Flammer, 2015a, 2015b). While Spicer (1978) reports that 'greener' firms perform better financially, Mahapatra (1984) and Jaggi and Freedman (1992) conclude the opposite, and Aupperle et al. (1985) do not find any relationship between CSR and profitability. Cochran and Wood (1984) report a weak correlation between a firm's CSR reputation index and operating profitability within industry groups, and emphasize the trade-off between industry-focused study and small sample size, because the significance of environmental concerns and managers' perceptions of social responsibilities vary across industries. In addition, the inter-industry variation can be driven by CSR demands from different stakeholders (e.g., consumers, regulators, non-governmental organizations) who often play different roles, more or less proactively in different industrial sectors (Steger et al., 2007). If this were the case, we would not expect to observe much market premium in portfolios consisting of equity securities of 'CSR-oriented' firms randomly drawn from the entire spectrum of industries. The lack of evidence that ethical mutual funds, or more broadly called socially responsible investment funds, underperform their conventional counterparts in most countries as reported in Renneboog et al. (2008) to some extent supports this view.

Given the conflicting results reported so far, determining the extent of firm performance attributable to social and environmental concerns has important implications for the corporate social responsibility arguments. Existing studies using data from all sectors to relate environmental to financial performance may well reflect the significant variations in characteristics of different industries. In this chapter we take a more focused approach to examine firms in a very special sector of the economy often associated with a strong social mission – health-care – and how their environmental reputation is valued, at a premium or discount, in the marketplace compared to other types of firms. Our examination of the market premium of sustainability in health-care-related companies is broadly related to studies of corporate social responsibility (CSR) using data from for-profit companies in the health-care sector, for example, Bear et al. (2010). They consider the health-care firms' KLD rating, an index developed by Kinder, Lydenberg, Domini & Co. (a financial advisory firm specializing in the assessment of CSR), as a key variable influencing corporate reputation. Within the literature studying the relationship between sustainability and financial performance, there are generally two categories: the changes in a firm's financial performance in response to the changes in its environmental performance over time (i.e., time-series analysis) and the changes in the stock price of a publicly traded firm in response to environment-related news such as a US Environmental Protection Agency (EPA) penalty for an oil spill (i.e., event study). For example, when firms announce voluntary participation in climate change programs they experience negative abnormal stock returns, and this could be due to investors' perception of additional costs associated with carbon reduction activities (Fisher-Vanden and Thorburn, 2011). Both Hamilton (1995) and Khanna et al. (1998) report short-term (e.g., 1-day period) negative abnormal returns for firms that reported high levels of emissions in the EPA's Toxics Release Inventory (TRI) database. These studies suffer from several limitations, including small sample size, lack of objective measure of environmental performance,[2] biased estimation using event study of market value,[3] and lack of the detailed control of industry characteristics.

Rather than studying the impact of a firm's environmental performance on its financial performance in a variety of industries, we examine a single sector of firms (publicly-traded for-profit health-care business) to circumvent these deficiencies by eliminating the need to control for industry characteristics that often represent the central features of sustainability and business outcomes. To measure the market valuation of a firm's financial condition and growth potential, we disaggregate the market value of a for-profit health-care firm into its tangible assets and intangible assets and regress the intangible assets (Tobin's q minus one)[4] on this firm's environmental performance measured by total toxic emissions (reported in the TRI) along with variables that control for firm characteristics. In previous studies a firm's aggregate measure of Tobin's q has been used to proxy for firm value and performance. For example, Gao and Zhang (2015) show that income-smoothing firms with higher levels of corporate social responsibility have a greater Tobin's q. The disaggregation of firm valuation into tangible and intangible measures permits us to focus on the intangible or forward-looking effects of corporate social responsibility. Our results, based on accounting information from Compustat, stock returns from CRSP (the Center for Research in Security Prices), and environmental quality data from TRI, show that health-care sector firms are valued at a premium relative to those in other industries; however, within the health-care sector, the market premium is dramatically reduced for firms that produce a higher level of toxic emissions.

The remainder of the chapter is organized as follows. Section 2 reviews the relevant prior research on corporate social responsibility and provides background information on sustainability in the health-care sector. Section 3 conducts empirical analysis and presents the findings. Section 4 discusses the channels through which sustainability practices affect financial performance. Section 5 concludes.

2. SUSTAINABILITY PERFORMANCE IN THE HEALTH-CARE SECTOR

Although, historically, not-for-profit organizations play a unique role in providing health-care services in the US, growing criticism has been raised towards this type of voluntary organization in providing health-care-related products and services. Most of these concerns are centered on cost control (Vladeck, 1981; Brown, 1981), production efficiency (Rossett, 1984), lack of market discipline (Herzlinger and Krasker, 1987), and the exploitation of tax exemption (Hirth, 1997). Therefore, the future success in providing health services and producing health-care products would depend upon a complex, interdependent and synergistic relationship between nonprofit and for-profit sectors (Berman, 2002). Unlike a tax-exempt, nonprofit business, a for-profit enterprise maximizes its profits and distributes them to private investors (i.e., shareholders), and this is what distinguishes for-profits from nonprofits. In recent years, the health-care industries have undergone a number of major transitions as new types of business entities, such as ambulatory care centers, preferred provider organizations, public-private partnerships and not-for-profit pharmaceutical companies, have been created, resulting in blurred boundaries between for-profit and not-for-profit organizations (Wolfson, 1996).

What is more interesting is the phenomenon, as suggested in the quote at the beginning of this chapter, that for-profit health-care businesses are maximizing profits and at the same time motivated by their social goals, although this is not explicitly stated in their mission statements. While 'doing well' is required for a business to survive, it also enables 'doing good' because profitability generates slack resources that can be devoted to social responsibilities (Preston and O'Bannon, 1997). Gradually, more and more for-profit businesses are involved in directly addressing community-wide social welfare issues or corporate social responsibility (Matten and Moon, 2008), and more importantly, 'doing good and doing well have found their perfect meeting place in American health care' (Quinn, 2000, p. 285).

The health-care sector has several unique characteristics that distinguish it from other sectors. First, in health-care, the results of business activities directly affect not only an organization's staff members but also its customers, the patients. Indeed, Anshari et al. (2013) show that the use of an electronic service platform can improve not only patients' satisfaction but also their level of health literacy. Second, managerial behavior is often influenced, if not controlled, by the health-care professions (i.e., physicians and nurses). Health-care professionals can create principles and guidelines for action (Scott and Backman, 1990) and have the power to block changes in this industry (Denis et al., 1996; Ferlie et al., 2005). Third, this sector has generally faced a challenging public relations environment because public reactions to health-care-related issues, such as drug failure, device malfunction, medical malpractice litigation, or simply rising health-care costs, often result in legislative measures to constrain market power that could potentially affect the bottom line. Therefore, senior managers of these companies may be more proactive in managing corporate responsibility initiatives, such as reducing environmental impact and improving clinical outcomes, and at the same time, enhancing financial performance and stakeholder relations (Worley, 2012; Bear et al., 2010; Bartlett, 1974).

Ironically, although the health-care sector has the goal of 'doing no harm', its waste and pollution often pose a real threat to our environment in the forms of toxic chemicals and medical waste, greenhouse gases, air and water pollution and land misuses (Turley et al., 2011; Dussault et al., 2008; Kolpin et al., 2002; Ternes, 1998). For example, the World Health Organization estimates that in a given year, about 15 percent of the total amount of waste generated by health-care activities is considered hazardous material that may be infectious, toxic or radioactive, and which can infect hospital patients, health workers and the general public (Halsen and Kramer, 2011; Weisz et al., 2011). Of the 16 billion injections administered worldwide, many needles and syringes are not properly disposed of afterwards (World

Health Organization, 2015). Because of these negative impacts that health-care has on the environment, it is expected that health-care companies that are committed to sustainable development and effective public-private partnerships in medical and pharmaceutical waste management are playing an increasingly important role in environmental protection (Mohrman et al., 2012; San Francisco Healthcare Working Group, 2007). Indeed, the situation has improved, at least in the for-profit health-care sector. The recent industrial pollution data from the TRI has shown that the total amount of toxic emissions in the US has been rising since 2004 and peaked in 2010, when on average, 0.05 pounds of toxic chemicals per dollar of revenue earned were released into the air, water and land (Figure 10.1).

The lowest rate of pollution (less than 0.005 pounds per dollar of revenue) was produced in the period of economic recession (2001–2003). During the same 17-year period (1998–2014), the level of toxic releases

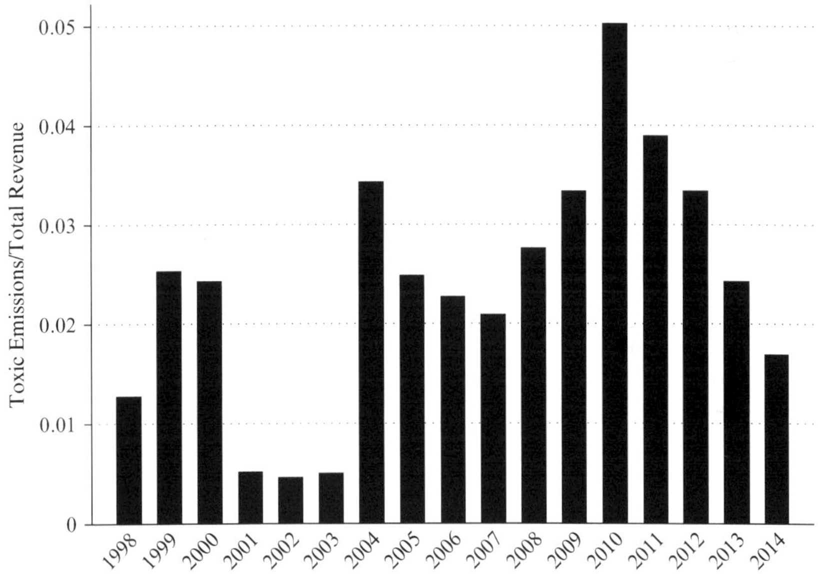

Notes: The emission level of a firm is calculated using the pounds of toxic chemicals released into the air, water and land each year scaled by the firm's total revenues in the same year. The pollution data is from the Environmental Protection Agency's Toxics Release Inventory (TRI). The bars in the graph show the average emission level (pounds per dollar of revenue earned) of all publicly traded firms in the US in each year over the period from 1998 to 2014.

Figure 10.1 Time-series plots of toxic emissions of all publicly traded firms

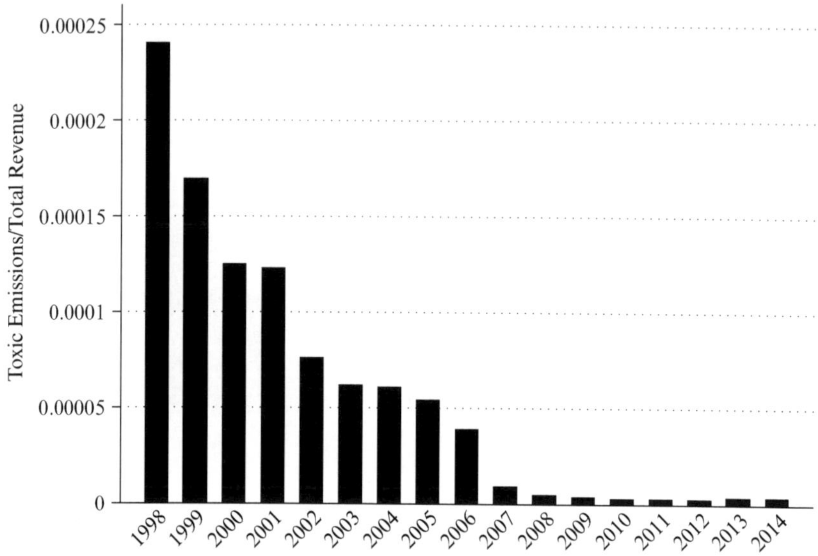

Notes: The emission level of a firm is calculated using the pounds of toxic chemicals released into the air, water and land each year scaled by the firm's total revenues in the same year. The pollution data is from the Environmental Protection Agency's Toxics Release Inventory (TRI). The bars in the graph show the average emission level (pounds per dollar of revenue earned) of publicly traded health-care sector firms in the US in each year over the period from 1998 to 2014.

Figure 10.2 Time-series plots of toxic emissions of publicly traded health-care-related firms

by an average health-care-related firm had been decreasing from 0.00024 pounds per dollar of revenue in 1998 to less than 0.00001 pounds per dollar of revenue in 2014 (Figure 10.2).

Apparently, the rising level of pollution is mainly caused by companies in non-health-care sectors. Figure 10.3 shows that the average level of toxic chemical releases has increased from a little over 0.01 pounds per dollar of revenue earned in 1998 to over 0.06 pounds per dollar of revenue in 2011, and decreased to 0.02 pounds per dollar of revenue in 2014, nearly double the level almost two decades ago.

3. EMPIRICAL ANALYSIS

The Compustat/CRSP databases from WRDS (Wharton Research Data Services) provide detailed financial accounting and stock market

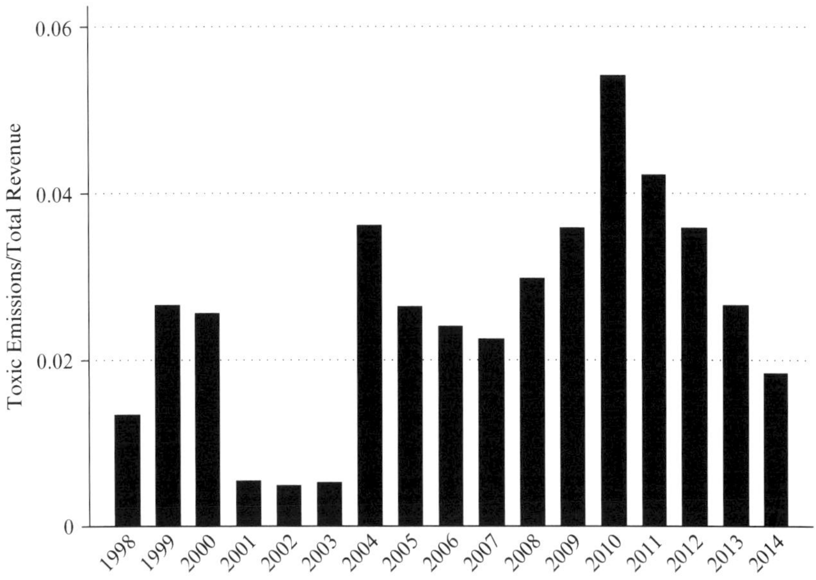

Notes: The emission level of a firm is calculated using the pounds of toxic chemicals released into the air, water and land each year scaled by the firm's total revenues in the same year. The pollution data is from the Environmental Protection Agency's Toxics Release Inventory (TRI). The bars in the graph show the average emission level (pounds per dollar of revenue earned) of publicly traded non-health-care firms in the US in each year over the period from 1998 to 2014.

Figure 10.3 Time-series plots of toxic emissions of publicly traded non-health-care firms

information on publicly traded companies. The TRI database from the US EPA contains data on annual emissions into the environment for more than 300 toxic chemicals. Companies that produce more than 25,000 pounds or handle more than 10,000 pounds of a listed toxic chemical must report it to the TRI. From these databases we create three samples for the period from 1998 to 2014. The first one includes all publicly traded companies in the US by matching firms that reported pollution data to the TRI database to the firms that have financial statement data in the Compustat database and stock returns in the CRSP database. This full sample has 17,186 firm-year observations with 1,558 unique firms over the period of 17 years. The second one is a subsample of the full sample and it includes 904 firm-year observations in the health-care sector. These companies are for-profit hospitals, clinics, long-term care centers, pharmaceuticals, drug wholesalers and retailers, insurers, medical product makers and other

Table 10.1 Health-care sector

SIC code	Industry description
2833	Medicinal Chemicals and Botanical Products
2834	Pharmaceutical Preparations
3841	Surgical and Medical Instruments and Apparatus
3842	Orthopedic, Prosthetic and Surgical Appliances and Supplies
3844	X-ray Apparatus and Tubes & Related Irradiation Apparatus
3845	Electromedical and Electrotherapeutic Apparatus
3851	Ophthalmic Goods
5122	Wholesale-drugs, Proprietaries and Druggists' Sundries
5912	Retail-drug Stores and Proprietary Stores
6321	Accident and Health Insurance
6324	Hospital and Medical Service Plans
8011	Services – Offices and Clinics of Doctors of Medicine
8050	Services – Nursing and Personal Care Facilities
8051	Services – Skilled Nursing Care Facilities
8060	Services – Hospitals
8062	Services – General Medical and Surgical Hospitals
8071	Services – Medical Laboratories
8082	Services – Home Health-care Services
8090	Services – Misc Health & Allied Services
8093	Services – Specialty Outpatient Facilities

Notes: The Standard Industrial Classification Codes that appear in a company's disseminated EDGAR filings indicate the company's type of business. Publicly traded companies of the 4-digit SIC codes above are included in the sample of health-care sector firms.

advanced medical device manufacturers. Detailed SIC code and industry descriptions of these health-care sector firms are shown in Table 10.1. The third one is also a subsample of the full sample, but excluding companies in the health-care sector.

We need to emphasize that our samples do not include not-for-profit organizations, such as not-for-profit hospitals, public health research institutes and foundations, because they are not publicly traded companies and hence we do not have a direct measure of market equity value. To specifically measure the market valuation of a firm's financial condition and growth potential, we follow Konar and Cohen (2001) to define the value of Tobin's q for firm *i* in year *t* as:

$$Tobin's\ q_{i,t} = \frac{Firm\ Value_{i,t}}{Replacement\ Cost_{i,t}}$$

$$= \frac{Equity\ Market\ Value_{i,t} + Preferred\ Stock_{i,t} + Debt\ Book\ Value_{i,t}}{Plant + Equipment_{i,t} + Inventory_{i,t} + Short\ Term\ Assets_{i,t}}$$

Based on Lindenberg and Ross (1981)'s disaggregation of firm value into tangible and intangible assets, the market value of firm i in year t, can be represented as the sum of firm value attributable to the tangible and firm value attributable to the intangible assets:

$$Firm\ Value_{i,t} = Tangible\ Asset\ Value_{i,t} + Intangible\ Asset\ Value_{i,t}$$

By rearranging terms, we can obtain the following relationship:

$$\frac{Firm\ Value_{i,t}}{Tangible\ Asset\ Value_{i,t}} = 1 + \frac{Intangible\ Asset\ Value_{i,t}}{Tangible\ Asset\ Value_{i,t}}$$

Assuming the *Tangible Asset Value* of the firm can be measured as the *Replacement Cost*, meaning the value of intangible assets will reflect the value in addition to the costs to replace tangible assets, Tobin's q is the intangible asset value plus one:

$$Tobin's\ q_{i,t} = 1 + \frac{Intangible\ Asset\ Value_{i,t}}{Tangible\ Asset\ Value_{i,t}} = 1 + Market\ Premium_{i,t}$$

This type of market premium can be due to monopoly power, research and development, advertising effort, brand equity and corporate social responsibility (Lindenberg and Ross, 1981; Jaffe, 1986; Simon and Sullivan, 1993; Konar and Cohen, 2001). In other words, if a firm has none of these, its market value is equivalent to the replacement cost, and Tobin's q will be one. If Tobin's q is greater than one, the market value is greater than the replacement cost, suggesting that it is worth more than the recorded value of the company's tangible assets. In this chapter, we are interested in the 'premium' portion of the valuation and define the market premium or financial performance of firm i in year t as follows:

$$Market\ Premium_{i,t} = Tobin's\ q_{i,t} - 1$$

We calculate the market premium using the firm's market value of equity and book values of preferred stock, debt, plant, equipment, inventory and short-term assets, plotting the change in the average market

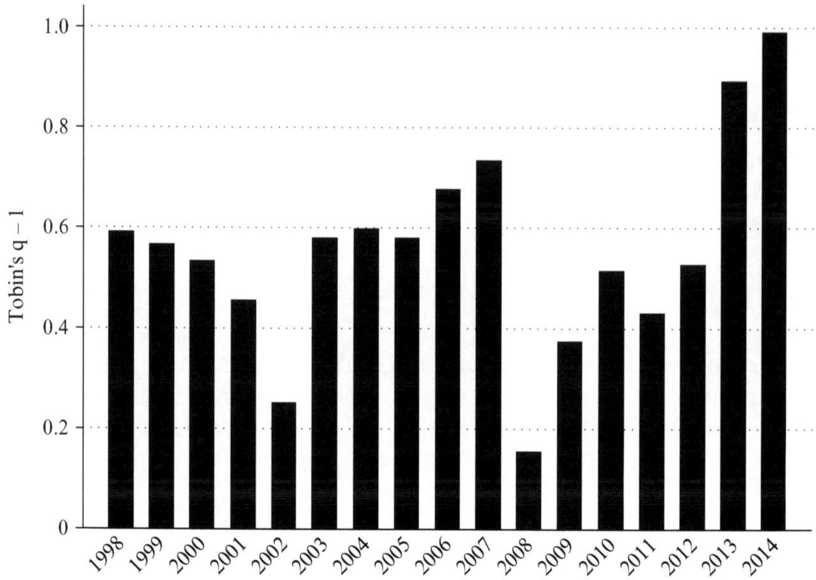

Notes: Market premium of a firm is measured using its intangible asset value, which is the Tobin's q minus one. The market data is from the Compustat/CRSP database. The bars in the graph show the average market premium of all publicly traded firms in the US in each year over the period from 1998 to 2014.

Figure 10.4 Time-series plots of market premium for all publicly traded firms

premium (Tobin's q – 1) of all publicly traded firms in the US from 1998 to 2014 in Figure 10.4. The time-series variation is largely correlated with economic fluctuations. For example, the two lowest observations of market premium are in the recession years of 2002 and 2008.

In the health-care sector, the market premium has been stable over time although the level is almost five times higher than that of firms in other sectors of the economy (Figures 10.5 and 10.6). For example at the peak of the recession in 2008, the market premium is 1.5 for an average health-care sector firm compared to less than 0.1 for an average non-health-care firm.

To estimate the effect of a firm's environmental performance on its market premium, we regress the firm's intangible asset value (Tobin's q – 1) on its environmental performance measured by total toxic emissions (reported in the TRI database) along with variables that control for firm characteristics. The basic specification of our regression analysis is given by:

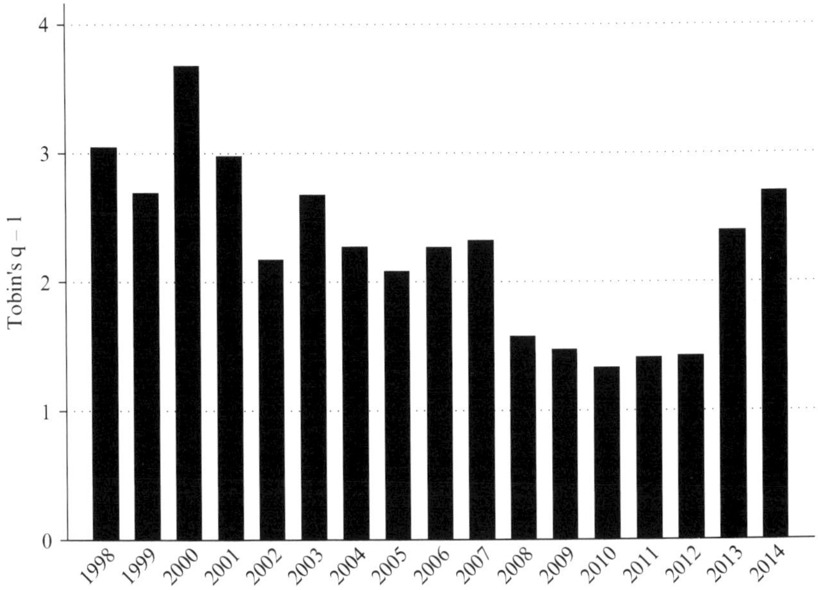

Notes: Market premium of a firm is measured using its intangible asset value, which is the Tobin's q minus one. The market data is from the Compustat/CRSP database. The bars in the graph show the average market premium of all publicly traded health-care sector firms in the US in each year over the period from 1998 to 2014.

Figure 10.5 *Time-series plots of market premium of publicly traded health-care-related firms*

$$Intangible\ Assets_{i,t} = \beta_0 + \beta_1\ Healthcare + \beta_2\ Pollution_{i,t} + \beta_3\ Healthcare \times Pollution_{i,t} + \gamma\ Controls + \varepsilon_{i,t}$$

where $IntangibleAssets_{i,t}$ is firm *i*'s Tobin's q in year *t* minus one. $Healthcare_i$ is an indicator variable with a value of one if the firm has an SIC code listed in Table 10.1 and zero otherwise. $Pollution_i$ is the firm's total toxic emissions (in pounds) divided by its total revenue (in dollars) in year *t*. The social responsibility effect (of being a health-care-related firm) is measured by β_1 and the sustainability effect is given by β_2. The coefficient of the interaction term (β_3) represents the joint effect of social responsibility (health-care business) and environmental performance. We include other variables to control for firm characteristics: size (total revenue, the natural logarithm of total assets), financial risk (financial leverage), growth opportunities (market to book, research and development expenditures), profitability (return on equity) and operating efficiency (return on assets).

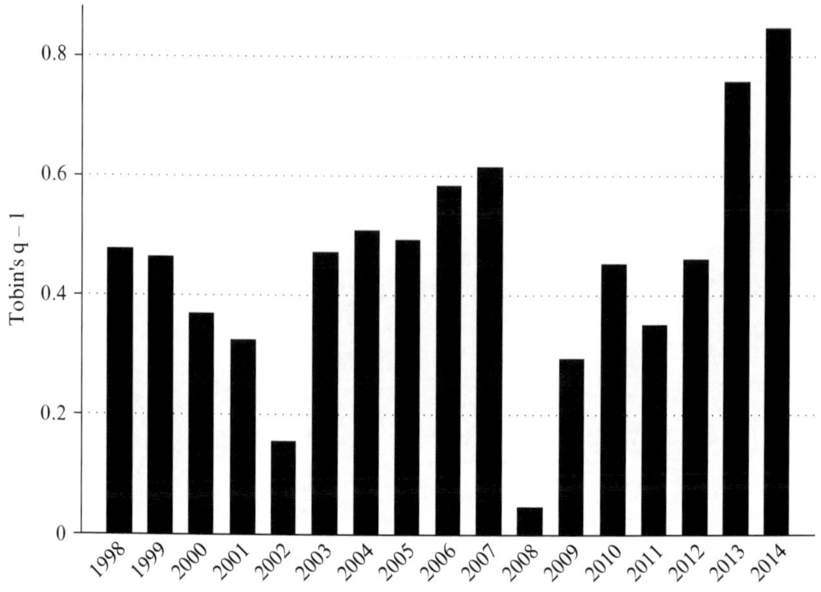

Note: Market premium of a firm is measured using its intangible asset value, which is the Tobin's q minus one. The market data is from the Compustat/CRSP database. The bars in the graph show the average market premium of all publicly traded non-health-care firms in the US in each year over the period from 1998 to 2014.

Figure 10.6 Time-series plots of market premium of publicly traded non-health-care firms

Table 10.2 shows the variable definition and summary statistics. Overall, health-care sector firms are larger, more profitable and efficient, and have more R&D investment, but less risky in terms of financial leverage than non-health-care firms. More importantly, they have fewer toxic chemicals released to the environment than their counterparts in other sectors of the economy, and at the same time have a higher market premium. The average amount of toxic releases of a health-care firm is 0.00059 pounds per dollar of revenue compared to 0.0218 pounds per dollar of revenue of a non-health-care firm, and the t-test statistic of mean difference (-0.0212) is significant at the 1 percent level. On average a health-care firm has a market premium of 1.91, whereas a typical non-health-care firm has a market premium of 0.35, and the t-test statistic of mean difference (1.56) is significant at the 1 percent level.

While the graphic and univariate comparisons indicate that firms in the health-care sector have better sustainability and financial performance,

Table 10.2 Variable definitions and summary statistics

Variable	Definition	N	Mean	Standard deviation	Minimum	Maximum
Revenue	Total revenue	17,186	4360	10,452	3.465	86,656
	Health-care firm	904	8183	$\text{Difference}^{\text{t-test significance}} = 4036$***		
	Non-health-care firm	16,282	4147			
Natural logarithm of total assets	Log(total assets)	17,186	6.798	1.982	1.580	11.67
	Health-care firm	904	7.803	$\text{Difference}^{\text{t-test significance}} = 1.0160$***		
	Non-health-care firm	16,282	6.743			
Financial leverage	Total assets ÷ book equity	17,186	3.074	3.611	1.107	36.22
	Health-care firm	904	2.323	$\text{Difference}^{\text{t-test significance}} = -0.7920$***		
	Non-health-care firm	16,282	3.115			
Market to book	Stock market value ÷ book equity	17,186	2.783	3.269	0.1598	30.83
	Health-care firm	904	4.754	$\text{Difference}^{\text{t-test significance}} = 2.080$***		
	Non-health-care firm	16,282	2.674			
Return on asset	Net income ÷ total assets	17,186	0.04041	0.09519	−0.5428	0.2860
	Health-care firm	904	0.06979	$\text{t-test}_{\text{Mean Difference}} = 0.03101$***		
	Non-health-care firm	16,282	0.03878			
Return on equity	Net income ÷ book equity	17,186	0.07266	0.3855	−2.944	1.819
	Health-care firm	904	0.1403	$\text{Difference}^{\text{t-test significance}} = 0.07147$***		
	Non-health-care firm	16,282	0.06890			
R&D expenditures	R&D expenditures ÷ total assets	17,186	0.02628	0.03953	0	0.2529
	Health-care firm	904	0.06601	$\text{Difference}^{\text{t-test significance}} = 0.04193$***		
	Non-health-care firm	16,282	0.02408			

Table 10.2 (continued)

Variable	Definition	N	Mean	Standard deviation	Minimum	Maximum
Tobin's q	Tobin's q	17,186	1.434	1.177	0.2185	8.109
Market premium	Tobin's q – 1	17,186	0.4345	1.177	−0.7814	7.109
	Health-care firm	904	1.911	$\text{Difference}^{\text{t-test significance}} = 1.559^{***}$		
	Non-health-care firm	16,282	0.3525			
Pollution	Toxic emissions ÷ revenue	17,186	0.02064	0.4125	0	15.32
	Health-care firm	904	0.0005941	$\text{Difference}^{\text{t-test significance}} = -0.02116^{***}$		
	Non-health-care firm	16,282	0.02176			
Health-care firm indicator	1 if a firm in the health-care sector and 0 otherwise	17,186	0.05260	0.2232	0	1
Health-care firm × pollution	Health-care firm × environmental performance	17,186	0.0000312	0.0005456	0	0.02545

Notes: This table reports the summary statistics of variables in the full sample and two subsamples: health-care firms and non-health-care firms. The differences in means between the two subsamples are reported with ***, ** and * indicating the t-test statistically significant levels of 1%, 5% and 10% respectively.

multivariate regression analysis allows us to examine the relationship after controlling for the potential impact of important firm characteristics such as size, leverage, profitability, operating efficiency, growth opportunities, sub-industry and time. Before we present our regression results, we first report the Pearson's correlations of all variables in Table 10.3. An examination of the correlation matrix indicates that correlations between independent variables are generally small. However, there are two pairs of variables having a high positive correlation: (1) total revenue and the natural logarithm of total assets and revenue (0.61); and (2) return on assets and return on equity (0.77). It is not surprising because firms with a larger asset size often generate more sales revenue and both return on assets (ROA) and return on equity (ROE) measure profitability. However including both variables in the model leads to concerns about multicollinearity: as the independent variables become more highly correlated, it becomes more difficult to determine which independent variable is actually producing the effect on the dependent variable (market premium). To be cautious, we remove two variables (total revenue and ROE) from our regression specifications.

The coefficient estimates for the variables of interest and other firm-level controls are reported in Table 10.4. Although we do not find a significant association between the amount of toxic emissions and the market value of intangible assets using all firms in the sample, the positive and significant coefficient (0.918) for the indicator of being in the health-care sector in specification (1) does suggest that health-care sector firms, presumably with strong social responsibility, receive a higher market premium measured by the value of intangible assets (Tobin's q – 1). More importantly, this social responsibility premium is reduced when these firms emit more toxic materials into the environment (coefficient estimate = −9.554). A useful way to interpret these coefficients is to examine the effect of changes in the environmental performance on the changes in the market premium. For example, a 10 percent increase in pollution levels, from 0.00059 to 0.00053 pounds per dollar of revenue, by an average health-care firm in the sample will offset its market premium entirely ($0.918 - 9.554 \times 10\% = -0.037$). This suggests that the market penalizes those whose environmental performance contradicts their social objectives by lowering the valuation that reflects weaker growth potential and management quality. In specifications (2) and (3), we break down the sample into two subsamples – health-care sector firms and non-health-care firms – and investigate the variation of the sustainability effects in both groups of firms. Within the health-care sector, the economic significance is such that a 10 percent reduction in toxic chemical releases will benefit the firm's intangible asset value by 0.24 ($- 2.393 \times 10\%$ in specification 2). Such an

Table 10.3 Correlation matrix

	Revenue	Log total assets	Financial leverage	Market to book	Return on asset	Return on equity	R&D expenditures	Tobin's q	Market premium	Pollution	Health-care firm indicator
Log total assets	0.61***										
Financial leverage	0.03***	0.09***									
Market to book	0.08***	0.12***	0.51***								
Return on asset	0.09***	0.16***	−0.16***	0.13***							
Return on equity	0.09***	0.17***	−0.15***	0.15***	0.77***						
R&D expenditures	0.05***	0.01	−0.06***	0.23***	−0.11***	−0.12***					
Tobin's q	0.06***	0.13***	−0.07***	0.55***	0.23***	0.14***	0.29***				

Market premium	0.06***	0.13***	−0.07***	0.55***	0.23***	0.14***	0.29***				
Pollution	−0.02***	−0.12***	−0.01	0.00	−0.06***	−0.05***	−0.01	0.00	0.00		
Health-care firm indicator	0.09***	0.12***	−0.05***	0.14***	0.07***	0.04***	0.24***	0.30***	0.30***	−0.01	
Health-care firm × environmental performance	−0.02**	−0.06***	−0.00	0.02**	−0.00	−0.01	0.05***	0.03***	0.03***	−0.00	0.24***

Notes: Pearson's correlation matrix is shown with ***, ** and * indicating the statistical significant level of 1%, 5% and 10% respectively.

Table 10.4 Regression analysis of intangible assets and toxic emissions

Dependent variable: Tobin's q − 1	(1) All firms	(2) Health-care firms	(3) Other firms
Pollution	−0.00494	−2.393**	−0.00197
	(−0.36)	(−2.80)	(−0.15)
Firm in health-care sector	0.918***		
	(5.91)		
Firm in health-care × pollution	−9.554***		
	(−2.70)		
Natural log of total assets	−0.108***	−0.0658	−0.0992***
	(−3.67)	(−0.77)	(−2.81)
Financial leverage	−0.00509***	−0.0639	−0.00508***
	(−11.95)	(−1.46)	(−11.86)
Market to book	0.00887***	0.0584	0.00887***
	(10.82)	(1.36)	(10.75)
Return on assets	−1.310***	−4.176*	−1.026***
	(−3.32)	(−2.37)	(−5.77)
R&D expenditures	1.370	−5.646	2.166
	(1.15)	(−1.12)	(1.43)
Constant	0.157	1.994**	0.0650
	(0.38)	(2.94)	(0.15)
Industry fixed-effects	Yes	Yes	Yes
Year fixed-effects	Yes	Yes	Yes
Clustered SE on industry (2-digit SIC Code)	Yes	Yes	Yes
N	17,186	904	16.282
Adj. R-squared	0.539	0.543	0.497

Notes: This table reports the regression results for the relation between a firm's environmental performance and its market premium with industry (2-digit SIC code) and year fixed-effects. The dependent variable is the firm's intangible asset value (Tobin's q minus one) and the independent variable is the firm's total toxic emissions reported in the TRI database. Other control variables include the natural logarithm of total assets, financial leverage, market to book, return on assets and R&D expenditures. Specification (1) uses all publicly traded firms with reported TRI data and the regression includes an indicator variable with a value of one for firms operating in the health-care sector and its interaction term with the firm's total toxic emissions. Specification (2) includes only firms in the health-care sector and specification (3) includes only firms in other industries. Standard errors are clustered at the industry level (2-digit SIC Code) in all specifications and the t-statistics of coefficient estimates are displayed in parentheses. ***, ** and * indicate significance at the 1%, 5% and 10% levels.

effect does not seem to be present for firms in other industries because the coefficient estimate for the pollution variable is not statistically significant in specification (3).

Clearly the results in specifications (1) and (2) in Table 10.4 suggest the existence of a market premium in health-care sector firms; however, these cross-sectional estimates may be subject to self-selection bias, i.e., unobserved heterogeneity in selection is correlated with unobserved heterogeneity in financial performance and business strategy. For example, firms in better financial condition to begin with are likely to engage in socially responsible investment that supports environmental sustainability. Therefore we use the within estimator to difference out firm-level fixed effects as follows:

$$\begin{aligned}Intangible\ Assets_{i,t} &= \alpha_i + \beta_1\, Healthcare + \beta_2\, Pollution_{i,t} \\ &+ \beta_3\, Healthcare \times Pollution_{i,t} + \gamma\, Controls + \varepsilon_{i,t}\end{aligned}$$

where α_i is the fixed effect for firm *i*, which implicitly controls for all unobservable differences across firms. Essentially this method demeans the level of intangible assets of each firm by its average, and therefore, β_3 measures the change in health-care firm *i*'s intangible assets in response to the change in its own environmental performance. Table 10.5 reports the results with firm fixed-effects, and for the full sample in specification (1) the coefficient estimates on many variables fall dramatically in magnitude, compared to the results in Table 10.4. More importantly, the health-care firm indicator, firm size (the natural log of total assets) and return on assets are no longer statistically significant factors in explaining the intangible asset value of the firm. Whilst the overall market premium no longer exists for health-care sector firms, the penalty for deviating from the common sustainability practices is still present (coefficient estimate = −3.599). Specifically in specification (2) which includes only health-care sector firms, when a firm emits 10 percent more toxic materials into the environment, its market premium as measured in Tobin's q − 1 is reduced by 0.1 (−0.970 × 10% in specification 2), meaning the market is willing to pay below the economic replacement costs of a firm's tangible assets. This could imply poor management performance, diminished growth opportunities, and reduced market power associated with the firm's sustainability practices; or it may simply reflect the investors' perception that when a firm pollutes more it tends to have worse prospects than when it doesn't. For firms in non-health-care sectors, this sustainability effect on market premium simply does not exist where the coefficient estimate of the pollution variable is not statistically significant in specification (3).

Table 10.5 Regression analysis of intangible assets and toxic emissions with firm fixed-effects

Dependent variable: Tobin's q – 1	(1)	(2)	(3)
	All firms	Health-care firms	Other firms
Pollution	0.0156	−0.970**	0.0149
	(0.60)	(−3.06)	(0.58)
Health-care firm	−0.00357		
	(−0.08)		
Health-care firm × pollution	−3.599***		
	(−2.99)		
Natural log of total assets	0.0518	0.387***	0.0615
	(0.76)	(36.18)	0.86)
Financial leverage	−0.00163*	−0.338***	−0.00145*
	(−1.73)	(−22.12)	(−1.86)
Market to book	0.00581*	0.291***	0.00519*
	(1.90)	(5.02)	(1.96)
Return on assets	0.320	3.335***	0.278
	(1.12)	(8.03)	(1.12)
R&D expenditures	0.520	2.857***	−0.705
	(0.75)	(8.71)	(−0.70)
Constant	1.004***	−1.780***	1.131***
	(3.40)	(−41.58)	(2.98)
Firm fixed-effects	Yes	Yes	Yes
Year fixed-effects	Yes	Yes	Yes
Clustered SE on industry (2-digit SIC Code)	Yes	Yes	Yes
N	17,186	904	16.282
Adj. R-squared	0.778	0.805	0.762

Notes: This table reports the regression results for the relation between a firm's environmental performance and its market premium with industry (2-digit SIC code) and firm fixed-effects. The dependent variable is the firm's intangible asset value (Tobin's q minus one), and the independent variable is the firm's total toxic emissions reported in the TRI database. Other control variables include the natural logarithm of total assets, financial leverage, market to book, return on assets and R&D expenditures. Specification (1) uses all publicly traded firms with reported TRI data and the regression includes an indicator variable with a value of one for firms operating in the health-care sector and its interaction term with the firm's total toxic emissions. Specification (2) includes only firms in the health-care sector and specification (3) includes only firms in other industries. Standard errors are clustered at the industry level (2-digit SIC Code) in all specifications and the t-statistics of coefficient estimates are displayed in parentheses. ***, ** and * indicate significance at the 1%, 5% and 10% levels.

4. DISCUSSION

The evidence reported thus far indicates better sustainability performance and market valuation of firms in the health-care sector compared to those in other sectors of the economy. However, it would be difficult to attribute the substantial gains in shareholders' wealth directly to the reduction of toxic chemical released into the environment. In the following, we discuss several plausible channels through which the adoption of environmental sustainability practices may improve the financial performance of health-care sector firms.

From the supply side of the market, there are numerous incentives for companies in this sector to adopt greener production methods and processes. In health-care, the influence of physicians, nurses and other clinical practitioners, and the challenging public relations environment have forced health-care business executives to be more proactive in managing environmental responsibility initiatives. In addition, for-profit health-care-related firms are competing with a large sector of not-for-profit businesses partially subsidized by the government (tax subsidization) in terms of customers. Therefore, environmental efficiency improvement is a way to reduce costs (Porter and Van der Linde, 1995). Of course, there is also the possibility of strategic over-compliance (Reinhardt, 2000). Pollution reduction can be a result of over-investment in the environmentally efficient technologies, and the 'overachieved' benefits can be used to influence regulatory authorities to set tighter industrial standards, thereby raising the cost of compliance for other firms (Klassen and McLaughlin, 1996). In the case of proactive management and cost reduction, one might expect a higher level of operating efficiency in this sector, whereas in the circumstances of overinvestment and over-compliance, one might expect a lower level of operating efficiency in these industries. We compare the return on assets (ROA), a measure of asset productivity, in the health-care and other sectors, and find that the average ROA of health-care sector firms is 7.0 percent compared to only 3.9 percent for firms in other industries (the t-test of mean difference 3.1 percent is statistically significant, as shown in Table 10.2).

There are many incentives from the demand side of the market as well; for example, the need to cater to customers, often the patients, who are very sensitive to socially responsible practices and believe that sustainable management is a signal of product quality (Baron, 2008; McWilliams and Siegel, 2001; Reinhardt, 1998; Servaes and Tamayo, 2013), and to satisfy employees who might be committed to an unstated mission of social responsibility and hence to achieve higher employee morale (Peterson, 2004; Vogel, 2005). In the first case, one might expect an increase in sales growth following the adoption of sustainable practices, and in the second case, if employee satisfaction is the underlying mechanism behind the increase in firm valuation, one might expect a higher level of labor productivity in the sector (Turban and Greening, 1997). While it is clearly hard to find a direct measure of higher (or lower) labor productivity from financial statements, the end result will be a better (or worse) profitability. From our results in Table 10.2, the average revenue and return on equity (ROE) of health-care sector firms are 8.2 billion dollars and 14 percent respectively, compared to 4.1 billion dollars and 6.8 percent for firms in other industries (the t-test of mean differences are statistically significant).[5]

5. CONCLUSION

We believe that closely examining the relationship between a company's sustainability practices and intangible asset value in the health-care sector will provide insight into the overall question of whether and how a firm's environmental performance is priced by the market. This sector is competing against both for-profit and nonprofit businesses for scarce economic and societal resources, and is facing trade-offs between financial viability and quality and value for money. Firms in the health-care sector are no different from other firms in the economy with objectives of maximizing both social and financial benefits. Still, companies in this sector are more concerned with social responsibility (Darr, 1997) and devoting more resources to socially responsible initiatives (Hansen et al., 2011). If health-care-related businesses provide products and services with more attention to the needs of society and the environment, the associated costs would reduce the value of shareholders' equity. While the need for social responsibility is apparent, this research does not find a negative relationship between the firms' toxic chemical releases into the environment and the market value of their intangible assets. Instead, health-care sector firms are valued at a premium relative to their counterparts in other industries; however, deviations from the presumed mission (e.g., higher levels of pollution) would have a negative impact on market valuation. This evidence demonstrates the potential and importance of understanding the sustainability and financial performance relationship using an intra-sector study. Although the conclusion drawn in this chapter is based on a sample of publicly traded firms operating in the health-care sector, it is not really unique to the areas of business or industry that these organizations participate in. Rather, the beneficial properties of social responsibility and sustainability objectives and the detrimental effects of strategic deviation from them documented in this chapter extend to other businesses alike, thus providing a basis for all companies to align strategies with sustainability objectives.

NOTES

1. Excerpt from Gray and McNerney (1986).
2. Summarized in Konar and Cohen (2001).
3. Discussed in Binder (1998).
4. Tobin's q can be viewed as measuring the intangible assets of the firm, such as potential growth opportunities, monopoly power, goodwill and the quality of management (Morck, Shleifer and Vishny, 1989).
5. Because on average health-care sector firms have lower financial leverage, 2.3 (i.e., the total assets are 2.3 times the book equity) compared to 3.1 in other sectors (the t-test of mean difference -0.79 is statistically significant as shown in Table 10.2), the higher ROE of health-care firms suggests higher profitability in this sector.

REFERENCES

Agle, B.R., T. Donaldson, R.E. Freeman, M.C. Jensen, R.K. Mitchell and D.J. Wood (2008), 'Dialogue: Toward Superior Stakeholder Theory', *Business Ethics Quarterly*, 18(2), 153–190.

Anshari, M., M.N. Almunawar, P.K.C. Low, Z. Wint and M.Z. Younis (2013), 'Adopting Customers' Empowerment and Social Networks to Encourage Participations in E-Health Services', *Journal of Health Care Finance*, 40(2), 17–42.

Aupperle, K.E., B.C. Archie and J.D. Hatfield (1985), 'An Empirical Examination of the Relationship between Corporate Social Responsibility and Profitability', *Academy of Management Journal*, 28(2), 446–463.

Barney, J. (1991), 'Firm Resources and Sustained Competitive Advantage', *Journal of Management*, 17(1), 99–120.

Baron, D.P. (2008), 'Managerial Contracting and Corporate Social Responsibility', *Journal of Public Economics*, 92(1–2), 268–288.

Bartlett, R. (1974), 'A Plea for Clinical Relevance in Medical Microbiology', *American Journal of Clinical Pathology*, 61(6), 867–872.

Bear, S., N. Rahman and C. Post (2010), 'The Impact of Board Diversity and Gender Composition on Corporate Social Responsibility and Firm Reputation', *Journal of Business Ethics*, 97(2), 207–221.

Berman, H.J. (2002), 'Doing "Good" vs. Doing "Well": The Role of Nonprofits in Society', *Inquiry*, 39(1), 5–11.

Binder, J. (1998), 'The Event Study Methodology Since 1969', *Review of Quantitative Finance and Accounting*, 11, 111–137.

Branco, M.C. and L.L. Rodrigues (2006), 'Corporate Social Responsibility and Resource-Based Perspectives', *Journal of Business Ethics*, 69, 111–132.

Brown, L.D. (1981), 'Competition and Health Cost Containment: Cautions and Conjectures', *Milbank Memorial Fund Quarterly*, 59, 145–189.

Carroll, A.B. (1979), 'A Three-Dimensional Conceptual Model of Corporate Social Performance', *Academy of Management Review*, 4(4), 497–505.

Carroll, A.B. (1991), 'The Pyramid of Corporate Social Responsibility: Toward the Moral Management of Organizational Stakeholders', *Business Horizons*, 34(4), 39–48.

Carroll, A.B. (1999), 'Corporate Social Responsibility? Evolution of a Definitional Construct', *Business and Society*, 38, 268–295.

Cochran, P.L. and R.A. Wood (1984), 'Corporate Social Responsibility and Financial Performance', *Academy of Management Journal*, 27(1), 42–56.
Crane, A., A. McWilliams, D. Matten, J. Moon and D. Siegel (2008), *The Oxford Handbook of CSR*, Oxford: Oxford University Press.
D'Amato, A., S. Henderson and S. Florence (2009), *Corporate Social Responsibility and Sustainable Business: A Guide to Leadership Tasks and Functions*, The Center for Creative Leadership: Greensboro, NC.
Darr, K. (1997), 'Social Responsibility in Hospitals', *Hospital Topics*, 75(1), 4–7.
Denis, J.L., A. Langley and L. Cazale (1996), 'Leadership and Strategic Change under Ambiguity', *Organization Studies*, 17(4), 673–699.
Dentchev, N.A. (2004), 'Corporate Social Performance as a Business Strategy', *Journal of Business Ethics*, 55, 397–412.
Dussault, E.B., V.K. Balakrishnan, E. Sverko, K.R. Solomon and P.K. Sibley (2008), 'Toxicity of Human Pharmaceuticals and Personal Care Products to Benthic Invertebrates', *Environmental Toxicology and Chemistry*, 27(2), 425–432.
Dyllick, T. and K. Hockerts (2002), 'Beyond the Business Case for Corporate Sustainability', *Business Strategy and the Environment*, 11, 130–141.
Elkington, J. (1997), *Cannibals with Forks: The Triple Bottom Line of 21st Century Business*, Oxford: Capstone Publishing.
Ferlie, E., L. Fitzgerald, M. Wood and C. Hawkins (2005), 'The Nonspread of Innovations: The Mediating Role of Professionals', *Academy of Management Journal*, 48(1), 117–134.
Fisher-Vanden, K. and K.S. Thorburn (2011), 'Voluntary Corporate Environmental Initiatives and Shareholder Wealth', *Journal of Environmental Economics and Management*, 62(3), 430–445.
Flammer, C. (2015a), 'Does Corporate Social Responsibility Lead to Superior Financial Performance? A Regression Discontinuity Approach', *Management Science*, 61(11), 2549–2568.
Flammer, C. (2015b), 'Does Product Market Competition Foster Corporate Social Responsibility? Evidence from Trade Liberalization', *Strategic Management Journal*, 36(10), 1469–1485.
Freeman, R.E. (2010), *Strategic Management: A Stakeholder Approach*, Cambridge: Cambridge University Press.
Friedman, M. (1962), *Capitalism and Freedom*, Chicago: University of Chicago Press.
Friedman, M. (1970), 'Social Responsibility of Business is to Increase its Profits', *New York Times*, September 13.
Gao, Lei and J.H. Zhang (2015), 'Firms' Earnings Smoothing, Corporate Social Responsibility, and Valuation', *Journal of Corporate Finance*, 32, 108–127.
Gray, B.H. and W.J. McNerney (1986), 'For-Profit Enterprise in Health Care', *New England Journal of Medicine*, 314, 1523–1528.
Halsen, G. and I. Kramer (2011), 'Assessing the Risk to Health Care Staff from Long-term Exposure to Anticancer Drugs – the Case of Monoclonal Antibodies', *Journal of Oncology Pharmacy Practice*, 17(1), 68–80.
Hamilton, J.T. (1995), 'Pollution as News: Media and Stock Market Reactions to the Toxics Release Inventory Data', *Journal of Environmental Economics and Management*, 28(1), 98–113.
Hansen S.S., B. Dunford, A. Boss, R.R. Boss and I. Angermeier (2011), 'Corporate Social Responsibility and the Benefits of Employee Trust: A Cross-disciplinary Perspective', *Journal of Business Ethics*, 102, 29–45.
Hart, S.L. (1995), 'A Natural-Resource-Based View of the Firm', *Academy of Management Review*, 20(4), 986–1014.
Herzlinger, R.E. and W.S. Krasker (1987), 'Who Profits from Non-Profits?', *Harvard Business Review*, 65, 93–106.
Hirth, R.A. (1997), 'Competition between For-profit and Nonprofit Health Care Providers: Can it Help Achieve Social Goals?', *Medical Care Research and Review*, 54(4), 414–438.

Holme, R. and P. Watts (2000), 'Corporate Social Responsibility: Making Good Business Sense', World Business Council for Sustainable Development: Geneva.
Jaffe, A.B. (1986), 'Technological Opportunity and Spillovers of R & D: Evidence from Firms' Patents, Profits, and Market Value', *American Economic Review*, 76(5), 984–1001.
Jaggi, B. and M. Freedman (1992), 'An Examination of the Impact of Pollution Performance on Economic and Market Performance: Pulp and Paper Firms', *Journal of Business Finance and Accounting*, 19(5), 697–713.
Jones, T.M. (1995), 'Instrumental Stakeholder Theory: A Synthesis of Ethics and Economics', *Academy of Management Review*, 20, 404–437.
Khanna, M., W.R.H. Quimio and D. Bojilova (1998), 'Toxics Release Information: A Policy Tool for Environmental Protection', *Journal of Environmental Economics and Management*, 36(3), 243–266.
Klassen, R.D. and C.P. McLaughlin (1996), 'The Impact of Environmental Management on Firm Performance', *Management Science*, 42(8), 1199–1214.
Kolpin, D.W., E.T. Furlong, M.T. Meyer, E.M. Thurman, S.D. Zaugg, L.B. Barber and H.T. Buxton (2002), 'Pharmaceuticals, Hormones, and Other Organic Wastewater Contaminants in U.S. Streams, 1999–2000: A National Reconnaissance', *Environmental Science and Technology*, 36, 1202–1211.
Konar, S. and M.A. Cohen (2001), 'Does the Market Value Environmental Performance', *Review of Economics and Statistics* 83, 281–289.
Lindenberg, E.B. and S.A. Ross (1981), 'Tobin's q Ratio and Industrial Organization', *Journal of Business*, 54(1), 1–32.
Lockett, A., J. Moon and W. Visser (2006), 'Corporate Social Responsibility in Management Research: Focus, Nature, Salience and Sources of Influence', *Journal of Management Studies*, 43, 115–136.
Mahapatra, S. (1984), 'Investor Reaction to Corporate Social Accounting', *Journal of Business Finance and Accounting*, 11(1), 29–40.
Matten, D. and A. Crane (2005), 'Corporate Citizenship: Toward an Extended Theoretical Conceptualization', *Academy of Management Review*, 30, 166–179.
Matten, D. and J. Moon (2008), '"Implicit" and "Explicit" CSR: A Conceptual Framework for a Comparative Understanding of Corporate Social Responsibility', *Academy of Management Review*, 33(2), 404–424.
McWilliams, A. and D. Siegel (2001), 'Corporate Social Responsibility: A Theory of the Firm Perspective', *Academy of Management Review*, 26(1), 117–127.
Mohrman, S., A.B. Shani and A. McCracken (2012), 'Organizing for Sustainable Healthcare: The Emerging Global Challenge', in S.A. Mohrman and A.B. Shani (eds), *Organizing for Sustainable Health Care*, Vol. 2, Bingley, UK: Emerald Group Publishing, pp. 1–39.
Moon, J., A. Crane and D. Matten (2005), 'Can Corporations be Citizens? Corporate Citizenship as a Metaphor for Business Participation in Society', *Business Ethics Quarterly*, 15, 427–451.
Morck, R., A. Shleifer and R.W. Vishny (1989), 'Alternative Mechanisms for Corporate Control', *American Economic Review*, 79, 842–852.
Peterson, D.K. (2004), 'The Relationship between Perceptions of Corporate Citizenship and Organizational Commitment', *Business & Society*, 43(3), 296–319.
Porter, M.E. and M.R. Kramer (2006), 'Strategy and Society: The Link between Competitive Advantage and Corporate Social Responsibility', *Harvard Business Review*, 84(12), 78–92.
Porter, M.E. and C. Van der Linde (1995), 'Toward a New Conception of the Environment-Competitiveness Relationship', *Journal of Economic Perspectives*, 9(4), 97–118.
Preston, L.E. and D.P. O'Bannon (1997), 'The Corporate Social-Financial Performance Relationship', *Business and Society*, 36(4), 419–429.
Quinn, K.P.S.J. (2000), 'Viewing Health Care as a Common Good: Looking Beyond Political Liberalism', *Southern California Law Review*, 73(2), 277–376.
Reinhardt, F.L. (1998), 'Environmental Product Differentiation: Implications for Corporate Strategy', *California Management Review*, 40(4), 43–73.

Reinhardt, F.L. (2000), *Down to Earth: Applying Business Principles to Environmental Management*, Boston: Harvard Business School Press.

Renneboog, L., J. Ter Horst and C. Zhang (2008), 'The Price of Ethics and Stakeholder Governance: The Performance of Socially Responsible Mutual Funds', *Journal of Corporate Finance*, 14, 302–322.

Rossett, R.N. (1984), 'Doing Well by Doing Good: Investor-Owned Hospitals', *Frontiers of Health Services Management*, 1, 2–9.

Russo, M.V. and P.A. Fouts (1997), 'A Resource-Based Perspective on Corporate Environmental Performance and Profitability', *Academy of Management Journal*, 40(3), 534–559.

San Francisco Healthcare Working Group (2007), Source Reduction Assistance – San Francisco Healthcare Working Group, Annual Grant Report, Report Period October 2004–October 2007.

Scott, W.R. and E.V. Backman (1990), 'Institutional Theory and the Medical Care Sector', in S.S. Mick (ed.), *Innovations in Health Care Delivery: Insights for Organization Theory*, San Francisco: Jossey Bass/Aha Press, pp. 20–52.

Servaes, H. and A. Tamayo (2013), 'The Impact of Corporate Social Responsibility on Firm Value: The Role of Customer Awareness', *Management Science*, 59(5), 1045–1061.

Simon, C.J. and M.W. Sullivan (1993), 'The Measurement and Determinants of Brand Equity: A Financial Approach', *Marketing Science*, 12(1), 28–52.

Spicer, B.H. (1978), 'Investors, Corporate Social Performance and Information Disclosure: An Empirical Study', *Accounting Review*, 53(1), 94–111.

Steger, U., A. Ionescu-Somers and O. Salzmann (2007), 'The Economic Foundations of Corporate Sustainability', *Corporate Governance*, 7(2), 162–177.

Ternes, T.A. (1998), 'Occurrence of Drugs in German Sewage Treatment Plants and Rivers', *Water Research*, 32(11), 3245–3260.

Turban, D.B. and D.W. Greening (1997), 'Corporate Social Performance and Organizational Attractiveness to Prospective Employees', *Academy of Management Journal*, 40(3), 658–672.

Turley, M., C. Porter, T. Garrido, K. Gerwig, S. Young, L. Radler and R. Shaber (2011), 'Use of Electronic Health Records can Improve the Health Care Industry's Environmental Footprint', *Health Affairs*, 30(5), 938–946.

Vladeck, B.C. (1981), 'The Market vs. Regulation: The Case for Regulation', *Milbank Memorial Fund Quarterly*, 59, 209–223.

Vogel, D.J. (2005), 'Is There a Market for Virtue? The Business Case for Corporate Social Responsibility', *California Management Review*, 47(4), 19–45.

Weisz, U., W. Haas, J. Pelikan and H. Schmied (2011), 'Sustainable Hospitals: A Socio-Ecological Approach', *GAIA – Ecological Perspectives for Science and Society*, 20(3), 191–198.

Wolfson, J. (1996), 'Overcoming Challenges to Tax-exempt Status', *Healthcare Financial Management*, 50(4), 58–63.

World Health Organization (2015), 'Waste from Health-care Activities', Fact Sheet no. 253, retrieved from http://www.who.int/mediacentre/factsheets/fs253/en

Worley, C.G. (2012), 'Organizing for Agile and Sustainable Health Care', in S.A. Mohrman and A.B. Shani (eds), *Organizing for Sustainable Health Care*, Vol. 2, Bingley, UK: Emerald Group Publishing, pp. 41–76.

11. Environmental sustainability and inter- and intra-industry variation in stock returns: international evidence

Harjap Bassan, Kartick Gupta and Ron P. McIver

1. INTRODUCTION

Whether, and, if so, where and when, engaging in environmentally sustainable practices is rewarded by the market are debates in the current literature (Dixon-Fowler et al., 2013; Martínez-Ferrero and Frías-Aceituno, 2015). One strand suggests that engaging in environmentally sustainable practices benefits a firm directly through increases in sales, productivity, and efficiency (e.g. Porter and van der Linde, 1995; Russo and Fouts, 1997), increasing firm cash flow and value. Another strand contends that due to the costs associated with engagement in environmentally sustainable practices financially constrained firms are unlikely to benefit from such activity (McGuire et al., 1988), suggesting that such investments are, in net terms, cash flow and value decreasing. However, while the existing studies enhance our understanding of the risk-return trade-off associated with environmentally sustainable practices (e.g. Mănescu, 2011; Girerd-Potin et al., 2014), inter-industry differences in environmental impact are potentially important determinants of their risk-return trade-off (Moura-Leite et al., 2012). Specifically, we argue that the activities of some industries strongly impact the environment, potentially attracting greater attention, while the activities of other industries may not have as great an impact on the environment. This suggests that the direct net benefit available from engaging in environmental-sustainability activities may vary significantly by industry. Therefore, it is not clear whether the undertaking of environmentally sustainable practices will potentially be treated more favorably by the market for some industry clusters than for others, impacting the potential net returns available from engaging in these practices.

In addition to the direct costs and benefits associated with engagement in environmentally sustainable practices, firm's improvements to environmental sustainability may provide indirect benefits by reducing the expected future losses associated with poor environmental performance (Gupta, 2018). Where positive, net indirect benefits available from these activities will increase the relative value of such firms, and in doing so reduce the riskiness and required return of the firm. However, an uneven geographical distribution of activity by industry and differences in the relative concentration of industry sectors by country are features of the global market (McIver, 2012). In countries with lower institutional quality, the expected benefits of engaging in environmentally friendly practices may be reduced, suggesting that the cost of initiating environmental-sustainability practices may outweigh the expected future benefits (Bahttarai and Hammig, 2004; Fredriksson et al., 2004; Welsch, 2004). We therefore posit that country-level determinants may influence both the reward from and incentives to engage in environmentally sustainable practices. This suggests that in understanding the effect on firm-level returns of engaging in environmentally sustainable practices, we need to account for intra-industry variations related to country-level determinants in addition to identifying inter-industry differences.

We investigate the extent to which stock returns differ between firms according to their level of environmental sustainability, and the extent to which differences within the stock returns of these firms are explained by inter-industry and intra-industry (country-level) determinants. In addressing these latter determinants we address several gaps in the literature in this chapter. One is a lack of studies linking industry factors to the financial performance benefits from firms engaging in higher levels of corporate environmental practices. Another is to address the potential for country-level factors, specifically differences in institutional quality, to be associated with intra-industry variation in the firm-level financial performance benefits derived from these practices. Finally, following the call by Gupta (2018), our multi-country study complements the relatively limited literature that provides an assessment of the impact of firm-level environmental performance on corporate financial performance for data samples that include both developing and developed economies.

In order to address the gaps identified, we utilize firm-level data from 45 countries, and construct firm-level environmental performance indices. Our analysis employs a fixed-effects panel data regression model. Our results confirm the importance of industry as a determinant of financial performance outcomes (as per McGahan and Porter, 1997; Powell, 1996; Rumelt, 1991; Short et al., 2015), as well as the impact of country-level differences in institutions on the returns available from improving corporate environmental practices (complementing the results of Martínez-Ferrero and Frías-Aceituno, 2015). We find statistically significant negative relationships between firm-level environmental performance and stock returns for firms located in some industry sectors, as well as a statistically significant negative relationship between high levels of institutional quality and stock returns in some industry sectors.

The remainder of the chapter is structured as follows. We next provide a brief review of the extant literature and develop our hypotheses. Following this, we discuss our data and methodology, including sample statistics for the key variables. Discussion of the panel data regression model results follows. We then conclude the chapter.

2. LITERATURE REVIEW AND HYPOTHESIS DEVELOPMENT

In the following we develop a brief overview of insights from a range of the extant literature on inter-industry and country-level differences in environmental performance in order to develop testable hypotheses.

A firm's environmental practices, actions to reduce the impact of the firm's activities on the environment (Molina-Azorín et al., 2009; Brammer et al., 2006), provide a signal of the firm's social responsiveness to stakeholder relationships (Wood, 1991). With respect to the shareholders as a key stakeholder group, it has been argued that the extent of adoption of environmentally sustainable practices should be reflected in a firm's performance, and so in its stock price. However, the research on the direct relationship between environmental practice and stock returns is inconclusive. Due to considerations such as increases in costs, higher revenues, operating efficiencies, risk and waste reduction, it is possible to justify any type of relationship – positive, negative, or none (Brammer et al., 2006; Girerd-Potin et al., 2014). In addition, any analysis of the impact of environmentally sustainable practices on firm performance needs to take into account the factors that indirectly influence this relationship. Mediators may include sustainable competitive advantage, reputation and customer satisfaction (Saeidi et al., 2015). Given the variety of permutations associated with theoretical considerations of the impact of environmentally sustainable practices, empirical evidence is required.

Dowell et al. (2000) find higher market values, as measured by Tobin's Q, for a sample of US-based multinationals that adopted a single global environmental standard. Using an event study methodology, Klassen and McLaughlin (1996) find positive returns from the announcement of environmental performance awards. Gupta and Goldar (2005) find that weak environmental ratings announcements lead to negative abnormal returns and a positive correlation between abnormal returns and the level of environmental ratings. In a study of the release of information linked to the pollution tendencies of nine paper companies, Fogler and Nutt (1975) find no effect on the valuation of these companies. Gilley et al. (2000) find no overall effect of announced environmental initiatives on stock returns, in contrast to their hypothesis, although reactions differ between product-driven and process-driven initiatives.

Brammer et al. (2006), examining the constituents of corporate social responsibility for a sample of UK companies, find that the environmental indicators are negatively correlated with returns. Mănescu (2011) finds that an environmental score has no significant effect on risk-adjusted returns, indicating that either its information content was reflected in stock returns or that it was not relevant. Cai et al. (2012), using long horizon stock returns, find a strong positive correlation between environmental responsibility and stock returns.

The effects of firm and industry factors on financial performance have been examined in many studies. However, less attention has been given to the connection of these factors to corporate social responsibility and corporate social performance (Short et al., 2015; Moura-Leite et al., 2012), and, in particular, we contend, to environmental practices. Banerjee (2002) calls for studies of sustainability practices and behavioral outcomes in a variety of industries, as much of the research has focused on the firm level, while Wagner et al. (2001) suggest that the evidence of economic benefits from environmental performance improvement across several industries is inconclusive. Furthermore, research on corporate environmental and financial performance has largely focused on US firms. As many studies employ data from developed countries, including the US, the results may not apply broadly (Gupta, 2018).

Finally, while much of the extant empirical research suggests a positive relationship between corporate environmental and financial performance (Dixon-Fowler et al., 2013; Molina-Azorín et al., 2009; Goglic and Smith, 2013), the operationalization of these factors moderates this positive association (Orlitzky et al., 2003). We contend that continued uncertainty over the impact of environmentally sustainable practices on corporate financial performance, along with the limited cross-country or inter-industry focus in many studies, supports the need to consider the potential impact of inter- and intra-industry factors on the nature of the relationship. It also suggests the use of a more broadly drawn sample of data.

The importance of industry structure as a determinant of firm performance has found support in many studies (e.g., McGahan and Porter, 1997; Powell, 1996; Short et al., 2015; Rumelt, 1991), with the industry framework being a central feature of Porter's (1980) *Competitive Strategy*. The five forces that shape industry competition are stated as threat of new entrants, bargaining power of suppliers, threat of substitutes, bargaining power of buyers, and rivalry among existing competitors. Thus, the relationship between stock returns and corporate social responsibility (CSR), including environmentally sustainable practices, may vary across industry sectors. In fact, Porter and van der Linde (1995, p. 116) maintain that 'success must involve innovation-based solutions that promote both environmentalism and industrial competitiveness'. However, activities regarded as best practice in some industries may be regarded as value-destroying in others (Brammer et al., 2006, p. 106).

We would expect, therefore, that environmentally friendly practices vary systematically at the industry level (Hart, 1995; Moura-Leite et al., 2012). This is supported by studies that decompose the variance in corporate social performance between firm and industry factors. For example, Moura-Leite et al. (2012) indicate that 14 percent of the variance is attributable to industry factors, with the environmental dimension showing a larger industry effect, whereas Short et al. (2015) find industry factors explain about 17 per cent of the variance in corporate social performance between firms.

Within the strategic management research, firms' resources and capabilities are viewed as sources of competitive advantage, environmental social responsibility being one such resource or capability, and so of performance. There are also likely to be common reasons for firms within industries to engage or not engage in similar environmental practices due to these firms facing similar regulatory and stakeholder pressures, similar operating processes and the ease of imitating the practices (Ramus and Montiel, 2005). Firms in the same industries are likely to have similar competitive strategies.

Institutional pressures lead to mimetic behavior as firms adopt similar behaviors from monitoring their competitors, especially when industry leaders practice environmental innovations (Varadarajan, 2017). Due to the shared competitive context for firms and mimicry, we expect that industry factors influence environmental practices within industries (Moura-Leite, 2012). In addition, Ramus and Montiel (2005), using institutional theory, infer that industry dynamics motivate industries to follow similar environmental management practices because of the process of isomorphism. Regulative, normative, and cognitive aspects of isomorphism 'may drive organizations to commit to the same environmental policies' (Ramus and Montiel, 2005, p. 385). Indeed, Ramus and Montiel (2005) find common levels of commitment to environmental policies across the four industries they study, as would be expected from mimetic behavior. However, their results show that services companies, while just as likely to commit to policies as other sectors, are less likely to implement most of the specific environmental policies due to economic disincentives – a case of greenwashing.

In light of the above discussion of industry effects on the returns from investment in environmentally-sustainable practices, we propose the following:

H1: Differences in the cost-benefit profile for engaging in environmentally sustainable practices by industry lead to industry variation in the return from investment in these practices.

In an interconnected global economy with multinational corporations, we might expect the globalization of social practices to eventually converge. However, countries are likely to have different social expectations from business – including environmental responsibility and their stewardship of natural resources. Mechanisms and processes of social engagement may differ and change over time. Differences in institutional settings would be expected to affect these processes. Supporting this view, Cormier and Magnan (2007) find that national institutional contexts are important in explaining the relationship between environmental reporting and the earnings valuation multiple.

Regulatory regime, cultural setting, customer behavior (Schaltegger and Synnestvedt, 2002), social norms, public pressure, and public expectations (Dixon-Fowler et al., 2013), along with reputation (Dasgupta et al., 2001), will influence firms' actions related to environmentally sustainable practices. For example, '[t]he majority of developing countries have piecemeal legislation, evolving policy agendas, and under-resourced government departments, which gives a . . . company little incentive to perform at a high level environmentally' (Hilson and Haselip, 2004, p. 26). However, differences in institutional contexts and their effect on environmental practices are still not well understood, especially in emerging economies (Wang et al., 2016).

National culture reflects behaviors, attitudes, and cognition, all of which affect the actions of business decision makers (Lewellen and Bao, 2015). This suggests that culture, to some extent a country-specific factor, will influence actions related to environmentally-sustainable practices and hence stock returns.

Governance mechanisms, which include a country's laws, its culture and norms, and the institutions that enforce the laws, are critical determinants of country-level differences in these mechanisms (Aggarwal et al., 2009). For example, Martínez-Ferrero and Frías-Aceituno (2015) identify a divergence in institutional settings based on classification by Anglo-Saxon, Germanic, Latin, and Asian governance systems. Their results indicate environmentally sustainable practices generate a positive effect on market value, although the relationship differs between these governance systems.

In identifying the relevance of institutional factors to the practice of social responsibility – sociocultural, national, industry, firm and intra-firm, and individual – Jones (1999) stresses their interrelatedness. In addressing the relationship between institutional conditions and social responsibility, Jones (1999) indicates that industry effects are based on factors such as the industry's location, its activities (primary, secondary or tertiary sectors), competitive structure, its public profile and visibility, culture, and degree of regulation. In addition, government and public pressure is often directed at entire industries which may respond cohesively in response (Jones, 1999). In particular, regulatory authorities operate at the industry level, thus often affecting each industry separately, resulting in differences in corporate social performance among industries (Moura-Leite et al., 2012; Short et al., 2015). Each of these factors suggests that country-level issues may generate intra-industry variation in the returns available from investment in environmentally sustainable practices.

Capital markets can act to monitor, enforce, and create incentives to adopt, environmentally sustainable practices, even in emerging markets (Gupta and Goldar, 2005). However, at the national level, Jones (1999, p. 166) suggests that modernization or the economic development of a nation and particular institutional arrangements affect the level of 'social responsibility discourse'. Thus, the development of institutions and their quality may impact expectations regarding the level and quality of corporate social responsibility within a country, including expectations regarding minimum standards for and specific levels of environmentally sustainable practices, impacting the financial returns available from corporate engagement in these areas. For example, in countries with highly developed institutions, expected standards for environmental (and other aspects of corporate social) performance may be high, with the converse applying to expected standards in countries with poorly developed institutions.

In light of the above considerations relating country-level institutional quality to corporate environmentally-sustainable practices and financial performance, we propose:

H2: The impact of higher levels of environmentally sustainable practices on corporate financial performance will vary intra-industry due to differences in country institutional quality and country risk.

3. DATA AND METHODOLOGY

We utilize stock returns (RET) as our measure to capture corporate financial performance. This reflects that the stock price represents a forward-looking metric and is the basis for the calculation of the equity return earned by stockholders, the key financial stakeholders, on an annual basis (Scholtens and Zhou, 2008).

Our data on environmental performance is derived from the Thomson Reuters Asset4 dataset, which is extensively used within the global investment community. An advantage of the Asset4 data is that it allows analysis of firm-level performance on environmental, social, and governance matters. The Asset4 data is constructed from publicly available primary data, being sourced from the company. The quality and accuracy of the data are verified via extensive use of stock exchange filings, media reports, etc. The Appendix to this chapter provides information on the 38 questions of which the Asset4 environmental indicator set is comprised.

The Asset4 dataset provides binary information based on each company's response to each of the 38 questions. Consistent with a range of the prior literature (e.g., Aggarwal and Goodell, 2009), we have utilized information on each company's binary coded response to each question to construct our environmental sustainability index (ESI). We score one where the company affirms that it meets the requirement specified in the question and zero otherwise. All scores are then added for each company and divided through by 38 (the total number of questions). By construction this gives an ESI taking a value between zero and one; zero would indicate no compliance in any area, while one would indicate a 100 percent compliance in all 38 environmental performance areas.

Table 11.1 highlights that the sample, which covers the 2002 to 2013 time period and is comprised of 28,459 firm-year observations, provides comprehensive coverage of firms in high-income, middle-income and low-income countries. This includes firms from emerging market and transition economies. However, consistent with expectations regarding the extent of stakeholder pressure to report on corporate social and environmental outcomes, the sample has a high representation of firms located in high-income western economies.

In addition to the use of ESI as an independent variable in the empirical modelling presented in this chapter, we use a range of control variables. These include: the size of the firm measured in terms of the log value of its total assets (ASSETS); the debt-equity ratio measured at market prices (LEVER); the price-to-book value (PTBV); profitability in the form of the return on assets (ROA); the realized volatility/standard deviation of returns over the previous year (VOL); and illiquidity, measured as the daily ratio of absolute stock return to dollar volume (ILLIQUID) (see Amihud and Mendelson, 1986). Finally, we use the World Bank Governance Indicators and The PRS Group's International Country Risk Guide risk indicator to separate samples into high and low institutional

Table 11.1 Sample distribution: firm-year observations by country

No	Country	Firm-years	No	Country	Firm-years	No	Country	Firm-years
1	Australia	1769	16	Hungary	19	31	Philippines	84
2	Austria	151	17	India	379	32	Poland	94
3	Belgium	253	18	Indonesia	114	33	Portugal	107
4	Brazil	245	19	Ireland	228	34	Russia	152
5	Canada	1718	20	Israel	72	35	Singapore	386
6	Chile	95	21	Italy	444	36	South Africa	446
7	China	382	22	Japan	3901	37	South Korea	455
8	Colombia	42	23	Luxembourg	46	38	Spain	424
9	Denmark	221	24	Malaysia	179	39	Sweden	507
10	Egypt	43	25	Mexico	129	40	Switzerland	629
11	Finland	258	26	Morocco	15	41	Taiwan	517
12	France	904	27	Netherlands	381	42	Thailand	105
13	Germany	729	28	New Zealand	96	43	Turkey	116
14	Greece	196	29	Norway	168	44	United Kingdom	2805
15	Hong Kong	428	30	Panama	22	45	United States	8,005
						Total		28459

quality groups to capture country-level institutional quality effects on industry-level stock returns.

Each of the control variables can be argued to potentially impact firm-level stock returns, and all are common in studies of corporate governance and asset pricing. For example, given their larger asset base, organizational structures, and volume of trading, larger firms are likely to have lower levels of stock return. Firms that demand a higher market-to-book valuation, based on expectations of faster growth in earnings, are likely to have higher levels of stock return. High levels of leverage may be associated with either higher or lower returns. Finally, relatively higher riskiness is likely to be associated with a need for higher returns to compensate shareholders.

Table 11.2 provides summary statistics, in the form of the mean, standard deviation, and key percentiles for the dependent and each of the main control variables. A brief examination of Table 11.2 identifies the considerable diversity in the firm-year characteristics possessed by the sample firms. For example, in examining returns, firms with firm-year observations in the lowest five percentile have returns less than or equal to −49.3 percent, while firms with firm-year observations in the highest five percentile have returns of greater than or equal to 88 percent. Realized volatility of stock returns varies between 2.8 percent and 44.7

Table 11.2 Descriptive statistics of dependent and independent variables (2002–2013 period)

			Distribution				
Variable	Mean	Std. Dev.	5th	25th	50th	75th	95th
RET	0.142	0.417	−0.493	−0.117	0.109	0.349	0.880
ESI	0.313	0.261	0.000	0.079	0.263	0.526	0.789
ASSETS	8.903	1.674	6.381	7.812	8.751	9.885	11.859
LEVER	0.277	0.229	0.000	0.092	0.227	0.418	0.734
PTBV	2.630	2.484	0.660	1.210	1.910	3.130	7.040
ROA	0.059	0.080	−0.031	0.021	0.053	0.093	0.182
VOL	0.146	0.145	0.028	0.057	0.098	0.176	0.447
ILLIQUID	0.072	0.058	0.019	0.042	0.054	0.088	0.172

Notes: RET are the realized annual stock returns; ESI is the environment sustainability index score calculated for each firm using 38 indicators; ASSETS is the logarithm of total assets; LEVER is calculated as long-term debt divided by the sum of the market value of the equity and book value of debt; PTBV is the price-to-book value ratio; ROA is calculated as net income scaled by total assets; VOL measures riskiness as calculated from the volatility of returns over the last 1 year; and ILLIQUID is calculated as the ratio of zero trading days to the total number of trading days over the last 1 year to capture illiquidity.

Table 11.3 *Return and realized volatility by level of environmental performance*

Quartile	ESI	RET	VOL	N
1	0.013	0.177	0.155	6415
2	0.157	0.161	0.149	6163
3	0.377	0.142	0.143	6912
4	0.678	0.090	0.138	6724

Notes: RET are the realized annual stock returns; ESI is the environment sustainability index score calculated for each firm using 38 indicators; and VOL measures riskiness as calculated from the volatility of returns over the last 1 year.

percent per annum. With respect to environmental performance, as measured by our ESI, firms in the lowest five percentile report zero affirmative responses to requirements specified in the Asset4 questionnaire, while those in the highest five percentile have provided a positive company response to at least 78.9 percent of the 38 requirements specified in the Asset4 questionnaire.

Table 11.3 highlights the average return and realized volatility characteristics of our sample stocks by ESI quartile. Consistent with Brammer et al. (2006), Table 11.3 suggests that higher levels of environmental performance (as captured in a higher ESI) are negatively related to the level of stock returns. Additionally, stocks with a higher ESI generally display a lower realized volatility in their stock returns, suggesting that these firms are, on an ex-post basis, lower risk over the 2002–2013 sample period.

To test the two hypotheses discussed in this chapter, we develop the following empirical models:

$$\begin{aligned}\mathrm{RET}_{\mathrm{it}} = {} & \alpha_i + \beta_1 \mathrm{ESI}_{\mathrm{it}} + \beta_2 \mathrm{ASSETS}_{\mathrm{it}} + \beta_3 \mathrm{LEVER}_{\mathrm{it}} + \beta_4 \mathrm{PTBV}_{\mathrm{it}} + \beta_5 \mathrm{ROA}_{\mathrm{it}} \\ & + \beta_6 \mathrm{VOL}_{\mathrm{it}} + \beta_7 \mathrm{ILLIQUID}_{\mathrm{it}} + \sum_{j=1}^{11} \gamma_j Year_j + \sum_{k=1}^{N} \lambda_k Industry_{ik} \\ & + \sum_{m=1}^{45} \varphi_m Country_{im} + \varepsilon_{\mathrm{it}} \qquad \text{(eqn. 1)}\end{aligned}$$

$$\begin{aligned}\mathrm{RET}_{\mathrm{ikt}} = {} & \alpha_i + \beta_1 \mathrm{ESI}_{\mathrm{ikt}} + \beta_2 \mathrm{ASSETS}_{\mathrm{ikt}} + \beta_3 \mathrm{LEVER}_{\mathrm{ikt}} + \beta_4 \mathrm{PTBV}_{\mathrm{ikt}} \\ & + \beta_5 \mathrm{ROA}_{\mathrm{ikt}} + \beta_6 \mathrm{VOL}_{\mathrm{ikt}} + \beta_7 \mathrm{ILLIQUID}_{\mathrm{ikt}} + \sum_{j=1}^{11} \gamma_j Year_j \\ & + \sum_{m=1}^{45} \varphi_m Country_{ikm} + \varepsilon_{\mathrm{ikt}} \qquad \text{(eqn. 2)}\end{aligned}$$

$$\mathrm{RET}_{ikt}^{INSTQUAL} = \alpha_i + \beta_1 \mathrm{ESI}_{\mathrm{ikt}} + \beta_2 \mathrm{ASSETS}_{\mathrm{ikt}} + \beta_3 \mathrm{LEVER}_{\mathrm{ikt}} + \beta_4 \mathrm{PTBV}_{\mathrm{ikt}}$$

$$+\beta_5 \text{ROA}_{\text{ikt}} + \beta_6 \text{VOL}_{\text{ikt}} + \beta_7 \text{ILLIQUID}_{\text{ikt}} + \sum_{j=1}^{11} \gamma_j Year_j$$
$$+ \varepsilon_{\text{ikt}}; \; INSTQUAL = High, Low \qquad \text{(eqn. 3)}$$

In eqn. 1, RET*it* is the rate of return achieved by firm *i* in year *t*. ESI_{it} is the value taken by the environmental performance index constructed for firm *i* in year *t*. ASSETS_{it}, LEVER_{it}, PTBV_{it}, ROA_{it}, VOL_{it}, and ILLIQUID_{it}, represent the values of the control variables for firm *i* in year *t*. As indicated in the regression model of eqn. 1, we control for year, industry and country fixed effects.

With eqn. 2, we separate our sample by industry, with *k* identifying whether firm *i* belongs to the Basic Materials, Consumer Goods, Consumer Services, Financials, Health Care, Industrials, Oil & Gas, Technology, Telecommunications, or Utilities sector. We then control for year and country fixed effects in each industry regression.

Finally, eqn. 3 identifies that we further divide our sample, undertaking the industry-based regressions for sub-samples of countries identified as having high and low institutional quality, respectively, based on their World Bank Governance Indicators scores. This is repeated for country risk ratings. Again we control for year fixed effects.

4. RESULTS

Table 11.4 provides statistical results on the effect of level of environmental performance on stock returns, firstly for all firms (Column (1)) and by industry (Column (2) through Column (11)).

Consistent with Brammer et al. (2006), and based on the eqn. 1 regression, the coefficient on ESI, our measure of environmental performance, is negative and statistically significant. We thus find that higher levels of reported environmental performance are negatively related to the level of stock returns when considered for the full sample of firms (Column (1)). Higher levels of leverage (LEVER) are associated with lower ex post returns, while higher levels of return on assets (ROA) and price-to-book value (PTBV) are associated with higher levels of ex-post stock returns. The coefficients on the other control variables (ASSETS, VOL, ILLIQUID) are not statistically significant for the full sample of firms.

Columns (2) to (11) of Table 11.4 are based on the eqn. 2 regressions. These provide results relevant to the first of our hypotheses (**H1**) that industry-level differences in the costs versus benefits from engaging in environmentally sustainable practices will lead to industry variation in

Table 11.4 Effect of level of environmental performance on stock returns, all firms and by industry

Stock Returns	(1)	(2)	(3)	(4)	(5)	(6)
	All firms	Basic Materials	Consumer Goods	Consumer Services	Financials	Health Care
ESI	−0.039***	0.048	0.044	−0.113***	−0.058**	−0.065
	(−3.59)	(1.09)	(1.31)	(−3.34)	(−2.52)	(−1.45)
ASSETS	0.002	−0.010	−0.003	0.023***	0.004	−0.016*
	(0.92)	(−1.12)	(−0.28)	(3.05)	(1.54)	(−1.81)
LEVER	−0.116***	−0.109**	−0.240***	−0.214***	−0.059***	−0.108
	(−9.12)	(−2.15)	(−5.03)	(−5.33)	(−2.93)	(−1.35)
PTBV	0.026***	0.053***	0.0105***	0.017***	0.032***	0.020***
	(20.28)	(8.44)	(4.32)	(6.89)	(8.24)	(4.89)
ROA	0.368***	0.678***	0.344***	0.331***	0.288***	0.209*
	(8.98)	(6.08)	(2.65)	(2.67)	(2.93)	(1.86)
VOL	−0.007	0.077	0.417***	0.258**	−0.106**	−0.274*
	(−0.26)	(0.96)	(3.62)	(2.50)	(−1.99)	(−1.73)
ILLIQUID	0.070	0.133	−0.110	0.337**	0.177**	0.062
	(1.33)	(0.80)	(−0.62)	(2.25)	(2.32)	(0.19)
Fixed effect?						
Country	Included	Included	Included	Included	Included	Included
Industry	Included	N/A	N/A	N/A	N/A	N/A
Year	Included	Included	Included	Included	Included	Included
N	28459	2757	3141	3686	5520	1659
Adj. R^2	0.336	0.444	0.321	0.320	0.408	0.303

Table 11.4 (continued)

Stock Returns	(7)	(8)	(9)	(10)	(11)
	Industrials	Oil & Gas	Technology	Telecommunications	Utilities
ESI	−0.025	−0.186***	0.007	−0.114	−0.097**
	(−1.07)	(−3.43)	(0.17)	(−1.05)	(−2.12)
ASSETS	0.003	0.005	−0.007	0.012	0.011
	(0.55)	(0.57)	(−0.85)	(0.66)	(0.95)
LEVER	−0.091***	−0.138**	−0.194***	−0.496***	−0.191***
	(−2.93)	(−2.51)	(−3.13)	(−4.61)	(−3.10)
PTBV	0.022***	0.079***	0.034***	0.036***	0.047***
	(7.15)	(8.97)	(7.54)	(4.74)	(4.53)
ROA	0.370***	0.437***	0.302***	−0.660	0.667***
	(3.30)	(2.78)	(3.63)	(−1.24)	(3.12)
VOL	0.193**	−0.163**	−0.006	0.395*	−0.124
	(2.47)	(−2.15)	(−0.06)	(1.76)	(−0.74)
ILLIQUID	0.242**	0.052	−0.024	0.634	0.079
	(2.14)	(0.25)	(−0.12)	(1.45)	(0.31)
Fixed effect?					
Country	Included	Included	Included	Included	Included
Industry	N/A	N/A	N/A	N/A	N/A
Year	Included	Included	Included	Included	Included
N	5544	2028	2020	743	1361
Adj. R^2	0.389	0.465	0.452	0.305	0.330

This table shows the impact of environmental performance on realized annual stock returns. ESI is the environment sustainability index score calculated for each firm using 38 indicators; ASSETS is the logarithm of total assets; LEVER is calculated as long-term debt divided by the sum of the market value of equity and book value of debt; PTBV is the price-to-book value ratio; ROA is calculated as net income scaled by total assets; VOL measures riskiness as calculated from the volatility of returns over the last 1 year; and ILLIQUID is calculated as the ratio of zero trading days to the total number of trading days over the last 1 year to capture illiquidity. * Statistically significant at 10%, ** statistically significant at 5 %, *** statistically significant at 1% level. N/A indicates not applicable.

the return from investment in these practices. Our results, therefore, are consistent with the findings on the importance of industry factors in explaining the variance between firms in corporate social performance (Moura-Leite et al., 2012; Short et al., 2015).

Expanding on, and consistent with, the results of earlier studies which identify that environmentally friendly practices vary systematically by industry (Hart, 1995; Russo and Fouts, 1997; Moura-Leite et al., 2012), we find that returns from such investments differ in the level of their impact on firms' stock returns by industry. In particular, our results suggest that, with the exception of firms in the Basic Materials, Consumer Goods, and Technology sectors, which have positive but statistically insignificant coefficients, the coefficients on ESI for each of the industry-based regression models are negative.

Of the industry-based regressions for which the coefficients on ESI are negative, those for the Health Care, Industrials, and Telecommunications sectors are statistically insignificant. Finally, for those sectors with statistically significant negative coefficients on ESI we identify substantial variation in the size of the coefficient – Consumer Services (−0.1130), Financials (−0.0584), Oil & Gas (−0.1860), and Utilities (−0.0969). We thus tentatively conclude that **H1** is supported.

Consideration of the likely industry differences to the cost of being able to affirm that a company meets the requirements specified in a number of the 38 Asset4 Environmental Indicators (Appendix), suggests that differences in the size of the coefficients may reflect industry factors. For example, firms in the Financials sector may be able to more efficiently embed processes and measurement systems to allow affirmation of Indicator 8: Does the company monitor its resource efficiency performance?

As with the regression on the full sample of firms, we find that for each industry higher levels of leverage (LEVER) are associated with lower ex-post returns. All industry-level coefficients are negative, and, with the exception of the Health Care sector, all are statistically significant. We also find again that, with the exception of the Telecommunications sector, higher levels of return on assets (ROA) and price-to-book value (PTBV) are associated with statistically significant increases in the level of ex-post stock returns. With the exception of Consumer Services (0.0232) and Health Care (−0.0155), the coefficients on firm size (ASSETS) are statistically insignificant. For all industries where the coefficient on illiquidity (ILLIQUID) is statistically significant – Consumer Services, Financials, and Industrials – it is also positive in sign. Finally, results for realized volatility (VOL), our measure of riskiness, are mixed for those industries where the coefficients are statistically significant. For Consumer Goods, Consumer Services, Industrials, and Telecommunications, the coefficients on VOL are positive. Coefficients on VOL for the Financials, Health Care, and Oil & Gas sectors are negative.

Table 11.5 summarizes results based on the eqn.3 format for regression models, where the firm sample is divided not just by industry but also into two country groups reflecting either the level of the institutional quality indexes or country risk rating. We have used the World Bank Governance Indicators to allocate countries to the high and low institutional quality groups based on their scores. We also utilize The PRS Group's *International Country Risk Guide* risk indicator to separate industries by high and low country risk. In order to conserve space, we report only the coefficient on ESI, the number of firm-years in each groups' sub-sample, and adjusted R-square, for each group. Finally, we focus on those industry sectors for which we identified a statistically significant coefficient on ESI.

The results of Table 11.5 highlight the potential importance of intra-industry factors, as captured through variations in country-level institutional quality (see also Martínez-Ferrero and Frías-Aceituno, 2015) and risk measures, on the impact on stock returns of increases in environmental performance by industry.[1]

For the Consumer Services and Oil & Gas sectors we find that high levels of institutional quality, indicated by high levels for indexes of Government Effectiveness, Regulatory Quality, Rule of Law, Corruption Control, and Accountability, and a low level of country risk rating (ICRG), are associated with a statistically significant and large negative impact of high levels of environmental performance outcomes on stock returns. In the case of the Oil & Gas sector, increases in ESI are also associated with a large negative impact on returns for countries with a high country risk rating. Low levels of Political Stability are also associated with a negative impact on stock returns of increases in ESI for both the Consumer Services and Oil & Gas sectors.

With respect to Financials and Utilities, each of which is a heavily regulated sector, with Utilities likely to be subject to environmental performance oversight, we identify a different impact from factors related to the country institutional quality indicators and country risk rating. For Financials, increases in ESI are only statistically significant in reducing stock returns where Regulatory Quality and country risk ratings are low. The negative impact of increases in ESI on returns in the Utilities sector are statistically significant only for low levels of Government Effectiveness, Political Stability and Regulatory Quality, and for low levels of country risk rating.

In light of the observed variation in the impact of country-level institutional quality and country risk rating by industry on the impact of higher levels of ESI, we suggest support for **H2**. Thus country-level factors

Table 11.5 Effect of level of environmental performance on stock returns, by industry and country institutional quality index

	Consumer Services		Financials		Oil & Gas		Utilities	
	High	Low	High	Low	High	Low	High	Low
Government Effectiveness								
ESI	−0.121***	0.064	−0.005	−0.068	−0.179***	0.0271	−0.034	−0.194*
	(−3.17)	(0.62)	(−0.19)	(−1.16)	(−2.82)	(0.17)	(−0.71)	(−1.66)
N	2861	400	3913	949	1488	293	914	293
Adj. R^2	0.322	0.446	0.435	0.577	0.488	0.553	0.427	0.419
Political Stability								
ESI	−0.091	−0.133***	−0.014	−0.025	−0.155	−0.189***	−0.116	−0.099*
	(−1.59)	(−3.01)	(−0.38)	(−0.79)	(−1.58)	(−2.58)	(−1.27)	(−1.81)
N	1235	2026	2005	2857	775	1006	318	889
Adj. R^2	0.312	0.377	0.460	0.458	0.456	0.533	0.368	0.401
Regulatory Quality								
ESI	−0.167***	0.014	−0.004	−0.101**	−0.224***	−0.033	−0.054	−0.188*
	(−3.84)	(0.24)	(−0.16)	(−2.14)	(−3.37)	(−0.25)	(−1.14)	(−1.71)
N	2505	756	3565	1297	1434	347	852	355
Adj. R^2	0.344	0.361	0.442	0.511	0.494	0.532	0.448	0.354

Table 11.5 (continued)

	Consumer Services		Financials		Oil & Gas		Utilities	
	High	Low	High	Low	High	Low	High	Low
Rule of Law								
ESI	−0.126***	0.036	−0.009	−0.048	−0.179***	0.008	−0.049	−0.131
	(−3.29)	(0.36)	(−0.32)	(−0.84)	(−2.81)	(0.05)	(−1.06)	(−1.02)
N	2,848	413	3,877	985	1,486	295	921	286
Adj. R^2	0.321	0.447	0.433	0.579	0.489	0.550	0.412	0.451
Corruption Control								
ESI	−0.163***	0.063	−0.008	−0.079	−0.201***	0.003	−0.044	−0.155
	(−4.13)	(0.74)	(−0.31)	(−1.47)	(−3.08)	(0.02)	(−0.94)	(−1.27)
N	2734	527	3756	1106	1473	308	913	294
Adj. R^2	0.333	0.444	0.439	0.584	0.490	0.553	0.415	0.438
Accountability								
ESI	−0.139***	−0.017	−0.009	−0.040	−0.200***	−0.009	−0.064	−0.123
	(−3.61)	(−0.21)	(−0.33)	(−0.79)	(−3.02)	(−0.06)	(−1.37)	(−1.11)
N	2649	612	3558	1304	1473	308	931	276
Adj. R^2	0.361	0.367	0.440	0.557	0.480	0.564	0.462	0.277
ICRG								
ESI	−0.064	−0.158***	0.004	−0.112***	−0.183**	−0.166**	−0.046	−0.100*
	(−1.32)	(−3.44)	(0.11)	(−3.57)	(−2.01)	(−2.40)	(−0.52)	(−1.80)
N	1,521	2,165	2,408	3,112	869	1,159	397	964
Adj. R^2	0.320	0.340	0.439	0.396	0.477	0.474	0.319	0.368

Note: This table shows the impact of environmental performance on realized annual stock returns by industry and grouped according to country institutional quality, using each of the World Bank Governance Indicators: Government Effectiveness, Political Stability, Regulatory Quality, Rule of Law, Corruption Control, and Accountability. As a robustness test we also use The PRS Group's International Country Risk Guide (ICRG) risk indicator to group firms by country institutional quality. ESI is the environment sustainability index score calculated for each firm using 38 indicators. The control variables indicated in Table 11.4 – ASSETS, LEVER, PTBV, ROA, VOL, and ILLIQUID – are used in the regressions, but results are not reported to conserve space. * Statistically significant at 10%, ** statistically significant at 5%, *** statistically significant at 1% level.

are significant in generating intra-industry variation in the response of firm-level stock returns to increases in firm environmental performance outcomes. This may reflect, as suggested by Jones (1999), that the development of a nation and its particular institutional arrangements affect the level of 'social responsibility discourse' and so expectations regarding environmental performance by its firms.

5. CONCLUSION

In this chapter we empirically examine whether there are inter-industry and intra-industry variations in firm-level financial performance from engaging in environmentally sustainable practices. In doing so we contribute to a literature where a lack of consensus exists as to the impact of environmental performance on financial performance, and in which there exists limited multi-industry and/or multi-country studies. The study in this chapter addresses each of these last deficiencies. Our data, which covers the 2002 to 2013 time period, is comprised of 28,459 firm-year observations for firms in ten industries across 45 countries. This provides a comprehensive coverage of firms in high-income, middle-income and low-income countries, with coverage of the basic materials, consumer goods, consumer services, financials, health care, industrials, oil and gas, technology, telecommunications, and utilities sectors.

To capture financial performance we utilize firm stock returns, a forward looking measure. Firm engagement in environmentally sustainable practices is measured through firm-level environment performance/sustainability indices (ESIs) constructed from 38 environmental indicators included in the Thomson Reuters' Asset4 CSR dataset. In addition to the use of ESI as an independent variable we control for a number of factors including: firm size; use of financial leverage (debt-to-equity); the price-to-book value (PTBV); profitability (ROA); stock return riskiness; and trade illiquidity. The World Bank Governance Indicators and The PRS Group's *International Country Risk Guide* risk indicator are used to separate industry-level sub-samples into high and low institutional quality groups to capture the impact of country-level institutional factors on industry-based firm stock returns. Finally, empirical results are based on a set of panel fixed-effects regression models based on a division of the data into full sample, industry-based sub-samples, and industry-based sub-samples grouped by high versus low country institutional quality.

Consistent with some of the extant literature, we find a statistically significant negative relationship between stock returns and firm-level environmental performance as captured in the ESIs. However, our industry-level sub-sample regressions reveal that the impact of higher levels of ESI is industry specific, with higher levels of ESI having a statistically significant negative impact on returns in only four sectors – consumer goods, oil & gas, financials and utilities. The coefficients on ESI are not statistically significant for the other six industries included in our sample.

Our use of sub-samples regression based on division of the dataset by both industry and high/low institutional quality, reveals additional, country-level, sources of variation in the impact of increases in environmental performance on industry-based, firm-level stock returns. In the case of the consumer goods and oil and gas sectors, higher ESI is only significant in reducing returns where the institutions related to government effectiveness, regulatory quality, rule of law, corruption control, and accountability are strong. However, for the financials and utilities sectors, we only find a significant relationship where a sub-set of these institutional quality factors are weak. Low levels of political stability are also found to be associated with a negative impact of ESI on stock returns for the consumer goods, oil & gas, and utilities industries.

Finally, we find that low levels of country risk rating are associated with a negative relationship between ESI and stock returns in the consumer goods, financials, and utilities, sectors. For the oil and gas sector ESI has a negative impact on stock returns in both low and high country risk rating environments.

Our results provide support for calls to undertake further study of the impact of sustainability practices across a variety of industries (Banerjee, 2002). Also, they support the importance of ensuring that greater attention is paid to the consideration of differences in institutional contexts and their potential effect on environmental practices, especially in less economically developed countries (Gupta, 2018; Wang et al., 2016).

NOTE

1. The above results, however, should be interpreted with care. One of the limitations of the current chapter is that the endogeneity issue may bias the results.

REFERENCES

Aggarwal, R. and Goodell, J. (2009). Markets and institutions in financial intermediation: National characteristics as determinants. *Journal of Banking and Finance*, 33: 1770–1780.

Aggarwal, R., Erel, I., Stulz, R. and Williamson, R. (2009). Differences in governance practices between U.S. and foreign firms: Measurement, causes, and consequences. *The Review of Financial Studies*, 22(8): 3131–3169.

Amihud, Y. and Mendelson, H. (1986). Asset pricing and the bid-ask spread. *Journal of Financial Economics*, 17: 223–249.

Bahttarai, M. and Hammig M. (2004). Governance, economic policy and the environmental Kuznets curve for natural tropical forest. *Environment and Development Economics*, 9(3): 367–382.

Banerjee, S. (2002). Organisational strategies for sustainable development: Developing a research agenda for the new millennium. *Australian Journal of Management*, 27(Special Issue): 105–117.

Brammer, S., Brooks, C. and Pavelin, S. (2006). Corporate social performance and stock returns: UK evidence from disaggregate measures. *Financial Management*, Autumn: 97–116.

Cai, Y., Hoje, J. and Pan, C. (2012). Doing well while doing bad? CSR in controversial industry sectors. *Journal of Business Ethics*, 108: 467–480.

Cormier, D. and Magnan, M. (2007). The revisited contribution of environmental reporting to investors' valuation of a firm's earnings: An international perspective. *Ecological Economics*, 62: 613–626.

Dasgupta, S., Laplante, B. and Mamingi, N. (2001). Pollution and capital markets in developing countries. *Journal of Environmental Economics and Management*, 42: 310–335.

Dixon-Fowler, H., Slater, D., Johnson, J., Ellstrand, A. and Romi, A. (2013). Beyond 'Does it pay to be green?' A meta-analysis of moderators of the CEP–CFP relationship. *Journal of Business Ethics*, 112: 353–366.

Dowell, G., Hart, S. and Yeung, B. (2000). Do corporate global environmental standards create or destroy market value? *Management Science*, 46: 1059–1074.

Fogler, H. and Nutt, F. (1975). A note on social responsibility and stock valuation. *Academy of Management Journal*, 18(1): 155–160.

Fredriksson, P, Damania, R. and Muthukumara, M. (2004). The persistence of corruption and regulatory compliance failures: Theory and evidence. *Public Choice*, 121(3): 363–390.

Gilley, K., Worrell, D. and El-Jelly, A. (2000). Corporate environmental initiatives and anticipated firm performance: The differential effects of process-driven versus product-driven greening initiatives. *Journal of Management*, 26(6): 1199–1216.

Girerd-Potin, I., Jimenez-Garcès, S. and Louvet, P. (2014). Which dimensions of social responsibility concern financial investors? *Journal of Business Ethics*, 121: 559–576.

Goglic, S. and Smith, C. (2013). A meta-analysis of environmentally sustainable supply chain management practices and firm performance. *Journal of Supply Chain Management*, 49(2): 78–95.

Gupta, K. (2018). Environmental sustainability and implied cost of equity: International evidence. *Journal of Business Ethics*, 147(2): 343–365.

Gupta, S. and Goldar, B. (2005). Do stock markets penalize environment-unfriendly behaviour? Evidence from India. *Ecological Economics*, 52: 81–95.

Hart, S. (1995). A natural-resource-based view of the firm. *Academy of Management Review*, 20: 986–1014.

Hilson, G. and Haselip, A. (2004). The environmental and socioeconomic performance of multinational mining companies in the developing world economy. *Minerals and Energy*, 19(3): 25–47.

Jones, M. (1999). The institutional determinants of social responsibility. *Journal of Business Ethics*, 20(2): 163–179.

Klassen, R.D. and McLaughlin, C.P. (1996). The impact of environmental management on firm performance. *Management Science*, 42(8): 1199–1216.

Lewellen, K. and Bao, S. (2015). R&D investment in the global paper products industry: A behavioral theory of the firm and national culture perspective. *Journal of International Management*, 21: 1–17.

Mănescu, C. (2011). Stock returns in relation to environmental, social and governance performance: Mispricing or compensation for risk? *Sustainable Development*, 19: 95–118.

Martínez-Ferrero, J. and Frías-Aceituno, J. (2015). Relationship between sustainable

development and financial performance: International empirical research. *Business Strategy and the Environment*, 24: 20–39.
McGahan, A. and Porter, M. (1997). How much does industry matter, really? *Strategic Management Journal*, 18(Summer Special Issue): 15–30.
McGuire, J., Sundgren, A. and Schneeweis, T. (1988). Corporate social responsibility and firm financial performance. *Academy of Management Journal*, 31(4): 854–872.
McIver, R. (2012). Global financial crisis and the changing geography and industrial composition of large, listed companies: Evidence on China's ascent. *Journal of Business Management*, 6: 5–18.
Molina-Azorín, J., Tarí, J., Claver-Cortés, E. and López-Gamero, M. (2009). Quality management, environmental management and firm performance: A review of empirical studies and issues of integration. *International Journal of Management Reviews*, 11(2): 197–222.
Moura-Leite, R., Padgett, R. and Galan, J. (2012). Is social responsibility driven by industry or firm-specific factors? *Management Decision*, 50(7): 1200–1221.
Orlitzky, M., Schmidt, F. and Rynes, S. (2003). Corporate social and financial performance: A meta-analysis. *Organization Studies*, 24(3): 403–441.
Porter, M. (1980). *Competitive Strategy: Techniques for Analysing Industries and Competitors*. Free Press: New York.
Porter, M. and van der Linde, C. (1995). Toward a new conception of the environment-competitiveness relationship. *Journal of Economic Perspectives*, 9(4): 97–118.
Powell, T. (1996). How much does industry matter? An alternative empirical test. *Strategic Management Journal*, 17: 323–334.
Ramus, C. and Montiel, I. (2005). When are corporate environmental policies a form of greenwashing? *Business and Society*, 44(4): 377–414.
Rumelt, R. (1991). How much does industry matter? *Strategic Management Journal*, 12: 167–185.
Russo, M. and Fouts, P. (1997). A resource-based perspective on corporate environmental performance and profitability. *Academy of Management Journal*, 40: 534–559.
Saeidi, S., Sofian, S., Saeidi P., Saeidi, S. and Saeidi, S. (2015). How does corporate social responsibility contribute to firm financial performance? The mediating role of competitive advantage, reputation, and customer satisfaction. *Journal of Business Research*, 68: 341–350.
Schaltegger, S. and Synnestvedt, T. (2002). The link between 'green' and economic success: Environmental management as the crucial trigger between environmental and economic performance. *Journal of Environmental Management*, 65: 339–346.
Scholtens, B. and Zhou, Y. (2008). Stakeholder relations and financial performance. *Sustainable Development*, 16(3): 213–232.
Short J., McKenny A., Ketchen, D., Snow, C. and Hult, G. (2015). An empirical examination of firm, industry, and temporal effects on corporate social performance, *Business & Society*, 54(1): 1–35.
Varadarajan, R. (2017). Innovating for sustainability: A framework for sustainable innovations and a model of sustainable innovations orientation. *Journal of the Academy of Marketing Science*, 45: 14–36.
Wagner, M., Schaltegger, S. and Wehrmeyer, W. (2001). The relationship between the environmental and economic performance of firms. *Greener Management International*, 2001: 94–111.
Wang, H., Tong, L., Takeuchi, R. and George, G. (2016). From the editors – corporate social responsibility: An overview and new research directions. *Academy of Management Journal*, 59(2): 534–544.
Welsch, H. (2004). Corruption, growth, and the environment: a cross-country analysis. *Environment and Development Economics*, 9(5): 663–693.
Wood, Donna J. (1991). Corporate social performance revisited. *Academy of Management Review*, 16: 691–718.

APPENDIX: ASSET4 ENVIRONMENTAL INDICATORS

1 Does the company have a policy for reducing the use of natural resources?
2 Does the company describe the implementation of its resource efficiency policy through the processes in place?
3 Does the company have a policy for reducing environmental emissions or their impacts on biodiversity?
4 Does the company report on initiatives to increase its energy efficiency overall?
5 Does the company describe the implementation of its emission reduction policy through the processes in place?
6 Does the company have a policy for maintaining an environmental management system?
7 Does the company report on initiatives to recycle, reduce, reuse, substitute, treat or phase out total waste, hazardous waste or wastewater?
8 Does the company monitor its resource efficiency performance?
9 Does the company describe the implementation of its resource efficiency policy through a public commitment from a senior management or board member?
10 Does the company have a policy to lessen the environmental impact of its supply chain?
11 Does the company report on partnerships or initiatives with specialized NGOs, industry organizations, governmental or supragovernmental organizations that focus on improving environmental issues?
12 Does the company have an environmental product innovation policy (eco-design, life cycle assessment, dematerialization)?
13 Does the company report about take-back procedures and recycling programs to reduce the potential risks of products entering the environment? OR Does the company report about product features and applications or services that will promote responsible, efficient, cost-effective and environmentally preferable use?
14 Does the company use environmental criteria (ISO 14000, energy consumption, etc.) in the selection process of its suppliers or sourcing partners?
15 Is the company aware that climate change can represent commercial risks and/or opportunities?
16 Does the company report on initiatives to reduce the environmental impact of transportation of its products or its staff?

17 Does the company report on initiatives to use renewable energy sources?
18 Does the company set specific objectives to be achieved on emission reduction?
19 Does the company monitor its emission reduction performance?
20 Does the company report on initiatives to protect, restore or reduce its impact on native ecosystems and species, biodiversity, and protected and sensitive areas?
21 Does the company describe the implementation of its environmental product innovation policy?
22 Does the company describe, claim to have or mention the processes it uses to accomplish environmental product innovation?
23 Does the company report on its environmental expenditures or does the company report making proactive environmental investments to reduce future risks or increase future opportunities?
24 Does the company report on initiatives to reuse or recycle water? OR Does the company report on initiatives to reduce the amount of water used?
25 Does the company report on at least one product line or service that is designed to have positive effects on the environment or which is environmentally labelled and marketed?
26 Does the company set specific objectives to be achieved on resource efficiency?
27 Does the company show an initiative to reduce, reuse, recycle, substitute, phase out or compensate CO2 equivalents in the production process?
28 Does the company report or provide information on company-generated initiatives to restore the environment?
29 Does the company describe the implementation of its emission reduction policy through a public commitment from a senior management or board member?
30 Does the company have environmentally friendly or green sites or offices?
31 Does the company report on the concentration of production locations in order to limit the environmental impact during the production process? OR Does the company report on its participation in any emissions trading initiative? OR Does the company report on new production techniques to improve the global environmental impact (all emissions) during the production process?
32 Has the company received product awards with respect to environmental responsibility? OR Does the company use product labels (e.g.,

FSC, Energy Star, MSC) indicating the environmental responsibility of its products?

33 Does the company report on specific products which are designed for reuse, recycling or the reduction of environmental impacts?

34 Does the company develop products or technologies for use in clean, renewable energy (such as wind, solar, hydro and geo-thermal and biomass power)?

35 Does the company report on initiatives to reduce, substitute, or phase out ozone-depleting (CFC-11 equivalents, chlorofluorocarbon) substances?

36 Does the company set specific objectives to be achieved on environmental product innovation?

37 Does the company report or show itself to be ready to end a partnership with a sourcing partner, if environmental criteria are not met?

38 Does the company comment on the results of previously set objectives?

Source: Thomson Reuters Asset4 dataset.

12. The role of financial markets in promoting sustainability – a review and research framework

Mohammed Amidu and Haruna Issahaku

1. INTRODUCTION

Despite the fact that the term 'sustainability' has become a buzz word, the world is still far from safety. According to the *Living Planet Report 2014* (McLellan et al., 2014), the humans' demands on the planet are 50 per cent in excess of what nature can renew, putting the lives of both man and other biological species at risk. According to the report, since 1961, the ecological footprint[1] of mankind has doubled. Even more frightening is the revelation that 1.5 Earths would be required to generate resources to support mankind's present ecological footprint. These statistics suggest that previous and current efforts at addressing the sustainability challenge have not yielded the desired results. A lesson from these statistics is that for global sustainable development to be attained, it will require galvanising the support of all, including but not limited to policy makers, global and multilateral institutions, civil society, citizens and the research community. And for the research community, the matter should not be left for only ecologists to deal with, rather, an integrated and multidisciplinary approach will be imperative.

Consequently, after several decades of neglect, the attention of economists, ecologists and financial experts is now turning towards the implications of financial markets, institutions, systems and processes for sustainable development. Notwithstanding this recent attention, the relationship between financial markets and the environment is not properly understood (Galaz et al., 2015). Mainstream finance journals have yet to fully incorporate finance and sustainability as an area of research. Even the most authoritative and widely accepted classification system used in categorizing research issues in economics and its sub-disciplines, the JEL Classification System produced by the Journal of Economic Literature (JEL), surprisingly, has no category for financial markets and sustainability in its 20-subject category list. Thus, we have yet to properly frame and categorize finance and sustainability research, which is one of the gaps this chapter aims to fill.

Previous reviews related to the present one include those of Renneboog et al. (2008), Busch et al. (2015) and Mattsson (2016). The work of

Renneboog et al. (2008) looks at the issues and research gaps in the area of Socially Responsible Investments (SRIs). Renneboog et al. (2008) show that current research is unable to answer the question of whether investors are willing to accept less than optimal returns from SRI funds. They suggest an examination of the direction of causality between Sustainability Investing (SI) and firm value, and how SI affects the cost of capital and investment decisions at the firm level as areas for future research. Busch et al. (2015) explore the extant literature on finance and sustainability and provide the way forward. They arrive at the conclusion that financial markets have made only a 'modest' contribution to sustainability. Busch et al. (2015) further unravel a paradox whereby investors increasingly factor Environmental, Social and Governance (ESG) issues into their decisions, while at the same time there is no discernible shift by businesses towards practising sustainability. Going forward, the authors make two critical suggestions: first, actors in the financial system should adopt a long-term approach towards sustainable business practices, and second, there is a need to build accurate and reliable data on sustainable investments. Mattsson (2016) reflects on how to bridge the gap between sustainable market policies and market practices. The author finds sustainable policy initiatives to be diverse, multidimensional and sometimes conflicting. Mattsson asks future research to investigate how the application of sustainable policies interacts with markets to shape sustainable development.

These studies have certainly contributed to our understanding of the implications of financial practices for sustainability. There are however still a number of unanswered questions. For instance, how is finance and sustainability research framed? What are the channels by which research on financial markets and sustainable development is disseminated? Which region(s) of the world is (are) given more attention in terms of research effort and which one(s) is (are) being neglected, and why? Which issues are deemed critical and require the attention of various actors? How should finance and sustainability research be conceptualised? The contribution of this chapter to the literature lies in finding answers to the above-mentioned questions – a quest the study has fulfilled. Specifically, the objectives the chapter addresses include the following:

1. To provide a literature review and analysis of research related to financial markets and sustainable development.
2. To classify financial market and sustainability research and identify its dissemination.
3. To build a conceptual framework for finance and sustainability research.
4. To identify and describe key research trends, and gaps pertaining to:

(a) conceptual approaches; (b) issues addressed and burning issues and (c) pointers for future research.

This chapter's contribution differs from the works of Renneboog et al. (2008), Busch et al. (2015) and Mattsson (2016) in a number of ways. First, unlike these studies, the chapter provides a classification system for finance and sustainability research and shows which areas require further research. Second, the chapter analyses the various channels by which finance and sustainability research are disseminated and the regions of the world that have received the most (least) attention so far as sustainability research is concerned. Finally, the chapter provides a research framework which emphasises a holistic approach to studying finance and sustainability to guide future research.

The study finds that, generally, there has been an upward trend in the number of articles published on finance and sustainability over the research period (January 2005 to August 2016). Europe and North America received the most research attention with 20.0 per cent and 16.7 per cent respectively of financial markets and sustainability research being conducted there. The least researched continents are Asia (3.3 per cent), South America (1.7 per cent) and Africa (1.7 per cent). Based on classification and analysis of research issues, it is found that the bulk of the research is concentrated on Financing Sustainability & Responsible Investing and Sustainability & Performance. The relatively less addressed research areas include Theory, Method & Measurement Issues in Sustainability Finance; International Finance & Sustainability; Islamic Finance & Sustainability; and Policy, Regulation & Sustainability.

The rest of the chapter is structured as follows. Section 2 presents a classification system for research on financial markets and sustainability. Section 3 details the methodology used for the review. Section 4 presents findings from the literature review. Section 5 unravels the evidence and burning issues on finance and sustainability research. Section 6 proposes a research framework to guide future research. Section 7 reveals research gaps and provides pointers to future research while Section 8 concludes.

2. FRAMING FINANCIAL MARKETS AND SUSTAINABILITY RESEARCH

Financial markets and sustainability research requires a proper classification of research themes or frames and a clear description of terms and concepts. This section elucidates some terms and concepts, and on that basis classifies financial market and sustainability research.

2.1 Financial Markets and Sustainability Defined

Something is said to be sustainable if it can last for a long time by being able to renew itself without causing harm to itself and others. The term sustainable development remains amorphous and has been variously defined. Whichever way we define sustainability some key ingredients are imperative and almost universally agreeable. Sustainable development has a time dimension (for how long?), an object dimension (the thing(s) to be sustained), and a beneficiary dimension (the thing(s) to be developed) (see Mattsson, 2016). The World Summit on Sustainable Development in 2002 proposed three pillars of sustainable development, namely, social, environmental and economic. In this light, sustainable development includes but is not limited to Corporate Social Responsibility (CSR) and ESG.

Badiru (2010) calls for a systems approach to the understanding of sustainability. The author sees sustainability to simply mean a prudent utilization of resources. Based on this systems view, Badiru (2010) enumerates different types of sustainability: environmental sustainability, operational sustainability, energy sustainability, health and welfare sustainability, safety and security sustainability, market sustainability, financial sustainability, economic sustainability, health sustainability, family sustainability and social sustainability.

Based on the foregoing discussion, we define financial markets and sustainability research as any research work that seeks to show how financial markets, institutions, instruments, investors, processes and systems impact on and or are impacted by sustainable development.

2.2 Description of Concepts

Sustainable Investments (SIs): these refer to investments that promote sustainable development by incorporating long-term ESG criteria into investment decisions (Busch et al., 2015). Sustainable investment therefore has an economic angle which requires that profits made are fair and responsible, and have intergenerational and intragenerational consciousness; an ecological perspective which requires investments in renewable resources, productivity enhancement, and the promotion of ecological balance and biodiversity, as well as a socio-cultural angle which seeks to foster human resource development, create sustainable jobs, and promote cultural diversity and human rights.

Socially Responsible Property Investment (SRPI): Pivo and McNamara (2005, p. 128) define SRPI as ‘maximizing the positive effects of property ownership, management and development on society and the natural environment in a way that is consistent with investor goals and fiduciary responsibilities'.

2.3 Classification of Research on Financial Markets and Sustainability

There is a need to categorise finance and sustainability research to enable a proper analysis of the research efforts in the area to further unravel which areas are receiving more attention and which are not. To accomplish this task, we had to examine the themes and contents of each of the 60 articles included in the study, matching each against the other and categorising them based on similarities of purpose. On the basis of this, financial markets and sustainability research is classified as follows.

2.3.1 International finance and sustainability

This category of research examines the role of international finance and capital flows in sustainable development. It embraces research on the sustainability implications of capital flows such as Foreign Direct Investments (FDIs), private portfolio investments, remittances, Official Development Assistance (ODA), external debt and cross-border banking. It also embodies research on the role of international financial and development institutions such as the World Bank, the International Monetary Fund (IMF), the United Nations, regional development banks and the World Trade Organization, among others, in promoting sound environmental practices and sustainable livelihoods. Lastly, international finance and sustainability research also covers research on the impact of environmental degradation, carbon emissions and other sustainable development issues on multilateral financial institutions and international capital flows.

2.3.2 Financing sustainability and responsible investments

This embodies research works that emphasise the options for financing sustainable development through financial markets as well as the issues, instruments, stakeholders and mechanisms involved in responsible investments. It encompasses the role of corporate disclosure, corporate governance, investment advisors, rating agencies and institutional and individual investors in sustainable development efforts.

2.3.3 Sustainability and performance

Research under this category investigates how being sustainability sensitive will affect the bottom line of firms as well as how the performance of a firm defines its involvement in sustainability initiatives. Such research assesses the link (either unidirectional or bidirectional) between sustainable development and performance indicators such as the market value of a firm, risk and return, executive compensation, competition and diversification.

2.3.4 Policy, regulation and sustainability

Studies under this category probe the role of financial policy and financial sector regulation in promoting sustainable development. They also examine how climate change and other ecological issues shape financial policy and regulatory environment.

2.3.5 Islamic finance and sustainability

Research in this area focuses on the implications of Sharia law for SRIs and how to bridge the gap between conventional financial markets and Islamic funds.

2.3.6 Finance and sustainability: theory, method and measurement

Under this category, the focus of research is on the development of theories for the study of SRIs, the introduction of new methods for analysing the finance and sustainability link and the development and construction of indices for assessing responsible investments.

2.3.7 General finance and sustainability issues

Research work in this category deals with cross-cutting issues on finance and sustainability such as tackling in a single paper the roles of financial openness, FDI and stock markets in environmental preservation. It also covers works on agencing markets and financial innovation for sustainability.

3. METHODOLOGY FOR THE REVIEW

Boundaries had to be defined for the literature search to ensure that only materials that were directly related to the area and thorough were included in the analysis. The following principles drove the review:

- *Timeframe*: The review covers the period January 2005 to August 2016. This timeframe was chosen to ensure that the review captures the burning issues and currently unanswered questions in the research area. Also, it ensures that we track the research trajectory on the subject.
- *Database*: The search was limited to the following recognised databases: Science Direct, Emerald Full Text, JSTORE, Wiley, Google Scholar, Oxford Journals, EBSCOhost and Sage.

- *Relevance*: The full text of each paper was screened to ensure that only papers that related to sustainability and financial markets, institutions, processes, instruments, systems and investors were included.
- *Geographical boundary*: Search words were not limited in terms of geographic boundary.
- *Type of material*: In order to limit materials for the review and to ensure that materials covered are of a high standard, the review has been limited to only refereed and peer reviewed journals. Working papers, books, reports, commentaries, non-peer reviewed journals, book reviews, conference proceedings, masters and doctoral dissertations have accordingly been excluded.
- *Language*: Only articles written in the English language have been included since this is the means of instruction the authors have control over.
- *Search descriptors*: The keywords used for the search include 'financial markets and sustainability', 'financial markets and sustainable development' and 'financial markets and environmental sustainability'. Each article produced from the search was scanned to ensure that only those directly related to the topic were included in the review.

Using these principles, 60 research articles were identified and used for the review.

4. PRESENTATION OF LITERATURE REVIEW FINDINGS

Sixty research articles published in 41 different journals across seven subdisciplines were reviewed and assessed. The articles were grouped based on global geographic regions, year of publication, research focus, journal outlets, discipline background, and the segment of financial market. In the ensuing subsections we will present and analyse the findings.

4.1 Distribution of Articles in Top Journals in Finance, Economics and Ecology

In this subsection, we show the avenues through which research on finance and sustainability is disseminated. This will guide emerging scholars as to where to seek quality research in the area and the avenues that are available for them to ventilate their research findings.

One of the best guides to the comparative quality of journals in business and management research is the Association of Business Schools (ABS) Journal Quality Guide (JQG), hereafter referred to as ABS JQG. Being a hybrid-based journal quality indicator, the ABS JQG ranks journals based on a combination of factors such as peer review, citation impact factor, and detailed editorial judgements and evaluation of research articles over a long period of time. The ABS JQG ranks journals from 4* to 1 with the following descriptions: 4* – world elite journal, 4 – top journal, 3 – a highly regarded journal, 2 – a well-regarded journal, and 1 – a recognised journal. Journals were classified according to ABS JQG, but due to the strict standards in the selection of journals for the list, some journals of appreciable quality are not included in the ABS JQG. Most of the journals in the ABS JQG list are in the Thomson Reuters/ISI Web of Knowledge list. The chapter classifies ISI journals not in ABS JQG as Non ABS ISI journals. We used the ABS JQG for 2015 and the ISI list of journals for 2015 to do the classification. The details of the breakdown of articles by top journals is found in Table 12.1. The journals included in this study fall into seven out of the 22 subject areas covered by the ABS JQG.

Among the finance journals that published research on sustainability over the period, the *Journal of Banking & Finance* has the largest number of articles, 5 (8.3 per cent). It specialises in publishing both theoretical and applied research in all areas of finance and banking. Its goal is to reduce the communication gap between and within academics and researchers on one hand, and policy makers and practitioners on the other. The journal has been in operation since 1977 and has become a household name among financial economists. The finance journals with the second largest number of papers are *Corporate Governance: The International Journal of Business in Society*, and *Qualitative Research in Financial Markets*, with 2 (3.3 per cent) articles published by each. The remaining finance journals which are 6 in number, published 1 article each.

None of the three elite journals in finance (*Journal of Finance*, *Review of Financial Studies* and *Journal of Financial Economics*) appear in Table 12.1. A direct search of our descriptors in the websites of these journals returned results not directly linked to financial markets and sustainability. Clearly, there seems to be a lack of interest from mainstream finance journals in sustainability issues. There is only one grade 4 finance journal (*Journal of Corporate Finance*) that published an article on the subject. A similar search at the sites of elite economics journals such as *American Economic Review*, *Quarterly Journal of Economics*, *Econometrica*, *Journal of Political Economy* and *Review of Economic Studies* also did not yield studies on the topic. Indeed, the two elite journals (*Journal of International Business Studies*, which is categorised under International Business and

Table 12.1 Distribution of articles by top journals in economics, finance and other disciplines

Top journals	Number of articles	ABS JQG grade
Finance		
Journal of Banking & Finance	5 (8.3%)	3
Corporate Governance: The International Journal of Business in Society	2 (3.3%)	2
Qualitative Research in Financial Markets	2 (3.3%)	1
Journal of Corporate Finance	1 (1.7%)	4
Research in International Business & Finance	1 (1.7%)	2
Pacific-Basin Finance Journal	1 (1.7%)	2
Journal of Financial Regulation and Compliance	1 (1.7%)	1
Managerial Finance	1 (1.7%)	1
International Journal of Islamic & Middle Eastern Finance & Management	1 (1.7%)	1
Economics		
Journal of Economic Surveys	1 (1.7%)	2
Accounting		
Accounting, Auditing & Accountability Journal	2 (3.3%)	3
Sustainability Accounting, Management & Policy Journal	1 (1.7%)	2
Accounting & Finance	1 (1.7%)	2
Accounting Research Journal	1 (1.7%)	2
International Business & Area Studies		
Journal of International Business Studies	1 (1.7%)	4*
Sector Studies		
Energy Policy	6 (10.0%)	2
Marine Policy	1 (1.7%)	2
General Management, Ethics & Social Responsibility		
Business & Society	2 (3.3%)	3
Business Ethics: A European Review	2 (3.3%)	2
Journal of Business Ethics	2 (3.3%)	3
Academy of Management Journal	1 (1.7%)	4*
Competition and Change	1 (1.7%)	2
Regional Studies, Planning & Environment		
Environment & Planning A	1 (1.7%)	4
Environment & Planning D: Society and Space	1 (1.7%)	4
Business Strategy & the Environment	2 (3.3%)	3
Corporate Social Responsibility and Environmental Management	1 (1.7%)	1
Public Sector & Health Care		
Environment and Planning C: Government & Policy Strategy	1 (1.7%)	3

Table 12.1 (continued)

Top journals	Number of articles	ABS JQG grade
Journal of Economics & Management Strategy	1 (1.7%)	2
Non ABS ISI		
International Journal of Climate Change Strategies & Management	1 (1.7%)	
Energy	1 (1.7%)	
Total ABS/ISI	**46 (76.6%)**	
Non-listed		
Social Responsibility Journal	2 (3.3%)	
Journal of Property Investment & Finance	2 (3.3%)	
Humanomics	2 (3.3%)	
Corporate Governance	2 (3.3%)	
Management of Environmental Quality: An International Journal	1 (1.7%)	
Sustainable Development	1 (1.7%)	
Annals in Social Responsibility	1 (1.7%)	
Journal of Cleaner Production	1 (1.7%)	
Trends in Ecology & Evolution	1 (1.7%)	
Copernican Journal of Finance & Accounting	1 (1.7%)	
Total non-listed journals	**14 (23.3%)**	
Total of all journals	**60 (100.0%)**	

Notes: This table shows the distribution of 60 articles published on financial markets and sustainability according to top journals in disciplines such as Economics, Finance, Accounting, International Business & Area Studies, Sector Studies, General Management, Ethics & Social Responsibility, Regional Studies, Planning & Environment and Public Sector & Health Care. Non ABS ISI journals are journals on the ISI list but not included on the ABS list. Non-listed journals are journals not found in either the ABS or ISI list. Column 2 shows the number of articles on finance and sustainability published by a specific journal. Column 3 describes the rank of the journal in the Association of Business Schools (ABS) Journal Quality Guide (JQG).

Area Studies, *Academy of Management Journal*, which is categorised under General Management, Ethics and Social Responsibility) in the ABS list that published research on the finance sustainability link are outside mainstream economics and finance journals. The Regional Studies, Planning and Environment area recorded two grade 4 journals, each having published a paper.

Interestingly, *Energy Policy* which is classified under Sector Studies boasts of the largest number of articles included in the study, 6 (10.0 per cent). The publishers state on the journal's website that it focuses on the 'policy implications of energy supply and use from their economic, social, planning and environmental aspects'.[2] Thus environmental and market issues are consciously being addressed by the journal. Little wonder it has become an important means of disseminating finance and sustainability research.

Altogether, journals in the ABS/ISI lists contributed 46 (76.4 per cent) out of the 60 articles included in the study. This testifies to the high quality of the journals included in the review. The remaining 14 (23.3 per cent) articles came from other peer reviewed journals not captured in the ABS/ISI lists.

4.2 Distribution of Articles by Year

Figure 12.1 shows the percentage of articles published per year from 2005 to 2016. Generally, there has been an upward trend in the number of articles published on finance and sustainability over the research period. The second highest percentage of articles published occurred in 2009 when the global financial crisis that started in 2007 had reached its zenith. The crisis may have drawn the attention of researchers to the potential implications of an unstable financial sector for sustainable development. The year 2015 boasts of the largest number of articles published per year. The year 2015

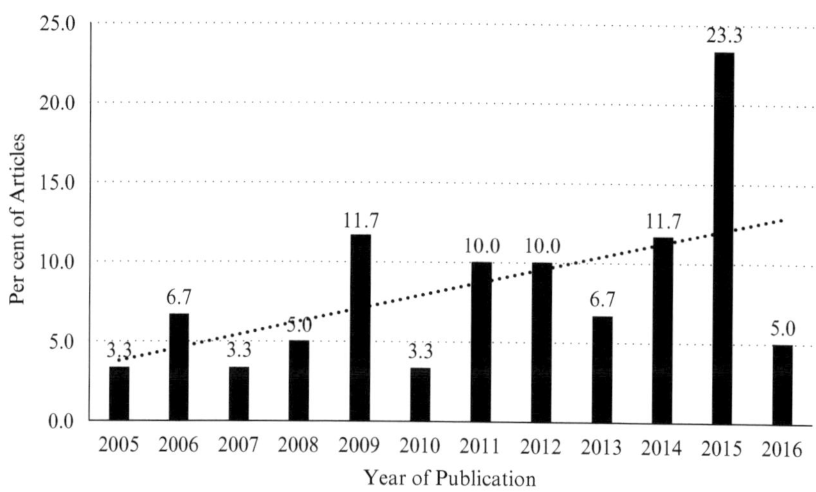

Notes: The figure shows the percentage of articles on the finance-sustainability nexus published in each year from January 2005 to August 2016. The vertical axis reveals the per cent of published articles while the horizontal axis shows the year of publication.

Figure 12.1 Distribution percentage of articles by year: 2005–2016

marked the end of the Millennium Development Goals (MDGs), under which member countries of the UN were to have achieved some lofty developmental targets including sustainable development. This may have triggered research on the role of finance in ensuring sustainability. With the Sustainable Development Goals (SDGs) replacing the MDGs, it is hoped that research efforts will be stepped up in the area of the contribution of financial markets to natural resource preservation, the promotion of biodiversity and reductions in carbon emissions.

4.3 Distribution of Research Focus

The distribution of articles according to the various segments of the financial system is shown in Figure 12.2. The majority of the research on finance and sustainability focuses on either stock markets or multiple sectors (other), with 18 (30 per cent) articles published in each sector. Research work on stock markets often deals with issues regarding responsible investment disclosures, market reaction to stocks issued by socially

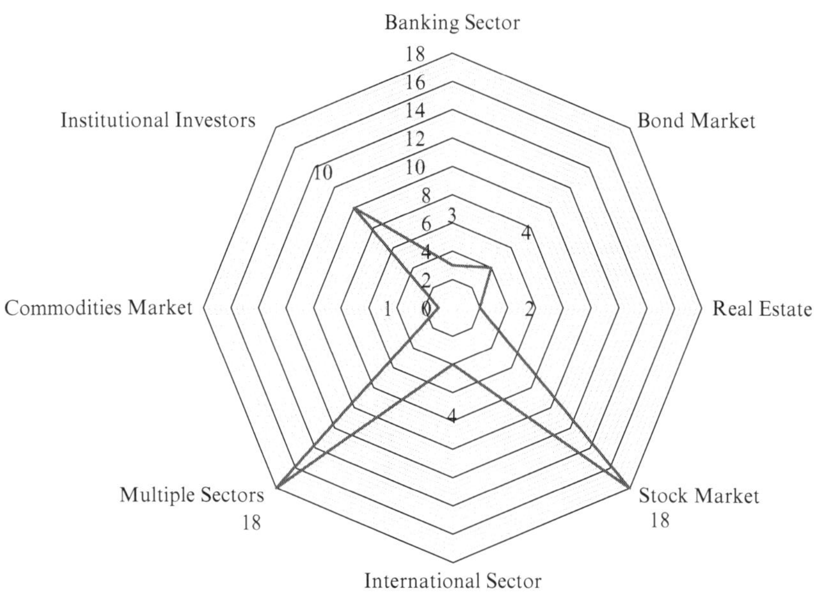

Notes: The figure describes the number of articles on finance and sustainability published in relation to the various sectors of the financial system. 'Multiple Sectors' refers to a piece of research that covers two or more sectors.

Figure 12.2 Distribution of articles by sector

responsible firms, the development of stock market infrastructure to support sustainability investing and the construction of market indices for measuring responsible investing. Since most big firms are listed on stock exchanges, this market constitutes an important channel through which sustainable business practices can be engineered and enforced.

A sizable amount of sustainability research (10 articles representing 16.7 per cent of all articles) has been conducted on institutional investors such as mutual funds, pension funds and insurance companies. The bulk of the research on this segment of the financial market focuses on whether institutional investors employ ESG criteria in making their investment decisions. The bond market, international sector and banking sector received comparatively less attention in terms of sustainability research, with each recording 4 (6.7 per cent), 4 (6.7 per cent) and 3 (5.0 per cent) articles respectively. The commodities market consisting of trading of commodities (such as cocoa, coffee, precious metals such as gold, diamonds and silver, and hydrocarbons such as crude oil) received the least attention in terms of sustainability research, followed by the real estate (mortgage) sector. Therefore, future research could explore research opportunities in the less and least research areas to broaden our understanding of the interaction between financial markets and sustainable development.

4.4 Distribution of Research by Geographical Location

We present results on the distribution of articles on finance and sustainability across the regions of the world in Figure 12.3. Most of the research has a global appeal (33.3 per cent), cutting across continental boundaries. In terms of continents, Europe and North America received the most research attention, with 20.0 per cent and 16.7 per cent, respectively, of financial markets and sustainability research being conducted there. Oceania has experienced a moderate amount of research focus. The least researched continents are Asia (3.3 per cent), South America (1.7 per cent) and Africa (1.7 per cent).

Clearly, the research effort is focused on high income countries, while middle and low income countries are given little attention. Meanwhile, according to the *Living Planet Report 2014* (McLellan et al., 2014), though low income countries have the smallest ecological footprint, they are the most affected by ecosystem losses. According to the report, for over five decades, the demand for ecological goods and services by most high income countries has exceeded their existing biocapacity. For this reason, most high income countries are living on middle and low income countries to satisfy their lifestyles. Therefore, much as we require research on how the life choices and financial markets of developed countries impact or

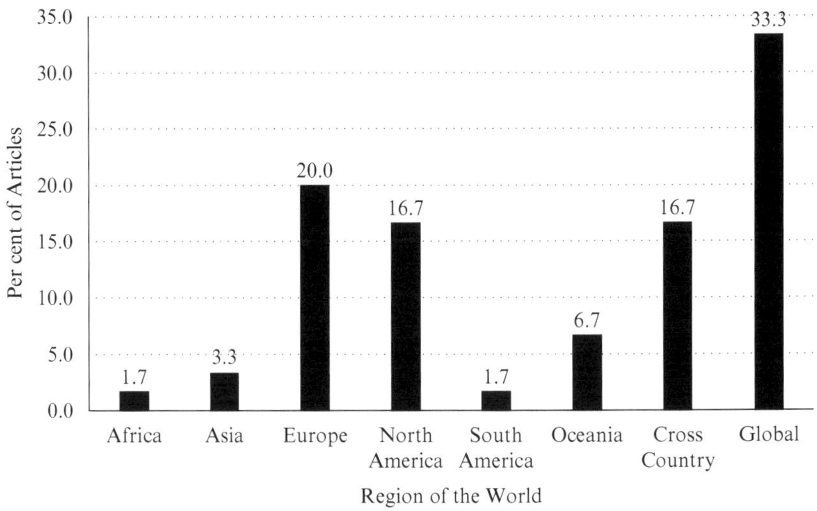

Notes: The figure describes the percentage of articles on finance and sustainability published in each of the major regions of the world. The vertical axis shows the per cent of articles published while the horizontal axis shows the major regions of the world. 'Global' refers to research which covers two or more continents.

Figure 12.3 Percentage of articles published in each region

are impacted by the environment, in the same manner we require research on the implications of advanced country environmental deterioration on the financial sector and general living conditions in developing countries. Again, even though developing countries are the least degrading of the ecosystem, it does not mean they do not have serious environmental concerns. There is a need in these countries to conduct more research on how financial markets can impact carbon emissions, forest preservation, sustainable livelihoods and general biodiversity preservation.

5. MAPPING FINANCIAL MARKETS AND SUSTAINABILITY RESEARCH: BURNING ISSUES AND EVIDENCE

5.1 Mapping Research Issues

From Table 12.2 it can be seen that the bulk of the research is concentrated on Financing Sustainability & Responsible Investing (19 articles, 31.7 per cent) and Sustainability & Performance (18 articles, 30.0 per cent).

Table 12.2 Distribution of articles on financial markets and sustainability

Research focus	Sub-issue	Number of articles	(Frequency)
International Finance and Sustainability			5 (8.3%)
	FDI	2 (3.3%)	
	Official Development Assistance	0 (0.0%)	
	Remittances	0 (0.0%)	
	Private Portfolio Investment	0 (0.0%)	
	External Debt	0 (0.0%)	
	Other	3 (8.3%)	
Financing Sustainability and Responsible Investing			19 (31.7%)
	Responsible Investing	7 (11.7%)	
	Financing Sustainability	5 (8.3%)	
	Disclosure	2 (3.3%)	
	Governance	4 (6.7%)	
	Financial Crises	1 (1.7%)	
Sustainability and Performance			18 (30.0%)
	Market Valuation	4 (6.7%)	
	Risk and/or Return	11 (18.3%)	
	Diversification	1 (1.7%)	
	Executive Compensation	1 (1.7%)	
	Several	1 (1.7%)	
Policy, Regulation and Sustainability			3 (5.0%)
	Sustainability Policies	0 (0.0%)	
	Financial Regulation	3 (5.0%)	
Islamic Finance and Sustainability			4 (6.7%)
	Sharia Compliant Sustainable Investing	3 (5.0%)	
	The Gap between Islamic and Conventional Market	1 (1.7%)	
Theory, Method and Measurement Issues in Sustainability Finance			7 (11.7%)
	Theory	1 (1.7%)	
	Method	1 (1.7%)	

Table 12.2 (continued)

Research focus	Sub-issue	Number of articles	(Frequency)
	Measurement	5 (8.3%)	
General			4 (6.7%)
	Stocks, FDI, Financial Openness		
Total			**60 (100.0%)**

Notes: The table describes how research on finance and sustainability is distributed across research themes. Column 1 specifies the research focus themes; column 2 describes the sub-themes under each theme; column 3 shows the number of articles per sub-theme; column 4 shows the number of articles per major research theme.

The relatively less addressed research areas include Theory, Method & Measurement Issues in Sustainability Finance (7 articles, 11.7 per cent), International Finance & Sustainability (5 articles, 8.3 per cent), Islamic Finance & Sustainability (4 articles, 6.7 per cent) and Policy, Regulation & Sustainability (3 articles, 5.0 per cent). The majority of the articles on Financing Sustainability & Responsible Investing focuses on Responsible Investing (11.7 per cent), Financing Sustainability (8.3 per cent) and Governance (6.7 per cent). The knowledge gap lies in how Disclosure (3.3 per cent) by financial markets can affect sustainability and how sustainable business practices are affected by or affect Financial Crises (1.7 per cent).

Most of the research work on Sustainability & Performance investigates the Risk and/or Return (18.3 per cent) implications of sustainable business practices and to a moderate extent the Market Valuation (6.7 per cent) of sustainability funds. The links between Diversification (1.7 per cent), Executive Compensation (1.7 per cent) and sustainable development however, require critical investigation. Under the relatively less researched issue of Theory, Method & Measurement Issues in Sustainability Finance, the research has mainly focused on measurement where indices for measuring sustainable business practices are developed. Studies on theories concerning the finance sustainability nexus and innovative methodologies are however insufficient.

With regards to International Finance & Sustainability, the bulk of the research deals with mixed issues ('Other'; 8.3 per cent) that describe the role of several sources of international finance or multilateral financial institutions in a single study. FDI (3.3 per cent) has also received some modest research attention. However, the sustainability implications of

Remittances, ODA, Private Portfolio Investment and External Debt are yet to engage the attention of researchers.

Within the less researched area of Islamic Finance & Sustainability more research is required on how to bridge the gap between Islamic and conventional markets through ethical and sustainability investing. Regarding the research on the role of financial Policy, Regulation & Sustainability, there is a modest amount of research on how the regulation of financial markets (5.0 per cent) can impact sustainable development. What is lacking in the literature is how sustainability policies by businesses and policy makers affect sustainable development in real life.

5.2 Burning Issues and Evidence

In this section, we highlight some interesting papers and some critical issues they raised.

5.2.1 Financing sustainability and responsible investments

Schaefer et al. (2012) investigate the demand for Socially Responsible Property Investments (SRPIs) in Germany. They find that institutional investors who already have a history of investing in socially responsible assets have a greater knowledge of SRIs and SRPIs. Again, institutional investors with a higher asset quota of SRI have a better knowledge of SRI but those investors with a higher asset quota of SRIs do not necessarily have more knowledge on SRPIs. Rather, investors with a higher asset quota in general property investments have a superior knowledge of SRPIs. The authors conclude that there is low demand for SRPIs in Germany due to the lack of innovative products on SRPIs or the opaqueness of the SRPIs market, or because institutional investors do not view the SRPIs asset class as a viable investment opportunity.

In a related study, de Zwaan et al. (2015) examine the perceptions of superannuation scheme members on ESG investing. They find that although the majority of superannuation fund members find ESG investments attractive, they lack adequate information about the ESG investment strategy of their fund. However, the study shows that scheme members pay more attention to governance issues than social and environmental issues. These two papers emphasise the need to develop innovative SRI and SRPI products and to involve investors in the formulation and implementation of ESG strategies.

Ng and Tao (2016) discuss how local currency corporate bonds, green bonds and asset backed bonds can be used to finance renewable energy projects in Asia. They find that although these bonds have the potential to help bridge the financing gap in renewable energy markets, critical issues such as the development of a renewable energy policy, the deepening of fixed income markets and the lack of standardisation for green bonds must be addressed.

5.2.2 Sustainability and performance

Strike et al. (2006) test the hypothesis that a firm can be both socially responsible and socially irresponsible at the same time. Their results show that, indeed, a firm can in one vein act in a socially responsible manner and in the other vein act in a manner that is socially irresponsible. According to the study, both corporate social responsibility and corporate social irresponsibility increase with the degree of international diversification. Corporate reputation and organisational learning enable international firms to engage in more CSR. At the same time, as the firm gets bigger as a result of international diversification, it becomes unwieldy and may find some of its subsidiaries compromising on social responsibility and environmental integrity. Hence, the authors reject a straight categorisation of firms into 'good' or 'bad' firms based on CSR since the same firm can exhibit both features.

The work of Galema et al. (2008) seeks to resolve the difference between theory and practice when it comes to the relationship between SRI and risk and return. While neoclassical theory predicts that responsible firms will receive lower returns than their irresponsible counterparts, earlier empirical results provided no support for this fact. The theoretical proposition is based on the thinking that investors will demand more of responsible stocks than irresponsible ones; this will lead to an overpricing of responsible stocks and an underpricing of irresponsible stocks. Galema et al. (2008) attribute the contradictions to 'misinterpretations' by empirical studies. After correcting for the misrepresentations, they find evidence consistent with the neoclassical theory.

In a related study, Liesen (2014) examines whether the stock market correctly prices systematic risk arising from climate change. They show that financial markets in Europe fail to correctly price climate driven systematic risk. The risk adjusted return of firms with low climate driven systematic risk was found to be higher than that of the risk adjusted return on stocks of companies with high climate induced systematic risk. Weber (2012) investigates whether Canadian financial institutions are proactive in factoring environmental risk in their credit decisions. The results show that Canadian financial institutions consider environmental credit risk in their corporate lending activities to the point that some firms have started integrating environmental and sustainability related issues in their business strategy. The study recommends that future research looks at computing the costs and benefits of integrating environmental and sustainability issues into business strategy.

5.2.3 Theory, method and measurement issues in sustainability finance

Studies that are based on measurement and sustainability focus on constructing an Environmental Risk Index (ERI) for financial firms (Prorokowski, 2016; Hoti et al., 2007), whether social ratings indeed measure CSR (Chatterji et al., 2009), the financialisation of sustainability (Hiss, 2013), and assessing business sustainability (Svensson and Wagner, 2015). The ERI constructed by Prorokowski (2016) contains 44 variables grouped into vectors such as carbon neutrality, water management, waste management, paper management, ESG-specific funds, employee engagement, environmental training and collaboration with NGOs. The findings show a positive relationship between ERI and revenues, suggesting that being green is profitable. In an examination of whether social ratings (in particular those of Kinder, Lydenberg, Domini Research & Analytics (KLD)) truly measure CSR, Chatterji et al. (2009) show that the KLD captures the past environmental performance of firms well. Also, firms with KLD concerns are more likely to pollute the environment and violate regulations in the future. The KLD is, however, unable to predict the propensity of firms with KLD environmental strengths to pollute or violate regulations. According to the authors, the KLD does not optimally incorporate the available data. Therefore, there is a need to broaden the scope of the index. The authors suggest that future research should examine the ability of social ratings to predict good environmental performance such as the development of green products.

In terms of method-based studies, Bilbao-Terol and Cañal-Fernández (2014) use the hedonic price model to assess the valuation of ethical funds in Spain. The results show that the Spanish market rewards firms that value 'environmental sustainability, the enforcement of labour rights, sustainable production and consumption and non-abusive market practices' (Bilbao-Terol and Cañal-Fernández, 2014, p. 1).

Theory-wise, Thistlethwaite and Paterson (2016) look at sustainability accounting in the light of three theoretical constructs – privatised neoliberal governance; professional epistemic authority; and experimentation and experimental governance. It is argued that while neoliberal governance portrays a platform where capital and civil society interact, professionalisation and experimentation deal with actions of individuals that obscure the capital–civil society link.

5.2.4 International finance and sustainability

With regards to international finance and sustainability, Lv and Spigarelli (2015) examine the role of Chinese FDI in integrating Chinese and European renewable energy markets and find that Chinese firms are more likely to invest in countries with similar legal structures to those of China.

The study further finds that firms with weak governance structures tend to gravitate towards countries with weak institutions and lax regulatory frameworks. Pao and Tsai (2011) look at the nature of causality among FDI, carbon emissions, energy consumption and economic growth in BRIC countries. In the end, a bidirectional relationship between FDI and carbon emissions is established. The authors advise developing countries to screen multinationals properly to ensure environmental soundness compliance, so that they can attain low emissions without sacrificing competitiveness.

Boakye-Agyei (2011) focuses the discussion on environmental due diligence by Multilateral Financial Institutions (MFIs) such as the World Bank, the African Development Bank, the Inter-American Development Bank and the European Bank for Reconstruction and Development. The study finds that although the banks integrate climate change into their general business strategies, most of their environmental safeguards (such as environmental impact assessments and strategic environmental assessments) do not formally incorporate climate change. Consequently, it is recommended that MFIs formally include climate change issues in their environmental safeguards.

5.2.5 Islamic finance and sustainability

Monzurul Hoque et al. (2015) and BinMahfouz and Kabir Hassan (2013) show that Islamic funds do not underperform when compared to conventional responsible investment funds or the broader market. In fact, Hassan (2009) finds that *Sharia* investments can even outperform conventional funds. These results imply that ethical and green investors can pursue their sustainability goals without fear of losing out financially and that *Sharia* funds should not seek to mimic conventional funds but, rather, should seek to replace them (Hassan, 2009). Bennett and Iqbal (2013) propose the use of the *Sukuk* to bridge the gap between Islamic and conventional funds. In their opinion, the use of the *Sukuk* can help deepen the fixed income segment of Islamic markets which is underdeveloped at the moment. Bennett and Iqbal (2013, p. 214) define a *Sukuk* as 'a certificate that represents the right to receive payments from an underlying asset or business venture'.

5.2.6 Policy, regulation and sustainability

Diaz-Rainey et al. (2011) and Nijman (2012) examine the role of the EU in crafting sustainability regulations for financial markets. Nijman (2012) particularly looks at the impact of newly proposed financial regulations on energy markets and finds that the regulations have no clear effect on energy markets, implying that the desired outcome of the regulations may not be realised. Richardson (2008) advocates the introduction of new regulations for socially responsible funds, especially by incorporating what he calls the 'fiduciary duties' of stakeholders into the financial system. In Richardson's view, linking such fiduciary duties will serve to encourage investments in sustainable funds.

6. BUILDING A RESEARCH FRAMEWORK FOR FINANCIAL MARKETS AND SUSTAINABILITY RESEARCH

We propose the framework in Figure 12.4 to guide research work on financial markets and sustainable development. A double-headed arrow connects sustainability and financial markets suggesting a two-way relationship between them. We suggest a conscious effort by researchers to ensure that a balanced and multidirectional view of the relationship is always considered. The framework is proposing a holistic consideration of sustainability in research efforts. Thus the system view of sustainability is what is modelled in the framework. Sustainability is divided into three main categories, namely, natural resource sustainability, business sustainability and sustainable human development. *Natural resource sustainability* embodies environmental sustainability, energy sustainability and water sustainability. Environmental sustainability research covers soil, birds, plants (crops, trees, timber and flowers), animals, minerals and atmosphere. Energy sustainability entails the judicious utilisation of energy resources such as solar, wind, natural gas, oil and fossil fuels. *Water sustainability* embodies the sustainable management and use of water resources such as seas, oceans, dams, streams, sea plankton, fish and other water living organisms.

Business sustainability is concerned with sustainable business practices that ensure market sustainability, financial sustainability, economic sustainability and operational sustainability. Thus research work in this area will examine how the different segments of financial markets affect the various dimensions of business sustainability. *Sustainable human development* takes a wider view of human development and embodies safety and security, income security, family sustainability, socio-cultural sustainability and health sustainability.

Again, a double-headed arrow connects the three categories of sustainability, indicating that sustainability is a continuum and, for that matter, achieving just one or two categories will not guarantee true sustainability. This consciousness must be integrated into finance and sustainability research. Such research work could look at how financial markets recon-

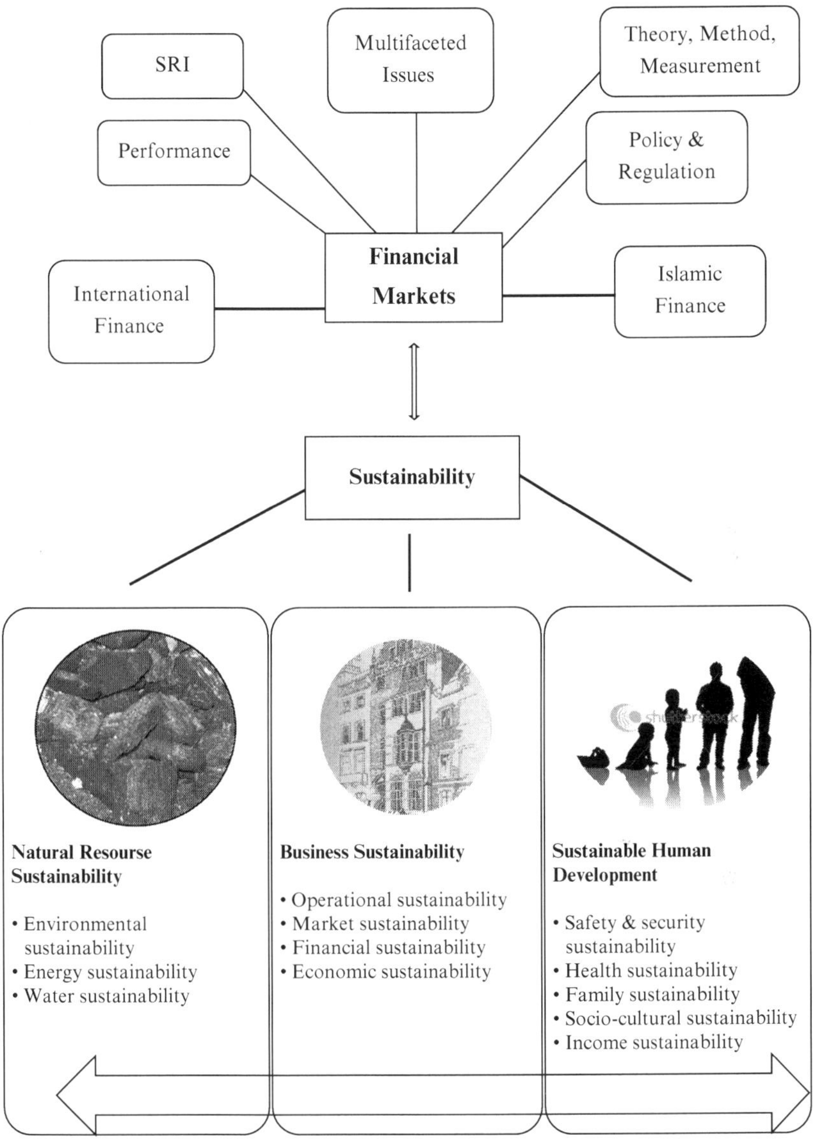

Notes: The figure shows a research framework for finance and sustainability. A double-headed arrow connects sustainability and financial markets, suggesting a two-way relationship between them. Sustainability has three major components each with sub-components. Again, a double-headed arrow connects the three categories of sustainability, indicating that sustainability is a continuum. The category 'Financial Markets' has seven main components, which are indicated in the topmost part of the diagram.

Figure 12.4 Research framework for financial markets and sustainability

cile say, natural resource sustainability with sustainable human development; whether there are trade-offs among the dimensions of business sustainability; whether the pursuit of sustainable human development goals will compromise financial market development and vice versa, and to what extent?

Our proposed research framework links the system view of sustainability to various segments of the financial system comprising international finance, firm performance, SRI, Islamic finance, financial policy and regulation, multifaceted issues and theory, method and measurement. Each of the components of the financial system has the subcomponents shown in Table 12.2. Multifaceted issues encompass research work that cuts across several segments of the financial system or deals with cross-cutting issues not specified in the framework.

While the framework captures the extant literature it opens up the scope for finance and sustainability research going forward. For instance, the links between finance and water resources, human safety and security, health, biodiversity and energy conservation are either ignored completely or have not been given sufficient attention in the literature. The framework embodies these issues and more.

7. RESEARCH GAPS AND FUTURE RESEARCH DIRECTIONS

A number of research gaps have been identified based on the mapping of the literature presented earlier. We identify some under-researched and inconclusive research issues regarding the finance–sustainability link. These gaps and issues can be taken up for future research. They include:

- The role of remittances, portfolio investment, external debt and ODA in ensuring sustainability;
- How financial crises affect sustainability and how climate change affects financial crises;
- The ways in which executive compensation, diversification and ESG disclosure impact on the sustainability drive of firms and the costs and benefit of such efforts;
- Explaining the development and implementation of firm- and market-level sustainability policies;
- Developing theories linking finance to the system view of sustainability;
- The application of rigorous econometric methodology and mixed methods to the finance–sustainability link;

- An assessment of the potential for using the *Sukuk* as a bridge between Islamic finance and conventional finance, and the sustainability gains from such a move;
- Clarification of the costs and benefits of integrating environmental and sustainability issues into business strategy.

Other critical research opportunities include the following questions. Can ESG and CRS indices accurately predict good sustainability performances of firms? How do developing countries screen multinational companies to ensure effective ESG without making such multinationals less competitive? What is/are the role(s) of commodity markets in ensuring sustainability (for example cocoa, coffee, rubber, gold, silver, diamonds and crude oil)? How do financial markets develop innovative products to encourage SRI?

8. CONCLUSION

The study elaborated in this chapter explores the literature on the link between financial markets and sustainable development. It analyses the trend of the research on this interesting subject from January 2005 to August 2016, as well as revealing the channels through which such research works are disseminated. We find that research on finance and sustainability peaked in 2015 when the MDGs came to an end. The study also shows that research on finance and sustainability is disseminated through a wide range of journals across several disciplines. We find that the elite journals in economics and finance do not pay so much attention to sustainability issues. The chapter identifies research themes that have received attention and those that have not. The chapter further classifies the prevailing literature and explores the empirical evidence and issues raised under each research category. On the basis of the review we propose a framework for studying the finance–sustainability nexus. The framework endorses a system view of sustainability and how it connects with the whole financial system. Drawing on the analysis of issues and the proposed framework, we identify research gaps and offer suggestions to guide future research on the finance–sustainability link.

ACKNOWLEDGEMENTS

Mohammed Amidu and Haruna Issahaku would like to thank the VolkswagenStiftung Foundation and Funddacao Calouste Gulbenkian for funding this research, which is part of a research project on 'Knowledge for Tomorrow – Cooperative Research Projects in Sub-Saharan Africa'. However, we state that the funding did not interfere with the research process in any way.

NOTES

1. Ecological footprint is defined in the *Living Planet Report 2014* (McLellan et al., 2014) as 'the ecological goods and services people demand that compete for space'.
2. See details at http://www.journals.elsevier.com/energy-policy/

REFERENCES

Alonso-Almeida, M., J. Llach and F. Marimon (2014), 'A closer look at the "Global Reporting Initiative" sustainability reporting as a tool to implement environmental and social policies: A worldwide sector analysis', *Corporate Social Responsibility and Environmental Management*, **21**(6), 318–335.

Badiru, A.B. (2010), 'The many languages of sustainability', *Industrial Engineer*, **42**(11), 31–34.

Bauer, R., K. Koedijk and R. Otten (2005), 'International evidence on ethical mutual fund performance and investment style', *Journal of Banking & Finance*, **29**(7), 1751–1767.

Bauer, R., R. Otten and A.T. Rad (2006), 'Ethical investing in Australia: Is there a financial penalty?', *Pacific-Basin Finance Journal*, **14**(1), 33–48.

Bennett, M.S. and Z. Iqbal (2013), 'How socially responsible investing can help bridge the gap between Islamic and conventional financial markets', *International Journal of Islamic and Middle Eastern Finance and Management*, **6**(3), 211–225.

Berrone, P. and L.R. Gomez-Mejia (2009), 'Environmental performance and executive compensation: An integrated agency-institutional perspective', *Academy of Management Journal*, **52**(1), 103–126.

Bianchi, R.J., R. Copp, M.L. Kremmer and E. Roca (2010), 'Should funds invest in socially responsible investments during downturns?', *Accounting Research Journal*, **23**(3), 254–266.

Bilbao-Terol, C. and V. Cañal-Fernández (2014), 'The market valuation of ethical assets in Spain: An application of the hedonic pricing method', *Business Ethics: A European Review*, **23**(4), 343–363.

BinMahfouz, S. and M. Kabir Hassan (2013), 'Sustainable and socially responsible investing', *Humanomics*, **29**(3), 164–186.

Boakye-Agyei, K. (2011), 'Approaching climate adjusted environmental due diligence for multilateral financial institutions', *International Journal of Climate Change Strategies and Management*, **3**(3), 264–274.

Busch, T., R. Bauer and M. Orlitzky (2015), 'Sustainable development and financial markets: Old paths and new avenues', *Business & Society*, **55**(3), 303–329.

Carnicer, J. and J. Peñuelas (2012), 'The world at a crossroads: Financial scenarios for sustainability', *Energy Policy*, **48**, 611–617.

Chatterji, A.K., D.I. Levine and M.W. Toffel (2009), 'How well do social ratings actually measure corporate social responsibility?', *Journal of Economics & Management Strategy*, **18**(1), 125–169.

Chen, J.-L., J.-Y. Chen, C.-T. Chuang, H.-J. Lu, H.-H. Liu and Y.-S. Lin (2014), 'Developing a co-management financing mechanism to enhance the financial sustainability of marine protected areas in Taiwan', *Marine Policy*, **48**, 126–133.

Clark, G.L. and T. Hebb (2005), 'Why should they care? The role of institutional investors in the market for corporate global responsibility', *Environment and Planning A*, **37**(11), 2015–2031.

Dangelico, R.M. and P. Pontrandolfo (2015), 'Being "green and competitive": The impact of environmental actions and collaborations on firm performance', *Business Strategy and the Environment*, **24**(6), 413–430.

de Zwaan, L., M. Brimble and J. Stewart (2015), 'Member perceptions of ESG investing through superannuation', *Sustainability Accounting, Management and Policy Journal*, **6**(1), 79–102.

Derwall, J., K. Koedijk and J. Ter Horst (2011), 'A tale of values-driven and profit-seeking social investors', *Journal of Banking & Finance*, **35**(8), 2137–2147.

Diaz-Rainey, I., M. Siems and J.K. Ashton (2011), 'The financial regulation of energy and environmental markets', *Journal of Financial Regulation and Compliance*, **19**(4), 355–369.

DiSegni, D.M., M. Huly and S. Akron (2015), 'Corporate social responsibility, environmental leadership and financial performance', *Social Responsibility Journal*, **11**(1), 131–148.

Dorfleitner, G. and S. Utz (2014), 'Profiling German-speaking socially responsible investors', *Qualitative Research in Financial Markets*, **6**(2), 118–156.

Fieseler, C. (2011), 'On the corporate social responsibility perceptions of equity analysts', *Business Ethics: A European Review*, **20**(2), 131–147.

Frisari, G. and M. Stadelmann (2015), 'De-risking concentrated solar power in emerging markets: The role of policies and international finance institutions', *Energy Policy*, **82**, 12–22.

Galaz, V., J. Gars, F. Moberg, B. Nykvist and C. Repinski (2015), 'Why ecologists should care about financial markets', *Trends in Ecology & Evolution*, **30**(10), 571–580.

Galema, R., A. Plantinga and B. Scholtens (2008), 'The stocks at stake: Return and risk in socially responsible investment', *Journal of Banking & Finance*, **32**(12), 2646–2654.

Hassan, A. (2009), 'After the credit crunch: The future of Shari'ah compliant sustainable investing', *Humanomics*, **25**(4), 285–296.

Hiss, S. (2013), 'The politics of the financialization of sustainability', *Competition & Change*, **17**(3), 234–247.

Hoti, S., M. McAleer and L.L. Pauwels (2007), 'Measuring Risk in Environmental Finance', *Journal of Economic Surveys*, **21**(5), 970–998.

Kalinowski, M. (2014), 'Stock exchanges sustainability support assessment', *Copernican Journal of Finance and Accounting*, **3**(2), 37–48.

Lenssen, G., A. Nijhof, L. Roger, H. Kievit, A. Sreekumar Nair and R. Ladha (2014), 'Determinants of non-economic investment goals among Indian investors', *Corporate Governance: The International Journal of Business in Society*, **14**(5), 714–727.

Lewis, A. and C. Juravle (2009), 'Morals, markets and sustainable investments: A qualitative study of "champions"', *Journal of Business Ethics*, **93**(3), 483–494.

Liesen, A. (2014), 'Climate change and financial market efficiency', *Business & Society*, **54**(4), 511–539.

Lourenço, I.C. and M.C. Branco (2013), 'Determinants of corporate sustainability performance in emerging markets: The Brazilian case', *Journal of Cleaner Production*, **57**, 134–141.

Lv, P. and F. Spigarelli (2015), 'The integration of Chinese and European renewable energy markets: The role of Chinese foreign direct investments', *Energy Policy*, **81**, 14–26.

Mattsson, L.-G. (2016), 'Bridging gaps between policies for sustainable markets and market practices', *IMP Journal*, **10**(2), 339–356.

McLellan, R., Iyengar, L., Jeffries, B. and Oerlemans, N. (2014). *Living Planet Report 2014: Species and spaces, people and places*, World Wide Fund for Nature.

Monzurul Hoque, D., M. Dah, M. Hoque and S. Wang (2015), 'Constrained investments and opportunity cost – evidence from Islamic funds', *Managerial Finance*, **41**(4), 348–367.

Moroney, R., C. Windsor and Y.T. Aw (2012), 'Evidence of assurance enhancing the quality of voluntary environmental disclosures: An empirical analysis', *Accounting & Finance*, **52**(3), 903–939.

Murray, A., D. Sinclair, D. Power and R. Gray (2006), 'Do financial markets care about social and environmental disclosure?', *Accounting, Auditing & Accountability Journal*, **19**(2), 228–255.

Newell, G. and C. Lin Lee (2012), 'Influence of the corporate social responsibility factors and financial factors on REIT performance in Australia', *Journal of Property Investment & Finance*, **30**(4), 389–403.

Ng, T.H. and J.Y. Tao (2016), 'Bond financing for renewable energy in Asia', *Energy Policy*, **95**, 509–517.

Nijman, L. (2012), 'The impact of the new wave of financial regulation for European energy markets', *Energy Policy*, **47**, 468–477.

Onyas, W.I. and A. Ryan (2015), 'Agencing markets: Actualizing ongoing market innovation', *Industrial Marketing Management*, **44**, 13–21.

Paetzold, F., T. Busch, and M. Chesney (2015), 'More than money: Exploring the role of investment advisors for sustainable investing', *Annals in Social Responsibility*, **1**(1), 195–223.

Pao, H.-T. and C.-M. Tsai (2011), 'Multivariate Granger causality between CO2 emissions, energy consumption, FDI (foreign direct investment) and GDP (gross domestic product): Evidence from a panel of BRIC (Brazil, Russian Federation, India, and China) countries', *Energy*, **36**(1), 685–693.

Peneda Saraiva, P. and Z.M. Silva Serrasqueiro (2007), 'Corporate sustainability in the Portuguese financial institutions', *Social Responsibility Journal*, **3**(2), 82–94.

Petersen, H. and H. Vredenburg (2009), 'Corporate governance, social responsibility and capital markets: Exploring the institutional investor mental model', *Corporate Governance: The International Journal of Business in Society*, **9**(5), 610–622.

Pivo, G. and P. McNamara (2005), 'Responsible property investing', *International Real Estate Review*, **8**(1), 128–143.

Prorokowski, L. (2016), 'Environmental Risk Index for financial services firms', *Qualitative Research in Financial Markets*, **8**(1), 16–44.

Renneboog, L., J. Ter Horst and C. Zhang (2008), 'The price of ethics and stakeholder governance: The performance of socially responsible mutual funds', *Journal of Corporate Finance*, **14**(3), 302–322.

Richardson, B.J. (2008), 'Keeping ethical investment ethical: Regulatory issues for investing for sustainability', *Journal of Business Ethics*, **87**(4), 555–572.

Rydin, Y. (2016), 'Sustainability and the financialisation of commercial property: Making prime and non-prime markets', *Environment and Planning D: Society and Space*, **34**(4), 745–762.

Schaefer, H., C. Gromer and A. Neligan (2012), 'The demand of sustainable property investments in Germany', *Journal of Property Investment & Finance*, **30**(1), 5–17.

Schinckus, C. (2017), 'Financial innovation as a potential force for a positive social change: The challenging future of social impact bonds', *Research in International Business and Finance*, **39**(Part B), 727–736.

Scholtens, B. (2011), 'Corporate social responsibility in the international insurance industry', *Sustainable Development*, **19**(2), 143–156.

Shaoul, J., A. Stafford and P. Stapleton (2010), 'Financial black holes: The disclosure and transparency of privately financed roads in the UK', *Accounting, Auditing & Accountability Journal*, **23**(2), 229–255.

Slager, R. and W. Chapple (2016), 'Carrot and stick? The role of financial market intermediaries in corporate social performance', *Business & Society*, **55**(3), 398–426.

Stellner, C., C. Klein and B. Zwergel (2015), 'Corporate social responsibility and Eurozone corporate bonds: The moderating role of country sustainability', *Journal of Banking & Finance*, **59**, 538–549.

Strike, V.M., J. Gao and P. Bansal (2006), 'Being good while being bad: Social responsibility and the international diversification of US firms', *Journal of International Business Studies*, **37**(6), 850–862.

Svensson, G. and B. Wagner (2015), 'Implementing and managing economic, social and environmental efforts of business sustainability', *Management of Environmental Quality: An International Journal*, **26**(2), 195–213.

Tamazian, A., J.P. Chousa and K.C. Vadlamannati (2009), 'Does higher economic and financial development lead to environmental degradation: Evidence from BRIC countries', *Energy Policy*, **37**(1), 246–253.

Thistlethwaite, J. and M. Paterson (2016), 'Private governance and accounting for sustainability networks', *Environment and Planning C: Government and Policy*, **34**(7), 1197–1221.

Van Velsor, E. and G. Caspary (2009), 'Improving sustainability in the financing of large infrastructure projects: What role for leaders?', *Corporate Governance: The International Journal of Business in Society*, **9**(1), 58–72.

Weber, O. (2012), 'Environmental credit risk management in banks and financial service institutions', *Business Strategy and the Environment*, **21**(4), 248–263.

Wu, M.-W. and C.-H. Shen (2013), 'Corporate social responsibility in the banking industry: Motives and financial performance', *Journal of Banking & Finance*, **37**(9), 3529–3547.

13. Financial innovation with a social purpose: the growth of Social Impact Bonds

Frédéric de Mariz and José Roberto Ferreira Savoia

1. INTRODUCTION

Corporate governance and market pressure have evolved to include social responsibility in the day-to-day running of large corporations and banks. In this chapter, we take stock of the existing body of knowledge around responsible finance and Social Impact Bonds (SIBs). While there is ample literature on the features and advantages of SIBs, our contribution focuses on lessons learned from existing SIBs, especially regarding the financial aspects of the instrument, and we make recommendations to grow this investment type.

Most of the existing literature on Social Impact Bonds belongs to three currents. Due to the recent creation of SIBs, the first current is rather descriptive and analyzes common features of existing instruments and reasons for success and failure, following Gustafsson-Wright et al. (2015) and Eccles (2016). The second current takes a financial approach and adds to the large literature on financial innovation as an ambiguous tool for economic development and growth, including Allen and Gale (1994), Beck et al. (2016) and de Mariz et al. (2016), among others. A third approach takes the angle of public policy and analyzes the relationship between public and private entities for the provision of public services, including Williamson (1999), de Mariz et al. (2014), and Hefetz and Warner (2012).

After taking stock of the existing literature and lessons learned from more than 60 existing SIBs, our chapter consists in an in-depth analysis of the financial structuring of SIBs, a theme not well covered. Finally, we note that there is a growing literature in finance that analyzes the value proposition of social or impact investing, following Humphrey et al. (2012), Reeder and Colantonio (2013) and Kaplan (2015). Authors question the rigor of impact measurement and the objective of impact investing to offer financial returns while at the same time aiming at other goals. Since data on SIBs are still too few and far between, testing the hypotheses of this impact literature with SIBs is impossible at this stage.

We show that SIBs are an example of financial innovation that can bridge the gap between providers of social services and capital, under certain conditions. Contrary to the existing literature, with its focus on targets, which treats SIBs as simple private placements (Gustafsson-Wright et al., 2015; Eccles, 2016), we find that financial structuring is complex and involves four key steps: a legal structure; the definition of the desired risk-return-impact; the placement of the SIB; and a governance model. We highlight that gaining scale remains a severe challenge and necessity for the sector. We also make four recommendations to grow the sector, consisting of: the creation of SIB Funds; the wide dissemination of knowledge; standardization in processes; and the definition of favorable regulations.

We divide the remainder of this chapter into four sections. Section 2 reviews the literature, starting with a short description of Social Impact Bonds, and we consider their advantages and drawbacks. We analyze aspects of impact bonds from the point of view of the outcome payer, most often a government. In this section, we ask why governments are shifting their focus to impact. Section 3 analyzes the viewpoint of investors who are socially-minded and focused on returns. We define a roadmap for the financial structuring of SIBs, a key contribution to the literature. We advocate an ambitious role for financial intermediaries and characterize the profile of investors, their risk appetite and expected returns. In section 4, we define a roadmap for SIBs' success. After explaining the motivations of the outcome payer and the investors, we highlight the main hurdles faced by SIBs in section 5. We end the chapter with a brief conclusion, presenting four actionable recommendations to pave the way for the issuance of more SIBs.

2. PAYING FOR OUTCOMES: LESSONS LEARNED WITH SOCIAL IMPACT BONDS

2.1 Social Impact Bonds Build on Existing Results-based Mechanisms

SIBs allow socially-motivated investors to provide working capital to social sector service providers. The investors receive a financial return on their investment from the outcome payer, most often a government, based on the social outcome that has been attained, which is measured independently.

Before we delve into the specifics of SIBs, we ask why payers are shifting their attention to the impact or outcome of some intervention. The change in focus from input (or money spent) to impact (result being produced) and outcome (the true social benefit) is a shift in paradigm for policy-makers but is not entirely new in the fields of aid or public policy. A large body of research has focused on the delivery of public services and the decision of governments to provide the services directly or through contracts. Williamson (1999) highlights that the public agency is well suited for some purposes and poorly suited for others, based on a perspective of transaction costs, and analyzes for which types of transactions the public bureaucracy is adapted. OECD (2008) stresses that public aid could and should be producing better impacts, detailing what works and what doesn't in aid. De Mariz et al. (2014) explain why and how governments can resort to effective procurement strategies, stressing some challenges for public managers. Hefetz and Warner (2012) analyze the drivers of public delivery or contracting, with a group of variables expanding beyond transaction costs to include important market, citizen and place characteristics. Analyzing SIBs, Chiodo (2015) discusses the ability of SIBs to reform the social procurement practice and the limits of the instrument.

Several societal changes have helped the gradual shift towards impact. The fiscal balance of governments has been challenged with rising levels of debt, while the current form of international aid and poor use of public spending have faced criticism. On the positive side, in some fields, access to public services, such as schooling, has made considerable progress in recent decades, suggesting authorities can focus on the quality of service and not just access itself, under the now common thought that schooling is not education. The Sustainable Development Goals (SDGs) agreed on at the United Nations (2015) have highlighted the need to establish bridges between different actors, as existing social challenges cannot be met by tax revenues alone.

Social Impact Bonds build on the experience of other mechanisms where the payer agrees on a cash transfer if a preset result is achieved, also known as payment-for-outcome. Among the most common payment-for-outcome instruments, we note that of cash on delivery. Savedoff, Perakis and Schwanke (2015) explain that under cash-on-delivery aid, donors pay governments for a specific outcome that can be measured and verified, such as $100 for every child who completes primary school and takes a test. For Leventhal (2013), the question of the effectiveness of public spending is essential to the growth of SIBs, which are a modality of contract between public authorities and the private sector. As a result, Burand (2013) describes how they share common characteristics with the model of public-private partnerships (PPPs), which have been used to fund public services for a long time.

However, CGD (2013) details how impact bonds differ in several ways from other results-based mechanisms. First, impact bonds provide working capital upfront, as opposed to when results are reached, therefore making a number of interventions viable. Second, results in social impact bonds are usually related to outcomes as opposed to outputs. Third, impact bonds can focus on the delivery of human services as opposed to infrastructure, which is most often the object of PPPs. Finally, SIBs attract private funding and therefore broaden the capital available to social projects, while also bringing in private sector efficiency, creating potential for innovation and rigor.

2.2 Basics of Social Impact Bonds

Social Impact Bonds are also known as Pay for Success projects in the US, Social Benefit Bonds in Australia, and Social Impact Contracts in France and Brazil. Development Impact Bonds (DIBs) are a variation on the theme where the outcome payer is not a government but can include foundations or not-for-profit entities. In this chapter, we use SIBs to refer to those different instruments.

The first step of a SIB consists in a feasibility study to identify the target population, the outcome and cost savings. The second step involves the structuring of the deal, where a series of contracts are signed between parties, and the SIB is placed with investors. The third step consists in the intervention itself – it includes feedback mechanisms to adjust the service delivery. The final step involves the measurement of outcomes, evaluation and potential repayment of investors. Social Impact Bonds propose a new model for delivery of public services. The focus on output and outcome helps to shift some of the risks from service providers and governments to private investors.

There are five key participants in a typical SIB (see Figure 13.1):

- *Outcome payers:* The outcome funder is willing to pay for predefined results and the eventual payment is tied to the achieved outcomes. In high-income countries, outcome payers have been municipal, state or government agencies. In low- and middle-income countries, outcome payers may be governments, but could also be foundations, development institutions, or a combination of these. Outcome payers are willing to repay the investor's principal and some interest because they derive financial savings from a successful intervention.
- *Service providers:* SIBs give service providers access to new pools of funding for upfront capital. Service providers propose innovative solutions for complex social issues where outcomes can be measured.

- *Investors:* These can include philanthropic investors, such as foundations, development institutions and high net worth individuals. As the sector matures, the group will broaden to include more traditional private sector investors. Investors assume risk for the performance of the project.
- *Specialized intermediaries:* These actors facilitate the creation of the deal, bringing together the service providers, outcome payers and investors. The intermediary has flexibility to select the service provider and define and adapt the details of the intervention. Financial intermediaries help with the due diligence process, investors' materials and the placement of the SIB.
- *Independent auditors or evaluators:* Independent from other parties, these parties measure the outcomes achieved by the intervention, an essential condition to trigger investors' payment.

Though SIBs address issues in traditional sectors of government service provision, such as education, access to employment and protection for the elderly, the interventions used in the existing SIBs are not traditional government interventions and involve unique combinations of services. SIBs have been used as a tool to fund interventions where inputs are fairly complex but outcomes are simple to measure (Gustafsson-Wright et al., 2015).

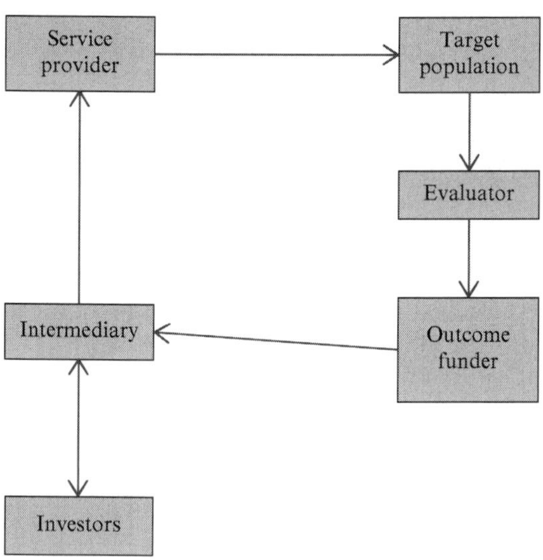

Figure 13.1 Anatomy of a SIB

There is a wide literature on the ambiguous relationship between financial innovation and economic growth. We do not try to exhaust this body of knowledge. We highlight the seminal work of Allen and Gale (1994), who emphasize the virtues of financial innovation relating to risk sharing. Authors also note that innovation can help reduce agency costs and improve allocative efficiency. On the flip side, research notes that innovation played a role in the 2008–9 financial crisis, in particular via excessive leverage or structured products whose risks were poorly understood (Johnson and Kwak, 2012).

Beck et al. (2016) tested this hypothesis by analyzing data from 32 countries over the period 1996–2010, and found that financial innovation is generally associated with a higher level of economic growth. In the case of SIBs, de Mariz et al. (2016) stress that SIBs bring several benefits, but are appropriate in certain situations only, and add another instrument to the government's toolkit (see Table 13.1).

Considering the innovation brought by SIBs, we add four conditions – SIBs are recommended in areas where: (1) outcomes can be clearly defined; (2) a proven track record of successful service provision exists; (3) political support exists; and 4) an intervention involving innovation and the private sector is socially acceptable. Existing cases involve early childhood, recidivism, homelessness, workforce development and preventive health care.

2.3 SIBs in Practice

There have been 64 social impact bonds launched globally, and more than 90 are in the works, according to Gustafsson-Wright (2016). The first SIB was implemented in 2010 in the United Kingdom for the purpose of reducing prison recidivism among short-term male prisoners at Peterborough prison, as detailed in Government of the UK (2011). In 2010, Social Finance UK raised £5 million from 17 investors to provide comprehensive assistance to three cohorts of 1,000 men (3,000 in total) released after serving short-term jail sentences in Peterborough prison. Their recidivism rates were tracked for 12 months following discharge and compared to the rates of a control group. If rates fell by at least 7.5 percent across all three cohorts compared to the control group, the British government would repay the investors' principal plus interest. The higher the drop in recidivism rates, the higher the government payment to investors, capped at 13 percent per year. If the threshold were not to be met, investors would lose their investment. The Peterborough SIB will take eight years to complete, with the potential for some intermediary payments. The Government of the UK (2014) released the preliminary results of the Peterborough SIB,

Table 13.1 Advantages and drawbacks of SIBs

Advantages	Drawbacks
SIBs have proven their flexibility, being applied in various sectors and under a variety of legal forms.	The complexity and number of parties involved makes the structuring of SIBs an expensive and complex exercise, especially as select rules of public procurement may apply.
Through a focus on impact (actual benefit) as opposed to input (euros spent), SIBs allow for a more effective public service.	Innovation is only limited, as entirely new solutions are unlikely to be tested by private investors.
SIBs infuse some degree of innovation as the outcome payer can test new solutions of public service delivery.	Scale is unproven as of now, as interventions require tailored services. Scale may be reached by standardization of SIB structures as opposed to a massification of intervention.
SIBs draw a pool of private capital into the solution of public issues.	Even though savings will be booked by the outcome payer, the possibility of a future payment demands a commitment by the outcome payer, and, in some cases, funds to be escrowed, depending on applicable public finance rules.
SIBs bring cashable savings to the outcome payer, as only successful SIBs trigger a payment.	In some geographies, impact investing remains a small investment niche, making SIB placement more complex, especially in emerging markets.
Impact investing is a growing industry, as a class of investors looks for a double or triple bottom line.	

showing that the services funded by the SIB led to a reduction of 8.4 percent in reconviction rates for ex-offenders from Peterborough compared to a national comparison group. Although the results were positive and are above the minimum threshold set by the project of a 7.5 percent reduction, the reduction was below 10 percent and therefore not sufficient to earn investors an early return.

Gustafsson-Wright et al. (2015) notes the enormous variation in the deals with respect to the structure, mechanics and stakeholder roles. This confirms the inherent flexibility of SIBs. Twenty-five of the 38 SIBs analyzed in the Brookings study (Gustafsson-Wright et al., 2015) serve populations equal to or smaller than 1,000 individuals. The smallest SIB was launched in Canada and aims at keeping 22 children and their mothers together. The largest SIB targets 10,000 youth in the US criminal justice system, while the DIB launched in India encompasses 15,000 children. Of the 38 SIBs, 16 have contract durations of three years or less, 14 have contract durations of four to five years, and seven have contracts that are longer than five years. The shortest contract duration is 20 months, and the longest 120 months (Instiglio, 2015).

DIBs are an interesting vehicle in developing countries where the government may not have the resources to fund the intervention. The Educate Girls Development Impact Bond is a joint project between the Children's Investment Fund Foundation (CIFF), Educate Girls, the UBS Optimus Foundation, IDinsight and Instiglio to provide and improve education for boys and girls in the district of Bhilwara in rural Rajasthan, India. The project was established for three years from mid-2015 until mid-2018. UBS Optimus acted as the investor, financing the project implementation, while CIFF will pay for enrollment and learning outcomes as ascertained by IDinsight, an independent evaluator. Instiglio is the manager for the project and will provide performance management services to Educate Girls. The DIB targets a dual outcome: enrollment and learning. According to Instiglio, 40 percent of girls do not reach the 5th grade in Rajasthan, and evidence suggests that, for each additional year a female is educated, household incomes rise 10–25 percent. Educated girls are also three times less likely to be HIV positive, will marry three years later, have healthier and fewer children, and educate their daughters (Instiglio, 2015).

3. FINANCIAL ASPECTS OF SIBs

After analyzing the motivations for public entities and outcome payers, we look into the motivation of investors. In this section, we provide a detailed analysis of the financial structuring of Social Impact Bonds, a step that is not well covered in the literature.

3.1 Equity or Debt? Financial Characteristics of SIBs

Where do SIBs fit? SIBs are results-based contracts and have characteristics of both fixed income and equity instruments. This is one of the reasons why they are called 'projects' or 'contracts' in some countries. The traditional financial definition differentiates equity and debt instruments based on three key characteristics: the existence of pre-defined fixed payments, voting rights and seniority. Payments of bonds are typically fixed, while equity holders' gains vary based on the performance of the company, and dividend payments can be reduced or suspended. Equity holders gain ownership of the business and also the right to vote on certain matters, contrary to bondholders. Finally, bondholders have a priority to receive their claims over equity holders. SIBs pay a return to investors that depends on a pre-agreed formula, similar to bonds. That return varies depending on the outcomes attained, which is similar to the logic of equities. In some cases, the instrument does not pay a return during a period of time, similar to a zero dividend payout policy, so that retained earnings are 'recycled' to finance the intervention, which is reminiscent of equity structures. SIBs do not provide voting rights and the question of their seniority depends on the legal status of the intermediary. Even though this is not a universal rule, bonds are usually seen as less risky than equity, especially in developed markets. The level of risk can help to differentiate bonds from equity-like investments. In the case of most SIBs, investors can lose the totality of their upfront investment, in the absence of guarantees.

The existing SIBs show a variety of investment structures, adapted to various investors' risk profiles. Most deals establish caps on returns and various cases follow a structure in tranches, with a scale of risk and returns. The different tranches may include senior investment (first tranche to be repaid), subordinated investment (riskier than senior), recoverable grants and non-recoverable grants. Recoverable grants essentially return the capital to investors, in the case of success. We do not treat non-recoverable grants as an investment type.

Some financial intermediaries have also added guarantees or mitigating instruments, which serve to protect part or all of the capital put to work by investors. In traditional finance, this could be compared to the investor buying a put option at the same time as buying the SIB. Guarantees are often provided by foundations to incentivize the development of the nascent SIB sector. In the case of the NYC ABLE Project for Incarcerated Youth, Bloomberg Philanthropies guaranteed 75 percent of the total investment made by senior investor Goldman Sachs' Urban Investment Group. As the intervention did not reach its pre-defined target, the investor lost just 25 percent of its commitment.

The smallest amount of upfront capital commitment is in the SIB in Portugal, with $148,000, and the largest is in the SIB in Massachusetts, with $24.5 million in upfront capital commitment, though the vast majority of this is from grants. The largest upfront capital commitment not including grants is the Child-Parent Center Pay for Success Initiative in the US in Chicago ($16.9 million), according to Gustafsson-Wright et al. (2015). Grants and guarantees have been mostly used in the US. It is worth highlighting that considering upfront capital only can underestimate the size of the intervention, as some SIBs, especially in the UK, 'recycle' funds in order to reduce the upfront capital commitment.

The size of the investment covers a range of expenses and the inclusion of costs varies depending on the structure. All SIBs cover the provision of the intervention with the committed capital. However, the remuneration of intermediaries and other providers, such as the evaluation agent, financial intermediary or legal counsel is not always contemplated and is often provided on a *pro bono* or concessionary basis. In some cases, the intermediary is paid a success fee. As a result, the cost of developing a pipeline lies mostly with intermediaries. International organizations such as the Inter-American Development Bank have played a key role in funding the early steps of the sector. As the market develops and matures, intermediaries and other specialized providers will look for sustainable payment structures closer to market rates.

3.2 What is the Profile of Investors?

According to J.P. Morgan and the Global Impact Investing Network (GIIN, 2016), an estimated US$77.4 billion is being managed in impact investing globally. Sixty percent of investors principally target 'risk-adjusted, market rate returns', while 25 percent target 'below market rate returns: closer to market rate' and 16 percent target 'below market rate returns: closer to capital preservation'. If we except grants, SIBs have attracted a slightly different investor base than the broader impact sector, including mostly philanthropic capital, foundations and 'impact first' investors, who are willing to accept below-market returns to favor social returns or impact. Such investors typically include development finance institutions, corporate social responsibility units of companies and high net worth individuals who are sensitive to social issues, while opportunities for retail investors are limited (Hochstadter and Scheck, 2014). Impact investors are mostly motivated to make an investment in the impact segment to test an innovative financial model for social services. Lastly, positive publicity has also played a role in attracting new sources of capital.

A growing body of research analyzes the value proposition of social or impact investing. Humphrey et al. (2012) investigate whether UK firms' corporate social performance ratings impact their performance and risk and find no meaningful difference. As a result, the authors suggest that investors can implement social strategy without sacrificing a financial return or increasing risk. Cambridge Associates (2015) create an impact investing benchmark and conclude that the performance of impact investing strategies is close to the performance of traditional comparable private investing, suggesting there is no trade-off between financial return and social impact. On a more cautious side, Reeder and Colantonio (2013) stress the lack of rigor around impact measurement, with a critical eye on industry participants. Kaplan (2015) explains that excluding some investments from the pool of options reduces diversification and potential returns by nature; he also flags the difficulty of measuring impact and additionality.

As the sector matures, the pool of investors will expand. Impact investing is gradually becoming part of the mainstream investment universe, as the sector becomes more well-known and a track record emerges. For new sources of impact capital, financing proven interventions will be easier than testing new models. Moreover, the design of SIBs with different tranches can attract investors with different risk profiles, including 'finance first' investors. It will become mainstream to consider a tripod of characteristics for every investment: its risk, return and impact. Over time, the structure of SIBs could become more standardized, especially as expiring SIBs are rolled over, and we note that the definition of common templates, investment sheets and impact metrics will help expand the investor base.

We define a spectrum of investors with different objectives and risk appetites (see Figure 13.2). At one end of the spectrum are investors focused mostly on impact. Contrary to what appears sometimes in the literature, we do not treat non-recoverable grants as an investment type, even though we recognize the key role they play in the sector. Investors concerned with impact can seek capital protection, or below-market returns. At the other end are investors who expect market returns, without necessarily focusing on the additionality of a social return.

SIBs' financial returns have been within the expected range. Research (Social Finance, 2016a) shows that out of 60 SIBs launched in 15 countries, 22 projects have reported performance data, 21 projects indicate positive social outcomes, 12 have made outcome payments, and four have fully repaid investors' capital. Social Finance provided a full summary of the returns of existing SIBs. In the One Service SIB in Peterborough UK, interim payments, as noted previously, are made for each of three cohorts if the percentage difference in outcomes between the treatment and control groups is greater than 10 percent, or a payment is made at the end of the program if the percentage difference between the treatment and control group exceeds 7.5 percent across all of the three cohorts. The first cohort achieved a reduction in recidivism of 8.4 percent, and did not meet the threshold for early payment but is on track for the overall payment at the end of the program (Social Finance UK, 2014). In the case of

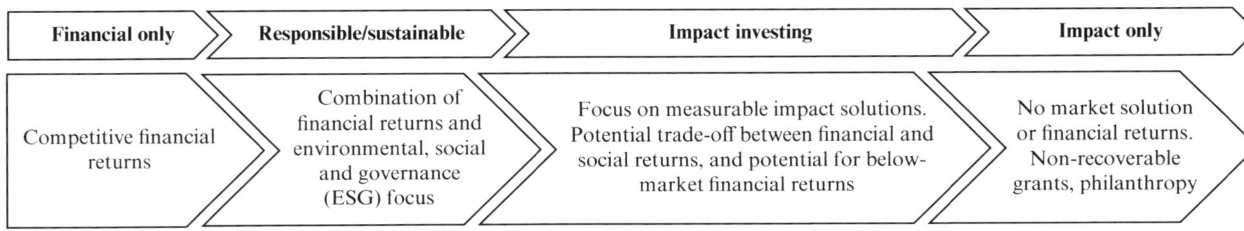

Figure 13.2 The spectrum of capital goes from investors focused on financial returns only, to impact only

the Newpin Social Benefit Bond in Australia, which raised AU$7 million to assist vulnerable families (Social Ventures Australia, 2015), investors target a return of 10 to 12 percent over the seven-year term (Government of New South Wales, 2015). In the case of the DIB in Rajasthan, early results suggest the bond is on track to deliver a financial return of up to 15 percent (UBS Optimus Foundation, 2016). The SIB for criminal justice in Rikers Island in New York City was below target in the third year of the intervention, leading to a loss for the senior investor, Goldman Sachs, of $1.2 million, and a loss for the loan guarantor, Bloomberg Philanthropies, of $6 million (Anderson and Phillips, 2015). While the outcome was below target, the termination of the SIB shows that the instrument behaved as expected (Eccles, 2016), since the intervention had not met with success. Early termination right due to poor performance is a common feature in SIBs.

Twelve programs had a cap on the annual return to investors. Seven of those caps on financial returns were below 7.5 percent. The German SIB defined a cap of 3 percent, while the SIB in Canada and the SIB for adult homelessness in the US have caps of 5 percent and 5.33 percent, respectively. The SIB for juvenile criminal recidivism in Massachusetts and the SIB for family support in Ohio in the US have set caps of 5 percent for senior investors and 2 percent for subordinated investors, but investors have the opportunity to earn significant additional success fees. Three SIBs have disclosed a target or maximum internal rate of return (IRR), amounting to 2 percent for the SIB in Portugal, 13 percent for the Peterborough SIB and 12.5 percent for the SIB in New York State.

4. ROADMAP FOR FINANCIAL STRUCTURING OF SIBs

We do not view SIBs as a new asset class, rather they are a mechanism of public service delivery. The existing literature on social impact bonds is quite evasive on the financial structuring of the deal and often only mentions the placement function of financial intermediaries, since most placements have been agreed by small numbers of participants. In larger traditional transactions, such as public offerings, the financial structuring would naturally be the role of an investment bank, potentially helped by other players such as legal counsels and auditors. As the sector matures, deals will evolve away from the format of small private placements, the number of investors will increase and structuring will rely less on *pro bono* service, while investors will rely more and more on an intermediary to support them. Financial structuring will gain relevance.

In this chapter, we contribute to the current knowledge on SIBs with an in-depth analysis of the financial structuring of a SIB, its constituents and risks. As an example, one of the five key recommendations for the growth of a social investment market in Portugal is to promote specialist intermediaries to facilitate access to capital. According to the Portuguese Social Investment Taskforce, social investment intermediaries speak the language of the different stakeholders and can navigate their diverse range of skills and expectations. Intermediaries can contribute by advising social organizations on financial and business issues, they can attract investors, structure financial products, manage performance and disseminate evidence on financial instruments (Portuguese Social Investment Taskforce, 2016).

We define four key pillars in the role of a financial intermediary:

- *Legal structure:* define the legal characteristics of the instrument;
- *Tripod of SIB characteristics:* define the desired risk-return-impact structure;
- *Placement:* identify investors and place the SIB;
- *Governance model:* define the feedback structure, governance and potential conflict resolution of the SIB during the life of the intervention.

First, defining the *legal structure* will allow investors to identify how they can be involved. This will require legal counsel, as for traditional public offerings. The delivery of funds to the intermediary will vary according to the corporate structure of the intermediary. For example, under Brazilian regulations, associations or foundations cannot receive equity investments, but only grants and, in very limited cases, loans. In this case, the intermediary may have to set up a new legal entity to be able to issue the instrument. In some locations, the involvement of a public entity as an outcome payer may involve special advice. In Brazil, for most cases but not all, the contract will require a public tender, which can be waived if there is limited competition, in the case of low-value contracts, or if the personnel being hired possess specific skills (Instiglio et al., 2014).

SIBs follow different types of models, depending on the role played by the service provider. Under the direct model, the outcome payer contracts the service provider directly. Under an intermediated model, the outcome payer contracts an intermediary, which then finds the service providers. The majority of SIBs follow the intermediated model (Goodall, 2014). A financial intermediary such as a bank can play a role in the due diligence on this intermediary. Information available to investors will have to be drafted and follow a standardized format, similar to the term sheets used in other placements, such as a prospectus and investor presentations. Some types of instrument may also lead to tax advantages.

The *tripod* of risk-return-impact characteristics will be defined in collaboration with the intermediary. The risks to investors should be clearly described in the term sheet. A key feature of the SIB is the transfer of select risks from the government to the intermediary (for the provision of a service) and to investors (for the upfront payment of the intervention). The most common risks to investors include a loss in the investment due to the failure of the intervention (outcome is not reached), or a failure in repayment by the outcome payer. The private sector may require some assurance that the government will honor its financial obligations in future budget cycles. De-risking mechanisms can be contemplated, such as the use of full or partial guarantees on principal and interest, or a lower outcome threshold for payment. The creation of outcome funds is also helpful to signal the commitment of a government and sets aside a pool of money for the repayment of successful SIBs. As a parallel, Colombia established a contingency fund for public-private partnerships (PPPs), so that the private sector will feel more confident that the government will honor its contractual obligations (Bloomgarden et al., 2014). Risks also involve reputation in the case that the intervention is not successful or backfires. The financial intermediary can play a key role in the due diligence to assess risks and in the education process of investors. A structure in tiers or tranches can be used to attract a wider investor base.

The terms of the contract will detail the financial returns based on a pre-set formula and the maturity of the instrument. Returns are defined as a percentage of the upfront capital or as a payment per unit of outcome, known as rate cards, as in the case of the rate cards defined by the Department of Work and Pensions. The literature and discussion with practitioners show there is a debate about what should be fair returns and whether there is a trade-off between financial and social returns. International comparisons make it less useful to focus on the absolute rate of return being paid. We prefer to use a classification with four categories: capital protection (0% return); inflation protection (rate of return equal to inflation); return below cost of capital (using the domestic policy rate as cost of capital); and return above cost of capital. In developed markets, where rates are currently at low levels, those categories will overlap. Talking about market returns is complex as there is no clear peer market for SIBs, and private equity investments are of a different nature and target higher rates of return. The term of SIBs spans over three to five years, on average. That said, several SIBs have built financial models that allow for early payments following early success, such as the youth unemployment and care SIBs (Social Finance, 2016a).

Finally, the impact (sometimes referred to as social return) should be measured by an independent agent, as in the case of the Newpin Bond in Australia, where Deloitte served as the outcome evaluator. Metrics indicating whether the outcome has been reached should be clearly defined before the investment is offered, so that investors can appropriately price the risk. As the sector matures, the SIB issuer will most likely be required to pay fees for structuring services, which will increase the demand for funding.

Placement is the traditional role of a financial intermediary. In some cases, the intermediary will market the investment to a number of investors or an investment bank that manages investments on behalf of its clients. For example, in the case of the Increasing Employment and Improving Public Safety bond in New York State, Bank of America Merrill Lynch distributed the investment to investors through its wealth management platform and raised $13.5 million (Social Finance, 2014; Social Finance, 2016b). An intermediary with access to investor networks and the necessary regulatory authorization (such as the SEC in the US) can help market the investment proposition to investors. An investor agreement will specify the terms under which payments will be made if outcomes are attained. To manage their investment risk, investors would ensure that qualified personnel and robust systems are in place to provide performance management of the portfolio of service providers.

The *governance* considers the SIB during its lifetime. Governance will define rules to allow the positive feedback loop of information and adjustments to the intervention. We believe it is appropriate to define a Board of the SIB with representatives from different stakeholders. The Board could play a key role in case the intervention needs to be re-oriented or even terminated. It may also be the case that further capital needs to be deployed during the life of the SIB. The governance also includes key aspects of disclosure and information release. Stakeholders will define the frequency and format of information releases that is desirable, realistic and cost efficient for their SIB. Governance will also define rules in case of potential conflicts between different stakeholders.

Finally, stakeholders should be ready to envision what comes after the SIB: after a repayment in the case of a successful SIB, should the intervention be rolled over with a new SIB, potentially with a larger scope or scale or should the policy be included in the traditional public policy tools? If the SIB is rolled over, should the rate of return be reduced, since the risk of the intervention is lower, potentially becoming less attractive for traditional investors?

5. OVERCOMING THE BARRIERS OF SIBs AND THE WAY AHEAD

5.1 Common Issues Raised in Existing SIBs

With just over 60 SIBs launched to date mostly in developed countries, the segment is still in its infancy. The possibility of financial or social returns should not be overstated. We identify four types of limitations or issues, relating to: government support, outcome, scale and complexity.

First, the main driver of successful SIBs is *government support*. Governments, in their roles of policy-maker, regulator and outcome payer, are the essential element for the growth of the segment. In particular, governments must be willing to let go of some of their power in the provision of basic services. It is important also to note that even though the intervention is performed by a third party, the government continues to bear a reputation risk, in case the service does not reach its desired outcome. Government can play a key role in funding feasibility studies and pipeline development (White House, 2015). The success of the first SIBs, social support and government engagement are paramount for the growth of SIBs.

Another set of issues relates to the *outcome*, which needs to be measurable, clear and properly designed. SIBs are particularly attractive where the intervention is complex, requires innovation and brings measurable outcomes. Cashable benefits must be estimated. Measuring the outcome is therefore a critical limitation for SIBs. Metrics must be well defined at the onset of the projects, in order to avoid perverse incentives or gaming (teaching to the test). A SIB may not be relevant if funding the activity is more appropriate than funding the outcome (Barclay and Symons, 2013). Many service providers may not be equipped to measure their impact, while many complex issues may not lead to the calculation of savings (Rangan and Chase, 2015).

Scale has been flagged by the literature as a limitation of SIBs, and a promise still to be met. Research shows that the first 38 impact bonds did not achieve substantial scale but SIB Funds have the potential to facilitate scale by funding multiple innovative organizations at once. Of the 38 SIBs, 25 serve populations of up to 1,000 individuals, according to Gustafsson-Wright (2016). Reaching scale can signify that successful SIBs are expanded to tackle broader issues or larger populations, such as the SIB on diabetes in Israel. Scaling, in turn, requires a standardization of instruments, and also a wider pool of investors.

Finally, *complexity* and hidden costs are a key hurdle for the sector. For example, the legal counsel to the intermediary in the Massachusetts recidivism SIB reported that '27 contracts were written and more than

1,100 legal hours were billed' to develop the bond (Olson, 2014). Additional costs are today not included in SIBs as third parties provide *pro bono* services. Moreover, as the sector grows, relying on philanthropic capital to provide guarantees to senior investors may not prove scalable (Godeke and Resner, 2012). The first SIBs have been time-intensive and costly operations, with two years being mentioned in several cases as a minimum timeframe to structure a SIB.

5.2 Recommendations to Grow the Acceptance of SIBs

SIBs have passed the first phase of testing and do not need a proof of concept anymore. The sector is now ready to learn lessons from existing interventions and prepare for its expansion (see Table 13.2). In order to widen the scope of SIBs into new themes and countries, SIBs will have to overcome some barriers. Building capacity remains essential, and we list below four key recommendations for the sector.

Setting up *SIB Funds* can contribute largely to the growth of the sector. Outcome funds dedicate money and they pool and maintain knowledge. Importantly, they send a strong signal that the government is willing to

Table 13.2 Recommendations for policy-makers and financial intermediaries

Participants	Outcome payer, service provider, private investors, specialized intermediaries, independent auditor
Challenges of Financial Structuring	(1) Legal structure (2) Definition of the desired risk-return impact (3) Placement of the SIB (4) Governance model
Recommendations	(1) Create Social Impact Bond Funds. SIB Funds set aside funding from outcome payers, pool knowledge, and send a strong signal to investors. (2) Disseminate knowledge. As track record grows, lessons learned and best practices need to be shared in various languages. (3) Standardize processes. Standardization stems from common templates and processes for due diligence, valuation and disclosure. (4) Leverage favorable regulations. Regulations can serve to protect investors and attract new capital into SIBs.

pay for successful intervention. In the UK, two funds exist: the Innovation Fund and the Fair Chance Fund. At the same time, the commissioning government departments have produced rate cards. After service provision began, service providers and intermediaries could submit claims of outcomes on a regular basis to the commissioner, using defined forms of administrative data. Portugal's Inovação Social, with its Eur150 million budget provided by the European Structural Funds, will serve four pillars: a Social Innovation Fund; a SIB program; capacity building; and a Venture Philanthropy program (Portugal Social Investment Taskforce, 2016).

Widely *disseminating takeaways and outcomes* in several languages is another recommendation, especially when it comes to developing countries, which has been done in countries such as Chile and Brazil (Gatica et al., 2015; de Mariz et al., 2016). The limited track record of the instruments provides an opportunity for academia with technical assistance labs (Harvard University, 2015), intermediaries and financial institutions to improve awareness. As sustainability is a rising concern of investors and a trend for financial intermediaries, they have an opportunity to accelerate the growth of this market.

Standardization is essential as the market matures. By standardization, we mean the definition of a common template to perform tasks such as running a due diligence, building financial models for valuation and evaluating risks, writing term sheets, educating investors and disclosing periodic information to investors. Standardization is essential to mobilize the 'multi-billion source of growth capital' initially expected (Social Finance US, 2012). Standardization should not come at the cost of the flexibility of SIBs, but will accelerate and streamline the launch of new instruments. The replication of successful SIBs will naturally streamline processes as participants have acquired the necessary skills, concepts and terminology relating to SIBs.

Finally, the role of the *regulator* could be enhanced and best practices shared. Regulators have supported the impact sector in several ways. Financial regulations can define the minimum standards for disclosure of information on SIBs. Tax incentives can be critical to attract new capital. For example, the Government of the UK (2016) set up a social investment tax relief in 2015, which includes SIBs. The Japan National Advisory Board (2014) recommends considering a law to allocate dormant funds (around US$1 billion) to social projects in the form of grants, loans and equity, following the model of the UK's Big Society Capital. Italy has recently defined the status of a B-corp (benefit corporation) in the law, which could open the door to offering benefits to companies that register under this status (B Corp, 2016). Countries could also establish incentives for foundations or pension funds to allocate capital to impact investments. Canada allowed foundations to invest in Limited Partners (LPs), allowing impact investment funds to receive capital from donations, as recommended by the Canadian Impact Investment National Advisory Board (MaRS, 2015).

6. CONCLUSION

SIBs represent a key innovation in the field of social finance and change the way public service can be delivered. They bring two advantages in particular: the incentive for service providers to improve their intervention, and a positive feedback loop during the life of the SIB. From the first Social Impact Bond in 2010 to today, more than 60 contracts have been signed across countries and social issues.

SIBs have passed the phase of the proof of concept and the segment is now sharing lessons and best practices. SIBs face key challenges in order to grow, including continuous government support. SIBs also present a high degree of complexity, with long structuring timeframes and a large number of parties involved. Challenges relating to their outcomes have been raised, such as their definition, measurement and validation. Finally, scale was one of the early claims of SIBs, and the instrument still has to prove its ability to fulfill this promise.

As the sector grows and matures, we make four recommendations. They include the creation of Social Impact Bond Funds so that outcome payers set aside capital. The dissemination of knowledge as well as the standardization of processes are essential for the sector to reach maturity. Finally, governments can draft regulations that support the SIB segment and impact sector at large, to protect investors and attract a wider base of capital.

REFERENCES

Allen, F. and D. Gale (1994), *Financial Innovation and Risk Sharing*, Cambridge, MA: MIT Press.

Anderson, J. and A. Phillips (2015), 'What We Learned from the Nation's First Social Impact Bond', Huffington Post, Impact What's Working (blog), accessed 6 July 2016, at huffingtonpost.com/james-anderson/whatwe-learned-from-the-_1_b_7710272.html

B Corp (2016), 'Italian Parliament Approves Benefit Corporation Legal Status', accessed 22 July 2016, at http://bcorporation.eu/blog/italian-parliament-approves-benefit-corporation-legal-status

Barclay, L. and T. Symons (2013), *A Technical Guide to Developing Social Impact Bonds*. Social Finance UK.

Beck, T., T. Chen, C. Lin and F.M. Song (2016), 'Financial Innovation: The Bright and the Dark Sides', *Journal of Banking & Finance*, 72(C), 28–51.

Bloomgarden, D., M. Eddy and Z. Levey (2014), *Social Impact Bonds and Education in Latin America*. GEMS Education Solutions.
Burand, D. (2013), 'Globalizing Social Finance: How Social Impact Bonds and Social Impact Performance Guarantees Can Scale Development', *NYU Journal of Law and Business.*
Cambridge Associates (2015), *Introducing the Impact Investing Benchmark*, accessed 22 July 2016 at http://www.cambridgeassociates.com/our-insights/research/introducing-the-impact-investing-benchmark/
CGD (2013), *Investing in Social Outcomes: Development Impact Bonds.* Center for Global Development and Social Finance.
Chiodo, V. (2015), 'Social Impact Bonds: New Finance or New Procurement?', *ACRN Oxford Journal of Finance and Risk Perspectives*, 4(4), 168–189.
de Mariz, C.L, C. Menard and B. Abeille (2014), *Public Procurement Reforms in Africa: Challenges in Institutions and Governance*, Oxford: Oxford University Press.
de Mariz, F., E. Souto, A. Menezes and R. Patriarca (2016), *Investing in Social Outcomes: UBS White Paper on Social Impact Bonds – Perspectives for Brazil.*
Eccles, T. (2016), Presentation at the Global Impact Investment Plenary Conference, Gulbenkian Foundation, Lisbon, 7 July.
Gatica, S., G. Carrasco and R. Mobarec (2015), *Bonos de Impacto Social: El Contexto en Chile*, FOMIN.
GIIN (2016), *2016 Annual Impact Investor Survey.*
Godeke, S. and L. Resner (2012), *Building a Healthy & Sustainable Social Impact Bond Market: The Investor Landscape*, Godeke Consulting.
Goodall, E. (2014), *Choosing Social Impact Bonds: A Practitioner's Guide*, Bridges Impact +.
Government of New South Wales (2015), *Social Impact Investment Policy*, Government of New South Wales, accessed 25 July 2016, at: www.dpc.nsw.gov.au/__data/assets/pdf_file/0011/168338/Social_Impact_Investment_Policy_WEB.pdf
Government of the UK (2011), *Social Impact Bond at HMP Peterborough*, Her Majesty's Government, accessed 21 July 2016, at https://www.gov.uk/government/publications/social-impact-bond-at-hmp-peterborough
Government of the UK (2014), *Final Results for Cohorts 1 Payment-by-results Prison Pilots*, Her Majesty's Government, accessed 21July 2016, at https://www.gov.uk/government/statistics/final-results-for-cohorts-1-payment-by-results-prison-pilots
Government of the UK (2016), *Social Investment Tax Relief*, Her Majesty's Government, accessed 25 July 2016, at https://www.gov.uk/government/publications/social-investment-tax-relief-factsheet/social-investment-tax-relief
Gustafsson-Wright, E. (2016), Presentation at the Global Impact Investment Plenary Conference, Gulbenkian Foundation, Lisbon, 7 July. [Emily Gustafsson-Wright counts 62 SIBs as of June 2016 and 2 DIBs globally.]
Gustafsson-Wright, E., S. Gardiner and V. Putcha (2015), *The Potential and Limitations of Impact Bonds: Lessons from the First Five Years of Experience Worldwide*, Brookings, accessed 21 July 2016, at http://www.brookings.edu/research/reports/2015/07/social-impact-bonds-potential-limitations
Harvard University (2015), 'State and Local Governments Receive Assistance to Launch Pay for Success Projects Across the Country', Harvard University Kennedy School of Government, accessed 25 July 2016, at https://www.hks.harvard.edu/news-events/news/press-releases/sib-lab-winners-2015
Hefetz, A. and M.E. Warner (2012), 'Contracting or Public Delivery? The Importance of Service, Market and Management Characteristics', *Journal of Public Administration Research and Theory*, 22(2), 289–317.
Hochstadter, A.K. and B. Scheck (2014), *Mapping the Social Impact Investing Market in Germany*, The Rockefeller Foundation.
Humphrey, J., D. Lee and Y. Shen (2012), 'Does It Cost to be Sustainable?', *Journal of Corporate Finance*, 18(3), 626–639.
Instiglio (2015), *Educate Girls Development Impact Bond, Improving Education for 18,000 Children In Rajasthan.*

Instiglio, Thomson Reuters Foundation, and Baker & McKenzie (2014), *A Legal Roadmap for Social Impact Bonds in Developing Countries*, Thomson Reuters Foundation.
Japan National Advisory Board (2014), *The Social Impact Investment Landscape in Japan.*
Johnson, S. and J. Kwak (2012), 'Is Financial Innovation Good for the Economy?', in J. Lerner and S. Stern (eds), *Innovation Policy and the Economy*, Volume 12, University of Chicago Press, National Bureau of Economic Research.
Kaplan, S. (2015), 'Is Impact Investing More Than Charity?', Debate at Chicago Booth, 8 September 2015, accessed 10 January 2017, at http://review.chicagobooth.edu/economics/2015/video/big-question-impact-investing-more-charity?cat=business&src=Video
Leventhal, R. (2013), 'Effecting Progress: Using Social Impact Bonds to Finance Social Services', *NYU Journal of Law and Business*, 9, 511.
MaRS (2015), 'MaRS Centre for Impact Investing Welcomes the Government of Canada's Support for Impact Investment and Social Finance', accessed 22 July 2016, at https://www.marsdd.com/media-centre/mars-centre-for-impact-investing-welcomes-the-government-of-canadas-support-for-impact-investment-and-social-finance/
OECD (2008), *Paris Declaration and Accra Agenda for Action*, accessed 21 July 2016, at http://www.oecd.org/dac/effectiveness/parisdeclarationandaccraagendaforaction.htm
Olson, A. (2014), 'The Complex Anatomy of Social Impact Bonds', Presentation, SOCAP Conference Panel. San Francisco, California, 12 September.
Portuguese Social Investment Taskforce (2016), *A Blueprint for Portugal's Emerging Social Investment Market.*
Rangan, V.K. and L.A. Chase (2015), *The Payoff of Pay-for-Success*, SSIR, 30 August, accessed 25 July 2016, at http://www.sibreview.com/media/2015/8/30/the-payoff-of-pay-for-success-ssir
Reeder, N. and A. Colantonio (2013), 'Measuring Impact and Non-financial Returns in Impact Investing: A Critical Overview of Concepts and Practice', EIBURS Working Paper 2013/01, London School of Economics and Political Science, October.
Savedoff, W., R. Perakis and B. Schwanke (2015), *Shifting the Foreign Aid Paradigm: Paying for Outcomes*, Washington DC: Center for Global Development, accessed 21 July 2016, at http://www.cgdev.org/publication/ft/shifting-foreign-aid-paradigm-paying-outcomes
Social Finance (2014), *Investing in What Works: 'Pay for Success' in New York State, Increasing Employment and Improving Public Safety.*
Social Finance (2016a), *Social Impact Bonds, The Early Years* [data as of June 2016].
Social Finance (2016b), *Increasing Employment and Improving Public Safety in New York State*, accessed 22 July 2016, at http://socialfinance.org/focus-areas/criminal-justice/nys-pay-for-success-financing/
Social Finance UK (2014), 'Peterborough Social Impact Bond Reduces Reoffending by 8.4%; Investors on Course for Payment in 2016', accessed 22 July 2016, at www.socialfinance.org.uk/wp-content/uploads/2014/08/Peterborough-First-Cohort-Results.pdf
Social Finance US (2012), *A New Tool for Scaling Impact: How Social Impact Bonds Can Mobilize Private Capital to Advance Social Good.*
Social Ventures Australia (2015), *Newpin Social Benefit Bond*, accessed 21 July 2016, at http://www.socialventures.com.au/work/newpin-social-benefit-bond/
UBS Optimus Foundation (2016), 'World's First Development Impact Bond On Track to Deliver Social Impact and Financial Returns', UBS.
United Nations (2015), *Sustainable Development Goals, 17 Goals to Transform Our World*, accessed 21 July 2016, at http://www.un.org/sustainabledevelopment/education/
White House (2015), 'Improving Outcomes through Pay for Success', accessed 25 July 2016, at www.whitehouse.gov/sites/default/files/omb/budget/fy2016/assets/fact_sheets/improving-outcomes-through-pay-for-success.pdf
Williamson, O.E. (1999), 'Public and Private Bureaucracies: A Transaction Cost Economics Perspective', *Journal of Law, Economics, & Organization*, 15(1), 306–342.

14. Asset allocation and the green bond market

K. Thomas Liaw

1. INTRODUCTION

Green bonds are a growing category in fixed-income securities that raise capital for projects to support the climate. The funded projects typically involve renewable energy, energy efficiency, sustainable land use and clean water. In the academic literature, there are large volumes of publications on environmental, social and governance (ESG) criteria and financial performance. Research on the labeled green bond market, however, has been limited, as this is a relatively new market. This chapter reviews the returns and volatilities of the four green bond indices. The chapter also examines the correlation of the returns and discusses the implications of asset allocation in green bonds.

1.1 Labeled Green Bonds

Green bonds are similar to traditional bonds with an added bonus of green benefits. The use of proceeds is defined for specific green projects. Most green bonds are general obligation or 'green use of proceeds' bonds, backed by the full credit of the issuer. In addition, there are green revenue bonds, green project bonds and green securitized bonds.

In order to label a bond green, the bond has to meet the requirements of the Green Bond Principles or Climate Bonds Standard (the Appendix provides a detailed description of the basic principles and the certification standards). The requirements include use of proceeds, a process for evaluation and selection of the nominated projects, management of proceeds and reporting. The prospective issuer generally appoints an approved independent verifier to provide a statement that the bond meets the standards.[1] Issuers use the certification in marketing materials and roadshows to launch the green bond. After the bond has been issued, the issuer tracks and reports annually eligible projects or assets. For investors, the green bond label is a signaling mechanism of climate-aligned investments. They use the disclosed information to evaluate the environmental impacts of their investments. The pre-issuance independent review and post-issuance disclosure are helpful to the confidence of investors and to the growth of the market.

The third party certification costs are in the $10,000–$50,000 range, depending on the project complexity. But, the benefits outweigh the costs. Issuers have saved several basis points in issuing green bonds. For example, Ludvigsen (2016) reported that the Australian based FlexiGroup issued green asset-backed securities in April 2016 at 5 basis points lower than non-green notes backed by the same pool of consumer receivables. Vornado Real Estate green bonds in 2015 saved 10–15 basis points, DC Waters 2015 green bond issue saved 2–6 basis points and HSBC green bond issue in 2016 saved 7 basis points. In the secondary market, green bonds traded at a premium as well. Preclaw and Bakshi (2015) showed that, on an option adjusted spread basis, the premium was 17 basis points as of mid-2015. They offered several reasons to explain such a premium. First, demand is strong because investors with an ESG mandate or focus have large sums of money to invest and the annual issuance of green bonds is still limited. Second, green bond prices are less volatile. This is due to the fact that supply is still small and thus most investors buy and hold. The limited amount available for sale in the secondary market results in few trades, leading to reduced volatility. The third reason is that investors are willing to accept a lower yield because they gain benefits for being green.

Green bond indices have also contributed to the growth of the market. They give investors a means to evaluate performance and assess risk when allocating funds to green bonds. Adding this new asset to a portfolio will move northwest the efficient frontier where the expanded portfolio offers a higher expected rate of return for each level of risk, provided that the correlations of green bonds with other assets in the portfolio are not perfectly positive.[2] There are currently four green bond indices by Solactive, S&P Dow Jones, Bank of America Merrill Lynch (BoA Merrill Lynch) and Barclays MSCI.

1.2 Select Literature Review

There are large volumes of publications that cover the relation between ESG factors and various measures of corporate financial performance. For example, Albertini (2013) investigated the inconsistent results from prior studies and showed a positive relationship between firm environmental performance and financial performance. Performance measures, regional differences and sample periods all impacted on the relationship. Dixon-Fowler et al. (2013) concluded that environmental factors had a strong influence on financial performance, small firms benefited as much or more than large firms and US firms benefited more than their international counterparts. Climent and Soriano (2011) found that environmental mutual funds underperformed conventional funds with similar characteristics during the 1987–2009 sample period. However, for a sub-sample period of 2001–2009, there was no significant difference in their performance. In socially responsible investing, analysis by Galema et al. (2008) concluded that socially responsible investing impacted on stock returns positively by lowering the book-to-market ratio and not by generating positive alphas. Kempf and Osthoff (2007) implemented a trading strategy that purchased stocks with high socially responsible ratings and sold those with low ratings. This strategy resulted in high abnormal returns of up to 8.7 percent per year. In the corporate governance area, Gillan and Starks (2007) concluded that there was little evidence of improvement in the long-term operating or stock performance of the companies targeted by shareholder activism, even though some prior studies indicated positive short-term reactions to the activism announcements. Similarly, Love (2010) found most studies in the literature provided evidence of a positive relation between corporate governance and valuation, operating performance or stock returns. But, the author argued that studies showing such a positive relation suffered from endogeneity problems. Corporate governance is likely to develop endogenously, affected by the specific characteristics of the firm and the environment.

Friede et al. (2015) provided an exhaustive overview of academic research on the linkage between ESG criteria and corporate financial performance. Based on 2,200 individual studies, the authors documented that a large majority of studies reported a positive ESG impact on corporate financial performance, and that such positive relation was stable over time. In developed markets, more than 38.0 percent of studies showed a positive relation, while only 7.7 percent found a negative impact of ESG on corporate financial performance. In studies of emerging markets, 65.4 percent showed a positive while 5.8 percent found a negative relation. Among the three factors (E, S or G), studies on the environmental factor (E) resulted in 58.7 percent positive findings, the social factor (S) 55.1 percent, the governance factor (G) 62.3 percent and all three criteria combined 35.3 percent. For asset classes, the positive linkage is 52.2 percent for equities, 63.9 percent for bonds, 71.4 percent for real estate and 15.5 percent for portfolio.

Morgan Stanley (2015) reviewed US-based mutual funds and separately managed accounts and concluded that investing in sustainability often exceeded the performance of comparable traditional investments, on both an absolute and a risk-adjusted basis. Sustainable equity mutual funds produced equal or higher median returns and equal or lower volatility than traditional funds for 64 percent of the sample periods. Furthermore, the MSCI KLD 400 Social Index outperformed the S&P 500 Index by 45 basis points per year since its inception in July 1990 to December 2014. The annual return for MSCI KLD 400 Social Index was 10.14 percent and that for the S&P 500 Index was 9.69 percent. Note that the MSCI KLD 400 Social Index includes firms meeting high ESG standards.

In the green bond area, duPont et al. (2015) examined the potential use of green bonds for financing sustainable land use and conservation projects. The authors interviewed issuers, banks, investors and environmental organizations to identify challenges and opportunities. Challenges include insufficient project cash flows to back the project-revenues-backed bonds and the mismatch in scales between the land-related deals and the green bond issuances. The identified opportunities for green bonds and land conservation were state and municipal issuances, and water and storm-water related projects. As mentioned previously, Preclaw and Bakshi (2015) performed a regression analysis and the results indicated that green bonds traded at a statistically significant 17 basis points tighter in options adjusted spread, after taking into consideration Moody's Weighted Rating Factors, spread duration and time since issuance. Those factors capture credit risk, investment length and the liquidity premium in off-the-run securities. Pham (2016) analyzed the volatility behavior of the S&P green bond indices for the period of April 2010 to April 2015. The empirical results indicated that the labeled green bond market segment experienced a larger volatility clustering than the unlabeled green bond segment. Additionally, the empirical results also provided evidence of shock spillover from the overall conventional bond market to the green bond market.

1.3 Summary and Chapter Organization

This study used data for the four green bond indices to review the return and volatility for each. The average monthly returns for Solactive, S&P, BoA Merrill Lynch and Barclays MSCI were −0.15 percent, 0.07 percent, 0.14 percent and −0.04 percent, respectively. The standard deviations for those indices were 1.68 percent, 2.20 percent, 2.40 percent and 1.46 percent, respectively. The data also showed the best and worst returns for each index. The range of returns for Solactive was from -3.29 percent to 4.48 percent, for S&P it was -8.08 percent to 5.52 percent, for BoA Merrill Lynch −9.17 percent to 7.47 percent and for Barclays MSCI −3.52 percent to 3.32 percent.

The study also examined correlations of those indices. The correlation coefficient between S&P and BoA Merrill Lynch was very high at close to 1. Other correlation coefficients were in the range of 0.20 to 0.36. If the returns relationships are linear, then investment allocations to both S&P and BoA Merrill Lynch index-based funds will produce limited benefits from diversification.

The rest of the chapter proceeds as follows. The next section covers the development of the green bond market. Section 3 reviews green bond indices and green bond funds. Section 4 discusses the index data and summary statistics. Section 5 examines the correlations between the four indices and the implications for asset allocation. Finally, Section 6 provides a concluding summary.

2. DEVELOPMENT OF THE GREEN BOND MARKET

The European Investment Bank (EIB) issued the first green bond in June 2007. This marked the beginning of this new category in fixed-income securities. In the first several years additional issuance was slow. During 2007–2009, new issuance was less than $1 billion a year. The amount increased to $3.9 billion in 2010, declined to $1.2 billion the next year and rebounded to $3.1 billion in 2012. A big jump came in 2013, with the entrance of corporate green bonds. Corporations such as EDF, Vasakronan and BoA Merrill Lynch started to tap the green bond market. That helped push the volume in 2013 to $11.0 billion, more than the combined total from all prior years. The market excelled to $36.6 billion in 2014 and continued up to $41.8 billion in 2015. The amount of issuance in 2016 was $81.0 billion, another record year. Table 14.1 lists the annual issuance data.

Table 14.1 Annual issuance of green bonds

Year	Volume ($ billion)
2007	0.8
2008	0.4
2009	0.9
2010	3.9
2011	1.2
2012	3.1
2013	11.0
2014	36.6
2015	41.8
2016	81.0

Source: Climate Bonds Initiative (https://www.climatebonds.net/).

2.1 Expanding Supply of Green Bonds

Supranational organizations (such as EIB, World Bank and International Finance Corporation (IFC)) have driven the market and they continue to be active. Other development banks are active as well. Asian Development Bank (ADB), Development Bank of Japan (DBJ) and German Development Bank (KfW) have issued billions of green bonds. As the market evolves, corporations, commercial banks, municipalities and government agencies have become important issuers as well.

Corporations issue green bonds to support the environment. Issuers have moved beyond the utilities, real estate, transport and waste sectors to other businesses. In February 2016, Apple raised $1.5 billion in green bonds for renewable energy, green building, water efficiency and waste management projects. Apple also planned to use the proceeds in projects that eliminate toxic substances in its products. Toyota, as another example, has raised billions since 2014 to fund new retail finance contracts and lease contracts for vehicles that meet specific criteria, including powertrain, fuel efficiency and emissions. It is expected that more corporates will come to market with green bonds to create positive image and to diversify their funding base.

Commercial banks have become very active in the green bond market. They utilize the green bond market to help close the financing gap for renewable energy, energy efficiency and other lower-carbon projects. They use the funds to finance or refinance eligible loans and mortgages with a positive impact on the climate. Robobank, ABN Amro, China Industrial Bank, Agricultural Bank of China, Credit Agricole CIB, Sumitomo Mitsui Banking Corp, Bank of America, Morgan Stanley and HSBC are just a few examples.

The municipal sector is a natural environment for green bonds to grow. State and local governments tap the green bond market to fund local green projects. For example, Paris, Ontario Province, the State of Massachusetts and New York City are among the many municipalities that have borrowed for environmentally beneficial capital projects. Local investors enjoy tax benefits and know that their money goes to support the climate. Universities such as MIT, the University of Virginia, Arizona State University, the University of Cincinnati and the University of Texas have all taken advantage of the opportunities for campus green projects.

Another source of growth comes from issuers of unlabeled climate-aligned bonds. The size of the unlabeled climate-aligned bond market is many times larger than the labeled green bond segment. At year-end 2015, the unlabeled climate-aligned bond outstanding was $531.8 billion and the total outstanding of labeled green bonds was $65.9 billion (Climate Bonds

Initiative, 2016). As some of the unlabeled issuers move to the labeled segment, the supply of labeled green bonds will increase. For example, Vestas Wind Systems started in 2015 to label its general-purpose bonds green with a EUR 500 million, 7-year note issue. It is interesting to note that the proceeds from this note were not earmarked for specific green projects. The independent second opinion provider DNV GL stated:[3]

> We understand that the net proceeds of the Notes will be applied by Vestas for general financing purposes and other general corporate purposes (including the production and sale of wind turbines, and service solutions to the wind energy sector). As the Notes are not linked to specific assets, they do not fall directly under the Green Bond Principles. However, the evidence we have reviewed indicates that the Notes are in line with the stated definition of green bonds within the Green Bond Principles, which is to 'enable capital-raising and investment for new and existing projects with environmental benefits' . . .

Some other issuers with qualified assets, projects or lines of business will take advantage of the green label to tap new investors.

2.2 Strong Government Support in Developing Countries

Strong policy support from developing countries adds success to the green bond market. Similar to the developed countries, the requirements in developing countries for climate targets are enormous. Many developing countries are also taking steps to grow their capital markets. Green bonds contribute to both. To assist emerging economies develop the market, supranational institutions such as the IFC have issued green bonds in emerging market currencies and participated as investors as well.

Emerging markets such as Brazil, Mexico, South Africa, India and China have promoted their green bond markets. Among them, India will add a substantial amount to this market and China is the most significant. After the 2015 Paris agreement (in which 195 countries reached a landmark accord in Paris to lower greenhouse gas emissions), Indian Prime Minister Modi in early 2016 released plans to boost renewable energy output and to increase the country's energy mix from clean sources such as wind and solar.[4] To move toward such a climate objective, large sums of investments in green projects will drive a surge in the issuance of green bonds.

In China, the Beijing government has established guidelines and taken initiatives to grow the green debt market (Kidney et al., 2015; International Institute for Sustainable Development and Development Research Center of the State Council, 2015). The People's Bank of China published its official green bond guidelines in 2015. Several significant developments took place in 2016. The 13th Five Year Plan endorsed a green financial system. The Shanghai and Shenzhen stock exchanges set up guidelines for green bond issuance pilot programs. Furthermore, EY Chinese Branch and SynTao Green Finance obtained approval as green bond certification verifiers. In addition to these policy initiatives, Chinese financial institutions have issued and will continue to issue green debt to meet the financing needs of large-scale environmental projects. The Bank of China and the Shanghai Pudong Development Bank raised $6.03 billion in 2016 (as of July 2016).[5] Financial regulators joined the efforts and announced in July 2016 that they would ban initial public offerings by companies that violated environmental protection rules. With all this, China is now seen as a leader in driving growth in the labeled green bond market (Climate Bonds Initiative, 2016).

2.3 Increasing Investor Demand

The demand started predominantly with institutional investors, especially those with an ESG focus or mandate. Over time, the investor base has expanded. Corporate treasurers and state or municipal investment funds have allocations in this asset category as well. In addition, retail investors have participated in this market. They purchase green bonds at issuance or invest in green bond mutual funds. State Street, TIAA-CREF, BlackRock and Aviva, just to name a few, all have funds in this segment. The World Bank, IFC and SolarCity have provided retail investors access to their new issues of green bonds.

Investors in green bonds provide funds to finance green projects without taking additional risks. Investors know how the issuer uses the proceeds. In most cases, there is an independent third party to verify that the issuer has met the certification requirements under the Green Bond Principles or the Climate Bonds Standard. In addition to the independent second opinion, Moody's started to provide green bond assessments in 2016 to help standardize and improve transparency on an ongoing basis.[6] Moody's evaluates each green bond issue on five factors to arrive at a composite grade. Those five criteria are organization, use of proceeds, disclosure of use of proceeds, management of proceeds and ongoing reporting. The composite grade is used to determine the overall assessment that runs from GB1 (Excellent) to GB5 (Poor). This annual assessment tracks issuers for the life of the funded projects. Such assessment is likely to add a ranking matrix in green bond space helpful to the investor's decision-making process.

3. GREEN BOND INDICES AND GREEN BOND FUNDS

With the introduction of green bond indices and green bond funds, green bond investing becomes part of index asset allocation and thus deepens and broadens the investor base. Each green bond index has its own methodology for choosing the component bonds. The index allows investors to invest in a portfolio of green bonds to diversify company-specific risks, while maintaining a green investment focus. There are four green bond indices: Solactive Green Bond Index; S&P Green Bond Index; BoA Merrill Lynch Green Bond Index; and Barclays MSCI Green Bond Index. There are more than a hundred green bond funds offered by various investment management companies. Many are index-based funds.

3.1 Green Bond Indices

The first index to provide exposure to green bonds was the Solactive Green Bond Index (Solactive, 2015). It is a rules-based, market value weighted index calculated to track the performance of the component green bonds. This index is composed of green bonds that have an amount outstanding of at least $100 million and a minimum remaining maturity of six months. Convertible bonds and inflation-linked bonds are excluded. Each bond is weighted by its market value with a maximum of 5 percent per bond.

The S&P Green Bond Index includes labeled green bonds whose issuers have clearly disclosed information about the use of proceeds or the issuers have obtained an independent second opinion about compliance with the Green Bond Principles (S&P Dow Jones, 2016). The index includes bonds issued by multilateral, government and corporate issuers. Each component bond must have maturity greater than one month from the rebalancing date. No bond matures in the index. Bills, STRIP and inflation-linked instruments are excluded.[7]

The BoA Merrill Lynch Green Bond Index includes debt of corporate and quasi-government issuers, but excludes securitized and collateralized securities (Bank of America, 2014). Qualified component bonds must have an investment grade rating, at least 18 months to final maturity at the time of issuance and at least one month remaining to final maturity as of the rebalancing date. The index selection methodology also requires a fixed coupon schedule. General debt obligations of corporations that are involved in green industries are not included.

Barclays MSCI Green Bond Index includes corporate, government-related and securitized green bonds with an investment grade and fixed coupon rate (Barclays MSCI, 2015). The index holds bonds until maturity and is rebalanced every month. In addition, Barclays MSCI offers separately the US Green Bond Index and Euro Green Bond Index.

3.2 Green Bond Funds

Green bond funds are a convenient way for investors to access this new asset class to expand their investment choice. Calvert Investments, Natixis and State Street are among the many asset managers to offer green bond funds in recent years. Table 14.2 lists green bond funds offered by various managers in different currencies and countries. The listing does not include separate classes of the same fund.

Some are actively managed green bond funds and others are passive index funds. We discuss one of each type as an illustration. The Calvert Green Bond Fund uses a relative value strategy and invests at least 80 percent of its net assets in green bonds of any maturity. Similar to other green bond funds, the size was still small. Total assets under management (AUM) was $69.09 million as of 30 June 2016. The annual return since inception (31 October 2013) was 3.17 percent, behind the Barclays US Aggregate Bond Index at 4.05 percent. For the first half of 2016, the Calvert Green Bond Fund return was 4.87 percent, again lower than the 5.31 percent from Barclays US Aggregate Bond Index.

State Street launched the State Street Green Bond Index Fund on 29 April 2015. This fund tracks the Barclays MSCI Green Bond Index. The AUM was only EUR 23.80 million in May 2016. The return since inception was 0.97 percent, slightly behind the 1.02 percent from the index. In 2015, the fund returned investors −3.76 percent, while the index produced −3.26 percent. It reversed in 2016. The return of the fund was 4.92 percent and that of the index was 4.43 percent.

4. DESCRIPTION AND SUMMARY STATISTICS OF DATA ON GREEN BOND INDICES

The previous section briefly describes each of the four indices that track the green bond market. This section discusses the sample periods and the summary statistics. As the history for this market is relatively short and the indices were introduced in 2014, the availability of data varies among those indices. We searched data sources from Bloomberg, Factset and S&P Dow Jones. We determined on using monthly data for two sample periods. The first is from December 2013 to March 2016 for all four indices. Data were not available for Solactive Green Bond Index before

Table 14.2 Samples of green bond funds

Fund Name	Currency	Domicile
Allianz Green Bond	EUR	LU
Aviva Nikko AM Shenton World Bank Green Bond Fund	SGD	SG
CJ New Green Long-Term Government and Corporate Bond Investment Trust	KRW	KR
CROWD – Green Bond Impact Fund	EUR	LU
Calvert Green Bond Fund	USD	US
Green Koushasai Toushin	JPY	JP
Green World Bank Bond Fund/Nikko	JPY	JP
HI Shale Gas Focus 10 Securities Feeder Investment Trust 1 – Bond Balanced	KRW	KR
Hanwha Dream & Green Securities Investment Trust 1 – Bond	KRW	KR
Hanwha Dream & Green Securities Master Investment Trust – Bond	KRW	KR
KB Star Green Bond Investment Trust	KRW	KR
NH-CA SK Group Green Energy Securities Investment Trust – Bond Balanced	KRW	KR
NN L – Euro Green Bond	EUR	LU
Natixis Asset Management Mirova Green Bond – Global	EUR	FR
Nikko AM Shenton World Bank Green Bond Fund	SGD	SG
SEB Green Bond Fund	EUR	LU
Samsung Global Green Growth 30 Securities Investment Trust – Bond Balanced	KRW	KR
ShinYoung Short-Term Green Government and Corporate Bond Investment Trust	KRW	KR
Shinko Green Mid-term Government Bond Fund	JPY	JP
State Street Global Advisors SICAV – State Street Global Green Bond Index Fund	EUR	LU
State Street Green Bond Fund	USD	US

Source: Bloomberg, 21 June 2016.

December 2013. Thus, the longer sample period (December 2010 to March 2016) is for the other three indices.

All four indices were launched in 2014. The Solactive Green Bond Index was first, on 12 March. S&P launched its green bond index on 31 July. BoA Merrill Lynch followed on 30 October and Barclays MSCI was last on 13 November. Data prior to an index launch date were provided and back tested by the index provider.

Table 14.3 Annual returns (in percent)

Time	Solactive	S&P	BoA Merrill Lynch	Barclays MSCI
2016Q1*	6.23	4.95	5.28	4.16
2015	−9.13	−7.12	−7.32	−2.79
2014	−2.85	−2.31	−2.19	5.28
2013		−2.23	−1.80	−8.45
2012		9.16	8.66	−0.42
2011		1.14	5.52	−0.16

Note: * Returns for 2016Q1 are not annualized.

The average monthly return and standard deviation for Solactive were −0.15 percent and 1.68 percent, respectively. The maximum return was 4.48 percent in March 2016, while the largest loss was −3.29 percent in January 2015. For S&P Green Bond Index, the average return was 0.07 percent and the standard deviation was 2.20 percent. The best month was 5.52 percent in October 2011 and the worst was -8.08 percent in September 2011. BoA Merrill Lynch Green Bond Index followed a pattern similar to S&P's index. The average return was 0.14 percent with a standard deviation of 2.40 percent. The highest monthly return was 7.47 percent in October 2011 and the deepest decline was −9.17 percent in September 2011. Barclays MSCI Green Bond Index showed slightly different results. The average return and standard deviation were −0.04 percent and 1.46 percent, respectively. The best was 3.32 percent in January 2015 and the biggest monthly losses were −3.52 percent in May 2013.

Examination of data indicated that the best period was the first quarter of 2016 for all indices. For 2013 and 2015, the returns were negative. During the period 2011–2012, S&P and BoA Merrill Lynch indices produced positive returns while Barclays MSCI posted a slight negative. Table 14.3 shows the annual returns for each index.

5. ANALYSIS OF DATA ON GREEN BOND INDICES

This section examines the correlations of the indices and discusses the asset allocation implications. As this is a new asset class, investment allocation to it has the potential of improving the risk-return profile of a portfolio. The degree of the benefits depends on the correlation of this asset class with other assets in the portfolio. Investors can invest in the new asset either by active strategies or via passive indexed green bond funds.

Table 14.4 Correlation matrix during December 2013 to March 2016

	Solactive	S&P	BoA Merrill Lynch	Barclays MSCI
Solactive	1.00	0.32	0.31	0.36
S&P		1.00	0.98	0.23
BoA Merrill Lynch			1.00	0.20
Barclays MSCI				1.00

Table 14.5 Correlation matrix during December 2010 to March 2016

	S&P	BoA Merrill Lynch	Barclays MSCI
S&P	1.00	0.97	0.30
BoA Merrill Lynch		1.00	0.28
Barclays MSCI			1.00

For investors investing in passive index funds, it is helpful to examine the correlations among those indices. Two correlation matrixes are provided. The first correlation matrix covers the data period from December 2013 to March 2016. This shorter time period accommodates the limitation of data availability for the Solactive Green Bond Index. Table 14.4 shows the correlation matrix among those four green bond indices. As the table shows, all correlation coefficients are in the range of 0.20 to 0.36, except that between the S&P and BoA Merrill Lynch indices at 0.97.

The second correlation matrix covers a longer sample period (December 2010 to March 2016) for three indices. The S&P and BoA Merrill Lynch indices are again highly correlated. The correlation coefficients of those two indices with the Barclays MSCI Green Bond Index are much lower at 0.30 and 0.28, respectively. Table 14.5 shows the correlation matrix for the extended period for those three indices.

The returns between the S&P and BoA Merrill Lynch green bond indices are almost perfectly correlated (0.98 and 0.97 for two different time periods). The standard deviation of the portfolio returns with both included is very similar to that of the portfolio with just one of those two added. Diversification in the case of investing in both with almost perfect correlation is not efficient. Thus, investing in both at the same time does not improve the efficient frontier. Investors will enjoy the standard diversification benefits when they choose among the S&P, Solactive and Barclays MSCI indices or among the BoA Merrill Lynch, Solactive and Barclays MSCI indices. With knowledge of correlations, investors who choose to invest in both the S&P and BoA Merrill Lynch indices base their decisions on non-financial factors.

6. CONCLUSIONS

The green bond market is growing rapidly. It started with supranational organizations. Over time, banks, corporates and municipalities have also tapped into this new funding source. Government initiatives and policies, especially in developing counties, have played and will continue to play an important role in the development of the market as well. Seven years after the inception of the market, the introduction of the Green Bond Principles in early 2014 provided a foundation for a rapid increase in labeled green bond issuance. This is because the principles established the defined use of proceeds and relevant compliance measures. The guidelines added comfort to investors because they know they can use green bonds to advance their sustainability mandate.

Green bond funds allow investors to integrate this new asset category into their portfolios. If this new category is not perfectly correlated with other assets, adding green bonds to a portfolio will improve the risk-return profile. Only in the special case of perfect positive correlation, are there no gains from diversification. The mean return and the standard deviation of the expanded portfolio are just the weighted averages. The four indices provide a benchmark in green bond market exposures. The chapter reviewed summary statistics for those indices and calculated the correlation coefficients. Among the four green bond indices, monthly returns between S&P and BoA Merrill Lynch are highly and positively correlated. Adding both at the same time in a portfolio results in limited diversification benefits for investors. Adding other index-based investments will result in diversification benefits, as the correlation coefficients are at 0.36 or lower.

The issuance of bonds with a green label was $0.8 billion in 2007 and rose to $81 billion in 2016. In 2017, global green bond issuance totaled $155.5 billion. Even with such rapid growth, the market is still relatively small and has tremendous potential to grow. A global sustainability initiative like the Paris Agreement will drive large sums of issuance in green bonds to support the climate objective. There are currently several guidelines or standards that issuers use to label bonds green. The convergence of those certification schemes will provide uniform and transparent criteria that are necessary for green bonds to become a significant segment of the global fixed-income market. On the other hand, investors building green bond portfolios require credible, regular information to verify and assess the intended green use of funds. Moody's green bond assessments are an important step in this direction. Investors use such assessment ratings to evaluate issuers' green compliance on an ongoing basis. There are various reasons that investors allocate funds in green bonds. A common motive is to support the climate. This chapter has offered an additional financial incentive. Adding green bonds to a portfolio will improve the risk-return profile if the relation is not perfectly positive.

With more issuers taking advantage of this new funding source and more investors focusing on sustainability and diversification, the market will continue to grow. As the market grows in size, more issuers will enter and green bonds will become a common vehicle for bond investing. The trading of green bonds will be more active and liquidity in the secondary market will thus improve. That will further expand the market.

ACKNOWLEDGMENTS

I thank the editors for their helpful comments and suggestions. I also thank Allen Qu for assistance in data collection.

NOTES

1. For example, KPMG, EY, DNV GL, Sustainalytics, Oekom, Vigeo EIRIS, Cicero, Bureau Veritas, Trucost and SynTao Green Finance are approved verifiers under the international Climate Bonds Standard and Certification Scheme.
2. There are limits to our use of correlations here. The correlation coefficient is a numerical way to represent the linear relationship between the returns of those indices in the data. However, the result is inaccurate if the relationship is not linear. The estimated correlation coefficient does not imply future relationship, either.
3. DNV GL (2015), 'Vestas green bond: DNV GL second party opinion', news release, 23 March, accessed 25 July 2016 at https://www.vestas.com/~/media/vestas/investor/investor%20pdf/bond/second_party_opinion.ashx
4. K. Ross (2016), 'India charts a roadmap to achieve ambitious solar targets', World Resources Institute blog, 31 May, accessed 18 June 2016 at http://www.wri.org/blog/2016/05/india-charts-roadmap-achieve-ambitious-solar-targets
5. D. Weinland (2016), 'Bank of China issues $3 bn in international green bonds', ft.com, 6 July, accessed 8 July 2016 at https://www.ft.com/content/2034d8a0-4370-11e6-9b66-0712b3873ae1
6. Moody's Investors Service (2016), 'Moody's publishes methodology on green bond assessment', New York, USA: Moody's Investor Service, news release, 3 June.
7. STRIP securities are zero-coupon bonds that separate individual coupons and principal components of eligible instruments as separate securities.

REFERENCES

Albertini, E. (2013), 'Does environmental management improve financial performance? A meta-analysis review', *Organization & Environment*, **26**(4), 431–457.

Bank of America (2014), 'BoA Merrill Lynch Global Research launches green bond index', New York, USA: Bank of America, news release, 3 November.

Barclays MSCI (2015), 'Barclays MSCI Green Bond Index: Index factsheet', New York, USA: Barclays; and New York, USA: MSCI, January.

Climate Bonds Initiative (2016), 'Bonds and climate change: the state of the market in 2016', London, UK: Climate Bonds Initiative.

Climent, F. and P. Soriano (2011), 'Green and good? The investment performance of US environmental mutual funds', *Journal of Business Ethics*, **103**(2), 275–287.

Dixon-Fowler, H.R., D.J. Slater, J.L. Johnson, A.E. Ellstrand and A.M. Romi (2013), 'Beyond "Does it pay to be green?" A meta-analysis of moderators of the CEP-CFP relationship', *Journal of Business Ethics*, **112**(2), 353–366.

duPont, C.M., L.N. James and L.J. Bilmes (2015), 'Green bonds and land conservation: the evolution of a new financing tool', Faculty Research Working Paper Series RWP15–075, Harvard Kennedy School, December.

Friede, G., T. Busch and A. Bassen (2015), 'ESG and financial performance: aggregated evidence from more than 2000 empirical studies', *Journal of Sustainable Finance & Investment*, **5**(4), 210–233.

Galema, R., A. Plantinga and B. Schotens (2008), 'The stocks at stake: return and risk in socially responsible investment', *Journal of Banking and Finance*, **32**(12), 2646–2654.

Gillan, S. and L. Starks (2007), 'The evolution of shareholder activism in the United States', *Journal of Applied Corporate Finance*, **19**(1), 55–73.

International Capital Market Association (2015), *Climate Bonds Standard*, Zurich, Switzerland: International Capital Market Association.

International Capital Market Association (2016), *Green Bond Principles*, Zurich, Switzerland: International Capital Market Association, 16 June.

International Institute for Sustainable Development and Development Research Center of the State Council (2015), *Greening China's Financial System*, Geneva, Switzerland: International Institute for Sustainable Development.

Kempf, A. and P. Osthoff (2007), 'The effect of socially responsible investing on portfolio performance', *European Financial Management*, **13**(5), 908–922.

Kidney, S., B. Sonerud and P. Oliver (2015), 'Growing a green bonds market in China', London, UK: Climate Bonds Initiative; and Geneva, Switzerland: International Institute for Sustainable Development.

Love, I. (2010), 'Corporate governance and performance around the world: what we know and what we don't', *The World Bank Research Observer*, **26**(1), 42–70.

Ludvigsen, P. (2016), 'Advanced topics in green bonds: maximizing rewards', London, UK: Environmental Finance, 10 June.

Morgan Stanley (2015), 'Sustainable reality', New York, USA: Morgan Stanley Institute for Sustainable Investing, March.

Pham, L. (2016), 'Is it risky to go green? A volatility analysis of the green bond market', *Journal of Sustainable Finance & Investment*, **6**(4), 263–291.

Preclaw, R. and A. Bakshi (2015), 'The cost of being green', *Credit Research: US Credit Focus*, New York, USA: Barclays, 18 September, 1–12.

S&P Dow Jones (2016), *S&P Green Bond Index Methodology*, New York, USA: S&P Dow Jones LLP.

Solactive AG (2015), *Guidelines Relating to Solactive Green Bond Index*, Frankfurt, Germany: Solactive AG.

APPENDIX: DESCRIPTION OF THE GREEN BOND PRINCIPLES AND THE CLIMATE BONDS STANDARD

The Green Bond Principles set forth four high-level criteria for labeled green bonds. The Climate Bonds Standard establishes sector-specific criteria to verify the green credentials of a bond. It provides detailed description of the requirements and certification. The following provides a description of the Green Bond Principles and Climate Bonds Standard.

The Green Bond Principles

The Green Bond Principles (GBP) are capital market industry voluntary guidelines for the issuance of labeled green bonds to fund eligible projects. The GBP include four high-level criteria. The first specifies the qualified use of proceeds for environmentally sustainable activities. The second requirement relates to the process for project evaluation and selection. The third criterion recommends the management of the proceeds in a traceable fashion. The last component regards the annual reporting on the use of proceeds.

1. Use of proceeds

Proceeds from the green bond issuance are to be used to finance or refinance, in part or in full, existing or new projects with environmental benefits. The eligible categories aim to address concerns in areas such as climate change, natural resources depletion, loss of biodiversity and/or pollution control. Those projects include, but are not limited to: renewable energy, energy efficiency, pollution prevention and control, sustainable management of living natural resources, terrestrial and aquatic biodiversity conservation, clean transportation, sustainable water management, climate change adaptation and eco-efficient products' production technologies and processes.

2. Process for project evaluation and selection

The issuer of a green bond should outline how the funded projects meet the eligibility requirements of green projects and the environmental sustainability objectives. The GBP encourage issuers to provide transparency on the use of proceeds. The issuer includes an external review for project evaluation and selection as well. In addition to the issuer's disclosed information, investors may also evaluate the issuer's overall profile and track record in supporting environmental sustainability.

3. Management of the proceeds

Under the GBP, the green bond issuer establishes an internal process tracking the movement of funds and provides transparency on how the proceeds are managed. During the time period when the bond is outstanding, the issuer should provide information to investors on the transitional management of the to-be-allocated proceeds. The GBP encourage the use of an auditor or a third party to verify the internal tracking method and the allocation of funds.

4. Reporting

Issuers will document and make available information on the use of proceeds annually until full allocation. The disclosure should include any new developments as well. Such disclosure documents the allocation of funds in eligible projects and a description of their expected or achieved impact. The International Capital Market Association provides templates for impact reporting (https://www.icmagroup.org/green-social-and-sustainability-bonds/). It is helpful that the report includes an external review to confirm that the proceeds are allocated in accordance with the key features of the GBP.

The Climate Bonds Standard

The Climate Bonds Standard (CBS) establishes a verifiable process to certify the green credentials of a bond. The CBS provides sector-specific eligibility criteria. Under the CBS, certification currently covers solar, wind, geothermal, low carbon transport and low carbon building. Eligibility criteria for other areas are being developed. The Climate Bond Certified Mark is issued to a bond that has met the certification requirements. The CBS document covers pre-issuance requirements, post-issuance requirements and the certification process.

1. Pre-issuance requirements

Before the issuance, the issuer needs to demonstrate that the nominated projects and assets meet the eligibility requirements. In addition, the issuer is required to establish internal processes and controls to track the use of proceeds, manage the unallocated funds and earmark funds to the nominated projects and assets. The issuer shall disclose in the bond documents related information such as the management of funds prior to the intended uses and if the issuer has procedures in place to ensure continuous compliance with the CBS.

2. Post-issuance requirements

The requirements are for continued certification after the bond has been issued. These are to verify the use of funds, the internal process and the eligibility of projects and assets. Part A in this section of the CBS document lists requirements that the issuer has to meet to continue post-issuance certification, including the nominated projects and assets, the use of proceeds, annual reports on how the funds had been allocated to nominated assets and the expected environmental objectives.

Part B in this section of the CBS document outlines a process to determine the eligibility of projects and assets that contribute to a low-carbon and climate-resilient economy. The current version of the CBS includes five sector-specific eligibility standards. Those sectors are wind energy, solar energy, geothermal energy, low carbon buildings and a bus rapid transit system.

Part C in this section of the CBS document deals with the requirements for specific types of bonds such as the use of proceeds bonds, the use of proceeds revenue bonds, project bonds and securitized bonds. Specific requirements are set for each type of bond in project holding, settlement period and earmarking.

3. The certification process

The first phase of the certification process evaluates the issuer's selection process for projects and assets as well as internal processes of tracking and allocation of funds. It allows the qualified issuer to use the climate bond certified mark during the marketing and pricing of the bond. The second phase of the certification aims at ensuring the integrity of the certified mark post issuance. The requirements include the assurance from the independent verifier about the issuer's compliance with the post issuance requirements.

Sources: International Capital Market Association (2015 and 2016).

15. Demystifying green bonds

Kathrin Berensmann, Florence Dafe and Nannette Lindenberg

1. INTRODUCTION

Governments, investors and the media have hailed green bonds – debt instruments intended to finance environmentally friendly projects – as a key instrument of climate finance because they could efficiently tap the trillions of dollars held in global bonds markets and by institutional investors. Representatives from development banks (DBs), for instance, often portray green bonds as 'essential to confronting climate change' (World Bank, 2015b) while institutional investors emphasize that green bonds make it possible to invest for sustainability and also achieve the financial performance that shareholders and policyholders expect (Zurich Insurance Group, 2014: 26).

A quick glance at the data does indeed indicate that global bonds markets are 'greening'. Two categories of green bonds have emerged in bond markets, namely green bonds which are labelled, that is certified as green, and unlabelled green bonds, which are not.[1] A sub-category are climate bonds, where the proceeds are linked to projects that address climate change. Annual labelled green bonds issuance has risen steadily – from US$ 2.6 billion in 2012 to US$ 160 billion in 2017 (CBI, 2015a, 2017a, 2018a; 2018b). The Climate Bonds Initiative (CBI), a non-governmental organization (NGO) that promotes green bonds markets, estimates that in 2018 issuance of labelled green bonds will reach USD 250 billion (CBI, 2018b).

In this chapter we probe the potential of green bonds to contribute to sustainable development by financing investments that support the environment, notably through combating climate change and its impact. The extant literature on green bonds is limited. The vast majority of the literature has been published by three types of actors: issuers of green bonds; investors; and NGOs. There is hardly any academic research on the topic.[2] Moreover, while publications on green bonds are increasing, the authors of studies are barely addressing one another's work and often focus on one dimension of green markets development such as market size, while neglecting others.

This chapter contributes to the emerging literature on green bonds by connecting different strands of the literature and by providing a more holistic assessment of the potential contribution of green bonds to sustainable development. In assessing the potential contribution of green bonds to sustainable development, we examine the size of the green bonds market and the factors that have driven its development as well as those that impede further development. Particular emphasis is placed on delineating the governance structures of the green bonds market – which have been heavily criticized by institutional investors and other financial market experts – and their consequences. We also use data from a variety of secondary sources and semi-structured interviews with issuers, investors and scholars of climate finance to examine the claim that the green bonds market can significantly contribute to sustainable development.

Our conclusions only partly support this claim. We find that there is significant potential for growth in the green bonds market as suggested by the market's increase in size and geographic reach and the broadening of the investor base. However, there are also limitations such as shallow secondary markets, a narrow investor base and 'greenwashing', the risk of green bonds' proceeds not being used to finance genuinely green projects. A major reason for these limitations is the weakness of the framework that governs green bonds markets. In particular, there are shortcomings with respect to the rules for standardization and disclosure: the governance structures for green bonds have limited transparency and accountability. In order for the green bonds market to mature with integrity, these shortcomings must be addressed.

The chapter proceeds as follows. In section 2 we first briefly describe the major types of green bonds and issuers and then discuss the significant growth of the green bonds market. In section 3 we explain the major impediments to their further development and argue that addressing weaknesses in the framework for governing green bonds is essential for the development of green bonds markets. In the final section, we present policy implications with a particular focus on measures for improving the governance of the market for green bonds.

2. CAPITAL MARKETS, GREEN BONDS AND THE TRANSFORMATION TOWARDS A GREEN ECONOMY

There is broad agreement among scholars and policymakers that transitioning towards a low-carbon society requires significant investment of economic resources in ecologically sustainable development. It is estimated that in order to limit global warming to 2°C, annual investments in clean energy must be quadrupled to reach US$ 1 trillion each year until 2030 (Fulton and Capalino, 2014). At the same time, investments must be reduced in carbon-intensive sectors that lock in greenhouse gas emissions for decades. In 2015, leaders from 195 countries and the European Union (EU) negotiated a climate agreement to limit global warming to at least 2°C (UNFCCC, 2015). In order to channel savings into sectors and projects that support economically sustainable development it will be important to intensify the use of adequate financing instruments (Berensmann and Lindenberg, 2018). One such instrument – the green bond – has been hailed as key to green financial markets for increasing the share of green investments.

2.1 What Are Green Bonds?

Green bonds have no universal definition: they are self-labelled and have no legal parameters. In 2014, a group of major green bonds issuers, underwriters and investors developed the Green Bond Principles (GBPs) – voluntary process guidelines intended to promote integrity in the green bonds market. The GBPs broadly define green bonds as any type of bond instrument whose revenues are exclusively used to partly or completely finance or re-finance new and/or existing 'eligible' green projects.

To delineate developments in the global market for green bonds, it is helpful to consider five different characteristics: (1) the type of green bond; (2) the size of the market and targeted areas; (3) the issuer; (4) the objective of the issuance; and (5) the market regulations (ICMA, 2017).

2.2 Types of Green Bonds

Green bonds markets trade four major types of bonds, which mainly differ in the way the assets that securitize the bond are grouped (ICMA, 2017). The majority are green 'use-of-proceeds' bonds, which means that the proceeds of this type of bond are earmarked for green projects in the issuer's portfolio, and the bond's recourse is to the issuer's entire balance sheet. When a green 'use-of-proceeds' bonds is issued, net revenues from issuances are moved to a sub-portfolio of the issuer's general account or otherwise tracked. The net proceeds from these bonds are then disbursed to any eligible green projects. Since use-of-proceeds bonds are backed by the issuer's complete balance sheet, credit-rating agencies do not rate individual bonds: green bonds of this type receive the same credit rating as their issuer.[3]

The other types of green bonds are also generally earmarked for green projects. However, the recourse of the second type, the 'use-of-proceeds revenue' bond, is limited to the issuer's pledged revenue streams. The third type is the 'green project' bond, which is used for specific green projects whose recourse is restricted to the project's assets and balance sheet. The fourth type is the 'green securitized' bond, whose revenues are used for a group of green projects with recourse to a certain group of assets on the issuer's balance sheet.

It is important to note that green bonds may be issued as 'covered' and 'uncovered' bonds. Covered bonds are bonds backed by assets on the issuer's balance sheet; most investors of a covered bond have preferential claims in the event of default. Although most green bonds have been issued as uncovered bonds, covered bonds have several advantages, one of which is their reduced investment risk. Since covered bonds tend to be highly regulated, they usually have better credit ratings than uncovered bonds and lower funding costs. Moreover, covered bonds are subject to stricter legislation and their assets must be transparent – guaranteeing the quality of their collaterals. Green bonds could be used as covered bonds if public sector guarantees were added to existing legislation (Damerow et al., 2012; Kreditanstalt für Wiederaufbau, 2016). A rare example of a covered green bond is that issued by the Berlin Hyp in 2015 (Berlin Hyp, 2016).

2.3 The Size of the Market and the Targeted Areas

Developments in the green bonds market are also revealed by the size and areas financed through bonds issuance. According to the GBP, to assure that the financed projects actually provide sustainable environmental benefits, projects to be financed by green bonds must fall into one of the following broad categories: renewable energy, energy efficiency, sustainable waste management, sustainable land use, biodiversity conservation, clean transportation, sustainable water management or climate-change adaptation (ICMA, 2017).

The CBI is the most-cited source of estimations related to the size of the green bonds market. According to the CBI US$ 82 billion of labelled green bonds were issued in 2016 (CBI, 2018b). In the same year, outstanding labelled and unlabelled green bonds which CBI calls climate aligned bonds amounted to US$ 895 billion, 221 billion of which were labelled green bonds. In 2012, less than 5 per cent of climate aligned bonds were labelled green bonds. These data show that the green label has significant market potential (CBI, 2017a).

In 2016, the proceeds of labelled green bonds were mainly utilized for renewable energy and green buildings projects (64 per cent of total). The use of proceeds for transport amounted to 14 per cent and for water 10 per cent. Land use, waste management and adaptation each made up only 3–5 per cent of total use of proceeds in 2016 (CBI, 2017a: 18).

While these numbers are impressive, the green bonds market remains tiny in relation to the multi-trillion-dollar corporate bonds market.[4] Green bonds make up less than 1 per cent of global bonds (G20 GFSG, 2016: 3). Moreover, a lot hinges on the definition of what constitutes a 'green' or 'climate-aligned' project or sector. The 'greenness' of the targeted field or sector is often questioned, which makes it more difficult to objectively estimate the market's size. For instance, any estimations of the market volume based on the assumption that rail transportation cannot be labelled 'green' – regardless of the energy source and where the rails might be laid – would yield much smaller numbers for the market's size. The inclusion of nuclear power or even large hydropower projects in enumerating eligible 'green' projects is also contested.

Moreover, the bonds were partly issued in different currencies in 2016: labelled green bonds were mainly issued in US$ (36 per cent) and Euros (38 per cent), while climate aligned bonds including both unlabelled and labelled bonds were quite often also issued in emerging market currencies such as the Chinese currency (32 per cent). The US dollar and the Euro accounted for only 26 per cent and 20 per cent of total, respectively (CBI, 2017a: 5 and 18). The greater diversity of currencies in the unlabelled green bonds market can be explained by the fact that in emerging countries many issuers do not label their bonds 'green'.

2.4 The Issuers

The third aspect that describes the universe of green bonds are their sources. As Figure 15.1 shows, the landscape of issuers has become much more diversified in the last two years. After the European Investment Bank (EIB) issued the first green bonds in 2007, the number of labelled green bonds issuances grew slowly in the wake of the 2008 global financial crisis, when there was little appetite for new financial instruments. At first, DBs were the major players in the green bonds market. However, the share of green bond issuance from DBs in terms of total labelled green bond issuance decreased to about 21 per cent in 2017. Banks and municipalities began to enter the market in 2012, with corporations following a year later. Similarly, sub-sovereign issuance from Local Government and Government-backed Entities amounted to 21 per cent of total labelled green bond issuance in 2017. The increase of issuances by sovereigns was remarkable in 2017: while their issuance amounted to US$ 780 million in 2016, they went up to US$ 10.8 billion in 2017 (CBI, 2018a; 2018b).

Hence, the green bonds offer was much more complex in 2016 and 2017

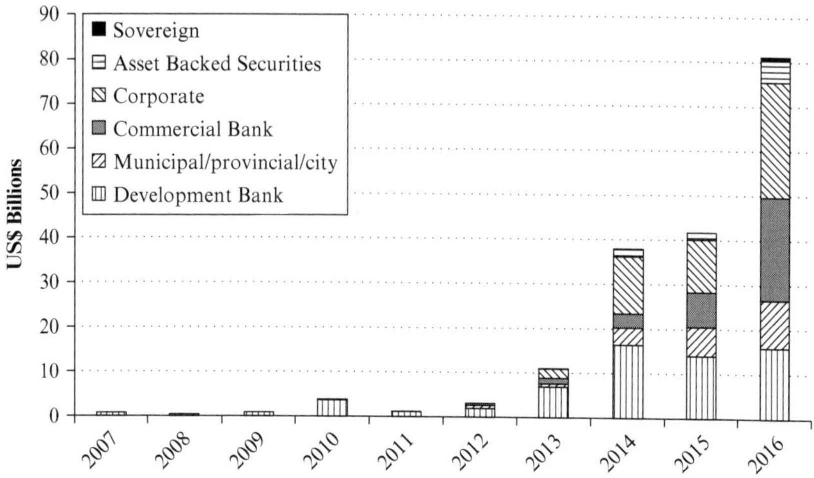

Source: Data provided by CBI.

Figure 15.1 Annual labelled green bonds issuance by issuer type

than it was in the pioneering years. This complexity is not only the result of the increase in volume and market participants; it results above all from the new types of issuers.

As a matter of fact, more and more professional investors are becoming convinced that sustainability considerations can help to improve their risk management tools and help them to make better decisions about investments.[5] The fear of assets being stranded due to the growing political, economic and environmental risks related to fossil fuel investments makes green investments more attractive. Unforeseen events like the Volkswagen emissions scandal in the automotive sector that came to light in 2015 and the risks of mass legal proceedings or loss of reputation are other strong drivers of this new dynamism.

2.5 The Objective of the Issuance

A final consideration for illustrating developments in the green bonds market and its potential is the underlying motivation for issuing green bonds. NGOs expect that green bonds will provide additional climate finance, while companies want to show that they are ecologically conscious by conducting 'green image campaigns'. Other important reasons to issue green bonds are to refinance existing projects and diversify the investor base.[6]

The diversification of the investor base is particularly relevant for

DBs against the backdrop of the bond-purchasing programmes of many central banks in the aftermath of the global financial crisis, which led to the dominance of central banks among potential buyers and a kind of 'monoculture' in the DBs' bonds market. A senior official from the KfW development bank explains that DBs view diversification of the investor base through green bonds issuances as a way of insuring against the time when central banks reduce their bond purchases.[7] They prioritize establishing good relationships with alternative purchasers to safeguard against a future lack of investor demand.

The experience of the African Development Bank (AfDB) suggests that the issuance of green bonds may indeed help to diversify the investor base by attracting new, socially responsible investors (Duru and Nyong, 2016). Usually central banks and other official bodies buy about 75 per cent of the AfDB's benchmark bonds, but in October 2013 socially responsible investors bought 84 per cent of its US$ 500 million green bonds issuance. Central banks and official institutions constituted only 28 per cent of the buyers: 43 per cent were asset managers, 28 per cent insurance companies and pension funds, and 1 per cent retail and private banks.

An additional motivation for DBs is raising awareness – altruistically, for the sake of climate-related investments, particularly in emerging and developing economies and to market their own climate-related activities. Furthermore, DBs wish and sometimes are mandated to build and scale up the market for green bonds, as in the case of the KfW.

However, it is not clear that mobilizing additional climate finance is the objective of green bonds issuers. Like traditional bonds, green bonds often serve to re-finance existing projects. We do not yet have enough evidence to suggest that green bonds attract more new financing than traditional bonds (Clapp et al., 2016: 8). In this sense, the terminology of the EIB, which in 2007 issued the first green bond called a 'climate awareness bond' (CAB) and continues to use this name, is actually more appropriate for DB's green bonds.

Nevertheless, the CBI argues that green bonds' true additionality is offering project developers simple, reasonably priced possibilities for refinancing which incentivize them to make an initial investment (Sonerud et al., 2015). According to the CBI, the leveraging effect of green bonds may be indirect rather than direct. The certainty of having good possibilities for offloading an initial investment after some years through the green bonds market eliminates the long holding period of the majority of green investments, which can deter investment.

2.6 Rules Governing the Green Bonds Market

A plethora of agents is involved in developing rules, especially regarding standards, for the green bonds market. Among the key actors are states and public and private issuers such as development and commercial banks, NGOs, research institutes and rating agencies. However, most of the impetus to formulate rules and standards has come from outside the public domain in the form of industry self-regulation.

The first standards designed for the green bonds market were the GBPs – voluntary guidelines for issuing green bonds, which were first formulated in 2014 and have been updated annually since then. The GBPs specify a number of categories for projects eligible for green bonds financing and recommend transparency and disclosure with respect to the use of the proceeds (ICMA, 2017). Issuers, investors and intermediaries in the green bonds market, as well as the International Capital Market Association (ICMA), formulate the GBPs. The guiding principle is industry self-regulation, with membership for the GBPs being restricted to organizations that have issued, underwritten (placed) or invested in a green bond. Others may apply for observer status regarding the formulation of guidelines but not be involved in the drafting process.

The GBPs are not the only effort to develop standards for the green bonds market. The CBI has also developed the 'Climate Bond International Standards and Certification Scheme', which includes a certification process, pre- and post-issuance requirements and a suite of sector-specific eligibility and guidance documents (CBI, 2017a). Working groups of technical and industry experts, supervised by an advisory board of institutional investors and environmental NGOs, develop the Climate Bond Standards. Another type of standard setter is the second opinion provider, often a research institute or consulting agency. Before a green bond is issued, its issuers can seek second opinions, independent assessments of their green credentials and the green bonds issuance framework. Credit-rating agencies that have developed green bonds indices have also promoted standards for green bonds by ensuring that only green bonds that fulfil certain criteria are included. Examples are the S&P Dow Jones, Solactive, Barclays MSCI and Bank of America Merrill Lynch (S&P, 2017).

At the end of 2017, the Association of Southeast Asian Nations (ASEAN) Capital Markets Forum (ACMF), including capital market regulators from ASEAN countries, implemented the ASEAN Green Bond Standards that are based on the GBP (ACMF, 2017).

The public sector has also attempted to formulate standards. Several DBs have not only sought to shape the GBPs by becoming members, but have also led efforts regarding post-issuance reporting. The AfDB, the EIB, the International Finance Corporation (IFC) and the World Bank (IBRD) have been working to create a harmonized framework for reporting the impacts of projects that have been allocated green bonds proceeds (AfDB et al., 2015; Reichelt and Davies, 2015; IDFC and MDB, 2015). These DBs recommend that core indicators be used to report their impacts on energy efficiency and renewable energy projects.

The People's Bank of China Green Finance Committee has published the Green Projects Catalogue, which establishes rules for evaluating projects to ensure their eligibility for green bonds financing (Green Finance Committee of the China Society of Finance and Banking, 2015). In November 2017, China's Green Finance Committee (CGFC) and the European Investment Bank (EIB) published a white paper with the aim of increasing the comparability of green bond standards in China and the EU that is based on the Chinese Green Bond Endorsed Projects Catalogue, the project eligibility criteria of EIB's climate Awareness Bonds and the MDB-International Development Finance Club's (IDFC) Common Principles for Climate Mitigation Finance Tracking (EIB and CGFC, 2017; IDFC and MDBs, 2015).

Another example of a public attempt to govern the green bonds market are the guidelines published by the Securities and Exchange Board of India (SEBI, 2016). These guidelines include rules about third-party verification of green bonds by independent auditors. Other states and the EU are also pondering whether they should regulate the green bonds market, since it is not clear that industry self-regulation suffices to ensure its quantitative and qualitative growth (Kretschmer, 2016).

Overall, however, the formulation of standards has been driven far more by markets than by states. Multilateral bodies like the United Nations Environment Programme (UNEP) or the G20 also have not taken the lead in efforts to improve the green bonds market's governance – which may reflect the broader governance vacuum with regard to steering the green economy (Tienhaara, 2016). States' hesitance to more actively govern green bonds markets may reflect broader concerns about stifling the market's growth through standards and regulations (Kretschmer, 2016).

3. CHALLENGES FOR DEVELOPING THE GREEN BONDS MARKET

While both quantitative and qualitative criteria indicate that significant progress has been made in developing the green bonds market, we should be wary of painting too rosy a picture. The literature on green bonds highlights a variety of obstacles to the sustainable growth of green bonds markets, notably, the weakly developed pipeline for green projects largely due to the absence of policies and regulations that create demand for green investments; the costs associated with labelling a bond 'green' – administrative certification, verification and monitoring; green investors' unwillingness to pay a 'green' premium and accept smaller returns for those bonds than for their traditional 'grey' alternatives; and in the case of emerging and developing economies, weakly developed capital markets and low credit ratings for potential green bonds issuers.[8]

The main challenge to the market's further development relates to the governance of the green bond market. While the academic literature examining the governance of the green bonds market is limited, there is a broad body of work by policymakers, market analysts, issuers and investors suggesting that the limited standardization and disclosure rules for green bonds are problematic.[9] Although the market's governance framework is developing dynamically, it still has deficiencies. It is not clear that voluntary guidelines for transparency and disclosure can ensure that the market will mature with integrity. What is more, there is still no universal agreement among market participants, such as issuers and investors, about what constitutes a green bond and the characteristics required for projects to be eligible for green bonds financing.

One core problem has been missing harmonised standards. While several international and national taxonomies have been established, including the GBPs and the Climate Bonds Standard, the architecture of green bond standards at the international and national level is fragmented. Similarly, a number of voluntary standards and various instruments for certifying green bonds has been implemented, including second opinions, green ratings and green bond indices (Berensmann, 2017).

Finally, the continued lack of transparency and disclosure makes it difficult for regulators, NGOs and research institutions to assess market developments (Schneeweiß, 2016). Similarly, there are no legally binding standards for disclosing how green bonds proceeds are used, reporting the impact of projects funded by green bonds proceeds or independently assuring the green credentials. Monitoring is often recklessly neglected.

How might limited rules regarding standardization and disclosure affect the development of the green bonds market? One could argue that more governance and standardization would slow the market's dynamic growth. However, there is some risk that the uncontrolled increase of green bonds without stringent standards creates a market bubble and that the insecurity due to this development may eventually cause it to burst.

Moreover, closer examination of the effects of limited governance and standardization reveals that potential green bonds issuers might be hesitant to issue a green bond due to the risk of having their green credentials challenged (KPMG, 2015). Universally accepted standards for projects financed by green bonds would reduce the likelihood that a particular bond's green credentials would be scrutinized. Enhanced standardization could also help to increase the pipeline of projects eligible for green bonds by providing potential issuers with clearer guidelines to design and select projects that could be financed through green bonds. Increased standardization and cheaper certification seem to be key to increasing the supply of green bonds.

In much the same way, enhanced standardization and disclosure rules might also be needed to broaden the investor base (Lindenberg, 2014). Investors may be hesitant to invest in green bonds because weak standards increase the possibility of challenges to a bond's green integrity and, by extension, its reputation (OECD, 2015). This is particularly true for institutional investors who have both huge amounts of money under management and strict investment criteria. In fact, in the Paris Green Bonds Statement, investors controlling US$ 11.2 trillion encouraged experts to support the green bonds market by creating clear and independent standards, as well as introducing transparency rules about the use of their proceeds and their impacts (CBI, 2015b).

Broadening the investors base, which is currently dominated by the 'buy-and-hold' types, would also help deepen the secondary market for trading green bonds. A deeper secondary market in turn would make the green bonds market more attractive to investors.

Another way that weak rules governing green bonds can inhibit investment in the green bonds market is by limiting the scope to legally enforce green integrity (OECD, 2015). Moreover, the green bonds market's lack of clear standards may hinder investments in green bonds because investors have to make special efforts to examine the green credentials of a bond and its issuer, and an extra due diligence may be difficult to fulfil. Many investors have limited capacities for analysing green investments (OECD, 2015).

Enhanced and more consistent standardization and rules regarding disclosure are not just important for the green bonds market to quantitatively develop by increasing the scale and depth of the market; standards and rules for disclosure also help to qualitatively develop the green bonds market by reducing the risk of greenwashing, thereby enhancing market integrity. For instance, highly polluting companies must be prevented issuing green bonds to finance green projects in order to free up funds to subsidize grey operations.

The projects currently financed by green bonds proceeds exhibit different shades of green, ranging from pale green projects, with very limited environmental impact, to dark green projects that significantly impact the environment. Weak standards and disclosure rules make it difficult to assess the environmental benefits of a particular bond. For instance, in 2014 a Massachusetts State agency sold green bonds and planned to use some of the proceeds to build a 725-space parking garage – one example of the risk of using green bonds proceeds for projects with dubious environmental benefits (Cherney, 2015). Another controversial case was a green bond sold by the French power company GDF Suez in 2014 to build a hydropower plant in Brazil that is deemed to have significant environmental and social costs, such as contributing to floods displacing tens of thousands of people and potentially significant greenhouse gas emissions (Banktrack, 2015; Cherney, 2015).

More comprehensive and binding governance is essential for the sustainable growth of green bonds markets. Moreover, with the increasingly global issuance of green bonds, international coordination to develop standards and disclosure rules are needed to avoid a 'race to the bottom' through regulatory arbitrage. It is also important to ensure that developing and emerging economies maintain some flexibility to adapt global standards to their local contexts, capacities and necessities (Berensmann, 2017). However, better global standards are still needed. Although improved financial governance through enhanced standardization and disclosure rules will not solve all the challenges in developing the green bonds market, without better governance it is unlikely to mature with integrity.

While better governance through enhanced and more consistent standardization and disclosure rules is essential for the green bonds market to develop, it will not solve all the challenges, such as that of pricing. At least in the primary market, green bonds are usually priced like their grey alternatives because investors are unwilling to assume a reduction of the bond's return for the sake of making a green investment, despite the higher costs of issuance caused by the costs of green labelling.[10] As a consequence, some companies with green credentials and projects have refused to issue green bonds because of the extra costs – and some highly polluting companies have issued green bonds (Jackson, 2016).

A study by Barclays (2015) suggests that enhanced demand for green bonds might allow green bonds to be more highly priced. Barclays found that investors are currently paying a premium to acquire green bonds in the secondary market, which is partly attributed to opportunistic pricing based on strong demand from environmental funds. Policies like improved standards and regulations to stimulate interest in green investments and raise the demand for green bonds may also help to address the pricing challenge.

One challenge for the development of the green bonds market that cannot fully be addressed by standardization and disclosure is that of extending the geographic reach of issuances and green-bonds-eligible projects to emerging and developing countries. In developing countries, weak capital markets and low credit ratings for potential green bonds issuers limit the geographic reach of green bonds markets – and green bonds' contribution to sustainable development.

In fact, green bonds proceeds have rarely been allocated to low-income countries (LICs). Development banks like the IFC have focused on middle-income countries. There are several reasons that green bonds are rarely allocated to LICs, for instance, the institutions responsible for LICs at some of the major multilateral DBs, such as the World Bank's International Development Association and the AfDB's African Development Fund, do not issue bonds in capital markets because they use aid allocations to finance projects. Another reason is that in poorer countries, projects that could be eligible for financing through green bonds are often just too small.

However, as we have noted, green bonds have been issued in several emerging economies and the geographic reach of green bonds markets is expanding. As green bonds markets develop in emerging economies, enhanced standardization and disclosure rules will be as important for them as for the global green bonds market.[11] In fact, in developing and emerging countries, where capital markets are weakly developed and governance structures are just now being designed, there may be a window of opportunity for developing green standards since there are no costs from changing governance structures and there may also be fewer vested interests that benefit from weak governance.

4. CONCLUSION AND RECOMMENDATIONS: QUO VADIS, GREEN BONDS MARKET?

In the past decade there has been an explosive growth in the market for green bonds. Government efforts to tackle global warming, the increase in the number of socially responsible investors, rising concerns about stranded assets and great enthusiasm in debt capital markets because of extremely low interest rates have all contributed to the popularity of green bonds as an asset class. Recognition that environmental and financial issues are intimately linked has also grown.

To realize the enormous potential of green bonds, several challenges must be addressed, notably the risk of greenwashing, limited standardization, an undiversified investor base, the time lag from directing proceeds from a bond sale to green projects or assets, narrow secondary markets, the high costs of green bonds issuance and the development of a green project pipeline. An improved governance framework could help to address several of these challenges. What should policymakers, issuers, investors and other groups who seek to contribute to the greening of bond markets do? We see considerable potential for reforms in six areas.

4.1 Transparency and Disclosure

The first area is transparency and disclosure. For the green bonds market to contribute to ecologically sustainable development, there must be greater transparency about how green bonds are defined. For instance, the GBPs should be elaborated to provide a clearer definition of green bonds that leaves less room for greenwashing. Second opinions could provide more detailed assessments of the greenness of particular projects the way Cicero does with its 'three shades of green' approach (Clapp et al., 2016; Nanji et al., 2014; Schneeweiß, 2016). Cicero's approach should be emulated. To make it easier to compare second opinions, the evaluation criteria – including information about the issuer's core business activities – and their rating scales must be standardized and adopted by all second opinion providers.

Disclosure reforms should aim to ensure publication of details about the intended use of proceeds and the annual reporting of the actual use of proceeds and second opinions. Covered bonds could increase transparency because they are more strictly regulated than uncovered bonds.

Green bonds indices may also increase transparency on the green bonds market for both issuers and investors by defining specific criteria.[12] Indeed, more green bonds indices have been established, such as those of S&P Dow Jones, Solactive, Barclays MSCI and Bank of America Merrill Lynch. One good example is the Barclays MSCI Green Bond Index which is based on various criteria for green bonds, including the definition of the eligible use of proceeds and the evaluation and project selection methods; it also stipulates regular reporting (Reichelt and Davies, 2015). Other examples are the S&P Green Project Bond and the S&P Green Bond indices (Standard and Poors, 2016). That said, more transparency and clarity is needed with regard to the selection criteria used to compile indices.

4.2 Compliance with Standards

The second area concerns compliance with standards. Several measures could help to improve that. For instance, bodies that design green bonds indices could more closely monitor the bonds included in any index of bonds that are claimed to adhere to the strictest industry standards. Rating agencies could explicitly consider the environmental aspects of green bonds in their evaluations. Financial authorities could regulate the green bonds market, and institutional investors could integrate green investment criteria in their guidelines.

Industry self-regulators should stop recommending compliance with standards and require it. Public disclosure will help to ensure compliance. If the green bonds market is to mature with integrity, clearer monitoring responsibilities must be defined, with sanctions for violating the rules. It will be equally important to eliminate market monitors' conflicts of interest. For instance, rating agencies and some second opinion providers could face a conflict of interest because of their need to maintain good relations with the bond issuers who commission the opinions.

4.3 Reduction of Complexity

The third area regards the need to reduce the complexity of the green bonds asset class. Financial products must be simple to attract investors. Green bonds' growing diversity, which results from more and more issuers in a broad range of sectors designing their own bonds, must somehow be reversed in order to make green bonds appeal to the mass market.

4.4 Cost of Green Bonds Issuance

The fourth area relates to the costs of issuing green bonds. Smaller green projects may be aggregated to enable lower-cost access to the green bonds market. Tax benefits for green bonds issuers or investors are one way to reduce costs. However, cost reductions for green bonds issuance should be granted to small and medium-sized companies rather than to large entities.

According to a senior banker at HSBC, larger institutions with more sophisticated funding operations, such as banks, can more easily incorporate green bonds into their borrowing plans (Jackson, 2016). The informant argues that larger institutions can spread the cost of running a green policy over many issues by maintaining a presence in the bond markets. Public schemes to reduce the price of green bonds must also be weighed against other climate policies (Shishlov et al., 2016).

4.5 Research

The fifth important area is the support of research. There is very little academic research which links developments in green bond markets to wider theories of finance. Few scholars have examined the political and economic drivers of green bonds market development and the political and economic consequences of green bonds issuances. Among the important research questions are: What are the risks of aggregating green bonds projects through securitization? To what extent does the green bonds market help to mobilize additional climate finance? Which governance mechanisms would help the green bonds market to develop qualitatively? Scholars from business and management studies, economics and international politics could cluster around these questions. It will also be important to track green bonds financing provided by and in developing economies – 'South-South climate finance' – in order to foster such flows and more effectively align them with traditional climate finance (Ha et al., 2016).

4.6 Expand Governance Inclusiveness

Sharing more detailed information between the various stakeholders will make governance more inclusive. Round tables of investors, issuers, governments, NGOs and regulators should be organized to discuss what and how much regulation and policy support is needed to foster the development of green bonds. Such an approach could help the market to mobilize climate finance while also meeting the needs of the finance industry. The establishment of the GBP Executive Committee was an important step in the right direction. The committee gathers together issuers, investors and intermediaries in the green bonds market to assess its development and formulate best practices.

The ICMA similarly operates as a secretariat supporting the GBP, for example, by facilitating the exchange of information among stakeholders and offering advice about its governance (ICMA, 2017). However, it will be important to ensure that stakeholder dialogues are inclusive. One recent initiative is the CBI Climate Bond Standards, where working groups consisting of technical and industry experts and an advisory board of institutional investors and environmental NGOs collaborate to develop standards. When the development of standards becomes a more inclusive process, the resulting standards may also be considered more legitimate.

NOTES

1. Note that green bonds do not necessarily imply a limited exposure of investors to environmentally related financial risks such as Ehlers and Packer (2016) highlight.
2. There are notable exceptions. See for instance Bracking (2015), duPont et al. (2015) and Flaherty et al. (2016).
3. For instance, both the World Bank and its green use-of-proceeds bonds are rated 'AAA'.

4. The volume of the worldwide bond market amounts to about USD 100 trillion (Schneeweiß, 2016).
5. See also Dietz et al. (2016) for the impact of climate change on asset values.
6. Interview with a senior official from the African Development Bank, Abidjan, 21 January 2016. Interview with a senior official of the KfW in Bonn, 13 November 2015.
7. Interview with a senior official of the KfW in Bonn, 13 November 2015.
8. Interviews with senior officials from the KfW, the EIB and the AfDB.
9. See for instance Ceres (2015), Cort and Krosinsky (2015), KPMG (2015) and OECD (2015). The Paris Green Bonds Statement, a document published by existing and potential green bonds investors, also emphasizes that enhanced standardization and disclosure rules are essential for the green bonds market to develop (CBI, 2015b).
10. There may be exceptions. For instance, the AfDB reports that feedback from investors indicates that AfDB's Swedish Krona green bonds issuance was executed at a price that would not have been possible without a green label (Duru and Nyong, 2016: 4).
11. This holds notably for green bonds targeted at financing projects which support climate change adaptation, which is of major concern to developing and emerging economies. Because the policy debate and bond issuance have focused on green credentials in relation to climate-change mitigation, the criteria for assessing the climate-change adaptation benefits of a green bond have received little attention in international discussions about standardization. For instance, as of June 2015, the IBRD had committed 78 per cent of green bonds proceeds to mitigation and 22 per cent to adaptation projects (World Bank, 2015a).
12. Extant research suggests that responsible investment indices like the FTSE4Good Index might also have a positive impact on environmental management (Mackenzie et al., 2013).

REFERENCES

AfDB (African Development Bank), EIB (European Investment Bank), IFC (International Finance Corporation) and WB (World Bank) (2015), 'Green Bonds – Working Towards a Harmonized Framework Impact Reporting', accessed 30 May 2018 at http://www.afdb.org/fileadmin/uploads/afdb/Documents/Generic-Documents/Green_Bonds_-_Working_Towards_a_Harmonized_Framework_for_Impact_Reporting_-_March_2015.pdf

ASEAN Capital Markets Forum (ACMF) (2017), 'ASEAN Green Bond Standards', Kuala Lumpur, assessed 30 May 2018 at http://www.theacmf.org/ACMF/upload/ASEAN_Green_Bond_Standards.pdf

Banktrack (2015), 'Open Letter on the 2015 Update of the Green Bond Principles', accessed 30 May 2018 at http://www.icmagroup.org/Regulatory-Policy-and-Market-Practice/green-bonds/other-gbp-resources/

Barclays (2015), 'The Cost of Being Green', New York: Barclays.

Berensmann, K. (2017), 'Upscaling Green Bond Markets: The Need for Harmonised Green Bond Standards' (Briefing Paper 10/2017), German Development Institute, accessed 30 May 2018 at http://www.die-gdi.de/briefing-paper/article/upscaling-green-bond-markets-the-need-for-harmonised-green-bond-standards/

Berensmann, K. and Lindenberg, N. (2018), 'Green Finance across the Universe', in S. Boubaker, D. Cumming and D. Nguyen (eds) *Ethics, ESG and Sustainable Prosperity*, London: World Scientific Publishing, forthcoming.

Berlin Hyp (2016), 'Press Release', accessed 30 May 2018 at http://www.berlinhyp.de/uploads/media/2016-02-04_Green_Bond_Award_D.pdf

Bracking, S. (2015), 'Performativity in the Green Economy: How Far Does Climate Finance Create a Fictive Economy?', *Third World Quarterly*, 36(12), 2337–2357.

CBI (2015a), '2015 Green Bond Market Roundup', accessed 30 May 2018 at https://www.climatebonds.net/files/files/2015%20GB%20Market%20Roundup%2003A.pdf

CBI (2015b), 'The Paris Green Bonds Statement', accessed 30 May 2018 at https://www.climatebonds.net/files/files/Paris_Investor_Statement_9Dec15.pdf.
CBI (2017a), 'Bonds and Climate Change: The State of the Market in 2016', accessed 30 May 2018 at https://www.climatebonds.net/files/reports/cbi-sotm_2017-bondsclimatechange.pdf
CBI (2017b), *Labelled Green Bonds Dataset*, London: Climate Bonds Initiative.
CBI (2018a), 'Green Bond Highlights 2017', London: Climate Bonds Initiative, accessed 30 May 2018 at https://www.climatebonds.net/resources/reports/green-bond-highlights-2017
CBI (2018b), website, accessed 30 May 2018 at https://www.climatebonds.net/
Ceres (2015), 'A Statement of Investor Expectations for the Green Bond Market', accessed 30 May 2018 at http://www.emergingmarketsdialogue.org/wp-content/uploads/2018/02/Statement_of_Investor_Expectations_for_Green_Bonds.pdf
Cherney, M. (2015), '"Green Bonds" for a Parking Garage?', accessed 30 May 2018 at http://www.wsj.com/articles/green-bonds-for-a-parking-garage-1426176294
Clapp, C., Alfsen, K.H., Lund, H.F. and Pillay, K. (2016), 'Green Bonds and Environmental Integrity: Insights from Cicero Second Opinions', Policy Note 2016:01, Oslo: CICERO (Center for International Climate and Environmental Research), May.
Cort, T. and Krosinsky, C. (2015), 'To Thrive, Green Bonds Need Standards for Environmental Impact', accessed 30 May 2018 at https://insights.som.yale.edu/insights/to-thrive-green-bonds-need-standards-for-environmental-impact
Damerow, F., Kidney, S. and Clenaghan, S. (2012), 'How Covered Bond Markets Can Be Adapted for Renewable Energy Finance and How This Could Catalyse Innovation in Low-Carbon Capital Markets', accessed 30 May 2018 at https://www.climatebonds.net/files/uploads/2012/05/Climate-Bonds_RE-covered-bonds_22May20121.pdf
Dietz, S., Bowen, A., Dixon, C. and Gradwell, P. (2016), '"Climate Value at Risk" of Global Financial Assets', *Nature Climate Change*, 6(7), 676–679.
duPont, C.M., Levitt, J.N. and Bilmes, L.J. (2015), 'Green Bonds and Land Conservation: The Evolution of a New Financing Tool', HKS Faculty Research Working Paper 5–072. Cambridge, MA: John F. Kennedy School of Government, Harvard University.
Duru, U. and Nyong, A. (2016), *Why Africa Needs Green Bonds*, Tunis: African Development Bank.
Ehlers, T. and Packer, F. (2016), *Green Bonds – Certification, Shades of Green and Environmental Risks. Contribution to the G20 Green Finance Study Group*, Basel: Bank for International Settlements.
European Investment Bank and China's Green Finance Committee (2017), 'The Need for a Common Language in Green Finance. Towards a Standard-Neutral Taxonomy of the Environmental Use of Proceeds', Phase I Report, 11 November, accessed 30 May 2018 at http://www.eib.org/attachments/press/white-paper-green-finance-common-language-eib-and-green-finance-committee.pdf
Flaherty M., Gevorkyan A., Radpour S. and Semmler, W. (2016), 'Financing Climate Policies through Climate Bonds – A Three Stage Model and Empirics', New York: Schwartz Center for Economic Policy Analysis and Department of Economics, The New School for Social Research, Working Paper Series 2016–3.
Fulton, M. and Capalino, R. (2014), 'Investing in the Clean Trillion: Closing the Clean Energy Investment Gap. A Ceres Report', Boston, MA: Ceres.
G20 GFSG (2016), 'G20 Green Finance Synthesis Report. 5 September 2016', accessed 30 May 2018 at http://unepinquiry.org/wp-content/uploads/2016/09/Synthesis_Report_Full_EN.pdf
Green Finance Committee of the China Society of Finance and Banking (2015), 'Preparation Instructions on Green Bond Endorsed Project', accessed 30 May 2018 at https://webcache.googleusercontent.com/search?q=cache:Jxs4kgwd5JsJ:https://www.bourse.lu/documents/brochure-GB_endorsed_project_catalogue_2015.pdf+&cd=1&hl=de&ct=clnk&gl=de
Ha, S., Hale, T. and Ogden, P. (2016), 'Climate Finance in and between Developing Countries: An Emerging Opportunity to Build On', *Global Policy*, 7(1), 102–108.
ICMA (2017), 'Green Bond Principles 2017', accessed 30 May 2018 at https://www.icmagroup.org/assets/documents/Regulatory/Green-Bonds/GreenBondsBrochure-JUNE2017.pdf

International Development Finance Club (IDFC) and Multilateral Development Banks (MDBs) (2015), 'Common Principles for Climate Mitigation Finance Tracking', accessed 30 May 2018 at https://www.ifc.org/wps/wcm/connect/65d37952-434e-40c1-a9df-c7bdd8ffcd39/MDB-IDFC+Common-principles-for-climate-mitigation-finance-tracking.pdf?MOD=AJPERES

Jackson, G. (2016), 'Green Bond Market Faces Growing Pains. Market's Rapid Growth Will Raise Questions about Regulation', accessed 30 May 2018 at https://next.ft.com/content/fc537c36-2982-11e6-8b18-91555f2f4fde

KPMG (2015), *Sustainable Insight: Gearing up for Green Bonds*, Zurich: KPMG.

Kreditanstalt für Wiederaufbau (2016), 'Kfw Green Bond Portfolio'.

Kretschmer, B. (2016), 'Green Finance and Green Bonds – Preliminary Results. Presentation at the Suedwind Seminar, Bonn 30 June', Brussels: European Commission.

Lindenberg, N. (2014), *Public Instruments to Leverage Private Capital for Green Investments in Developing Countries*, Bonn: German Development Institute/Deutsches Institut für Entwicklungspolitik (DIE).

Mackenzie, C., Rees, W. and Rodionova, T. (2013), 'Do Responsible Investment Indices Improve Corporate Social Responsibility? Ftse4good's Impact on Environmental Management', *Corporate Governance: An International Review*, 21(5), 495–512.

Nanji, A., Calder, A. and Kolodzie, M. (2014), 'Green Bonds: Fifty Shades of Green', accessed 30 May 2018 at http://www.rbc.com/community-sustainability/_assets-custom/pdf/Green-Bonds-Fifty-Shades-of-Green.pdf

OECD (2015), *Green Bonds. Mobilizing Debt Capital Markets for a Low-Carbon Transition: Policy Perspectives*, Paris: OECD.

Reichelt, H. and Davies, C. (2015), 'Getting to Know the Green Bond Market', Pension Fund Service: Local Government, accessed 30 May 2018 at http://treasury.worldbank.org/cmd/pdf/GettingtoKnowtheGreenBondMarket_PensionFundService.pdf

Schneeweiß, A. (2016), *Green Bonds – Black Box Mit Grünem Etikett?* Bonn: SÜDWIND e.V. – Institut für Ökonomie und Ökumene.

SEBI (2016), 'Disclosure Requirements for Issuance and Listing of Green Bonds', accessed 30 May 2018 at https://www.sebi.gov.in/sebi_data/meetingfiles/1453349548574-a.pdf

Shishlov, I., Morel, R. and Cochran, I. (2016), *Beyond Transparency: Unlocking the Full Potential of Green Bonds*, Paris: I4CE – Institute for Climate Economics.

Sonerud, B., Kidney, S. and Tripathy, A. (2015), 'Scaling up Green Bond Markets for Sustainable Development: A Strategic Guide for the Public Sector to Stimulate Private Sector Market Development for Green Bonds. Consultation Paper', accessed 30 May 2018 at https://www.climatebonds.net/files/files/GB-Public_Sector_Guide-Final-1A.pdf

Standard & Poors (2016), 'S&P Green Bond Index', accessed 30 May 2018 at http://eu.spindices.com/indices/fixed-income/sp-green-bond-index

Standard & Poors (2017), 'Aligning Impact and Income: The Next Generation of Green Bond Indices', accessed 30 May 2018 at http://us.spindices.com/indexology/esg/aligning-impact-with-income-the-next-generation-of-green-bond-indices

Tienhaara, K. (2016), 'Governing the Global Green Economy', *Global Policy*, 481–490.

UNFCCC (2015), *Adoption of the Paris Agreement. Proposal by the President*, Geneva: United Nations Office at Geneva.

World Bank (2015a), *Green Bond Impact Report*, Washington, DC: World Bank.

World Bank (2015b), 'Green Bonds Attract Private Sector Climate Finance', accessed 30 May 2018 at http://www.worldbank.org/en/topic/climatechange/brief/green-bonds-climate-finance

Zurich Insurance Group (2014), *Annual Review 2013*, Zurich: Zurich Insurance Group.

PART III

CSR AND SOCIALLY RESPONSIBLE INVESTMENT

16. Models of corporate socially responsible banks: financial cooperatives, Islamic banks, and microfinance institutions

Narjess Boubakri and Jocelyn Grira

1. INTRODUCTION

Corporate Social Responsibility (CSR) has been a topic of growing interest in the last decade. KPMG's (2017) survey shows the increasing importance of CSR to investors, and global corporations nowadays disclose extensive information related to their CSR activities. Investors in turn seem to integrate the disclosed CSR information in their decision-making process (Attig et al., 2016; Sievänen et al., 2013; among others). Only 8 percent of global corporations reported CSR content in their disclosed information in 2008 compared to 51 percent in 2013. Furthermore, CSR gained more importance following the recent global financial crisis (GFC), and has emerged as a spontaneous response to social, economic, and political pressure (Paulet et al., 2015). Ho et al. (2016) cite the cases of Apple Inc. and ExxonMobil as global corporations that exemplify their commitment toward CSR. ExxonMobil makes claims concerning its engagement with education, public health, human rights, community and social work, employee safety, and environment preservation. Similarly, Apple embraces environmental responsibilities, and social and ethical engagement. Moreover, Di Giuli and Kostovetsky reported in 2014 that around 80 percent of Global Fortune 250 companies disclose detailed CSR information compared to 50 percent in 2005. Recent research shows that CSR has an impact on the cost of capital and firm value (El Ghoul et al., 2011; Servaes and Tamayo, 2013), and that corporations adopt CSR investments because they believe that the perceived benefits will outweigh the costs, thereby improving their performance in the long run (Margolis et al., 2007).

From a theoretical point of view, two opposite theories/hypotheses have been proposed in relation to CSR: the shareholder value maximization hypothesis and the shareholder expense hypothesis (Deng et al., 2013; Jha and Cox, 2016). The first hypothesis builds on contract theory and the theory of the firm (Alchian and Demsetz, 1972; Jensen and Meckling, 1976; Cornell and Shapiro, 1987; Hill and Jones, 1992; among others), where shareholders are related to firms' stakeholders by contracts, so as to provide resources to support firms' operations. Consequently, CSR activities increase stakeholders' awareness about the need of resources for firms' operations, hence positively impacting firm performance. In contrast, the second hypothesis asserts that managers engage in CSR activities for the benefit of other stakeholders at the expense of the shareholders (Pagano and Volpin, 2005; Surroca and Tribo, 2008; Cronqvist et al., 2009), which results in wealth transfer from shareholders to the different stakeholders. Empirical evidence is mixed though, with some studies being supportive of the first hypothesis (El Ghoul et al., 2011; Goss and Roberts, 2011; Cheng et al., 2014; Kim et al., 2014; Lin et al., 2014; among others),[1] whereas others are in favor of the second (Di Giuli and Kostovetsky, 2014; McWilliams and Siegel, 2001).

The financial literature on the role of CSR in the banking sector has been relatively scarce. While prior studies generally underscore the important role of the banking system in economic development (Levine, 2005; Shen and Lee, 2005; Beck et al., 2010), by showing that a healthy banking system is the key to sustained prosperity (King and Levine, 1993), contrasting evidence demonstrates that, even if banks started being aware of the importance of ethics, financial institutions keep using considerable resources at the expense of society. For example, in periods of financial distress, governments bail out the failing institutions or take them over at the expense of taxpayers. As financial institutions employ public resources paid for by the society, they are required to provide feedback to the community more often than other industries, and are, consequently, highly scrutinized by the media, government, and academia regarding their CSR activities. The implicit guarantee against default offered by governments to banks during periods of financial distress reflects the ethical challenge of banks, as discussed in Iannotta et al. (2013) and Shen et al. (2016). Scholtens (2009) mentions that in member countries of the Organisation for Economic Cooperation and Development (OECD), specialized financial institutions offer savings accounts to the public while promising that the money will be used to finance so-called community investments in the environment. Thus, in most countries, financial institutions are involved in economic activities aimed at sustainable development. For instance, Goss and Roberts (2011) show that CSR firms enjoy lower costs of banking debt than their non-CSR peers. Besides, Paulet et al. (2015) argue that CSR banks react differently to financial distress and behave distinctively compared to non-CSR banks in terms of credit policy and risk appetite. In an interesting short paper, Green (1989) discusses the ethical issues in the banking industry and argues that it goes far beyond the letter of the law and of contract. To the author, banks have corporate social responsibilities toward the different stakeholders:

governments, customers, shareholders, employees, and the community. Fulfilling these responsibilities enhances banks' reputations, provides legitimacy to their operations, and, somehow, ensures their long-term success. Finally, Harvey (1995) discusses the challenge of CSR for economists and managers as it widens the range of the stakeholders to satisfy, going from only shareholders, as stated in the theory of the firm, to a larger set of interested parties. He argues that the CSR paradigm implies the acceptance of the legitimate rights of others, other than the shareholders, with respect to firms' tangible or intangible outcomes.

This chapter discusses three well-established, and corporate socially responsible, banking models. The first model relates to cooperative financial institutions where the ownership structure is spread over the owners instead of being relatively concentrated and mainly owned by institutional portfolios. The cooperative model differs fundamentally from the conventional banking model as per the historical underlying reasons for its inception, the specificities related to its corporate governance, and the extent of its involvement in the community. The second model is the Islamic banking model. In its construction, it is built to comply with a set of moral rules driven from Islamic principles. For example, speculation, over-charging interest, investing in non-ethical industries (tobacco, gambling, etc.) are examples of financial practices that do not comply with the moral principles in the Islamic banking model. The distinguishing profit-and-loss sharing feature allows for an easier access to capital facilities and achieves a higher involvement of the financial institution in the economy and the community. The third model relates to microfinance institutions. It provides financial accessibility to small-sized economic agents that may not have the opportunity to initiate their projects otherwise. Microfinance institutions' counterparties are usually low-revenue individuals and small firms with no, or almost no, formal credit records as generally required by conventional banks. In many countries, these firms represent a large proportion of the economic network. This stresses the importance of microfinance institutions in the socio-economic development of these countries.

This chapter sheds more light on the distinctive characteristics of corporate socially responsible financial institutions, highlights their contributions to socio-economic development, and emphasizes the role they play in promoting ethical business standards and practices, as well as their contribution to the community. The next section discusses the areas in which banks usually implement most of their CSR practices. The subsequent sections handle each of the individual banking models and provide an overview of the factors that catalyze CSR and help in promoting an effective culture of sustainability. The last section concludes.

2. CSR IN BANKING

The most widely accepted definition of CSR is 'the social responsibility of business encompassing the economic, legal, ethical, and discretionary expectations that society has of organizations at a given point in time' (Carroll, 1979, p. 500). An alternative commonly used definition is provided by McWilliams and Siegel (2000) and presents CSR as 'actions that appear to further some social good, beyond the interests of the firm and that which is required by law'. These definitions apply to a broad range of firm types, including financial institutions. Now, why do banks engage in CSR activities? Viewed as rational economic agents, banks decide to commit to society if the benefits of CSR engagement are greater than the costs. However, the financial literature has been inconclusive about the relationship between CSR and financial performance, even if recent studies document a positive relationship more often than otherwise (Chih et al., 2010; Kopel and Brand, 2012; Lambertini and Tampieri, 2015; Nollet et al., 2016; Wu and Shen, 2013; among others).

Financial institutions adopting CSR activities do so for different reasons. First, CSR-engaged banks invest in their reputation. This directly enhances their image and strengthens their relationship with their customers. Ultimately, it may be rewarding through a premium that the customers may be willing to pay. Second, banks' commitment to CSR may be viewed as a way to give back to society as a form of compensation for the considerable use of public resources instead of those of shareholders. In fact, governments' implicit guarantees, which were effectively operationalized during the GFC in many countries, through public funding facilities, full coverage deposit insurance for the period of distress, and injection of liquidities, represent a net positive cost for society and the community. Finally, the need to comply with new standards other than those required by regulatory agencies has emerged, and, as a reply, some banks have adhered to them. Equator principles are examples of such standards. Also, the classification of some industries as unethical (e.g. weapons, casinos, pollution, tobacco, blood diamonds) impacted the lending business in many jurisdictions.

Regardless of the type of financial institutions considered in this chapter, whether they are cooperative financial services, Islamic banks, or microfinance financial institutions, those adopting CSR practices take a strategic decision that impacts their operations, financials, governance, and reputation. In fact, operations are impacted because CSR investments necessarily imply the avoidance of some sectors and niches commonly defined as unethical or non-CSR. Implementing a CSR culture in the banking sector incorporates the inclusion of CSR dispositions in its risk policies and risk management frameworks, as well as the adjustment of credit practices to account for the CSR dimension in banks' business. Moreover, financials are also impacted because the changes in business practices constitute a costly investment where banks try to obtain some benefit out of them. Corporate philanthropy and social involvement are not necessarily for-free activities, financially speaking. Using the new branding where the CSR etiquette is highlighted is a characteristic feature of the quest for return on investment in CSR. As argued in McCarthy et al. (2017), CSR may be considered as a hedge against extreme losses. Finally, CSR differently shapes the governance of the banks that effectively implement CSR practices. In fact, a large part of the trauma caused by the GFC was attributed to major failures in banks' governance, to important information asymmetries regarding banks' activities, operations, and products, hence forcing CSR banks to invest considerable resources in improving the quality and scope of the information disclosed to financial markets.

3. MODELS OF CSR FINANCIAL INSTITUTIONS

3.1 Cooperative Financial Institutions

As argued in Birchall (2013), the antecedents of cooperative banking have a history that can be traced back to 1798 with the establishment of a cooperative bank on the Solway Firth in the South West of Scotland. Historically, most cooperative businesses have been created as a natural response to social inequalities and economic tensions, since periods of economic distress and social upheaval often represent occasions of paradigm shifts and organization restructuring. For example, Jones (2006) states that the experience of poverty motivates individuals to establish local credit unions as a solution to the financial needs of the poor. The inability to access mainstream credit facilities pushed low-income economic agents to find community financial solutions and ended up by initiating local cooperatives of financial services (Jones, 2008). Another example is the so-called *Mouvement Desjardins*, or *Desjardins Group*, launched by Alphonse Desjardins in 1900 when he co-founded, along with his wife, Dorimène Roy-Desjardins, the first *Caisse d'epargne Desjardins*. The idea of launching the first North American version of credit unions came as a reaction to the social and economic distress of the economically vulnerable French Canadians, set against the wealthy and prosperous English Canadians. Today, the Desjardins Group has 335 cooperative financial institutions, called *caisses populaires*, and more than $260 billion in assets. As argued by Emelianoff (1948), the diversity of cooperative forms necessarily implies infinite ways of defining a cooperative. However, the most commonly used definition was introduced by The International Co-Operative Alliance (ICA), a globally recognized organization founded in 1895 that actually counts 224 active cooperatives-members from more than 100 countries. The ICA defines a cooperative as 'an autonomous association of persons united voluntarily to meet their common economic, social, and cultural needs and aspirations through a jointly owned and democratically controlled enterprise'.[2]

According to Banerjee et al. (1994), two main reasons explain why financial services cooperatives might be an interesting and viable alternative to conventional banks. The first stresses the importance of the community in sustaining non-opportunistic behavior among the cooperators, usually referred to as *members* (Besley and Coate, 1995). The second reason relies on the fact that a cooperative is sustained by the interactions among its members (Bontems and Fulton, 2009). Furthermore, Hansmann (1996) argues that cooperatives only emerge as a viable organizational alternative when the cost of collective decision-making is low. Moreover, Talbot et al. (2015) discuss the advantages and challenges of mutualism and assert that cooperative financial institutions correct some market failure related to information asymmetry and the financial exclusion of small and medium-sized borrowers. By providing credit to small and medium-sized firms, local cooperative financial institutions alleviate information asymmetry (Nofsinger and Wang, 2011). Access to more complete information about the borrowers reduces the risk for lender financial institutions, hence reducing potential moral hazard and adverse selection (Denis, 2004). Finally, Baas and Schrooten (2006) argue that borrowers are also less likely to endanger the survival of the community-owned cooperative bank for social and community reasons.

The ICA also enunciates the underlying values of cooperation:

- Empowerment of personal and mutual responsibility;
- Democracy;
- Equality;
- Fairness;
- Solidarity.

Moreover, the members of cooperatives adhere to an ethical behavior based on honesty, transparency, social responsibility and altruism.

Furthermore, the underlying principles of cooperation as enunciated by the ICA are:

- Voluntary and open membership;
- Democratic member control;

- Member economic participation;
- Autonomy and independence;
- Education, training and information;
- Cooperation among cooperatives;
- Concern for the community.

The ICA's values and principles are consistent with the content and substance of the definitions of CSR provided by Carroll (1979) and McWilliams and Siegel (2000), since the involvement of cooperatives of financial institutions in CSR activities is not required by law (it is fully voluntary), and is done for the betterment of society.

Having said that, besides cooperatives' engagement in CSR practices, they also face specific challenges due to the uniqueness of their governance structure (Hillier et al., 2008), their disclosure and information costs (Talbot et al., 2015), and cost efficiency issues (Servin et al., 2012), which affect their profitability (Ely, 2014; Rubin et al., 2013) and, ultimately, their competitiveness. Responses to international regulatory standards, usually set on the assumption that they are dealing with a relatively homogeneous banking system, need to be adapted by national supervisory agencies to fit within the cooperative banking model. Furthermore, finding the expertise specialized in cooperative matters (e.g. attorneys, financial analysts, developers) will remain a continuous challenge. Finally, preserving the cooperative identity is a challenge in itself. In fact, the co-existence of the cooperative model along with the conventional model puts pressure on cooperative financial institutions to cope with conventional banks' offers in order to remain competitive. This issue is more challenging for small and medium-sized cooperatives because they have limited access to capital, which stresses the importance of maintaining adequate capital reserves in all times.

3.2 Islamic Finance Institutions

Why would Islamic Finance Institutions (IFIs) be considered as CSR financial institutions? What do we know about IFIs as far as CSR is concerned? What are the challenges faced by IFIs? We attempt in this section to provide answers to these questions.

Williams and Zinkin (2010) assert that religion influences personal values, which in turn play an important role in shaping business practices. They discuss how Abrahamic faiths impact business behavior and how they relate to ethical values. The literature documents how religious people have more awareness and pay more attention to CSR than non-religious people (Weaver and Agle, 2002). According to Chapra (1992),

Islam stresses the importance of having a balance between the needs of this life and the demands of the afterlife. Consistently, Azzi and Ehrenberg (1975) had already introduced the idea of afterlife utility, where religious individuals directly gain utility from adopting religious behavior consistent with their religious beliefs. Moreover, the Islamic faith encourages commercial and economic activity (Lewis, 2001), and requires every individual to work in order to contribute to society (Rahman, 1994). As a matter of fact, Prophet Muhammad was a successful businessman. Besides, he was married to a wealthy and very successful businesswoman, Aisha. Beekun and Badawi (2005) discuss how Muslims need to obey the Quran's precepts and simultaneously fulfill their responsibility as God's stewards on earth. Equilibrium between life and afterlife is required for the harmony of society and environment, and is embedded in the ethical basis of the Islamic faith.

Beck et al. (2013) discuss the differences between Islamic financial institutions (IFI) and conventional ones. First, Islamic principles prohibit IFIs from charging interest or at least excessive interest on capital because this would be considered as *riba* (usury), hence raising a concern for the moral, social and economic well-being of society, since it creates profit without work, and without sharing the risk between the lender and the borrower (Williams and Zinkin, 2010). El-Gamal (2006) argues that the prohibition of *riba* facilitates improvements in both economic efficiency and social justice. Second, the same principles forbid speculation because it is based on a selfish interest to make money by taking advantage of risk or uncertainty at the expense of society as a whole, hence leading people with low revenues to pay more. This recalls the repercussions of the recent financial crisis, where banks took undue risks and were later bailed out by the government using taxpayers' money. Speculation is commonly referred to as *gharar* by Muslim scholars and is totally forbidden. Islamic principles call for a fair pricing of assets' value since Islam discourages price fixing, monopolies, information asymmetry, and price manipulation. Third, Sharia[3] principles do not allow IFIs to invest in illicit sectors (e.g. casinos, weapons, alcohol); financing projects in these sectors would be considered as *haraam*, i.e. forbidden, by Islamic principles. Fourth, Sharia principles prescribe the adoption of the profit and loss sharing principle when it comes to financing projects, whereas conventional financial institutions do not take part voluntarily in the projects' losses. Finally, all IFI operations should be backed by projects involving tangible assets.

Ali et al. (2013) argue that, unlike conventional banks, profit maximization is not to be the only objective of Islamic financial institutions. Moreover, Belal et al. (2015) compare the tenets of Islam with the principles of responsible business outlined in the United Nations Global

Compact,[4] and show that both converge. In other words, IFIs are, in their construction, CSR financial institutions. For example, IFIs can reduce financial exclusion, hence promoting national efforts for poverty alleviation (Rajan, 2006). As argued in Dusuki (2007), IFIs are expected to promote social welfare and to contribute to the fulfillment of the socio-economic objectives of the society, such as providing financing facilities and promoting entrepreneurship to weak segments of society such as the poor and women. Interestingly, Sidani and Al Ariss (2015) present the thinking of Al-Ghazali and show that Islam had already introduced the concept of *Ihsan*, meaning benevolence and being charitable to others, an early reference to CSR. According to Al-Ghazali, it is not enough to restrict oneself to following the law and avoiding transgression, since *Ihsan* means doing what is good for the other party, society, community, environment, economy, and individuals, beyond what is required by the rules of law.

As CSR financial institutions, Islamic banks operate on the same market as other financial institutions, the conventional (non-Islamic) financial institutions, regardless of their adoption of CSR practices. Market dynamics require the different players to perform and compete for market shares and, ultimately, for survival. Prior literature documents the specificities of Islamic financial institutions compared to their conventional peers in terms of investment financing (Aggarwal and Yousef, 2000), stability and business cycle (Čihák and Hesse, 2010; Ibrahim, 2015), efficiency (Johnes et al., 2014; Saeed and Izzeldin, 2014), asset quality (Baele et al., 2014; Farook et al., 2014; Narayan and Bannigidadmath, 2017), financing cost and pricing (Grira et al., 2016, 2017), and risk and valuation (Abedifar et al., 2013, 2016; Elnahass et al., 2014; Belkhir et al., 2017). In terms of performance, the literature shows that Islamic banks are better capitalized and have better asset quality than conventional banks (Beck et al., 2013; Rosman et al., 2014). The likelihood of insolvency for Islamic banks is consequently lower than the likelihood of insolvency for conventional banks, *ceteris paribus*. Čihák and Hesse (2010) find that small Islamic banks are more stable than small conventional banks and large Islamic banks. Baele et al. (2014) show that default rates for Islamic banks portfolios are lower than for conventional banks. Khan (2010) finds that Islamic banks enjoy higher deposit growth rates than conventional banks during normal times as well as periods of distress. On the profitability side, prior research shows that Islamic banks achieve higher returns than conventional banks (Iqbal, 2001; Hassoune, 2002), and that Islamic banks recorded superior performance during the recent financial crisis (Belanes et al., 2015; Hasan and Dridi, 2010).

The challenges faced by IFIs with regard to CSR are related to compliance, cost efficiency, and risk-taking. First, IFIs need to be compliant with Islamic principles because the CSR dimension is implicitly embedded in Sharia rules. Critics argue that products engineered by IFIs are exact replicas of those offered by conventional financial institutions. Warde (2013) refers to this issue as the prevalence of 'form-over-substance'. For IFIs to be considered and viewed as a form of CSR, they necessarily need to focus on substance, otherwise IFIs would suffer from an image issue as they are selling what may not be. Second, IFIs have a cost efficiency issue since they are less cost efficient than their conventional peers. The differential may be viewed as a premium to be paid by Muslim customers who ask for Islamic-compliant products and may be willing to pay such a premium. However, it may also be viewed as a result of the mimicking dynamic adopted by IFIs toward conventional, non-Islamic, products. This leads to an image issue that was nicely summarized by Khan (2010) who asked the question 'How Islamic is Islamic Banking?' Finally, risk-taking is a distinctive feature of IFIs: they finance projects on a profit-and-loss sharing basis. This necessarily implies a higher risk for IFIs' loan portfolios. Risk assessment processes in IFIs are, again, very similar to those of conventional banks as well as credit policies and standards. IFIs need then to come back to the Islamic principles as they relate to risk and hence allow for a more legitimate link with CSR.

3.3 Microfinance Institutions

Van Rooyen et al. (2012) define microfinance as the provision of financial services to low-income clients. Some of the main objectives of microfinance institutions are to alleviate poverty, reduce income inequalities (Beck and Demirgüç-Kunt, 2008), sustain economic growth (Stevens and Morris, 2001), and strengthen sustainable development initiatives (Busch et al., 2016). Microfinance initiatives have gained growing public attention and academic interest (Beisland et al., 2015; García-Perez et al., 2017). In fact, an emerging body of research investigates the impact of microfinance institutions on economic aggregates (Armendariz de Aghion and Morduch, 2005; Feigenberg et al., 2013), environmental outcomes (Allet and Hudon, 2015), social concerns (Mosley, 2001), and governance issues (Mersland and Strom, 2009; Hartarska and Mersland, 2012).

The modern microfinance experience started with Muhammad Yunus, who shaped today's microfinance paradigm. The experience quickly spread out all over the world: Bolivia, Chile, China, Ethiopia, Honduras, India, Malaysia, Mali, the Philippines, Sri Lanka, Tanzania, Thailand, and Vietnam (Morduch, 1999). Yunus (1995) presents how things started:

> Bangladesh had a terrible famine in 1974. I was teaching economics in a Bangladesh University at that time. You can guess how difficult it is to teach the elegant economic theories when people are dying of hunger all around you. Those theories appeared like cruel jokes. I became a drop-out from formal economics. I wanted to learn economics from the poor in the village next door to the university campus.

As a result of this initiative, Hermes (2014) and Imai et al. (2012) show that countries in which microfinance institutions have significant loan portfolios tend to have lower levels of poverty. This is consistent with Clarke et al.'s (2006) findings showing that an increase of 1 percent in financial development reduces the level of income inequality by 0.31 percent. Moreover, Lopatta and Tchikov (2016) show that the success and performance of microfinance institutions have a significant impact on economic development.

Microfinance institutions implicitly obey some principles that were formalized in 2004 by the Consultative Group to Assist the Poor, a global independent policy and research center, in collaboration with the World Bank, and then endorsed by the Group of Eight leaders at the 2004 G8 Summit. These principles, ten in number, are briefly listed as follows:

- Poor people need not just loans but also savings, insurance and money transfer services.
- Microfinance must be useful to poor households, helping them raise income, build up assets and/or cushion themselves against external shocks.
- Microfinance can pay for itself.
- Microfinance means building permanent local institutions.
- Microfinance means integrating the financial needs of poor people into a country's mainstream financial system.
- The job of government is to enable financial services, not to provide them.
- Donor funds should complement private capital, not compete with it.
- The key bottleneck is the shortage of strong institutions and managers.
- Interest rate ceilings hurt poor people by preventing microfinance institutions from covering their costs, which chokes off the supply of credit.
- Microfinance institutions should measure and disclose their performance, both financially and socially.

Similar to the financial services cooperatives and Islamic financial institutions, microfinance institutions complement the conventional banking system and co-exist with far larger structures, even though more concentrated in poor and low-revenue countries. Further, financial services cooperatives, Islamic financial institutions and microfinance institutions are not mutually exclusive, in the sense that some microfinance institutions are Islamic in nature and others are built within a cooperative framework.

Similar to small and medium-sized cooperatives and IFIs, microfinance institutions face challenges related to their access to capital markets and to the cost of financing. Without the sort of access that provides greater financial flexibility, microfinance institutions have to rely mostly on savings. However, being oriented to help low-revenue individuals, raising large amounts of savings becomes a major hurdle. Moreover, microfinance institutions operate as depository institutions and commercial banks in the sense that they accept deposits (savings) and lend money as allowed by their charter. Consequently, they have to comply with similar regulatory requirements as conventional financial institutions in regard to capital adequacy and liquidity. Regulatory costs can hardly be amortized as in larger financial institutions, due to the lack of economies of scale. Furthermore, the risk dimension is important for microfinance institutions because the quality of their portfolio relies on the ability of their customers, low revenue individuals, to pay back their loans. Microfinance institutions might mitigate that risk through the social proximity and network channel. However, the fact is that borrowers with low liquidity ratios show higher default rates on average, in the long run. Finally, the question of human capital remains an important issue, needing continuous efforts to train and retain qualified resources that specialize in microfinance institutions, a situation which significantly differs from mainstream finance in conventional financial institutions. This implies higher unitary HR costs incurred by microfinance institutions compared to their conventional peers.

4. CONCLUSION

Financial institutions usually engage in CSR activities with the expectation of receiving, directly or indirectly, future economic benefits from such an engagement. Some financial institutions embed, by construction, CSR goals in their culture, mission, and vision. This is the case for the three banking models we discussed in this chapter: financial services cooperatives, Islamic financial institutions, and microfinance institutions. Nevertheless, conventional financial institutions also engage in CSR activities: CSR being a universal concept.

The financial institutions presented in this chapter face important challenges. Their size, smaller compared to their conventional peers, their particular structure and their impact on daily operations represent major hurdles in regard to business development, the growth of their portfolios, the preservation of their market shares and, ultimately, their survival alongside traditional mainstream finance. Consequently, innovation becomes a crucial channel through which they can gain a competitive advantage, hence strengthening their market position. Investing in innovation should be done consistently with their fundamental mission, that is, consistently with CSR principles and goals. Moreover, regulatory agencies and supervisory authorities have difficulties in adapting the international standards to their specific business context. International regulation should adopt a wider and more inclusive approach throughout the standard-setting process, as described in Grira and Labidi (2016), so as to account for the specificities of these financial institutions. This would allow for the embedding of more CSR principles into the spirit of banking regulation, which may be considered as a self-regulatory mechanism per se.

Financial institutions' engagement in CSR remains a heterogeneous practice. In fact, the CSR focus differs from developed countries to emerging countries: environment, transparency, and ethics being major concerns in the former; economic and social problems being important issues in the latter. How CSR practices differ from one country to another, depending on the differences in socio-economic, cultural, and institutional contexts, is a question that would be interesting to answer in future research.

NOTES

1. Research shows that high CSR is associated with a lower cost of equity (El Ghoul et al., 2011), lower cost of debt (Goss and Roberts, 2011), easier access to credit (Cheng et al., 2014), lower risk of a stock price crash (Kim et al., 2014), and better access to political relations (Lin et al., 2014).
2. https://ica.coop/en/whats-co-op/co-operative-identity-values-principles (retrieved May 7, 2018).
3. Sharia is the legal framework that regulates the different aspects of Muslims' lives, including business and finance.
4. http://www.unglobalcompact.org (retrieved January 2, 2017).

REFERENCES

Abedifar, P., Hasan, I., and Tarazi, A., 2016. Finance-growth nexus and dual-banking systems: Relative importance of Islamic banks. Journal of Economic Behavior and Organization, 132, 198–215.

Abedifar, P., Molyneux, P., and Tarazi, A., 2013. Risk in Islamic banking. Review of Finance, 17, 2035–2096.
Aggarwal, R.K. and Yousef, T., 2000. Islamic banks and investment financing. Journal of Money, Credit and Banking, 32, 93–120.
Alchian, A.A. and Demsetz, H., 1972. Production, information costs, and economic organization. American Economic Review, 62, 777–795.
Ali, A., Al-Aali, A., and Al-Owaihan, A., 2013. Islamic perspectives on profit maximization. Journal of Business Ethics, 117, 467–475.
Allet, M. and Hudon, M., 2015. Green microfinance: Characteristics of microfinance institutions involved in environmental management. Journal of Business Ethics, 126, 395–414.
Armendariz de Aghion, B. and Morduch, J., 2005. *The Economics of Microfinance*. Cambridge, MA: MIT Press.
Attig, N., Boubakri, N., El Ghoul, S., and Guedhami, O., 2016. Firm internationalization and corporate social responsibility. Journal of Business Ethics, 134, 171–197.
Azzi, C. and Ehrenberg, R., 1975. Household allocation of time and church attendance. Journal of Political Economy, 83, 27–56.
Baas, T. and Schrooten, M., 2006. Relationship banking and SMEs: A theoretical analysis. Small Business Economics, 27, 127–137.
Baele, L., Farooq, M., and Ongena, S., 2014. Of religion and redemption: Evidence from default on Islamic loans. Journal of Banking and Finance, 44, 141–159.
Banerjee, A., Besley, T., and Guinnane, T.W., 1994. Thy neighbor's keeper: The design of a credit cooperative with theory and a test. Quarterly Journal of Economics, 109, 491–515.
Beck, T. and Demirgüç-Kunt, A., 2008. Access to finance: An unfinished agenda. World Bank Economic Review, 22, 383–396.
Beck, T., Demirgüç-Kunt, A., and Levine, R., 2010. Financial institutions and markets across countries and over time: The updated financial development and structure database. World Bank Economic Review, 24, 77–92.
Beck, T., Demirgüç-Kunt, A., and Merrouche, O., 2013. Islamic vs. conventional banking: Business model, efficiency and stability. Journal of Banking and Finance, 37, 433–447.
Beekun, R.I. and Badawi, J.A., 2005. Balancing ethical responsibility among multiple organizational stakeholders: The Islamic perspective. Journal of Business Ethics, 60, 131–145.
Beisland, L.A., Mersland, R., and Strom, O., 2015. Audit quality and corporate governance: Evidence from the microfinance industry. International Journal of Auditing, 19, 218–237.
Belal, A.R., Abdelsalam, O., and Nizamee, S., 2015. Ethical reporting in Islami Bank Bangladesh Limited (1983–2010). Journal of Business Ethics, 129, 769–784.
Belanes, A., Fitti, Z., and Regaieg, R., 2015. What can we learn about Islamic banks efficiency under the subprime crisis? Evidence from GCC region. Pacific Basin Finance Journal, 33, 81–92.
Belkhir, M., Grira, J., Hassan, M.K., and Soumaré, I., 2017. Islamic banks and political risk: International evidence. Working Paper, UAE University.
Besley, T. and Coate, S., 1995. Group lending, repayment incentives, and social collateral. Journal of Development Economics, 46, 1–18.
Birchall, J., 2013. *Resilience in a Downturn: The Power of Financial Cooperatives*. Geneva: International Labour Office.
Bontems, P. and Fulton, M., 2009. Organizational structure, redistribution and the endogeneity of cost: Cooperatives, investor-owned firms and the cost of procurement. Journal of Economic Behavior and Organization, 72, 322–343.
Busch, T., Bauer, R., and Orlitzky, M., 2016. Sustainable development and financial markets: Old paths and new avenues. Business Society, 55, 303–329.
Carroll, A.B., 1979. A three-dimensional conceptual model of corporate performance. Academy of Management Review, 4, 497–505.
Chapra, M.U., 1992. *Islam and the Economic Challenge*. Leicester: International Institute of Islamic Thought.

Cheng, B., Ioannou, I., and Serafeim, G., 2014. Corporate social responsibility and access to finance. Strategic Management Journal, 35, 1–23.
Chih, H.L., Chih, H.H., and Chen, T.Y., 2010. On the determinants of corporate social responsibility: International evidence on the financial industry. Journal of Business Ethics, 93, 115–135.
Čihák, M. and Hesse, H., 2010. Islamic banks and financial stability: An empirical analysis. Journal of Financial Services Research, 38, 95–113.
Clarke, G., Colin Xu, L., and Zou, H.F., 2006. Finance and income inequality: What do the data tell us? Southern Economic Journal, 72, 578–596.
Cornell, B. and Shapiro, A.C., 1987. Corporate stakeholder and corporate finance. Financial Management, 16, 5–14.
Cronqvist, H., Heyman, F., Nilsson, M., Svaleryd, H., and Vlachos, J., 2009. Do entrenched managers pay their workers more? Journal of Finance, 64, 309–339.
Deng, X., Kang, J., and Low, B., 2013. Corporate social responsibility and stakeholder value maximization: Evidence from mergers. Journal of Financial Economics, 110, 87–109.
Denis, D.J., 2004. Entrepreneurial finance: An overview of the issues and evidence. Journal of Corporate Finance, 10, 301–326.
Di Giuli, A. and Kostovetsky, L., 2014. Are red or blue companies more likely to go green? Politics and corporate social responsibility. Journal of Financial Economics, 111, 158–180.
Dusuki, A.W., 2007. The ideal of Islamic banking: A survey of stakeholder's perceptions. Review of Islamic Economics, 2, 29–52.
El-Gamal, M.A., 2006. *Islamic Finance: Law, Economics and Practice*. Cambridge: Cambridge University Press.
El Ghoul, S., Guedhami, O., Kwok, C.C.Y., and Mishra, D.R., 2011. Does corporate social responsibility affect the cost of capital? Journal of Banking and Finance, 35, 2388–2406.
Elnahass, M., Izzeldin, M., and Abdelsalam, O., 2014. Loan loss provisions, bank valuations and discretion: A comparative study between conventional and Islamic banks. Journal of Economic Behavior and Organization, 103, 160–173.
Ely, D., 2014. Credit unions and risk. Journal of Regulatory Economics, 46, 80–111.
Emelianoff, I., 1942. *Economic Theory of Cooperation: Economic Structure of Cooperative Organizations*. PhD thesis, Columbia University.
Emelianoff, I.V., 1948. *Economic Theory of Cooperation: Economic Structure of Cooperative Organizations*. Reprinted by the Center for Cooperatives, University of California, 1995.
Farook, S., Hassan, M.K., and Clinch, G., 2014. Islamic bank incentives and discretionary loan loss provisions. Pacific-Basin Finance Journal, 28, 152–174.
Feigenberg, B., Field, E., and Pande, R., 2013. The economic returns to social interaction: Experimental evidence from microfinance. Review of Economic Studies, 80, 1459–1483.
García-Perez, I., Munoz-Torres, M.J., and Fernandez-Izquierdo, M.A., 2017. Microfinance literature: A sustainability level perspective survey. Journal of Cleaner Production, 142, 3382–3395.
Goss, A. and Roberts, G.S., 2011. The impact of corporate social responsibility on the cost of bank loans. Journal of Banking Finance, 35, 1794–1810.
Green, C.F., 1989. Business ethics in banking. Journal of Business Ethics, 8, 631–634.
Grira, J. and Labidi, C., 2016. How international standards apply to emerging countries. In Boubaker, S., Buchanan, B., and Nguyen, D.K. (eds), *Risk Management in Emerging Markets: Issues, Framework and Modeling*. Bingley, UK: Emerald Publishing.
Grira, J., Hassan, M.K., Labidi, C., and Soumaré, I., 2017. Equity pricing in Islamic banks: International evidence. Working Paper, UAE University.
Grira, J., Hassan, M.K., and Soumaré, I., 2016. Pricing beliefs: Empirical evidence from the implied cost of deposit insurance for Islamic banks. Economic Modelling, 55, 152–168.
Hansmann, H., 1996. *The Ownership of Enterprise*. Cambridge, MA: Harvard University Press.
Hartarska, V. and Mersland, R., 2012. Which governance mechanisms promote efficiency in reaching poor clients? Evidence from rated microfinance institutions. European Financial Management, 18, 218–239.

Harvey, B., 1995. Ethical banking: The case of the cooperative bank. Journal of Business Ethics, 14, 1005–1013.
Hasan, M. and Dridi, J., 2010. The effects of the global crisis on Islamic and conventional banks: A comparative study. IMF Working Paper # WP/10/201.
Hassoune, A., 2002. Islamic banks' profitability in an interest rate cycle. International Journal of Islamic Financial Services, 4, 1–13.
Hermes, N., 2014. Does microfinance affect income inequality? Applied Economics, 46, 1021–1034.
Hill, C.W.L. and Jones, T.M., 1992. Stakeholder-agency theory. Journal of Management Studies, 29, 131–154.
Hillier, D., Hodgson, A., Stevenson-Clarke, P., and Lhaopadchan, S., 2008. Accounting window dressing and template regulation: A case study of the Australian credit union industry. Journal of Business Ethics, 83, 579–593.
Ho, S.S.M., Li, A.Y., Tam, K., and Tong, J.Y., 2016. Ethical image, corporate social responsibility, and R&D valuation. Pacific-Basin Finance Journal, 40, 335–348.
Iannotta, G., Nocera, G., and Sironi, A., 2013. The impact of government ownership on bank risk. Journal of Financial Intermediation, 22, 152–176.
Ibrahim, M.H., 2015. Issues in Islamic banking and finance: Islamic banks, Shari'ah-compliant investment and sukuk. Pacific-Basin Finance Journal, 34, 185–191.
Imai, K.S., Gaiha, R., Thapa, G., and Annim, S.K., 2012. Microfinance and poverty – A macro perspective. World Development, 40, 1675–1689.
Iqbal, M., 2001. Islamic and conventional banking in the nineties: A comparative study. Islamic Economic Studies, 8, 1–27.
Jensen, M.C. and Meckling, W.H., 1976. Theory of the firm: Managerial behavior, agency costs, and ownership structure. Journal of Financial Economics, 3, 305–360.
Jha, A. and Cox, J., 2016. Corporate social responsibility and social capital. Journal of Banking and Finance, 60, 252–270.
Johnes, J., Izzeldin, M., and Pappas, V., 2014. A comparison of performance of Islamic and conventional banks 2004–2009. Journal of Economic Behavior and Organization, 103, 93–107.
Jones, P.A., 2006. Giving credit where it's due: Promoting financial inclusion through quality credit unions. Local Economy, 21, 36–48.
Jones, P.A., 2008. From tackling poverty to achieving financial inclusion – The changing role of British credit unions in low income communities. The Journal of Socio-economics, 37, 2141–2154.
Khan, A.K., 2010. How 'Islamic' is Islamic Banking? Journal of Economic Behavior and Organization, 76, 805–820.
Kim, Y., Li, H., and Li, S., 2014. Corporate social responsibility and stock price crash risk. Journal of Banking and Finance, 43, 1–13.
King, R.G. and Levine, R., 1993. Finance and growth: Schumpeter might be right. The Quarterly Journal of Economics, 108, 717–737.
Kopel, M. and Brand, B., 2012. Socially responsible firms and endogenous choice of strategic incentives. Economic Modelling, 29, 982–989.
KPMG, 2017. The KPMG Survey of Corporate Responsibility Reporting 2017. KPMG. https://assets.kpmg.com/content/dam/kpmg/xx/pdf/2017/10/kpmg-survey-of-corporate-responsibility-reporting-2017.pdf (retrieved 6 May 2018).
Lambertini, L. and Tampieri, A., 2015. Incentives, performance and desirability of socially responsible firms in a Cournot oligopoly. Economic Modelling, 50, 40–48.
Levine, R., 2005. Finance and growth: Theory and evidence. In Aghion, P. and Durlauf, S. (eds), *Handbook of Economic Growth*, 1st edn, vol. 1, Amsterdam: North Holland, 865–934.
Lewis, M.K., 2001. Islam and accounting. Accounting Forum, 25, 103–127.
Lin, H., Zeng, S.X., Ma, H.Y., Qi, G.Y., and Tam, V.W.Y., 2014. Can political capital drive corporate green innovation? Lessons from China. Journal of Cleaner Production, 64, 63–72.

Lopatta, K. and Tchikov, M., 2016. Do microfinance institutions fulfil their promise? Evidence from cross-country data. Applied Economics, 48, 1655–1677.
Margolis, J., Elfenbein, H., and Walsh, J., 2007. Does it pay to be good? A meta-analysis and redirection of research on the relationship between corporate social and financial performance. Working paper, Harvard University, Cambridge, MA.
McCarthy, S., Oliver, B., and Song, S., 2017. Corporate social responsibility and CEO confidence. Journal of Banking and Finance, 75, 280–291.
McWilliams, A. and Siegel, D., 2000. Corporate social responsibility and financial performance: Correlation or misspecification? Strategic Management Journal, 21, 603–609.
McWilliams, A. and Siegel, D., 2001. Corporate social responsibility: A theory of the firm perspective. The Academy of Management Review, 26, 117–127.
Mersland, R. and Strom, O., 2009. Performance and governance in microfinance institutions. Journal of Banking and Finance, 33, 662–669.
Morduch, J., 1999. The microfinance promise. Journal of Economic Literature, 37, 1569–1614.
Mosley, P., 2001. Microfinance and poverty in Bolivia. Journal of Development Studies, 37, 101–132.
Narayan, P.K. and Bannigidadmath, D., 2017. Does financial news predict stock returns? New evidence from Islamic and non-Islamic stocks. Pacific-Basin Finance Journal, 42, 24–45.
Nofsinger, J.R. and Wang, W., 2011. Determinants of start-up firm external financing worldwide. Journal of Banking and Finance, 35, 2282–2294.
Nollet, J., Filis, G., and Mitrokostas, E., 2016. Corporate social responsibility and financial performance: A non-linear and disaggregated approach. Economic Modelling, 52, 400–407.
Pagano, M. and Volpin, P.F., 2005. Managers, workers, and corporate control. Journal of Finance, 60, 841–868.
Paulet, E., Parnaudeau, M., and Relano, F., 2015. Banking with ethics: Strategic moves and structural changes of the banking industry in the aftermath of the subprime mortgage crisis. Journal of Business Ethics, 131, 199–207.
Rahman, Y.A., 1994. *Interest Free Islamic Banking*. Kuala Lumpur: Al-Hilal Publishing.
Rajan, R.G., 2006. Has finance made the world riskier? European Financial Management, 12, 499–533.
Rosman, R., Abd Wahab, N., and Zainol, Z., 2014. Efficiency of Islamic banks during the financial crisis: An analysis of Middle Eastern and Asian countries. Pacific Basin Finance Journal, 28, 76–90.
Rubin, G.M., Overstreet Jr., G.A., Beling, P., and Rajaratnam, K., 2013. A dynamic theory of the credit union. Annals of Operations Research, 205, 29–53.
Saeed, M. and Izzeldin, M., 2014. Examining the relationship between default risk and efficiency in Islamic and conventional banks. Journal of Economic Behavior and Organization, 132, 127–154.
Scholtens, B., 2009. Corporate social responsibility in the international banking industry. Journal of Business Ethics, 86, 159–175.
Servaes, H. and Tamayo, A., 2013. The impact of corporate social responsibility on firm value: The role of customer awareness. Management Science, 59, 1045–1061.
Servin, R., Lensink, R., and Berg, M., 2012. Ownership and technical efficiency of microfinance institutions: Empirical evidence from Latin America. Journal of Banking and Finance, 36, 2136–2144.
Shen, C.H. and Lee, C.C., 2005. Same financial development yet different economic growth – and why? Journal of Money, Credit, and Banking, 38, 1907–1944.
Shen, C.H., Wu, M.W., Chen, T.H., and Fang, H., 2016. To engage or not to engage in corporate social responsibility: Empirical evidence from global banking sector. Economic Modelling, 55, 207–225.
Sidani, Y. and Al Ariss, A., 2015. New conceptual foundations for Islamic business ethics: The contributions of Abu-Hamid Al-Ghazali. Journal of Business Ethics, 129, 847–857.

Sievänen, R., Rita, H. and Scholten, B., 2013. The drivers of responsible investment: The case of European pension funds. Journal of Business Ethics, 117, 137–151.
Stevens, K. and Morris, J., 2001. Struggling towards sustainability: Considering grassroots development. Sustainable Development, 9, 149–164.
Surroca, J. and Tribo, J.A., 2008. Managerial entrenchment and corporate social performance. Journal of Business Finance and Accounting, 35, 748–789.
Talbot, S., Bhaird, C.M., and Whittam, G., 2015. Can credit unions bridge the gap in lending to SMEs? Venture Capital, 17, 113–128.
Van Rooyen, C., Stewart, R., and de Wet, T., 2012. The impact of microfinance in Sub-Saharan Africa: A systematic review of the evidence. World Development, 40, 2249–2262.
Warde, I., 2013. *Islamic Finance in the Global Economy*. Dubai: CFA Institute Middle East Investment Conference.
Weaver, G.R. and Agle, B.R., 2002. Religiosity and ethical behavior in organizations: A symbolic interactionist perspective. Academy of Management Review, 27, 77–97.
Williams, G. and Zinkin, J., 2010. Islam and CSR: A study of the compatibility between the tenets of Islam and the UN global compact. Journal of Business Ethics, 91, 519–533.
Wu, M.W. and Shen, C.H., 2013. Corporate social responsibility in the banking industry: Motives and financial performance. Journal of Banking and Finance, 37, 3529–3547.
Yunus, Muhammad, 1995. Testimony before the House [of Representatives of the U.S.] Committee on International Relations. Fed. News Services. June 27.

17. CSR implementation in French SMEs: an adapted framework

Karen Delchet-Cochet and Linh Chi Vo

1. INTRODUCTION

The corporate social responsibility (CSR) movement has attracted considerable attention from academics and has quickly moved up in the corporate agenda. In this context, SME (small and medium enterprise) engagement in CSR has recently emerged in mainstream academic research. So far, CSR in SMEs has attracted a considerable number of dedicated scholars (e.g. Spence, 1999; Spence & Schmidpeter, 2003; Moore & Spence, 2006; Spence & Painter-Morland, 2010; Perrini, 2006; Perrini et al., 2007; Jenkins, 2006). It has also been the topic of two special issues in the *Journal of Business Ethics*[1] and a special issue of *Business Ethics: A European Review*.[2]

However, the knowledge on CSR in SMEs is still fragmented (Lepoutre & Heene, 2006). One important gap in this literature involves the lack of CSR implementation procedures that are tailored to SMEs. Although current CSR theories and practices are insightful for large corporations, they are far from applicable for SMEs (Davies & Crane, 2010; Jenkins, 2004; Spence & Rutherfoord, 2003). SMEs have particular qualities pertaining to size, resources, management style and personal relationships (Jenkins, 2004), which makes it difficult for them to adopt large firm practices. Not much is known about what approaches might be adopted to guarantee that CSR implementation has a real impact on SMEs' management and functioning (Murillo & Lozano, 2009).

The purpose of this chapter is to contribute to filling this gap. It does so by investigating a case study to develop a framework for CSR implementation in SMEs. This case study is composed of two projects, in which we acted as practitioners to implement CSR in French SMEs. These projects are the Global Performance procedure and the SD21000 implementation guideline.

Our recommended framework particularly pertains to the context of SMEs. Compared to the extant literature, it differs to the extent that it engages in a double perspective that embraces both the content and process of CSR implementation. Furthermore, the suggested framework has a pedagogical nature that enables the SMEs to not only define their CSR strategy but also learn about CSR. It also takes into consideration the role of different stakeholders related to CSR, including government bodies, networks organizations, and so forth. Overall, the framework emphasizes the need to link CSR implementation to the core strategy of SMEs.

Our chapter is organized as follows. First, we discuss the need for specific CSR implementation tools for SMEs. We then review the discussion about CSR implementation for SMEs that has been developed in the literature, showing that it is still fragmented. We also present the work related to CSR implementation in SMEs around the globe. That section is followed by the presentation of our two projects for CSR implementation in French SMEs. We then discuss our recommended framework. In terms of implementation content, the framework puts forward the need for an auto-evaluation, a diagnosis linked to core businesses, the pedagogical nature of CSR implementation tools, and the avoidance of using performance indicators. In terms of the implementation process, the framework emphasizes dialogues and networks, the participation of stakeholders, and support from government bodies and sponsoring organizations. The chapter ends with a conclusion.

2. THE NEED FOR CSR IMPLEMENTATION TOOLS SPECIFIC TO SMEs

There is a need for specific implementation tools for CSR in SMEs. This need can be justified by three reasons: (1) SMEs play a crucial role in the economy; (2) their CSR practices remain informal due to lack of support for CSR implementation; and (3) the implementation of CSR within SMEs cannot rely on formal tools that have been developed for large corporations because they differ from each other in many aspects. We will now discuss these points in more detail.

First, SMEs are by far the most common form of private business in both developed and developing economies (Spence, 2007). They are often dynamic and longstanding players in local communities (Castka et al., 2004). They make up a sizable portion of the European economy. Of the Europe-19 firms, 99.8 percent are SMEs and they employ nearly 70 percent of the total employed workforce (Davies and Crane, 2010). Practitioners are recognizing the strong influence SMEs have on their surrounding communities (Perrini, 2006).

Second, despite their important role in the economy, the actual implementation of CSR in SMEs in practice can be described as an ad hoc issue (Jenkins, 2006). SMEs often do not have a person appointed to manage CSR (Sweeney, 2007). The responsibility for CSR tends to rest with the owner/manager or a senior manager of the firm. Research shows that SMEs are deterred from implementing CSR activities because of the lack of appropriate support services on CSR for SMEs, their fear of doing things wrong, and the lack of appropriate information (Roberts et al., 2006). Thus, there is a clear demand in the SME sector for assistance in improving understanding of the CSR issue and its relevance for SMEs, especially advice that focuses on determining CSR priorities, developing action plans, and assessing resource requirements (Roberts et al., 2006).

Third, SMEs cannot rely on the current CSR agenda, in which most research focuses on large organizations and their characteristics (Castka et al., 2004; Jenkins, 2006; Perrini, 2006; Spence et al., 2003; Spence, 2007). The conventional argument is that SMEs are 'little big companies' (Tilley, 2000), and CSR theory can simply be scaled down to 'fit' (Jenkins, 2004; Morsing & Perrini, 2009). However, in SMEs, control remains in the hands of the owners (Spence, 1999), whose acceptance of CSR depends largely on their personal attitudes (Perez-Sanchez, 2003). In comparison to large firms, SMEs confront a unique set of issues, such as the stress of just surviving, a more local market, and less stakeholder pressure. Smaller businesses do not have the resources or prioritization to engage in CSR. The CSR motives and initiatives of SMEs often take different forms to those of larger firms (Jenkins, 2004; Kusyk & Lozano, 2007; Lepoutre & Heene, 2006; Spence, 2007; Vives, 2006). Thus, the implementation of standardized CSR concepts in SMEs needs to adapt to their specific context and organizational conditions (Avram & Kuhne, 2008).

CSR has become a paradigm that is not easy to translate into the day-to-day management of SMEs (Castka et al., 2004; Murillo & Lozano, 2009). The call for the development of CSR tools for SMEs is common in the literature. The CSR agenda needs to move towards particularization, answering the particular needs and challenges that face SMEs (Murillo & Lozano, 2009). There is an obvious need to have CSR implementation tools tailored to their specificities (Jenkins, 2004; Moore & Spence, 2006; Spence, 1999; Spence & Lozano, 2000). 'More is needed than a simple extension of the existing concepts' (Spence et al., 2003). Moore and Spence (2006) argued that one of the biggest gaps in CSR research is the development of tools for responsible business practice in SMEs. A vast array of reports on CSR, including European Commission (2001) and *CSR Magazine* (2002), conclude with a clear direction for further research in CSR: provide SMEs with guidance and tools that enable them to implement and report on their corporate social responsibility policies, processes, and performance in an effective manner (Castka et al., 2004).

3. THE EXISTING CSR IMPLEMENTATION DISCUSSION

The current discussion on CSR implementation in SMEs can be described as sparse and in need of further development. Empirical work often continues to draw from 'large-firm' perspectives to identify good examples of CSR implementation in SMEs, implying an underlying lack of understanding of the SME context (Spence, 2007).

A common approach for CSR implementation in SMEs is to rely on stakeholder theory, which has been largely mobilized in the literature about CSR in big corporations (Jenkins, 2006). In this theory (Freeman, 1984), progress in terms of CSR must inevitably bring with it a parallel stakeholder approach (European Commission, 2001, 2002). This perspective argues that enhancing responsiveness to stakeholders' legal, ethical, social, and environmental expectations can help the company achieve its business objectives and improve its social responsibility (Perrini, 2006). It has been agreed upon by different stakeholder theorists that CSR is a means to increase SME competitiveness (Battaglia and Frey, 2014).

Several authors have used this theory to propose implementation tools for CSR in SMEs. For example, Castka et al. (2004), based on the investigation of a SME in the UK, developed a model for CSR implementation that relies on stakeholder theory and aims at choosing the right balance between ethical and entrepreneurial practices. Jenkins (2006) also proposed stakeholder theory as a framework to implement CSR in SMEs, as SMEs prefer to learn through networking and from their peers. The process is composed of four key steps: developing an understanding of CSR and translating this into business principles, targeting CSR activities appropriately, overcoming challenges, and business benefits. Maignan et al. (2005) provided a comprehensive managerial framework to understand and provide a well-balanced and integrated stakeholder orientation for implementing corporate social responsibility in marketing. Madueño et al. (2016) argued that CSR practices and quality management should be implemented in accordance with each other, since they both respond to stakeholders' needs. However, the applicability of stakeholder theory to SMEs remains questionable, as the nature of stakeholder relationships for SMEs may not be drastically different, but it is the case for the management of such relationships (Jenkins, 2004). Perrini (2006) argued that stakeholder theory is more appropriate for large corporations.

Related to the stakeholder perspective is the community-based approach. In this approach, businesses are not separate from their civil society but an integral part of it (Lawrence et al., 2006). Fisher et al. (2009) explored a case study of one Canadian SME that uses a community development framework called Asset Based Community Development (ABCD) for its CSR programming. The ABCD framework is characterized by a three-step process, which involves asset mapping, visioning, and mobilizing. The framework emphasizes stakeholder participation in the process and refrains from utilizing external resources until local resources have been exhausted. It is argued that the ABCD framework is an effective means to encourage the development of social capital and help strengthen a company's CSR strategy and program.

Another conceptual foundation that has been employed to develop CSR implementation tools in SMEs is strategic management theory. For example, Avram and Kuhne (2008) developed a framework based on this theory, suggesting taking into consideration the strategic position within the industry of the SME, its intended strategic focus, and its consumer needs. Lamberti and Noci (2012), based on their empirical study of the relationship between CSR and the strategy of Italian medium-sized companies, argued that a comprehensive theory of SMEs' approach to CSR and of the role of CSR in SMEs' strategy is needed. Perrini and Minoja (2008), acknowledging the growing emphasis on the integration of CSR into corporate strategy, explored the antecedents of this process and the dynamics underlying it in a medium-sized company. Their findings showed that CSR strategies must be explicit and codified into specific managerial procedures if CSR practices are to be widely adopted in SMEs.

However, Graafland, van de Ven, and Stofelle (2003) found that SMEs and large businesses differ in many aspects of their use and integration of strategies into ethical activities. In order to engage SMEs, it may be better to build on what they are already doing (Vives, 2006). Jenkins (2009) suggested that integrating CSR into the core of a company is crucial to its success. The author's paper proposed a way for CSR to be built into a company's systems and become 'just the way we do things' through a 'business opportunity' model of CSR for SMEs. Such research confirms the need for implementation tools that are developed specifically for SMEs.

The network approach is also used by Murillo and Lozano (2009) in the promotion and implementation of CSR in SMEs. It involves the establishment of a working network, in which the issues of inclusion, representativity, and legitimacy are the key elements for its success. The role of intermediate organization, network management and leadership is crucial in running the network. Enderle (2004) demonstrated that carefully designed and persistently developed networks are an effective means to strengthen SMEs, not only in their economic performance but also in their social and environmental performance. The author offered seven recommendations for SMEs to successfully face global competition and fulfill their economic, social, and environmental responsibilities, one of which is to unite with like-minded partners by forming a variety of networks.

In short, Jeppesen (2005) correctly stressed the importance of understanding the specific context and distinguishing between the actual and potential role of different kinds of enterprises. Only on such a basis is it possible to identify the resources and policies most appropriate for promoting CSR implementation in SMEs. Tools for CSR implementation that are tailored to the characteristics of SMEs need further development.

4. CSR IMPLEMENTATION IN SMEs AROUND THE WORLD

There has been a wide range of studies about CSR practices adopted by SMEs around the world. The book edited by Spence and Painter-Morland (2010) is an example. However, these studies do not focus on developing CSR implementation tools that are appropriate to the nature of SMEs. Many of them are simply descriptive. For example, Bevan and Yung (2015) examined the levels of CSR implementation among Australian construction SMEs and the role of awareness level and concerns for the economic aspect in such implementation. They found that Australian construction SMEs incorporated some aspects of CSR into their business activities even though they did not refer to these practices as CSR, and none of them had a formal CSR policy in place. Mehta and Sharma (2016) also obtained similar findings among SMEs in India. With regard to SMEs in Sweden, Lee et al. (2016) indicated that they adopted a profit-seeking rather than a profit-sacrificing CSR approach. Furthermore, the perception, the motivation, and part of the CSR activities were well incorporated into the decision of these SMEs to engage in CSR.

Some other studies focus on the results and antecedents of CSR implementation in SMEs. For example, Martínez-Martínez et al. (2017) did not investigate the actual implementation process among Spanish SMEs. They rather considered the strategic impact of CSR practices and found that companies adopting CSR had better competitive performance, relational marketing, and innovative capacity. On the other hand, El Baz et al. (2016) examined the influencing role of national institutions on the implementation of CSR among French and Moroccan SMEs in the food processing industry. Their study showed that there was a distinct difference between the CSR practices adopted by SMEs in France and Morocco due to the difference between the rule-based governance system in the former and the relationship-based governance system in the latter. Iatridis et al. (2016) studied the motivating factors at a more micro level by investigating how the motives and commitment of Greek SMEs influenced their subscription to certified CSR-related standards. Similarly, Johnson (2015) considered how the CSR awareness of managers had an impact on CSR implementation among German SMEs. Papasolomou-Doukakis et al. (2005) found that the CSR approach of Cypriot businesses depends on the importance of managerial initiative, and that financial gain is a key motive for the adoption of CSR by the business sector in Cyprus in terms of tax deduction.

Most of the studies focus on different issues related to CSR in SMEs, providing recommendations for CSR implementation within SMEs as part of their discussion or conclusion. The most commonly heard recommendations include: active support from governmental bodies (Perrini, 2006; Roberts et al., 2006; Southwell, 2004; Tilley, 2000; Vives, 2006), simple tools and language used for CSR practices in SMEs (Graafland et al., 2003; Murillo & Lozano, 2006; Roberts et al., 2006; Southwell, 2004; Vives, 2006). Similar recommendations are education for SME entrepreneurs (Yu & Bell, 2007), consideration of the nature of SMEs, such as diversity (Battisti & Perry, 2011; Graafland et al., 2003; Spence & Rutherfoord, 2001), and the involvement of employees (Davies & Crane, 2010).

Our literature review found only one study that truly focuses on the CSR implementation process – Nguyen et al. (2015). The authors applied a system thinking approach and suggested intervention at three levels: personal development, organizational development, and institutional development. This conceptual model helps to enhance Vietnamese SMEs' adaptive capacity in response to environmental requirements in Vietnam.

5. OUR PROJECTS

The first project is the Global Performance procedure. The Center of Young Entrepreneurs, a French association of employers, developed it in 2002. Their member enterprises are almost all SMEs: 85 percent are enterprises of fewer than 100 employees and 96 percent have fewer than 300. The Global Performance procedure was developed to help SME members implement CSR by addressing, at the same time, economic, social, and environmental issues. In 2011, we were in charge of revising the procedure to ensure coherence with ISO26000, published in 2011. Another objective

Table 17.1 Steps to revise the Global Performance procedure in 2011

Step	Data collection	Objectives	Outcomes
Step 1	2 interviews with 5 members of Global Performance's steering committee (3 SME owners and 2 employees of the Center of Young Entrepreneurs)	To understand the Global Performance procedure and the SME members' specificities	First proposition of revision
	1 meeting with all members of Global Performance's steering committee (10 people)	Discuss the first proposition of revision	Second proposition of revision
Step 2	2 meetings with 5 members of Global Performance's steering committee (3 SME owners and 2 employees of Center of Young Entrepreneurs)	Discuss the second proposition of revision	Final report

Notes: The Global Performance procedure was developed by the Center of Young Entrepreneurs, a French association of employers, in 2002. It aimed at helping SME members implement CSR by simultaneously addressing economic, social, and environmental issues. In 2011, the authors were in charge of making revisions and improvements to the procedure.

was also to improve it further. Table 17.1 represents the actions that we undertook to accomplish our goals.

The second project is the SD21000 implementation guideline. SD21000 is a French norm published in 2003 for the integration of CSR into the management and strategy of firms. To facilitate its implementation in SMEs, the French association for standardization (AFNOR) launched a project to develop a version of the SD21000 implementation guideline adapted to SMEs. We acted as the managers of this project over three years. Table 17.2 summarizes the actions we undertook during this time.

These two projects constitute our case study (Yin, 2003). This method has been used elsewhere (e.g. Murillo & Lozano, 2009). Moreover, the use of a case study is appropriate for our research for several reasons. First, it is particularly recommended in situations where a phenomenon is still insufficiently understood, since it allows a thick description that leads to an understanding of what is important about that case within its own world (Preuss & Perschke, 2010). Second, the use of cases has been justified by Ghauri (2004) for studies where the goal of the research is to

Table 17.2 Steps to develop the SD21000 implementation guideline for SMEs – a 3-year project

Step	Data collection	Objectives	Outcomes
Step 1	1 interview with 3 SME owners	Discuss the first version of the SD21000 implementation guideline for SMEs	Finalize the first version and conduct experimental implementation in 83 SMEs
Step 2	3 interviews with 3 SMEs owners participating in the experimental implementation 3 interviews with 3 consultants participating in the experimental implementation	Revise the first version	Final version that is implemented in 150 SMEs

Notes: SD21000 is a French norm published in 2003 for the integration of CSR into the management and strategy of firms. To facilitate its implementation in SMEs, the French association for standardization (AFNOR) launched a project to develop a version of the SD21000 implementation guideline adapted to SMEs. The authors were in charge of this project.

extend existing theory. The framework for CSR implementation in SMEs was developed based on insights from these two projects. As the aim of this article is to contribute to theory building rather than to produce generalizable findings, the use of two projects seems appropriate. In this way, we followed an 'exemplar' approach, in which the exemplar may be variously described as something or someone to be copied, or is perceived as ideal or in some way commendable (Jenkins, 2006).

6. FINDINGS

In this section, we present how CSR should be implemented in SMEs, as identified in our two projects.

6.1 Global Performance Procedure

The Global Performance procedure helps to implement CSR in SMEs through two phases: START and JUMP. They are carried out over a period of two years, with one year allowed for each phase.

During the START phase, the participating SMEs gather once a month. As there are more than 300 SME members participating in this project, the meetings are organized on a regional basis to take advantage of proximity and the similar environmental and social conditions of SMEs from the same area. Each SME takes it in turn to host the meetings. The sequential activities of this phase are presented below:

- In the very first meeting, the SME entrepreneurs present their firms and their vision of CSR. They also have to identify the principal actors of stakeholder groups that the Global Performance procedure has listed (including employees, shareholders, clients, suppliers and the community).
- A general questionnaire is then sent to these stakeholders to obtain a general understanding of their expectations in terms of the CSR activities of the SMEs.
- The seven following meetings are used to conduct the Global Performance diagnosis. This diagnosis is composed of 100 questions having three answer choices and covering ten themes: five related to the strategic issues (values, vision and strategy, pilot strategic programs, innovation, and environment) and five others related to the stakeholder issues (employees, shareholders, clients, suppliers, and the community). In each meeting, the SME entrepreneurs discuss one or two themes with an animator, who is an expert in CSR, and their SME peers. Moreover, the SME entrepreneurs have to compare their answers with the expectations of stakeholders expressed in the completed questionnaire. At the end of each meeting, the SME entrepreneurs have to conclude the main CSR and strategic issues to be addressed based on their discussion.
- In the final meeting of the START phase the SMEs summarize all the strategic CSR issues defined during the year and finalize the CSR vision they presented in the first meeting.

The purpose of the START phase is to provide the SMEs with an opportunity to conduct a well-rounded analysis of their CSR practices and then develop a more formalized CSR strategy. This phase also allows for the sharing of experience between the SMEs about their CSR practices and how those practices are related to the strategy and the operation of their companies. It is important to note that the SME entrepreneurs do not have to be experts in CSR to understand and be able to answer the questions. All the ten themes are explicit and the three choices of each answer are well explained.

The purpose of the JUMP phase is to define a CSR strategy and action plan based on the results of the START phase. The meetings are organized in the same way as in the START phase. The sequential activities of this phase are presented below:

- In the very first meeting, the SME entrepreneurs rank the CSR and strategic issues finalized at the end of START phase in order of importance. They then retain the five top priorities.
- Based on these top priorities, the SMEs set up their own strategic committees, which are composed of major stakeholders, including members of an executive committee, employees, and service providers. They work with these committees to develop the action plan for implementation.
- In each of the seven following meetings of the JUMP phase, they present their progress in developing their plan.
- In the final meeting, they present their CSR reports, which have been approved by their strategic committee.

The Global Performance procedure for CSR implementation in SMEs is represented in Figure 17.1.

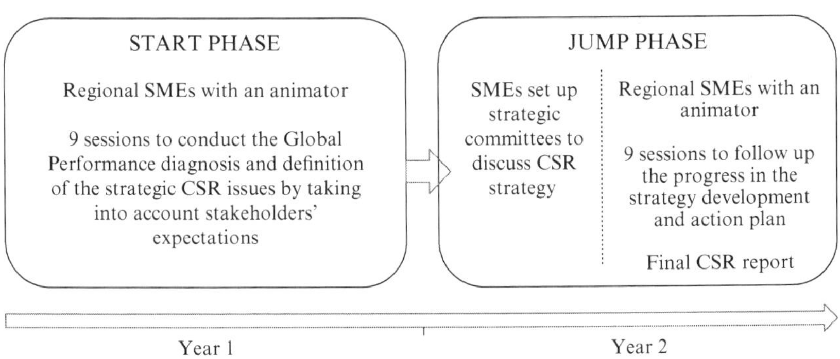

Figure 17.1 Global Performance procedure to implement CSR in the SMEs' strategy according to the Centre des Jeunes Dirigeants d'Entreprise

6.2 SD21000 Implementation Guideline

This guideline helps to implement CSR in SMEs by relying on two components: individual and collective. The individual component consists of 6.5 days of activity, which are spread over two years. CSR consultants animate the activities. The sequential activities of this component are presented below:

- The first 2.5 days are devoted to conducting CSR diagnosis and strategic analysis as required by AFNOR. The SMEs work with the consultants in this activity. The CSR diagnosis has the following characteristics:
  - There are 34 themes related to different CSR issues. They are analyzed in terms of performance and importance levels on a scale from 1 to 5.
  - The SMEs then revise their analysis of the 34 themes by discussing them with their stakeholders and taking into account their opinions. There are around 50 stakeholders for each SME.
  - The SMEs finalize their analysis and the themes are listed based on their priority. This process of prioritization is carried out without participation of the stakeholders.
- Based on this final list of themes, an action plan is developed over the four remaining days. The plan has a classic format, with the following content:
  - List of actions
  - The themes addressed by each of the actions
  - The stakeholders.

The collective component enables the SMEs to network with each other. It starts when the SMEs begin developing their action plan. The SMEs are required to form communities among themselves on a regional basis, which are called enterprise circles ('cercle des enterprises' in French). Each regional enterprise community has about ten participants. The communities organize meetings of three hours over two years, in which they exchange their experience and ideas with CSR experts. The collective component has two objectives. The first is to allow the SMEs to share with each other lessons learned and successes achieved, as well as building networks. The second is to provide the SMEs with expert information and competences that they do not have due to their limited time, resources, and access to CSR specialists. The SD21000 implementation guideline is represented in Figure 17.2.

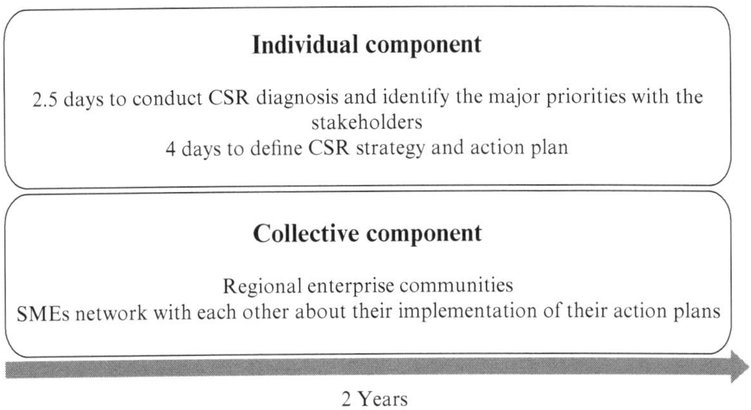

Figure 17.2 *SD2100 implementation guideline to implement CSR in SMEs' strategy according to AFNOR*

7. DISCUSSION: RECOMMENDATIONS FOR CSR IMPLEMENTATION IN SMEs

In this section, we will discuss the recommendations for CSR implementation in SMEs based on an analysis of the Global Performance procedure and the SD2100 implementation guideline. Both tools are composed of two main components: content and process. The discussion below will present how these components are adapted to the specificities of SMEs and discuss them in relation to the extant literature. From this discussion, our recommendations will be then summarized in a table.

7.1 Implementation Content

As presented above, Global Performance procedure starts with an analysis of the context (START phase). This analysis takes into account the stakeholders' expectations, the company's strategic issues, and its perspective on CSR. The SMEs are then required to finalize their CSR visions and identify the priorities for strategic and CSR issues. An action plan is then developed accordingly (JUMP phase). Similarly, the SD21000 implementation guideline also starts with a diagnosis of the context. This is followed by a prioritization of major strategic and CSR issues and an action plan. It can be seen that both procedures are composed of three main components: analysis of the context, identification of major CSR and strategic issues to be addressed, and an action plan. These components are not particularly adapted to the SMEs: all implementations would necessitate a thorough understanding of the context before taking concrete actions. The themes addressed in the two procedures, although slightly different, are also commonly seen in big corporations' sustainable development reports.

However, the content is adapted to SMEs to the extent that the diagnosis is an auto-evaluation process linked to their core businesses. It has a pedagogical nature and does not rely on formal indicators of CSR. We will discuss these points below.

7.1.1 Nature of the diagnosis: auto-evaluation

In both implementation tools, SME entrepreneurs themselves conduct the diagnosis of the context. We believe that an auto-evaluation is of crucial importance. First, managerial choices reflect the attributes and personal characteristics of the managers of SMEs (Hammann et al., 2009). They are a crucial factor in influencing the success of CSR implementation. Second, an auto-evaluation is critical since it allows the SME entrepreneurs to be aware of their CSR practices. Indeed, Murillo and Lozano (2006) argued that any attempt to establish tools for implanting CSR in SMEs needs to incorporate the SMEs' organizational characteristics.

7.1.2 Nature of the diagnosis: linked to core businesses

The auto-evaluation takes into account not only CSR issues but also the strategic issues of the SMEs. The ten themes covered by the Global Performance procedure and the 34 themes of the SD21000 implementation guidelines enable the SMEs' entrepreneurs to conduct a CSR analysis that takes into consideration their core businesses. CSR practices among SMEs seem to start in those activities that are more associated with the core business of the company (Murillo & Lozano, 2006). Profit maximization is their primary goal, and investment in CSR is only considered when the investment positively affects the financial performance (Battisti & Perry, 2011).

Scholars have supported the argument for the link between CSR framework and core businesses of SMEs. For instance, Morsing and Perrini (2009) stated that a CSR practice must not be considered as an ad hoc expense; rather it should be integrated into the company's core business activities in such a way that it positively affects the company's performance and its competitiveness. Jenkins (2009) pointed out that it is crucial to develop a business strategy that aligns the company's business goals with a strong commitment to CSR values and principles. Grayson and Hodges (2004) suggested seven steps for integrating CSR into business strategy – identifying the triggers, scoping what matters, making the business case, committing to action, integrating and gathering resources, engaging stakeholders, and measuring and reporting. The importance of linking CSR issues with core business strategies, although not a new concept, should not be taken lightly. It has been commonly observed that SMEs fail to incorporate the two aspects together and fail to gain the maximum competitive advantage from CSR (Jenkins, 2009).

7.1.3 Nature of the diagnosis: pedagogical

The questions used for the contextual diagnosis in both implementation procedures are pedagogical in nature. As presented, in the Global Performance procedure, each question has three answer choices, reflecting different levels of commitment to CSR by the firm; while in the SD21000 guideline, the SMEs analyze each theme using a performance scale and an importance scale with five levels. Such detailed and specific questions are useful for the SMEs in two ways. On the one hand, the SME entrepreneurs do not have to be experts in CSR to be able to conduct the diagnosis. On the other hand, doing the diagnosis is inherently a learning process. By doing the diagnosis, the SME entrepreneurs learn not only about the actual CSR situation in their organizations but also about CSR itself. The diagnosis is like a pedagogical tool for the SMEs. This is very important, since SME entrepreneurs tend to lack an appropriate understanding of CSR (Petts et al., 1999). Many of them have never thought about CSR, or believe that its social and environmental impacts are negligible (Lepoutre & Heene, 2006).

7.1.4 Nature of the diagnosis: practices without indicators

The diagnoses of both procedures do not contain any quantitative, formal, and well-accepted indicators of CSR activities. This absence of indicators may be surprising, given the fact that CSR indicators have been well developed by large corporations. This is an adaptation to CSR in SMEs because most of the time, SMEs have only limited (financial) resources and few formal processes (Hammann et al., 2009). They are less likely to report CSR activities (Graafland et al., 2003; Perrini et al., 2007). They reflect to a great extent the personality, values, character, attitudes, education or background of the entrepreneur or the owner-manager (Vives, 2006). The absence of indicators allows the participating SMEs to focus on the issue of CSR implementation rather than on developing indicators specific to CSR in their company.

7.2 Implementation Process

As the content components are carried out sequentially, the process contains three corresponding steps in the same order: analysis of the context, identification of major CSR and strategic issues to address, and an action plan. These steps are not unknown for any implementation process. However, the way these steps are carried out is adapted to SMEs. It emphasizes dialogue and networking between the SMEs, as well as between the SMEs and CSR experts; it allows the participation of stakeholders in CSR implementation, especially local authorities; and it calls for support from government bodies and sponsoring organizations. This section will present these points in detail.

7.2.1 Dialogue and networking

Both procedures provide SMEs with an opportunity to network and have discussions with their peers and an animator about their strategic issues, their CSR vision, and how they plan to put the CSR norms into action. This is crucial for CSR implementation in SMEs. In the Global Performance procedure, the SMEs meet and discuss the issues in the monthly meetings during START and JUMP phases. In the SD21000 implementation guideline, the SMEs develop networks with their peers through the regional enterprise communities. The participation of animators, who are CSR experts, aims to provide CSR knowledge. They also ensure the discussion takes place between SMEs and urge them to truly engage in the diagnosis.

The development of networks between SMEs and CSR experts is important because CSR is a new and complex subject. SMEs do not have a sound understanding of CSR, but they cannot afford to hire experts/consultants for help. The lack of knowledge about CSR issues among SME entrepreneurs has been described extensively (Lepoutre & Heene, 2006). For example, a study by Sweeney (2007) showed that SMEs tend to describe CSR vaguely as conducting business in a responsible manner. According to Jenkins (2006), the term CSR means something, but not always the same thing, to everybody. Tilley (2000) pointed out clearly that SMEs must rely on external experts to guide their decision-making processes and to provide them with appropriate solutions to environmental problems.

Moreover, a special characteristic of SMEs is the fact that their engagement in CSR practice depends largely on their owners, who lack time and have to take care of a wide variety of organizational activities. Therefore, their limited knowledge of CSR is not only a contextual consequence, but also a result of the cognitive limitations of the owners (Lepoutre & Heene, 2006). This problem can be solved when businesses are engaged in certain networks (Meredith, 2000), especially networks with their peers. Indeed, there is a tremendous desire to learn from others amongst SME businesses, which are aware that the most effective learning comes from sharing experience among themselves (Roberts et al., 2006). Jenkins (2009) stated that external networks are crucial to have access to all the skills and information needed to adopt CSR practices. Networks have been cited as the key media through which SMEs can learn on a wide variety of topics (Lepoutre & Heene, 2006).

7.2.2 Participation of stakeholders

Both implementation procedures take into consideration stakeholders' interests and expectations. This is understandable, as stakeholder theory has been well acknowledged as an important theoretical foundation for CSR implementation. Where SMEs are concerned, the need to follow a multi-stakeholder approach is solid advice (Murillo & Lozano, 2009).

What is adapted to SMEs in the two procedures is the participation of stakeholders in the auto-evaluation process, albeit in different ways and at different levels. SMEs collaborate with their stakeholders in the JUMP phase of the Global Performance procedure. In the SD21000 implementation guideline, SMEs discuss with their stakeholders when they conduct the diagnosis of the CSR issues. The relationship with stakeholders is managed differently in SMEs. Large companies are likely to engage in carefully planned and formal strategic stakeholder management. But stakeholder relationships for an SME may be based on a more informal, trusting basis and characterized by personal engagement (Jenkins, 2004). It has been argued that stakeholder pressure is the most frequent encouragement for many SMEs to improve their social initiatives (Morsing & Perrini, 2009). Thus, their participation in the diagnosis is not only feasible but also desirable.

Similarly, the local authorities, a special type of stakeholder, also participate in both procedures. On a regional basis, SMEs, consultants, and local stakeholders from the same regions are gathered. Again, we see a feature adapted to the specificities of SMEs. SMEs have close and direct relationships with the local authorities (Longo et al., 2005). Local authorities usually receive more attention from SMEs than from large corporations (Jenkins, 2004; Murillo & Lozano, 2006; Spence, 2007; Vives, 2006). Thus, involving local government bodies in the CSR implementation process enables the SMEs to better understand local authorities' expectations and manage their relationships with them more effectively.

7.2.3 Support from the government bodies and sponsoring organizations

In both procedures, we see the participation of government bodies and sponsoring organizations. Their role is crucial in assisting the SMEs' implementation of CSR practices. This is in line with the results found by Worthington et al. (2006), who stated that SMEs in their study expressed the need for support from the government in their CSR endeavors.

Governments provided funding and facilitated networking between SMEs and their stakeholders. There are several ways in which they contribute to a successful CSR implementation.

First, they provide financial support. The SD21000 implementation was financed by public funds made available by a national program for sustainable development. The Global Performance procedure did not receive any public funding, but the participating SMEs just had to pay the logistical costs, such as meeting rooms and meals during meeting days. This was very helpful because SMEs have limited financial resources (Kusyk & Lozano, 2007; Lepoutre & Heene, 2006; Sweeney, 2007). SME entrepreneurs often cite the lack of financial resources as one of the most important barriers for engaging in CSR (Hillary, 2000; Ludevid, 2000; Sweeney, 2007). The costs for investing in CSR may be too large for them to carry (Tilley, 1999).

Second, it is only with assistance from government bodies and sponsoring organizations that SMEs can be brought together in a common project and form a network. One common problem of SME owners is their solitary position in managing their firms. Their role in this regard is also very important. While SMEs may be keen to learn about CSR from peers and to network with them, they do not often seek CSR-related support (Jenkins, 2009).

Finally, SMEs need guidance in CSR implementation due to their organizational characteristics, which present barriers to CSR practice (Lepoutre & Heene, 2006; Sweeney, 2007; Vives, 2006). Jenkins (2004) described SMEs as being untidy, informal, trusting, overlapping, intuitive, 'tactically strategic', personally monitoring, ambiguous, holistic, owner managed, and customer/network exposed. Moreover, SMEs tend to focus on the short term, which means long-term investment projects in CSR are not of immediate concern (Spence, 1999). When they implement CSR practice under the umbrella of sponsor organization, there is a pressure not to put CSR issues aside to take care of more short-term problems. Thus, we can be sure that CSR is well adopted and implemented.

7.3 Framework for Implementation

From our discussion, the following framework for CSR implementation in SMEs can be proposed. In implementing CSR activities in SME, there are two aspects to be considered: implementation content and implementation process. In terms of implementation content, this should enable SMEs to conduct an auto-evaluation of their organization and CSR orientation. The diagnosis should be pedagogical in nature, meaning it is at the same time an implementation guideline and a source of learning about CSR. Also, for SMEs, including indicators in implementation is not recommended. In terms of implementation process, we suggest that SMEs should not carry out the implementation on their own. They should form networks with other SMEs, with whom they can share their experience and also learn with each other. Assistance from CSR experts, who can provide guidance along the way, is needed. Stakeholders should be involved in the process, since their role and expectations in terms of CSR activities are very important. The implementation of CSR activities must receive support from governmental bodies. Only with the sponsorship of local authorities can they finance their CSR implementation, form their networks, and feel the pressure to keep track of their CSR implementation. The framework is summarized in Table 17.3.

8. CONCLUSION

CSR in SMEs is an important area of study, as SMEs are different from large corporations and they need CSR implementation tools tailored to their particular characteristics. However, the literature on CSR in SMEs is still underdeveloped. While articles have been calling for research on CSR in SMEs since the 1990s, the work to date has been limited and a considerable amount of research needed (Sweeney, 2007).

There is a major need for CSR implementation tools that are adapted to SMEs. The current CSR implementation discussions that have been put forth are in need of further development. They mostly rely on stakeholder theory, strategic management theory, and the network approach, which have been largely employed for CSR implementation in large corporations. Thus, their application in SME conditions is questionable.

In this context, we contribute to the literature by proposing a set of recommendations for effective CSR implementation in SMEs. Our recommendations are drawn from our analysis of two successful implementation procedures in France. The output of this research also has important managerial implications. Following our recommended implementation

Table 17.3 Framework for CSR implementation in SMEs

Implementation content	Implementation process
Auto-evaluation	Dialogue and network
Diagnosis linked to core businesses	Participation of stakeholders
Pedagogical nature	Support from government bodies and sponsoring organizations
No indicators	

content and process, SMEs can develop CSR implementation programs that are adapted to their particular context and characteristics.

A limitation of our study is the lack of information on how SMEs actually implemented CSR activities after having defined their action plan. The two procedures were considered successful based on the large number of SMEs adopting and following them. This represents a direction for future research, in which a follow-up of SMEs' CSR activities after their action plans is conducted.

NOTES

1. Vol. 47, No. 1, 2003; Vol. 67, No. 3, 2006.
2. Vol. 18, No. 1, 2009.

REFERENCES

Avram, D. and Kuhne, S. (2008), 'Implementing responsible business behavior from a strategic management perspective: developing a framework for Austrian SMEs'. *Journal of Business Ethics*, **82**, 463–475.

Battaglia, M. and Frey, M. (2014), 'Public policies of promotion of CSR amongst SMEs and effects on competitiveness: the case of Tuscany region'. *International Journal of Business Governance and Ethics*, **9**(1), 1–26.

Battisti, M. and Perry, M. (2011), 'Walking the talk? Environmental responsibility from the perspective of small-business owners'. *Corporate Social Responsibility and Environmental Management*, **18**, 172–185.

Bevan, E. and Yung, P. (2015), 'Implementation of corporate social responsibility in Australian construction SMEs'. *Engineering, Construction and Architectural Management*, **22**(3), 295–311.

Castka, P., Balzarova, A. and Bamber, C. (2004), 'How can SMEs effectively implement the CSR agenda? A UK case study perspective'. *Corporate Social Responsibility and Environmental Management*, **11**(3), 140–149.

CSR Magazine (2002), 'Starting small: Europe's SMEs and social responsibility', October, 4–7.

Davies, I. and Crane, A. (2010), 'Corporate social responsibility in small- and medium-size enterprises: investigating employee engagement in fair trade companies'. *Business Ethics: A European Review*, **19**(2), 126–139.

El Baz, J., Laguir, I., Marais, M. and Stagliano, R. (2016), 'Influence of national institutions on the corporate social responsibility practices of small- and medium-sized enterprises in the food-processing industry: differences between France and Morocco'. *Journal of Business Ethics*, **134**, 117–133.

Enderle, G. (2004), 'Global competition and corporate responsibilities of small and medium-sized enterprises'. *Business Ethics: A European Review*, **13**(1), 51–63.

European Commission (2001), *Promoting a European Framework for Corporate Social Responsibility, Green Paper (COM 366, July)*. Luxembourg: Office for Official Publications of the European Communities.

European Commission (2002), *Corporate Social Responsibility: A Business Contribution to Sustainable Development. Communication from the Commission (COM 347, July)*. Luxembourg: Office for Official Publications of the European Communities.

Fisher, K., Geenen, J., Jurcevic, M., McClintock, K. and Davis, G. (2009), 'Applying

asset-based community development as a strategy for CSR: a Canadian perspective on a win–win for stakeholders and SMEs'. *Business Ethics: A European Review*, **18**(1), 66–84.
Freeman, R.E. (1984), *Strategic Management: A Stakeholder Approach*. Boston, MA: Pitman.
Ghauri, P. (2004), 'Designing and conducting case studies in international business'. In Marschan-Piekkari, R. and Welch, C. (eds), *Handbook of Qualitative Research Methods for International Business*. Cheltenham: Edward Elgar Publishing, 109–124.
Graafland, J., van de Ven, B. and Stofelle, N. (2003), 'Strategies and instruments for organizing CSR by small and large businesses in the Netherlands'. *Journal of Business Ethics*, **47**, 45–60.
Grayson, D. and Hodges, A. (2004), *Corporate Social Opportunity! 7 Steps to Make Corporate Social Responsibility Work for Your Business*. Sheffield, UK: Greenleaf.
Hammann, E.-M., Habisch, A. and Pechlaner, H. (2009), 'Values that create value: socially responsible business practices in SMEs – empirical evidence from German companies'. *Business Ethics: A European Review*, **18**(1), 37–53.
Hillary, R. (2000), 'The Eco-Management and Audit Scheme, ISO 14001 and the smaller firm'. In R. Hillary (Eds), *Small and Medium-Sized Enterprises and the Environment*. Sheffield, UK: Greenleaf, 128–147.
Iatridis, K., Kuznetsov, A. and Whyman, P. (2016), 'SMEs and certified management standards: the effect of motives and timing on implementation and commitment'. *Business Ethics Quarterly*, **26**(1), 67–94.
Jenkins, H. (2004), 'A critique of conventional CSR theory: an SME perspective.' *Journal of General Management*, **29**(4), 37–57.
Jenkins, H. (2006), 'Small business champions for corporate social responsibility'. *Journal of Business Ethics*, **67**, 241–256.
Jenkins, H. (2009), 'A "business opportunity" model of corporate social responsibility for small- and medium-sized enterprises'. *Business Ethics: A European Review*, **18**(1), 21–37.
Jeppesen, S. (2005), 'Enhancing competitiveness and securing equitable development: can small, micro, and medium-sized enterprises (SMEs) do the trick?' *Development in Practice*, **15**(3–4), 463–474.
Johnson, M. (2015), 'Sustainability management and small and medium-sized enterprises: managers' awareness and implementation of innovative tools'. *Corporate Social Responsibility and Environmental Management*, **22**, 271–285.
Kusyk, S. and Lozano, J. (2007), 'SME social performance: a four-cell typology of key drivers and barriers on social issues and their implications for stakeholder theory'. *Corporate Governance*, **7**(4), 502–515.
Lamberti, L. and Noci, G. (2012), 'The relationship between CSR and corporate strategy in medium-sized companies: evidence from Italy'. *Business Ethics: A European Review*, **21**(4), 402–416.
Lawrence, S.R., Collins, E., Pavlovich, K. and Arunachalam, M. (2006), 'Sustainability practices of SMEs: the case of NZ'. *Business Strategy and the Environment*, **15**, 242–257.
Lee, K.-H., Herold, D. and Yu, A.-L. (2016), 'Small and medium enterprises and corporate social responsibility practice: a Swedish perspective'. *Corporate Social Responsibility and Environmental Management*, **23**(2), 88–99.
Lepoutre, J. and Heene, A. (2006), 'Investigating the impact of firm size on small business social responsibility: a critical review'. *Journal of Business Ethics*, **67**, 257–273.
Longo, M., Mura, M. and Bonoli, A. (2005), 'Corporate social responsibility and corporate performance: the case of Italian SMEs'. *Corporate Governance*, **5**(4), 28–43.
Ludevid, M. (2000), 'Small and medium-sized enterprises' perceptions of the environment: a study from Spain'. In Hillary, R. (Eds), *Small and Medium-Sized Enterprises and the Environment*. Greenleaf Publishing, Sheffield, UK, 61–74.
Madueño, J.H., Larrán Jorge, M., Martínez Conesa, I. and Martínez-Martínez, D. (2016), 'Relationship between corporate social responsibility and competitive performance in Spanish SMEs: Empirical evidence from a stakeholders' perspective'. *BRQ Business Research Quarterly*, **19**(1), 55–72.

Maignan, I., Ferrell, O.C. and Ferrell, L. (2005), 'A stakeholder model for implementing social responsibility in marketing'. *European Journal of Marketing*, **39**(9–10), 956–980.

Martínez-Martínez, D., Madueño, J., Jorge, M. and Sancho, M. (2017), 'The strategic nature of corporate social responsibility in SMEs: a multiple mediator analysis'. *Industrial Management & Data Systems*, **117**(1), 2–31.

Mehta, K. and Sharma, R. (2016), 'SMEs and corporate social responsibility: Indian perception'. *Journal of Indian Management*, July–September, 58–69.

Meredith, S. (2000), 'Environmental innovation and small and medium-sized enterprises'. In Hillary, R. (eds), *Small and Medium-Sized Enterprises and the Environment*. Greenleaf, Sheffield, UK, 171–182.

Moore, G. and Spence, L. (2006), 'Editorial: Responsibility and small business'. *Journal of Business Ethics*, **67**, 219–226.

Morsing, M. and Perrini, F. (2009), 'CSR in SMEs: Do SMEs matter for the CSR agenda?' *Business Ethics: A European Review*, **18**(1), 1–6.

Murillo, D. and Lozano, J. (2006), 'SMEs and CSR: an approach to CSR in their own words'. *Journal of Business Ethics*, **67**, 227–240.

Murillo, D. and Lozano, J. (2009), 'Pushing forward SME CSR through a network: an account from the Catalan model'. *Business Ethics: A European Review*, **18**(1), 7–22.

Nguyen, N.H., Beeton, R. and Halog, A. (2015), 'A systems thinking approach for enhancing adaptive capacity in small- and medium-sized enterprises: causal mapping of factors influencing environmental adaptation in Vietnam's textile and garment industry'. *Environment Systems and Decisions*, **35**(4), 490–503.

Nooteboom, B. (1994), 'Innovation and Diffusion in Small Firms: Theory and Evidence'. *Small Business Economics*, **6**(5), 327–347.

Papasolomou-Doukakis, I., Krambia-Kapardis, M. and Katsioloudes, M. (2005), 'Corporate social responsibility: the way forward? Maybe not'. *European Business Review*, **17**(3), 263–279.

Perez-Sanchez, D. (2003), 'Implementing environmental management in SMEs'. *Corporate Social Responsibility and Environmental Management*, **10**(2), 67–77.

Perrini, F. (2006), 'SMEs and CSR theory: evidence and implications from an Italian perspective'. *Journal of Business Ethics*, **67**, 305–316.

Perrini, F. and Minoja, M. (2008), 'Strategizing corporate social responsibility: evidence from an Italian medium-sized, family-owned company'. *Business Ethics: A European Review*, **17**(1), 47–63.

Perrini, F., Russo, A. and Tencati, A. (2007), 'CSR strategies of SMEs and large firms: evidence from Italy'. *Journal of Business Ethics*, **74**(3), 285–300.

Petts, J., Herd, A., Gerrard, S. and Horne, C. (1999), 'The climate and culture of environmental compliance within SMEs'. *Business Strategy and the Environment*, **8**(1), 14–30.

Preuss, L. and Perschke, J. (2010), 'Slipstreaming the larger boats: social responsibility in medium-sized businesses'. *Journal of Business Ethics*, **92**, 531–551.

Roberts, S., Lawson, R. and Nicholls, J. (2006), 'Generating regional-scale improvements in SME corporate responsibility performance: lessons from Responsibility Northwest'. *Journal of Business Ethics*, **67**, 275–286.

Southwell, C. (2004), 'Engaging SMEs in community and social issues'. In Spence, L., Habisch, A. and Schmidpeter, R. (eds), *Responsibility and Social Capital: The World of Small and Medium Sized Enterprises*. New York: Palgrave Macmillan, 96–111.

Spence, L.J. (1999), 'Does size matter? The state of the art in small business ethics'. *Business Ethics: A European Review*, **8**(3), 163–174.

Spence, L. (2007), 'CSR and small business in a European policy context: The five "C"s of CSR and small business research agenda 2007'. *Business and Society Review*, **112**(4), 533–552.

Spence, L. and Lozano, J.F. (2000), 'Communicating about ethics with small firms: experiences from the UK and Spain.' *Journal of Business Ethics*, **27**, 43–53.

Spence, L. and Painter-Morland, M. (eds) (2010), *Ethics in Small and Medium Sized Enterprises: A Global Commentary*. Dordrecht: Springer.

Spence, L. and Rutherfoord, R. (2001), 'Social responsibility, profit maximisation and the

small firm owner-manager'. *Journal of Small Business and Enterprise Development*, **8**(2), 126–139.
Spence, L. and Rutherfoord, R. (2003), 'Small business and empirical perspectives in business ethics: editorial'. *Journal of Business Ethics*, **47**, 1–5.
Spence, L. and Schmidpeter, R. (2003), 'SMEs, social capital and the common good'. *Journal of Business Ethics*, **45**, 93–108.
Spence, L., Schmidpeter, R. and Habisch, A. (2003), 'Assessing social capital: small and medium sized enterprises in Germany and the UK'. *Journal of Business Ethics*, 47, 17–29.
Sweeney, L. (2007), 'Corporate social responsibility in Ireland: barriers and opportunities experienced by SMEs when undertaking CSR'. *Corporate Governance*, **7**(4), 516–523.
Tilley, F. (1999), 'The gap between the environmental attitudes and the environmental behavior of small firms'. *Business Strategy and the Environment*, **8**(4), 238–248.
Tilley, F. (2000), 'Small firm environmental ethics: how deep do they go?' *Business Ethics: A European Review*, **9**(1), 31–40.
Vives, A. (2006), 'Social and environmental responsibility in small and medium enterprises in Latin America'. *Journal of Corporate Citizenship*, Spring, 39–50.
Worthington, I., Ram, M. and Jones, T. (2006), 'Giving something back: a study of corporate social responsibility in UK South Asian small enterprises'. *Business Ethics: A European Review*, **15**(1), 95–109.
Yin, R.K. (2003), *Case Study Research: Design and Methods*. Thousand Oaks, CA: Sage.
Yu, J. and Bell, J. (2007), 'Building a sustainable business in China's small and medium-sized enterprises (SMEs)'. *Journal of Environmental Assessment Policy and Management*, **9**(1), 19–43.

18. The performance, volatility, downside risk and persistence of socially responsible investments in Korea and the impact of the Korean Green New Deal

Wei Rong Ang and Olaf Weber

1. INTRODUCTION

Korea is one of the countries in Asia advocating sustainability. In 2009,[1] for instance, Korea implemented the Korean Green New Deal that supports a transition to a greener economy. Korea has invested intensively in renewable energy, energy-efficient buildings, low-carbon vehicles, and water and waste management through this Green New Deal policy. Overall, a total of $38.1 billion was spent to stimulate the green economic growth. Eighty percent of the investment was allocated to environmental issues. Furthermore, the Korean government has planned to expand the use of renewable energy from 5 percent in 2011 to 11 percent by 2030.[2]

As emphasized by the Korean government, Korea's Green New Deal aims to create a new era of green growth which encompasses four elements: the green energy paradigm; green technology as a new growth engine; a contribution to the global community; and improvement in the quality of life.[3] This shows that Korea's Green New Deal is not just an environmental policy but also strives to create jobs and revenues. This policy has funded nine key projects as well as supporting projects, including four major river restorations, green transportation, integrated land use management, one water resource catchment, green automobile and clean energy development, a waste resource reuse project, sustainable forestry, green homes, green schools and an ecological river project. Based on the statistics and indicators published by OECD, it can be stated that Korea is on the path to sustainable and green growth.[4]

In Asia, assets invested in socially responsible investment (SRI) comprise $53 billion, an amount that is relatively small compared to the amount of SRI assets in North America and Europe. This, however, poses a unique opportunity for investors, since the SRI industry is relatively new in Asia and also in Korea (Global Sustainable Investment Alliance, 2015). SRI assets in Korea were lower than $2 billion in 2011.[5] Although the

Korean SRI market is relatively small compared to other countries, Korea actively advocates sustainability and socially responsible investment in the country and has raised awareness for SRI. Consequently, SRI increased to $8 billion in 2013.[6]

A number of studies, such as those by Ang and Lean (2013a) and Lean et al. (2014), have analyzed the performance of SRI in the Asia-Pacific region. Both studies found that the performance of Asia-Pacific SRI funds is not significantly different to conventional market benchmarks. Ang and Lean (2013b), however, found that SRI funds in Luxembourg, a country in which many European funds are located, underperformed the conventional market benchmark. In addition, Lean et al. (2014) did not find persistence for SRI assets in the Asia-Pacific region. Furthermore, studies on North American and European SRI (Ang et al., 2014; Lean et al., 2015) suggest an outperformance of SRI. Furthermore, Ang et al. (2014) suggest that market timing skills exist for fund managers in Europe and North America when handling SRI funds, and, consequently, found performance persistence for European SRI funds (Lean et al., 2015).

With regard to different market performance characteristics, Leite and Cortez (2015) found that French SRI funds underperformed conventional funds during non-crisis periods, but matched the performance of their conventional funds during crisis periods. Similar results based on a global sample of funds have been found by Weber et al. (2011). The underperformance of SRIs during bullish phases is largely caused by funds that use negative screening processes. In contrast, Bertrand and Lapointe (2015) suggest that firms with high environmental, social and governance performance contribute positively to the risk-adjusted performance of European equity portfolios. However, Mollet and Ziegler (2014) suggest that SRI firms in both Europe and North America are large sized firms and it is their size rather than their ESG performance that influences the risk-adjusted return of SRI portfolios. A recent study on emerging markets by Weber and Ang (2016) found that an emerging market SRI index performed similarly to the conventional market index.

With regard to institutional investments, Marlowe (2014) found that pension funds that followed an SRI approach performed similarly to pension funds that did not take SRI into account. Finally, a review study that analyzed more than 2,000 academic and non-academic studies found that SRI assets perform at least as well as conventional investments (Friede et al., 2015). Although previous studies have investigated SRI in several regions, such as North America, Europe and Asia-Pacific, there are no studies on the persistence and downside risks of Korea's SRI assets, and in particular the impact of the Korean Green New Deal on SRI performance. Therefore, this research fills a gap by investigating the performance, persistence, risk and downside risk of SRI indexes in Korea, as well as the impact of the Korean Green New Deal.

This chapter has five objectives: investigating the performance of SRI assets in Korea, understanding the impact of the Korean Green New Deal on Korean SRI, and analyzing the volatility, the downside risk, and the persistence of Korean SRI by segregating the sample into two sub-periods, where one of the sub-periods includes the 2008 global financial crisis. We examined how Korean SRI has performed compared with conventional investments during the period between January 2006 and December 2015. SRI is often considered a limited investment opportunity portfolio, with higher risks and lower return because of its limitations with regard to stock selection in order to fulfil the social, environmental and governance thresholds (Chegut et al., 2011). Because other studies presented contrary findings (Friede et al., 2015; Milevsky et al., 2006), we explored the financial performance of Korean SRI assets compared to conventional benchmarks.

We analyzed the performance of the DJSIK, with regard to its financial performance compared to conventional indexes for a span of ten years, using daily returns from January 2006 to December 2015. This period includes the time of implementation of the Korean Green New Deal that was implemented in 2009. Our findings suggest that the DJSIK performed equally to the market benchmark. Generally, we found a relatively stable performance and persistence for the SRI index, whereby its performance is no different from most of the conventional Korean portfolios. We found, however, that the Korean Green New Deal policy had a positive impact on the performance of SRI in Korea. Based on the assessment of downside risks, we conclude that the DJSIK has a lower sensitivity to market returns during bearish conditions. Furthermore, the results also suggest that neither negative nor positive shocks have stronger impacts on the volatility of the DJSIK than on conventional indexes.

The rest of the chapter is organized as follows. Section 2 describes the data used for the study. Section 3 explains the methodology. Section 4 reports and discusses the empirical findings and section 5 presents the conclusions.

2. DATA

We analyzed data between January 2006 and December 2015 based on daily returns. This time span included the 2008 financial crisis. Data about the price series of the DJSIK were taken from the Dow Jones website.[7] The Korean conventional stock indexes that have been used to benchmark the performance of the DJSIK were the Korean Composite Stock Price Index

(KOSPI), KOSPI LargeCap, KOSPI MidCap and KOSPI SmallCap. The data were taken from Google Finance. As in Hammoudeh et al. (2014), Ajmi et al. (2014), Ang (2015), and Weber and Ang (2016), indexes were used as benchmarks for analyzing SRI performance. KOSPI 200, KOSPI 100 and KOSPI 50 were used as market benchmarks for robustness tests. As the risk-free rate we used the return on the US Treasury bill. The size (SMB), value (HML) and momentum (MOM) factors were taken from Kenneth French's website.[8]

3. METHODOLOGY

We used Carhart's (1997) model to compare the performance of the Dow Jones Sustainability Index Korea (DJSIK) against several conventional Korea-based stock indexes as market benchmarks. The Carhart (1997) model is presented in Function 1.

$$R_t - R_{ft} = \alpha_0 + \beta_0 (R_{mt} - R_{ft}) + \beta_1 SMB_t + \beta_2 HML_t + \beta_3 MOM_t + \varepsilon_t \quad (1)$$

where
R_{it} = Return of DJSIK at time t
R_{ft} = US T-bill rate at time t
R_{mt}= Return of market benchmark at time t
SMB_t = The difference in return between small and large sized portfolios
HML_t = The difference in return between value and growth portfolios
MOM_t = The difference in return between past winner and loser portfolios.

α_0 is a measure of underperformance or outperformance of DJSIK against the market benchmarks. Moreover, β_0 represents the sensitivity of DJSIK compared to market benchmarks. β_1, β_2 and β_3 are the coefficients for size, value/growth and momentum variables.

Next, we determined whether the Korean Green New Deal has an impact on the performance of DJSIK. Because the policy was implemented between 2009 and 2013, we added a dummy variable (KGND) to capture the time of implementation of the Korean Green New Deal (see Function 2):

$$R_t - R_{ft} = \alpha_0 + \beta_0 (R_{mt} - R_{ft}) + \beta_1 SMB_t + \beta_2 HML_t + \beta_3 MOM_t + KGND + \varepsilon_t \quad (2)$$

where KGND is a dummy variable with the value '1'for the time KGND has been implemented and '0' otherwise. As a robustness test, we applied Racicot et al.'s (2014) model, which was also used by Weber and Ang

(2016) to examine the performance of DJSIK against the market benchmarks. The model shows a higher adjusted-r^2 than the Carhart (1997) model. Therefore, we extended the Carhart (1997) model by adding the quadratic and cubic function of the excess market return (see Function 3):

$$\alpha_0 + \beta_0(R_{mt} - R_{ft}) + \beta_1(R_{mt} - R_{ft})^2 + \beta_2(R_{mt} - R_{ft})^3 + \beta_3 SMB_t + \beta_4 HML_t + \beta_5 MOM_t + KGND + \varepsilon_t \quad (3)$$

where
$(R_{mt} - R_{ft})^2$ = quadratic function of the excess market return at time t
$(R_{mt} - R_{ft})^3$ = cubic function of the excess market return at time t.

All equations were corrected for the standard error through the Newey-West method if a serial correlation or heteroscedasticity was found (Newey and West, 1987). The EGARCH model (Brandt and Jones, 2006; Nelson, 1991) has been selected to accommodate the important stylized facts (asymmetric return, volatility clustering and leverage effect) of portfolio returns (Ang, 2015; Weber and Ang, 2016). The model has been developed by Nelson (1991) to measure leverage effects that exist when negative facts and news contribute more to volatility than positive facts and news. The leverage effect can be determined by testing the value of γ_2. If the leverage effect exists and bad news increases the volatility more than good news, then $\gamma_2 < 0$ and vice versa. The EGARCH model is defined as:

$$log(\sigma_t^2) = \gamma_0 + \gamma_1 \left| \frac{\varepsilon_{t-1}}{\sigma_{t-1}} \right| + \gamma_2 \frac{\varepsilon_{t-1}}{\sigma_{t-1}} + \gamma_3 \, log(\sigma_{t-1}^2) \quad (4)$$

Lastly, we used Ang et al.'s (2006) model to estimate the downside risk and to understand how the DJSIK reacts during downturn markets. Downside risk is defined as the covariance of excess fund return relative to the market return, given that the market excess return is negative. Hayat and Kraeussl (2011) also used this method to measure the downside risk (see Function 5):

$$\beta_0^- = \frac{cov(r_i, r_m) | r_m < 0}{var(r_m) | r_m < 0} \quad (5)$$

where r_m and r_i represent the excess returns of the SRI index and the market benchmark index respectively. β_0^- is the sensitivity of a portfolio excess return to the market's excess return given that the latter is negative. We follow Lean et al. (2015) and Weber and Ang (2016) to calculate the downside risk by removing positive excess returns of the market index.

Subsequently, the excess return of the DJSIK is regressed against the negative excess market return, expressed by SMB, HML and MOM.

To analyze performance persistence, we followed Weber and Ang (2016) and used Grinblatt and Titman's (1992) model (see Function 6). The sample period is split into two equal sub-periods. Then, the return of the two sub-periods is calculated. Finally, the return of the first sub-period is regressed against the return of the second sub-period. A significant positive value of the coefficient (β) indicates that positive performance persistence exists. A negative significant coefficient indicates negative persistence. Moreover, a non-significant β symbolizes that there is no persistence during the ten years of measurement.

$$R_1 = \alpha + \beta R_2 \tag{6}$$

where
R_1 = return of first sub-period
R_2 = return of second sub-period.

4. RESULTS

Table 18.1 presents the descriptive statistics of the DJSIK's and the conventional indexes' daily returns. The returns of both SRI and conventional investments are lower than those of the risk-free US Treasury Bill. However, the standard deviation of DJSIK is about the same as KOSPI 200, KOSPI 100 and KOSPI Large. The returns are negatively skewed and have fatter tails than a normal distribution (excess kurtosis), meaning that their probability distributions are skewed to the left and show a leptokurtic behavior. The Jarque-Bera test for normality confirms the non-normality of the distribution ($p < 0.00001$).

Table 18.2 presents the performance evaluated by applying the Carhart (1997) model. At a first glance, the performance of DJSIK is not significantly different from KOSPI and KOSPI LargeCap. There is also no significant difference in α_0 between KOSPI and KOSPI LargeCap, and the DJSIK, which means that the performance of DJSIK is on par with KOSPI and KOSPI Large. However, compared to KOSPI MidCap and MOSPI SmallCap, the DJSIK underperforms significantly ($\alpha_0 < .001$). For the robustness analysis we used three more KOSPI series indexes, KOSPI 200, KOSPI 100 and KOSPI 50. However, the DJSIK only underperforms when compared to KOSPI 50, whereas no significant performance difference has been found compared to KOSPI 200 and KOSPI 100 as market benchmarks. Therefore, the results suggest that

Table 18.1 Descriptive statistics

	Mean	Standard deviation	Skewness	Kurtosis	Jarque-Bera
DJSIK	0.0001	0.0136	−0.3288	9.9796	5342.72^{+} (<0.00001)
KOSPI	0.0001	0.0132	−0.5710	12.1431	9229.34^{+} (<0.00001)
KOSPI 200	0.0001	0.0136	−0.4187	11.0043	7041.01^{+} (<0.00001)
KOSPI 100	0.0001	0.0137	−0.3818	10.7906	6661.16^{+} (<0.00001)
KOSPI 50	0.0001	0.0142	−0.1514	13.6399	12316.52^{+} (<0.00001)
KOSPI LargeCap	0.0001	0.0136	−0.4549	11.4185	7794.18^{+} (<0.00001)
KOSPI MidCap	0.0002	0.0135	−1.0737	13.7265	13009.05^{+} (<0.00001)
KOSPI SmallCap	0.0003	0.0117	−1.7223	16.6915	21668.01^{+} (<0.00001)
USTBILL	0.0028	0.0045	1.3795	3.1206	829.05^{+} (<0.00001)

Notes: Values in parentheses indicate p-value and $^{+}$ denotes significance at 1%.

the performance of the DJSIK index is not significantly different to the performance of conventional indexes. Our results, presented in Table 18.2, are in line with the results of Auer and Schuhmacher (2016). These authors found that highly rated SRI stocks in the Asia-Pacific region as well as in the United States did not contribute higher returns compared with market benchmarks.

Next, we split the ten-year period into two sub-periods, with the first period being January 2006 to December 2010, and the second period January 2011 to December 2015. For the first period Table 18.3 demonstrates little evidence of underperformance for the DJSIK compared to KOSPI LargeCap and KOSPI 50 because the majority of the α_0's are not significant. There is no size effect for the DJSIK when compared to all market benchmarks. But, the large sized portfolio contributes more return when the market benchmark is KOSPI, KOSPI MidCap and KOSPI SmallCap. Nevertheless, the performance recovered in the second sub-period (see Table 18.4). During the second period the DJSIK performed similarly to all market benchmarks.

Table 18.2 Performance evaluation by Carhart (1997) model (Equation (1))

Panel A	α_0	β_0	β_1	β_2	β_3	Adjusted-R^2
KOSPI	−1.50×10−06	0.9949***	−3.36×10−05	2.44×10−05	−8.15×10−06	0.9407
	(0.9829)	(0.0000)	(0.1392)	(0.3959)	(0.6465)	
KOSPI LargeCap	−3.81×10−05	0.9732***	−3.26×10−06	2.85×10−06	−6.52×10−06	0.9568
	(0.5235)	(0.0000)	(0.8662)	(0.9074)	(0.6667)	
KOSPI MidCap	−0.0005***	0.8165***	−0.0001**	4.85×10−05	−7.00×10−05*	0.6570
	(0.0027)	0.0000)	(0.0170)	(0.4826)	(0.0906)	
KOSPI SmallCap	−0.0005***	0.8303***	−0.0001*	6.02×10−05	−4.06×10−05	0.5335
	(0.0055)	(0.0000)	(0.0619)	(0.4551)	(0.4149)	
Panel B	α_0	β_0	$\beta 1$	β_2	β_3	Adjusted-R^2
KOSPI 200	−2.95×10−05	0.9755***	1.73×10−06	5.39×10−06	−8.56×10−06	0.9581
	(0.6165)	(0.0000)	(0.9275)	(0.8234)	(0.5659)	
KOSPI 100	−3.90×10−05	0.9709***	1.16×10−05	6.33×10−07	−8.51×10−06	0.9595
	(0.4991)	(0.0000)	(0.5361)	(0.9787)	(0.5617)	
KOSPI 50	−0.0001*	0.9123***	3.28×10−05	−1.29×10−05	−2.55×10−05	0.9150
	(0.0757)	(0.0000)	(0.2267)	(0.7077)	(0.2299)	

Notes: Values in parentheses indicate p-value. The sample relates to January 2006–December 2015. ***, ** and * denote significance at 1%, 5% and 10% respectively.

Table 18.3 Performance evaluation for first sub-period by Carhart (1997) model (Equation (1))

Panel A	α_0	β_0	β_1	β_2	β_3	Adjusted-R^2
KOSPI	4.85×10−05	0.9909***	−6.41×10−05**	3.12×10−05	1.21×10−05	0.9539
	(0.6423)	(0.0000)	(0.0337)	(0.3967)	(0.5825)	
KOSPI LargeCap	−5.25×10−05	0.9737***	−2.97×10−05	9.39×10−06	7.59×10−06	0.9636
	(0.5711)	(0.0000)	(0.2676)	(0.7740)	(0.6968)	
KOSPI MidCap	−0.0008***	0.8120***	−0.0002***	3.66×10−05	−6.38×10−05	0.7137
	(0.0023)	(0.0000)	(0.0316)	(0.6899)	(0.2428)	
KOSPI SmallCap	−0.0003	0.9059***	−0.0002**	0.0001	1.78×10−05	0.5947
	(0.3182)	(0.0000)	(0.0420)	(0.3389)	(0.7853)	
Panel B	α_0	β_0	β_1	β_2	β_3	Adjusted-R^2
KOSPI 200	−3.48×10−05	0.9789***	−2.67×10−05	1.24×10−05	4.41×10−06	0.9674
	(0.6921)	(0.0000)	(0.2923)	(0.6883)	(0.8111)	
KOSPI 100	−4.42×10−05	0.9783***	−1.66×10−05	9.01×10−06	6.75×10−06	0.9702
	(0.5978)	(0.0000)	(0.4929)	(0.7606)	(0.7018)	
KOSPI 50	−0.0003**	0.9097***	1.80×10−05	−1.69×10−05	−2.66×10−05	0.9130
	(0.0176)	(0.0000)	(0.6499)	(0.7386)	(0.3776)	

Notes: Values in parentheses indicate p-value. The sample relates to January 2006–December 2015. ** and ** denote significance at 1% and 5% respectively.

Table 18.4 Performance evaluation for second sub-period by Carhart (1997) model (Equation (1))

Panel A	α_0	β_0	β_1	β_2	β_3	Adjusted-R^2
KOSPI	−2.60×10−05	1.0117***	−3.87×10−06	8.39×10−06	−4.27×10−05	0.9033
	(0.7907)	(0.0000)	(0.9152)	(0.8589)	(0.1966)	
KOSPI LargeCap	1.48×10−05	0.9724***	2.58×10−05	−1.17×10−05	−3.33×10−05	0.9361
	(0.8528)	(0.0000)	(0.3834)	(0.7613)	(0.2149)	
KOSPI MidCap	−0.0001	0.7984***	−8.62×10−05	5.66×10−05	−0.0001	0.4861
	(0.4641)	(0.0000)	(0.3042)	(0.6083)	(0.1442)	
KOSPI SmallCap	−0.0003	0.6674***	−6.85×10−06	2.77×10−05	−0.0001	0.3697
	(0.2750)	(0.0000)	(0.4608)	(0.8182)	(0.1603)	
Panel B	α_0	β_0	β_1	β_2	β_3	Adjusted-R^2
KOSPI 200	2.30×10−05	0.9675***	3.51×10−05	−7.50×10−06	−3.04×10−05	0.9317
	(0.7800)	(0.0000)	(0.2507)	(0.8500)	(0.2742)	
KOSPI 100	3.51×10−05	0.9529***	4.23×10−05	−1.33×10−05	−3.58×10−05	0.9300
	(0.6740)	(0.0000)	(0.1714)	(0.7408)	(0.2032)	
KOSPI 50	4.70×10−05	0.9116***	5.58×10−05	−1.42×10−05	−3.71×10−05	0.9118
	(0.6159)	(0.000)	(0.1081)	(0.7524)	(0.2400)	

Notes: Values in parentheses indicate p-value. The sample relates to January 2006–December 2015. *** denotes significance at 1%.

We suggest that the underperformance of DJSIK during the first sub-period could have been caused by the global financial crisis in 2008. We agree with Becchetti et al. (2015) that financial crises have a smaller impact on the financial performance of SRI than on conventional investment. This provides an insurance cushion that is able to prevent a performance decrease. The covered performance in the second sub-period is mainly caused by a resilience effect, as also mentioned by Soler-Domínguez and Matallín-Sáez (2016).

Next, we added KGND as a dummy variable to Carhart's model to capture the effect of the Korean Green New Deal on the performance of DJSIK (see Table 18.5). We found that the performance of DJSIK increased compared to the market benchmarks KOSPI MidCap, KOSPI SmallCap and KOSPI 50, suggesting that the policy has an impact on SRI in Korea (see also Ang, 2015). This result shows that the performance of SRI in Korea has been increased through the implementation of the Korean Green New Deal.

To test the robustness of the results, we used Racicot et al.'s (2014) test to evaluate the performance of DJSIK and the impact of KGND. At a first glance, Table 18.6 suggests that the adjusted-R^2 has increased compared to the Carhart model. The result also demonstrates that the DJSIK underperformed and KGND had an effect for the benchmarks KOSPI MidCap and KOSPI SmallCap. Nevertheless, there is scant evidence for a size effect for KOSPI 50. This result reaffirms that KGND has a positive impact on the performance of SRI in Korea.

We present the analysis of the conditional volatility of the DJSIK using an EGARCH model as the conditional mean equation (see Table 18.7). The results indicate that the EGARCH model successfully captures the dynamics of conditional volatility of the DJSIK since all the ARCH and GARCH coefficients (γ_1 and γ_3, see Table 18.7) are significant regardless of the market benchmarks. With respect to the volatility leverage effect, it is worth noting negative shocks have a stronger impact on the conditional volatility of the DJSIK than positive shocks compared with KOSPI MidCap and KOSPI SmallCap. Likewise, neither negative nor positive shocks have greater impact on the volatility of DJSIK compared to KOSPI, KOSPI LargeCap, KOSPI 200, KOSPI 100 and KOSPI 50.

Table 18.8 presents the downside risk of the DJSIK against its market benchmarks. In general, the DJSIK has a lower sensitivity to market returns during bearish conditions than during bullish conditions. This result reaffirmed the result presented in Table 18.3 that SRI in Korea underperforms slightly during the first sub-period. Also, negative shocks only have small impacts on the performance of the DJSIK, as shown

Table 18.5 Performance evaluation by Carhart (1997) model with KGND dummy variable (Equation (2))

Panel A	α_0	β_0	β_1	β_2	β_3	KGND	Adjusted-R^2
KOSPI	3.27×10−05	0.9954***	−3.33×10−05	2.42×10−05	−8.02×10−06	−6.59×10−05	0.9407
	(0.7449)	(0.0000)	(0.1430)	(0.3989)	(0.6515)	(0.6351)	
KOSPI LargeCap	−3.34×10−05	0.9732***	−3.22×10−06	2.83×10−06	−6.51×10−06	−9.11×10−06	0.9568
	(0.6967)	(0.0000)	(0.8681)	(0.9082)	(0.6676)	(0.9386)	
KOSPI MidCap	−0.0012***	0.8079***	−0.0001**	5.10×10−05	−7.43×10−05*	0.0013***	0.6589
	(0.0000)	(0.0000)	(0.0131)	(0.4592)	(0.0807)	(0.0001)	
KOSPI SmallCap	−0.0011***	0.8206***	−0.0001*	6.18×10−05	−4.33×10−05	0.0011***	0.5349
	(0.0001)	(0.0000)	(0.0538)	(0.4431)	(0.3839)	(0.0039)	
Panel B	α_0	β_0	β_1	β_2	β_3	KGND	Adjusted-R^2
KOSPI 200	−2.25×10−05	0.9756***	1.80×10−06	5.35×10−06	−8.54×10−06	−1.35×10−05	0.9581
	(0.7897)	(0.0000)	(0.9249)	(0.8245)	(0.5672)	0.9079)	
KOSPI 100	−2.39×10−05	0.9711***	1.17×10−05	5.63×10−07	−8.45×10−06	−2.92×10−05	0.9595
	(0.7725)	(0.0000)	(0.5313)	(0.9811)	(0.5644)	(0.7992)	
KOSPI 50	−0.0003**	0.9104***	3.14×10−05	−1.22×10−05	−2.60×10−05	0.0003*	0.9151
	(0.0125)	(0.0000)	(0.2482)	(0.7236)	(0.2206)	(0.0792)	

Notes: Values in parentheses indicate p-value. The sample relates to January 2006–December 2015. ***, ** and * denote significance at 1%, 5% and 10% respectively.

Table 18.6 Performance evaluation by Racicot et al. (2014) model (Equation (3))

Panel A	α_0	β_0	β_1	β_2	β_3	β_4	β_5	KGND	Adjusted-R^2
KOSPI	3.21×10−07	1.0138***	0.3887***	−6.3169***	−1.51×10−05	1.89×10−05	−7.52×10−07	−0.0001	0.9414
	(0.9975)	(0.0000)	(0.0014)	(0.0001)	(0.5097)	(0.5090)	(0.9661)	(0.4645)	
KOSPI LargeCap	−3.44×10−05	0.9849***	0.1569	−4.6180***	5.85×10−06	−4.36×10−08	−2.86×10−06	−4.01×10−05	0.9571
	(0.6969)	(0.0000)	(0.1150)	(0.0005)	(0.7651)	(0.9986)	(0.8504)	(0.7349)	
KOSPI MidCap	−0.0014***	0.8467***	1.3796***	−4.2750	−7.43×10−05	3.92×10−05	−5.07×10−05	0.0014***	0.6632
	(0.0000)	(0.0000)	(0.0000)	(0.2149)	(0.1779)	(0.5671)	(0.2329)	(0.0000)	
KOSPI SmallCap	−0.0014***	0.8769***	2.2815***	−1.0368	−6.09×10−05	6.08×10−05	−1.02×10−05	0.0011***	0.5414
	(0.0000)	(0.0000)	(0.0000)	(0.8615)	(0.3410)	(0.4470)	(0.8380)	(0.0060)	
Panel B	α_0	β_0	β_1	β_2	β_3	β_4	β_5	KGND	Adjusted-R^2
KOSPI 200	−3.35×10−05	0.9826***	0.1392	−2.6842**	8.43×10−06	3.39×10−06	−5.94×10−06	−2.91×10−05	0.9582
	(0.7003)	(0.0000)	(0.1606)	(0.0433)	(0.6624)	(0.8884)	(0.6912)	(0.8035)	
KOSPI 100	−2.02×10−05	0.9753***	0.03818	−1.8375	1.44×10−05	−1.20×10−07	−7.30×10−06	−4.16×10−05	0.9595
	(0.8142)	(0.0000)	(0.6947)	(0.1593)	(0.4487)	(0.9960)	(0.6198)	(0.7178)	
KOSPI 50	1.09×10−04	0.9903***	−0.4077***	−30.6983***	4.42×10−05*	−7.62×10−06	−1.08×10−05	−7.92×10−05	0.9321
	(0.3239)	(0.0000)	(0.0001)	(0.0000)	(0.0706)	(0.8044)	(0.5686)	(0.5952)	

Notes: Values in parentheses indicate p-value. The sample relates to January 2006–December 2015. ***, ** and * denote significance at 1%, 5% and 10% respectively.

in Table 18.7. Furthermore, our results regarding persistence suggest that the performance of SRI and of conventional investments in Korea is not persistent over the sample period of ten years (see Table 18.9). Consequently, we agree with Lean et al. (2015) that SRI tends to have a stronger degree of persistence in markets with higher demands, such as in Europe.

Table 18.7 Conditional volatility using an EGARCH model (Equation (4))

Panel A	α_0	β_0	β_1	β_2
KOSPI	−0.7071***	0.2125***	−0.0087	0.9522***
	(0.0000)	(0.0000)	(0.3264)	(0.0000)
KOSPI LargeCap	−0.9525***	0.1877***	−0.0032	0.9307***
	(0.0000)	(0.0000)	(0.7555)	(0.0000)
KOSPI MidCap	−0.2384***	0.1143***	−0.0426***	0.9844***
	(0.0000)	(0.0000)	(0.0000)	(0.0000)
KOSPI SmallCap	−0.2266***	0.1134***	−0.0539***	0.9851***
	(0.0000)	(0.0000)	(0.0000)	(0.0000)
Panel B	α_0	β_0	β_1	β_2
KOSPI 200	−1.6419***	0.2035***	−0.0039	0.8731***
	(0.0000)	(0.0000)	(0.7529)	(0.0000)
KOSPI 100	−1.8094***	0.2134***	−0.0048	0.8599***
	(0.0000)	(0.0000)	(0.7242)	(0.0000)
KOSPI 50	−8.4434***	0.5018***	−0.0216	0.2960***
	(0.0000)	(0.0000)	(0.2835)	(0.0000)

Notes: Values in parentheses indicate p-value. The sample relates to January 2006–December 2015. *** denotes significance at 1%.

Table 18.8 Downside risk by Ang et al.'s (2006) model (Equation (5))

	KOSPI	KOSPI 200	KOSPI 100	KOSPI 50	KOSPI LargeCap	KOSPI MidCap	KOSPI SmallCap
β_0^-	0.3168***	0.2991***	0.2967***	0.2680***	0.3010***	0.3259***	0.4086***
	(0.0000)	(0.0000)	(0.0000)	(0.0000)	(0.0000)	(0.0000)	(0.0000)

Notes: Values in parentheses indicate p-value. The sample relates to January 2006–December 2015. *** denotes significance at 1%.

Table 18.9 Performance persistence by Grinblatt and Titman's (1992) model (Equation (6))

	KOSPI	KOSPI 200	KOSPI 100	KOSPI 50	KOSPI LargeCap	KOSPI MidCap	KOSPI SmallCap
β	−0.0139	−0.015	−0.0151	−0.0065	−0.0124	−0.0125	0.0086
	(0.7344)	(0.7598)	(0.7124)	(0.8758)	(0.7659)	(0.8000)	(0.8219)

Notes: Values in parentheses indicate p-value. The sample relates to January 2006–December 2015.

5. CONCLUSION

We analyzed the performance of the DJSIK with regard to its financial performance compared to conventional indexes during a span of ten years using daily returns between January 2006 and December 2015. This time span includes the implementation of the Korean Green New Deal. Our analyses suggest little evidence of underperformance of the DJSIK. Generally, we found a relatively stable performance and persistence for the SRI index, whereby its performance is no different from most of the conventional Korean portfolios. Furthermore, we could not find persistence for the DJSIK. This result is consistent with Ang and Lean (2013a), Lean et al. (2014) and Ang (2015).

All β_0 in Table 18.2 (sensitivity of the DJSIK compared with conventional indexes) are significant and less than 1, suggesting that the DJSIK has a lower systematic risk than conventional indexes. This result is consistent with Ang (2015) and Ur Rehman et al. (2016). There is also no size and value/growth effect for DJSIK regardless of the market benchmarks. However, the large sized portfolio contributed more to returns than the small sized portfolio when KOSPI Mid and KOSPI Small are used as market benchmarks because β_1 is negative and significant (Table 18.2 and Table 18.5). This result is in line with Lean et al. (2015), who analyzed North American SRI funds. Finally, we found that a contrarian strategy added more returns to the DJSIK compared to the KOSPIMid. This result is consistent with Ang et al. (2014) for European SRI funds in their study. This implies that small sized stocks do not contribute more returns to SRI in Korea. Hence, a contrarian strategy based on buying past losers and selling past winners could contribute more returns to SRI in Korea.

Next, we split the time period into two sub-periods, the first period being from January 2006 to December 2010 and the second period from

January 2011 to December 2015 in order to investigate the influence of market phases on the financial performance of the DJSIK. While the DJSIK slightly underperformed during the first phase, its performance recovered during the second sub-period. This result is consistent with Weber and Ang (2016), who suggest that the performance of SRI in emerging markets is not significantly different compared to conventional benchmarks between June 2011 and December 2014, the phase after the financial crisis of 2008.

Furthermore, we found that the Korean Green New Deal has a positive impact on the performance of SRI in Korea. Based on the measurement of downside risk, we conclude that the DJSIK has a lower sensitivity to market returns during bearish conditions. This result is consistent with Weber and Ang (2016), who found that SRI indexes in emerging markets have lower returns during bearish conditions. This implies that the returns of SRI in Korea are resistant to downward pressure, which could serve as a hedging tool during economic turbulence. Our results also suggest that neither negative nor positive shocks have a stronger impact on the volatility of the DJSIK compared to conventional benchmarks (see also Lean et al., 2014; Weber and Ang, 2016).

With regard to financial policy, we suggest that the Korean government may consider implementing a second SRI-related economic policy to stimulate the sustainable growth of the country in the future. In addition, SRI investors may consider Korea as an alternative investment destination for international diversification purposes. With regard to future research, we suggest the analysis of economic, financial and policy-related factors that influence the financial performance of SRI in Korea.

NOTES

1. Global Green New Deal (An Update for the G20 Pittsburgh Summit), http://unep.ch/etb/publications/Green%20Economy/G%2020%20policy%20brief%20FINAL.pdf
2. *Low Carbon Green Growth Roadmap for Asia and the Pacific: Turning Resource Constraints and the Climate Crisis into Economic Growth Opportunities*, http://www.unescap.org/sites/default/files/Full-report.pdf
3. Green Growth Initiative of Korea, http://www.infodev.org/infodev-files/resource/InfodevDocuments_861.pdf
4. *Korea's Green Growth based on OECD Green Growth Indicators*, https://www.oecd.org/greengrowth/Korea's%20GG%20report%20with%20OECD%20indicators.pdf
5. Asia Socially Responsible Investment Roundtable Summary Transcript, http://www.bsr.org/reports/Asia_SRI_Roundtable_Summary_Transcript.pdf
6. South Korea's socially responsible investment estimated at US$8 billion, http://english.yonhapnews.co.kr/business/2015/02/03/0501000000AEN20150203002600320.html?6088ccb0
7. Data for Dow Jones Sustainability Index Korea (DJSIK) series, http://www.sustainability-indices.com/

8. Data for size, value/growth and momentum factors, http://mba.tuck.dartmouth.edu/pages/faculty/ken.french/

REFERENCES

Ajmi, A.N., Hammoudeh, S., Nguyen, D.K. and Sarafrazi, S. (2014), 'How strong are the causal relationships between Islamic stock markets and conventional financial systems? Evidence from linear and nonlinear tests', *Journal of International Financial Markets, Institutions and Money*, 28, 213–227.

Ang, A., Chen, J. and Xing, Y. (2006), 'Downside risk', *Review of Financial Studies*, 19(4), 1191–1239.

Ang, W.R. (2015), 'Sustainable investment in Korea does not catch a cold when the United States sneezes', *Journal of Sustainable Finance and Investment*, 5(1–2), 16–26.

Ang, W.R. and Lean, H.H. (2013a), 'Socially responsible investing funds in Asia Pacific', in Hooy, C.W., Ali, R. and Ghon Rhee, S. (eds), *Emerging Markets and Financial Resilience: Decoupling Growth from Turbulence*, Basingstoke, UK: Palgrave Macmillan, pp. 169–180.

Ang, W.R. and Lean, H.H. (2013b), 'Market Timing Ability of Socially Responsible Investing Funds in Luxembourg', in Mirdala, R. (ed.), *Financial Aspects of Recent Trends in the Global Economy (FINART)*, Vol. 2. Craiova: ASERS Publishing, pp. 127–135.

Ang, W.R., Gregoriou, G.N. and Lean, H.H. (2014), 'Market-timing skills of socially responsible investment fund managers: The case of North America versus Europe', *Journal of Asset Management*, 15(6), 366–377.

Auer, B.R. and Schuhmacher, F. (2016), 'Do socially (ir)responsible investments pay? New evidence from international ESG data', *The Quarterly Review of Economics and Finance*, 59, 51–62.

Becchetti, L., Ciciretti, R., Dalò, A. and Herzel, S. (2015), 'Socially responsible and conventional investment funds: performance comparison and the global financial crisis', *Applied Economics*, 47(25), 2541–2562.

Bertrand, P. and Lapointe, V. (2015), 'How performance of risk-based strategies is modified by socially responsible investment universe?', *International Review of Financial Analysis*, 38, 175–190.

Brandt, M.W. and Jones, C.S. (2006), 'Volatility forecasting with range-based EGARCH models', *Journal of Business and Economic Statistics*, 24(4), 470–486.

Carhart, M.M. (1997), 'On persistence in mutual fund performance', *The Journal of Finance*, 52(1), 57–82.

Chegut, A., Schenk, H. and Scholtens, B. (2011), 'Assessing SRI fund performance research: best practices in empirical analysis', *Sustainable Development*, 19(2), 77–94.

Friede, G., Busch, T. and Bassen, A. (2015), 'ESG and financial performance: aggregated evidence from more than 2000 empirical studies', *Journal of Sustainable Finance and Investment*, 5(4), 210–233.

Global Sustainable Investment Alliance (2015), accessed 20 April 2016 at http://www.gsialliance.org/wpcontent/uploads/2015/02/GSIA_Review_download.pdf

Grinblatt, M. and Titman, S. (1992), 'The persistence of mutual fund performance', *Journal of Finance*, 47(5), 1977–1984.

Hammoudeh, S., Mensi, W., Reboredo, J.C. and Nguyen, D.K. (2014), 'Dynamic dependence of the global Islamic equity index with global conventional equity market indices and risk factors', *Pacific-Basin Finance Journal*, 30, 189–206.

Hayat, R. and Kraeussl, R. (2011), 'Risk and return characteristics of Islamic equity funds', *Emerging Markets Review*, 12(2), 189–203.

Lean, H.H., Ang, W.R. and Smyth, R. (2014), 'Performance persistence of socially responsible investment funds in the Asia Pacific region', in Gregoriou, G. and Lee, D.

(eds), *Handbook of Asian Finance REITs, Trading, and Fund Performance*, Vol. 2, Oxford: Academic Press Inc., pp. 377–392.
Lean, H.H., Ang, W.R. and Smyth, R. (2015), 'Performance and performance persistence of socially responsible investment funds in Europe and North America', *The North America Journal of Finance and Economics*, 34, 254–266.
Leite, P. and Cortez, M.C. (2015), 'Performance of European socially responsible funds during market crises: evidence from France', *International Review of Financial Analysis*, 40, 132–141.
Marlowe, J. (2014), 'Socially responsible investing and public pension fund performance', *Public Performance and Management Review*, 38(2), 337–358.
Milevsky, M., Aziz, A., Goss, A., Comeault, J. and Wheeler, D. (2006), 'Cleaning a passive index: how to use portfolio optimization to satisfy CSR constraints', *The Journal of Portfolio Management*, Spring, 110–118.
Mollet, J.C. and Ziegler, A. (2014), 'Socially responsible investing and stock performance: new empirical evidence for the US and European stock markets', *Review of Financial Economics*, 23(4), 208–216.
Nelson, D.B. (1991), 'Conditional heteroskedasticity in asset returns: a new approach', *Econometrica*, 59(2), 347–370.
Newey, W.K. and West, K.D. (1987), 'A simple, positive semi-definite, heteroskedasticity and autocorrelationconsistent covariance matrix', *Econometrica*, 55, 703–708.
Racicot, F.E., Theoret, R. and Gregoriou, G.N. (2014), 'The hedge fund alpha puzzle with an application to Asian hedge funds', in Gregoriou, G. and Lee, D. (eds), *Handbook of Asian Finance REITs, Trading, and Fund Performance*, Vol. 2, Oxford: Academic Press Inc., pp. 343–362.
Soler-Domínguez, A. and Matallín-Sáez, J.C. (2016), 'Socially (ir)responsible investing? The performance of the VICEX Fund from a business cycle perspective', *Finance Research Letters*, 16, 190–195.
Ur Rehman, R., Zhang, J., Uppal, J., Cullinan, C. and AkramNaseem, M. (2016), 'Are environmental social governance equity indices a better choice for investors? An Asian perspective', *Business Ethics: A European Review*, 25(4), 440–459.
Weber, O. and Ang, W.R. (2016), 'The performance, volatility, persistence, and downside risk characteristics of sustainable investments in emerging market', *ACRN Oxford Journal of Finance and Risk Perspectives*, 5(2), 1–13.
Weber, O., Mansfeld, M. and Schirrmann, E. (2011), 'The financial performance of RI funds after 2000', in Vandekerckhove, W., Leys, J., Alm, K., Scholtens, B., Signori, S. and Schaefer, H. (eds), *Responsible Investment in Times of Turmoil*. Berlin, Germany: Springer, pp. 75–91.

19. Are SRI funds conventional funds in disguise or do they live up to their name?

Christin Nitsche and Michael Schröder

1. INTRODUCTION

In recent years, driven by overhauling capital investment decision-making, the socially responsible investing (SRI) industry has become an important segment of international capital markets. Globally, in 2014, more than US$ 21.4 trillion of professionally managed assets incorporated ESG (environmental, social and governance) factors into their selection and management process, and in Europe – by far the most important region – the figure was US$ 13.6 trillion (63.7 percent of the known SRI assets under management (AuM)) (see GSIA, 2014).[1] The SRI fund industry plays an increasingly large role in this evolving segment. For investors it is important to know whether these funds invest in line with their objectives or whether they are, rather, conventional funds in disguise. As Osthoff (2016) shows, SRI investors are also attracted by the high ethical standards of mutual funds.

Today's academic literature on SRI mainly focuses on the financial performance of ESG-screened funds and compares their risk-adjusted returns to those of conventional funds. The majority of these studies finds no difference in the respective performance of fund returns, which raises the question of whether portfolios of SRI funds are any different from the portfolios of conventional funds (see Schroeder, 2014). However, hitherto, academics have paid little attention to the portfolio compositions and ESG performance of SRI mutual funds. To mention a few studies, Bello (2005) and Benson et al. (2006) compare general fund characteristics of SRI and non-SRI funds, in particular the total AuM, asset class focus, sector allocation and the market capitalization of companies invested in. The ESG performance of SRI funds and indices compared to their conventional benchmarks is addressed in only a few studies. Statman (2006) and Kempf and Osthoff (2007) measure the ESG performance by applying the social and environmental scores of the rating institution KLD Research and Analysis, Inc. (KLD) to the equities held by the analyzed indices and funds. Both studies find that sustainable investments have higher mean social scores than standard investments. Utz and Wimmer (2014) show instead that SRI funds traded in the US do not exhibit a higher ethical investment structure. But investors choosing these SRI funds can reduce the risk of investing in the least ethical funds.

Our study will significantly expand the existing literature on the relative ESG performance of SRI funds. On the one hand, the analysis covers two fund data sets – one includes funds that invest in the European market, and the other funds with a global investment universe, whereas the existing literature focuses primarily on US-based funds. On the other hand, ESG corporate ratings of three rating agencies, and not only one, are applied to the fund holdings, in order to investigate whether the results are driven by only one ESG rating agency or whether the findings can be generalized.

The aim of this study is to investigate whether SRI funds are conventional funds in disguise or if they live up to their names and invest in more sustainable equities. The following main research questions are addressed:

1. Are the Top fund holdings of SRI funds different from the holdings of conventional funds? Our finding is that these holdings are relatively similar between conventional and SRI fundings, either for the European and the global funds. This confirms the results of earlier studies for the US.
2. Do SRI funds have higher ESG rankings than conventional funds? If SRI funds invest in line with their objectives they should have higher ESG rankings than standard funds. Our analysis finds that both European and global SRI funds exhibit higher ESG ratings.
3. If SRI funds have higher ESG rankings, are the absolute rating differences between SRI and conventional funds statistically significant? We run cross-sectional regressions in order to test whether SRI funds show significantly positive rating differences compared to standard funds. Our study shows that the ESG ratings of SRI funds are significantly higher. Thus, most SRI funds are not conventional funds in disguise but seem really to invest according to their SRI principles.

The remainder of the chapter is structured as follows. Section 2 gives a review of the literature on ESG performance of mutual funds. Then, sections 3 and 4 describe the data used in our study. Section 3 concentrates on the ESG data, whereas section 4 gives information on the fund data. Section 5 is the main part of the study. In this part the empirical methodology is explained and the results are presented. Section 6 concludes and summarizes the main findings of the empirical research.

2. LITERATURE REVIEW

In recent years, driven by the increasing demand for responsible investing, the SRI fund industry has evolved into an important part of the international capital markets and attracts interest from researchers, investors and the financial services industry. Their interest is particularly directed towards the financial and non-financial performance of sustainability funds (see Schroeder, 2014), whereas this study focuses on the assessment of the non-financial performance of SRI compared to non-SRI funds. The following gives a short summary of the current state of academic research in this field.

When studying ethical investments or SRI, the first discussion evolves around the question of which investments deserve this label. Schwartz (2003) claims that the ethical mutual fund industry is not acting in an ethical manner, meaning moral standards or principles such as transparency, accountability and integrity are not met. Investment decisions are based on negative screens, reflecting the investors' intended social, religious, or political beliefs rather than any ethical reasoning. Moreover, Schwartz argues that most funds do not meet the additional ethical obligations of full and complete disclosure of portfolio selection criteria and fair and non-deceptive marketing (Schwartz, 2003).

A similar distinction was proposed by Mackenzie (1998), who argues that there are ethically significant differences in the way portfolio selection criteria are chosen by funds. While 'deliberative' funds choose criteria on the basis of ethical discussion and reasoning, usually carried out by advisory committees, 'market-led' funds choose criteria based on their opinion of market demand (Mackenzie, 1998). The two use different portfolio selection methods: value-driven ethical investments use negative or sin screens in order to avoid controversial stocks, and profit-driven SRI funds invest in companies that pass positive screens with high scores on ESG indicators (Derwall et al., 2011). The standard portfolio selection in SRI consists of two steps, first screening sustainability and second financial optimization (Dorfleitner and Utz, 2012). Studies suggest how SRI funds could include ESG scores in the portfolio optimization in the second stage (Dorfleitner and Utz, 2012; Barracchini and Addessi, 2012).

The study of Chieffe and Lahey (2009) shows that most SRI mutual funds utilize a combination of positive and negative screens, summarized under the screening concept called 'best-in-class'. This strategy focuses on sustainability leaders of sectors or industries and is often index-based or oriented towards benchmarks with a wide sector allocation (Von Flotow, 2008). Funds that utilize this portfolio selection method are often criticized, because even the most sustainable company in an industry may not avoid environmental pollution (Schwartz, 2003; Faust and Scholz, 2008). Moreover, it is argued that the portfolio holdings of such funds may show virtually no difference compared to conventional funds.

This leads to a number of studies that compare general fund characteristics as well as the portfolio composition of SRI mutual funds with conventional funds.

Bello (2005) analyzes the portfolio characteristics of 42 SRI funds and 84 randomly selected conventional funds. He finds no significant difference between the two groups of funds, neither in the percentage of bonds and stocks in the portfolios nor in the market capitalization of the companies in which they invest. The portfolio constraints of SRI funds do not influence the number of portfolio holdings or the percentage of total assets invested in the top 10 holdings.

Benson et al. (2006) examines the question of whether the portfolio allocation of SRI funds across industries is any different from conventional funds. The study finds that the two types of funds invest different percentages of their AuM in different industries, but these differences are not consistent across the time period analyzed, encompassing the years 1994 to 2003.

The studies of Statman (2006) and Kempf and Osthoff (2007) analyze the portfolio compositions of SRI and conventional indices and funds by applying sustainability scores to the companies included in the index or fund. These scores are provided by the rating institution KLD Research and Analysis, Inc. and are calculated as the sum of a company's scores on the following indicators: corporate governance, community, diversity, employee relations, environment, human rights, product, alcohol, firearms, gambling, military, nuclear and tobacco.

Statman (2006) compares the constituents of the S&P 500 index to four indices of socially responsible companies: the Domini 400 Social Index, the Calvert Social Index, the Citizens Index, and the US Dow Jones Sustainability Index. He finds that each SRI index has a higher mean score than that of the S&P 500 index. The study concludes that the list of companies included in SRI indices shows a wide range of scores and a high degree of overlap with the S&P 500 (Statman, 2006).

Kempf and Osthoff (2007) similarly utilize KLD company scores to compare the portfolio holdings of SRI funds to conventional funds concerning their social and environmental standards. The study ranks US equity funds in the time period of 1991 to 2004, according to their KLD scores and shows that SRI funds have a significantly higher ethical ranking than conventional funds. Moreover, the funds are ranked higher with respect to every qualitative characteristic analyzed, and the results are stable over time and after controlling for additional fund characteristics (Kempf and Osthoff, 2007).

However, Chieffe and Lahey (2009) find that there are only small differences between the content of the two fund types. They analyze the top 10 holdings of 78 SRI funds and count how many times each firm appears. From the 37 most frequently counted companies, 33 are in the S&P 500 index and also part of the Fortune 500 firms and 13 are constituents of the Dow Jones Industrial Average (Chieffe and Lahey, 2009).

While the studies of Statman (2006) and Kempf and Osthoff (2007) apply KLD scores to evaluate companies' social and environmental performance, an analysis of Wimmer (2013) utilizes the ESG scores of the ASSET4 database of the Thomson Reuters Datastream to analyze the persistence of 27 SRI mutual fund ESG scores in the time period between 2003 and 2009. His study shows that ESG scores of funds remain high for approximately two years, but no empirical evidence of persisting ESG scores after three and four years is found. This lack of persistence is not caused by adverse changes in firms' ESG scores, but is driven by a change of funds' portfolio holdings towards lower rated companies.

In addition, Utz and Wimmer (2014) analyze 150 SRI funds traded in the US and show that these funds do not exhibit a better ethical investment structure than conventional funds. But investors choosing these SRI funds can reduce the risk of investing in the least ethical funds, which means that SRI funds have lower ESG downside risk compared to their conventional counterparts.

Our study expands the literature in several ways. We analyze not only US-based funds (which in most cases invest primarily in US stocks), but investigate relatively large samples of funds investing in European stocks and worldwide. We apply not only ratings of one (US based) rating agency, but use a variety of ratings by applying the ESG ratings of ASSET4, Oekom and Sustainalytics, thus analyzing whether the results are not only driven by one ESG rating agency but are more general in nature.

3. DATA: ESG RATINGS

The aim of this chapter is to provide an overview of the ESG data used in the empirical part of the analysis. Like most rating agencies, the three institutions in the focus of our study, i.e. oekom research AG (Oekom), Sustainalytics and ASSET4, assess the sustainability of companies based on three pillars: environmental, social and governance. In the first subsection the concepts of the ESG ratings are described, whereas the second subsection discusses the characteristics of the ESG rating data.

3.1 Concepts of the ESG Ratings

Oekom distinguishes between the two main dimensions: *social* and *environmental*. Both dimensions are further subdivided into three categories each. The social rating is comprised of the sub-ratings for staff & suppliers, society & product responsibility and corporate governance & business ethics. The environmental pillar is broken down into the categories environmental management, products & services and eco-efficiency. The assessment of a company's performance in these categories is based on 700 criteria out of which 100 are specifically selected, partially depending on the industry. The relation between industry-specific indicators and criteria used across all industries is approximately 35:65 (Windorfer, 2011).

Sustainalytics' corporate ratings are similarly based on the three ESG pillars subdivided into different numbers of categories. *Environmental* evaluations are based on the assessment of a company's operations and supply chain as well as its products. Indicators around employees, customers, supply chain and the community are reviewed under the *social* pillar. The *governance* score results from the analysis of the company's governance, business ethics and public policies. All described categories subordinated to the ESG pillars are evaluated based on a total of approximately 60 to 100 indicators, depending on the industry in which the company operates (ORSE, 2012). In this process, Sustainalytics distinguishes between core indicators that are used for the evaluation of every company in all peer groups and industry-specific indicators applied to a particular peer group (van den Heuvel, 2012).

ASSET4's company research includes over 750 criteria covering all aspects of sustainability reporting, which are subsequently summarized into 280 key performance indicators (KPIs). The categories resource reduction, emission reduction and product innovation are subcomponents of the *environmental* rating. The *social* score is based on seven categories: employment quality, health & safety, training & development, diversity, human rights, community and product responsibility. The board structure, compensation policy, board functions, shareholder rights and vision & strategy are reviewed for the assessment of the company's corporate *governance*. In addition to the ESG pillars used by all three analyzed rating agencies, ASSET4 adds a fourth *economic* pillar to its company analysis, which is based on the categories client loyalty, performance and shareholder loyalty.

All three agencies base their company assessment exclusively or at least mainly (ASSET4) on the three ESG pillars. Table 19.1 summarizes the ratings and the subcategories for the three rating agencies.

The *environmental* performance is measured by comparable categories

Table 19.1 Comparison of corporate rating criteria for the three ESG rating agencies Oekom, Sustainalytics and ASSET4

Corporate Rating Criteria	Oekom	Sustainalytics	ASSET4
Environmental	Environmental Management	Operations	Resource Reduction
	Products & Services	Products & Services	Product Innovation
	Eco-efficiency	Supply Chain	Emission Reduction
Social	Staff	Employees	Employment Quality
			Health & Safety
			Training & Development
			Diversity
	Suppliers	Supply Chain	Human Rights
	Society Responsibility	Community & Philanthropy	Community
	Product Responsibility	Customers	Product Responsibility
Governance	Corporate Governance	Corporate Governance	Board Structure
			Compensation Policy
			Board Functions
			Shareholders Rights
	Business Ethics	Business Ethics	
		Public Policy	Vision & Strategy
Economic			Client Loyalty
			Performance
			Shareholder Loyalty

Source: Authors' compilation, based on information from Oekom, Sustainalytics and ASSET4.

that cover the environmental impacts of a company's products and services as well as the impacts of production processes (e.g. emissions, resource consumption). The granularity of *social* rating criteria used by ASSET4 is much higher compared to Oekom's and Sustainalytics' criteria. While Oekom's and Sustainalytics' categories mainly focus on the three company's stakeholders, employees, suppliers and customers or society, ASSET4 uses four separate categories to assess the social performance related to the staff and only analyzes the suppliers with respect to their compliance with human rights (e.g. child labor). A similar pattern can be found when comparing the categories evaluated under the *governance* pillar. Oekom and Sustainalytics use the broad category corporate governance for the review of a company's board independence and compensation policy, whereas ASSET4 applies more detailed categories for these aspects. In addition, Oekom and Sustainalytics cover the category business ethics, under which, for example, corruption policies and controversies like bribery and lobbying are analyzed. In ASSET4's rating, these topics are included in only one KPI in the community category under the social pillar. A review of a company's sustainability strategy and reporting standard is carried out in Sustainalytics' and ASSET4's framework, while Oekom has not defined a specific category for these topics. As not all corporate rating indicators used by Oekom are publicly available, it cannot be clarified if these aspects are covered in one of the other categories.

In summary, all three agencies cover the ESG pillars in their corporate assessments and strong overlaps of the categories subordinated to the environmental and social pillar can be identified. The aspects of corporate governance are only part of the social pillar in Oekom's ratings, while Sustainalytics and ASSET4 analyze this pillar in more detail.

3.2 Characteristics of the ESG Rating Data

The data set provided by **Oekom** for research purposes comprises corporate ratings of 682 companies as of March 2012. Oekom, being a German rating agency, has a European focus, with more than 59 percent of the rated companies located in Europe, the Middle East and Africa (EMEA), and only 22 percent and 19 percent from the American and Asia Pacific areas, respectively. Besides the overall ratings, scores for the environmental and social pillar are also available for all companies in the 12-notch rating system (A+ to D−) as well as in numeric ratings ranging from 0 to 4, with 4 being the highest score. In order to reflect the precise corporate ratings, the numeric scores are used for the analysis and converted into point scores ranging from 0 to 100, e.g. a rating of 3.5 equals 87.5 (= 3.5 / 4 * 100).

Sustainalytics' corporate rating data for the three ESG pillars are publicly accessible on the website of STOXX,[2] because both companies, Sustainalytics and STOXX, partnered to launch the STOXX Global ESG Leaders Indices, which are based on Sustainalytics' sustainability data. The data set includes 1,792 companies, while ESG pillar scores (point scores between 0 and 100) were only available for 1,484 companies as of September 2013. The overall company scores, which are not included in the original data set, are calculated by equally weighting the three pillar scores.

ASSET4's ESG research data are available on Thomson Reuters Datastream in any degree of detail (by pillar, category, KPIs, indicators). The total and the four pillar scores are retrieved for the current ASSET4 universe of 3,894 companies for year-end 2012 and 2013. While only 1,021 company scores (point scores between 0 and 100) can be found for the year 2013, rating data for 3,360 companies are available for 2012. The data as of December 2012 will be used for further analysis to allow the application of as many corporate ratings as possible to the fund holdings, in order to reliably evaluate the funds' ESG performance. In comparison to Oekom and Sustainalytics, ASSET4 includes an economic pillar score in the total corporate ratings. In order to align the rating data and evaluate companies solely based on non-financial information, this pillar will be excluded. Similarly to Sustainalytics' overall company scores, ASSET4's ESG scores will be calculated using equal weights for the three remaining subcategories without including the economic subcategory.

When looking at the total ESG and pillar scores (Table 19.2) of the three rating agencies, several things are worth noting. First, Oekom (O) scores have a smaller range of total [30.9, 81.2] and pillar scores [26.0, 87.5], compared to Sustainalytics (S) and ASSET4 (A), which almost use the entire rating spectrum [0, 100]. Consequently, the two data sets show a much higher standard deviation in total ESG ($\sigma_S = 22.2$ and $\sigma_A = 24.2$) and pillar scores, while the average scores of all three agencies are still close together ($\mu_O = 55.0$, $\mu_S = 50.0$ and $\mu_A = 54.0$). Bearing in mind that Oekom's rating universe is much narrower, with a geographical focus on European companies, one could argue that the range and standard deviation differences are the results of dissimilar rating universes.

In the next step, only the 458 companies that are rated by all three agencies are included in the analysis.[3] In addition to the descriptive statistics, correlations of the total and pillar scores amongst the rating agencies are summarized in Table 19.3. While Oekom scores still show a smaller range of total [34.9, 77.9] and pillar scores [29.8, 87.5] compared to Sustainalytics' and ASSET4's scores, the standard deviations $\sigma_S = 17.1$ and $\sigma_A = 12.8$ (Table 19.3) of Sustainalytics and ASSET4 significantly decrease compared to the total universe analysis with $\sigma_S = 22.2$ and $\sigma_A = 24.2$ (Table 19.2). However, the standard deviations are still considerably larger compared to those ($\sigma_O = 8.0$) of Oekom's scores (Table 19.3). Interestingly, the geographical focus of the matched universe on European companies significantly increases the average ratings of Sustainalytics

Table 19.2 Descriptive statistics ofESG ratings and sub-ratings for the total universe by rating agency

Total Universe by Rating Agency	Descriptive Statistics	Oekom	Sustainalytics	ASSET4
	N	682	1484	3360
ESG	Minimum	30.9	3.6	4.7
	Maximum	81.2	98.4	94.9
	Mean	55.0	50.0	54.0
	Standard Deviation	8.3	22.2	24.2
Environmental	Minimum	26.0	0.0	8.3
	Maximum	87.5	100.0	94.2
	Mean	54.6	50.0	53.5
	Standard Deviation	10.5	28.9	31.9
Social	Minimum	33.2	0.0	3.6
	Maximum	82.0	100.0	97.3
	Mean	55.4	49.9	53.0
	Standard Deviation	8.4	28.9	30.7
Governance	Minimum		0.0	1.3
	Maximum		100.0	96.8
	Mean		50.2	55.5
	Standard Deviation		28.9	29.3

Notes: N = number of observations; Minimum = smallest rating value in the sample; Maximum = highest rating value in the sample; Mean = arithmetic average of the ratings.

Source: Author's calculations.

and ASSET4 to μ_S = 66.9 and μ_A = 79.5, respectively. This shows that European firms achieve on average higher ESG ratings than their American and Asian-Pacific counterparts that drive down the average Sustainalytics and ASSET4 scores. Oekom's average score for the same matched universe is still around μ_O = 55.7, which shows that Oekom seems to apply a more rigorous ESG definition and evaluation compared to Sustainalytics and ASSET4.

When correlating Oekom's scores with the ratings of Sustainalytics and ASSET4, the Pearson coefficient is around 0.35 with significance at the 0.001 level (2-tailed). This translates into R^2 of around 0.13, which means that only 13 percent of the variance in Oekom's total ESG scores is explained by the variation in Sustainalytics' and ASSET4's ESG scores. The low correlations in the social pillar scores can be explained by the fact

Table 19.3 Descriptive statistics of ESG ratings and sub-ratings for the Oekom matched universe

Oekom Matched Universe	Descriptive Statistics (n=458)	Total Score (ESG)	Environmental	Social	Governance
Oekom	Minimum	34.9	29.8	36.3	
	Maximum	77.9	87.5	79.2	
	Mean	55.7	55.5	55.8	
	Standard Deviation	8.0	10.1	8.2	
Sustainalytics	Minimum	*19.7*	5.4	0.0	0.6
	Maximum	98.4	100.0	99.9	100.0
	Mean	66.9	70.8	65.4	64.6
	Standard Deviation	17.1	22.9	25.4	26.5
ASSET4	Minimum	18.3	15.7	11.2	4.6
	Maximum	94.5	94.2	97.1	96.8
	Mean	79.5	86.3	84.0	68.1
	Standard Deviation	12.8	11.8	15.6	26.4
Oekom vs. Sustainalytics	Pearson	0.353**	0.224***	0.376 ***	
	R^2	0.125	0.050	0.142	
Oekom vs. ASSET4	Pearson	0.356**	0.249***	0.403 ***	
	R^2	0.127	0.062	0.162	
Sustainalytics vs. ASSET4	Pearson	0.474**	0.398***	0.349 ***	0.319 ***
	R^2	0.224	0.159	0.122	0.102

*** correlation significant at the 0.001 level (2-tailed)

Notes: 'Matched' means that only those ratings of ASSET4 and Sustainalytics are used which fit to the Oekom universe, which is the smallest universe of all three rating agencies under consideration.

Source: Author's calculations.

that Oekom includes governance indicators in this pillar, while the other agencies report separate governance scores. For the given universe, the Pearson correlation coefficient of Sustainalytics' and ASSET4's total ESG scores is 0.47, with R^2 of 0.22, considerably higher than their correlations with Oekom's scores. As mentioned before, this was expected as Oekom's scores are based on only two pillars, with industry-specific weightings for the total scores. In addition, governance factors are included as one of three categories of the social pillar, thereby receiving significantly less weight in the total rating.

In summary, the analysis has shown that Oekom seems to use a more rigorous ESG definition (following the Frankurt-Hohenheimer guidelines), which leads to lower average ESG scores, smaller ranges and lower correlations with the ratings of Sustainalytics and ASSET4. The ESG scores of these two agencies show stronger relationships (higher correlations), both with large ESG ranges and standard deviations, and different average scores. One should bear in mind these fundamental rating differences when applying ratings to the equity holdings of European and global funds.

4. DATA: FUNDS

The analysis is based on two main fund data sets, both focusing on active, open-end funds with an asset class focus on equities. The Bloomberg fund database is used for the fund selection and the retrieval of the portfolio holdings. The first data set is limited to equity funds with a geographical focus on the 'European Region', 'Eurozone' and 'European Union'. For the second data set, the geographical criterion is set to 'International' and 'Global' funds. Both data sets consist of an equal number of SRI and conventional funds. SRI funds are selected by applying positive screens for the general attribute 'ESG' and 'Socially Responsible'. Vice versa, negative screens for these two attributes are used to create the conventional European and global fund universe. Table 19.A1 in the Appendix shows the resulting number of SRI and conventional funds in both data sets after the application of the described filter criteria. Some subsequent adjustments had to be applied in order to ensure the comparability of the data sets:

European funds

- Out of the 67 selected *European SRI funds*, seven funds are excluded as portfolio holdings are not available for five funds. The remaining 60 SRI funds are part of the final European fund data set.
- Out of the 175 filtered *European conventional funds*, 60 funds are randomly selected, in order to generate a balanced European fund data set comprised of an equal number of SRI and conventional funds.

Global funds

- Out of the 130 selected *global SRI funds*, 11 funds are excluded because of holding data availability issues, resulting in 119 SRI funds included in the final global fund data set.
- For the *global conventional fund* universe the asset class allocation filter is adjusted to 100 percent equities to downsize the fund universe. Out of the remaining 362 global conventional funds, 119 funds are randomly selected, yielding a balanced global fund data set.

The portfolio holdings of all funds including equity name, international securities identification number (ISIN) and the weightings of the equities within the funds as of 31 December 2013 are retrieved from Bloomberg. The ESG corporate ratings of Oekom, Sustainalytics and ASSET4 will be subsequently combined with the funds' data using the ISIN as a matching criterion. The detailed research methodology and analysis results will be discussed in the next section.

The fund data for a total of 358 funds are combined with the ESG ratings using the companies' ISIN codes. For each fund, the portfolio weights for the equities for which rating data is available are computed. If not all portfolio holdings are rated, the portfolio weights for rated equities are adjusted so that they sum up to 100 percent.

Using this approach implicitly assumes that the holdings, which are not rated by the respective rating agency, obtain the average rating of the rated assets in the fund.[4] The value-weighted pillar and ESG ratings of the funds are calculated using the adjusted equity weights. The pillar and total ESG ratings of all SRI and conventional funds included in the European and global fund data set are calculated using Oekom's, Sustainalytics' and ASSET4's data. Funds that cannot be rated by a rating agency because ESG corporate rating data for the fund's holdings are not available will be subsequently excluded in the respective fund analysis of that rating agency. Based on the ESG fund rating data sets, the following research question (Q) will be investigated, for the European fund universe and the global funds separately.

5. EMPIRICAL ANALYSIS

This section combines the theoretical considerations regarding ESG corporate ratings with the fund data analysis by applying the rating data to the selected funds in order to evaluate their non-financial performance. The aim is to investigate whether SRI funds are conventional funds in disguise or invest in line with their objectives. First, the research questions are summarized, accompanied by the methodologies applied during the data analysis. Next, the research results will be discussed.

5.1 Hypotheses

Research Question 1: *Are the Top portfolio holdings of SRI funds any different from the holdings of conventional funds?*

Investors are usually interested in which companies a fund invests in and may gain a first impression by looking at the Top fund holdings. Consequently, this study aims to analyze if the holdings of SRI and conventional funds are any different at first glance. For that purpose, it is determined how frequently a company is included in the Top fund holdings of SRI and non-SRI funds. The 20 most often counted companies in each fund type will be compared with each other.

Research Question 2: *Do SRI funds have higher ESG rankings on average than conventional funds?*

In this step of the analysis, all SRI and conventional funds in the respective data set are ranked based on their total ESG fund ratings. The ranking is normalized so that the ranks are equally distributed between 0 and 1. The fund with the highest ESG rating obtains the 1st rank and the fund with the lowest rating rank 0. Next, the SRI and conventional funds are clustered into 10-quantiles (deciles) according to their rankings. Finally, the percentage of funds in each decile is calculated. These steps are repeated for the ESG fund ratings based on each rating agency. If SRI funds invest in line with their objective, one would expect that these funds would have higher ESG rankings than their conventional counterparts. Consequently, the percentage of SRI funds in the top deciles should be above the share of conventional funds.

Research Question 3: *If SRI funds have higher ESG rankings, are the absolute rating differences between SRI and conventional funds statistically significant?*

While *Q1* and *Q2* only give a first impression of the differences between SRI and conventional funds with respect to their sustainability, next a formal test, analyzing whether the differences in the ratings are statistically significant, will be conducted. The statistical significance of rating differences is not only tested for the total ESG ratings of the three agencies studied, but also for each pillar score by running the following cross-sectional regression:

$$Rating_{i;j} = \beta_{0;j} + \beta_{1;j} * D_i + \varepsilon_{i;j} \quad (1)$$

The $Rating_{i;j}$ denotes the rating in the category j of fund i, and D_i is a dummy variable that takes on the value 1 for SRI funds and 0 otherwise.[5] The constant $\beta_{0;j}$ takes on the value of the average rating for the analyzed category j of the conventional funds, and the coefficient $\beta_{1;j}$ measures the rating difference in the respective pillar or the total score between SRI and non-SRI funds. The statistical significance of the constant $\beta_{0;j}$ and the coefficient $\beta_{1;j}$ is tested at the 0.1%, 1% and 5% level, indicated by ***, ** and * respectively.

5.2 Results

In the following section, the fund data sets are analyzed following the research methodologies described above and the results are discussed for the European and the global fund universe.

The European fund data set is comprised of 60 SRI funds; for the global funds we identified 119 SRI funds. As described in section 4 we randomly selected 60 and 119 conventional funds, respectively, to represent the characteristics of the European and global funds not focusing on SRI. After combining the funds' holdings data with the ESG ratings, funds without any ESG rating are excluded from the respective analysis.[6]

5.2.1 Research question 1: differences in the Top fund holdings

Firstly, the research question is addressed if the Top SRI fund holdings of European and global sustainability funds are different from conventional funds. For that purpose, the Top fund holdings of European and global funds are analyzed with respect to the most popular companies in SRI and non-SRI funds. The 20 equities that are most often counted in European funds are reported in Table 19.4 for SRI funds and Table 19.5 for conventional funds. The companies' counts as well as the ESG ratings they received from the ratings agencies Oekom, Sustainalytics and ASSET4 are listed in columns 3–6.

Table 19.4 shows that Sanofi is under the Top fund holdings of more than half of the analyzed European SRI funds, closely followed by BNP Paribas (27 counts) and Roche (22 counts). However, Oekom and ASSET4 have actually given SAP, with 68.3 points (pts) and 92.4pts, the maximum ESG score of the 20 most frequently counted companies, and Sustainalytics evaluates Allianz (96.1pts) as the most sustainable company. These two companies are found in approximately one third of the analyzed European SRI funds. Based on Oekom's rating, the 20 most counted companies have an average rating of $\mu_{O;ESG} = 60.4$, which is 5.4pts

Table 19.4 Top fund holdings of European SRI funds

Top Fund Holdings	European SRI Funds	Count	Oekom Rating	Sustain-alytics Rating	ASSET4 Rating
1	SANOFI	31	63.8	80.6	87.7
2	BNP PARIBAS	27	46.7	91.9	91.7
3	ROCHE HOLDING AG-GENUSSCHEIN	22	62.3	72.6	80.0
4	SAP SE	21	68.3	72.9	92.4
5	AXA SA	21	60.0	82.2	89.9
6	ALLIANZ SE-REG	20	62.9	96.1	89.7
7	SIEMENS AG-REG	19	67.6	69.4	89.4
8	NOVARTIS AG-REG	19	64.2	72.5	83.8
9	BAYER AG-REG	17	57.6	65.5	77.8
10	BASF SE	15	66.6	75.6	80.6
11	VODAFONE GROUP PLC	15	n/a	n/a	n/a
12	TOTAL SA	14	67.6	39.4	81.9
13	BANCO BILBAO VTZCAYA ARGENTA	12	52.7	82.4	87.4
14	BG GROUP PLC	11	62.8	87.4	83.4
15	DAIMLER AG-REGISTERED SHARES	10	64.1	69.0	83.1
16	NESTLE SA-REG	10	59.3	74.9	84.8
17	ING GROEP NV-CVA	9	44.4	85.6	89.2
18	UNILEVER NV-CVA	9	62.1	79.3	86.7
19	HSBC HOLDINGS PLC	8	47.5	n/a	85.3
20	GLAXOSMITHKLINE PLC	7	67.11	68.9	91.2
	Minimum		44.4	39.4	77.8
	Maximum		68.3	96.1	92.4
	Mean		60.4	75.9	86.1

Notes: 'Count' gives the number of funds in which the respective company is part of the Top companies. Columns 4–6 show the company rating of the ESG rating agencies. The highlighted companies are those that are not part of the Top list of conventional funds (= Table 19.5).

Source: Author's calculations.

above the average rating of the total Oekom universe. Sustainalytics' and ASSET4's assessments yield an average rating of $\mu_{S;ESG} = 75.9$ and $\mu_{A;ESG} = 86.1$, actually 25.9pts and 32.1pts above their total universe averages. These huge differences are mainly driven by the fact that their total

Table 19.5 Top fund holdings of European conventional funds

Top Fund Holdings	European Conventional Funds	Count	Oekom Rating	Sustain-alytics Rating	ASSET4 Rating
1	SANOFI	25	63.8	80.6	87.7
2	TOTAL SA	18	67.6	39.4	81.9
3	ROCHE HOLDING AG-GENUSSCHEIN	17	62.3	72.6	80.0
4	NOVARTIS AG-REG	16	64.2	72.5	83.8
5	BNP PARIBAS	15	46.7	91.9	91.7
6	ALLIANZ SE-REG	13	62.9	96.1	89.7
7	BAYER AG-REG	13	57.6	65.5	77.8
8	HSBC HOLDINGS PLC	13	47.5	n/a	85.3
9	SIEMENS AG-REG	12	67.6	69.4	89.4
10	VODAFONE GROUP PLC	12	n/a	n/a	n/a
11	AXA SA	11	60.0	82.2	89.9
12	BP PLC	10	50.5	n/a	84.9
13	NESTLE SA-REG	9	59.3	74.9	84.8
14	AIRBUS GROUP NV	8	58.9	n/a	84.3
15	ANHEUSER-BUSCH INBEV NV	8	48.9	56.6	78.8
16	GLAXOSMITHKLINE PLC	8	67.1	68.9	91.2
17	VIVENDI	6	60.0	72.3	90.6
18	DAIMLER AG-REGISTERED SHARES	6	64.1	69.0	83.1
19	UNILEVER NV-CVA	6	62.1	79.3	86.7
20	BRITISH AMERICAN TOBACCO PLC	6	63.11	66.9	93.4
	Minimum		46.7	39.4	77.8
	Maximum		67.6	96.1	93.4
	Mean		59.71	72.4	86.0

Notes: 'Count' gives the number of funds in which the respective company is part of the Top companies. Columns 4–6 show the company rating of the ESG rating agencies. The highlighted companies are those that are not part of the Top list of ESG funds (= Table 19.4).

Source: Author's calculations.

universe is comprised of significantly more non-European companies, which generally have lower ESG ratings than European companies.

In comparison to Table 19.4, Table 19.5 reports the 20 most frequently counted companies in the Top holdings of European conventional funds. It is remarkable that Sanofi and Roche are again at the top of the list and included in the Top fund holdings of 25 and 17 conventional funds, respectively. The average ESG ratings of the 20 listed companies are below those of the most counted companies in SRI funds, but still above the universe averages of the three rating agencies. This finding suggests that also fund managers of conventional funds select companies with above average ESG ratings. However, the companies may not be chosen by conventional fund managers because of sustainability considerations but because of good risk-return profiles.

When comparing both lists, it becomes clear that 15 out of 20 companies show up under the most often counted companies of SRI and conventional funds. Consequently, at first glance, an investor may have difficulties in recognizing differences in the Top fund holdings, when comparing SRI and non-SRI funds. The tables can only be distinguished by the five companies marked in the above tables by gray-shaded fields. Here, it can at least be seen that SRI funds seem to avoid companies that generate revenues from alcohol (Anheuser-Busch) and tobacco (British American Tobacco) and which may cause environmental harm (BP and Airbus), while these companies frequently show up in conventional funds. However, one may raise the question of why so many European SRI funds invest in Total, an oil and gas company similar to BP. The 2013 returns of Total compared to BP could be an argument for a purely return-driven investor, but this is a questionable approach for SR investors. Overall, the holding-based analysis suggests that SRI funds are perhaps disguised conventional funds, as the frequently included equities in the Top holdings of SRI and non-SRI funds are very similar.

For the global fund universe Table 19.6 and Table 19.7 show the 20 equities that are most often counted in each of the fund types. Table 19.6 shows that Google leads the list of the most often counted companies under the Top fund holdings of the analyzed global SRI funds with 28 counts (included in 23.5% of the funds). This is surprising when looking at the average ratings and ranges of the 20 listed companies. With respect to this benchmark, Google is rated below average by Oekom ($Google_O = 46.0$, $\mu_O = 54.7$) and is the worst rated company by Sustainalytics ($Google_S = 31.5$) and ASSET4 ($Google_A = 52.4$). Microsoft (24 counts), Nestle (22 counts) and Apple (21 counts) follow Google in the list of the frequently included equities in SRI funds, and are rated better by all three agencies. Out of the top listed companies, Microsoft ($Microsoft_A = 93.9$)

Table 19.6 Top fund holdings of global SRI funds

Top Fund Holdings	Global SRI Funds	Count	Oekom Rating	Sustain-alytics Rating	ASSET4 Rating
1	GOOGLE INC-CL A	28	46.0	31.5	52.4
2	MICROSOFT CORP	24	54.2	42.5	93.9
3	NESTLE SA-REG	22	59.3	74.9	84.8
4	APPLE INC	21	58.7	37.9	72.1
5	JOHNSON & JOHNSON	19	57.1	63.5	92.9
6	VODAFONE GROUP PLC	18	n/a	n/a	n/a
7	ROCHE HOLDING AG-GENUSSCHEIN	18	62.3	72.6	80.0
8	JPMORGAN CHASE & CO	17	43.8	60.2	80.3
9	PROCTER & GAMBLE CO/THE	16	62.1	62.5	92.2
10	NOVARTIS AG-REG	14	64.2	72.5	83.8
11	CITIGROUP INC	13	43.9	62.8	78.3
12	WELLS FARGO & CO	13	n/a	49.0	79.7
13	BG GROUP PLC	12	62.8	87.4	83.4
14	GENERAL ELECTRIC CO	12	59.2	73.7	91.7
15	EXXON MOBIL CORP	11	51.9	38.4	83.1
16	BNP PARIBAS	10	46.7	91.9	91.7
17	PEPSICO INC	9	55.1	72.6	81.0
18	PFIZER INC	9	54.9	66.4	76.4
19	HSBC HOLDINGS PLC	8	47.5	n/a	85.3
20	PENTAIR PLC	8	n/a	n/a	n/a
	Minimum		43.8	31.5	52.4
	Maximum		64.2	91.9	93.9
	Mean		54.7	62.4	82.4

Notes: 'Count' gives the number of funds in which the respective company is part of the Top companies. Columns 4–6 show the company rating of the ESG rating agencies. The highlighted companies are those that are not part of the Top list of conventional funds (= Table 19.7).

Source: Author's calculations.

received the best rating from ASSET4, BNP Paribas ($BNP_S = 93.9$) from Sustainalytics, and Novartis ($Novartis_O = 64.2$) from Oekom.

Overall, the 20 most counted companies have an average Oekom rating of $\mu_{O;ESG} = 54.7$, which is 0.3pts below the total universe average. This can be anticipated as Oekom's universe includes more companies from the EMEA regions, which achieve on average higher ESG scores. Consequently,

Table 19.7 Top fund holdings of global conventional funds

Top Fund Holdings	Global Conventional Funds	Count	Oekom Rating	Sustain-alytics Rating	ASSET4 Rating
1	GOOGLE INC-CL A	25	46.0	31.5	52.4
2	ROCHE HOLDING AG-GENUSSCHEIN	19	62.3	72.6	80.0
3	APPLE INC	18	58.7	37.9	72.1
4	TENCENT HOLDINGS LTD	13	n/a	n/a	n/a
5	VODAFONE GROUP PLC	12	n/a	n/a	n/a
6	NESTLE SA-REG	11	59.3	74.9	84.8
7	MICROSOFT CORP	11	54.2	42.5	93.9
8	SAMSUNG ELECTRONICS CO LTD	10	62.2	n/a	72.7
9	NOVARTIS AG-REG	9	64.2	72.5	83.8
10	TAIWAN SEMICONDUCTOR MANUF.	9	62.4	n/a	71.0
11	EXXON MOBIL CORP	9	51.9	38.4	83.1
12	JOHNSON & JOHNSON	9	57.1	63.5	92.9
13	CHINA MOBILE LTD	8	49.1	42.5	86.7
14	AMAZON.COM INC	8	n/a	11.8	29.9
15	GAZPROM OAO-SPON ADR	7	n/a	n/a	n/a
16	CHEVRON CORP	7	51.8	n/a	80.1
17	CHINA CONSTRUCTION BANK-H	7	n/a	n/a	56.0
18	CITIGROUP INC	7	43.9	62.8	78.3
19	HSBC HOLDINGS PLC	7	47.5	n/a	85.3
20	TOTAL SA	7	67.6	39.4	81.9
	Minimum		43.9	11.8	29.9
	Maximum		67.6	74.9	93.9
	Mean		55.9	49.2	75.6

Notes: 'Count' gives the number of funds in which the respective company is part of the Top companies. Columns 4–6 show the company rating of the ESG rating agencies. The highlighted companies are those that are not part of the Top list of conventional funds (= Table 19.6).

Source: Author's calculations.

it is expected that a global company portfolio performs below average. Sustainalytics' and ASSET4's assessments yield an average rating of μ_S = 62.4 and μ_A=82.4, actually 12.4pts and 28.4pts above their total universe averages. This suggests that the most frequently included companies in global SRI funds are at least more sustainable than the average company.

In comparison to Table 19.6, Table 19.7 reports the 20 most frequently counted companies in the Top holdings of global conventional funds. Google is once more at the top of the list and included in the Top holdings of 25 out of 119 global conventional funds. When looking at the average ESG ratings of the 20 listed companies, it can be observed that the Oekom average for the conventional fund list ($\mu_{O;C}$ = 55.9) is above that of the SRI fund list ($\mu_{O;SRI}$ = 54.7). This is astonishing, as one would expect that the Top holdings of SRI funds are on average more sustainable than those of non-SRI funds.

Using Sustainalytics' and ASSET4's rating data, this expectation is fulfilled with $\mu_{S;C} = 49.2 < \mu_{S;ESG} = 62.4$ and $\mu_{A;C} = 75.6 < \mu_{A;ESG} = 82.4$. The average ratings of the frequently included companies in conventional funds are 0.8pts below the total universe averages of Sustainalytics and 21.6pts above the averages of ASSET4's total universe.

In order to test if investors would be able to distinguish SRI and non-SRI funds by the Top portfolio holdings, the two company lists will be compared with each other. The companies that show up in only one of the lists are again marked in the above tables by gray-shaded fields. More than half of the listed companies (11 out of 20) show up under the most frequently counted companies in the top holdings of SRI *and* non-SRI funds. Investors may only be able to distinguish the two types of funds by the fact that global SRI funds, similar to European sustainability funds, seem to avoid companies that may cause environmental harm. For example, companies like Gazprom, Taiwan Semiconductor Manufacturing Company and Chevron are not that frequently included in SRI funds. However, following this line of argument, one may also call into question why Exxon Mobil, a multinational oil and gas company, is more often included in the Top fund holdings of SRI than non-SRI funds.

To summarize, the global fund analysis also shows that the portfolio holdings of both fund types are very similar and the fund lists can hardly be distinguished by investors at first glance.

5.2.2 Research question 2: comparison of average ESG rankings

In the next step, the holding-based results are further tested using a fund ranking analysis. All funds are ranked based on their total ESG fund ratings. The ranking is normalized and equally distributed between 0 (fund with worst ESG rating) and 1 (fund with best ESG rating). If SRI

Table 19.8 European funds sorted in ESG Deciles (from '0–0.1' = lowest ESG value until '0.9–1.0' = highest ESG value) by rating agency

European Funds Sorted in Deciles	Oekom		Sustainalytics		ASSET4	
	Conventional Funds	SRI Funds	Conventional Funds	SRI Funds	Conventional Funds	SRI Funds
0.0–0.1	19.0%	1.7%	20.7%	0.0%	16.7%	3.3%
0.1–0.2	13.8%	6.8%	15.5%	5.1%	20.0%	0.0%
0.2–0.3	13.8%	5.1%	12.1%	6.8%	6.7%	13.3%
0.3–0.4	5.2%	15.3%	12.1%	8.5%	11.7%	8.3%
0.4–0.5	13.8%	5.1%	13.8%	5.1%	10.0%	10.0%
0.5–0.6	10.3%	10.2%	10.3%	10.2%	5.0%	15.0%
0.6–0.7	6.9%	13.6%	3.4%	16.9%	8.3%	11.7%
0.7–0.8	5.2%	13.6%	5.2%	13.6%	8.3%	11.7%
0.8–0.9	5.2%	15.3%	3.4%	16.9%	8.3%	11.7%
0.9–1.0	6.9%	13.6%	3.4%	16.9%	5.0%	15.0%
Mean Rank	0.39%	0.61%	0.34%	0.65%	0.40%	0.60%

Notes: The percent values show how many percent of the funds are in the respective decile. The 'Mean Rank' is the arithmetic mean of the ranking position.

Source: Author's calculations.

funds live up to their names, it is expected that they have higher ESG rankings than conventional funds. In order to test this hypothesis, SRI and conventional funds are clustered into deciles based on their rankings, whereby the percentage of funds in each cluster is calculated. This ranking analysis is carried out separately for each rating agency and the results are summarized in Table 19.8.

The first column shows the ten clusters between 0 and 1 and the following columns report the percentage of conventional and SRI funds in the respective deciles for each of the rating agencies. For example, the fund rankings based on Oekom's ESG rating data indicate that 19 percent of all analyzed conventional funds show up in the lowest decile, while only 1.7 percent of the SRI funds are ranked in this decile. A similar distribution in this decile is reported when the fund rankings are based on Sustainalytics' and ASSET4's data. Based on Oekom's and ASSET4's ratings, around 65 percent, and based on Sustainalytics' ratings even 74 percent of all conventional funds rank in the bottom half (0–0.5). In contrast, SRI funds are primarily ranked in the high deciles and only a few sustainability funds rank in the lower deciles.

The ranking-based analysis indicates that SRI funds have on average higher ESG rankings than their conventional counterparts. The average rank of SRI funds is between 0.60 and 0.65 ($\mu_O^{SRI} = 0.61$, $\mu_S^{SRI} = 0.65$, $\mu_A^{SRI} = 0.60$) depending on the rating agency. The respective average rank of standard funds is between 0.34 and 0.40 ($\mu_O^C = 0.39$, $\mu_S^C = 0.34$, $\mu_A^C = 0.40$).

In order to further illustrate this result, the probability is calculated that an investor, who randomly chooses one of the European SRI funds, gets a higher ranked fund than an investor who randomly chooses one of the European conventional funds. To this end 50,000 pairs of SRI and non-SRI funds are drawn randomly for each rating agency. Based on Oekom, Sustainalytics and ASSET4, the SRI funds have a higher ranking in 72.2 percent, 80.8 percent and 69.7 percent of all cases, respectively.

Similar to the European fund analysis, the fund ranking analysis is used to investigate the global funds. The global SRI and non-SRI funds are clustered into 10-quantiles based on their ESG rankings, whereby the percentage of funds in each group is calculated. The results of the ranking analysis based on the total ESG fund ratings of Oekom, Sustainalytics and ASSET4 are summarized in Table 19.9.

Table 19.9 Global funds sorted in ESG deciles (from '0−0.1' = lowest ESG value until '0.9−1.0' = highest ESG value) by rating agency

European Funds Sorted in Deciles	Oekom		Sustainalytics		ASSET4	
	Conventional Funds	SRI Funds	Conventional Funds	SRI Funds	Conventional Funds	SRI Funds
0.0−0.1	14.9	5.1	16.4	5.1	13.7	6.8
0.1−0.2	14.0	6.0	16.4	2.6	18.8	0.8
0.2−0.3	14.0	6.0	12.1	7.7	13.7	6.8
0.3−0.4	9.6	10.3	8.6	11.1	7.7	11.9
0.4−0.5	8.8	11.1	10.3	9.4	9.4	10.2
0.5−0.6	8.8	11.1	9.5	11.1	6.0	14.4
0.6−0.7	9.6	10.3	6.0	13.7	7.7	11.9
0.7−0.8	7.0	12.8	10.3	9.4	12.0	8.5
0.8−0.9	8.8	11.1	5.2	14.5	6.0	13.6
0.9−1.0	4.4	16.2	5.2	15.4	5.1	15.3
Mean Rank	0.41	0.58	0.40	0.60	0.41	0.59

Notes: The percent values show how many percent of the funds are in the respective decile. The 'Mean Rank' is the arithmetic mean of the ranking position.

Source: Author's calculations.

For each decile between 0 and 1, the percentage of conventional and SRI funds for each rating agency is reported. While 14 percent to 16 percent of the conventional funds are ranked in the lowest decile (0–0.1), only 5 percent to 7 percent of the SRI funds are ranked in that decile depending on the rating agency. A similar trend is observed in the second and third worst categories (0.1–0.3). Based on Oekom's ratings, around 61 percent, and based on Sustainalytics' and ASSET4's ratings, even around 64 percent of all conventional funds rank in the bottom half (0–0.5). In contrast, SRI funds are primarily ranked in the high deciles. The lower the decile, the fewer SRI funds are in it.

The ranking-based analysis of global funds comes to the same conclusion as the European fund analysis, namely that sustainability funds have on average higher ESG rankings than their conventional counterparts. The average rank of global SRI funds is between 0.58 and 0.60 ($\mu_O^{SRI} = 0.58$, $\mu_S^{SRI} = 0.60$, $\mu_A^{SRI} = 0.59$) depending on the rating agency. The respective average rank of conventional funds is between 0.40 and 0.41 ($\mu_O^{C} = 0.41$, $\mu_S^{C} = 0.40$, $\mu_A^{C} = 0.41$).

One can translate this result again into the probability for an investor, who randomly chooses one of the global SRI funds, to get a higher ranked fund than an investor who randomly chooses one of the global non-SRI funds. Again, 50,000 pairs of global SRI and non-SRI funds are drawn randomly for each rating agency. The SRI fund investor would invest in 68.1 percent of all cases in a higher ranked fund when Oekom's rating data is used. The respective probabilities that the investor chooses a better ESG ranked fund using Sustainalytics' and ASSET4's data sets are 67.0 percent and 69.3 percent, respectively.

All in all, the ranking-based analysis for European and global funds finds no evidence that sustainability funds are standard funds in disguise, but proves that these funds have on average higher ESG rankings. Nevertheless, sustainability investors should take a closer look at ESG fund ratings because more than one third of the analyzed SRI funds are ranked in the bottom half (0–0.5).

5.2.3 Research question 3: are ESG rating differences significant?

The results so far have given an impression of the similarities and differences between SRI and non-SRI funds. While the top 10 portfolio holdings of both fund types show significant overlaps, SRI funds obtain on average better ESG rankings than conventional funds. In the last step of the analysis, a formal test is conducted in order to investigate if the rating differences between SRI and non-SRI funds are statistically significant. This test is not only performed for the total ESG ratings of the three agencies, but also for each pillar score. The results of the cross-sectional

Table 19.10 ESG ratings of European SRI and conventional funds by rating agency for the total rating and sub-ratings

European Funds	Category (j)	$\beta_{0;j}$	$\beta_{1;j}$	R^2
Oekom	Environmental	57.234 ***	2.546 ***	0.145
	Social	56.732 ***	1.315 ***	0.102
	Total Score	57.082 ***	1.940 ***	0.139
Sustainalytics	Environmental	69.074 ***	6.784 ***	0.148
	Social	65.181 ***	6.416 ***	0.221
	Governance	66.351 ***	5.190 ***	0.133
	Total Score	66.869 ***	6.130 ***	0.233
ASSET4	Environmental	82.214 ***	4.779 **	0.085
	Social	81.002 ***	6.546 ***	0.135
	Governance	68.582 ***	2.410 ***	0.020
	Total Score	77.482 ***	4.363 **	0.082

* p <0.05, ** p <0.01, *** p <0.001

Notes: The analysis is based on the regression equation: $Rating_{i;J} = \beta_{0;j} + \beta_{1;j} * D_i + \varepsilon_{i;J}$. With $D_i = 1$ if ESG Fund and $D_i = 0$ if Conventional Fund. $\beta_{0;j}$ is the average rating of Conventional Fund and $\beta_{1;j}$ is the difference of the average rating of ESG Funds relative to Conventional Funds. A positive $\beta_{1;j}$ means that the ESG funds exhibit a higher average ESG rating than the Conventional Funds. The significance levels are 5% (*), 1% (**) and 0.1% (***).

Source: Author's calculations.

regressions for the European fund universe following equation (2) are summarized in Table 19.10.

The first column shows the agencies that provide the ESG corporate ratings applied to the fund holdings. The second column lists the categories (pillar and total ESG score) in which the funds are rated. The estimated constant $\beta_{0;j}$ is reported in column 3 and takes the value of the average conventional fund score in the respective category *j*. The coefficient $\beta_{1;j}$ in column 4 measures the rating difference between SRI and non-SRI funds as the dummy variable D_i takes on the value of 1 if a fund is an SRI fund and the value 0 otherwise. ***, ** and * indicate the significance of the constant $\beta_{0;j}$ and the coefficient $\beta_{1;j}$ at the 0.1 percent, 1 percent and 5 percent level. For reasons of completeness, the last column shows the R^2 of the respective regression.

Table 19.10 reveals that the average score of European conventional funds using Oekom's rating data is around 57pts for both pillar scores ($\beta_{0;E}$ = 57.234, $\beta_{0;S}$ = 56.732) and the total ESG score ($\beta_{0;ESG}$ = 57.082).

The parameter of interest, $\beta_{1;j}$, is significantly positive at the 0.1 percent level for all Oekom scores ($\beta_{1;E} = 2.546$, $\beta_{1;S} = 1.315$, $\beta_{1;ESG} = 1.940$). Using Sustainalytics' ESG ratings, the average conventional fund total score is around 67pts ($\beta_{0;ESG} = 66.869$), with higher average scores in the environmental pillar ($\beta_{0;E} = 69.072$) and lower ratings in the social and governance pillars ($\beta_{0;S} = 65.181$, $\beta_{0;G} = 66.351$). SRI funds show significantly positive deviations (at the 0.1 percent level) in all pillar scores ($\beta_{1;E} = 6.784$, $\beta_{1;S} = 6.416$, $\beta_{1;G} = 5.190$) and in the total ESG score ($\beta_{1;ESG} = 6.130$). The European conventional funds obtain an average total ESG score of 77pts ($\beta_{0;ESG} = 77.482$) using ASSET4's rating data. They score $\beta_{0;E} = 82.214$ and $\beta_{0;S} = 81.002$ in the environmental and social pillar and $\beta_{0;G} = 68.582$ in the governance pillar. The sustainable counterparts have significantly positive coefficients in the social score (at 0.1 percent level) and in the environmental and total score (at the 1 percent level). The impact of the ESG dummy D_i is not significantly different from 0 for the governance pillar.

Based on Table 19.10, one can conclude that SRI funds have significantly higher ratings than conventional funds. This result holds not only for the total ESG scores, but for all pillar scores. The rating differences between SRI and non-SRI funds are smaller when Oekom's ratings are applied, compared to Sustainalytics' and ASSET4's fund rating differences. This can be explained by the fact that Oekom's rating distribution has a significant lower range and standard deviation. In contrast, Sustainalytics' and ASSET4's fund rating distributions are widely spread, driven by higher ranges and standard deviations on the corporate ESG rating level.

Next, it is tested whether similar conclusions can be drawn for the global fund data set. The results for the global funds are shown in Table 19.11.

The cross-sectional regressions using Oekom's rating data show that the average total ESG score of global conventional funds is around 55pts ($\beta_{0;ESG} = 55.471$), with an average environmental score of $\beta_{0;E} = 56.037$ and a social score of $\beta_{0;S} = 54.918$. The coefficient $\beta_{1;j}$ is significantly positive at the 0.1 percent level for all three scores ($\beta_{1;E} = 1.793$, $\beta_{1;S} = 2.011$, $\beta_{1;ESG} = 1.959$). This means that a global SRI fund is rated on average approximately 2pts better than a conventional fund by Oekom, which is in line with the difference between both fund types in the European fund data set. Using Sustainalytics' ESG ratings, the average conventional fund total score is around 53pts ($\beta_{0;ESG} = 52.818$), with higher average scores in the environmental pillar ($\beta_{0;E} = 56.492$) and lower ratings in the social and governance pillars ($\beta_{0;S} = 50.504$, $\beta_{0;G} = 51.457$). The sustainable counterparts show significantly positive coefficients (at 0.1 percent level) in all three pillar scores ($\beta_{1;E} = 7.379$, $\beta_{1;S} = 7.439$, $\beta_{1;G} = 4.722$) and the total ESG score ($\beta_{1;ESG} = 6.513$). The global conventional funds obtain an

Table 19.11 ESG ratings of global SRI and conventional funds by rating agency for the total rating and sub-ratings

Global Funds	Category (j)	$\beta_{0;j}$	$\beta_{1;j}$	R^2
Oekom	Environmental	56.037 ***	1.793 ***	0.054
	Social	54.918 ***	2.011 ***	0.088
	Total Score	55.471 ***	1.959 ***	0.084
Sustainalytics	Environmental	56.492 ***	7.379 ***	0.092
	Social	50.504 ***	7.439 ***	0.107
	Governance	51.457 ***	4.722 ***	0.058
	Total Score	52.818 ***	6.513***	0.117
ASSET4	Environmental	68.666 ***	7.525 ***	0.106
	Social	65.697 ***	7.328 ***	0.092
	Governance	66.260 ***	3.296 *	0.022
	Total Score	66.874 ***	6.050 ***	0.104

*p<0.05, ** p<0.01, ***p<0.001

Notes: The analysis is based on the regression equation: Ratingi;j = $\beta_{0;j} + \beta_{1;j} * D_i + \varepsilon_{i;j}$. With $D_i = 1$ if ESG Fund and $D_i = 0$ if Conventional Fund. $\beta_{0;j}$ is the average rating of Conventional Fund and $\beta_{1;j}$ is the difference of the average rating of ESG Funds relative to Conventional Funds. A positive $\beta_{1;j}$ means that the ESG funds exhibit a higher average ESG rating than the Conventional Funds. The significance levels are 5% (*), 1% (**), and 0.1% (***).

Source: Author's calculations.

average total score of 67pts ($\beta_{0;ESG} = 66.874$) using ASSET4's rating data. They score $\beta_{0;E} = 68.666$ and $\beta_{0;S} = 65.697$ in the environmental and social pillar and $\beta_{0;G} = 66.260$ in the governance pillar. The SRI funds show significantly positive deviations at the 0.1 percent level in the environmental ($\beta_{1;E} = 7.525$), social ($\beta_{1;S} = 7.328$) and total ESG scores ($\beta_{1;ESG} = 6.050$) and at the 5 percent level in the governance rating ($\beta_{1;G} = 3.296$).

Three main conclusions can be drawn from Table 19.11. First, global SRI funds have significantly higher ESG ratings than standard funds. This result is very robust as it holds for all pillars and the total ESG scores as well as across the different ratings applied. Secondly, the absolute rating averages of conventional funds ($\beta_{0;Oekom} = 55.471$, $\beta_{0;Sustainalytics} = 52.818$, $\beta_{0;ASSET4} = 66.874$) are all above the universe averages of the respective rating agency ($\mu_O = 55.0$, $\mu_S = 50.0$, $\mu_A = 54.0$). This finding suggests that conventional fund managers also overweigh companies with above average ESG ratings, being driven either by sustainability considerations or more likely by attractive risk-return profiles. Thirdly, rating differences between the two types of funds measured by the coefficient $\beta_{0;j}$, are smaller for the Oekom fund ratings compared to the differences when Sustainalytics' or ASSET4's ratings are applied. This is driven by the characteristics of Oekom's ESG ratings, i.e. low ranges and standard deviations. Consequently, the fund rating distributions for global funds are also expected to show lower ranges and rating differences between both fund types. The fund rating distributions of Sustainalytics and ASSET4 are widely spread, driven by higher ranges and standard deviations on the corporate ESG rating level.

In summary, the results of the European and global fund analysis strengthen the findings of the previous sections that SRI funds are not standard funds in disguise. They have on average higher ESG rankings compared to their conventional counterparts. In addition, it seems that European funds (both SRI funds and conventional funds) are on average more sustainable than global funds.

6. RESEARCH SUMMARY

This section summarizes the main analysis results by following the three research questions.

The study focuses on equity mutual funds with a geographical focus either on the European area or on a global investment universe. For both groups of funds, those with the classification 'ESG' and 'Socially Responsible', are compared with conventional funds. The analysis aims to examine whether sustainable investment funds are conventional funds in disguise or whether they live up to their names. Three specific research questions have been analyzed and the main findings will be summarized below.

Research Question 1: *Are the portfolios of SRI funds different from the holdings of conventional funds when focusing on the Top fund holdings?*

The study analyzed and compared the equity holdings which are most frequently included under the Top holdings of both types of funds. More than half of the most frequently counted companies in global conventional funds also appeared on the list of SRI funds, with the European fund analysis displaying even more matches. Therefore, at first glance, an investor may have difficulties distinguishing SRI and non-SRI funds by the Top fund holdings.

Socially responsible investors could be satisfied with this outcome, if all of these companies were sustainable companies with respect to the ESG criteria. However, the ESG corporate ratings of the three agencies are very mixed for some of the companies, and SRI funds can be criticized for frequently investing in companies that have relatively low ESG ratings.

On the other hand, one could give SRI fund managers credit for excluding companies from the investment universe which generate revenues from alcohol and tobacco or cause environmental harm. However, even here, negative examples were found. This may be explained by the best-in-class concept used by many sustainable investment funds.

In short, at the first glance, the fund holdings of SRI and non-SRI funds are very similar. From an investor's point of view, it seems doubtful that SRI funds really invest in more sustainable companies than standard funds when looking at the Top fund holdings.

Research Question 2: *Do SRI funds have higher ESG rankings than conventional funds?*

In the second step of the analysis, all funds were ranked based on their total ESG ratings. The rankings are distributed between 0 (worst ESG rated fund) and 1 (best ESG rated fund). The study compared the percentage of sustainable and conventional funds in ten calculated quantiles. If SRI funds invest in line with their objectives, they are expected to have on average higher ESG rankings than standard funds.

This hypothesis was confirmed for the European as well as the global fund data set, in which SRI funds ranked on average around 0.20 better than their conventional counterparts, independent of the rating agency. While more than 60 percent of the conventional funds ranked in the bottom half (0–0.5) at any given point in time, SRI funds are primarily ranked in the higher deciles. The lower the decile, the fewer SRI funds are in it.

Nevertheless, from an investor's point of view, it is worthwhile looking at the ranking of the SRI fund of her choice as there are also sustainable funds that rank even below conventional funds. For the European data set an investor choosing randomly amongst SRI and conventional funds has a probability of about 30 percent and for the global funds about 33 percent of selecting an SRI fund with an ESG rating that is below the conventional fund.

Research Question 3: *If SRI funds have higher rankings, are the absolute rating differences between SRI and conventional funds statistically significant?*

While the previous research findings suggest that SRI funds have on average higher ESG rankings compared to non-SRI funds, a formal test, analyzing whether the differences in the ratings are statistically significant, was conducted in the last step of the analysis. Cross-sectional regressions were run for each category *j* by rating agency yielding a constant $\beta_{0;j}$ and a coefficient $\beta_{1;j}$ (see equation (1)).

The constant $\beta_{0;j}$ reports the average ESG rating of conventional funds, which is higher for the European fund data set compared to the global funds, irrespective of the rating agency.

The parameter of main interest, $\beta_{1;j,}$ measures the rating difference between SRI and non-SRI funds for the analyzed sub-scores and the total ESG rating. If socially responsible investment funds keep to what their names promise, the coefficient $\beta_{1;j}$ should be significantly positive. This hypothesis was confirmed for the total ESG ratings of the European as well as global fund data sets for all ESG ratings applied. In general, SRI funds are rated better than their conventional benchmarks, independent of the geographical focus of the fund. In addition, the reported coefficients $\beta_{1;j}$ are not only significantly positive for the total ESG scores, but for almost all sub-scores analyzed.

At first glance, the absolute rating differences between both fund types seem to be small. This is mainly due to the best-in-class approach applied by many SRI funds. Following this concept, sustainability funds may invest in the best rated company of an industry with on average poor sustainability measures, while conventional funds may also include, for example, the second and third best companies. Thus, SRI funds are only able to outperform conventional funds with respect to ESG ratings by some rating points (between the first and second/third best company), as the ESG company ratings in one industry are often narrowly distributed. Hence, larger rating differences between the two fund types cannot be expected as long as most funds rely on best-in-class concepts.

Nevertheless, the cross-sectional regressions show that the rating differences between SRI funds and conventional funds are highly significantly positive, i.e. SRI funds are not conventional funds in disguise but exhibit a significantly higher weight on those companies with a relatively high ESG rating.

NOTES

1. According to the Global Sustainable Investment Review 2014 (GSIA, 2014), this represents 30.2% of the total global assets managed professionally (excluding Latin American regions).
2. See http://www.stoxx.com
3. This universe, consisting of 458 companies, is referred to as the 'Oekom Matched

Universe' as the Oekom universe with the lowest number of rated companies is used as the basis.
4. The process of replacing missing data with the mean of that variable for all other cases is called 'mean imputation'.
5. The analyzed categories *j* are the three pillars ('E' = environmental pillar; 'S' = social pillar; 'G' = governance pillar) and the total score ('ESG').
6. Number of exclusions from the European fund universe: Oekom and Sustainalytics = 1 SRI, 2 conventional, ASSET4: no exclusion. Number of exclusions from global fund universe: Oekom = 2 SRI, 5 conventional, Sustainalytics: 2 SRI, 3 conventional, ASSET4: 1 SRI and 2 conventional funds.

REFERENCES

Barracchini, C. and M. Addessi (2012), 'Ethical Portfolio Theory: A New Course', *Journal of Management and Sustainability*, **2**(2), 35–42.

Bello, Z. (2005), 'Socially Responsible Investing and Portfolio Diversification', *Journal of Financial Research*, **28**(1), 41–57.

Benson, K., T. Brailsford and J. Humphrey (2006), 'Do Socially Responsible Fund Managers Really Invest Differently?', *Journal of Business Ethics*, **65**(4), 337–357.

Chieffe, N. and K. Lahey (2009), 'Helping Clients Select SRI Mutual Funds and Firms', *Journal of Financial Planning*, **22**(2), 60–70.

Derwall, J., K. Koedijk and J. Ter Horst (2011), 'A Tale of Values-Driven and Profit-Seeking Social Investors', *Journal of Banking & Finance*, **35**(8), 2137–47.

Dorfleitner, G. and S. Utz (2012), 'Safety First Portfolio Choice Based on Financial and Sustainability Returns', *European Journal of Operational Research*, **221**(1), 155–164.

Faust, M. and S. Scholz (2008), 'Nachhaltige Geldanlagen', in M. Faust and S. Scholz (eds), *Nachhaltige Geldanlagen: Produkte, Strategien und Beratungskonzepte*, Frankfurt am Main, Germany: Frankfurt School Verlag, pp. 133–156.

Global Sustainable Investment Alliance (GSIA) (2014), *Global Sustainable Investment Review 2014*, accessed 11 January 2017 at http://www.ussif.org/Files/Publications/GSIA_Review.pdf

Kempf, A. and P. Osthoff (2007), 'SRI Funds: Nomen est Omen', *Journal of Business Finance & Accounting*, **35**(9–10), 1276–1294.

Mackenzie, C. (1998), 'The Choice of Criteria in Ethical Investment', *Business Ethics: A European Review*, **7**(2), 81–86.

Observatoire sur la Responsabilité Sociétale des Entreprises (ORSE) (2012), *Guide to Sustainability Analysis Organisations: Sustainalytics*, Paris, France: ORSE.

Oekom Research AG (2014), *Oekom Corporate Rating: IBM*, Munich, Germany: Oekom Research AG.

Osthoff, P. (2016), 'What Matters to SRI Investors?', in T. Hebb, J. Hawley, A. Hoepner, A. Neher and D. Wood (eds), *The Routledge Handbook of Responsible Investment*, London: Routledge, pp. 705–723.

Schroeder, M. (2014), 'Financial Effects of Corporate Social Responsibility: A Literature Review', *Journal of Sustainable Finance & Investment*, **4**(4), 337–350.

Schwartz, M. (2003), 'The "Ethics" of Ethical Investing', *Journal of Business Ethics*, **43**(3), 195–213.

Statman, M. (2006), 'Socially Responsible Indexes: Composition, Performance, and Tracking Error', *Journal of Portfolio Management*, **32**(3), 100–109.

Sustainalytics (2014), *HSBC Holdings plc ESG Report*, Amsterdam, Netherlands: Sustainalytics.

Utz, S. and M. Wimmer (2014), 'Are They Any Good At All? A Financial and Ethical Analysis of Socially Responsible Mutual Funds', *Journal of Asset Management*, **15**(1), 72–82.

van den Heuvel, R. (2012), 'How Robust are CSR Benchmarks? Comparing ASSET4 with Sustainalytics', Tilburg University, Netherlands, accessed 11 January 2017 at http://arno.uvt.nl/show.cgi?fid=127705

Von Flotow, P. (2008), 'Nachhaltige Publikumsfonds im deutschsprachigen Markt: Konzepte und gute Gründe', in M. Faust and S. Scholz (eds), *Nachhaltige Geldanlagen: Produkte, Strategien und Beratungskonzepte*, Frankfurt am Main, Germany: Frankfurt School Verlag, pp. 293–309.

Wimmer, M. (2013), 'ESG-persistence in Socially Responsible Mutual Funds', *Journal of Management and Sustainability*, **3**(1), 9–15.

Windorfer, R. (2011), 'Das Nachhaltigskeitsrating der oekom research AG' (PowerPoint presentation from 18 July 2011), Munich, Germany: TU Munich, accessed 11 January 2017 at: http://fwl.wzw.tum.de/fileadmin/Downloads/TUM_Bwl/TUM_2011_07_18_RW.ppt.pdf

APPENDIX

Table 19A.1 Fund selection criteria for building the research sample and results for the number of funds

Fund Selection	Filter	Criterion	SRI Funds	Conventional Funds
European Funds	Market Status	Active	224,669	224,669
	Fund Primary Share Class	Yes	105,824	105,824
	Fund Type	Open-End Funds	76,834	76,834
	Asset Class Focus	Equity	18,766	18,766
	Asset Class Allocation	Equity > 95%	11,795	11,795
	Fund Geographical Focus	European Region, Eurozone, European Union	1,209	1,209
	General Attribute	+/− ESG, Socially Responsible	67	175
	Adjustments	After Exclusions/ Random Selection	60	60
Global Funds	Market Status	Active	224,669	224,669
	Fund Primary Share Class	Yes	105,824	105,824
	Fund Type	Open-End Funds	76,834	76,834
	Asset Class Focus	Equity	18,766	18,766
	Asset Class Allocation	Equity > 95%/ Equity > 100%	11,795	1,510
	Fund Geographical Focus	Global, International	3,144	375
	General Attribute	+/− ESG, Socially Responsible	130	362
	Adjustments	After Exclusions/ Random Selection	119	119

Source: Author, based on data from Bloomberg data base, https://www.bloomberg.com (accessed 2014).

20. Socio-psychological motives of socially responsible investors

Julia M. Puaschunder

1. BACKGROUND

In the aftermath of the world financial crisis and the subsequent age of austerity, social responsibility has evolved into an *en vogue* topic for the corporate world and the finance sector. Contrary to classic finance theory that sees investments as primarily based on expected utility and volatility, the consideration of social responsibility in financial investment decisions has gained unprecedented momentum (Aja, Bustillo, Darity, & Hamilton, 2013; *The Economist*, 2008; Boyer, 2012; Dymski, 2013; Ghilarducci, 2013; *The Wall Street Journal*, August 21, 2008).

Financial Social Responsibility is primarily addressed in Socially Responsible Investment (SRI), which integrates personal values and social concerns into financial investments (Schueth, 2003). SRI is an asset allocation style, by which securities are not only selected on the basis of profit return and risk probabilities, but mainly in regards to the social and environmental contributions of the issuing entities (Beltratti, 2003; Williams, 2005).

Socially responsible investors allocate financial resources based on profit maximization goals as well as societal implications. Pursuing economic and social value maximization alike, socially responsible investors incorporate CSR into financial decision making (Renneboog, Horst, & Zhang, 2007; Schueth, 2003; Steurer, Martinuzzi, & Margula, 2012). Socially conscientious investors fund socially responsible corporations based on evaluations of the CSR performance as well as the social and environmental risks of corporate conduct. Thereby, SRI becomes an investment philosophy that combines profit maximization with intrinsic and social values (Ahmad, 2008; Livesey, 2002; Matten & Crane, 2005; Wolff, 2002). SRI allows the pursuit of financial goals while catalyzing positive change in the corporate, finance and political arenas alongside minimizing financial crises' emergent risks (Centeno, Cinlar, Cloud, Creager, DiMaggio, Dixit, Elga, Felten, James, Katz, Keohane, Leonard, Massey, Mian, Mian, Oppenheimer, Shafir, & Shapiro, 2013; Centeno & Tham, 2012; Mohr, Webb, & Harris, 2001; Schueth, 2003).

The various forms of expression of SRI leverage Financial Social Responsibility into a multi-stakeholder phenomenon. By combining social, environmental and financial aspects in investment options, SRI encompasses a broad variety of stakeholder interests (Dupré, Girerd-Potin, & Kassoua, 2008; Harvey, 2008; Steurer, 2010). Building the relationship between the financial world and society, SRI embraces multiple stakeholders, ranging from *economic* (e.g., institutional and private investors), *organizational* (e.g., labor union representatives, banking executives, fiduciaries) and *societal* (e.g., representatives of international organizations and non-governmental organizations, governmental officials, public servants, nonprofits, media representatives, academics) *actors* (Binder, Kriebaum, Marboe, Nowak, Reinisch, & Wittich, 2014; Fraser, 2014).

Today the range of shareholder engagement possibilities is more sophisticated than ever and trends forecast a further maturation of SRI. The SRI market has reached unprecedented diversity, featuring a wide range of multi-faceted SRI activities and a variety of stakeholder engagement possibilities. Financial Social Responsibility comprises commercial SRI retail to the public in socially screened separate accounts, mutual and pension funds, bonds and community development, as well as hybrid instruments that undergo financial and ethical value tests (Mathieu, 2000; Rosen, Sandler, & Shani, 1991; Sparkes & Cowton, 2004). The establishment and advancement of SRI retail and the adoption of SRI by major institutional investors has matured SRI from a marginal to a more mainstreamed asset allocation style (Mathieu, 2000; Rosen et al., 1991; Sparkes & Cowton, 2004). SRI has been adopted by a growing proportion of investors around the world. In light of the growing attention paid to climate stability, the incorporation of social, environmental and global governance factors into investment options has increasingly become an element of fiduciary duty, particularly for investors with long-term horizons that oversee international portfolios (Barnosky, Matzke, Tomiya, Wogan, Swartz, Quental, Marshall, McGuire, Lindsey, Maguire, Mersey, & Ferrer, 2011; Foley, 2009; Puaschunder, 2016a).

The rise of SRI has been accompanied by a change in the qualitative nature of social investments for the sake of doing good to others and the environment (Foley, 2009). The current SRI notion is very different from the earlier 'ethical investment' based on negative screenings (McCann, Solomon, & Solomon, 2003). Although a moral touch remains, the establishment of SRI retail funds and the adoption of SRI by institutional investors have turned SRI into a proactive positive screening option. The growth of Financial Social Responsibility expressions has transformed SRI into an investment philosophy adopted by a growing proportion of investment firms and governmental agencies around the world (Knoll,

2008; Mohr et al., 2001; Sparkes & Cowton, 2004). The sophistication of socially responsible shareholder engagement has triggered the emergence of social and environmental stock exchange rating agencies, SRI impact measurement tools, corporate social and environmental reporting and certifications on social, ethical and environmental corporate performance (Steurer, Margula, & Martinuzzi, 2008). This trend goes hand in hand with business professionals and analysts monitoring, as well as academia documenting Financial Social Responsibility.

Information on the socio-psychological motives of socially responsible investors will add behavioral insights to classic financial market theories. Potential underlying SRI causes and triggers will be presented to become empirically tested in behavioral economics research on Financial Social Responsibility. Gaining a more sophisticated understanding of Financial Social Responsibility will help in finding repeatable patterns and crafting policies to trigger SRI within financial markets, and thus foster a more effective social responsibility implementation. In particular, depicting socio-psychological SRI factors may help to delineate triggers and impact success factors for SRI.

Overall, the research is targeted at unraveling the dynamics of social responsibility to increase the social conscientiousness of the finance world. Engaging in the current discussion on Financial Social Responsibility will allow predicting future global trends in order to aid a productive interplay of public and private sector forces. Research on SRI in the aftermath of the 2008/09 World Financial Crisis will help in understanding SRI as a means to re-establish trust in financial global governance to ensure financial market stability as a prerequisite for sustainable market economies and a future guarantee of societal progress (Puaschunder, 2015c). Contributing to a successful rise of social responsibility within modern market economies is aimed at SRI becoming a mainstream feature of financial decision making serving the greater goal of fostering positive societal change.

2. SOLUTIONS AND RECOMMENDATIONS

Traditional financial market theory holds that investment decisions are based on rationality (Baron, 2000; Carswell, 2002; Michelson, Wailes, van der Laan, & Frost, 2004). Classical portfolio theory depicts investment allocations dependent on profit maximization of expected utility and volatility (Dupré et al., 2008; Harvey, 2008). The recent boom in socially responsible investment options, but also the heightened attention to Financial Social Responsibility in the aftermath of the 2008/09 financial meltdown, has leveraged the demand to understand irrational socio-psychological motives of investment behavior with an unprecedented momentum (Beltratti, 2003). With the current body of SRI studies focusing on the supply side and financial performance, scarce is the understanding of socio-psychological motives for SRI (Brenner, 2001; De la Cuesta & Valor, 2007; Mohr et al., 2001).

Investors potentially consider SRI for economic, psychological and social reasons (Slaper & Hall, 2011; Slawinski & Bansal, 2012). SRI grants multifaceted utilities to investors – some of them rational, others less in sync with classic *homo oeconomicus* assumptions. Monetary gratification may very likely be accompanied by socio-psychological values and human-imbued wishes for compliance with common goals (Waldman, Siegel, & Javidian, 2004). The underlying socio-psychological motives for investors exhibiting social responsibility and integrating ethicality in their portfolio choice are as yet opaque. As classic finance theories have blacked out moral and ethical dimensions, a descriptive framework for Financial Social Responsibility has yet to be built (Dupré et al., 2008). In a first attempt to shed light on socio-psychological SRI facets, the following investor motives are proposed and described in detail in the rest of the chapter:

1. The intention to maximize profits.
2. Altruism as a concern for the societal well-being.
3. The need for innovation and entrepreneurship.
4. Strategic leadership advantages through social status elevation.
5. Utility derived from transparency and information disclosure.
6. Self-enhancement through identification and self-consistency.
7. Expression of social values.
8. Long-term considerations.

3. THE INTENTION TO MAXIMIZE PROFITS

Empirical investigations of the relationship between SRI and profitability offer no generalizable pattern (Butz, 2003; Hamilton, Hoje, & Statman, 1993; McWilliams & Siegel, 2000). Up to now no absolute answer concerning the performance of SRI in relation to the overall market has been identified (Dixon, 2002; Jones, van der Laan, Frost, & Loftus, 2008; Little, 2008; Mackey, Mackey, & Barney, 2004). While some evidence supports SRI (e.g., Kempf & Osthoff, 2007), others see it as underperforming in the market (e.g., Fowler & Hope, 2007), and some studies report no difference between SRI and conventional market indices at all (e.g.,

Abramson & Chung, 2000; Boutin-Dufresne & Savaria, 2004). There is no definitive answer as to whether SRI is associated with an increase or decrease in shareholder return and volatility (Berman, Wicks, Kotha, & Jones, 1999). Sometimes socially responsible financial market options increase shareholder value, in some cases SRI reduces shareholder profits, and sometimes SRI does not deviate from ordinary financial options (Hamilton et al., 1993; Maux & Saout, 2004).

This inconsistency of findings is attributed to manifold SRI forms of expression and measurement deficiencies. Positively screened SRI funds – that more likely feature IT-technology and alternative energy industries attracting innovative venture capital – tend to be more volatile, yet, if successful, offer high profitability; for example, solar energy funds have significantly outperformed the market in recent years and remained relatively stable during the 2008/09 World Financial Crisis.

As for excluding high-return, high-volatility industries such as petroleum, defense and addictive substances, negatively screened options are more likely to underperform in the market. At the same time, negative screened market options are robust to overall market changes. Negative screening asset holders are more loyal to their choice in times of crises, which contributes to the stability of these options. Data on the profitability of political divestiture indicates a potential first mover advantage for early divestiture.

In a cost-benefit analysis, SRI implies short-term expenditures, but grants long-term sustainable investment streams. In the short run, screened funds have a higher expense ratio in comparison to unscreened ones – that is, social responsibility imposes an instantaneous 'ethical penalty' of decreased immediate shareholder revenue (Mohr & Webb, 2005; Tippet, 2001). In addition, searching for information and learning about CSR is associated with cognitive costs. Screening requires an extra analytical decision-making step – positive screens especially are believed to be more cognitively intensive than negative ones (Little, 2008). In addition, screening out financial options lowers the degrees of freedom of a full-choice market spectrum and risk diversification possibilities (Biller, 2007; Mohr & Webb, 2005; Williams, 2005).

In the long run, however, SRI options offer higher stability and lower turnover and failure rates compared to general assets (Dhrymes, 1998; Geczy, Stambaugh, & Levin, 2003; Guenster, Derwall, Bauer, & Koedijk, 2005; Schroeder, 2003; Stone, Guerard, Gületkin, & Adams, 2001). Being based on more elaborate decision making, once investors have made their socially responsible decision, they are more likely to stick with their choice (Little, 2008). As a matter of fact, SRI options are less volatile and more robust regarding cyclical changes (Bollen & Cohen, 2004).

The unclear picture of whether SRI leads to an increase or decrease in market value may stem from Financial Social Responsibility measurement deficiencies, including intangible and time-inconsistent pay-offs. SRI studies are methodologically limited by small sample sizes due to the relative novelty of Financial Social Responsibility, inconsistencies in the short time frames under scrutiny, and the differing modeling techniques used to estimate investment returns (Jones et al., 2008; McWilliams & Siegel, 1996; Mohr et al., 2001; Ngassam, 1992; Teoh, Welch, & Wazzan, 1999). Most SRI studies do not take externalities on the wider constituency group into consideration, which lowers the external validity of the results and calls for a more well-rounded examination of SRI (McWilliams, Siegel, & Teoh, 1999).

When widening the interdisciplinary lens for SRI motives, it becomes apparent that the socio-psychological motives of socially conscientious investors have not been studied sufficiently. Apart from the intention to maximize profits, the following framework proposes socio-psychological mechanisms that may impact on financial social conscientiousness. Altruism as a concern for societal well-being, as well as the need for innovation and entrepreneurship, are potential SRI triggers. Financial Social Responsibility may also grant strategic leadership advantages through social status elevation prospects and utility derived from transparency and information disclosure. SRI options may allow self-enhancement through identification and self-consistency and an expression of the social values of future-oriented, long-term-focused socially-conscientious investors.

4. ALTRUISM AS THE CONCERN FOR THE SOCIETAL WELL-BEING

A mixture of egoistic and altruistic acts constitutes human behavior, as both are features of human nature (Becker, 1976). The duality of altruism and egoism in human behavior is addressed in sources as early as in ancient Greek writings. Socrates had already connected egoistic individual responsibility to altruism (Sichler in Weber, Pasqualoni, & Burtscher, 2004). The altruism versus egoism predicament is also captured by Adam Smith (Beinhocker, 2007). In *An Inquiry into the Nature and Causes of the Wealth of the Nations*, Smith (1776/1976) proposes self-interest as the motivating force for all economic activity to cumulatively enhance societal well-being (Jones & Pollitt, 1998). In *The Theory of Moral Sentiments*, Smith (1759/1976) argues for all human beings being selflessly interested in the well-being of others and for altruistic moral sentiments (Zak, 2008).

Altruism is captured as a state, by which individuals increase the well-being of others at the expense of their own (Wilson, 1975). As a source of value for those who give, altruism is associated with selfish pleasure (Brooks, 2008). The short-term intangible gratification of altruism is related to the warm glow – an internally rewarding positive feeling derived from the giver being conscientious of their pro-social behavior (Brammer, Williams, & Zinkin, 2005; Frey & Stutzer, 2002; Heyman & Ariely, 2004). Granting meaning to the individual beyond the self, altruism contributes to the positive self-perception and well-being of the giver. As one of the most enduring human traits, altruism is evolutionary explained by the increased survival likelihood of those who are supported by others and the dominance of supportive networks (Becker, 1976).

Today, classic market fundamentalism is challenged by findings of the importance of altruism in decision making (Osnabrugge & Robinson, 2000). Contrary to classical economic assumptions of pure self-interest driving all human action, behavioral economists find altruism to be a part of economic decision making in experiments (Frank, 2007). Behavioral economics introduces altruism and pro-social behavior in financial decision-making analyses. Challenging classic portfolio theory that holds investments as purely based on rationality, business ethics describe affluent societies as exhibiting altruism in investment choices deviating from pure profit maximization (Becker, 2008; Brooks, 2008; Frey & Stutzer, 2007). Economic psychology finds altruism to be a pivotal motivation factor for investment allocations as investors exhibit pro-social concerns (Brooks, 2008; Csikszentmihalyi, 2003; Kirchler, 2001). Market behavior is captured to serve pro-social, altruistic endeavors. As socially conscientious investors are found to be willing to sacrifice profits for the sake of altruism, SRI is portrayed as an investment strategy that combines profit intentions with social considerations (Little, 2008). Within society, altruism breeds cooperation and creates long-term beneficial societal ties. Altruism contributes to collective trust and social capital as implicit prerequisites for any economic market activity and societal prosperity (Brooks, 2005; Frey, 2008).

Extended investors' altruism is expressed in investor philanthropy, which stems from a combination of tax exemptions for charity but also the decline of marginal utility leading to the search for a warm glow in giving beyond personal profit maximization (Holman, New, & Singer, 1985). Investor philanthropy is most common in the US due to a combination of financial wealth accumulation, cultural values of giving and tax exemptions for charity. Prominent US investor philanthropists are Warren Buffett – who has donated over 85 percent of his fortune to charity – and George Soros, who couples economic investments with philanthropy by leading the Soros Fund Management alongside the non-profit Open

Society Institute and Soros Foundation (Bernstein & Swan, 2007; Soros, 1997, 2003).

5. THE NEED FOR INNOVATION AND ENTREPRENEURSHIP

Innovations are as old as humankind. Since industrialization, entrepreneurial activities and innovations have been the mainspring of societal progress and economic prosperity (Drucker, 1985; Schumpeter, 1951/1989). Karl Marx had already described the constant diffusion of innovations driving capitalism. Joseph Schumpeter (1934, 1951/1989) refined the idea of profit stemming from innovations. Entrepreneurs were perceived to uniquely combine the means of production to generate new products for innovation-seeking consumers. By efficiently using resources in an unprecedented, productive way, entrepreneurs spur innovative change. Entrepreneurial innovations drive productivity, create and extend markets and steer economic development in open market societies (Handy, 2006).

Entrepreneurs are in need of a supportive environment and advantageous societal settings that support their endeavors. While entrepreneurial activities are reported in various historical contexts and exist in almost all cultures, their degree of success depends on external, culture-related factors of institutional and regulatory frameworks, investment capital and societal values (Brooks, 2008; De Woot, 2005). As incubators for entrepreneurship, innovative milieus attract entrepreneurs and prosper innovations (Aydalot & Keeble, 1988). Libertarian, open market societies breed innovation through economic freedom, investment capital, private property securitization and social capital (Camagni, 1991; Fromhold-Eisebith, 2004; Rodrik, 2007). In innovative milieus, knowledge dissemination in sync with collective learning processes and expertise platforms stimulate entrepreneurial activities.

While innovations flourish best under regulatory leeway, the 2008/09 World Financial Crisis has drawn attention to an additional essential feature for the long-term success of entrepreneurial innovations in free-market hubs – social responsibility. The 2008 world financial meltdown underlined that creative entrepreneurs featuring dynamic energy, an extraordinary striving for innovative progress and high levels of risk acceptance can impose emergent and systemic risks on unregulated markets (Drucker, 1985; Goleman, 2006; Kirchler, 2001). While unregulated markets are essential for fostering an innovative climate, the past 2008/09 regulatory watchful eye over the marketplace has created an 'Age of

Angst,' featuring shied liquidity and corporate capital hoarding that may only be overcome by renewed attention to the importance of risky entrepreneurs driving innovation, yet who are also socially conscientious, allowing free market innovations to prosper sustainably. Social responsibility as an essential safety protection beyond legal regulation ensures the correct performance of contracts coupled with additional conscientiousness for social needs. In these functions, Financial Social Responsibility serves societal goals beyond the regulatory control.

Within the financial market in particular, SRI is an innovative and entrepreneurial investment option that allows sustainable free market economic growth protected by a personal social responsibility which tames the personal excesses that can impose potential risks onto the economy (Waldman et al., 2004). As a means of stakeholder activism, SRI allows investors to reward societal progress and innovatively tackle social and environmental concerns (Chakrabarty & Wang, 2012). In particular, positively screened SRI funds feature innovative corporations that proactively administer social responsibility beyond the legal requirements (Aiken & Hage, 1971; Little, 2008). Positively screened environmentally friendly corporations contribute to future-oriented funds that attract innovative and entrepreneurial investors (Blank & Carty, 2002; Coulson, 2002; Meyers & Nakamura, 1980; Nordhaus, 2008; Russo & Fouts, 1997; Ziegler, Rennings, & Schröder, 2002). In shareholder advocacy, SRI becomes a means to address social concerns (Little, 2008).

As an innovative capital allocation form for entrepreneurial spirits, SRI is preferred by venture capitalists and business angel investors. These future-oriented investors have an interest in innovative market options that steer societal change and sustainably improve societal conditions (Schueth, 2003). Social venture capitalists are prone to screen financial options for entrepreneurial opportunities. Venture capitalists seek to finance social entrepreneurs and early-stage business innovations. Venture funds feature relatively high risks in combination with extraordinary return expectations. Apart from high growth outlooks, venture capital funds serve as a source for innovative economic growth and international development within society (Gompers, Kovner, Lerner, & Scharfstein, 2005).

Business angel investors are the oldest and most influential external entrepreneurial start-up funding source. In the US close to three million business angels invest more than US$ 50 billion in entrepreneurial corporations per year (Little, 2008). Business angels fund 30–40 times as many entrepreneurial start-ups than venture capitalists (Little, 2008). As innovative investors, business angels are attracted to entrepreneurial ideas, and are willing to take high risks and accept lower returns. Angel investors primarily finance early-stage projects that may require hands-on managerial involvement. As for interests in start-up corporations and early-stage ventures, business angels are less likely to make follow-up investments in the same entities. In the US individual angel investors are predominantly male and 35 to 40 years old – which is significantly older than the average venture capitalist – while their European counterparts are slightly older (Wetzel & Freear, 1996). Business angels are well-educated, with 60 percent holding postgraduate degrees and 13 percent PhDs in various disciplines. Having more corporate exposure than venture capitalists, around 90 percent of business angels have prior corporate experience. Business angels tend to be more flexible than venture capitalists and make industry-wide investments. In recent decades, the overall market for business angels has grown quantitatively and qualitatively in the Western world.

6. STRATEGIC ADVANTAGES THROUGH SOCIAL STATUS ELEVATION

Social status superiority is favorable in terms of attached rights, honors and prestige (Berger, Fisek, Norman, & Zelditch, 1977; Cole, Mailath, & Postlewaite, 1992; Huberman, Loch, & Önçüler, 2004; Postlewaite, 1998). Adam Smith (1759/1976) had already related social status advantages to consumption opportunities (Roussanov, 2009). Sociologists depict the economic utility of status expression through conspicuous consumption (Bolton & Ockenfels, 2000; Coelho & McClure, 1993; Congleton, 1989; Galiani & Weinschelbaum, 2007; Hopkins & Kornienko, 2004; Kahneman & Thaler, 1991; Konrad & Lommerud, 1993; Veblen, 1899/1994).

Leaders express and distinguish themselves from others by their possessions and social empathy. Sociologists outline conspicuous consumption as a leadership distinction and social status elevation (Coleman, 1990; Veblen, 1899/1994). Leaders are willing to pay premium prices for trademarked high-end goods and innovative first editions to differentiate themselves from others (Becker & Murphy, 2000). In addition, pro-social giving grants leaders control over their social environment and discourages others from causing harm to givers. In pro-social activities, leaders thereby create strong interpersonal networks that lift their position in hierarchies (Brooks, 2008).

SRI implies social-status-enhancing leadership advantages for investors, when perceived as an innovative market option that allows investors to distinguish themselves from others and establish and maintain leadership positions through pro-social outcomes. As an innovative entrepreneurial financial market option, SRI implies first mover advantages as a competitive edge. The extra-step of screenings leverages SRI into high-end, branded products. Positive image transfer portrays socially responsible investors as pro-social leaders and therefore offers social mobility opportunities (Ait-Sahalia, 2004; Puaschunder, 2015b).

Related to advantageous power and wealth distributions, leaders are in a position to give to others, and those who give distinguish themselves as leaders. Altruistic social responsibility and charitable giving thus imply additional leadership advantages. Pro-social behavior of leaders is accompanied by positive feedback and a benevolent climate generated by their admirers (Brooks, 2008). As altruism contributes to the social reputation of the altruist, social responsibility enhances the social status of leaders (Becker, 1976; Brooks, 2008; Hermann, 2008; Sichler in Weber et al., 2004). Pro-social behavior thereby grows into value for those who give and leads to higher personal standing and status, leadership effectiveness and ultimately greater success. Because of their charitable giving, socially responsible investors enjoy a positive reputation and social status advantages (Ait-Sahalia, 2004; Brasington, Kato, & Semmler, 2010; Wright & Ferris, 1997).

SRI offers potential implicit or explicit strategies to express and enhance social status in the social arena. Based on Maslow's (1943) hierarchy of needs, one can only be uberethical if one has reached a certain social status (Puaschunder, 2016b). Not having to worry about food and shelter frees mental capacities to address higher societal, ethical needs and the future-oriented filling of current legal gaps (Puaschunder, 2017). As ethicality is perceived as a noble act that grants others' respect, individuals may use SRI as a conspicuous social status symbol in the social compound. Beyond governmental regulation and legal obligations, the nobleness of uberethical SRI may thus bestow individuals with social status elevation prospects (Puaschunder, 2017; Putnam, 2015).

SRI serving a need for ethicality captures when human are overdoing what is required by the law. In the natural human drive to do good to others, humans are outperforming legal regulation whilst incurring costs and imposing risks on themselves. Similar to Zimbardo's heroic imagination (2011a, 2011b) describing voluntary service to others that involves a risk to physical comfort, social stature or quality of life, this kind of uberethicality stems from the voluntarily filling of legal gaps or outperforming of legal goals that imposes costs and risks on the individual (Puaschunder, 2017). In closing current legal gaps, the evolutionary-based natural law of uberethicality is forerunning legal codifications if it considers laws to be the expression of our shared nature and the amalgamated sum of social norms in society (Benke & Meissel, 2008; Cicero in Keyes, 1966; Puaschunder, 2017). Socially responsible investors are foresightedly fulfilling future regulatory requirements, which grants them a first-mover leadership advantage (Young, 2011).

Given the natural respect for the voluntary willingness to incur risks for the sake of pro bono outcomes, as well as the leadership advantages attributed to proactively tackling ethical problems that will likely cover future regulation, SRI is thus an implicit means of social status elevation. Under the assumption that an individual's self-esteem is dependent on social status and that humans constantly wish to maintain or gain positive social status, uberethical SRI choices can thus serve as a powerful social status pedestal to claim or regain social status in the aftermath of the 2008/09 World Financial Crisis and to overcome inequality (Piketty, 2014; Puaschunder, 2017; 2016c).

7. UTILITY DERIVED FROM TRANSPARENCY AND INFORMATION DISCLOSURE

The basis for shareholder activism is transparency and information disclosure, the monitoring of corporate conduct and accountability for the implementation of corporate codes of social conduct, as well as internal and external CSR oversight. In the search for trustworthy information on CSR and corporate conduct externalities, socially conscientious investors primarily use corporate track records and shareholder resolutions on social and environmental performances (Graves, Rehbeim, & Waddock, 2001; Little, 2008). Access to CSR information is formally granted through fiduciary obligations and spearheaded by respective security and transparency legislations (Bazerman & Tenbrunsel, 2011). In the largest SRI market, fiduciary responsibility is attributed to a variety of stakeholders by the US Statement of Investment Principles (Goodpaster & Matthews, 2003). Since 2000 trustees have been required to disclose – as a part of their Statement of Investment Principles – the extent to which social, environmental or ethical considerations are taken into account in the selection, retention and realization of investments. This measure was introduced to encourage socially responsible investments in pension funds (Hennigfeld, Pohl, & Tolhurst, 2006). SRI selections are also influenced by information-sharing networks, word-of-mouth and emotional display (Thaler & Sunstein, 2008).

In the global arena, international organizations play a key role in defining transparency of SRI practices (Matten & Crane, 2005). From a global governance perspective, transnational entities are pivotal in institutionally supporting Financial Social Responsibility and streamlining SRI practices around the globe (Matten & Moon, 2004). International organizations define SRI standards and guidelines for the Financial Social Responsibility implementation in order to foster financial markets' global governance impetus on international development goals.

One instrument of CSR transparency is the United Nations Global Compact (UNGC), which helps in moving towards a universal consensus on the minimum standards of corporate social conduct in the areas of labor standards, human rights, poverty reduction, health and workplace safety, education and community engagement. The participation of corporations in the UNGC is primarily ensured through multi-stakeholder partnerships that target leveraging the quality of corporate commitment to UN principles. The partnerships integrate CSR into corporate practices at the operational level throughout all hierarchical layers. The UNGC participants are advised to change corporate policies in sync with the Ten Principles, which relate to topics such as human rights, labor standards, the environment and anti-corruption.[1]

Another effort targeted at ingraining CSR information into everyday investment decision making are the Principles for Responsible Investment (PRI). The United Nations Global Compact and the United Nations Environment Programme Finance Initiative launched the PRI at the New York Stock Exchange to ingrain social responsibility in asset owners and financial managers' investment decisions in April 2006. This public-private-partnership initiative was set up to increase the number of socially responsible investors and steer SRI by creating models for positive change within the investment community. The PRI are supported by the UNGC Conference Board, the chief executive officers of 20 global corporations, the International Finance Corporation of the World Bank Group, the Swiss Government, Columbia University and the UNEP Finance Initiative. Under the auspices of the UNGC and the UNEP Finance Initiative, the PRI invite institutional investors to consider SRI and mobilize chief executives of the world's largest pension funds to advance SRI on a global scale. The principles are designed to place Financial Social Responsibility at the heart of financial managers and asset owners' investment decision making regarding pension funds, foundation assets and institutional endowments. At the one-year anniversary of the PRI, more than 170 institutions representing approximately US$ 8 trillion in assets had committed to the PRI. Corporations that join the PRI report concomitant tangible (profit gain, efficiency, product innovations, market segmentation) and intangible (reputation, employee morale) benefits.

In February 2008 the UN Conference on Trade and Development (UNCTAD) launched the 'Responsible Investment in Emerging Markets' initiative at the Geneva PRI office. This public-private partnership (PPP) aims at fostering transparency and disclosure in emerging financial markets. The key constituents are stock exchange and financial analyst communities as future SRI drivers to support the UNGC goals and aid intergenerational responsibility (Puaschunder, 2015a). In addition, NGOs are invited to advance financial market transparency and accountability (Puaschunder, 2010).

In the wake of the 2008/09 World Financial Crisis, corporate governance failures and responsibility deficiencies of market actors have pushed stakeholder calls for transparency of corporate conduct, accountability of shareholder meetings, standardized tracking of proxy voting and accessibility of shareholder meetings (Gärling, Kirchler, Lewis, & Van Raaij, 2010). As a positive externality of the financial crisis, the drive towards transparency and accountability within financial markets is likely to foster SRI in the future. Access to information is believed to lower the economic default risks of socially irresponsible corporate conduct and contribute to an upswing in SRI trends.

8. SELF-ENHANCEMENT THROUGH IDENTIFICATION AND SELF-CONSISTENCY

While socially responsible investors are interested in financial profitability, at the same time they want their portfolio choices to conform with their personal opinions and societal norms (Little, 2008; Statman, 2007; Williams, 2005). Socially responsible investors are willing to sacrifice financial returns for aligning their investment allocations with personal and societal values (Statman, 2008). Financial Social Responsibility allows investors to benefit causes that are in line with their beliefs and societal values. As a means to integrate ethicality in economic decision making, SRI enables investors to address social norms that may resonate with their personal values (Knoll, 2008). SRI thereby serves intrinsic obligations to uphold protected values of morality (Alperson, Tepper-Marlin, Schorsch, & Wil, 1991; Frey & Irle, 2002; Sparkes & Cowton, 2004). When paying attention to protected values, decision makers depart from rationality (Bazerman & Moore, 2008). Socially responsible investors fund ethical causes about which they personally care and refrain from ethical infringements. These protected values of ethicality are relatively stable across cultures and the drive towards social responsibility in investment decisions is a natural behavioral law (Baron & Spranca, 1997; Puaschunder, 2011).

The integration of personal ethics into their portfolio decision making and the perception of the investment decisions being in sync with personal protected values let investors identify with their choice (Mohr & Webb, 2005). The alignment of beliefs and actions evokes identification with investments that grants investors the notion of self-consistency. Self-consistency contributes to the self-enhancement of socially responsible investors (Frey & Irle, 2002; Schueth, 2003).

Emotions related to protected values may play a key role. Emotionality makes individuals resistant to economic utility considerations (Horberg, Oveis, & Keltner, 2011). Honing social values with investments triggers positive feelings related to solidarity on common goals. Groups are bestowed with self-worth-elevating pride when members are complying with socially favorable goals, and shame arises when individuals act socially irresponsibly. Fear of social status losses breaks unfavorable anti-social habits. Forced trade-offs from deontological ethics result in resistance, anger and denial through wishful thinking. By serving as a positive self-reaffirmation for investors and creating a favorable mood in them, SRI contributes to a benevolent climate between the finance community and real economy actors.

9. EXPRESSION OF SOCIAL VALUES

Everyday economic decisions are influenced by social considerations. Social motives also underlie financial decision making (Frey & Stutzer, 2007; Hong & Kacperczyk, 2006). Social norms are a prerequisite for Financial Social Responsibility. In particular, SRI enables investors to align personal economic endeavors with social obligations and express their social conscientiousness to others (Hitsch, Hortaçsu, & Ariely, 2005).

Socially responsible economic activities can be leveraged into a form of expression of social conformity (Soros, 1995; Statman, 2000). When paying attention to SRI in their decision making, investors can express social conformity (Sichler, 2006). SRI signals attention to culturally endorsed social values that help connect investors with social reference groups. SRI thereby expresses accordance of personal values with the societal norms of the wider society. The expression of personal values in SRI is attributed to stem from an internal need for conformity of words and deeds with social norms and societal values (Hofmann, Hoelzl & Kirchler, 2008). Individuals who care about their pro-social images signal their conformity with societal norms in socially responsible investment choices (Huberman et al., 2004).

The accordance of market interactions with social norms expresses positive, meaningful social identities. Stemming from the positive image of socially responsible corporations and the social gratification of pro-social behavior, socially responsible investors benefit from reputation and prestige gains (Derwall & Koedijk, 2006; Hong & Kacperczyk, 2006;

Schroeder, 2003; Simons, Powers, & Gunnemann, 1972; Stone et al., 2001; Webster, 1975). Expressing social norms in their investment behavior empowers socially responsible investors with regard to the social gratification of their pro-social choice. Socially conscientious financial decision making also grants influential expressive powers to change corporate policies and practices. SRI gives investors the right to vote at the shareholders' general assembly, as well as the possibility to put forward resolutions on corporate governance. Shareholder advocacy influences corporate policies with positive societal implications (Mohr et al., 2001). As a positive externality, the expression of personal values in SRI positively contributes to overall long-term societal progress through pro-social transfers (Puaschunder, 2015a, 2015d).

10. LONG-TERM CONSIDERATIONS

Starting in the 1970s in the wake of shareholder activism, financial markets have increasingly become attentive to socio-political circumstances over the last decades. Concurrently, the diminishing power of nation states in a globalizing world has shifted social responsibility onto the private sector (Ahmad, 2008; Puaschunder, 2010). Since the 1990s capitalism has seen the triumph of the market system and upcoming financial market dominance was forecast. In the wake of financial markets' worldwide outreach into socio-political affairs and rising levels of social venture capital in international development, Financial Social Responsibility increasingly advanced into a means of global governance (*World Development Report*, 2015).

In general, investment decisions are based on reflections about future prospects. Investment strategies can build sustainable financial returns if considering lasting, long-term societal implications (Shaikh, 2013). The long-term viability of corporate conduct is ensured by CSR. Socially attentive corporate conduct features sustainability considerations of corporate executives who are mindful of the future risks and social impacts of their decision making. CSR grants long-term stability of corporate conduct in terms of creating a supportive business environment and decreasing stakeholder pressure and litigations risks (Little, 2008; Posnikoff, 1997; Sparkes, 2002). As socially responsible corporate conduct attributes long-term perspectives when taking rising CSR trends into consideration, SRI offers lasting financial prospects and an impact on society (Dupré et al., 2008; Little, 2008; McWilliams et al., 1999). From a multi-stakeholder perspective, SRI implies long-term positive societal outcomes (Sparkes, 2002). SRI ensures that corporations are held accountable for any social and environmental impacts and investments are in line with societal values (Sparkes, 2002). By shifting capital from socially disapproved to socially conscientious corporations, SRI fosters corporate social performances. Investors interested in 'social change' put their investments to work in ways that sustainably improve the overall quality of life. Socially conscientious investors thereby use SRI as a long-term strategy to contribute to society (Knoll, 2008; Schueth, 2003).

By offering long-term prospects, SRI also breeds economic stability and societal advancement. As for being incentivized by first mover leadership advantages, increasingly corporations may pay attention to social responsibility in the future. Accompanied by followers, the rising supply of SRI in combination with a heightened demand for the integration of personal values and social concerns into financial decision making may prospectively leverage social conscientiousness to become a standard feature of investment markets. In the long run, the integration of SRI into the overall competitive model will further add sophistication to social responsibility in corporate conduct (Starr, 2008; Stiglitz, 2003). Financial market demand and supply geared towards SRI will qualitatively sophisticate the option range in a more socially responsible way. In addition, if the majority of investors are socially conscientious, socially responsible corporations will continuously benefit from increasing investment streams. Directed capital flows to socially responsible market options will thereby sustainably contribute to CSR and SRI trends (Dupré et al., 2008). Overall, financial markets attuned to social responsibility will lift entire industries onto a more socially conscientious level (Trevino & Nelson, 2004). As such, SRI is attributed with the potential to positively impact on the financial markets and create socially attentive market systems that improve the overall standard of living and quality of life for this and the following generations.

11. FUTURE RESEARCH DIRECTIONS

Future research may study SRI in a qualitatively and quantitatively nested approach. Qualitative interviews on the social perception of SRI will help in resolving societal losses imbued in the novelty of the phenomenon and aligning incoherent viewpoints on SRI. Exploratory studies may capture predicted SRI trends with attention to the socio-economic success factors of Financial Social Responsibility and stakeholder-specific SRI nuances. Quantitative market assessments may feature the event study methodology as the state-of-the-art analysis technique for capturing the impact of SRI on corporate success. Financial market experiments may provide complementary tests for the microeconomic effects of divestment behavior. Research on bounded decision making could reveal implicit and accidental financial social irresponsibility, and may validate the proposed socio-psychological SRI framework to distinguish moderator variables of investors' willingness to trade off financial profits for social gratifications. The findings will reduce cognitive barriers of decision making predicaments and lead to educative means for steering behavioral patterns in a more socially conscientious direction.

Additional investigations of the perception of SRI in the aftermath of the crisis could determine in what way the financial crisis has changed the financial community's view of market responsibility. Paying attention to the 2008/09 World Financial Crisis may help in deriving recommendations for research-based transparency campaigns that promote SRI as a stable market option during times of crisis throughout the financial community, and thereby raise the stakeholders' confidence in Financial Social Responsibility. The predicted trend of the rising of SRI should be captured by additional research on up-to-date corporate and Financial Social Responsibility conduct, determining the strengths and weaknesses of private-sector contributions to social welfare (Puaschunder, 2016d). All these profound research findings will serve as a basis for stimulating SRI innovations that lead to concurrent economic prosperity and societal advancement (*World Development Report*, 2015).

12. CONCLUSION

Overall, the chapter has explored innovative corporate and financial market potentials to create value for society. A Financial Social Responsibility framework portrayed the manifold potentials of SRI to re-establish trust in financial markets by finding the optimum interplay of deregulated market systems and governmental control in ensuring market-driven social responsibility (Puaschunder, 2015d). The proposed socio-psychological SRI motives framework is targeted at outlining ways to better capture the effects of Financial Social Responsibility on economic markets and societal systems in order to provide recommendations for a successful rise of social responsibility within modern market economies. All these endeavors are aimed at fostering Financial Social Responsibility as a future guarantor of sustainable economic stability and societal progress throughout the world.

NOTE

1. https://www.unglobalcompact.org/what-is-gc/mission/principles

REFERENCES

Abramson, L., & Chung, D. (2000). Socially responsible investing: Viable for value investors? *Journal of Investing*, *9*(3), 73–81.

Ahmad, M. (2008). Global CEOs at World Economic Forum cite sovereign wealth funds as the new power broker. *BI-ME*, January 24.

Aiken, M., & Hage, J. (1971). The organic organization and innovation. *Sociology*, *5*, 63–82.

Ait-Sahalia, Y. (2004). Disentangling diffusion from jumps. *Journal of Financial Economics*, *74*, 487–528.

Aja, A., Bustillo, D., Darity, W., & Hamilton, D. (2013). Jobs instead of austerity: A bold policy proposal for economic justice. *Social Research: An International Quarterly*, *80*, 3, 781–794.

Alperson, M., Tepper-Marlin, A.T., Schorsch, J., & Wil, R. (1991). *The better world investment guide: One hundred companies whose policies you should know about before you invest your money*. From the Council on Economic Priorities. Prentice Hall: New York.

Aydalot, P., & Keeble, D. (1988). *High technology industry and innovative environments: The European experience*. London: Routledge.

Barnosky, A.D., Matzke, N., Tomiya, S., Wogan, G.O.U., Swartz, B., Quental, T.B., Marshall, C., McGuire, J.L., Lindsey, E.L., Maguire, K.C., Mersey, B., & Ferrer, E.A. (2011). Has the earth's sixth mass extinction already arrived? *Nature*, *471*, 51–57.

Baron, J. (2000). *Thinking and deciding*. Cambridge, MA: Cambridge University Press.

Baron, J., & Spranca, M. (1997). Protected values. *Organizational Behavior and Human Decision Processes*, *70*(1), 1–16.

Bazerman, M.H., & Moore, D. (2008). *Judgment in managerial decision making*. Hoboken: Wiley.

Bazerman, M.H., & Tenbrunsel, A.E. (2011). *Blind spots: Why we fail to do what's right and what to do about it*. Princeton: Princeton University Press.

Becker, G.S. (1976). *The economic approach to human behavior*. Chicago: The University of Chicago Press.

Becker, G.S. (2008). *Is corporate altruism viable in a competitive environment?* Retrieved from https://www.huffingtonpost.com/gary-becker/is-corporate-altruism-via_b_110726.html

Becker, G.S., & Murphy, K.M. (2000). *Social economics: Market behavior in a social environment*. Cambridge, MA: Harvard University Press.

Beinhocker, E.D. (2007). *The origin of wealth: The radical remaking of economics and what it means for business and society*. Cambridge, MA: Harvard Business School.

Beltratti, A. (2003). *Socially responsible investment in general equilibrium: Economic theory and applications*. Retrieved from https://papers.ssrn.com/sol3/papers.cfm?abstract_id=467240

Benke, N., & Meissel, F.-St. (2008). *Übungsbuch Römisches Sachenrecht*. Vienna: Manz.

Berger, J.M., Fisek, M., Norman, R.Z., & Zelditch, M. (1977). *Status characteristics in social interaction: An expectation states approach*. New York: Elsevier.

Berman, S.L., Wicks, A.C., Kotha, S., & Jones, T.M. (1999). Does stakeholder orientation matter? The relationship between stakeholder management models and firm financial performance. *Academy of Management Journal*, *42*(5), 488–506.

Bernstein, P.W., & Swan, A. (2007). *All the money in the world: How the Forbes 400 make – and spend – their fortunes*. New York: Knopf.

Biller, A. (2007). Socially responsible investing now part of the landscape. *Benefits & Compensation Digest*, *44*(12).

Binder, C., Kriebaum, U., Marboe, I., Nowak, M., Reinisch, A., & Wittich, S. (2014). *Völkerrecht*. Vienna: University of Vienna Faculty of Law Juridicum.
Blank, H.D., & Carty, C.M. (2002). *The eco-efficiency anomaly*. Innovest working paper retrieved from http://www.sristudies.org/Blank+and+Carty+(2002)?
Bollen, N.P.B., & Cohen, M.A. (2004). *Mutual fund attributes and investor behavior*. Working paper, Vanderbilt University.
Bolton, G., & Ockenfels, A. (2000). ERC: A theory of equity, reciprocity, and competition. *American Economic Review*, *90*(1), 166–193.
Boutin-Dufresne, F., & Savaria, P. (2004). Corporate social responsibility and financial risk. *Journal of Investing*, *13*(1), 57–66.
Boyer, R. (2012). The four fallacies of contemporary austerity policies: The lost Keynesian legacy. *The Cambridge Journal of Economics*, *36*(1), 283–312.
Brammer, S., Williams, G.A., & Zinkin, J. (2005). *Religion and attitudes to corporate social responsibility in a large cross-country sample*. Nottingham University Business School.
Brasington, D., Kato, M., & Semmler, W. (2010). Transitioning out of poverty. *Metroeconomica: International Review of Economics*, *61*(1), 68–95.
Brenner, R. (2001). *The force of finance: Triumph of the capital markets*. New York: Texere.
Brooks, A. (2005). *Gifts of time and money: The role of charity in America's communities*. New York: Rowman & Littlefield.
Brooks, A. (2008). *Social entrepreneurship. Course reader*, Spring, Maxwell School of Citizenship and Public Affairs, Syracuse University.
Butz, C. (2003). Decomposing SRI performance: Extracting value through factor analysis. *Pictet Quants*, September.
Camagni, R. (1991). *Innovation networks*. London: Routledge.
Carswell, A. (2002). Crisis of conscience. *Australian CPA*, *72*, 26–27.
Centeno, M.A., Cinlar, E., Cloud, D., Creager, A.N., DiMaggio, P.J., Dixit, A.K., Elga, A.N., Felten, E.W., James, H., Katz, St. N., Keohane, R.O., Leonard, T.C., Massey, W.A., Mian, A.R., Mian, Z., Oppenheimer, M., Shafir, E., & Shapiro, J.N. (2013). *Global systemic risk*. Unpublished manuscript for research community. Princeton Institute for International and Regional Studies, Princeton University, April.
Centeno, M.A., & Tham, A. (2012). *The emergence of risk in the global system*. Working paper, Princeton University.
Chakrabarty, S., & Wang, L. (2012). The long-term sustenance of sustainability practices in MNCs: A dynamic capabilities perspective of the role of R&D and internationalization. *Journal of Business Ethics*, *110*(2), 205–217.
Coelho, P.R.P., & McClure, J.E. (1993). Toward an economic theory of fashion. *Economic Inquiry*, *31*, 595–608.
Cole, H., Mailath, G., & Postlewaite, A. (1992). Social norms, savings behavior, and growth. *Journal of Political Economy*, *100*(6), 1092–1125.
Coleman, J. (1990). *Foundations of social theory*. Cambridge, MA: Harvard University Press.
Congleton, R.D. (1989). Efficient status seeking: Externalities, and the evolution of status games. *Journal of Economic Behavior and Organization*, *11*, 175–190.
Coulson, A. (2002). *A benchmarking study: Environmental credit risk factor in the pan-European banking sector*. London: ISIS Asset Management.
Csikszentmihalyi, M. (2003). *Good business: Leadership, flow, and the making of meaning*. New Baskerville: Penguin.
De la Cuesta, G.M., & Valor, C. (2007). Fostering corporate social responsibility through public initiative: From the EU to the Spanish case. *Journal of Business Ethics*, *55*(3), 275–293.
De Woot, A. (2005). *Should Prometheus be bound? Corporate social responsibility*. London: Palgrave Macmillan.
Derwall, J., & Koedijk, K. (2006). *Socially responsible fixed-income funds*. Working paper, Erasmus University.
Dhrymes, P.J. (1998). *Socially responsible investment: Is it profitable? The investment research guide to socially responsible investing*. The Colloquium on Socially Responsible Investing.

Dixon, F. (2002). *Financial markets and corporate environmental results*. Working paper, Innovest.
Drucker, P.F. (1985). *Innovation and entrepreneurship: Practice and principles*. New York: Harper Business.
Dupré, D., Girerd-Potin, I., & Kassoua, R. (2008). *Adding an ethical dimension to portfolio management*. Retrieved from https://papers.ssrn.com/sol3/papers.cfm?abstract_id=394101
Dymski, G. (2013). The logic and impossibility of austerity. *Social Research: An International Quarterly*, *80*(3), 665–696.
The Economist (2008), The next question: Does CSR work? January 17, Retrieved from https://www.economist.com/node/10491055
Foley, D.K. (2009). The economic fundamentals of global warming. In J.M. Harris & N.R. Goodwin (eds), *Twenty-first century macroeconomics: Responding to the climate challenge*, pp. 115–126, Cheltenham: Edward Elgar Publishing.
Fowler, S.J., & Hope, C. (2007). A critical review of sustainable business indices and their impact. *Journal of Business Ethics*, *76*(3), 243–252.
Frank, R.H. (2007). *The economic naturalist: In search of explanations for everyday enigmas*. New York: Perseus.
Fraser, N. (2014). Can society be commodities all the way down? Post-Polanyian reflections on capitalist crisis. *Economy and Society*, *43*(4), 441–458.
Frey, B.S. (2008). *Happiness: A revolution in economics*. Cambridge, MA: MIT Press.
Frey, D., & Irle, M. (2002). *Theorien der Sozialpsychologie*. Bern: Hans Huber.
Frey, B.S., & Stutzer, A. (2002). What can economists learn from happiness research? *Journal of Economic Literature*, *15*, 402–435.
Frey, B.S., & Stutzer, A. (2007). *Economics and psychology: A promising new cross-disciplinary field*. Cambridge, MA: MIT Press.
Fromhold-Eisebith, M. (2004). Innovative milieu and social capital: Complementary or redundant concepts of collaboration-based regional development? *European Planning Studies*, *12*(6), 747–765.
Galiani, S., & Weinschelbaum, F. (2007). *Social status and corruption*. Manuscript retrieved from http://citeseerx.ist.psu.edu/viewdoc/download?doi=10.1.1.504.2066&rep=rep1&type=pdf
Gärling, T., Kirchler, E., Lewis, A., & Van Raaij, F. (2010). Psychology, financial decision making, and financial crises. *Psychological Science in the Public Interest*, *10*(1), 1–47.
Geczy, C.C., Stambaugh, R.F., & Levin, D. (2003). *Investing in socially responsible mutual funds*. Philadelphia, PA: The Wharton School.
Ghilarducci, T. (2013). Austerity distorts the common economic interest between generations. *Social Research: An International Quarterly*, *80*(3), 953–976.
Goleman, D. (2006). *Social intelligence: The new science of human relationships*. New York: Bantam.
Gompers, P., Kovner, A., Lerner, J., & Scharfstein, D. (2005). *Venture capital investment cycles: The impact of public markets*. NBER Working Papers, 11385, Cambridge, MA: National Bureau of Economic Research.
Goodpaster, K.E., & Matthews, J.B. (2003). *Can a corporation have a conscience? Harvard Business Review on Corporate Responsibility*. Cambridge, MA: Harvard Business School.
Graves, S.B., Rehbeim, K., & Waddock, S. (2001). Fad and fashion in shareholder activism: The landscape of shareholder resolutions 1988–1998. *Business and Society Review*, *106*, 293–314.
Guenster, N., Derwall, J., Bauer, R., & Koedijk, K. (2005). *The economic value of corporate eco-efficiency*. Working paper, Erasmus University.
Hamilton, S., Hoje, J., & Statman, M. (1993). Doing well while doing good? The investment performance of socially responsible mutual funds. *Financial Analysts Journal*, *49*(6), 62–66.
Handy, C. (2006). *What's a business for?* Harvard Business Review on Corporate Responsibility. Cambridge, MA: Harvard Business School.
Harvey, C. (2008). *Campbell R. Harvey's hypertextual finance glossary*. Retrieved from http://www.duke.edu/~charvey/Classes/wpg/bfglosa.htm

Hennigfeld, J., Pohl, M., & Tolhurst, N. (2006). *The ICCA handbook on corporate social responsibility*. West Sussex: Wiley.
Hermann, M. (2008). *Political leadership*. Course Reader, Spring 2008, Maxwell School of Citizenship and Public Affairs, Syracuse University.
Heyman, J., & Ariely, D. (2004). Effort for payment: A tale of two markets. *Psychological Science, 15*(11), 787–793.
Hitsch, G.J., Hortaçsu, A., & Ariely, D. (2005). *What makes you click: An empirical analysis on online dating*. Retrieved from https://papers.ssrn.com/sol3/papers.cfm?abstract_id=895442
Hofmann, E., Hoelzl, E., & Kirchler, E. (2008). A comparison of models describing the impact of moral decision making on investment decisions. *Journal of Business Ethics, 82*(1), 171–187.
Holman, W.R., New, J.R., & Singer, D. (1985). The impact of corporate social responsiveness on shareholder wealth. In L. Preston (ed.), *Research in corporate social performance and policy*, pp. 265–280. Greenwich, CT: JAI.
Hong, H. & Kacperczyk, M. (2006). *The price of sin: The effects of social norms on markets*. Working paper, Princeton University.
Hopkins, E. & Kornienko, T. (2004). Running to keep the same place: Consumer choice as a game of status. *American Economic Review, 94*(4), 1085–1107.
Horberg, E.J., Oveis, C., & Keltner, D. (2011). Emotions as moral amplifiers: An appraisal tendency approach to the influences of distinct emotions upon moral judgments. *Emotion Review, 3*, 237–244.
Huberman, B.A., Loch, C. H., & Önçüler, A. (2004). *Status as a valued resource*. Working paper. Retrieved from https://papers.ssrn.com/sol3/papers.cfm?abstract_id=281211
Jones, I., & Pollitt, M. (1998). *The role of business ethics in economic performance*. London: Macmillan.
Jones, S., van der Laan, S., Frost, G., & Loftus, J. (2008). The investment performance of socially responsible investment funds in Australia. *Journal of Business Ethics, 80*(2), 181–203.
Kahneman, D., & Thaler, R. (1991). Economic analysis and the psychology of utility: Applications to compensation policy. *American Economic Review, 81*, 341–346.
Kempf, A., & Osthoff, P. (2007). The effect of socially responsible investing on portfolio performance. *European Financial Management, 13*(5), 908–922.
Keyes, C.W. (1966). *Cicero, M. T. De republica, De legibus.* The Loeb Classical Library. Cambridge: Harvard University Press.
Kirchler, E.M. (2001). *Wirtschaftspsychologie*. Göttingen: Hogrefe.
Knoll, M.S. (2008). *Socially responsible investment and modern financial markets*. Working paper, University of Pennsylvania Law School.
Konrad, K.A., & Lommerud, K.E. (1993). Relative standing comparisons, risk taking, and safety regulations. *Journal of Public Economics, 51*, 345–358.
Little, K. (2008). *Socially responsible investing: Put your money where your values are*. New York: Penguin.
Livesey, S. (2002). The discourse of the middle ground: Citizen Shell commits to sustainable development. *Management Communication Quarterly, 15*, 313–349.
Mackey, A., Mackey, T., & Barney, J. (2004). *Corporate social responsibility and firm performance: Investor preferences and corporate strategies*. Working paper retrieved from http://www.sristudies.org/Mackey+et+al+(2004)
Maslow, A.H. (1943). A theory of human motivation. *Psychological Review, 50*, 370–396.
Mathieu, E. (2000). *Response of UK pension funds to the SRI disclosure regulation*. London: UK Social Investment Forum.
Matten, D., & Crane, A. (2005). Corporate citizenship: Toward an extended theoretical conceptualization. *Academy of Management Review, 30*, 166–179.
Matten, D., & Moon, J. (2004). *'Implicit' and 'explicit' CSR: A conceptual framework for understanding CSR in Europe*. 20th EGOS Colloquium, 1–3 July 2004, Ljubljana, Slovenia.
Maux, J., & Saout, E. (2004). The performance of sustainability indexes. *Finance India*, April 1.
McCann, L., Solomon, A., & Solomon, J.F. (2003). Explaining the growth in UK socially responsible investment. *Journal of General Management, 28*(4), 15–36.

McWilliams, A., & Siegel, D. (1996). The use of event studies in management research. *Academy of Management Best Papers Proceedings*, 338–342.
McWilliams, A., & Siegel, D. (2000). Corporate social responsibility and financial performance: Correlation or mis-specification? *Strategic Management Journal, 21*, 603–609.
McWilliams, A., Siegel, D., & Teoh, S.W. (1999). Issues in the use of the event study methodology: A critical analysis of corporate social responsibility studies. *Organizational Research Methods, 2*, 340–365.
Meyers, J.G., & Nakamura, L. (1980). Energy and pollution effects on productivity: A Putty-Clay approach. In J. Kendrick (ed.), *New developments in productivity measurement and analysis*. Chicago: University of Chicago Press.
Michelson, G., Wailes, N., van der Laan, S., & Frost, G. (2004). Ethical investment processes and outcomes. *Journal of Business Ethics, 52*, 1–10.
Mohr, L.A., & Webb, D.J. (2005). The effects of corporate social responsibility and price on consumer responses. *Journal of Consumer Affairs, 39*(1), 121–147.
Mohr, L.A., Webb, D.J., & Harris, K.E. (2001). Do consumers expect companies to be socially responsible? The impact of corporate social responsibility on buying behavior. *Journal of Consumer Affairs, 35*(1), 45–72.
Ngassam, C. (1992). *An examination of stock market reactions to U.S. corporate divestitures in South Africa*. Newark, DE: University of Delaware.
Nordhaus, W.D. (2008). *A question of balance: Weighting the options on global warming*. New Haven: Yale University Press.
Osnabrugge, M.V., & Robinson, R.J. (2000). *Angel investing: Matching start-up funds with start-up companies: The guide for entrepreneurs, individual investors, and venture capitalists*. San Francisco, CA: Jossey-Bass.
Piketty, T. (2014). *Capital in the 21st century*. Cambridge, MA: Harvard University Press.
Posnikoff, J.F. (1997). Disinvestment from South Africa: They did well by doing good. *Contemporary Economic Policy, 15*(1), 76–86.
Postlewaite, A. (1998). The social basis of interdependent preferences. *European Economic Review, 42*(3–5), 779–800.
Puaschunder, J.M. (2010). *On corporate and financial social responsibility*. Unpublished doctoral thesis. University of Vienna, Faculty of Psychology.
Puaschunder, J.M. (2011). *Intergenerational equity as a natural behavioral law*. Library of Congress United States of America Copyright Office, Copyright Catalogue TXu001743422/2011-03-08.
Puaschunder, J.M. (2015a). *Intergenerational transfer model*. Working paper, New York: The New School for Social Research.
Puaschunder, J.M. (2015b). *Meritocracy and intergenerational mobility*. The Worldly Philosopher Blog. Schwartz Center for Economic Policy Analysis. Retrieved from http://www.economicpolicyresearch.org/insights-blog/meritocracy-builds-equality
Puaschunder, J.M. (2015c). On the social representations of intergenerational equity. *Oxford Journal of Finance and Risk Perspectives, 4*(4), 78–99.
Puaschunder, J.M. (2015d). *Trust and reciprocity drive social common goods allocation norms*. Cambridge, UK: Cambridge University, Proceedings of the 2015 6th International Conference of the Association of Global Management Studies at Columbia University, New York: The Association of Global Management Studies.
Puaschunder, J.M. (2016a). Intergenerational climate change burden sharing: An economics of climate stability research agenda proposal. *Global Journal of Management and Business Research: Economics and Commerce, 16*(3), 31–38.
Puaschunder, J.M. (2016b). On eternal equity in the fin-de-millénaire: Rethinking capitalism for intergenerational justice. *Journal of Leadership, Accountability and Ethics, 13*(2), 11–24.
Puaschunder, J.M. (2016c). The beauty of ivy: When inequality meets equality. *Global Journal of Management and Business Research: Economics and Commerce, 16*(3), 1–11.
Puaschunder, J.M. (2016d). The call for global responsible intergenerational leadership in the corporate world: The quest for an integration of intergenerational equity in contemporary Corporate Social Responsibility (CSR) models. In D. Jamali (ed.), *Comparative*

Perspectives in Global Corporate Social Responsibility, pp.275–288, Hershey: IGI Global Advances in Business Strategy and Competitive Advantage Book Series.
Puaschunder, J.M. (2017). Ethical decision-making under social uncertainty: An introduction of Überethicality. *Sustainable Production and Consumption*, *12*, 78–89.
Putnam, R.D. (2015). *Our kids: The American dream in crisis*. New York: Simon & Schuster.
Renneboog, L.D.R., Horst, J.R.T., & Zhang, C. (2007). *Socially responsible investments: Methodology, risk and performance*. Tilburg University Center for Economic Research Discussion Paper 2007–2031, Tilburg, the Netherlands.
Rodrik, D. (2007). *One economics, many recipes*. Princeton: Princeton University Press.
Rosen, B.N., Sandler, D.M., & Shani, D. (1991). Social issues and socially responsible investment behavior: Preliminary empirical investigation. *Journal of Consumer Affairs*, *25*(2), 221–234.
Roussanov, N. (2009). *Diversification and its discontents: Idiosyncratic and entrepreneurial risk in the quest for social status*. Working paper, Wharton School, University of Pennsylvania.
Russo, M.V., & Fouts, P.A. (1997). A resource-based perspective on corporate environmental performance and profitability. *Academy of Management Journal*, *40*, 534–559.
Schroeder, M. (2003). *Socially responsible investments in Germany, Switzerland, and the United States*. Centre for European Economic Research Discussion Paper 03–10, March.
Schueth, S. (2003). Socially responsible investing in the United States. *Journal of Business Ethics*, *43*, 189–194.
Schumpeter, J.A. (1934). *The theory of economic development*. Cambridge, MA: Harvard University.
Schumpeter, J.A. (1951/1989). *Essays on entrepreneurs, innovations, business cycles, and the evolution of capitalism*. New Jersey: Transaction.
Shaikh, A. (2013). Crisis, austerity, and the role of economic theory in policy. *Social Research: An International Quarterly*, *80*(3), 653–664.
Sichler, R. (2004). Autonomie: Ihre Konstitution und Ambivalenz im Kontext von Arbeit und Lebensführung. In W.G. Weber, P. Pasqualoni & C. Burtscher (eds), *Wirtschaft, Demokratie und soziale Verantwortung. Psychologie und Beruf*. Göttingen: Vandenhoeck & Ruprecht.
Sichler, R. (2006). *Autonomie in der Arbeitswelt. Psychologie und Beruf*. Göttingen: Vandenhoeck & Ruprecht.
Simons, J.G., Powers, C.W., & Gunnemann, J.P. (1972). *The ethical investor: Universities and corporate responsibility*. New Haven: Yale University Press.
Slaper, T.F., & Hall, T.J. (2011). *The triple bottom line: What is it and how does it work?* Retrieved from http://www.ibrc.indiana.edu/ibr/2011/spring/article2.html
Slawinski, N. & Bansal, P. (2012). A matter of time: The temporal perspectives of organizational responses to climate change. *Organization Studies*, *33*(11), 1537–1563.
Smith, A. (1759/1976). *The theory of moral sentiments*. Oxford: Clarendon.
Smith, A. (1776/1976). *An inquiry into the nature and causes of the wealth of nations*. Oxford: Clarendon.
Soros, G. (1995). *Jan Patocka memorial lecture: A failed philosopher tries again*. Unpublished notes. New York: The Open Society Institute.
Soros, G. (1997). *The capitalist threat*. Tbilisi: Open Society Georgia Foundation.
Soros, G. (2003). *The alchemy of finance*. New York: Wiley.
Sparkes, R. (2002). *Socially responsible investment: A global revolution*. Chichester: Wiley.
Sparkes, R., & Cowton, C.J. (2004). The maturing of socially responsible investment: A review of the developing link with corporate social responsibility. *Journal of Business Ethics*, *52*, 45–57.
Starr, M. (2008). Socially responsible investment and pro-social change. *Journal of Economic Issues*, *42*(1), 51–73.
Statman, M. (2000). Socially responsible mutual funds. *Financial Analysts Journal*, *56*(3), 30–39.
Statman, M. (2007). *Socially responsible investors and their advisors*. Working paper, Santa

Clara University. Retrieved from https://papers.ssrn.com/sol3/papers.cfm?abstract_id=1328347
Statman, M. (2008). *The expressive nature of socially responsible investors*. Working paper, Santa Clara University. Retrieved from https://papers.ssrn.com/sol3/papers.cfm?abstract_id=1094068
Steurer, R. (2010). The role of governments in corporate social responsibility: Characterising public policies on CSR in Europe. *Policy Science, 43*, 49–72.
Steurer, R., Margula, S., & Martinuzzi, A. (2008). *Socially responsible investment in EU member states: Overview of government initiatives and SRI experts' expectations towards governments. Analysis of national policies on CSR, in support of a structured exchange of information on national CSR policies and initiatives*. Final report to the EU High-Level Group on CSR provided by the Research Institute for Managing Sustainability. Vienna University of Economics and Business.
Steurer, R., Martinuzzi, R.-A., & Margula, S. (2012). Public policies on CSR in Europe: Themes, instruments and regional differences. *Corporate Social Responsibility and Environmental Management, 19*, 206–227.
Stiglitz, J.E. (2003). *Globalization and its discontents*. New York: Norton.
Stone, B.K., Guerard, J.B., Gületkin, M.N., & Adams, G. (2001). *Socially responsible investment screening: Strong evidence of no significant cost for actively managed portfolios*. Working paper. Retrieved from https://community-wealth.org/content/socially-responsible-investing-screening-strong-evidence-no-significant-cost-actively
Teoh, S.H., Welch, I., & Wazzan, C.P. (1999). The effect of socially activist investment politics on the financial markets: Evidence from the South African boycott. *Journal of Business, 72*(1), 35–89.
Thaler, R.H., & Sunstein, C.R. (2008). *Nudge: Improving decisions about health, wealth, and happiness*. New Haven: Yale University Press.
Tippet, J. (2001). Performance of Australia's ethical funds. *Australian Economic Review, 34*(2), 170–178.
Trevino, L.K., & Nelson, K.A. (2004). *Managing business ethics: Straight talk about how to do right*. Hoboken: Wiley.
Veblen, T. (1899/1994). *The theory of the leisure class: An economic study of institutions*. New York: Dover.
Waldman, D.A., Siegel, D., & Javidian, M. (2004). *Transformational leadership and corporate social responsibility*. Working paper, January 2004. Retrieved from http://www.sristudies.org/Waldman+et+al+(2004)
Weber, W.G., Pasqualoni, P., & Burtscher, C. (2004). *Wirtschaft, Demokratie und soziale Verantwortung. Psychologie und Beruf*. Göttingen: Vandenhoeck & Ruprecht.
Webster, F.E. (1975). Determining the characteristics of the socially conscious consumer. *Journal of Consumer Research, 12*(2), 188–196.
Wetzel, W.E., & Freear, J. (1996). Promoting informal venture capital in the United States: Reflections on the history of the venture capital network. In R.T. Harrison & C.M. Mason (eds), *Informal venture capital: Evaluating the impact of business introduction services*. Hemel Hempstead: Woodhead-Faulkner.
Williams, G. (2005). *Are socially responsible investors different from conventional investors?* A comparison across six countries. Working paper, University of Bath.
Wilson, E.O. (1975). *Sociobiology*. Cambridge, MA: Harvard University Press.
Wolff, M. (2002). Response to 'Confronting the critics'. *New Academy Review, 1*, 230–237.
World Development Report: Mind, Society, and Behavior (2015). Washington, DC: World Bank.
World Economic Forum 2015 Report. Davos, Switzerland: World Economic Forum.
Wright, P., & Ferris, S. (1997). Agency conflict and corporate strategy: The effect of divestment on corporate value. *Strategic Management Journal, 18*(1), 77–83.
Young, I.M. (2011). *Responsibility for justice*. Oxford: Oxford University Press.
Zak, P.J. (2008). *Moral markets: The critical role of values in the economy*. Princeton: Princeton University Press.

Ziegler, A., Rennings, K., & Schröder, M. (2002). *Der Einfluss ökologischer und sozialer Nachhaltigkeit auf den Shareholder Value europäischer Aktiengesellschaften*. Diskussionspapier 02–32, Zentrum für Europäische Wirtschaftsforschung.
Zimbardo, P. (2011a). *My journey from evil to heroism*. Speech delivered at Webster University. May 31, Vienna, Austria, EU.
Zimbardo, P. (2011b). *Evil no! Heroes yes!* Speech delivered at Harvard Law School. October 26, Cambridge, MA, USA.

Index